THE CAMBRIDGE COMPANION
JEWISH THEOLOGY

The Cambridge Companion to Jewish Theology offers an overview of Jewish theology, an aspect of Judaism that is equal in importance to law and ethics. Covering the period from antiquity to the present, the volume focuses on what Jews believe about God and also about the relation of God to humans and the world. Parts I and II cover exciting new research in Jewish biblical and rabbinic theology, medieval philosophy, Kabbalah (mysticism), and liturgy. Parts III and IV turn to modern theology with an exploration of works by leading figures, such as Rabbi Abraham I. Kook, Franz Rosenzweig, and Emmanuel Levinas, as well as the relation of theology to issues such as feminism and the Holocaust, and the relation of Judaism to other world religions. In Part V, the book explores how the insights of analytic philosophy have been integrated with Jewish theology.

STEVEN KEPNES is Professor of Religion and Jewish Studies at Colgate University. He is the author of *The Future of Jewish Theology and Jewish Liturgical Reasoning* (2007).

CAMBRIDGE COMPANIONS TO RELIGION

This is a series of companions to major topics and key figures in theology and religious studies. Each volume contains specially commissioned chapters by international scholars, which provide an accessible and stimulating introduction to the subject for new readers and nonspecialists.

Other Titles in the Series

THE COUNCIL OF NICAECA Edited by *Young Richard Kim*

APOSTOLIC FATHERS Edited by *Michael F. Bird and Scott Harrower*

AMERICAN CATHOLICISM Edited by *Margaret M. McGuinness and Thomas F. Rzeznick*

AMERICAN ISLAM Edited by *Juliane Hammer and Omid Safi*

AMERICAN JUDAISM Edited by *Dana Evan Kaplan*

AMERICAN METHODISM Edited by *Jason E. Vickers*

ANCIENT MEDITERRANEAN RELIGIONS Edited by *Barbette Stanley Spaeth*

APOCALYPTIC LITERATURE Edited by *Colin McAllister*

AUGUSTINE'S "CONFESSIONS" Edited by *Tarmo Toom*

KARL BARTH Edited by *John Webster*

THE BIBLE, 2nd edition Edited by *Bruce Chilton*

THE BIBLE AND LITERATURE Edited by *Calum Carmichael*

BIBLICAL INTERPRETATION Edited by *John Barton*

BLACK THEOLOGY Edited by *Dwight N. Hopkins and Edward P. Antonio*

DIETRICH BONHOEFFER Edited by *John de Gruchy*

JOHN CALVIN Edited by *Donald K. McKim*

CHRISTIAN DOCTRINE Edited by *Colin Gunton*

CHRISTIAN ETHICS Edited by *Robin Gill*

CHRISTIAN MYSTICISM Edited by *Amy Hollywood and Patricia Z. Beckman*

CHRISTIAN PHILOSOPHICAL THEOLOGY Edited by *Charles Taliaferro and Chad V. Meister*

CHRISTIAN POLITICAL THEOLOGY Edited by *Craig Hovey and Elizabeth Phillips*

THE CISTERCIAN ORDER Edited by *Mette Birkedal Bruun*

CLASSICAL ISLAMIC THEOLOGY Edited by *Tim Winter*

JONATHAN EDWARDS Edited by *Stephen J. Stein*

EVANGELICAL THEOLOGY Edited by *Timothy Larsen and Daniel J. Treier*

FEMINIST THEOLOGY Edited by *Susan Frank Parsons*

FRANCIS OF ASSISI Edited by *Michael J. P. Robson*

THE GOSPELS Edited by *Stephen C. Barton*

(continued after index)

THE CAMBRIDGE COMPANION TO
JEWISH THEOLOGY

Edited by

Steven Kepnes
Colgate University

CAMBRIDGE
UNIVERSITY PRESS

CAMBRIDGE
UNIVERSITY PRESS

University Printing House, Cambridge CB2 8BS, United Kingdom

One Liberty Plaza, 20th Floor, New York, NY 10006, USA

477 Williamstown Road, Port Melbourne, VIC 3207, Australia

314–321, 3rd Floor, Plot 3, Splendor Forum, Jasola District Centre, New Delhi – 110025, India

79 Anson Road, #06–04/06, Singapore 079906

Cambridge University Press is part of the University of Cambridge.

It furthers the University's mission by disseminating knowledge in the pursuit of education, learning, and research at the highest international levels of excellence.

www.cambridge.org
Information on this title: www.cambridge.org/9781108415439
DOI: 10.1017/9781108233705

© Cambridge University Press 2020

This publication is in copyright. Subject to statutory exception and to the provisions of relevant collective licensing agreements, no reproduction of any part may take place without the written permission of Cambridge University Press.

First published 2020

A catalogue record for this publication is available from the British Library.

Library of Congress Cataloging-in-Publication Data
NAMES: Kepnes, Steven, 1952– editor.
TITLE: The Cambridge companion to Jewish Theology / edited by Steven Kepnes.
DESCRIPTION: 1. | New York : Cambridge University Press, 2021. | Series: Cambridge Companions to Religion | Includes bibliographical references and index.
IDENTIFIERS: LCCN 2020027276 (print) | LCCN 2020027277 (ebook) | ISBN 9781108415439 (hardback) | ISBN 9781108233705 (ebook)
SUBJECTS: LCSH: Judaism – Doctrines. | God (Judaism)
CLASSIFICATION: LCC BM602 .C36 2021 (print) | LCC BM602 (ebook) | DDC 296.3–dc23
LC record available at https://lccn.loc.gov/2020027276
LC ebook record available at https://lccn.loc.gov/2020027277

ISBN 978-1-108-41543-9 Hardback
ISBN 978-1-108-40143-2 Paperback

Cambridge University Press has no responsibility for the persistence or accuracy of URLs for external or third-party internet websites referred to in this publication and does not guarantee that any content on such websites is, or will remain, accurate or appropriate.

Contents

Notes on Contributors page vii
Acknowledgements xi

1 Introduction
   STEVEN KEPNES   1

2 What is Jewish Theology?
   DAVID NOVAK   20

   PART I   BIBLICAL-RABBINIC   39

3 Jewish Biblical Theology
   MARVIN A. SWEENEY   41

4 The God of the Rabbis
   MOSHE HALBERTAL   60

5 The Theology of the Daily Liturgy
   REUVEN KIMELMAN   77

   PART II   MEDIEVAL   103

6 Maimonides' Theology
   DANIEL RYNHOLD   105

7 Law and Order: The Birth of a Nation and the Creation of the World
   DANIEL FRANK   132

8 The Mystical Theology of Kabbalah: From God to Godhead
   ADAM AFTERMAN   149

   PART III   MODERN   183

9 R. Kook: A This-Worldly Mystic
   TAMAR ROSS   185

10 Rosenzweig's *Midrashic* Speech-Acts: From Hegel and German Nationalism to a Modern-day *Ba'al Teshuvah*
    JULES SIMON 213

11 Levinas' Theological Ethics
    RICHARD A. COHEN 239

PART IV CONTEMPORARY ISSUES 265

12 The Holocaust and Jewish Theology
    MICHAEL L. MORGAN 267

13 Theology and Halakhah in Jewish Feminisms
    RONIT IRSHAI 297

14 Jewish Models of Revelation
    ALAN BRILL 316

15 Jewish Theology of Religions
    ALON GOSHEN-GOTTSTEIN 344

PART V ANALYTIC PHILOSOPHY AND THEOLOGY 373

16 Can There Be a Positive Theology?
    KENNETH SEESKIN 375

17 Theological Realism and its Alternatives in Contemporary Jewish Theology
    CASS FISHER 392

18 A Defense of Verbal Revelation
    SAMUEL FLEISCHACKER 423

19 A Constructive Jewish Theology of God and Perfect Goodness
    JEROME YEHUDA GELLMAN 453

Index 467

Notes on Contributors

Adam Afterman is Associate Professor in Jewish Philosophy and Mysticism at Tel Aviv University and Chair of the Department of Jewish Philosophy and Talmud. He is a Senior Research Fellow at the Shalom Hartman Institute Kogod Research Center for Contemporary Jewish Thought in Jerusalem and the John Paul II Center for Interreligious Dialogue. His most recent book *"And They Be One Flesh": On the Language of Mystical Union in Judaism* (2016) explored the linguistic developments within Jewish mysticism concerning the mystical union of the human and divine.

Alan Brill is the Cooperman/Ross Endowed Chair for Jewish-Christian Studies at Seton Hall University, where he teaches Jewish studies in the graduate program. Brill is the author of *Thinking God: The Mysticism of Rabbi Zadok of Lublin* (2002), *Judaism and Other Religions: Models of Understanding* (2010), and *Judaism and World Religions* (2012). He was a Fulbright Senior Scholar awardee to research and teach at Banares Hindu University in Varanasi, India, which is the subject of a recent book, *Rabbi on The Ganges: A Jewish Hindu Encounter* (2019).

Richard A. Cohen is Professor of Jewish Thought, and of Philosophy, at the University at Buffalo (SUNY). He is author of *Out of Control: Confrontations between Spinoza and Levinas* (2016), *Levinasian Meditations: Ethics, Philosophy, and Religion* (2010), *Ethics, Exegesis and Philosophy: Interpretation after Levinas* (2001), *Elevations: The Height of the Good in Rosenzweig and Levinas* (1994); editor and author of many other writings in contemporary continental philosophy and Jewish thought; and Director of the annual Levinas Philosophy Summer Seminar.

Cass Fisher is an Associate Professor in Religious Studies at the University of South Florida. He is a philosopher of religion focusing on rabbinic theology and modern Jewish thought. His first book, *Contemplative Nation: A Philosophical Account of Jewish Theological Language* (2012), presents a new model for understanding Jewish theology that emphasizes the multiple forms and functions of Jewish theological language and grounds theological reflection within religious practice. He is currently working on a second book titled, *As If It Could Be Said: Realism, Reference, and the Limits of Jewish Theological Language*, sections of which have recently appeared in *Harvard Theological Review*, *AJS Review*, and *Religions*.

Samuel Fleischacker is LAS Distinguished Professor of Philosophy at the University of Illinois in Chicago and Director of Jewish Studies there. He is the author of nine books, including two on revealed religion: *The Good and the Good Book* (2015) and *Divine Teaching and the Way of the World* (2011). He has also edited a collection entitled *Heidegger's Jewish Followers* (2008), and written on revelation for Torah.com.

Daniel Frank is Professor of Philosophy and Jewish Studies at Purdue University. Among recent books are *Spinoza on Politics* (with Jason Waller, 2016), *Jewish Philosophy Past and Present: Contemporary Responses to Classical Sources* (co-edited with Aaron Segal, 2017), and *Cambridge Critical Guide to Maimonides' Guide of the Perplexed* (co-edited with Aaron Segal, forthcoming).

Jerome Yehuda Gellman is Professor Emeritus of the Department of Philosophy at Ben-Gurion University. He has published widely on analytic philosophy of religion, Jewish theology, and philosophical topics in Hasidism. His last three books present contemporary Jewish theologies on, respectively: the Jews as the Chosen People, Torah and the critique of history, and the perfect goodness and the God of the Hebrew Bible and rabbinic literature.

Alon Goshen-Gottstein is acknowledged as one of the world's leading figures in interreligious dialogue. He is founder and director of the Elijah Interfaith Institute since 1997. His work bridges the theological and academic dimension with a variety of practical initiatives, especially involving world religious leadership. His academic work is divided between contributions to early rabbinic thought, Jewish spirituality, interfaith theory, and Jewish Theology of Religions. He has held academic posts at Hebrew University of Jerusalem and Tel Aviv University, and has served as Director of the Center for the Study of Rabbinic Thought, Beit Morasha College, Jerusalem.

Moshe Halbertal is the John and Golda Cohen Professor of Jewish Thought and Philosophy at the Hebrew University and the Gruss Professor at NYU Law School, and a member of the Israel's National Academy for Sciences and the Humanities. His latest book *The Birth of Doubt: Confronting Uncertainty in Early Rabbinic Literature* (2020) was published in the Brown Judaic Series.

Ronit Irshai is an Associate Professor in the gender studies program at Bar Ilan University and a research fellow at the Shalom Hartman Institute in Jerusalem. Her first book *Fertility and Jewish Law – Feminist Perspectives on Orthodox Responsa Literature* was published in 2012. She is now working on two new books: The first examines modern halakhic texts, in order to show how male and female identities are constructed by contemporary halakhic rulings. The second book (together with Dr. Tanya Zion-Waldox and Banna Shoughry) compares Jewish Orthodox feminism and Islamic feminism in Israel.

Steven Kepnes is Professor of World Religions and Jewish Studies and Director of Chapel House at Colgate University, Hamilton, NY. He is the author of seven books including *The Future of Jewish Theology* (2013), *Jewish Liturgical Reasoning* (2007), and *The Text As Thou: Buber's Hermeneutics* (1993).

Reuven Kimelman is Professor of Classical Judaica at Brandeis University. His Ph.D. is from Yale University. He is the author of *The Mystical Meaning of 'Lekhah Dodi' and Kabbalat Shabbat* (2003), and forthcoming *The Rhetoric of the Liturgy: A Historical and Literary Commentary to the Jewish Prayer Book*. His audio course books are *The Hidden Poetry of the Jewish Prayer Book* (2006) and *The Moral Meaning of the Bible* (2006).

Michael L. Morgan is emeritus Chancellor's Professor of Philosophy and Jewish Studies at Indiana University, Bloomington, and emeritus Grafstein Chair in Philosophy and Jewish Studies at the University of Toronto. He has also taught at Yale, Princeton, Northwestern, and Stanford. He is the author or editor of over twenty books and the author of dozens of papers on the history of philosophy and Jewish philosophy. His most recent books are *Levinas's Ethical Politics* (2016) and *The Oxford Handbook of Levinas* (2019).

David Novak is the J. Richard and Dorothy Shiff Professor of Jewish Studies and Philosophy in the University of Toronto, and President of the Union for Traditional Judaism. He is a Fellow of the Royal Society of Canada and of the American Academy for Jewish Research. Among his many books are: *Natural Law in Judaism* (2008), *Covenantal Rights* (2009), and *Athens and Jerusalem: God, Humans, and Nature* (2019) (based on his 2017 Gifford Lectures at the University of Aberdeen).

Tamar Ross is Professor Emerita of the Department of Jewish Philosophy at Bar Ilan University. She has taught in many academic and religious settings in Israel and abroad and publishes widely on various topics relating to Jewish thought. Her particular areas of interest include: contemporary challenges to traditionalist Jewish theology (including feminism, historicism, biblical criticism, and postmodernity); concepts of God, divine revelation, religious epistemology, and hermeneutics; philosophy of halakhah; the Musar movement (a modern pietist movement devoted to the development of spiritual discipline and moral conduct); and the thought of the twentieth-century mystic, Rabbi A. I. Kook.

Daniel Rynhold is Professor of Jewish Philosophy and Dean at the Bernard Revel Graduate School of Jewish Studies, Yeshiva University. He has published on numerous topics in Jewish philosophy, and is the author of *Two Models of Jewish Philosophy: Justifying One's Practices* (2005), *An Introduction to Medieval Jewish Philosophy* (2009), and (co-authored with Michael J. Harris) *Nietzsche, Soloveitchik, and Contemporary Jewish Philosophy* (2018).

Kenneth Seeskin is Professor of Philosophy and the Philip M. and Ethel Klutznick Professor of Jewish Civilization at Northwestern University. He has taught at Northwestern since 1972 and has served as Chair of the Philosophy Department as well as the Religious Studies Department. He is the author of *Searching for a Distant God* (2000), *Maimonides on the Origin of the World* (2007), and *Jewish Messianic Thoughts in an Age of Despair* (2012). His most recent publications include *Thinking about the Torah: A Philosopher Reads the Bible* (2016) and *Thinking about the Prophets: A Philosopher Reads the Bible* (2020).

Jules Simon is a Professor in the Department of Philosophy at the University of Texas at El Paso in El Paso, Texas—on the border of Mexico and the USA. As a philosopher, he writes, teaches, and lectures in the areas of phenomenology, ethical theory, aesthetics, and Jewish philosophy. He has published extensively in the area of Jewish philosophy, including an original monograph, *Art and Responsibility: A Phenomenology of the Diverging Paths of Rosenzweig and Heidegger* (2011), two edited books focusing on ethics and genocide—*History, Religion, and Meaning: American Reflections on the Holocaust and Israel* (2000) and *The Double Binds of Ethics after the Holocaust: Salvaging the Fragments* (2009)—and a Festschrift for John Haddox, *Thought and Social Engagement in the Mexican-American Philosophy of John H. Haddox: A Collection of Critical Appreciations* (2010). He is currently finishing a co-translation of Franz Rosenzweig's *Hegel and the State* from German into English with his son, Josiah Simon.

Marvin A. Sweeney is Professor of Hebrew Bible at the Claremont School of Theology. He is the author of sixteen volumes in the fields of Bible and Jewish Studies, such as *Tanak: A Theological and Critical Introduction to the Jewish Bible* (2012) and *Reading the Bible After the Shoah: Engaging Holocaust Theology* (2008). His latest volume is *Jewish Mysticism: From Ancient Times Through Today* (2020). He currently serves as Past-President of the National Association of Professors of Hebrew.

Acknowledgements

I would like to thank first all the contributors to this volume, who have written wonderful pieces in a timely manner and to the highest of academic standards. I also need to thank Beatrice Rehl, editor at Cambridge University Press, together with Mary Bongiovi, and the copy editor Mary Morton. Special gratitude is due to Amy Sommers of Chapel House at Colgate University and its Fund for the Study of World Religions. Michael Fishbane was helpful in the initial conceptualization of this volume and there were two exciting seminars at the Association of Jewish Studies meetings in December 2014 and 2015 that Cass Fisher and I put together, as well as small conferences at Chapel House, Colgate University in August 2015 and one at the University of Illinois-Chicago that Sam Fleischacker organized in July of 2018. I also want to thank artist and Rabbi Matt Berkowitz for the cover design *Va'nitzak* "And We Cried Out," from his *Lovell Haggadah*, 2005.

The topic of God and theology is infinite so that any attempt at summary is bound to fail. This is an admittedly limited and even idiosyncratic attempt at a one-volume introduction that will hopefully inspire other future work on this very important and somewhat neglected subject in Jewish studies. Most authors follow tradition and Hebrew grammar in referring to God as "He" although this should not be taken as advocating the maleness of YHWH who, philosophically, transcends body and gender.

1 Introduction
STEVEN KEPNES

The reader will find here, in this *Cambridge Companion to Jewish Theology*, essays by leading Jewish Studies scholars that display the Jewish theological tradition as long, sustained, complex, and deep. This collection aims to cover the full historical span of Judaism from the biblical through to the contemporary periods. Each essay is a gem filled with not only an overview of a topic that employs and reviews the best in contemporary scholarship, but also brings important new insights to it. One thing that will become obvious for the reader is the variety of theological approaches that Jews have taken to presenting and understanding God. For example, on the crucial issue of revelation, Alan Brill presents us with seven models of revelation in modern Jewish theology.

I should also say, from the outset, that Jewish theology encompasses not only the issue of the nature of God but also the dynamic of interrelations between God and humans and God and the world. I have attempted to focus the attention of my authors mainly on God but, quite naturally, a number of authors also discuss the relations between God and humans, God and the world. Here, for example, a figure like Emmanuel Levinas stands out for wanting to focus almost exclusively on ethical relations between humans.

Although this volume intends to give a sense of the long history of Jewish theology, the reader will see an emphasis on modern and more recent times. Thus there are three sections here, one on modern figures, one on contemporary issues such as the Holocaust and feminism, and a final section on analytic philosophy and "positive or constructive" Jewish theology. This is done both because of the background of your editor and because of the recent flourishing of work in Jewish theology, which has been somewhat suppressed until recently. This is true certainly in relation to modern thinkers and issues, but it is also true in relation to ancient materials.

2   Steven Kepnes

Thus Marvin Sweeney tells us in "Jewish Biblical Theology" that it is a "relatively new field within the larger context of Jewish thought" (p. 41). This is so because of a number of reasons. First, the field of "Biblical Theology" was originally called "Old Testament Theology," which "originated within the context of Christian dogmatic theology" (p. 41). This theology included in it many anti-Jewish prejudices about the religious limitations of biblical law and other Israelite religious practices and the superiority of Christian grace and other Christian doctrines. Jewish scholars needed to identify, sort through, and rectify these Christian prejudices and place biblical theology on a new footing. Second, although much of traditional Jewish theology is based on interpreting the Hebrew Bible (Tanak), little of it takes into account the type of historical, philological, archeological, and literary critical insights available to the contemporary Bible scholar. Therefore, the field of Jewish biblical theology is "new" both in its attempt to investigate the Tanak without a Christian interpretive lens and in its utilization of academic methods of biblical scholarship.

THE STRUCTURE OF THIS BOOK

Given the long history of the Jewish theological tradition, together with a recent flourishing of new approaches, methods, and questions, it is not easy to put together a one-volume Companion to Jewish Theology. One can imagine different ways to organize such a volume: historically, geographically, thematically, and organizationally based on significant figures, texts, or issues. In this volume, I roughly follow a historical trajectory with an emphasis especially on the modern period and contemporary issues.

The volume begins with a general discussion of "What is Theology?" by David Novak followed by three essays that focus on traditional materials: biblical, rabbinic, and liturgical. We then move to the medieval period with two contributions on Maimonides' theology and one on Kabbalah or Jewish mysticism. The second part of the volume focuses on the modern period. We begin with essays on Abraham Isaac Kook, Franz Rosenzweig, and Emmanual Levinas. This is followed by discussions of four issues: Holocaust, feminism, revelation, and Judaism and world religions. The final section engages analytic philosophy with four essays on "constructive" Jewish theology.

Given my charge to attempt to cover the entire theological tradition from the Bible forward, there are obvious holes and extremely important figures, texts, and movements that I have left out. Any knowledgeable Jewish scholar can see these holes, imagine a different structure, and point to figures omitted or question those included. Here, I can only say that the figures and topics collected here represent one necessarily incomplete collection without any pretense to be exhaustive of the vast field of Jewish theology.

Having very briefly described the structure and nature of the chapters contained herein, I will now attempt to place them within both the larger intellectual contexts of Western thought and within the Jewish tradition. This begins with a defense of Jewish theology as a Jewish religious form together with an engagement with responses to the challenge that the modern Enlightenment posed to theology. I will also discuss the perennial issue of "negative theology" in Judaism, which poses another kind of challenge to Jewish theology. Here, I review some of the discussions in contemporary philosophical movements such as philosophical hermeneutics and analytical philosophy that are providing new ways to respond to negative theology with positive theologies. In what follows, the reader will often find references to the essays in this volume. Although this is not always done sequentially, in the order in which they appear, it is my hope that the reader will receive both one version of what one could call the "story of Jewish theology" and, also, a basic sense of what is contained in this volume.

JEWISH THEOLOGY?

Any book on Jewish theology must, unfortunately, include some discussion of the validity of the enterprise. This is because the assertion that Judaism contains a long and sustained tradition of Jewish theology has been questioned both within and without Judaism. And one way that this book responds to queries about the status of theology in Judaism is simply by displaying the theological riches that exist.

But some further argument must be given, if only because Jews themselves often deny that Judaism has a theology. If some do acknowledge a few theological doctrines and treatises, they often then point to the massive attention in Judaism given to Jewish law, halakhah, as opposed to theology. The study, discussion, systematization, and application of Jewish law certainly takes up more space than theology in the sacred texts and commentaries of Judaism. Furthermore, one can say that the covenant with God is built more on behaviors than beliefs. Certainly, the fact that Christianity focuses so much on theology and much less on law is another important factor here, with both Jews and Christians seeking to distinguish themselves from the other by asserting their different religious commitments—one to law and the other to theology. However, even if we take the distinction of law and theology seriously, the reader will see that for Jews there is an intricate connection between law and theology and many Jewish theologians seek to make that connection explicit. In this collection, David Novak argues that Jewish theology must have essentially to do with law, which means it needs to explain the best "grounds for intelligent obedience to the law," p. 23. Daniel Frank sees the connection between theology and law in the parallel between the creation of the world with its natural laws and the creation of the nation of Israel with its social and religious laws. And Ronit Irshai argues that feminist theology cannot avoid halakhah if it is to be relevant to the larger enterprise of Judaism.

But to continue on the issue of the question of theology, I would note that not only Jewish theology, but Christian theology as well, has received less scholarly attention in the contemporary non-sectarian university.[1] In the university, theology is sometimes seen as antithetical to the value-free standards of scholarly objectivity and an early modern fear of the proselytization of religion has surprising staying power even in the contemporary university.

Certainly, there has been significant attention to Jewish theology especially in the medieval period, but also in modernity. One strategy to make Jewish theology "kosher" for the academy has been to label it "Jewish philosophy" instead of theology. But even with this, the task of the scholar has largely been to trace the path of Jewish theology from Greek, Arabic, and Latin Christian materials to Jewish theological expressions, as well as placing Jewish philosophy and theology in its historical context. In this way, Jewish theology becomes a matter of intellectual history rather than a normative and constructive task of discerning and discussing the truth value of Jewish theological claims.

In reviewing the relation of Jewish theology to the academy, it is instructive to look at the example of the nineteenth-century German case. Jewish scholars who launched the Wissenschaft des Judentums or "The Science of Judaism" in Germany clearly wanted to distinguish their study from the ahistorical, reverential, and excessively apologetic

---

[1] Although it may not be surprising that Jewish theology finds little place in the modern secular university, even in Jewish rabbinical seminaries and Yeshivot (traditional institutions of study), Jewish theology is not well represented.

practices of traditional Jewish education. They sought to employ the most exacting, historical, and documentary methods of the academy to find, translate, and annotate the myriad of Jewish texts, commentaries, and treatises that were largely unknown in the non-Jewish academic world. At the same time, as George Y. Kohler of Bar-Ilan has shown, they saw their work as contributing not only to building the field of academic Jewish studies but also to the construction of a new form of universal and humanistic Judaism for the modern Jew.[2] Kohler argues that the focus was, precisely, on theology as an alternative to traditional halakhic practice on the one hand and a purely secular Judaism on the other. In addition, Kohler attempts to show that the models for a theological Judaism were not taken from Protestant Christian sources, as many have assumed,[3] but instead, from the medieval theological sources that the Wissenschaft scholars had unearthed.[4]

Contemporary Jewish Studies in Europe, America, and Israel has continued the historical, philological, and cataloguing activities of classic German Wissenschaft des Judentums adding to it sociological, ethnographic, and, recently, cultural studies, while largely dropping the theological agenda and normative concerns of the nineteenth-century German Jewish scholars. However, in this volume, a number of thinkers take up the later tasks again.

For an example of a normative presentation of Jewish theology we have a fine statement in the first chapter of this book by one of the leading theologians of our generation, David Novak. In "What is Theology?" Novak argues that the task of the Jewish theologian is to explicate Judaism in a way that "best intends its truth." p. 20. For Novak, theology as a normative practice involves "doing theology" as "a participant" from the inside (p. 20) of the Jewish community, rather than the study of theology or "talking about" theology from the outside. Still, while attempting to do theology from the inside, Novak's work

---

[2] George Y. Kohler, "Judaism Buried or Revitalised?, Wissenschaft des Judentums in Nineteenth Century Germany – Impact, Actuality, and Applicability Today," in Daniel Lasker, ed., *Jewish Thought and Jewish Belief*, (Beer Sheva: BGU Press, 2012) 27–63.

[3] See Leora Batnitzy for the position that highlights the role Christian thought plays in modern Judaism, *How Judaism Became a Religion* (Princeton: Princeton University Press, 2012).

[4] While Maimonides is the usual suspect pointed to for the origins of a modern Jewish theology, Adam Shear attempts to show how central is the figure of Yehudah Halevi, in *The Kuzari and the Shaping of Jewish Identity* (Cambridge: Cambridge University Press, 2008).

engages with the "outside" frameworks of classic and modern philosophy and also welcomes the comparative theology project wherein Jewish theology is placed in dialogue with Christian theology. The last section of this book on analytic Jewish theology has additional contributions of the normative type.

JEWISH THEOLOGY AS HERMENEUTICAL

In the later part of the twentieth century, especially in the US, spurred on by the celebrated "turn to language" in philosophy in both Continental and analytic thought, a more profound way to speak of Jewish theology and its difference from Christian theology has been to say that Jews do, after all, have theology, but that Jewish theology is different from Christian theology. Here, the difference is often described in terms of the asymmetrical role that Greek philosophy plays in Christianity and Judaism. Thus, Christian theology embraced Greek philosophy from the outset and Jewish theology, especially in the rabbinic period, eschewed Greek philosophy and embraced narrative strategies, such as those seen in the Bible, and the forms of exegesis and commentary.

Therefore, the argument goes, Jewish theology is more apt to follow narrative forms like parable and allegory than the syllogistic, systematic, and propositional forms of Christian theology. Given the Jewish focus on the Torah as the central expression of God's word and will and the nexus of the connection between God and Jew, the interpretation of the Torah is the central vehicle of Jewish theology and not philosophy. Thus some have argued that Jewish theology is interpretive or "hermeneutical theology" rather than "philosophical theology." So where Christian theology takes the form of systematic propositions about God, Jewish theology takes the form of commentary, or in rabbinic terms, "midrash."

In accordance with the hermeneutic theory of Hans Georg Gadamer and Paul Ricoeur,[5] hermeneutical theology interprets older texts for the needs of the contemporary situation. Thus, a hermeneutical approach to theology attempts to apply the truths of Torah to contemporary life. In this way, the sacred text remains alive and relevant, and God's word

---

[5] Hans Georg Gadamer, *Truth and Method* (New York: Crossroads, 1982); Paul Ricoeur, *Interpretation Theory* (Fort Worth: Texas Christian University Press, 1976).

becomes a living word that calls out across the generations. In his essay on Franz Rosenzweig, Jules Simon argues that the dynamic quality of Rosenzweig's theology is found precisely in its hermeneutic and "midrashic" quality. But we see the hermeneutical method appears in many of the other contributions on contemporary theology in this volume. Alan Brill reviews hermeneutical approaches to theology as his seventh model for revelation (p. 337ff.).

JEWISH PHILOSOPHICAL THEOLOGY

However, the claim that Jewish theology is hermeneutical and not properly philosophical is both too simple and inaccurate. This is because Greek and Western philosophy has played a not insignificant role in Jewish theology. Indeed, beginning with Philo in the first century and then Saadia Gaon in the ninth, through the great period of medieval philosophy, to modern and contemporary eras, Jewish thinkers have developed forms of theology based on propositions, deductive logic, correspondence and coherence theories of truth, and the full panoply of methods and logics found in Western philosophy.

Indeed, it is easy to argue, as many have, that the most sustained, disciplined, complex, and articulate forms of Jewish theology are found in the medieval period where Neoplatonic and Neoaristotelian philosophical paradigms were married to Jewish biblical and rabbinic thought in extremely creative ways that resulted in both the system of Maimonides and the Kabbalah. Here, in this collection, I would direct the reader to the essays on Jewish medieval theology by Daniel Frank, Daniel Rynhold, and Kenneth Seeskin, and also to that on the Kabbalah by Adam Afterman.

In the modern period, Enlightenment thinkers, especially Immanuel Kant, had a central role in Jewish theological formulations. And this resulted in an extremely influential form of theology often referred to as "Ethical Monotheism" with leading figures being Abraham Geiger, Hermann Cohen, Leo Baeck, and a significant group in Great Britain as well as in the United States.[6] Today a relatively new form of Jewish theology is being developed by Jewish theologians trained in

---

[6] Here we could include Solomon Schechter, J. H. Hertz, and C. G. Montefiore. Leora Batnitzky has a good discussion of Ethical Monotheism in her *Idolatry and Representation* (Princeton: Princeton University Press, 2000), ch. 1.

contemporary analytic philosophy. Here I would direct the reader to the contributions by Fisher, Fleischacker, and Gellman.

Certainly, not the least of the contributions of analytic philosophy to Jewish theology has been to advance the argument, implicit in the Tanak and rabbinic texts, and explicit in medieval Jewish thought, that Jewish theology deserves to be seen as a form of knowledge and not a matter of subjective opinion, communal myth, or non-rational thinking. Jewish theology has an important epistemological dimension and endeavors to make normative truth claims that deserve to take their place alongside other philosophical and religious epistemologies.

THE ENLIGHTENMENT CHALLENGE TO THEOLOGY

In some way the recent attempt to argue that theology deserves to be considered a form of knowledge was required by the severe challenge of Enlightenment thinkers to this very claim. In the eighteenth century, Locke, Hume, and Kant argued that philosophy needed to limit itself to what it could know with certitude on the basis of empirical science and a purified reason that was limited to articulating presuppositions of thinking and physical laws on the model of mathematics. In short, the Enlightenment sought to destroy medieval metaphysics with the result that theology of all kinds was presented as without rational warrant or justification. This meant that theological knowledge was false knowledge and it was the duty of the enlightened rational man to deny it. Especially, in Germany, where the most creative modern Jewish philosopher-theologians lived, the legacy of Kant's critique of religion had a very important effect that relegated all theological beliefs to the unknowable realm of the *noumena* and focused philosophy on the phenomenal realm alone.

It is important to say that the Kantian critique did not destroy Jewish theology. Kant left theology enough avenues to survive and play a productive role in Western culture and in the Jewish community, specifically. These avenues were first ethical (and then aesthetic), so that Judaism became, as previously mentioned, "Ethical Monotheism." In the words of one of the greatest representatives of this school, Hermann Cohen, Judaism is the origin of a "religion of reason" and its essence is its practical reason or ethics which makes Judaism best suited to provide not only Jews, but non-Jews as well, with a moral beacon for the modern world.

Following the Enlightenment hope of creating more democratic and culturally varied societies, post-Enlightenment Jewish theologies focused Jewish energies on issues of individual human rights and social justice. Like many Europeans in the early twentieth century, many Jews were attracted to the moral vision of socialism which they saw as a revival of the vision of the Israelite prophets. Both socialism and the vision of the prophets was then very much part of early Zionism. We see the strong emphasis on human rights and social ethics in many of the essays in this volume, but especially in those on Levinas and the feminist theologies covered by Ronit Irshai.

Certainly one of the most revolutionary and significant movements of contemporary Judaism is Jewish Feminism which begins with a critique of Judaism as patriarchal and religiously inhospitable to women, but then moves to develop highly creative new forms of Jewish theology that are both sensitive to the spiritual needs of women and seek continuity with Jewish tradition. The French feminist philosopher Julia Kristeva has said that the most compelling issues of culture in the twenty-first century revolve around matters of sexuality and gender. Jews have taken a central role in addressing these issues both in Judaism and the wider culture. Irshai's essay reviews just a few of the important ways in which this is being done in Jewish theology and also in Jewish law.

However, as powerful as the move to ethics in Jewish theology has been, the project to reduce the great textual, interpretive, legal, and ritual aspects of Judaism to ethics alone has its obvious drawbacks. It is spiritually quite thin and dry and it also fails to take into account the significant non-ethical or supra-ethical "holy" aspects of Judaism. This has led Jews, and also Christians, to explore aesthetics, textuality, and the "symbolic" realm along with mysticism as alternative ways to articulate a modern "post-Enlightenment" theology and religion. We can also include the earlier mention of hermeneutical theologies as a contemporary offshoot of the aesthetic strategy. Although there are some Jewish theologians that stay fairly close to ethics as the central vehicle of Jewish expression in the modern period, many have explored both ethical and aesthetic (and hermeneutical) strategies in their theologies. This we see particularly in Martin Buber, Abraham Isaac Kook, and Franz Rosenzweig.

NEGATIVE AND POSITIVE JEWISH THEOLOGIES

Another important issue for Jewish theology that is covered in this collection is the issue of "negative theology" and its opposite "positive theology." For examples of positive theology one need only look to the Hebrew Bible where God is portrayed with positive attributes such as power, knowledge, wisdom, and everlastingness. In the Bible, God is described also as walking, talking, loving, caring, judging, saving. Furthermore, at times, God is described as having arms, fingers, a face, and other body parts. Yehudah Halevi, the great medieval theologian and poet, described this God simply as the God of Abraham, Isaac, and Jacob.

However, the Bible also warns Israel against making images of God and the second commandment against idols inserts a strong aniconic tradition in Judaism. This tradition is developed in the Babylonian Talmud in Tractate Avodah Zarah and other places, but it received its most developed exposition in Maimonides' thought. Here, Maimonides sought to severely limit not only iconic but also conceptual expressions for God. Thus we have Maimonides' "negative theology."

Negative theology, in its first stage, states that one should not speak of God as having positive attributes of power, wisdom, eternality, etc., but one should say God is not powerless, not ignorant, not temporal, or embodied. However, in its full-blown expression, even these negative statements are prohibited because they suggest that God does, indeed, have positive attributes that compare, if only by negation, to human ones. As Daniel Rynhold says in his essay on Maimonides' theology: "It is important ... to specify the precise nature of the negation to which Maimonides refers, for clearly an ordinary negation would simply lead us back to the positive attribute that we had intended to avoid" (p. 123). Rynhold continues, "when we speak of God therefore, we are to take any attribution of an essential attribute as a negation in this sense. To say that God is not-dead, is not to positively describe Him as having 'life,' but to eliminate him from the category of things that can be living or dead" (p. 123). Finally, Rynhold explains that negative theology is a statement about the limitations of language itself: "When taken to its logical conclusion this means that human language is simply inadequate for representing God" (p. 123).

NEGATIVE THEOLOGY IN EXISTENTIALISM AND LEVINAS

Given the towering position of Maimonides in Jewish thought and theology, the legacy of negative theology extends into the modern period. We clearly see it in the thought of Hermann Cohen who argues that God's Oneness means that He is "unique," that is to say, essentially different from all that is. But, a different form of negative theology emerges in Jewish Existentialism which casts doubts on the ability of language to capture the divine reality. We see this in the work of Martin Buber who continued the tradition of negative theology by suggesting that God, as "Eternal Thou," could not be "expressed but only addressed."[7] By this he means that we can only speak *to* God but not speak *about* God. In Buber's terms, we can only address God in the second person, as "You" for instance in the standard blessing "Blessed are You." But we cannot speak *about* God, since that involves assigning God attributes and qualities. Indeed, all speech about God in the third person—He is x, y, z—and all theological formulations that attempt to describe God are to be prohibited. These formulations are prohibited since they turn the "Eternal Thou" into an object, in Buber's terms an "It," a thing, that can be encompassed by human terms.

Like many German romantic and existential thinkers of the nineteenth and early twentieth century, Buber was highly influenced by mystical accounts of God as infinite, ineffable, "nothing," and the mystical feeling and experience of the human as equally ineffable. Indeed, we can say that Existentialism liked to substitute the words "feeling," "experience," "encounter" for thought in Jewish theology. Alan Brill in his contribution articulates well the Buberian understanding of God in his sixth model of Revelation which he calls "revelation without content" (p. 335ff.)

Many others followed Buber with modern forms of negative theology, such as Abraham Joshua Heschel who spoke of the experiences of the "Sublime," "Wonder," and "Awe" in the presence of God.[8] As Samuel Fleischacker notes in this collection, Heschel wrote that "the nature of revelation is ineffable," and "human language will never be able to portray" it.[9]

Levinas, following in the ethical tradition of Kant and educated by the phenomenology of Husserl, expresses negative theology in a different way by arguing that "First Philosophy" is ethics. For

---

[7] Martin Buber, *I and Thou* [1923], trans. R. G. Smith (New York: Scribner, 1986), 81.
[8] Abraham Joshua Heschel, *God in Search of Man* (New York: Farrar, Straus & Giroux, 1955).
[9] Ibid., 184–5, as quoted in Fleischacker (p. 425) in this collection. We can summarize the theologies of Buber and Heschel by saying that they are positive on God but negative on theology as an expression of God. To capture this distinction, Cass Fisher, in this collection, refers to Buber and Heschel as "theo-realists" (p. 399) but not "theological realists."

Levinas all forms of theology that take us away from a focus on the needs of the suffering human "Other" are false. Richard A. Cohen, in his essay, makes it very clear that Levinas stands against all forms of Jewish metaphysics and mysticism and even epistemology. For Levinas these are detours that take us away from what he sees as the central quest of Judaism for interpersonal ethics and social justice.

Given that the twentieth century was witness to two world wars, the Holocaust, and many genocidal movements against minority populations, Jewish thinkers attempted to use the absolute moral standpoint of God and the ethical commands of the Torah as warrants to direct the energies of Jews and all humans toward practical moral issues in social and political life.

What all this meant and still means for many Jewish thinkers is that theologians need to practice a radical critique of traditional Jewish metaphysics and God talk and a redirection of thought toward action. This action is not behaving in accord with the mitsvot of the Torah, but with ethical, social, and political action in the world. Here, we are certainly far from Maimonidean negative theology. For Maimonides, negative theology only refers to the limitations of human language and concepts; it intends no limitations about God. Indeed, negative theology is an invitation to deeper and more profound contemplation of the grandeur and glory of God. And Maimonides also sees performance of mitsvot as an essential way for Jews to perfect themselves morally and to spiritually approach God.

NEGATIVE THEOLOGY, HOLOCAUST, AND MODERNITY

In his important book titled *Negative Theology as Jewish Modernity*, Michael Fagenblat[10] tries to show that the tradition of negative theology lives on in a different form in modernity. As he says, the Jews of modernity have established *"the via negativa"* as a "distinctively Jewish feature"[11] of Jewish culture, both secular and religious, in the modern period. Fagenblat describes this distinctive Jewish feature as "involving the negation, denial, or refusal of ultimate grounds and thereby the discovery of mysterious ruptures constitutive of its own legitimacy, authority, and even 'identity.'"[12] Therefore, Fagenblat

---

[10] Michael Fagenblat, ed., *Negative Theology as Jewish Modernity* (Bloomington: Indiana University Press, 2017).
[11] Ibid., 1.   [12] Ibid.

argues that Judaism for modern Jews, and for many Christians and secularists as well, is "negative theology." So that the mark of Judaism in modern life becomes precisely the denial of meaning, rational foundations, and even self-identity. Negative terms, such as absence, difference, deconstruction, abyss, lacunae, exile, then take center stage as expressions of Judaism in modernity.

Certainly for many people it was the Holocaust or Shoah that really marked the end of traditional metaphysics and theology and ushered us into the age of what Richard Rubenstein called "the death of God" and what Fagenblat calls the new *via negativa*. In the essay by Michael Morgan in our collection on "Holocaust Theology," Morgan quotes Rubenstein's famous statement: "I reached a theological point of no return – If I believed in God as the omnipotent author of the historical drama and Israel as His Chosen People, I had to accept ... [the] conclusion that it was God's will that Hitler committed six million Jews to slaughter. I could not possibly believe in such a God nor could I believe in Israel as the chosen people of God after Auschwitz."[13] Rubenstein's purposely provocative proclamation in 1962, together with the work of Elie Wiesel and also Emil Fackenheim, shocked many Jewish thinkers to respond to what can only be called a collective Jewish theological crisis. This call for a post-Holocaust theology then initiated a series of highly creative theological responses, a number of which Morgan presents here. Among a very long list of distinguished post-Holocaust thinkers, Morgan reviews the theologies of Eliezer Berkovits, Irving Greenberg, and Hans Jonas.

JEWISH THEOLOGY AND WORLD RELIGIONS

If the feminists, ethicists, and post-Holocaust theologians tried to focus Jewish energies on contemporary issues in the world, another issue that needed to be addressed was the other religions in the world. If there is one thing that the academic study of Judaism shows us about Jewish theology, it is that it was never fashioned in a vacuum, sealed off from the other religions and theologies of the world. Certainly, there are unique elements in Jewish theology that we must recognize, describe, and celebrate. Yet, from its origins in the Bible, we see Jewish religious leaders in relationship to other religions and worldviews, be they

---

[13] Richard Rubenstein, *After Auschwitz* (Indianapolis: Bobbs Merrill, 1966), 46, as quoted in Morgan in this collection (p. 268).

Canaanite, Egyptian, or Greek. And there is no doubt that Christian and Islamic theologies have had an extremely profound affect on Jewish theology. Thus, this collection necessarily contains an essay on Jewish theology and the world's religions. We are fortunate to have one of the leading figures in this discussion, Alon Goshen-Gottstein, with his, "A Theology of Religions."

In the Jewish world, the crucial issue here is the extent to which other religions are considered forms of idolatry or as "valid" religious expressions. The tradition includes two extreme positions—one is that all other religions are idolatrous, and the other is that if religions follow the seven universal ethical laws of Noah or the " Laws of Noah" (BTalmud Sanhedrin 59a) their adherents can be considered "righteous gentiles."

The most creative part of Goshen-Gottstein's essay is his review of the "pluralist" views of Rabbi Abraham Isaac Kook. Through R. Kook, Goshen-Gottstein is able to provide the justification for the creative enterprise of "comparative theology" that many Jewish theologians have recently entered into. This work of theological dialogue highlights both the differences and similarities between Jewish theology and the other theologies of the world's religions.[14] Goshen-Gottstein himself, through his *Elijah Institute*, has helped initiate important and interesting dialogue between Jewish theology and Hindu and Buddhist thinkers. This dialogue represents an extremely promising avenue for future interfaith relations between Jews and the religions of the East.

POSITIVE THEOLOGY

In his book, Fagenblat is not only interested in describing modern Jewish negative theology, but also in investigating and questioning it. He suggests a question which I find particularly compelling and which has led me to want to end this collection with some of the constructive work of those involved with "positive Jewish theology." Fagenblat's question is this: "Has the modern pairing of Judaism with negativity

---

[14] See *Jewish Theology and World Religions*, eds. Alon Goshen-Gottstein and Eugene Korn (Oxford: Littman Library of Jewish Civilization, 2012); Alan Brill, *Judaism and World Religions* (New York: Palgrave Macmillan, 2012). For a more hermeneutical approach, see Jacob Goodson, *The Journal of Scriptural Reasoning* (online) and M. Dakake, T. Greggs, and S. Kepnes, *Handbook of Scriptural Reasoning* (forthcoming).

reached a point of exhaustion? And if so, what comes after negative theology?"[15]

Here, we can learn a little bit from history. For what came after Maimonides' negative theology was a variety of forms of positive theology in the constructive work of his successors Levi ben Gershon or Gersonides (1288–1344) and also the Spanish Jewish thinkers Hasdai Crescas (1340–1411) and Joseph Albo (1380–1444).

Although the rational interpretation of Judaism by Maimonides managed to find its way into Judaism, many rabbinic figures sought to mute the effects of negative theology by pointing to the Torah itself as a central repository of positive images for God and presentations of God as wise, powerful, living, just, merciful etc. Thus the simplest response to negative theology is the positive theology present in the Torah revealed by God at Sinai.

Moshe Halbertal in his chapter, "The God of the Rabbis," asks the obvious question of the Jewish philosopher: "Who wants to be in relationship with an unmoved mover, with a being that cannot be changed and is not a responsive entity" (p. 75). Halbertal shows how, long before medieval philosophy, the rabbis of the mishna and midrash "deepened" and "extended" the tradition of biblical anthropomorphism with images of God as teacher and even servant (p. 67). This was done, he suggests, to present God as a "relational subject" with whom the Jew could interact.

We can also look to the tradition of Kabbalah, with its images, symbol, parables, and biblical interpretations (e.g., Zohar), as a constructive and positive response to the negative theology of Maimonides. Kabbalah, indeed, attempts to offer multiple positive avenues for the conceptualization of God that make it the ideal foil to Jewish philosophy.

The reader will find, in the essay on Kabbalah by Afterman, a splendid review of the central themes of Kabbalistic theology that culminates with an argument against the great pioneer in scholarship on Kabbalah, Gershom Scholem. Afterman argues, contra Scholem,

---

[15] Fagenblat, *Ibid.*, p.15. Jacques Derrida, the master of deconstruction and one of the leaders of the postmodern denial of meaning and the powers of reason to give us truth, calls deconstruction "a catastrophic consciousness" and he also argues that deconstruction marked the "end of philosophy," Jacques Derrida, *Writing and Difference*, translated by A. Bass (Chicago: University of Chicago Press, 1967), 3. On this, I think that Derrida was correct. But endings always call for new beginnings, the negative calls out to the positive. And so it is predictable that we are seeing, after the rash of negative theologies, the beginnings of creative new positive Jewish theologies.

who tried to preserve the distance between humans and God, that some Kabbalists developed theologies and practices of *unio mystica* or mystical union with God. Afterman also shows how the Kabbalists pushed beyond the philosophical notions of God by developing a concept of a "Godhead," that is, a God with multiple faces, aspects, and qualities.

In the contemporary world of Jewish theology one finds strong interest in Kabbalah for its positive theological portraits of God and its many concrete ways of envisioning the relationship between God and Jew. The Kabbalistic assertion that the dynamic attributes of God can be found in the very body of the human being and the idea that human action, in fulfilling mitsvot, can affect the "divine body" present a dramatic portrait of divine immanence and embodiment.

Here, I would direct the reader to the extremely complex but also illuminating essay by Tamar Ross on Abraham Isaac Kook, whom she calls a "this-worldly mystic." Kook, Ross says, attempts to synthesize Kabbalistic theology with modern philosophy to bring Jewish spirituality to the world. Ross speaks, at the end of her essay, of how attuned Kook is to the need to craft a theology that stresses the themes of theological immanence and embodied spirituality. For this he seeks to highlight the continuities between Kabbalah and contemporary science.

The move in hermeneutical theology toward Jewish texts, interpretation, and commentaries presents another avenue by which to construct positive Jewish theologies in allowing individual Jews to find meaning in biblical and rabbinic figures and extend links between older Jewish texts and the contemporary world. Perhaps no figures were more significant to the construction of a hermeneutic Jewish theology than Martin Buber and Franz Rosenzweig in their joint work on Bible translation and interpretation.[16]

The chapter by Jules Simon focuses specifically on Rosenzweig and his early contribution to a hermeneutical theology in *The Star of Redemption*. In addition, the chapter by Irshai on feminist theology

---

[16] Michael Fishbane articulated and developed the hermeneutical approach to theology in *Sacred Attunement: A Jewish Theology* (Chicago: University of Chicago Press, 2008). We also see it in feminist theology which Irshai shows us in this collection. And although the essay by Richard A. Cohen focuses mainly on Levinas' philosophical essays which stress the import of ethics, Levinas' Jewish writings, especially on the Talmud, present brilliant new interpretations of select talmudic *sugayot*, where some of his ethical insights are married to rabbinic thought: Emmanuel Levinas, *Nine Talmudic Readings* (Bloomington: Indiana University Press, 1994). Cf. Brill's seventh form of revelation in which he uses Levinas as an example of hermeneutical theology.

discusses a particularly creative group of female theologians who have endeavored to fashion fascinating feminist midrashim about God and women's spiritual experience.

A very important old/new avenue for Jewish theology is found in perhaps the most significant Jewish theological book after the Tanak, the Siddur or Prayerbook. In his chapter "The Theology of the Daily Liturgy," Reuven Kimelman provides convincing evidence that the Siddur contains the "richest vein for mining [Jewish] theology ... It shows how Judaism affirms its belief system by liturgizing it" p. 77. Kimelman masterfully employs historical and literary analyses of the daily prayer service to argue that the liturgy presents a theology of the "Sovereignty of God" (p. 77).

As I have said before, the hermeneutical strategy in Jewish theology allows the Kantian point that philosophy has no business with the articulation of knowledge of God in the traditional epistemological sense. Hermeneutics then turns to language and aesthetics for its theological categories. However, for some, this strategy is still lacking in that it cedes the grounding of theology in rational thought and abandons the epistemological task of defining theology as knowledge and the normative quest for theological truth. Taking on these epistemological and normative tasks is another way of articulating the project of a positive theology.

ANALYTIC JEWISH THEOLOGY

The end of this book includes a series of essays which use analytic philosophy instead of hermeneutics to present a positive theology. These tend to focus on epistemological and normative rather than textual and interpretive issues. The section begins with Kenneth Seeskin who discusses resources in Maimonides, the master of negative theology himself, to talk about God as "author" with "will and intelligence" and not merely cause of the universe. Seeskin also reviews Kant's practical theology, and Cohen's notions of "correlation" between God and human, to discuss how far traditional notions of reason can be stretched toward a positive and rational Jewish theology.

Cass Fisher then introduces us to a relatively new theological movement called "Theological Realism." Theological Realism, simply put, is the claim that God is real, independent of thought about Him. But, as Fisher suggests, Theological Realism goes beyond this simple assertion to "an inquiry into the power and limits of theological language and our ability to acquire knowledge of God" (p. 392). For Fisher, then, it is important to investigate both Theological Realism and its alternatives.

Given many modern attempts to reduce God to the natural world, beginning with Spinoza and running to Mordechai Kaplan, Theological Realism also involves the assertion that God is independent of the world. Theological Realism harks back to medieval theology with its notions of God as separate from but also creator of the world, but, as Fisher shows, many contemporary analytic philosophers are trying to support a Theological Realism through more contemporary philosophical resources.

The reader will find additional statements of positive theology in this section in Fleischacker's attempt to resurrect the view of God as giving a verbal revelation—the Torah—to the Jewish people. Fleischacker argues that modern views, like those of Buber and Heschel, that present revelation as non-verbal or wordless, together with the historical critical presentation of the Bible as composed by schools of human authors, undermine Jewish belief and mitsvot and "make it very hard to keep the [Jewish] tradition alive" (p. 424). Fleischacker points out that the basis of the "wordless theology" view is found in nineteenth-century German Romanticism and Religious Existentialism whose views of an "uninterpreted," "non-linguistic" experience have been radically challenged. He uses a series of arguments from analytic philosophers Willard van Orman Quine and Donald Davidson that challenge the very notion of "non-linguistic" or "prelinguistic" forms of communication.[17] Through these arguments, Fleischacker aims to articulate "what the advantages are" of the linguistic view of revelation for Jewish theology and Judaism (p. 425).

Rather than speak of a positive theology, Yehuda Gellman refers to his work as "constructive theology." The aim of this "is to construct Jewish theology for contemporary times" (p. 453). In his essay, Gellman performs a close reading of the central *"Shema"* prayer in the context of other biblical and rabbinic texts. The Shema requires Jews to love the Lord God with all their heart, strength, and might—that is to love him "maximally." Gellman argues that "maximal love of God will have two features (p. 454). It will entail gratitude and be grounded in perfect goodness." He then proposes that "a necessary and sufficient condition of God's being worthy of our utmost love is that God be a *perfectly good being*" (p. 457).

---

[17] Donald Davidson, "On the Very Idea of a Conceptual Scheme," in *Inquiries into Truth and Interpretation*, (Oxford: Clarendon Press, 1984), 189, 198, as quoted in Fleischacker in this collection (p. 439).

Therefore, what we see at the end of this book are the beginnings of promising new constructive work that aims to open a new chapter in Jewish theology in which Jews attempt to formulate public, communal, rational, and positive ways of speaking of God. This has the potential to clarify what Jewish theology is, that is what Jews, as a religious people, believe, for the good of themselves as a community and for the good of the world.

Selected Further Reading

Batnitzky, Leora. *How Judaism Became a Religion*. Princeton: Princeton University Press, 2012.

Batnitzky, Leora. *Idolatry and Representation*. Princeton: Princeton University Press, 2000.

Brill, Alan. *Judaism and World Religions*. New York: Palgrave Macmillan, 2010.

Buber, Martin. *I and Thou* [1923]. Translated by R. G. Smith. New York: Scribner, 1986.

Dakake, M., T. Greggs, and S. Kepnes. *Handbook of Scriptural Reasoning* (forthcoming).

Davidson, Donald. "On the Very Idea of a Conceptual Scheme." In *Inquiries into Truth and Interpretation*. Oxford: Clarendon Press, 1984.

Derrida, Jacques. *Writing and Difference*. Translated by A. Bass. Chicago: University of Chicago Press, 1978.

Fagenblat, Michael, ed. *Negative Theology as Jewish Modernity*. Bloomington: Indiana University Press, 2017.

Fishbane, Michael. *Sacred Attunement: A Jewish Theology*. Chicago: University of Chicago Press, 2008.

Gadamer, Hans Georg. *Truth and Method*. New York: Crossroads, 1982.

Goodson, Jacob, ed. *The Journal of Scriptural Reasoning*. https://jsr.shanti.virginia.edu.

Goshen-Gottstein, Alon and Eugene Kom, eds. *Jewish Theology and World Religions*. Oxford: Littman Library of Jewish Civilization, 2012.

Heschel, Abraham Joshua. *God in Search of Man*. New York: Farrar, Strauw & Giroux, 1955.

Kohler, George Y. "Judaism Buried or Revitalised? Wissenschaft des Judentums in Nineteenth Century Germany – Impact, Actuality, and Applicability Today." In *Jewish Thought and Jewish Belief*, 27–63. Edited by Daniel Lasker. Beer Sheva: BGU Press, 2012.

Levinas, Emmanuel. *Nine Talmudic Readings*. Bloomington: Indiana University Press, 1994.

Ricoeur, Paul. *Interpretation Theory*. Fort Worth: Texas Christian University Press, 1976.

Rubenstein, Richard. *After Auschwitz*. Indianapolis: Bobbs Merrill, 1966.

Shear, Adam. *The Kuzari and the Shaping of Jewish Identity*. Cambridge: Cambridge University Press, 2008.

2 What is Jewish Theology?

DAVID NOVAK

TWO VIEWS OF JEWISH THEOLOGY

Because the word "theology" is not part of the vocabulary of most Jews, even of most religiously learned Jews, those advocating that the enterprise of theology be acknowledged as an essential component of the Jewish tradition (now usually called "Judaism"), and thus an enterprise to be continued, must first define the concept "theology." They must then show the indispensability of theology for the Jewish tradition's ongoing intelligent operation. So, instead of simply surveying the thought of various Jewish thinkers who could be called "theologians" because they engage in "God-talk" (the literal meaning of "theology"), but not employing the approach of any one of them, this essay is an exercise of a certain kind of Jewish theology, plus at least implying why it is to be preferred to the alternatives by those who take theology seriously. "Doing" theology" rather than just "looking at" theology is a normative enterprise. It is the work of a participant in the ongoing Jewish tradition rather than that of a spectator outside it. Only participants in an enterprise have the right to apply its teachings normatively.[1] A spectator can say many true things *about* God-talk as it has been discussed in the history of Judaism. But only a participant can attempt to bespeak the truth *of* Jewish God-talk by explicating it in the way he or she thinks best intends its truth.

The double task of defining "theology," plus doing Jewish theology in a certain way, is clearly illustrated in the following incident.

---

[1] As philosopher Hans-Georg Gadamer wrote in *Truth and Method* (New York: Continuum, 2004), 275: "In both legal and theological hermeneutics there is the essential tension between the text set down ... and the sense arrived at by its application in the particular moment of interpretation, either in judgment or in preaching ... to be made concretely valid through being interpreted ... according to the claim it makes."

A number of years ago, a group of traditional Jewish students at Cambridge University invited a prominent rabbi and talmudic scholar to speak to them. The main thrust of his talk was on the primacy of halakhah or law in Judaism, and that Jews loyal to their tradition must learn and obey its legally formulated norms. However, Jews do not need to engage in what is commonly called "theology." In fact, he implied theology should be avoided. During the question and answer period following the talk, a young woman (herself a student of philosophy) asked the speaker why he himself is so engaged in learning Jewish law and so obedient of its specific norms, and why he thinks all Jews should do likewise. He answered that he is so engaged in and obedient of Jewish law *because* it is the law God commands every Jew to learn and obey. The student then asked: "Jewish law is what God commands every Jew to learn and obey. Is that a legal proposition or is that a theological proposition?" In other words, isn't the proposition with which the rabbi responded to the young woman's query *describing* something God *does*, which is then seen as the justification (the "because") of propositions *prescribing* what Jews *ought to do*? Indeed, by the rabbi's own justification of his insistence on learning and obedience of the law, doesn't the law's authority stand or fall on the truth or falsehood of that inherently theological proposition?

From this exchange, it seems that the rabbi and the student had two differing definitions of what "theology" is, and whether theology is genuinely "Jewish" or not. If theology is genuinely Jewish, then it seems it should be engaged in by faithful and thoughtful Jews. If not, it should be eschewed. On the other hand, nobody could deny halakhah being genuinely Jewish. Therefore, unlike theology, halakhah's Jewish authenticity is indisputable.[2] Indeed, as we shall see, showing how

---

[2] In his 1933 essay, "Was ist die jüdische Theologie" (now translated as "What is Jewish Theology?"), the late Alexander Altmann wrote: "[E]very Jewish theological system that does not do justice structurally to the central position of halakhah is wrong ... into which the factor of halakhah is built only secondarily and artificially ... that do not grant primacy to halakhah." *The Meaning of Jewish Existence*, trans. E. Ehrlich and L. H. Ehrlich, ed. A. L. Ivry (Hanover, NH: Brandeis University Press, 1991), 45. Even though an Orthodox rabbi himself, Altmann also seemed to be critical of the "undoubted unpopularity in Orthodox circles of the term Jewish theology" (42), probably because of theology's Christian connotation. Although admitting that "the function of theology is only of secondary importance" (ibid.), he nevertheless calls for "a theological understanding of the existence of Judaism" (ibid.). Eighty-five years later, this essay of mine attempts to take up Altmann's challenge, namely, to theologize in a way that by no means makes halakhah secondary to something more foundational in Judaism.

halakhah needs theology for its own integrity is probably the best way to advocate for the authenticity of Jewish theology. And, as we shall also see, theology needs halakhah to give its exercise normative force.[3]

While it is likely he was unaware of it, the rabbi was assuming that theology is what Aristotle who coined the term "theology" (*theologikē*) said it is, namely, what humans can theorize or speculate or philosophize about, that is, what humans can "say" (*logos*) about God (*theos*).[4] For Aristotle, there is no higher human pursuit than to philosophize at this most exalted level; and he was followed by Maimonides (albeit by reading Arabic versions of Aristotle's works) on the naturally rational inclination imperative of all humans that impels them to speculate about God.[5] However, the rabbi seemed to regard such speculation as being peripheral, perhaps even antithetical, to authentic Judaism. No doubt, the rabbi is part of a long tradition that regards any philosophical theology, even that of the great halakhist Maimonides, to be at best superficial apologetics, and at worst a dangerous diversion from the centrality of halakhah in the Jewish tradition.[6] Although Maimonides and the rabbi would agree as to *what* theology is, they would strongly differ as to whether theology so defined is valuable or dangerous for faithful Jews.

Nevertheless, doesn't the rabbi's refusal to take theology seriously leave open the question as to why it is so necessary to differentiate Jewish law as commanded by God from a law commanded by human authorities. Certainly, the Jewish tradition emphasizes the vital importance of this difference.[7] In fact, could a Jew actually fulfill many of the

---

[3] Somewhat along these lines, see Leo Strauss, *Philosophy and Law*, trans. E. Adler (Albany: State University of New York Press, 1995), 60.

[4] *Metaphysics*, 6.1/1026a20. Since philosophy's highest pursuit is to bespeak Being per se (*ontos ōn*) who is God, what Aristotle called "theology" is what we call "ontology." For Aristotelians like Maimonides, theology/ontology is the epitome of philosophy, which as theoretical reason is itself superior to halakhah as practical reason. See Maimonides, *Mishneh Torah* [hereafter "MT"]: Foundations, 4.13; *Guide of the Perplexed*, 1, intro., trans. S. Pines (Chicago: University of Chicago Press, 1963), 5–11.

[5] *Sefer ha-Mitsvot*, pos. no. 1 and MT: Foundations, 1.9 re Exodus 20:2; *Guide of the Perplexed*, 2.33. Re the "naturally rational inclination" of humans, see MT: Kings 8.11 and 9.1.

[6] For the whole controversy over philosophical theology, centered on Maimonides and those who followed him, see G. Stern, *Philosophy and Rabbinic Culture* (London: Routledge, 2009).

[7] Note this biblical denunciation of those who do not differentiate between divine law and human law: "Their fear of Me is a commandment of men [*mitsvat anashim*] ... the wisdom of their sages will perish." (Isaiah 29:13–14).

commandments if he or she did not have some notion of *who is* this God *who* commands every Jew to act one way and not act another way. In fact, it is generally accepted as indispensable for the proper performance of any of the positive commandments (*mitsvot ma`asiyot*) that the one performing the commandment intend (*kavvanah*) his or her action to be done *because* it is God who has so commanded it be done.[8]

Even if the rabbi were to take Maimonidean theological speculation seriously, can this kind of philosophical-theological speculation truly ground the normativity of the law? After all, speculative theology can only talk about what God *does* to the world as its Creator, but it cannot talk about what is uniquely divine about the commandments God reveals to humans *to do*. Therefore, theology cannot be cogently dismissed even by those whose legalism has been called "pan-halachic."[9] So, it would seem that another way of doing theology is needed to better ground intelligent obedience of the law, which nobody could deny lies at the core of the lives of Jews faithful to God, the Torah, and the Jewish tradition. The choice here is not between theology and no-theology; instead, the choice here is between which kind of Jewish theology better explains essentially Jewish normativity. That is, which kind of Jewish theology is more coherent than the others, and which kind better corresponds to the overall content of the Jewish tradition?

Now whether or not the student was aware of it, she was alluding to another way of doing theology in the Jewish tradition. In the oldest translation of the Bible into any non-Hebraic language, the Greek Septuagint, the Hebrew *davar* or "word" is rendered *logos*. Thus the Hebrew "the word of the Lord" (*dvar adonai*) is sometimes translated as *logos tou theou*, namely, "God's word."[10] As such, it might be said that Jewish reflection on the meaning of "God's word" is what best denotes Jewish theology as a legitimate, indeed fruitful, Jewish intellectual enterprise. That is, theology is not what humans can say about God, rather it is what God says to humans about ourselves. Revelation per se

---

[8] *Mishnah* [hereafter "M."]: Berakhot 2.1; *Babylonian Talmud* [hereafter "B."]: Berakhot 13a; Joseph Karo, *Shulhan Arukh*: Orah Hayyim, 60.4; Abraham Joshua Heschel, *God in Search of Man* (New York: Farrar, Straus & Cudahy, 1955), 317–19, n. 3.

[9] Heschel, *God in Search of Man*, 323. I cannot begin to describe the excitement I felt when first encountering this book as a boy of 15. I even wrote Prof. Heschel a fan letter at the time, to which he graciously replied.

[10] For example, LXX on Jeremiah 1:2. More often *dvar adonai*, namely, "the word of the Lord," is more literally translated as *logos kyriou* (e.g., LXX on Jeremiah 1:4).

is God's unmediated communication about, to, and with His people.[11] Moreover, revelation of God's word is only about the human condition insofar as God designates what enables humans to accept God's commandments and act according to them, which is because they speak to the human condition truthfully.[12]

THE PRIMACY OF REVELATION

Surely, revelation is absolutely central to Jewish theology as the methodological reflection thereon. Along these lines, my late revered teacher, Abraham Joshua Heschel (1907–1972), insightfully asserted that "the Bible is God's anthropology rather than man's theology."[13] I can think of no better statement of the theology implied by the Cambridge student's challenge to the rabbi. In fact, it could well be said that Abraham Joshua Heschel was the most significant practitioner of rabbinic theology in our time, which is the type of theology the Cambridge student's challenge was alluding to.[14] Let us now follow the implications of his own statement just quoted.

Calling biblical revelation "God's anthropology" can have two meanings, and it is important to see these two meanings separately and then how they are connected.

---

[11] At the core of revelation are the first two statements (*dibbrot*) of the Decalogue, which the people Israel "heard directly from the mouth of God," while the rest of the Torah is mediated through Moses. (B. Makkot 23b–24a re Deuteronomy 33:4 and Exodus 20:2–3). Cf. MT: Foundations, 8.1, 3; *Guide of the Perplexed*, 2.33 re Exodus 20:2–3. However, Maimonides seems to interpret the Sinai theophany as a mass ratiocination of eternal truth *about* God, rather than God's revelation *to* His people. In fact, God's message to the people is not only mediated *through* Moses, it is actually enunciated in words *by* Moses (*Guide* 1.65).

[12] B. Shabbat 88b–89a re Psalms 8:1–6.   [13] Heschel, *God in Search of Man*, 412.

[14] Kabbalah is another kind of Jewish theology that neither the rabbi nor the student even alluded to. Kabbalah takes revelation to be what God says *about* Godself *to* Godself, which is God's self-naming inasmuch as there is nothing real apart from God to talk about. Since God can talk of nothing but Godself, the Torah is nothing but permutations of the divine names. See Nahmanides' introduction to his *Commentary on the Torah*, trans. C. Chavel (New York: Shilo Publishing House, 1974), 6; *Zohar*: Yitro 87a; Gershom Scholem, *On the Kabbalah and Its Symbolism*, trans. R. Manheim (New York: Schocken, 1969), 35–41. Nevertheless, although great scholars like Scholem have been able to talk *about* Kabbalah using philosophical concepts, I wonder if anyone could actually speak kabbalistically in the first person and still address those outside the ultimately self-referential language of kabbalistic discourse, which is something I think those doing either rabbinic theology or rationalistic theology in more worldly language can do.

First, revelation as God's anthropology means what God tells (*logos*) us humans *about* ourselves. What God tells all of us humans in general is that we are made in God's image (tselem elohim) and thus we have the capacity for a mutual though unequal relationship with God.[15] As such, God tells each and every human *who* he or she essentially *is*. "Who I *am*" means that my unique personal identity as a human creature depends on *whom* I am inextricably related to.[16] Indeed, without that inextricable relation, I have no unique identity in the natural or created world.

What *is* unique *about* human nature? It is the capacity, innate in every human creature, to participate in the divine–human relationship. Furthermore, what God tells Israel or the Jewish people in particular *about* ourselves is that God has chosen us as a people to live that relationship called a "covenant" (*berit*) as a community and not just as individual persons.[17] As such, God tells us Jews *who* we essentially *are*, that is, what makes us a unique people in the history of the world. Being chosen is an historical event; it is a choice God made at a certain time, namely, at the time of the giving of the Torah at Sinai. Unlike being the image of God, being a chosen people is not an innate or natural property; rather, it is an acquired or received status given to the Jewish people at Sinai. Also, since the covenant between God and Israel presupposes the universal human capacity for the divine–human relationship, the difference between the Jewish people and the rest of humankind is one of degree rather than one of kind. The Jews and other humans are not two separate natural species. That is why gentiles can convert to Judaism and become full members of the Jewish people.[18] The election of Israel by God is not racist.

Second, the revealed Torah as God's anthropology does not tell us who we are so that we might regard our nature as our possession or some property we *have*; instead, revelation tells us who we *are*, that is, our innate capacity to *do* what God commands us to do with God as covenantal activity.[19] That is why the covenant is to be an *interactive* relationship, not a static fact. Knowing who we are tells us *that* we are capable of doing what God wants us to do in and for the covenantal relationship. Being told *what* God wants us to do specifically teaches us

---

[15] M. Avot 3.14 re Genesis 9:6.
[16] See Heschel, *Who is Man?* (Stanford, CA: Stanford University Press, 1965), 44–46.
[17] M. Avot 3.14 re Deuteronomy 14.1.   [18] See B. Yevamot 22a and parallels.
[19] *Palestinian Talmud* [hereafter "Y."]: Rosh Hashanah 1.3/ 57a–b re Leviticus 22:9.

exactly *how* that capacity or created potential is to be activated in the world.[20] Moreover, like any potential, the capacity for a relationship with God is only truly appreciated when viewed retrospectively from the time it has already been activated in the world. The constitution of that covenantal relationship is the Torah, which is to be learned. The consequence of that learning is supposed to be our being more likely to keep the content of that covenantal relationship, which are the commandments (*mitsvot*) God gives us as our ongoing task in the world. "Great is learning [*talmud*] Torah, for learning brings one to deeds [*ma`aseh*]."[21]

HALAKHAH AND AGGADAH

Revelation as the giving of the word of God to human recipients has two aspects: halakhah and aggadah. Halakhah literally means "law."[22] Aggadah literally means "narrative."[23] Aggadah *tells us who* God *is* by relating *how* God acts for and with the Jewish people.[24] Halakhah *instructs* us *what* God wants us to do and *how* to do it (*hora'ah*), ultimately, in response to what God has done, and is doing, and will do for and with us.[25] As such, aggadah is descriptive; halakhah is prescriptive. Nevertheless, aggadic speculation is not imparting information about God apart from God's relationship with us; rather, it tells us of the God who has the right to require our obedience because of what God does for us, and persuade us that this is for our good in this world

---

[20] B. Baba Batra 130b.
[21] B. Kiddushin 40b. Learning the specifics of the mitsvot of the Torah is halakhic learning. Learning the more general meaning that makes the overall doing of the mitsvot interactions with God is aggadic or theological learning. See Maimonides, *Commentary on the Mishnah*: Berakhot, ed. Kafih (Jerusalem: ha-Rav Kook, 1976), 1.53; Sanhedrin, ch. 10, intro., ed. Kafih, 133. Learning Torah (whether as halakhah or as aggadah) is a mitsvah to be done for its own sake (*li-shmah*), and is not just the means to the end of doing other more practical mitsvot (Maimonides, *Sefer ha-Mitsvot*, pos. no. 11). Nevertheless, even learning Torah and doing mitsvot for extraneous reasons is still encouraged since one could eventually learn and do them for their own sake (B. Nazir 23b; Y. Hagigah 1.7/76c).
[22] See my late revered teacher, Saul Lieberman, *Hellenism in Jewish Palestine*, 2nd ed. (New York: Jewish Theological Seminary of America, 1962), 83, n. 3.
[23] B. Pesahim 116b re Exodus 13:8.
[24] *Sifre*: Devarim, no. 49 re Deuteronomy 11:22, ed. Finkelstein (New York: Jewish Theological Seminary of America, 1969), 115.
[25] *Sifra*: Shemini, ed. Weiss (New York: Om Publishing Co., 1969), p. 46d and B. Keritot 13a re Leviticus 10:11.

and beyond.[26] It addresses us as participants in the covenant, not as spectators outside it. Thus it could be said that halakhah presupposes aggadah insofar as aggadah contextualizes halakhah by situating it in the narrative of God's ongoing covenantal relationship with Israel. But we can only live that relationship throughout our history as God's people by living according to the concrete norms structured by halakhah. Paraphrasing Kant: aggadah without halakhah is empty; halakakh without aggadah is blind.[27]

When aggadah becomes theoretical, it then becomes "theology" as method. Methodological theology is the reformulation of the narrative, telling of God's doings in our world. On the other hand, when halakhah becomes systematic, it becomes "theology" as the basic prescriptive content of the word of God. The interconnection of halakhah and aggadah is perhaps best expressed in a contemporary idiom in a famous article written by a Jewish law professor, the late Robert Cover, who wrote: "No set of legal institutions or prescriptions exists apart from the narratives that locate it and give it meaning."[28]

Halakhah, neither generally nor specifically, is directly derived from aggadah, that is, aggadah is not applied halakhah.[29] Halakhah is not "theological ethics," that is, it is not practice deduced from theory, which is what aggadah becomes when principles are abstracted from it by methodological theology and then applied practically "from the top down." Rather, aggadah *informs* halakhah by guiding halakhah's operation in the world, primarily by keeping halakhah's purposes in front of the halakhists so that they do not become narrow legalists. Nevertheless, while aggadah gives halakhah its "why," it does not give halakhah its "what" or its "how." For the determination of specific practice of the commandments, halakhists must turn to the normative experience of the covenanted communities (on the ground so to speak) for guidance. In that way, the Torah's immediate normative context is at hand, rather than coming down from what seems to be a remote, heavenly perspective,

---

[26] M. Peah 1.1; M. Kiddushin 1.10.
[27] Immanuel Kant, *Critique of Pure Reason* (Cambridge: Cambridge University Press, 1999), B75.
[28] R. Cover, "Nomos and Narrative" in *Narrative, Violence, and Law*, ed. M. Minow et al. (Ann Arbor, MI: University of Michigan Press, 1992), 95. The rabbinic background of Cover's article has been explored by his Yale colleague, Steven D. Fraade, "Nomos and Narrative," *Yale Journal of Law and Humanities* 17 (2005), 81–96.
[29] Y. Peah 2.4/17a.

one that seems to be oblivious to the immediate situation of the various Jewish communities. That is because people rely on the customary practice of their local community (*minhag*) as to what is to be done.[30] They are prone to reject what seems to have been imposed upon them by theorists, but not rooted in the history of their particular community.[31] In case of doubt as to what the proper practice is to be, what is to be done there and then is not supposed to be deduced from theory; rather, one is told to "go out and see how [*ha'ich*] the community are conducting themselves [*noheg*] and conduct yourself accordingly."[32] (Of course, that means that the community is generally law-abiding; if not, then popular practice is to be changed, that is, whenever possible.[33]) Therefore, it might be said that aggadah gives the commandments of the Torah their greater, more general, context in the historical relationship between God and Israel, while halakhah determined by local practice gives the commandments of the Torah their lesser, more specific, context in the histories of the various Jewish communities. Moreover, the particular practices of the people, although having no obvious basis in Scripture, nonetheless are considered to be a form of quasi-revelation.[34] So, while more general aggadah helps halakhists not "miss the forest for the trees"; more specific halakhah helps theologians not "miss the trees for the forest."

Torah is learnt by rational discernment of its content as halakhah, and of its meaning as aggadah. As aggadah, the Torah is more literally the *word of* God, that is, the aural experience of *hearing* God address us. The Torah as halakhah is more literally the concrete *thing from* God, that is to say, it is the word now written down.[35] To be sure, one could say that the Torah's content itself emerged out of a dialogue between

---

[30] M. Sukkah 3.10; M. Baba Metsia 7.1; also, M. Peah 8.1; B. Sukkah 38a–b.

[31] B. Avodah Zarah 35a–36a; B. Baba Batra 60b and *Tosafot*, s.v. "mutav"; MT: Rebels, 2.5–6.

[32] Y. Maaser Sheni 5.2/56b; B. Berakhot 45a. See, also, Y. Yevamot 12.1/12c and Y. Baba Metsia 7.1/11b.

[33] See, for example, B. Hullin 110a.   [34] B. Pesahim 66a.

[35] This distinction between "word" and "thing" comes out in the earliest translation of the Bible. Sometimes, when the Hebrew davar clearly means "word" and not "thing," the Septuagint does not translate it as *logos*, but by the more aural *rēma*, a noun coming from the verb *reō* ("flow"). See LXX on Jeremiah 1:1 and Deuteronomy 8:3. But when the Hebrew davar clearly means "thing," the Septuagint sometimes uses the noun *pragmatos* (lit. "what has been made," like *factum* in Latin) or just the pronoun *tauta* ("them"). See LXX on Leviticus 5:2 and Exodus 29:1 respectively.

God and Moses.[36] Nevertheless, Moses' dialogical relationship with God was *sui generis*.[37] Our dialogical relationship is between the text of the Torah and ourselves, that is, when the Torah seems to be calling upon us to understand it and explain it to others, and we respond accordingly by questioning the text before directly applying it.[38] This dialogue with the text of the Torah, though, is not primarily a private dialogue between an individual and the text; rather, it is public discourse among members of the Torah-discursive community. This discourse is conducted most immediately among ourselves here and now in the present (i.e., it is conducted synchronically).[39] Moreover, this public discourse with the Torah is also conducted (less immediately, to be sure) with members of the community from the past who have preceded us (i.e., it is conducted diachronically). As an ancient rabbi put it: "whoever says a tradition [*shemu`ah*] that came from the mouth of the one who first said it, the master of this tradition should be looked upon as if he were standing before [*ke-negdo*] this person."[40]

On the other hand, we can best experience the Torah as God's revealed word to us when we feel we are hearing it directly from God. This is the experience of certain specially graced individuals, which is intermittent and totally unpredictable. It should be very much desired and hoped for by those who want to truly appreciate the Torah as God's unmediated word to us, but it should not be a *sine qua non* of observance because it cannot be willed as one can will to understand the Torah and perform its commandments.[41] Nevertheless, our public

---

[36] *Midrash Tehillim*, 18.29 re Exodus 19:19, ed. Buber (Vilna: Romm, 1895), 156; Abraham Ibn Ezra, *Commentary on the Torah*, ed. Weiser (Jerusalem: Mosad ha-Rav Kook, 1977), Exodus 19:19.

[37] Maimonides, *Guide of the Perplexed*, 2.35.

[38] Y. Megillah 1.1/70a re I Chronicles 28:19.

[39] That is why, for example, one's participation in the public Torah-learning of the *bet ha-midrash* trumps private learning at home (M. Shabbat 16.1; B. Shabbat 115a and Rashi, s.v. "bayn," and 116b; MT: Shabbat 23.19 and Vidal of Tolosa, *Magid Mishneh* thereon). Furthermore, we are able to engage all those "fellows" who went before us diachronically, especially those whose words are recorded in the traditional commentaries and elaborations of the written Torah, because we are taught that everything true, learned, at whatever time, is considered to have been, at least potentially, given at Sinai (Y. Peah 2.4/17a re Ecclesiastes 1:10). And that is because we are also taught the souls of all Jews were present at Sinai (*Tanhuma*: Nitsavim, no. 3 re Deuteronomy 29:13–14). That is why strict chronological sequence is at times overlooked in talmudic discourse (see, e.g., B. Sanhedrin 84a).

[40] Y. Shabbat 1.2/3a re Ps. 39:7.

[41] We see this in Franz Rosenzweig's famous distinction between mitsvah as "commandment" (*Gebot*) and halakhah as "law" (*Gesetz*). Unlike Martin Buber, for

interaction with the text of the Torah itself is not dialogical in the way Moses' interaction with God was dialogical, because unlike Moses' personal relationship with God, no new content emerges from our personal relationship with God. Only out of our public dialogue with the text of the Torah does new content emerge, such as innovative enactments (*taqqanot*) like Hanukkah.[42] No new normative content, however, can emerge out of even a prophetic experience of the presence of God.[43] However, new theological insights can emerge from our aggadic reflection on what God has done for us and with us.[44] In that way, theoretical-theological reflection can be more "creative" than practical-halakhic discourse can be.

CREATION, REVELATION, REDEMPTION

Now since tasks are done in the present looking toward the future, whereas facts are discovered in the present looking back to the past, the living covenant ultimately looks forward to its total fulfillment by God's redemption (*ge'ulah*) of Israel and the rest of the world along with us. Just as the commandments of the Torah come from God, not from us humans, so does the final fulfillment of the covenant come from God, not from us humans. Only God, not any creature—not even any special creature like us humans—is "the first and the last" (Isaiah 44:6). In this overall cosmic story, humankind in general and even Israel in particular come into the world always in-between, neither at the beginning nor at the end. Thus the task of the interpreters of the Torah is to address the Torah to the present needs of the community, both intellectual and practical. That gives us humans enough liberty to function as God's active junior partners in the covenant rather than being merely passive pawns in an exclusively divine drama. Nevertheless, we are not to regard ourselves as either initiating or

---

whom *Gesetz* is the antithesis of *Gebot*, Rosenzweig only rejects the view of those who think of Jewish law as requiring but the affirmation of a remote first cause rather than the present affirmation of the ever-present (what he calls *Heutigkeit*, lit. "todayness") Giver of the mitsvah. See his exchange with Buber (and some others) in *On Jewish Learning*, trans. W. Wolf, ed. N. N. Glatzer (New York: Schocken, 1955), 109–24. In his 1923 essay, *Die Bauleute*, Rosenzweig wrote: "Law must become again immediate [*unmittelbar*] commandment." *Kleinere Schriften* (Berlin: Schocken, 1937), 116 (my translation).

[42] B. Shabbat 23a re Deuteronomy 17:11; also, B. Rosh Hashanah 30b re Leviticus 23:14.
[43] Y. Megillah 1.7/70d re Leviticus 27:34; B. Baba Metsia 59b re Deuteronomy 30:12.
[44] *Otsar ha-Geonim*: B. Hagigah 14a, ed. B. M. Lewin (Jerusalem: Hebrew University, 1931), 59–60.

consummating the covenant, of which the Torah is its constitution. Indeed, to regard ourselves as the initiators of the covenant (which is the position of many liberal Jewish thinkers) makes God into a kind of cosmic *facilitator* of an essentially human project, that is, God *becomes* our junior partner rather than we *becoming* God's junior partners. And, to regard ourselves as the consummators of the covenant (which is the position of some messianically oriented Jewish thinkers) makes God into the remote first cause, who began the world and then turned it over to humans to complete it without Him as it were, that is, as God's successors.

In this explication of theology as "the word (*davar* or *logos*) of God" rather than as "human God-talk," the rubric set up by Franz Rosenzweig (1886–1929) has been employed here (albeit somewhat differently from the way he formulated it). Rosenzweig saw the reality lived by Jews in the covenant (and hence the basic subject matter of Jewish theology) being demarcated by three irreducible events: creation, revelation, redemption.[45]

Creation can be seen as the source of the innate capacity for a relationship with God already given to us in the past before we become aware of it when actualizing it in the present. Creation is not a remembered past inasmuch as nobody has ever experienced it, no more than anybody has ever experienced their own birth. Thus creation is an event that transcends any power of ours to recollect it and use it as raw material, so to speak, for our own autonomous projects. Our invocation of creation only serves to give a universal background for the singular revelation of the Torah. As such, it limits any presumption that this singular revelation is particularistic or parochial.[46]

Revelation can be seen as God's ever-ready gift to us whereby we are able to actualize our potential for a content-filled relationship with God in the present, yet we can know that potential only retrospectively, that is, after it has been actualized. However, this is not self-caused actualization; it is not autonomous. Instead, our actualization of our capacity for a relationship with God can only be realized when God gives us the means proper to that end. Without doing the commanded content as revealed in the Torah, we can only accomplish what is ephemeral, which is a transient present that either sinks back into the

---

[45] Franz Rosenzweig, *The Star of Redemption*, trans. B. Galli (Madison, WI: University of Wisconsin Press, 2005), *passim*.

[46] See Nahmanides, *Commentary on the Torah*, ed. Chavel (Jerusalem: Mosad ha-Rav Kook, 1959), Genesis 1:1.

irretrievable past or is swallowed up into and thereby overcome by the novel, forgetful future.

Redemption can be seen as God's consummation of the covenant, which means that nobody who has not denied God will be excluded from the covenant.[47] There will be nobody nor anything outside of the covenant. The sphere of the covenant and the sphere of all creation will become one by a divine redemptive act. Redemption will not be the end-result of a present human projection into the future, however. The futurity of redemption is much more radical. Redemption will thus transcend even the imagined anticipation of what it could be like. It is infinitely more than anything we could infer in the present from our experience of the retrievable past.[48] Redemption is not an ideal to be realized by us. Instead, redemption will be the invasion of a future known only by God into the present. So, as regards redemption, there is nothing for us to do but wait impatiently for it to arrive. Our waiting for redemption only functions as a limitation of the pretension that the consummation of the covenantal relationship is somehow or other in our own hands to finalize.[49]

HALAKHAH AND AGGADAH AT SINAI

The center of the Torah is the revelatory event at Sinai, when the Ten Commandments or Decalogue is given to the entire people of Israel. One can see the interrelation of aggadah and halakhah in a famous rabbinic midrash dealing with the question of why the Decalogue begins with the words: "I am the Lord your God, who has brought you out of the land of Egypt, from out of slavery" (Exodus 20:2). Maimonides saw the first clause of this statement (*dibbur*), namely, "I am the Lord your God," to be a commandment to believe that God exists.[50] However, most other Jewish theologians follow Judah Halevi, seeing the statement to be God's telling the people of Israel *who God is in relation to us*, namely, *how* God has acted *for is* in their very recent experience.[51] The midrash puts forth the following parable:

> A king who entered a province said to the people: may I rule over you? The people said to him, have you done us any good [*tovah*] that

---

[47] M. Sanhedrin 10.1; B. Sanhedrin 105a re Psalms 9:18 (the opinion of Rabbi Joshua); MT: Kings 8.11.
[48] B. Berakhot 34b re Isaiah 64:3.
[49] B. Sanhedrin 97b re Isaiah 30:18 and re Jeremiah 3:14, and Rashi, s.v. "dyo" and "ba`alti."
[50] *Sefer ha-Mitsvot*, pos. no. 1; MT: Foundations. 1.6; *Guide* 2.33.   [51] *Kuzari* 1.25.

you should rule over us? So, what did he do? He built the city wall ... He said to them, now may I rule over you? They responded to him: yes, yes. So it is with God. He brought Israel out of Egypt ... when all Israel stood before Mount Sinai to accept the Torah, they became equally mindful of accepting God's kingship [*malkhut elohim*] with joy [*be-simhah*].[52]

This midrash has been interpreted to mean that God has benefitted the people, who then must be grateful in return by obeying His commandments.[53] However, doesn't this portray God as some sort of insecure parent (like King Lear), who indulges his children in order that they be forever beholden to him and thus obligated to gratefully obey his perpetual demands on them? However, children are usually resentful of this kind of gift to them because while the gift is finite, the grateful response demanded of them is infinite. In other words, what ought to be a finite symmetrical relationship is, in fact, an asymmetrical relation, benefitting the creditor and making the debtor's debt interminable. But debtors do not want a perpetual relationship with their creditor; rather, they want a finite repayment of a finite debt, which will then enable them to go their separate ways. In fact, shouldn't one avoid this type of dependency relationship at all?[54] Therefore, this interpretation of the midrash does not accurately depict the covenantal relationship between God and His people with which this midrash is so concerned. Isn't the covenant an unending, asymmetrical partnership between God and His people, which neither side wants to ever get over? God says to Israel: "My loyalty will not depart from you, and My covenant of peace will not move." (Isaiah 54:10).[55] And on behalf of the people Israel, Moses says to God: "If Your presence does not go [with us], do not take us up out of this [wilderness]." (Exodus 33:15) In the covenant, God is the senior partner and the Jews are the junior partners.

Furthermore, at the time this midrash was composed, the Jews were not experiencing God's saving beneficence to them. In fact, this midrash was composed at a time of Roman persecution of the Jewish people, when God did not seem to be vanquishing Rome for the Jewish people as God did vanquish Egypt for them.[56] Surely, seeing obedience to the

---

[52] *Mekhilta de-Rabbi Ishmael*: "Yitro," eds., H. Horovitz and I. Rabin (Jerusalem: Wahrmann 1960), 219. See *Shemot Rabbah* 29.2 re Exodus 20:2.
[53] *Mishnat Rabbi Eliezer*, ed. H. G. Enelow (New York: Bloch, 1933), ch. 7, 137–38.
[54] See MT: Gifts to the Poor, 10.18. [55] See B. Berakhot 32a re Exodus 32:13.
[56] See B. Gittin 56b re Exodus 15:11.

commandments as gratitude for God's salvation in this world is even more problematic today in view of recent Jewish experience of what seems to have been God's absence during the Holocaust. So, when doing theology, we must be aware of the immediate historical context of the classical sources being cited. Even more so, we must be aware of the historical context in which we are now citing them and reinterpreting them for our contemporaries "where ever they might be" (Genesis 21:17). Indeed, the two historical contexts, then and now, are quite similar.

To avoid these two problems, might there be another way to interpret this midrash? What if God is not asking the people for gratitude for what God *has done* for them in a past event? What if, instead, God is telling the people something like this: Just as I have been good to you in the recent past events you have experienced, so I will continue to benefit you by giving you "good [*tovim*] laws and commandments" (Nehemiah 9:13). I not only have taken you out of bondage, I will teach you how to survive, even flourish, by cooperating with My beneficent rule over you, which you must accept willingly if it is to be effective in the world.[57] Moreover, whereas what God has done for the people in past events can never be taken for granted as something ready at hand, but can only be commemorated and hoped for in the future, the Torah which God has given the people to learn and its commandments given to them to do are "these words I command you this day [*ha-yom*]" (Deuteronomy 6:6). The Rabbis take "this day" to mean every day, that the Torah's commandments are like a "new [*hadashah*] decree" that nobody should take as passé.[58] In other words, God is with us insofar as there is never a time when we cannot do some commandment there and then. Therefore, the initial acceptance of God's kingship is due to our being told (i.e., aggadah) how God has benefitted His people in the past, while the subsequent acceptance of the commandments to be obeyed can only be done properly through the halakhah informing us exactly how this obedience is to be achieved.[59]

A woman who survived Auschwitz once told me that when her fellow prisoners taunted her for saying the shema each day, she said back to them: "They [the Nazis] have taken everything away from me, but I won't let you take my God away from me." She was not counting

---

[57] B. Shabbat 88a re Esther 9:27.
[58] *Sifre*: Devarim, no. 33, ed. Finkelstein (New York: Jewish Theological Seminary of America), 59.
[59] M. Berakhot 2.2.

on what God had done for her in the past, nor was she counting on what God might do for her in the future. Instead, she was responding to what God requires her to do here and now, which is to proclaim God's uniqueness, even if only to herself, even if only in that Hell. As a covenantal act, this involves both God and the Jewish people, the senior partner and the junior partners of the covenant respectively.[60] Unlike many other Jewish survivors of the Holocaust, this woman did not lose her faith in the death camp; if anything her faith saved her from the kind of despair that plagued and even still plagues many of those who did survive. "The righteous live through their faith [*b'emunato*]." (Habakkuk 2:4).[61] Her existential story (her aggadah) best illuminates what I think the midrash we have been discussing is teaching us. Hers is a theological statement par excellence.

TWO TYPES OF COMMANDMENTS AND THEIR AGGADIC COMPONENTS

Halakhah as the structuring of two different types of commandments of the Torah governs two different, though intertwined, kinds of relationships: one, commandments that govern the God–human relationship (*bein adam le-maqom*); two, commandments that govern interhuman relationships (*bein adam le-havero*). In both types of commandments, aggadah as theology is needed in the attempt to discern the meaning or purpose for which the commandment was prescribed by God. Indeed, without this theological project, the commandments of the Torah would appear to be the orders of a capricious, even tyrannical, ruler.[62] This theological project is a human effort,

---

[60] B. Shabbat 119b re Genesis 2:1. Cf. *Tosefta*: Sanhedrin 8.7 and B. Sanhedrin 38a, where it is stated that the first human (*adam*) was the last creature created by God to refute the claim of those who could say "God had a partner [*shuttaf*] in the work of creation." However, in talmudic fashion, we might reconcile this seeming contradiction by arguing that this latter text is speaking of the presumption of humans being the *equal* partners of God at the beginning of the work of creation, while the former text is speaking of humans only imitating God as God's *junior* partners on the Sabbath at the conclusion of creation. Indeed, presuming to be God's equal was what the serpent tempted the first humans to consider themselves, in defiance of God, namely, "you shall be gods" (Genesis 3:5). See *Beresheet Rabbah* 19.4; also, B. Sukkah 45b re Exodus 22:19.

[61] Being faithful (*emunah*) is considered in one rabbinic text (B. Makkot 24a) to be the one act that can be done by anybody under any circumstances (Rashi, s.v. "ve-h'emidan"). See Y. Berakhot 9.7/14d re Psalms 119:164 and 34:8.

[62] Maimonides, *Guide of the Perplexed*, 3.26.

especially since the Torah itself rarely reveals the reasons for the commandments it presents (*ta'amei ha-mitsvot*).[63] Thus aggadah not only provides the reason for the whole body of the Torah's commandments, it also provides the reasons for many of the specific commandments of the Torah.

Now no commandment pertaining to the God–human relationship is without some connection to interhuman relationships inasmuch as the God–human relationship is with a community in which the human members are interrelated. And no commandment pertaining to interhuman relationships is without some connection to the God–human relationship inasmuch as the interhuman community is an elected covenantal community, whose very coming together with one another is for the sake of living the covenant with God. Nevertheless, theology functions differently in the two respective realms. In the realm of the God–human relationship, theology functions more precisely as aggadah, that is, interpreting and applying the narrative of the unique historical covenant between God and the Jewish people.

In the realm of interhuman relationships, however, theology functions more philosophically, that is, it deals ethically with natural human conditions that are not unique to the Jewish people. So, for example, when it was decided that only Jews, but not gentiles, ought to be required to keep the Sabbath, the reason given is that the Sabbath is what is exclusively "between Me and the children of Israel" (Exodus 31:17).[64] The reason for that seems to be that keeping the Sabbath is not a universally evident norm, but that it had to be revealed to the Jewish people during their sojourn in the Wilderness after leaving Egypt. Thus keeping the Sabbath is a prime example of God's unique care for His unique people. Here theology is functioning as aggadah.

On the other hand, when certain norms of the Torah pertaining to the interhuman realm could be interpreted so as to give Jews the right to take unjust advantage of gentiles, such a right is rescinded.[65] That is because, if such a right is exercised with impunity, Jewish law comes off looking immoral according to universal standards of morality that ought to be accepted and practiced by all humans as those created in the image of God, whether they be Jewish or gentile. The Torah is

---

[63] B. Sanhedrin 21a–b re Deuteronomy 17:16–17.
[64] B. Sanhedrin 58b re Gen. 8:22; *Devarim Rabbah* 1.18; *Shemot Rabbah* 25.16 re Exodus 16:29. Cf. *Guide of the Perplexed*, 2.31 and 3.43.
[65] B. Baba Kama 113a–b re Deuteronomy 22:3. Cf. ibid. 38a.

considered to be a further and higher specification of moral law that is universally normative, not a descent from it.⁶⁶ To interpret the law otherwise is considered to be "desecration of God's name" (*hillul ha-shem*). Here theology is functioning philosophically. Nevertheless, even here, the God–human relationship is the main factor, since the rights of every human being that the Torah legislates duties to enforce are because every human being is created in the image of God and thus deserves to have their rights so enforced by legally stipulated duties.⁶⁷

THE ENTERPRISE OF JEWISH THEOLOGY TODAY

Doing Jewish theology today requires one to take some method of articulation from the surrounding world. This is not, however, the type of obsequious thinking that subordinates the Jewish tradition to something foreign to it. And this is not the type of thinking that assumes the language of the Torah is *sui generis*, thus requiring nothing outside itself for its explication. Instead, the need to critically employ the language of the world goes back to the rabbinic principle: "The Torah speaks according to human language."⁶⁸ That is, the Torah came into a world already in place, and whose inhabitants could not very well receive it, let alone interpret it, were not the Torah given in a language they had already been hearing and speaking.

Now since philosophy seems to employ worldly language with greater precision than other disciplines, and since philosophy seems to deal with the deepest questions of human existence in the world, Jewish theology is, arguably, best articulated when Jewish theologians employ philosophically honed language critically.

When Jewish theology is aggadah, describing the experience of the covenantal relationship of the Jewish people with God, then the best philosophical method to be employed is phenomenology. By perceiving how we experience our personal encounter with God, and enabling us to reflect on how it occurs, phenomenology is most adequate for theology's task of telling, retelling, and formulating the meaning of irreducible experiences and the truth shown therein. This is especially so when dealing with the "reasons of the commandments" that pertain to the

---

[66] B. Yevamot 22a. [67] Y. Nedarim 9.4//41c re Genesis 5:1; M. Avot 3.14 re Genesis 9:6.
[68] The most profound treatment of the theological significance of this principle is Heschel, *Heavenly Torah: As Refracted Through the Generations*, trans. G. Tucker and L. Levin (New York: Continuum, 2005), 47–56, 659–68.

God–human relationship, and how discerning these reasons helps us interpret and judge practice in this part of the Torah's domain.

When Jewish theology is halakhah, prescribing how we are to actively respond to our encounters with God and our fellow humans, which is theology as the normative content of revelation, then the best philosophical method is that of current political philosophy. Analytic philosophers have been in the forefront of the discourse of current political philosophy, which is why their methods should be critically employed here. Jewish interest in this type of philosophy is because of its concern with justice. According to criteria of justice are the commandments pertaining to the political realm to be understood. Ultimately, they need to be justified by the justice by which God governs all creation. This is especially so when dealing with the "reasons of the commandments" that pertain to interhuman relationships, and how they help us to interpret and judge practice in this part of the Torah's domain.

Understanding the context (via aggadah) and the content (via halakhah) of revelation has been, is, and should be the ongoing task of Jewish theology and the theologians who practice it. There is still much much more to be done. Our task is "not to finish the work nor are we free to desist from doing it".[69]

Selected Further Reading

Baeck, Leo. *This People Israel*. Tanslated by A. H. Freidlander. New York: Holt, Rinehart and Winston, 1965.

Benamozegh, Elijah. *Israel and Humanity*. Translated by M. Luria. New York: Paulist Press, 1995.

Borowitz, Eugene B. *Renewing the Covenant*. Philadelphia: Jewish Publication Society, 1991.

Cohen, Hermann. *Religion of Reason Out of the Sources of Judaism*. Translated by S. Kaplan. New York: Frederick Ungar, 1972.

Diamond, James A. *Jewish Theology Unbound*. Oxford: Oxford University Press, 2018.

Goodman, Lenn E. *God of Abraham*. New York: Oxford University Press, 1996.

Hartman, David. *A Living Covenant*. New York: The Free Press, 1985.

Heschel, Abraham Joshua. *The Sabbath*. New York: Farrar, Straus and Giroux, 2005.

Jacobs, Louis. *A Jewish Theology*. London: Darton, Longman and Todd, 1973.

Novak, David. *The Election of Israel*. Cambridge: Cambridge University Press, 1995.

Soloveitchik, Joseph B. *The Lonely Man of Faith*. New York: Doubleday, 2006.

---

[69] M. Avot 2.21.

PART I

BIBLICAL-RABBINIC

3 Jewish Biblical Theology
MARVIN A. SWEENEY

I

Jewish biblical theology is a relatively new field within the larger context of Jewish thought. This is the case because the larger field of biblical theology and its sub-field of Old Testament theology originated within the context of Christian dogmatic theology as a means to interpret the Bible, including both the Old and New Testaments, in relation to the questions addressed in Christian theology.[1] In the case of Christian Old Testament theology, a major concern is to correlate the teachings of the Old Testament in relation to the teachings of the New Testament, particularly its focus on Jesus Christ as the means by which human beings relate to G-d and attain eternal salvation beyond life in this world. Prominent Jewish scholars have expressed concerns about Christian biblical theology; for example, Levenson points to the essential Christian character of biblical theology and its heavily anti-Jewish character.[2] But with the increasing role played by Jewish biblical scholars in the field of critical biblical studies since the 1960s, Jewish biblical studies has emerged as a recognized field within the larger context of Jewish thought and it has proved to be a useful and legitimate means with which to study the Bible's understanding of G-d in relation to Judaism and the Jewish people in particular and to humanity and the world of creation at large.

As the field of Jewish biblical theology has developed, a number of useful surveys and collections of essays have appeared, such as surveys

---

[1] Marvin A. Sweeney. "Biblical Theology. Hebrew Bible/Old Testament," in *Encyclopedia of the Bible and its Reception*, ed. H.-J. Klauck et al. (Berlin and Boston, MA: Walter de Gruyter, 2011), 3: 1137–49.

[2] Jon D. Levenson. "Why Jews are not Interested in Biblical Theology." *The Hebrew Bible, The Old Testament, and Historical Criticism: Jews and Christians in Biblical Studies* (Louisville, KY: Westminster John Knox, 1993), 33–61, 165–70.

by Ben Zvi, Kalimi, Sommer, Sweeney, and Zevit,[3] and collections edited or presented by Bellis and Kaminsky, Kalimi, Perdue et al., and Sweeney.[4]

Biblical theology is the systematic theological interpretation of the Bible, and Jewish biblical theology is the systematic theological interpretation of the Jewish Bible (Tanak). The reason for such qualification is that the Bible appears in multiple forms, most of which are Christian and are constructed to give expression to the concerns of the Christian Bible and Christian theology. But the Jewish Bible appears in its uniquely distinctive form as the Tanak, which enables the Jewish Bible to function as the essential and foundational work of Jewish thought and practice. In order to provide an overview of Jewish biblical theology, this essay treats several fundamental concerns, namely, the unique form of the Jewish Bible in contrast to the distinctive forms of the Christian Bible; the dialogical character of the Jewish Bible in relation to itself and to the larger context of Jewish thought; the eternal

---

[3] Ehud Ben Zvi, "The Recent History of Jewish Biblical Theology," in *Jewish Bible Theology*, ed., I. Kalimi (Winona Lake, IN: Eisenbrauns, 2012), 31–50; Isaac Kalimi, "History of Israelite Religion or Hebrew Bible/Old Testament Theology? Jewish Interest in Biblical Theology," in *Early Jewish Exegesis and Theological Controversies: Studies in Scripture in the Shadow of Internal and External Controversies* (Assen: Van Gorcum, 2002), 107–34; Benjamin D. Sommer, "Biblical Theology. Judaism," in *Encyclopedia of the Bible and its Reception*, ed. H.-J. Klauck et al. (Berlin and Boston, MA: Walter de Gruyter, 2011), 3: 1159–69, and "Dialogical Biblical Theology: A Jewish Approach to Reading Scripture Theologically," in *Biblical Theology: Introducing the Conversation*, ed. L. G. Perdue, et al. (Nashville, TN: Abingdon, 2009), 1–53; Marvin A. Sweeney: "Jewish Biblical Theology: An Ongoing Dialog," *Interpretation* 70 (2016): 314–25; *Tanak: A Theological and Critical Introduction to the Jewish Bible* (Minneapolis, MN: Fortress, 2012); "Biblical Theology. Hebrew Bible/Old Testament," in *Encyclopedia of the Bible and its Reception*, ed. H.-J. Klauck, et al. (Berlin and Boston, MA: Walter de Gruyter, 2011), 3: 1137–49; "Jewish Biblical Theology," in *The Hebrew Bible: New Insights and Scholarship* (New York and London: New York University Press, 2008), 191–208; "The Emerging Field of Jewish Biblical Theology," in *Academic Approaches to Teaching Jewish Studies*, ed. Z. Garber (Lanham, MD: University Press of America, 2000), 83–105; Ziony Zevit, "Jewish Biblical Theology: Whence? Why? And Whither?" *Hebrew Union College Annual* 49 (2005): 289–340.

[4] Alice Ogden Bellis and Joel S. Kaminsky, eds., *Jews, Christians, and the Theology of the Hebrew Bible* (SBL Symposium Series 8; Atlanta, GA: Society of Biblical Literature, 2000); Isaac Kalimi, Editor. *Jewish Bible Theology: Perspectives and Case Studies* (Winona Lake, IN: Eisenbrauns, 2012); Leo G. Perdue, et al., eds., *Biblical Theology: Introducing the Conversation* (Nashville, TN: Abingdon, 2009); Marvin A. Sweeney, ed., *Theology of the Hebrew Bible. Volume 1: Methodological Issues and Studies* (SBL Resources for Biblical Study; Atlanta, GA: Society of Biblical Literature, 2018).

covenant between G-d and the Jewish people; the construction of the Jewish people and its institutions, such as the land of Israel, the holy Temple, and the monarchy; and the problem of evil, particularly the exile and potential destruction of the Jewish people, that calls the eternal covenant between G-d and Israel into question.

II

The first issue for discussion is the distinctive form of the Jewish Bible or Tanak and the interpretation of this distinctive form as a key issue in understanding the theological outlook of the Tanak within the larger context of Jewish thought and practice.[5]

Many readers simply assume that the Christian Old Testament and the Jewish Tanak are one and the same work. Although the books of each canon may be largely the same, the distinctive organization of the Christian Old Testament and the Jewish Tanak points to substantive differences in their interpretation and worldview. Each distinctive structure took time to develop; they are not inherent in either form of the Bible. Rather these forms are imposed upon them by means of the influence of later Christian and Jewish interpretation of the books and the reading strategies employed in each tradition. For the most part, they are not fully formed until the advent of printing in the sixteenth century CE which facilitated the standardization of structure in a manner that was not always possible before. Even so, they are not always uniformly employed, particularly in Christian tradition, which understands a wide variety of textual forms to serve as witnesses to sacred scripture within the various Christian Churches around the world.

The Christian Bible comprises two basic parts, the Old Testament and the New Testament, that define the manner in which the Bible is read and interpreted in Christianity. Insofar as the English word "testament," means "covenant," in reference to the older Mosaic covenant between G-d and Israel and the newer covenant based on the revelation of Jesus as the Christ or Messiah in Christianity, this basic structure gives expression to the theological worldview of Christianity. Historically, Christian theology maintains that the new covenant based on the revelation of Jesus Christ fulfills or supersedes the older covenant, based on the revelation of divine law for Israel through Moses.

---

[5] Sweeney, *Tanak*.

Such a conceptualization entails that the prior revelation was somehow flawed or inadequate, particularly since Christians observed that Israel or Jews went into exile from the promised land of Israel due to the Bible's frequent allegations that they had somehow sinned against G-d and therefore suffered invasion by foreign powers and exile as divine punishments for those sins. In such a scenario, Christian interpreters tended to view the Old Testament or Mosaic covenant as an obsolete relationship that had failed and required replacement by a newer covenant and New Testament that would allegedly provide a more secure foundation in divine love and be open to all humanity. Recognition of the moral problems posed by the Shoah (Hebrew, for destruction; see Garber and Zuckerman 1989) or Holocaust, as well as the role of Christian persecution of Jews from late antiquity through to modern times, has prompted many Christian thinkers to rethink supersessionist models (Williamson 1993).[6] Indeed, such recognition has prompted many Christian theologians to recognize the continuing theological legitimacy of Judaism alongside Christianity.

Nevertheless, the formal structure of the Christian Bible as the Old and New Testament indicates a linear conceptualization of history in which divine revelation proceeds in stages, first by means of the Mosaic covenant at Mt. Sinai, based in large measure on the revelation of divine law to Israel by the agency of Moses, and second by means of the revelation of Jesus of Nazareth as the Christ or Messiah who would enable the potential salvation of all humanity. Insofar as the anticipated salvation is yet to be realized, Christianity looks forward to a third stage when Christ will return to the world to complete the redemption.

Such a conceptualization also has an impact on the organization of the Christian Old Testament, based especially on early Greek manuscripts of the Christian Bible, for example, the Codex Vaticanus and Codex Sinaiticus, which date roughly to the fourth century CE when Christianity emerged as the dominant religion of the Roman Empire. Although not all manuscripts follow the organization of Vaticanus and Sinaiticus, their organization is today widely employed in printed editions of the Bible.

---

[6] Shoah, "destruction," is the Hebrew designation for the Holocaust. For discussion of these terms, see Zev Garber and Bruce Zuckerman, "Why Do We Call the Holocaust 'the Holocaust?' An Inquiry into the Psychology of Labels," *Modern Judaism* 9 (1989): 197–211. For discussion of Christian supersessionism, see Clark M. Williamson. *A Guest in the House of Israel: Post-Holocaust Church Theology* (Louisville, KY: Westminster John Knox, 1993).

Jewish Biblical Theology 45

The Christian Old Testament comprises four major sections, namely, the Pentateuch, the Historical Books, the Poetic and Wisdom Books, and the Prophetic Books. This organization represents a linear progression in human history that within the larger context of the Christian Bible points to the ultimate redemption of humankind at the second coming of Christ.

This linear progression begins with the Pentateuch, that is, Genesis, Exodus, Leviticus, Numbers, and Deuteronomy, which recounts the earliest stages of human history. This includes the creation of the world and humanity, the divine election of the family of Abraham, the history of the descendants of Abraham and his wife Sarah until they ultimately formed the tribes of Israel, the enslavement of the Israelite tribes by Egypt and their exodus from Egyptian bondage under the leadership of Moses, the revelation of the divine covenant with Israel at Mt. Sinai in the wilderness, and the guidance of Israel to the borders of the promised land of Israel.

The second portion of the Old Testament canon comprises the Historical Books, namely, Joshua, Judges, Ruth, 1–2 Samuel, 1–2 Kings, 1–2 Chronicles, Ezra, Nehemiah, and Esther, as well as Tobit, Judith, and 1–2 Maccabees in the Deuterocanonical or Apocryphal Books. The Historical Books present the history of Israel from its initial settlement in the land through the Hellenistic period immediately prior to the time of the revelation of Christ. It therefore constitutes a second stage of history, which focuses especially on the exile of Israel from the land by Assyrian and Babylonian empires and anticipates exile once again following the Roman destruction of the Second Temple.

The third segment of the Christian Old Testament comprises the Wisdom and Poetic Books, namely, Job, Proverbs, Ecclesiastes, Song of Songs, and Psalms, as well as the Deuterocanonical or Apocryphal Books, Wisdom of Solomon and Sirach. These books take up questions of philosophy or worldview, human conduct in the world, and human worship and praise of G-d that represent the present in any given generation, insofar as they are concerns of human beings no matter in what historical context they might live.

Finally, the Prophetic Books constitute the fourth segment of the Christian Old Testament with the books of Isaiah, Jeremiah, Lamentations, Epistle of Jeremiah, Ezekiel, Daniel, and the Twelve Minor Prophets. Although these books look retrospectively at the past, they are understood to take up the future as well, and so point to the culmination of human history when Israel is restored to the land and the nations of the world will come to recognize G-d as the true master of the world. It is no accident that they immediately precede the New Testament in Christian Bibles to anticipate Jesus Christ as the figure who will usher in the final redemption.

Insofar as the Christian Old Testament lays out a progressive understanding of history, it also anticipates the structure of the New Testament in which the Gospels represent the earliest history of Christian revelation with Jesus, the Acts of the Apostles represent the subsequent early history of the Church, the Epistles of Paul and the other Apostles represent the ongoing present with issues pertaining to Christians in any generation, and the Apocalypse of John or Revelation which points to the future and the second coming of Christ.

The Jewish Tanak has a very different formal structure of three major portions, including the Torah or Instruction; the Nevi'im or Prophets, including the Nevi'im Rishonim or Former Prophets and the Nevi'im Aḥronim or Latter Prophets; and the Ketuvim or Writings. Indeed, the first letter of the Hebrew word for each section is employed with vocalization to create the acronym TaNaK, Torah, Nevi'im, Ketuvim.

The distinctive structure of the Tanak presents a cyclical understanding of human history in which Israel is formed, suffers reverses, but reconstitutes and restores itself for the future. Such a structure and conceptualization helps to explain Judaism's resilience and its ability to evolve and progress throughout its history.

The initial and foundational element of the Tanak is the Torah, which comprises Genesis, Exodus, Leviticus, Numbers, and Deuteronomy. The Hebrew term, *torah*, means, "instruction" or "teaching." This understanding of the term Torah is crucial for understanding the contents and conceptualization of the Torah within the Tanak. Christians are accustomed to translating Torah as "law," based on the writings of Paul in the New Testament and the typical translation of *torah* as *nomos*, "law," in Greek, but this is an inaccurate translation. The Hebrew word for "law" is *mishpat*. The books of the Torah include law, especially in Exodus, Leviticus, Numbers, and Deuteronomy, but they also include much more than law. Indeed, the basic form of the Torah is narrative, and it presents the earliest history of the people of Israel from the creation of the world in Genesis 1:1–2:3 through the ancestral period in which the eternal covenant with YHWH was established, the formation of the nation in the Exodus and Wilderness accounts, of which the revelation of law at Sinai and elsewhere is a part, and the account of Moses' last speeches to Israel prior to their entry into the promised land of Israel. Overall, the Torah provides instruction concerning the formation of the people, Israel, the people's relationship with YHWH, the G-d of Israel and Creation, and YHWH's expectations of Israel and Creation. It presents an ideal understanding of that relationship in which Israel is expected to create a holy and just society within the larger context of creation.

The second element of the Tanak is the Nevi'im, "Prophets," divided into the *Nevi'im Rishonim*, "Former Prophets," and the *Nevi'im Aḥronim*, "Latter Prophets." The Nevi'im Rishonim include Joshua, Judges, Samuel, and Kings, which present an account of Israel's history in the land from the initial entry by Joshua through the Babylonian exile. These books are understood within Judaism to have been written by prophets, Joshua by Joshua, Judges and Samuel by Samuel, and Kings by Jeremiah. The Nevi'im Aḥronim, which present the accounts and oracles of the prophets after whom they are named, include Isaiah, Jeremiah, Ezekiel, and the Book of the Twelve Prophets, which are especially concerned to explain the issues of exile and restoration. The Nevi'im address the question of evil, that is, what does it mean when Israel and Judah suffer punishment and exile from the land of Israel in the form of the Assyrian destruction of the northern kingdom of Israel and the Babylonian destruction of the southern kingdom of Judah"? Overall, they address the disruption of the ideals portrayed in the Torah insofar as they explain destruction and exile as the result of the people's failure to abide by the divine will and restoration as the result of YHWH's commitment to covenant.

Finally, the *Ketuvim*, Writings, contain the remainder of the books of the Tanak, including Psalms, Job, Proverbs, the Five Megillot or Scrolls (Song of Songs, Lamentations, Ruth, Qohelet, and Esther), Daniel, Ezra-Nehemiah, and Chronicles. This section is the least understood section of the Tanak insofar as some scholars presume that it is simply a catchall section for the remaining books. But closer examination indicates that the Ketuvim are understood as a means to address the possibilities of the restoration of the ideals expressed in the Torah. Psalms presents the songs employed in the Temple for the worship of YHWH. Proverbs and Job are wisdom books which reflect upon divine presence and human responsibility in the world. The Five Megillot are the books that are read at major holidays to give expression to the meaning of each holiday, namely, Song of Songs at Passover to express the intimate relation between G-d and Israel; Lamentations at Tisha b'Av to mourn for the loss of the Temple; Ruth at Shavuot to celebrate the revelation of Torah in relation to a convert; Qohelet at Sukkot to reflect upon the transitory nature of life in relation to the Wilderness wanderings; and Esther to celebrate the deliverance of Israel from attempted genocide. Daniel looks forward to the restoration of divine presence in the world from the context of the Babylonian Exile. Ezra-Nehemiah recounts the rebuilding and reestablishment of the holy Jerusalem Temple and the reinstitution of the holy Torah at the center of Jewish life. And Chronicles recaps the history of Israel in the world from the time of creation through Cyrus' decree concerning the return of exiled Jews to the land of Israel, apparently in anticipation that such an event will happen again. Altogether, Ketuvim are fundamentally concerned with the restoration of the ideals articulated in the Torah.

III

Another dimension of the Jewish Bible is the diversity of viewpoint expressed within and among its constituent books. Not all of the books of the Bible agree with each other in their views of G-d, Israel, human obligation, and any number of other topics. This diversity is often understood as a problem by interpreters who expend considerable effort to reconcile the differences in the laws of Exodus, Leviticus, and Deuteronomy; the historical accounts of Samuel or Kings versus Chronicles; the prophetic viewpoints of Isaiah and the Twelve Prophets; the views of Proverbs and Job concerning the nature of the world in which we live; and many other topics. But those who view the diversity of viewpoint within the Bible miss a fundamental point, namely, that such diversity is to be embraced, not explained away, as an aspect of the divine character and will and the means by which we understand G-d, ourselves, and the world in which we live.

A number of examples illustrate the point. With respect to biblical law, Exodus 21:1–11 presents a slave law in which a man becomes a slave for a period of six years to resolve a debt. At the end of his term of service, he can choose to go free or remain a slave forever. If he goes free, he gets no support from his master to begin life anew, and he is likely to go into debt and become a slave once again. If he is married while in slavery, his wife and children do not go free with him. If a woman is a slave, she never goes free because she is presumed to be given in marriage to a man of the master's house, unless her husband does not provide food, garments, and sexual relations to ensure the birth of children who will care for her in old age. These factors alone present considerable incentive for someone to remain a slave. Deuteronomy 15 is apparently written with these problems in mind and stipulates several changes.[7] First, a master is obligated to give his former slave a share of what the slave has produced to help him start life anew and avoid renewed debt and slavery. Also, women go free like men. These provisions help to address the problems inherent in the Exodus version of the law, and better enable Israelite law to achieve its ideals of holiness and justice in the world. Israelite law therefore functions as a living system of law in which changes in law may be made to address issues that may not have been anticipated in the original formulation of the law in question. Such diversity of viewpoint in the Bible teaches that change is necessary as experience and learning advance.

An analogous example appears in the presentation of King Manasseh of Judah in 2 Kings 21:1-18 and 2 Chronicles 33:1-20. According to 2 Kings 21, King Manasseh was the worst monarch of the House of David; his sins were so great that YHWH decided to destroy Jerusalem and exile its people some 60 years after his death, despite the efforts of the righteous King Josiah of Judah. In this view, later generations suffered for the sins of their ancestors. Second Chronicles 33 takes a different approach. Manasseh is as wicked in Chronicles as he was in Kings, but the outcome differs. YHWH does not decide to destroy Jerusalem due to Manasseh's sins. Instead, Manasseh is bound in chains by the Assyrian king and taken to Babylon to witness the efforts to put down the Babylonian revolt against Assyria. When Manasseh returned to Jerusalem, he repented from his sins and became a righteous monarch for the rest of his life. Josiah died in Chronicles because of his refusal to abide by YHWH's will, and Jerusalem was destroyed because the leaders and people of the time corrupted the city. In the view of Chronicles, people may repent, and those who suffer punishment do so for their own sins. The inclusion of both moral viewpoints in the Bible is quite deliberate as both realities appear in human life and both appear to represent the character of G-d.

Interpreters have long recognized that the prophets do not represent a single movement, but instead have different institutional settings and theological worldviews related to those settings. Isaiah was a monarchist based in the Davidic Zion tradition; Jeremiah was a priest of the line of Ithamar based in Mosaic Torah; and Ezekiel

---

[7] Bernard M. Levinson. *Deuteronomy and the Hermeneutics of Legal Innovation* (Oxford and New York: Oxford University Press, 1997).

was a Zadokite priest based in the sanctity of the Jerusalem Temple. Consequently, prophets disagree. Isaiah articulates a worldview in Isaiah 2 in which the nations and Israel will ascend together to Zion to learn divine Torah and end war. He holds that the Davidic kings must put their trust in YHWH's eternal promise in the first part of the book, but the second part of the book reassigns the eternal Davidic covenant to the people of Israel at large and names King Cyrus of Persia as YHWH's messiah and Temple builder (Isaiah 44:28, 45:1, 55). Prophets in the Book of the Twelve disagree. Micah also holds to Isaiah's vision of the nations and Israel ascending to Zion to learn Torah in Micah 4–5, but he also holds that each nation walks in the way of its own god and that a Davidic messiah will arise who will defeat the oppressor nations, much as Zechariah does. Jeremiah calls for adherence to Mosaic Torah in Jeremiah 7, and he reassigns the Davidic covenant to the city of Jerusalem and the Levitical priesthood in Jeremiah 33:14–26. Ezekiel maintains that there will be a Davidic King in Ezekiel: 40–48, but he acts under the authority of the holy Jerusalem Temple. Again, a variety of viewpoints exist, but all express the will of YHWH in the Tanak.

The Wisdom literature also expresses a variety of viewpoints. Proverbs envisions a stable creation in which one may learn YHWH's ways by observing creation. Job disagrees by holding that YHWH's justice in the world does not always make sense because it is so difficult to find and discern as indicated in Job 28, which questions Proverbs' principle, "the fear of YHWH is the beginning of wisdom." And Qohelet speaks of the futility of finding meaning in the world, which runs counter to Proverbs, but nevertheless affirms life in this world, which is consistent with Proverbs. Although these books express various viewpoints, all are consistent with the will of YHWH.

IV

A foundational concept of the Tanak is the notion of the *Berit Olam*, "the eternal covenant," generally understood as the eternal covenant between YHWH and Israel (Sweeney, forthcoming). The concept of a *Berit Olam* or eternal covenant between YHWH and Israel is foundational in the Torah, but its full understanding demands closer observation. The Hebrew word, *olam*, is generally and correctly understood to mean, "eternal," but the term also means "world," as in the world of creation. It appears in a number of texts, such as YHWH's covenant with Noah in Genesis 9:1–16; YHWH's covenant with Abraham in Genesis

17; the Shabbat covenant in Exodus 31:12–18; the covenant of Challah for the sons of Aaron in Leviticus 24:5–9; the covenant of the offerings for the sons of Aaron in Numbers 18:12–18; and the covenant of eternal priesthood for Phineas in Numbers 25:6–15. Interpreters oftentimes argue that each of these examples represents a different eternal covenant within the Torah based upon their respective parties, contents, and reconstructed diachronic or historical dimension, but when the Torah is read synchronically they emerge as different aspects of one fundamental covenant between YHWH and creation in which Israel plays a leading role. Such an understanding recognizes that the eternal covenant with Israel in all of its dimensions is set within the broader context of the world of creation, beginning with the account of creation in Genesis 1:1–2:3.

Genesis 1:1–2:3 presents the basic account of YHWH's creation of the world in the Torah and therefore of the context in which the covenant with Israel and creation at large will be established and function. As Rashi's exegesis of Genesis 1:1–2 demonstrates, G-d did not create the earth at the outset of creation.[8] Rashi showed that Genesis 1:1–2 could not be read as "in the beginning, G-d created the heavens and the earth, and the earth was formless and void," which meant that the earth came into being after G-d began the process of creation. Instead, close study of the grammar and syntax of the passage requires that it be read, "when G-d began to create the heavens and the earth, the earth was formless and void," indicating that the earth was already in existence, but it is characterized as *tohu va-bohu*, "formless and void," or in a state of chaos. G-d does not create the earth per se in Genesis 1:1–2:3; rather, G-d creates order out of the chaos in which the earth had previously existed. Such order can be disrupted, either by human beings or by G-d, as demonstrated by the early accounts of human life in the world, such as the Adam and Eve narratives in Genesis 2:4–4:26, in which Adam and Eve are expelled from the Garden of Eden and their son, Cain, murders his brother, Abel, or the flood narratives in Genesis 6–9 in which creation was destroyed due to the bloodshed committed by human beings. Creation was only reconstituted in the aftermath of the flood when Noah and company demonstrated their capacity for recognition of YHWH. It is at this point that the first reference to *Berit Olam* appears in Genesis 9:1–16 when G-d establishes the eternal covenant with

---

[8] Harry M. Orlinsky. *Notes on the New Translation of the Torah* (Philadelphia: The Jewish Publication Society of America, 1969), 49–55.

creation based on the understanding that human beings would be able to shed blood under controlled conditions, for example, sacrifice to YHWH and the limited eating of meat, which would become the basis on which Israel would present meat offerings to YHWH. Such practice recognized the sanctity of blood and therefore of life that is conveyed by blood as well as the responsibility of human beings to treat blood and therefore life properly in accordance with the will of YHWH. Such practice would be essential to maintaining the covenant between YHWH and humanity within the larger context of creation.

But from the standpoint of the Torah narrative, the simple treatment of blood as holy as envisioned in Genesis 9:1–16 is not sufficient. As human beings continued to demonstrate their capacity to overturn order in creation, for example, by their efforts to build a tower of Babel (Babylon) that would enable them to reach G-d in the heavens as narrated in Genesis 11:1–9, YHWH determined that it would be necessary to select Abram and Sarai, later known as Abraham and Sarah, to become the ancestors of a nation that would introduce G-d's expectations into the world so that human beings would assume responsibility for ensuring the sanctity and integrity of creation. Consequently, the *Berit Olam* is extended to Abraham and his descendants through Sarah and their son, Isaac, who will become the nation Israel and who are granted the right to live in the land of Israel and the obligation to observe YHWH's commandments.

The other aspects of the *Berit Olam* then follow in the Torah narrative, all of which will form key elements of Temple practice that are designed to express and maintain the sanctity and integrity of the relationship between YHWH and Israel to ensure the sanctity and integrity of the world. The first appears in Exodus 31:12–18, which builds upon the creation narrative in Genesis 1:1–2:3 to ensure that the Shabbat is observed as the means to sanctify YHWH's creation. The second appears in Leviticus 24:5–9, which calls for the presentation of Challah to symbolize the support due to the Israelite priesthood, that is, the sons of Aaron, for their holy service before YHWH. The third appears in Numbers 18:12–18, which likewise ensures support for the sons of Aaron who were selected to serve as YHWH's priests by granting them an appropriate share of the offerings presented to YHWH. The fourth appears in Numbers 25:6–15, which grants the covenant of eternal priesthood to Phineas, the grandson of Aaron and the founder of the Zadokite priestly line that would ultimately serve in the Jerusalem Temple.

Although the blessings and curses in both Leviticus 26 and Deuteronomy 28–30 anticipate the possibility of punishment and exile from the land should Israel fail to observe YHWH's expectations, both passages conclude with promises that YHWH will restore the relationship when the people confess their sins and repent of the wrongdoing that they have committed. Although many interpreters view Deuteronomy 28–30 as a conditional expression of covenant, Shechter calls attention to Deuteronomy 30, which anticipates the repentance and restoration of the people. Likewise, the Prophets, including both the *Nevi'im Rishonim* and the *Nevi'im Aḥronom*, charge Israel and Judah with wrongdoing and anticipate or report exile as the punishment for violation of the covenant with YHWH.[9] Although many interpreters view the prophets as recognizing the conditional nature of the covenant, the restorative elements in prophetic texts which anticipate restoration at an appropriate time cannot be dismissed in a synchronic reading of these books.

V

Although YHWH's *Berit Olam* is concerned with the world of creation at large, it is clearly focused upon the people or nation Israel, understood within the Bible to be the descendants of the ancestors, Abraham and Sarah, Isaac and Rebekah, Jacob, Rachel, Leah, Bilhah, and Zilpah, and the twelve sons of Jacob, including Reuben, Simeon, Levi, Judah, Zebulun, Issachar, Dan, Asher, Gad, Naphtali, Joseph (later divided into Manasseh and Ephraim), and Benjamin, who are ancestors of the twelve tribes of Israel. This is an ideal configuration of Israel as the ten northern tribes are exiled, leaving only Judah, Benjamin, and Levi to form the southern kingdom of Judah as the heir to northern Israel. Furthermore, it is clear from Deuteronomy, Ruth, and elsewhere that foreigners may reside within Israel and ultimately be recognized as converts. Israel and Judah are both ethnic or national identities as well as religious identities. Consequently, it is important to recognize elements of both national and religious identity in the construction of Israel and Judah as YHWH's partners in the *Berit Olam* in the Tanak.

Modern Western culture has learned to recognize religion as a separate identity from national identity, but Israelite and Judean

---

[9] Jack Shechter. *The Land of Israel: Its Theological Dimensions. A Study of a Promise and of a Land's Holiness* (Lanham, MD: University Press of America, 2010).

identity function as both. Observance of divine expectations in the form of legal revelation at Sinai constitutes national law for ancient Israel and Judah expressed in religious terms. Readers will note that law codes, such as the Covenant Code of Exodus 21–23 or the Deuteronomic Code among others, contain laws that pertain both to religious and civil law and are intended to provide the legal foundations for a society that strives for a combination of holiness and justice. Insofar as the Shabbat functions as the capstone of creation in Genesis 1:1–2:3, it is not surprising to find that the Shabbat principle of the holiness of the seventh day informs laws for the sustenance of the poor, the release of debt slaves, the return of land, etc., as means to ensure that human conduct conforms to this basic principle of creation.[10] The observance of such laws becomes obligatory for the people of Israel and Judah; insofar as these laws are defined as divine instruction, that is, Hebrew, *torah*, the expression of such laws in the Torah are foundational to the covenant. Violation of those laws then constitutes violation of the covenant, as exemplified by Amos' condemnation of northern Israel for violating the laws of the covenant code in Amos 2:6–16; Isaiah's condemnation of Ahaz and Hezekiah for turning to other nations—and therefore to their gods—in Isaiah 7–9; 28–32, 39; Jeremiah's condemnation of King Zedekiah for reneging on his release of slaves in Jeremiah 34; and Ezekiel's condemnation of those who violate laws of the Holiness Code (Leviticus 17–26) in Ezekiel 18. Indeed, observance of the laws of YHWH's Torah is obligatory to ensure life in the land of Israel and Judah as understood in the Torah and the Tanak at large, and so the land of Israel is a central aspect of the *Berit Olam* in the Torah and the Bible as a whole.[11] Failure to observe YHWH's laws or expectations is the typical explanation for exile and other forms of punishment for Israel and Judah throughout the Bible.

The Temple serves as the primary Israelite and Judean institution through which YHWH's presence and laws are revealed and taught to

---

[10] Marvin A. Sweeney, "Shabbat: An Epistemological Principle for Holiness, Sustainability, and Justice in the Pentateuch," in *Christian Origins and the New Testament in Greco-Roman Context. Essays in Honor of Dennis R. MacDonald*, ed. M. Froelich et al. (Claremont, CA: Claremont Press, 2016), 53–81.

[11] Harry M. Orlinsky, "The Biblical Concept of the Land of Israel: Cornerstone of the Covenant between G-d and Israel," in *The Land of Israel: Jewish Perspectives*, ed. L. Hoffman (Notre Dame, IN: Notre Dame University Press, 1986), 27–64; David Frankel, *The Land of Canaan and the Destiny of Israel: Theologies of Territory in the Hebrew Bible* (Siphrut 4; Winona Lake, IN: Eisenbrauns, 2011).

the people. Levenson (1985) points out that the portrayal of the revelation of divine Torah at Sinai is understood as parallel to the revelation of divine Torah at Mt. Zion, understood to be the site of YHWH's Temple in Jerusalem.[12] Although interpreters know less about the ideology of other Israelite sanctuaries, such as Shiloh, Beth El, Dan, Gilgal, and others, these sanctuaries likely functioned with similar theological and ideological conceptualizations. Readers may observe that the Israelite slave law in Exodus 21:1–11 calls upon a slave who would refuse release in the seventh year in favor of perpetual slavery to make his declaration before G-d at the doorpost, presumably of the Temple. Deuteronomy 16:18–22 calls for a judicial system that includes both secular magistrates and priests, but it also calls for the high priest of the Temple to serve as the chief justice. The kings of Israel and Judah are anointed by the priests, and there is a clear division between priestly and royal roles and responsibilities, as demonstrated by Saul's rejection as king of Israel in 1 Samuel 13–14 for the sin of performing priestly duties when it was not his prerogative to do so. Levenson also points out that the interior of the Temple is decorated with motifs pertinent to the Garden of Eden, and the designation of the high priest as Ben Adam, the Son of Adam, points to his role as the representative of humankind who appears before YHWH in the holy of holies of the Temple at Yom Kippur, the Day of Atonement, in an attempt to reenter the Garden of Eden.[13] Altogether, the Temple is both the holy center of creation and the holy center of Israel and Judah, and its role is to ensure the sanctity and integrity of both creation at large and Israel and Judah in particular.

The monarch also plays an important role as head of state, who rules over the people as YHWH's regent, designated and anointed by the priests. Royal abuse of power is certainly known in the Tanak and frequently provokes criticism in the Prophetic Books, whether they are the Former Prophets or the Latter Prophets. Indeed, the so-called Torah of the King in Deuteronomy 17:14–20 calls upon the monarch to keep a copy of YHWH Torah and to study it daily under the supervision of the Levitical priests, although there is little evidence that this actually happens. But interpreters must note that the monarchy is not a necessity; 1 Samuel 8 recognizes that it is a concession by

---

[12] Jon D. Levenson, *Sinai and Zion: An Entry into the Jewish Bible* (Minneapolis, MN: Winston, 1985).

[13] Levenson, *Sinai and Zion*, and "The Temple and the World," *Journal of Religion* 64 (1984): 275–98.

YHWH to the will of the people. As noted above, the Book of Isaiah is willing to abandon the role of a Davidic monarch, designate the people of Israel as the heirs to the Davidic covenant (Isaiah 55), and designate King Cyrus of Persia as YHWH messiah and Temple builder (Isaiah 44:28, 45:1). Ezra-Nehemiah appears to concur in this assessment. Likewise, Jeremiah assigns the eternal Davidic covenant to the city of Jerusalem and the Levitical Priesthood in Jeremiah 33:14–26. Others, such as Ezekiel and the Book of the Twelve Prophets, hold to a Davidic ideal, apparently supported by Psalms, albeit sometimes with the qualification that the king observe YHWH's expectations (e.g., Psalms 89, 132).

Altogether, Israel and Judah comprise both national and religious identity, and they are intended to exemplify YHWH's expectations for an ideally holy and just society under YHWH to the nations of the world.

VI

Jewish biblical theology must also consider what happens when things do not function ideally.[14] When humans fall short, they are punished, but the Bible also recognizes times when YHWH fails to protect Israel and Judah as promised and others when YHWH acts or proposes to act in a manner that contradicts expectations of holiness or righteousness. The Tanak addresses these issues as well. Several examples illustrate the issue.

G-d sometimes shows petulance as when G-d punishes humankind by mixing their languages and scattering them around the earth when they try to build a tower to heaven in Genesis 11. When G-d proposes to destroy Sodom and Gomorrah for their immorality in Genesis 18, it is left to Abraham to ask if G-d will destroy the righteous with the wicked, and only then does G-d relent if there are ten righteous in the cities. When the people of Israel rebel in the wilderness twice in Exodus 32–34 and Numbers 13–14, a frustrated G-d proposes to kill the people and create a new nation from Moses, but Moses reminds G-d that such action would be immoral and a violation of the covenant. G-d exiles

---

[14] Marvin A. Sweeney, *Reading the Hebrew Bible after the Shoah: Engaging Holocaust Theology* (Minneapolis, MN: Fortress, 2008); Jon D. Levenson, *Creation and the Persistence of Evil: The Jewish Drama of Divine Impotence* (Princeton: Princeton University Press, 1988).

northern Israel based on the sins of Jeroboam (1 Kings 12; 2 Kings 17) and Judah based on the sins of Manasseh (2 Kings 21), although Chronicles argues instead that Jerusalem was punished due to the sins of its priests, officers, and people at the time (2 Chronicles 36).

There are issues within the Latter Prophets as well. When G-d orders Isaiah in Isaiah 6 to render the people blind, deaf, and dumb so that they will not repent and interfere with G-d's plans for self-revelation to the world, Isaiah does not object like Abraham or Moses. Although YHWH's command might be justified in teleological ethics, it is ontologically immoral. And so by the end of the book, the ideals of the nations streaming to Zion to learn divine Torah and end war are not achieved (Isaiah 2:2–4), leaving the reader to ponder what might have happened had Isaiah said no. But when Jeremiah charges G-d with having raped him and impregnated him with the divine word in Jeremiah 20, YHWH shows no remorse, and Jeremiah is left to his task. And when Ezekiel depicts the destruction of Jerusalem and the killing of its old men, women, children, and babies in Ezekiel 8–11, there is no distinction between the fate of the righteous and the wicked; all suffer—which is exactly what happens in an event such as this.

The Ketuvim are a primary arena in which questions of divine failure are addressed. In the Psalms, human beings address their concerns to G-d. Although many Psalms are songs of praise and the like, the most common type of psalm in the Psalter is the lament or complaint in which the psalmist appeals to G-d for help in a time of crisis, often asking "where are you?" or "why do you hide your face?" in a time of distress (e.g., Psalms 6, 7, 44).[15] Lamentations portrays Jerusalem metaphorically as Bat Zion, the bride of G-d, who demands that G-d look upon her suffering and humiliation in the aftermath of the destruction of the city. Job raises questions of divine righteousness throughout the book, and Elihu posits in Job 28 that—unlike Proverbs—wisdom is almost impossible for humans to discern. By the end of the book, G-d affirms that Job was right (Job 42:7) and restores Job's fortunes, although Fackenheim points out that G-d can never restore Job's ten dead children.[16] The Book of Esther posits that G-d does not appear or act at a time much like the modern Shoah when the Persian government proposes to exterminate its Jewish population, and only Esther, an

---

[15] See esp. Eliezer Berkovits. *Faith after the Holocaust* (New York: KTAV, 1973).

[16] Emil Fackenheim, *The Jewish Bible after the Holocaust: A Rereading* (Bloomington and Indianapolis: Indiana University Press, 1990).

impious woman married to the Persian monarch, is able to save the people.[17] But readers should also note that G-d does not appear in the Song of Songs, which portrays human sexuality and thus the potential for humans to act like G-d by entering into intimate relationships and creating other human beings. Based on his study of Psalms, Blumenthal in response proposes that readers must view G-d as an abusive parent, who must be forgiven, not because G-d deserves it, but because forgiveness of the abuser is a key step in the recovery of the victim.[18] And, as the examples of Esther and the Song of Songs show, human beings must recognize their own responsibility to act in the world.

VII

Jewish Biblical Theology is part of a larger dialogue within Judaism with G-d, the Jewish people, and humankind at large concerning the experience of ancient Israel and Judah in the world and their reflection on the meaning of that world. It is part of the larger dialogue of Jewish thought as an ongoing whole. The Tanak has its own perspectives on G-d, creation, the nation Israel, covenant, exile and evil, and the potential restoration of Israel to Jerusalem and the land of Israel. As the foundational document of Jewish thought, the Tanak is bound to be in dialogue with the rest of Jewish tradition, although its reading and interpretation is not bound to be controlled by that tradition (contra Sommer 2015). Much like the rabbinic Kallah in which the Rabbis debated the meaning of Torah, made their decisions, and recorded both the positions that were accepted and rejected in that debate, the Tanak represents a debate between its own various elements as well as a voice in the larger dialogue of Judaism of which it is a part.[19]

---

[17] Isaac Kalimi, "Fear of Annihilation and Eternal Covenant: The Book of Esther in Judaism and Jewish Theology," in *Jewish Bible Theology: Perspectives and Case Studies*, ed. I. Kalimi (Winona Lake, IN: Eisenbrauns, 2012), 231–47; Marvin A. Sweeney, "Absence of G-d and Human Responsibility in the Book of Esther," in *Reading the Hebrew Bible for a New Millennium: Form, Concept and Theological Perspective. Volume 2: Exegetical and Theological Essays*, ed. W. Kim et al. (Harrisburg, PA: Trinity International, 2000), 264–75.

[18] David Blumenthal. *Facing the Abusing G-d: A Theology of Protest* (Louisville, KY: Westminster John Knox, 1993).

[19] Cf. Michael Fishbane. *Biblical Myth and Rabbinic Mythmaking* (Oxford, UK, and New York: Oxford University Press, 2003).

Selected Further Reading

Berkovits, Eliezer. *Faith after the Holocaust*. New York: KTAV, 1973.
Blumenthal, David. *Facing the Abusing G-d: A Theology of Protest*. Louisville, KY: Westminster John Knox, 1993.
Fackenheim, Emil. *The Jewish Bible after the Holocaust: A Rereading*. Bloomington and Indianapolis: Indiana University Press, 1990.
Frankel, David. *The Land of Canaan and the Destiny of Israel: Theologies of Territory in the Hebrew Bible*. Siphrut 4. Winona Lake, IN: Eisenbrauns, 2011.
Kalimi, Isaac, ed. *Jewish Bible Theology: Perspectives and Case Studies*. Winona Lake, IN: Eisenbrauns, 2012.
Levenson, Jon D. *Creation and the Persistence of Evil: The Jewish Drama of Divine Impotence*. Princeton: Princeton University Press, 1988.
Levenson, Jon D. *The Hebrew Bible, The Old Testament, and Historical Criticism: Jews and Christians in Biblical Studies*. Louisville, KY: Westminster John Know, 1993.
Levenson, Jon D. *Sinai and Zion: An Entry into the Jewish Bible* Minneapolis, MN: Winston, 1985.
Orlinsky, Harry M. "The Biblical Concept of the Land of Israel: Cornerstone of the Covenant between G-d and Israel." In *The Land of Israel: Jewish Perspectives*, 27–64. Edited by L. Hoffman. Notre Dame, IN: Notre Dame University Press, 1986.
Shechter, Jack. *The Land of Israel: Its Theological Dimensions. A Study of a Promise and of a Land's Holiness*. Lanham, MD: University Press of America, 2010.
Sommer, Benjamin D. "Dialogical Biblical Theology: A Jewish Approach to Reading Scripture Theologically." In *Biblical Theology: Introducing the Conversation*, 1–53. Edited by L. G. Perdue et al. Nashville: Abingdon, 2009.
Sommer, Benjamin D. *Revelation and Authority: Sinai in Jewish Scripture and Tradition*. New Haven, CT, and London: Yale University Press, 2015.
Sweeney, Marvin A. "Jewish Biblical Theology: An Ongoing Dialog." *Interpretation* 70 (2016): 314–25.
Sweeney, Marvin A. *Reading the Hebrew Bible after the Shoah: Engaging Holocaust Theology*. Minneapolis, MN: Fortress, 2008.
Sweeney, Marvin A. *Tanak: A Theological and Critical Introduction to the Jewish Bible*. Minneapolis, MN: Fortress, 2012.

4 The God of the Rabbis
MOSHE HALBERTAL

I

The Rabbis never produced a systematic theology but rather expressed their religious attitude and sensibility mainly through a creative interpretive encounter with Scripture. The rabbinic sources in the various midrashim reveal an intense attentiveness to God as a divine relational subject, a subject that resonated and sometimes stood in tension with the historical and personal experiences of the Rabbis. A freestanding philosophical inquiry of God's attributes and being, and the appeal to reason for refining, defining, or proving God's existence were thoroughly alien to the Rabbis.

Rabbinic culture spanned roughly eight centuries, from the end of the Persian occupation of the Land of Israel at the beginning of the second century BCE until the advent of the Muslim conquest of the Land of Israel in the seventh century CE. It flourished in diverse geographical and geopolitical settings: under the Hellenistic and Roman rule of Palestine and as part of the Sasanian Empire in Babylonia. The literature produced during this long period consisted of radically different genres; its major canonical compilation—the Mishnah—which is organized thematically, is of a different nature than the midrash, which follows the sequence of scriptural verses and interprets them creatively. The Jerusalem Talmud and the Babylonian Talmud, devoted to meticulously complex interpretations of the Mishnah, differ dramatically from the Mishnah and the midrash as well, in style, modes of thinking, and language. Dozens of scholars were part of this immense creative outburst, and its diversity in geopolitical settings and literary genres is matched by the multiplicity of opinions and stances expressed in this vast literature. This diverse body of texts and contexts produced, as well, different religious positions concerning God. Nevertheless, it exhibits coherence and unity in grasping God as a thoroughly relational subject, and in mainly shaping God's image through an intense and careful reading of Scripture.

One such interpretative encounter that is quoted in an early midrashic source will serve as a starting point to illuminate the rabbinic understanding of God, and the deep gap between the Rabbis' religious sensibilities and the theological metaphysical stance which dominated medieval Jewish philosophy. This midrash, quoted in the Mekhilta to Exodus, raises a difficulty evoked by the description of God in leading Israel after the great exodus from Egypt:

> "And the LORD went before them by day in a pillar of cloud, to lead them the way; and by night in a pillar of fire, to give them light; that they might go by day and by night" (Exodus 13, 21). Can this be said? Is it not written "Do I not fill the heavens and earth? Says the Lord"? (Jeremiah 23:22). And "One (seraph) called to the other Holy, Holy, Holy is the Lord of hosts – the earth is full of His Glory"? and "And behold the glory of the God of Israel came from the east, His voice is like the voice of many waters, the earth shines from his glory". How then am I to understand "And the Lord went before them by day ..."? (Mekhilta d'Rabbi Ishmael, Va-Yehi, Ptichta)

The question posed by the midrash sounds very similar to the metaphysical difficulties that philosophers were accustomed to raise when they so frequently encountered a bold anthropomorphic biblical description. How can God, who is an infinite being, beyond space and time, reside within a pillar of smoke by day and a pillar of fire by night traveling ahead of the Israelites? Abraham ibn Ezra, the great biblical interpreter of the twelfth century, made the following comment as he encountered this verse: "We know that God resides in eternity holy is His name. And the Torah spoke in the language of humans, since it was God's power that walked with Israel" (Commentary on the Torah, Exodus 13:21). Ibn Ezra proposed to resolve this problem by postulating an intermediary being in order to mediate between the transcendent God and the pillars of smoke and fire. Instead of "the Lord" residing in the pillar of smoke and fire, it was his force manifested in the pillar before the Israelites. We would have expected a similar approach from the midrash, but instead, a surprising parable is introduced as an answer:

> Rabbi said: A parable that provides an analogy: The emperor Antoninus was presiding at the dais when it got dark, his sons

remaining there. After he was finished, he took the lantern and lit (the way) for his sons – whereupon the nobles close to him said: "Let us take the lantern and light (the way) for your sons." At this, he said: "It is not that I have no one to take the lantern and light (the way) for my sons; but I want to impress upon you my love for my sons, that you treat them honorably."

The parable that was brought as an answer can teach us a great deal concerning the way in which the initial question in the midrash has to be properly understood. What troubled the midrash is not a metaphysical problem concerning the impossibility of the infinite to reside within the finite. If this was the initial concern, the parable provides no answer at all. It seems that the gravity of the question posed by the midrash was not whether such a representation of God is metaphysically *possible*, but rather, whether such a representation of the God's conduct is relationally *proper*.

I will provide my own parable to explain the opposition between the metaphysically *possible* representation and the relationally *proper* one. Let us imagine that a head of a state, a super-power, is invited for an official visit to another state. As his lodging he is provided with a room in a cheap youth hostel instead of a lavish suite at the most elegant hotel. The question raised by such handling is not how is it metaphysically possible for a head of a state to reside in a youth hostel—after all, nobody tried to squeeze the visiting dignitary into the tiny space of a matchbox. Rather, the bewilderment would have been directed toward the fact that such an act is relationally improper, a kind of insulting breach of protocol. In a similar vein, the initial question of the midrash was not aimed toward the metaphysical impossibility of God's residing in the pillar; God, if he so wishes, can reside in a pillar. But rather the midrash wonders why God himself had performed such a task given his capacity to send his emissaries to do it. And moreover, if God himself had decided to perform the task, he could have revealed himself in a spectacle better suited to his immense cosmic stature.

The answer to such a breach of protocol, implicit in the imperial parable provided by the midrash, is love. The great Roman emperor acts like a servant when it concerns his sons, since love undermines the strict protocol of authority and hierarchy. The emperor carries the lantern by himself not due to lack of servants, but because he seeks to exhibit care for his children directly.[1] The question, as one of wonder about the properness of such behavior, was thus raised within a relational expectation. God, the master of the universe, is not supposed to act in such a way; but given his love for his children, God is seeking an immediate, intimate, and caring attitude.[2]

A similar question, and a far more dramatic and haunting answer, is raised in a midrash that refers to another theophany in the book of Exodus—God's revelation to Moses within the burning bush (*sneh*) in the desert.[3] The midrash wonders why God, whose residence is the whole cosmos, would reveal himself to Moses in a little, thorny, burning bush. One of the answers provided for such a modest revelation refers to God's sharing in the pain of the enslaved Israelites:

> Rabbi Hiya and Rabbi Yehuda say: Come and See the mercy of the One who said and the world was created. So long that Israel are in distress, God is distressed. Since it is written: "In all their affliction he was afflicted" (Isaiah 63, 7). This is true about the affliction of the many, how do we know about the affliction of an individual? It is stated: "He shall call upon me and I will answer him, I will be with him in affliction" (Psalms 91, 15)." (Mekhilta d'Rabbi Shimon ben Yochai 3, 8).

---

[1] It is a major feature of the midrash that God is understood in comparison and contrast with the Roman emperor through an extensive use of imperial parables. For the work that still might be considered as the most important book on the historical background of the imperial parables in the midrash, see I. Ziegler, *Die Konigsgleichnisse des Midrasch* (Bresslau: S. Schottlaender, 1903). For the larger methodological questions relating to the historical reading of the parable, see Y. Frankel, *The Paths of Agada and Midrash* (in Hebrew) 1, (Givatayim: Yad la-Talmud, 1991), 379–83. And see as well Stern, *Parables in Midrash*.

[2] For other sources describing God's revelation in an intimate mild setting motivated by love, see Sifra Dibura de-Nedava 2, 12.

[3] "And the angel of the LORD appeared unto him in a flame of fire out of the midst of a bush; and he looked, and, behold, the bush burned with fire, and the bush was not consumed. And Moses said: 'I will turn aside now, and see this great sight, why the bush is not burnt.' And when the LORD saw that he turned aside to see, God called unto him out of the midst of the bush, and said: 'Moses, Moses.' And he said: 'Here am I.' And He said: 'Draw not nigh hither; put off thy shoes from off thy feet, for the place whereon thou standest is holy ground.' Moreover, He said: 'I am the God of thy father, the God of Abraham, the God of Isaac, and the God of Jacob.' And Moses hid his face; for he was afraid to look upon God" (Exodus 3:2–4). God's revelation within a burning bush in the desert might have been moderated by the verses themselves in introducing at the beginning "And the Angel of the Lord appeared to him in a flame of fire out of the midst of a bush." Though as the verses proceed it is clear that God himself dwelt within the small bush.

God's empathy with the pain of Israel was manifested in his lowly and painful revelation within a small, thorny, burning bush. The midrashic portrayal of God's revelation in the burning bush as the distressed God, who is in pain and in exile because of his beloved humans, is one of the rabbinic innovations in exploring the dimensions of God's personality.[4] Such an explicit and developed idea is not present in the biblical descriptions of God.

Unlike their predecessors in the Second Temple literature, the Rabbis introduced new names for God above and beyond the biblical names, among them the feminine name שכינה (Presence) and other names such as הקדוש ברוך הוא (The Holy One blessed be He).[5] But the ultimate expression of their religious outlook is manifested in the meaning that was given in the midrash to God's most important and proper name— י-הוה. The biblical literature presents us with diverse names for God, the most prevalent of them are— אלהים commonly translated as "God," and י-הוה commonly translated as "the Lord." In rabbinic law as in many other traditions, י-הוה is considered as the most important and sacred of God's names, to the degree that it can be uttered only in rare and extremely restricted circumstances, and it is therefore pronounced with the substitute of אדני (the Lord). The unique status of the name י-הוה among God's names is rooted within biblical tradition since it was revealed to Moses by God declaring it to be his own name in one of the most theologically potent and complex verses in the Bible.[6] The meaning of the name י-הוה is a matter of debate among biblical scholars, but for many readers the name resonated with the Hebrew term for being— היה. In line with such resonance, the name י-הוה was interpreted among the philosophers, starting with Philo onwards, as referring to the apersonal transcendent dimensions of God as a pure perfect being.[7] Maimonides, for example, claimed that, unlike all of God's names which are all adjectives, י-הוה is God's only proper name, and it gestures to God as a necessary being.[8] The midrash, in contrast to

---

[4] For an extensive analysis of the origin and history of this theme in rabbinic literature, see M. Eyali, "God who is Pained in the Pain of Israel," (in Hebrew) *Researches in Jewish Thought*, S. Heller Villensky and M. Idel eds. (Jerusalem: The Hebrew University Magnes Press, 1989), 29–50.

[5] On the rabbinic introduction of new names to God and their meaning, see Urbach, *The Sages: Their Concepts and Beliefs*, 37–96.

[6] Exodus 3:12–13.

[7] Philo, *Life of Moses*, I, 75. And see Wolfson, *Philo*, Vol. II, 120–22 and note 60.

[8] Maimonides, *Guide of the Perplexed*, I, 61.

this long metaphysical tradition, developed a radically different understanding of God's most sacred name. The meaning given to י-הוה in rabbinic literature was expressed for the first time in the following midrash:

> "The Lord (י-הוה)," in every place that it is said [in scripture] "The Lord" (י-הוה), this is the attribute of mercy, since it is said: "The LORD, the LORD, God, merciful and gracious" (י-הוה י-הוה אל רחום וחנון). And in every place that it is said "God" (אלוהים), this is the attribute of judgment, since it is said: "the cause of both parties shall come before God ((האלוהים, he whom God shall condemn shall pay double unto his neighbor" (Sifrei on Deuteronomy, 26)

This interpretation offered to the name י-הוה as mercy is the ultimate expression of the Rabbis' perception of God as a relational subject through and through, a subject whose essential most defining characteristic is mercy. The equation of God's proper name with mercy in the midrash, which had far-reaching echoes in Kabbalah and subsequent Jewish thought, is even more striking given the fact that within the Bible the name י-הוה appears as well in the context of punishment and judgment. The midrash was fully aware of these seemingly contradictory occurrences, and nevertheless insisted on reinterpreting them in order to preserve the sense that God's most intimate and direct name refers to his relational quality of mercy.[9] It is a testimony to the primacy of compassion over and above the aloofness of the pure impersonal perfect being.[10]

II

In their embrace of God as a fully relational subject, the Rabbis continued the biblical tradition in which the personality of God is articulated and manifested within an analogy to human institutions and hierarchical relationships. God is a king, a father, a husband, sometime a mother, and a judge, and the human counterpart is portrayed at the opposite pole of the hierarchical metaphor as a son and a daughter,

---

[9] On the rabbinic awareness for the appearance of the name י-הוה in the biblical context of judgment and punishment, see Bereshit Rabba 33, 3.

[10] On the status and meaning of the name י-הוה in rabbinic literature, see H. Ben Sasson and Moshe Halbertal, "The Tetramagon and Divine Mercy" (in Hebrew) in *Vezot le-Yehuda: Essays in Honor of Yehudah Liebes* (Jerusalem: Bialik Press, 2012), 53–69.

a wife, a subject, and a defendant. What gives the anthropomorphic paradigm its monotheistic mark is the fact that while the polytheistic religions can distribute these diverse roles to different gods that inhabit their pantheon, in the case of the one God all such roles and positions are located within one subject. These different human analogies determine different types of relationships, and they stand in tension with each other. Their simultaneous presence, or the temporal shift from one to the other, enriches the complexity and sometimes unpredictability of the God–human relationship. One such exploration of the complexities of God's personality in the midrash points to the tension that is inherent in God's inhabiting multiple simultaneous roles. It appears in the midrash in reference to Rosh Hashanah which is considered the day of judgment before God. In describing standing before God as a judge, the midrash offers the following relational analogy:

> Rabbi Levi in the name of Rabbi Hama son of Hanina, it is like a son of a king that had a trial before his father. His father told him: "if you wish to be acquitted before me in the trial, choose the following lawyer and you will be acquitted." In the same way God told Israel, "my sons if you will mention the merits of your forefathers you will be acquitted in my trial" (Pesikta de-Rav Kahana, ba-Chodesh ha-Sevi'i 23,7).

Rosh Hashanah, the day of judgment, has an ominous quality to it, but since the judge is also the loving father, the harsh quality of the day is mitigated. God the judge and the father offers the defendant a way to be acquitted, revealing to him ahead of the trial that there is a particular line of argumentation that will work for him, since God tends to be persuaded by the mentioning of the forefathers' merits. The duality of judgment and intimacy implied in the analogy captures the complex experience that defines Rosh Hashanah as a sacred day which is simultaneously a threatening day of judgment and a day that offers, as well, a great promise of acquittal in standing before God.[11]

The innovations in the rabbinic view of God were thus not expressed in an attempt to transcend the qualities of God as a relational subject, but rather to deepen and extend these qualities, sometimes bringing them to their utter limits. To the multiple analogies which the Rabbis explored and broadened, they added relational analogies of their own, among them God the teacher and Israel the

---

[11] Among other rabbinic sources that reflect a sense of hope and confidence in Rosh Hashanah, see Jerusalem Talmud, Rosh Hashanah 1: 3, 57b.

disciples.[12] And, in their bold anthropomorphism they did not shy away from inverting hierarchical analogies, portraying God as the defendant or as the servant.[13] One of the most important innovative rabbinic perceptions of God grew out of the inherent tension between the triumphant biblical God and the conditions of destruction and subjugation which defined the living historical reality of the Rabbis under the Roman Empire. The biblical tradition might have provided an answer to such a painful gap by claiming that exile and destruction are not signs of God's weakness but rather they are punishment issued by God for the sins of Israel. Certain rabbinic sources reject this form of theodicy and develop a different religious approach to the question, an approach which sheds a surprising new light on God's image.

An earlier and most precious formulation of this new emerging religious sensibility is articulated in the midrash on the biblical verses that recount the song of Israel in praise of God after Pharaoh and his army were drowned in the sea. Israel's song is one the strongest lyrical biblical portrayals of the triumphant warrior God. The song begins with the following verses: "I will sing unto the LORD, for He is highly exalted; The horse and his rider hath He thrown into the sea ... The LORD is a man of war; The LORD is His name. Pharaoh's chariots and his host hath He cast into the sea, and his chosen captains are sunk in the Red Sea." (Exodus 15:1, 3–4). Following the depiction of God the warrior, the song praises God as the mightiest of all: "Who is like unto Thee, O LORD, among the mighty [*ba-Elim*]? Who is like unto Thee, glorious in holiness, fearful in praises, doing wonders?" (15:11). Commenting on this verse that praises God as the mightiest, the most powerful, the midrash introduces a bold rereading of the term "among the mighty [*ba-Elim*]":

> Who is like unto Thee, O Lord among the mighty [ba- elim באלים]? Who is like you among the dumb [ba-ilmim באלמים]? Who is like you

---

[12] On God who studies and teaches Torah, see S. Rawidowicz's comments in this essay "On Jewish Learning," in *Israel the Ever Dying People and Other Essays*, B. Ravid, ed. (Rutherford, NJ: 1984), 134–37.

[13] The representation of God as a slave appears in the following talmudic reading: Rabbi Yochanan says: "What is the meaning of that which is written "He that graciously gives to the poor makes a loan to the to the Lord" (Proverbs 19, 17). Were it not written in the verse, it would be impossible to say this, "the borrower is a servant to the lender" (Babylonian Talmud, Baba Batra 10a). In giving charity, the giver pays God's debt and thus becomes God's lender which makes God his slave. And see as well the developed sequence in Pesikta D'Rav Kahana, Vayhei B'Shalach 8, which describes God caring for Israel as a disciple for his teacher.

that watches the humiliation of his children and keeps silent (Mekhilta be-Shalach, 7).

God is praised here not for his warrior's might but for his capacity for restraint. The midrash is using the phonetic similarity in the Hebrew between "the mighty"—אלים, and "the dumb"—אלמים. Through an addition of one letter to the word "mighty," a radical turn in God's image and reevaluation of power is introduced. In times of destruction and defeat, the triumphant warrior God turns into a silent, controlled, and unprovoked observer. God is praised for his silence, though the reader is kept in doubt whether such praise has more than a touch of bitterness or irony in it.

A later talmudic narrative extends this theme in an acute and instructive level of self-awareness:

> R. Joshua b. Levi said: Why were they called "Men of the Great Assembly" [the earlier generations of rabbinic culture are called הגדולה אנשי כנסת]? Because they restored the crown of the divine attributes to its ancient status. Moses had come and said: "The great God, the mighty, and the awesome" (Deuteronomy 10:7). Then Jeremiah came and said: Aliens [the armies of Nebuchadnezzar] are destroying His Temple. Where are, then, His awful deeds? Hence he omitted [the attribute] the "awesome." [Jeremiah in his prayer omitted the attribute of awesome: "The great God, the mighty Lord of Hosts, is His name." (Jeremiah 32:18)] Daniel came and said: Aliens are enslaving his sons. Where are His mighty deeds? Hence he omitted the word "mighty." [Daniel omits "the mighty" from his prayer in Daniel 9:5]. But they [the Rabbis of the Great Assembly who compiled the liturgy of prayer that states: "The God who is great, mighty and awesome"] came and said: On the contrary! Therein lie His might of his mightiness, that He conquers His inclination, that He exercises patience towards the wicked. Therein lie His awesomeness: For but for the fear of Him, how could one [single] nation persist among the [many] nations! But how could they [Jeremiah and Daniel] abolish something established by Moses? R. Eleazar said: Since they knew that the Holy One, blessed be He, is truthful, they would not ascribe false [attributes] to Him. (Yoma 69b)

This foundational talmudic narrative describes an imagined history in which God's attributes were reevaluated. At the center of this bold religious transformation stands the shift from triumphant Israel to the destroyed and exiled nation. Greatness was attributed to the Rabbis of the "Great Assembly" because of their ability to reinterpret the very idea of might and power, after a long historical process in which attributions of greatness, might, and awesomeness were gradually omitted from God in response to destruction and exile. The historical sequence constituted and imagined by the Talmud is of immense importance because it offers a large-scale reflection on the way in which God's image is shaped and understood in a dialectic of history and interpretation. Moreover, it points to an acute awareness in the Talmud of the transformative role of the founding fathers of rabbinic culture in reshaping and understanding the personality of God. The idea that God's power should be rather understood as his capacity for restraint and for self-overcoming was a rabbinic innovation. It is the mere endurance of Israel within such a troubled realm that attests to God's awesomeness rather than to Israel's triumph. This new understanding grew out of the clash between the triumphant warrior God of Exodus, and his defeated nation under Rome. And, as emerges from this narrative, the Rabbis are aware that this new sensibility is indeed their own innovative religious transformation. For this innovation, as talmudic figures claim, their earlier rabbinic predecessors deserve the title of greatness.

In further midrashic and talmudic sources a new picture of God emerges. God of the destruction and exile emerges as a character further away from the biblical vigorous, triumphant God or from the angry, punishing though loving God. In exilic form he is portrayed by the Rabbis as lamenting, crying, deprived of laughter and joy.[14] Unlike the Greek gods who are defined by playfulness, God deprived himself of such leisure.[15] He roars at night for the humiliation of his children—"Rav Yizhak Bar Shmuel said in the name of Rav, The night consists of three watches and over each and every watch the Holy One, blessed be He, sits and roars like a lion and says: Woe to me, that due to their sins I destroyed My house, burned My Temple and exiled them among the nation of the World" (Babylonian Talmud, Berachot 3a). This divine roar, that in the biblical imagery echoed a threatening destructive force, has turned into a roar of lament and regret, a roar that is burdened by his own guilt at being the source of their destruction.

---

[14] On God's weeping, see Babylonian Talmud, Hagiga 5b.
[15] On God's self-deprivation from laughter and leisure, see Babylonian Talmud, Avodah Zarah 3b.

The talmudic text concerning God's attributes that was analyzed above boldly ascribes to the prophets Jeremiah and Daniel the omissions of positive, praiseworthy attributes from God when they thought He was not deserving of them. Wondering how such behavior is possible, the Talmud answers: "Since they knew that the Holy One, blessed be He, is truthful, they would not ascribe false [attributes] to Him." This talmudic statement highlights a particular feature of rabbinic religious discourse that might seem surprising to other religious traditions. Among other components, rabbinic religious discourse has an irreverential tonality to it, a tonality that became part of Jewish religious expression at large. It grew out of a combination of intimacy and rage and from the confidence in faith that does not need pretense to sustain it. It grew from sorrow and distress and from a sense of honesty and trust.[16] One such midrashic text, maybe the boldest that I know from rabbinic literature, is an outcome of a subtle creative reading of the biblical text and exhibits a striking candor in questioning God's behavior. This midrashic reading concerns the killing of Abel by Cain and it refers to God's words to Cain after he has murdered his brother: "the voice of your brother's blood cries out to me from the earth" (Genesis 4:10):

> Rabbi Shimon ben Yochai said, it is a difficult thing to say and impossible for the mouth to utter. It is like two gladiators fighting before the king. Had the king wished to separate them, he could have. He did not, and the stronger overcame the other and killed him. As he was killed, he [the defeated gladiator about to be killed] cried and said "my lawful grievance is directed against the king," and so "the voice of your brother's blood cries out to me from the earth." (Genesis Rabbah 22, 9)

This imperial analogy, drawn from gladiatorial games, is not about love and care but rather draws attention to power and cruelty. Cain and Abel are described as two gladiators fighting before God, and God, as the emperor, could have saved Abel, the gladiator who is about to be killed.[17] In the bloody games in Rome the defeated party could not

---

[16] For an extensive and deep analysis of this theme, see D. Weiss, *Pious Irreverence: Confronting God in Rabbinic Judaism* (Philadelphia: University of Pennsylvania Press, 2016).

[17] For an extensive analysis of the parable and its meaning, see J. Levinson, "The Gladiator of Faith," *Tarbiz* 68, 1 (1999): 61–86.

The God of the Rabbis 71

have been killed without the approval of the emperor, who in a show of dominance while interacting with the cheers and desires of the crowd, provided the sign either to halt the killing or to proceed. Abel's blood, depicted in the verse as crying from the earth, is not crying for revenge against his brother Cain, but rather his cry is an accusation directed toward God the emperor, who caused the struggle between the brothers in the first place and approved the killing. The striking analogy produced by the midrash in order to explain the acute meaning of Abel's cry is preceded by a rare introductory statement that such a reading is introduced with grave difficulty. It reveals an awareness of the harsher dimensions of the human–God relationship.

III

These new religious sensibilities had an impact on the formation and rearticulation of legal practices as well. It would be worthwhile to examine an occasion of the intersection of law and the concept of God which seems to strike one of the deepest chords of the rabbinic religious imagination. This rabbinic reflection and reconstruction of a legal practice was anchored in the reinterpretation of a biblical law that prohibits leaving the body of an executed criminal unburied overnight:

> And if a man has committed a sin worthy of death, and he be put to death, and thou hang him on a tree; his body shall not remain all night upon the tree, but thou shalt surely bury him the same day; for he that is hanged is God's curse [קללת אלוהים תלוי]; that thou defile not thy land which the LORD thy God giveth thee for an inheritance (Deuteronomy 21:21–22).

While the biblical source prohibits leaving the body unburied overnight, the earlier rabbinic sources—the Mishnah, Toseftah, and the Midrash Halakhah—magnified the prohibition and prohibited leaving the body unburied even for the shortest of times. This is the way the Mishnah describes the ritual of hanging:

> How do they hang him? They sink the beam into the ground, and a [piece of wood protrudes from it, and one places his hands together and hangs him ... And then they undo him [from the gallows] immediately. (Mishnah Sanhedrin 6, 4)

While the Torah prohibits leaving the body all night long, according to the Mishnah the hanging has to be immediately undone. The

Toseftah sharpens the paradoxical nature of this construction of the hanging: "And when they hang him, while one ties, the other unties him" (Sanhedrin 9, 6). This far-reaching formation of the ritual, in which hanging is done and undone simultaneously, empties the content of the act completely. In the paradoxical structuring of the tying and the immediate untying, the exposure of the dead body and its humiliation in front of spectators are annulled at the moment that they might have been realized. Such a paradoxical construction of a ritual procedure, unknown to me in any other contexts, reflects the deepest ambivalence toward the performance of the hanging.

This peculiar innovative construction of the hanging is anchored in a creative reading of the verse in Deuteronomy, in particular the section in the verse that serves as the justification for the prohibition, and at this point the connection between the concept of God and the law is introduced. The justification provided in the verse for the prohibition states כי קללת אלוהים תלוי, a difficult text that can be translated in different ways. Earlier sources prior to the Mishnah, both Philo and Josephus as well as Paul in the Letter to the Galatians, read this verse in the following manner: "his body shall not remain all night upon the tree, but thou shalt surely bury him the same day; for the hanged is cursed by God." The obligation to bury the exposed body is based on the fact that such a body is cursed by God, and the executed person should not be excessively punished by leaving his corpse exposed all night long.[18] The Rabbis read the verse differently and thus loaded it with new urgency. In their reading, the expression קללת אלוהים תלוי means that hanging is a curse/reproach *to* God. The act of hanging has to come to an end immediately even as it is performed because such an act is a violation of God; it is like cursing God.

Three explanations are raised within the rabbinic material to explain why hanging the body constitutes a curse directed toward God. The first explanation stated in the Mishnah introduces the argument that since the hanged person is the one who cursed God, when people see him hanging they ask why is he hanged, and the description of his sin is a kind of repetition of the offence of cursing.[19] Punishment

---

[18] See Philo, *The Special Laws* III, 152; Paul's *Letter to the Galatians* 3:13 and Josephus, *Antiquities* 4, 265.

[19] "For he that is hanged is a reproach unto God ..." That is to say: why has he been hanged? Because he blessed [i.e., cursed] God, and God's name has become desecrated (Mishnah Sanhedrin 6, 5).

in that respect might turn self-defeating, since its public exposure might cause the repetition of the offence itself. The second and the third explanations for why hanging the human body is a curse directed toward God touch upon the deepest religious sensibilities of the Rabbis. The second explanation is brought in the continuation of the Mishnah:

> Said Rabbi Meir, when a human being is in distress, what expression does the Divine Presence use, as it were? "My head is in pain, My arm is in pain" (קלני מראשי קלני מזרועי). If so, God feels distress over the blood of the wicked that is spilled; how much more so does He over the blood of the righteous. (Sanhedrin 6, 5)

The body has to be immediately untied and buried because God is in distress due to the affliction of the executed. God's empathy extends even to the criminal who transgressed so severely as to be liable to the death penalty. If such is God's distress over the pain of the wicked, how much more so does He feel for the pain of the righteous. The urgency in stopping the possible humiliation of a human criminal is tied to God's suffering in encountering such pain. God, the sovereign, who commanded such an infliction of punishment cannot withstand its endurance. The tying is immediately followed by untying.

The third explanation is mentioned in the Toseftah following the section that constituted the paradoxical performance of hanging:

> Rabbi Meir said, what is the meaning of the verse: "for he that is hanged is a curse unto God ... [קללת אלוהים תלוי]"? It is comparable to two brothers who were identical twins. One became a king ruling the whole world, and the other deteriorated to banditry. After a while, the brother who became a robber had been caught, and he was crucified on the cross, and every passerby said "it looks like the king is crucified" [The king commanded to take him down immediately]. This is the meaning of verse: "the hanged is a curse unto God" (Toseftah Sanhedrin 9, 7).

Rabbi Meir's explanation of the verse begins with a common analogy drawn from the parables of kings. In the ordinary structure of such parables that are drawn from a hierarchical patriarchal and political relationship, the human counterpart to God, the king, is presented as the son, or the daughter, or the immediate circle of servants, or the subjects of the kingdom. What is unique about Rabbi Meir's parable is that the human counterpart is a brother, someone who is an equal to the king; God and the executed robber are represented as identical twins. Since humans are made in God's image, when the criminal is crucified, God the king is perceived as the one crucified on the cross; hence the immediacy and urgency in undoing such a form of punishment.[20] The ritual of hanging is thus structured in such a way that it is done not to humiliate the criminal, but rather to show that such a humiliation constitutes a direct offence to God, a tension that is enacted in the most ambivalent performance of the hanging.

This parable, that can be dated to the middle of the second century, seems to engage in an indirect or maybe in a direct dialogue with the central icon of Christianity—the suffering God on the cross. In its creative reading of the verse in Deuteronomy, the parable represents a stark difference from the Christian image. In Rabbi Meir's reading of the verse, the iconic relationship between God and humans is a feature of every human, and in this case the lowest of all humans—the criminal who was caught and executed. Crucifying the criminal represents the crucifixion of God. Within the Christian imagery it is only Christ the son of God who stands for God as his reincarnation on the cross. What had been the exclusive feature of Christ turns in the parable and the law into a feature of every human, who by virtue of his or her humanity is an iconic figure of God.

The legal rabbinic discourse surrounding the hanged, executed body presents a distilled combination of a creative reading of the biblical text, a paradoxical reconfiguration of an execution practice, while this legal and interpretive activity is informed and moved by a radical religious conception of the God–human relationship. Such a conception might have been amplified by a polemic edge about the meaning of the suffering God on the cross. In the parable that was produced by Rabbi Meir with its non-hierarchical horizontal analogy of the twin brothers, the rabbinic anthropomorphic imagination reached its most extreme and creative edge.

V

Generations of scholars saw the rabbinic conception of God as an affront to God's assumed perfection. Countless apologetic efforts were marshaled to salvage this religious embarrassment. The God of the midrash seemed human—all too human—vulnerable and flawed. But perfection is a category that needs to be clarified before uttering a clear judgment here.

---

[20] For an extensive analysis of this theme, see Halbertal, *Interpretative Revolutions in the Making*, 159–67; Lorberbaum, *God's Image: Halakhah and Aggadah*, 286–92.

There is no such thing as perfection independent of a goal or a context. Let us imagine a perfect ridge of mountains. It could be perfect for protecting a city or a territory, it could be perfect as a scenic spectacle, or it could be perfect as a track for climbing and walking. It would have to possess different qualities to answer for each of these functions, since perfection is relative to a function. There is no such thing as the perfect ridge, per se.

In the theological tradition nourished by the philosophers, God's perfection was constructed in the following way. What is a perfect being, perfect ontologically speaking, perfect in its "beingness"? From Ibn Sina to Spinoza, it was imagined that the existence of such a perfect being cannot be an accident, but is, rather necessary. God was thus defined as a necessary being. Furthermore, such a perfect being must, of necessity, be self-caused, hence its existence could not be derivative. And more important, such a perfect being, ontologically speaking, must be stable, unchanging, eternal, ontologically self-sufficient. As a supreme being, God must be imagined as well as the origin of all, the cause of all causes, the underlying principle that determines all that happens. All these features were ascribed to God as a being that stands for perfection, ontologically speaking. They are all relative to a particular aim or function—in this case the aim of constructing a perfect entity, a perfect being. But if we think of God not as an object but rather as a subject, or to put it more accurately as a relational subject, some of these ontological perfections would count as flaws. Who wants to be in a relationship with an unmoved mover, with a being that cannot be changed and is not a responsive entity? A greater and more troubling question might be raised concerning God's imagined ontological perfection. From the relational stance, God cannot be imagined as the cause of all, since in order to form an intersubjective relationship there must be place for human freedom. Without freedom no such relationship is possible. A complete deterministic world, all-governed by God's omnipotence, is thus a flaw, a false perfection that would put an end to the possibility of God as a relational subject. If a subject endowed with freedom other than God did not exist, God would not have anyone to relate to. Hence, in order for God to be a relational subject, he needs to give room to another "Other" free subject to confront Him. The biblical and rabbinic God is therefore marked by a human counterpart that is unpredictable. If the human counterpart were predictable or fully caused by God, he or she would not be worthy as relational subjects.

Lurianic Kabbalists imagined God's own self-contraction (*tsimtsum*) as a necessary step that preceded God's creative act since the infinite God had to allow space for the world to emerge. But the ultimate contraction in creation was the creation of humans, the unpredictable subject that can thus be worthy as a counterpart to God's relational being. God, we might say, contracted the power to cause; he formed an unpredictable human subject that keeps surprising him. Perfection as a concept must thus be relative to a function, and what might be perfection for this or that function might turn out to be a flaw for another function. The ultimate question is, therefore, not whether God is perfect or not, but whether God is understood within the paradigm of ontological being as the perfect "object," or whether God is understood as a relational subject. And if God is indeed a relational subject capable of intentionality and responsiveness seeking a partner, the perfections attributed to him by the philosophers are actually flaws and imperfections.

And here we might finish with a further last thought. Can we imagine, for example, the perfect parent, a father or a mother or a perfect friend? We can definitely think of better and worse parents, but wouldn't it be the case that a perfect parent would be rather a troubling parent? Is it the case that the very attempt at perfection when it comes to God, the relational subject, is flawed? Could the search for perfection within a relational paradigm be ultimately a self-defeating project?

Selected Further Reading

Halbertal, M. *Interpretative Revolutions in the Making.* Jerusalem: The Hebrew University Magnes Press, 1997.

Lorberbaum, Y. *God's Image: Halakhah and Aggadah.* New York: Schocken Publishing House, 2004.

Rawidowicz, S. "On Jewish Learning." In *Israel the Ever Dying People and Other Essays,* 134–37. Edited by B. Ravid. Rutherford, NJ: Fairleigh Dickinson University Press, 1984/1986.

Stern, D. *Parables in Midrash: Narrative and Exegesis in Rabbinic Literature.* Cambridge, MA: Harvard University Press, 1994.

Urbach, E. E. *The Sages: Their Concepts and Beliefs.* Translated by I. Abraham. Jerusalem: The Hebrew University Magnes Press, 1979.

Weiss, D. *Pious Irreverence: Confronting God in Rabbinic Judaism.* Philadelphia: University of Pennsylvania Press, 2016.

Wolfson, H. *Philo: Foundations of Religious Philosophy in Judaism 1–2.* Cambridge, MA: Harvard University Press, 1948.

5 The Theology of the Daily Liturgy

REUVEN KIMELMAN

The richest vein for mining theology is the Siddur. More than any other work, it reflects the consensual theology of Judaism. It shows how Judaism affirms its belief system by liturgizing it. Unlike standard credos, liturgical theology seeks to ground itself in life experience. Minimally, a theological insight is to be articulated; preferably, it is to be sung; maximally, it is to be performed in unison. As a communal performance, liturgy unifies the people Israel while confirming the collective theology of Israel.

INDIVIDUAL PRAYERS

The Siddur both articulates the consensual theology and makes the case for it.[1] Following the order of the Shaḥarit morning service, the best liturgical case for God's non-contingency and thus for the eternity of divine sovereignty is Adon Olam;[2] the best for the significance of the body in worship are the morning blessings; the best for the conjunction of body and soul are the adjacent blessings Elohai, Neshamah with regard to the soul and Asher Yaṣar with regard to

---

[1] This is a thesis of my upcoming book, *The Rhetoric of the Liturgy: A Historical and Literary Commentary to the Jewish Prayer Book* (subsequently, Kimelman, *RL*), slated for publication by Littman Press in 2021. The theological themes here are further developed there with greater attention to historical and literary development along with fuller bibliography. For pioneering surveys of the theology of the Siddur, see Issachar Jacobson, *Netiv Binah*, 5 vols. (Tel Aviv: Sinai, 1964–1978) I, 60–86; Abraham Milgram, *Jewish Worship* (Philadelphia: The Jewish Publication Society, 1971), 391–423; and especially Rosenzweig, *The Star of Redemption*, parts 2–3, with the insightful exposition of Steven Kepnes, *Jewish Liturgical Reasoning* (New York: Oxford University Press, 2007), 70–120. On his own, Kepnes (ibid., 152–56) provides a theological reading of the psalms of Pesuqei DeZimra.

[2] See below, 89–93; and Kepnes, *Jewish Liturgical Reasoning*, 177–79.

the body;[3] the best for speaking the world into being is Barukh SheAmar;[4] and the best for divine kingship is the Ashrei.[5] The best liturgical argument for creation is the first blessing of the ensuing Shema Liturgy; the best for the nature of divine love is the second blessing; and the best for past redemption is the third blessing. The first blessing adduces creation as evidence of divine sovereignty, the second blessing adduces God's teaching of Torah as evidence of God's love for us while using God's love of us to promote our love of God,[6] and the third blessing deploys past redemption to prod future redemption. The goals are the acceptance of divine sovereignty, the requital of God's love, and the realization of redemption.[7]

The first three blessings of the ensuing Amidah also constitute a theological program. The first blessing makes the case for God to engineer redemption, the second makes the case for resurrection, and the third ends with an acclamation of God's kingship on earth. As a three-stage redemptive scenario, the threefold unit advances from the redemption of Israel to the resurrection of humanity to the universalization of God's reign. The perception of God as first Lord over history, then Lord over nature and death, and finally Lord over humanity provides the theological wherewithal for the utopian hope in the ultimate redemption. Indeed, the best way of accounting for the rest of the Amidah, save for the added nineteenth blessing, is as a scenario of redemption starting with the individual (blessings 4–7), moving on to the nation (blessings 10–15/16), and culminating with all humanity (blessings 18).[8]

The best liturgical statement on the hoped-for universal acknowledgement of divine sovereignty is the ensuing Aleinu,[9] which itself is

---

[3] See Dalia Marx, "The Morning Ritual (Birkhot Hashahar) in the Talmud: The Reconstitution of One's Body and Personal Identity through the Blessings," *Hebrew Union College Annual*, 77 (2006), 103–29; Kimelman, *RL* "Preliminaries," ch. 3, and idem, "The Blessings of Prayerobics," *The B'nai Brith International Jewish Monthly* (February, 1986), 12–17. For the conjunction of body and soul, see idem, "The Rabbinic Theology of the Physical: Blessings, Body and Soul, Resurrection, Covenant and Election," 946–97, 952–56 (both available at academia.edu).

[4] See Kimelman, *RL*, ch. 5 "Pesuqei DeZimra,".   [5] See below, 93.

[6] See Reuven Kimelman, "'We Love the God Who Loved Us First': The Second Blessing of the Shema Liturgy," ed. I. Kalimi, *Bridging between Sister Religions: Studies of Jewish and Christian Scriptures Offered in Honor of Prof. John T. Townsend* (Leiden: Brill, 2016), 241–61 (available at academia.edu).

[7] See below, 81–89.   [8] See Kimelman, *RL*, ch. 7 "The Amidah."

[9] See below, 89–94.

based on blessing 18 (the Modim) of the Amidah and the rabbinic understanding of the Shema verse (see below). Accordingly, for both the Shema verse, the Amidah, and the Aleinu, the end goal of Judaism is the universal acknowledgement of the sovereignty of God. The Aleinu and the rest of the kingship section of the Rosh Hashanah Amidah is also the best statement on the transformation of the wicked in the eschaton, as opposed to their elimination in blessing 12 of the Amidah.[10] In scenarios of national redemption, the theological and moral deviant is slated for elimination; in those of universal redemption, they are slated for transformation by being redirected to God. In the Aleinu, a theology of monotheistic exclusivity broadens into an ideology of universalistic inclusivity. What begins as a manifesto of monotheism culminates in a program of universal redemption.

The theological program of specific prayers is quite explicit, whereas that of the whole daily liturgy is at most only implicit. This makes the construction of a theology of the liturgy a creative task. This is especially the case in a liturgy variegated in origin, authorship, and genre. Every stage of Jewish literary creativity contributed to the making of the current Siddur from the biblical, post-biblical, rabbinic, payetanic, geonic, Sephardic, Ashkenazic, philosophic, kabbalistic, Hasidic, to the modern. There is hardly a century of the last two millennia that did not contribute to the ongoing formation of the Siddur, as there is hardly a country of Jewish cultural significance that did not contribute to the growth of the daily liturgy. Israel-Palestine, Babylonia, Egypt, Syria, the Maghreb, Italy, Spain, Provence, France, Germany, Poland, possibly Persia, Yemen, and England all left their mark on the Siddur. For over twenty centuries in over ten lands the Siddur has been coming into being. The literary and theological cohesiveness of the Siddur, in the light of the temporal and geographical diversity is astonishing.

Proper conceptualization of the theology of the whole daily liturgy demands an enlargement of the theological imagination, without the relaxation of literary standards, historical method, and philological rigor. This study focuses on the theology of the liturgy by first disclosing through literary analysis the theology of a single prayer, then on a whole

---

[10] For blessing 12 and its historical context, see Reuven Kimelman, "Birkat Ha-Minim and the Lack of Evidence for an Anti-Christian Jewish Prayer in Late Antiquity," ed. E. P. Sanders, A. I. Baumgarten, and A. Mendelson, *Jewish and Christian Self-Definition*, 3 vols. (Philadelphia: Fortress Press, 1981), I, 226–44, 391–403 (available at academia.edu). For its later reception, see Ruth Langer, *Cursing the Christians: A History of the Birkat Haminim* (Oxford: Oxford University Press, 2012).

unit of the liturgy by adding the historical method, and finally on the thematic coherence of the whole daily liturgy through an expanded theological conceptualization.

The Emet VeYaṣiv-Ezrat Avoteinu section that links the recitation of the Shema lectionaries with the Amidah prayer is a parade example of a single prayer making its theology explicit. Its five asseverations, introduced by the word *emet* ("true"), cumulatively add up to a liturgical credo.[11] They are rattled off staccato-like:

1. *Emet!* the God of yore (*'olam*) is our king ...[12]
2. *Emet!* You Adonai are our God and God of our fathers; our king, king of our fathers; our redeemer, redeemer of our fathers.
3. *Emet!* You are the lord of Your people ...
4. *Emet!* You are the first and You are the last and besides You we have no king, redeemer, and savior ...
5. *Emet!* (following the sefardic version) You have redeemed us from Egypt ....

Save for the first where God is acclaimed "our king," they are all formulated in the language of direct address ("You" "You" "You" "You"). The first four follow a temporal order. The first affirms God from the beginning of time, the second from the time of our fathers, the third to the present, and the fourth to the future. The fifth details the redemptive acts of the everlasting God in the past as a warranty for future redemption. Between the first two asseverations, it is spelled out that in the acceptance of Adonai as king, one is also affirming His eternity, which, according to the prayer, entails His throne, His kingship, His promise, and His words. The eternity of God allows His promise of redemption to be integral to His kingship.

Three divine epithets lace the whole section together: "eternal," "king," and "redeemer." Indeed, God is designated both "king" and "redeemer" four times, first of our fathers, then of us. All the asseverations are professed in the context of the supporting structures of collective memory, for the credo itself is a coefficient of the collective experience. Thus, in the redemption of our fathers, it is proclaimed:

---

[11] See Naftali Wieder, *The Formation of Jewish Liturgy in the East and West* [Hebrew], 2 vols. (Jerusalem: Ben-Zvi Institute, 1998) II, 225; and Judah Halevi, *Kuzari* 3.17.

[12] God as *emet* means "He is the living God and eternal king [or: king of the world]"—*Leviticus Rabbah* 6, 6, ed. M. Margulies, 1953, p. 145 and parallels; see Jeremiah 10:10.

"*Emet* You have redeemed *us* from Egypt." The formulation generates an identification with the redemption of our fathers and their subsequent acceptance of divine sovereignty so that we, cognizant also of our redemption, will accordingly accept divine sovereignty. These asseverations correspond to the three lectionaries of the just-recited Shema. The first four correspond to the first (Deuteronomy 6:4–9) and the second (Deuteronomy 11:13–21); the fifth corresponds to the third (Numbers 15:37–41).

THE SHEMA LITURGY

An example of a whole unit tied together theologically is the Shema Liturgy. It consists of two blessings preceding the three biblical lectionaries and one succeeding. The linkage of the Shema verse, as rabbinically understood, with the motifs of creation, revelation, and redemption caps the whole liturgical composition as a rhetorical success. All three motifs are enlisted in the service of the theme of divine sovereignty. The oneness, or better the exclusivity and singularity, of God is supported by the representation of creation as an expression of divine sovereignty. It is further supported by the reenactment of revelation through the antiphonal mode of the recitation of the Shema, known as *Poreis et Shema*.[13] Finally, it is supported by the prefiguring of redemption through the call for God to be One for all, as the Shema verse was understood. Through the orchestration of all three, the liturgy discloses the evidence for divine sovereignty in all of reality to induce Israel to acclaim it as well.[14]

The Shema verse is more than the middle; it is the generative center of a layered composition on divine sovereignty. This needs underscoring lest we adopt an interpretive strategy of reading the liturgical composition only linearly from beginning to end. Such a reading following the order of events is likely to conclude that the beginning point is creation, the midpoint Shema, and the endpoint redemption. The problem with this emplotment is that it tends too easily to elide into culminations, if not climaxes. As goals give meaning to processes, so do literary endings control understandings. Since understanding so often turns out to be a "teleological process" whereby "a sense of totality is the end which governs the process,"[15] it becomes imperative to bear in mind the *telos*

[13] See Kimelman *RL*, ch. 6, "The Shema Liturgy," Excursus B.   [14] See ibid., part V.
[15] Jonathan Culler, *Structuralist Poetics* (Ithaca, NY: Cornell University, 1975), 171.

that controls the reading. It is one thing to note that the blessing of redemption comes at the end of the whole composition; it is another to see redemption as the *telos* of the whole composition.

A linear reading unduly privileges the theme of redemption. This is not to gainsay the significance of the redemptive motif, just its primacy. The hopes for redemption, inserted in some rites in the first blessing, and their connection with the realization of divine sovereignty in the second blessing attest to the resiliency of the motif.[16] Indeed, were we to undertake a phenomenological analysis of the liturgy incorporating all mentions of redemption, we would find in it "a figure for the integration of past, present and future which defies successive time." We would sense with regard to redemption something in the order of what Thomas Mann noted when he said: "in their beginning exists their middle and their end, their past invades the present, and even the most extreme attention to the present is invaded by concern for the future."[17] Moreover, with redemption as the *telos*, it could be argued that from the perspective of the consciousness of the worshiper, the unit as a whole makes the point that as ancient Israel acknowledged divine sovereignty and was redeemed, so contemporary Israel should do so to be redeemed.

Notwithstanding the lure of this reading and its applicability elsewhere, the reading does violence to the original order of the events of the Exodus where redemption preceded revelation. It also fails to give the theme of divine sovereignty its due. Although such a reading accounts for the parts of the composition that form a path from creation to redemption via the Shema, it does not account for the inclusion of the pre-Shema passage, Ahavat Olam/Ahavah Rabbah, on God's love, and the post-Shema passage, Emet VeYaṣiv, on the affirmation of the covenant. This deficiency argues for a more comprehensive interpretive strategy, a strategy that can account for all the components while resisting the identification of the purpose or *telos* of the composition with its end.

An alternative strategy to a linear reading is a chiastic one. The chiasmus is an ancient literary figure for structuring narratives. It pervades biblical, Christian, and rabbinic literature along with liturgical poetry.[18] The chiasmus, named after the Greek letter *chi* (x), signifies

---

[16] The requests for redemption appear to be a later interpolation; see Kimelman, *RL*, ch. 6, n. 379.

[17] Both citations are from Frank Kermode, *The Sense of an Ending: Studies in the Theory of Fiction* (London: Oxford University, 1975), 71–2.

[18] For bibliography on chiasmus in antiquity, see Kimelman, *RL*, ch. 6, nn. 381–82.

a crisscross arrangement in which the order of the first column is reversed in the second, as in the structure ABCBA. In chiastic structures, the elements form a thematic symmetry. Such organizational devices prove to be more than literary artifice. In making the middle the literary center, the chiasmus empties the ending of any privileged control over sense. Endings remain endings, not culminations.

In the case of the Shema Liturgy, the Shema verse is more than the middle. It is the generative center of the whole Shema Liturgy. The structure adheres to an organizational pattern that underscores the verse as center or pivot. By balancing the second part with the first part through inversion, the chiasmus of the Shema Liturgy accounts for all the parts, underscoring the centrality of the Shema as the spatial and ideological fulcrum of the whole structure.[19] Viewing the Shema and its blessings through this lens produces the following diagram:

A^1—Blessing for Creation with Angelic Acclamation of God
  B^1—Blessing for Torah: "With Eternal Love"
    C—Shema (the three biblical sections)
  B^2—Covenantal Pledge: "True and Firm"
A^2—Blessing for Redemption with Israelite Acclamation of God

The pyramid structure of the liturgy makes it obvious that the Shema is the literary as well as the theological centerpiece of the unit. The core composed of B^1, C, B^2 constitutes a covenantal ceremony.[20]

---

[19] As in the Qumran *1QHodayot* 7: 26–33, where it has been noted: "The theology of the psalm is enhanced by the recognition of the chiastic arrangement," Bonnie Kittel, *The Hymns of Qumran*, SBL Dissertation Series 50 (Atlanta, GA: Scholars Press, 1981), 108.

[20] If C is a single unit, it serves as the apex of the pyramidal structure. If C consists of the original first two paragraphs, the classic chiastic structure of A^1 B^1 C^1—C^2 B^2 A^2 emerges. An instructive parallel from Qumran, besides that of the previous note, is found in the structure of the *Sabbath Shirot* from Qumran Cave 4. According to Carol Newsom, the thirteen Sabbath Shirot are "constructed ... as a pyramidal structure" ("'He Has established For Himself Priests," Human and Angelic Priesthood in the Qumran Sabbath *Shirot*," ed. L. Schiffman, *Archaeology and History in the Dead Sea Scrolls* (Sheffield: JSOT Press, 1990), 101–20, p. 102), with six on each side, the seventh being the apex. She also notes that "the sixth through the eighth songs form a distinctive central structure, the top of the pyramid, so to speak, for the Sabbath Shirot" (109). Similarly, the common elements, especially the numerous lexical links between B^1 and B^2 as well as with C, form a distinctive central structure to top off the pyramid. Tellingly, the covenant ceremony of Deuteronomy 29:9–14 also adheres to a chiastic structure whose center is the similar verse "That He may establish you as His people and be your God" (29:12); see Jeffrey Tigay, *Deuteronomy, The JPS Torah Commentary* (Philadelphia: The Jewish Publication Society, 1996), 277.

Consisting totally of Deuteronomic material and motifs, it adheres to ancient treaty-covenantal models. There is, however, more to the Shema Liturgy than its core of a biblical-type covenantal ceremony. The Deuteronomy-based covenantal ceremony became flanked by the creation theme of Genesis and the redemption theme of Exodus. This produced an outer frame consisting of A¹ and A², which now brackets the original inner frame of B¹ and B². By the incorporation of the events of creation and redemption along with their heavenly and historical coronation ceremonies respectively, the appendage of A¹ and A² transforms an ancient pact form into a comprehensive rite for the realization of divine sovereignty.

To appreciate the significance of this transformation, one must realize that the original unit of B¹, C, B² lacked any reference to God as king. Subsequently, each component absorbed a reference to divine kingship. By late tannaitic times, C absorbed "Blessed be the name of His glorious *kingship* for ever and ever," after the Shema verse;[21] by early amoraic times, B² absorbed the kingship motif[22] as did B¹ by geonic times.[23] The result is that the biblical understanding of covenant was updated terminologically and conceptually to the rabbinic understanding of the acceptance of divine sovereignty. What the covenant was for biblical as for Second Temple theology and liturgy, especially at Qumran, the realization of divine sovereignty became for rabbinic theology and liturgy.[24]

The key element of a biblically based covenantal ceremony, namely the Decalogue, is absent. In Exodus 34:27–28 and Deuteronomy 4:11–13, the Decalogue is the document of the

---

[21] This formula resulted from the interpolation of the term "kingship" into the verse— "Blessed be His glorious name forever" (Psalm 72:19). The Shema verse alone does not qualify for the acceptance of God's sovereignty; see Jacob Molin, Sefer *Maharil* (Jerusalem: Machon Yerushalayim, 1989), 435 with n. 1; and Joseph Karo, *Beit Yoseif* with Joel Sirkes, B"Ḥ, to Jacob b. Asher, *Arba'ah Turim, Oraḥ Ḥayyim* 46.

[22] See Reuven Kimelman, "Blessing Formulae and Divine Sovereignty in Rabbinic Liturgy," eds. R. Langer and S. Fine, *Liturgy in the Life of the Synagogue: Studies in the History of Jewish Prayer* (Winona Lake, IN: Eisenbrauns, 2005), 1–39, 22–25 (available at academia.edu). Even early versions of the High Holiday liturgy lacked the kingship motif; see Kimelman, *RL*, ch. 6, "The Shema Liturgy" n. 387.

[23] Ibid. n. 159.

[24] Thus, the Qumran *Rule of the Community* alludes to the Shema by saying: "With the coming of the day and night I shall enter the covenant of God" (*1QS* 10:10), whereas *Mishnah, Berakhot* 2:2, 5 designates the twice-daily recitation of the Shema as "the acceptance of Divine sovereignty." The trope for the Shema shifts from covenant to kingship.

covenant. It thus preceded the Shema lectionaries in the Temple service, as recorded in *Mishnah Tamid* 5:1. In addition to the many links between the Shema verse and the Decalogue, there are also connections between the Decalogue and the third section from Numbers 15:37–41. According to the Rabbis, the first words of the concluding verse of the third section — "I am Adonai your [plural] God" — indicate the sovereignty of God,[25] and correspond to the opening of the Decalogue, "I am Adonai your [singular] God."[26] The two whole verses form a literary inclusion. The Decalogue begins: "I am Adonai your God who took you out of the Land of Egypt . . . " (Exodus 20:2); the third section ends: "I am Adonai your God, who took you out of the land of Egypt, to be your God. I am Adonai your God" (Numbers 15:41). This conforms to the widespread principle of liturgical composition that endings should recapitulate beginnings.[27] Moreover, the penultimate thought of the third section, "that you not be seduced by your heart or led astray by your eyes" (Numbers 15:39) was understood to refer "to heretical and idolatrous thoughts." It thus matches both the second saying of the Decalogue and the understanding of the end of the Shema verse, "Adonai is One," as also excluding idolatry. It is precisely the equivalence between the Shema and the Decalogue, as rabbinically understood, as acts of accepting divine sovereignty and the authority of the commandments that accounts for the exclusion of the Decalogue from the rabbinic liturgy.[28]

By ending with Numbers 15:41 and beginning with Deuteronomy 6:5, the three biblical sections of the Shema also comprise a liturgical construct based on an envelope figure that begins and ends on the two concomitant themes of the acceptance of divine sovereignty and the rejection of idolatry/polytheism. The difference between the Temple lectionary unit and the rabbinic unit is that the envelope figure of the former consists of a verbal tabulation, whereas that of the latter is

---

[25] See *Sifrei Numbers, Be-Ha'alotkha* 77, ed. M. Kahana, 2005, 1: 183, l. 16; *Shelaḥ* 115, 2:329, l. 95; *Sifra, Aḥarei Mot* 13, 3, ed. I. H. Weiss (1862, 85d; *J. Rosh Hashanah* 4:5, 58d; *B. Rosh Hashanah* 32a.

[26] *J. Berakhot* 1:4, 3c (R. Levi); see *Midrash Ḥadash Al Hatorah*, ed. G. Vachman, 2013, 224, with n. 37.

[27] See *B. Pesaḥim* 104a, Vatican Ms. ebr. 125; and *Tosafot, Berakhot* 46a, s. v., *kol*. For the frequency of the envelope figure in the liturgy, see Shulamit Elizur, "Towards a Description of Early Benedictions: Some Basic Considerations [Hebrew]," *Sidra* 32 (2017): 7–33; and Kimelman, *RL*, ch. 4, "The Ashrei," n. 55.

[28] See Kimelman, *RL*, Ch. 6 "The Shema Liturgy," part IV.

a conceptual one. This is consequential in determining the purpose behind the Rabbinic Shema Liturgy and its chiastic structure.

The retention of the Emet VeYaṣiv confirmation prayer in the rabbinic liturgy, after the third lectionary (Numbers 15:37–41), despite its independence of the redemption theme of the blessing, attests to the linkage between the recitation of the Shema and ancient loyalty pacts. The Shema-Decalogue connection may also have spawned the Shema-redemption connection. As the covenant at Sinai was grounded in the Exodus, "I am Adonai- your God who brought you out of the Land of Egypt," so the covenantal ceremony of the Shema came to invoke the Exodus.[29]

Once past redemption is evoked, hope for future redemption cannot lag far behind, except the future redemption encompasses all humanity, not just Israel. Thus, the end of the Shema verse "Adonai is one" was read in the light of Zechariah 14:9, "Adonai shall be king over all the earth. In that day, shall Adonai be one and His name o/One" to indicate that Adonai will be One for all.[30] The point is that the redemption of Israel, prefiguring the redemption of humanity, culminates in the universal acknowledgement of divine sovereignty.

Both literary structure and theological analysis confirm that the original blessing was an election-centered one on the order of the second blessing, rather than a creation-centered one on the order of the first. In fact, the second blessing was dubbed "the blessing of the Torah."[31] Such a Torah-centered blessing originally served to introduce the series of biblical lectionaries beginning with the Decalogue. In the absence of the Decalogue, it was adapted to the needs of introducing the Shema directly. Thus, the blessing became as much love-centered as Torah-centered.

The Qumran liturgy, *Daily Prayers*, also starts the morning service with an election-centered blessing. There, the response to the sun shining over the earth is "*Barukh* God of Israel who chose us from among all the nations."[32] The same terminology, "who chose us among all the

---

[29] See Yosef Soloveitchik, *Shiurim LeZekher Abba Mori Z"L*, 2 vols. (Jerusalem: Mossad HaRav Kook, 1983–1985), 1: 11.

[30] See *Sifrei Deuteronomy* 32, ed. L. Finkelstein (1969), 54; Rashi to Deuteronomy 6:4; and Judah b. Yaqar, *Peirush HaTefillot VeHaBerakhot*, 2 vols. (Jerusalem: Meorei Yisrael, 1968–69) 1: 115–16.

[31] *J. Berakhot* 1:8, 3c (in the name of R. Hamnunah); see Rashi, *B. Berakhot* 11b: "He already fulfilled his obligation through Ahavah Rabbah, as it is comparable to the blessing over the Torah."

[32] 4Q503 24–25, 4–5.

nations" characterizes the opening rabbinic blessing for biblical lectionary readings, a blessing considered on a par with the second blessing of the Shema. The motifs of the hymn of *The Rule of the Community* (*1QS* 10:10) that starts "With the coming of the day and night, I will enter the covenant of God; when evening and morning depart, I will recite His ordinances," also correlate exactly with the covenantal core of the Shema, specifically the second blessing and the first two lectionaries of the Shema.[33]

The first blessing of the Shema Liturgy, which precedes the covenantal core, also has Qumran parallels in the offering of a blessing at the turn of the day and in the incorporation of a combination of angelic and human praise. As the first blessing blesses God at the daily interchange of the luminaries, so the concluding hymn of *The Rule of the Community* states that the *Maskil* shall bless Him [with the offering of the lips] at the times ordained by Him:

> At the beginning of the dominion of light, and at its end when it retires to its appointed place; at the beginning of the watches of darkness when He unlocks their storehouse and spreads them out and at their end when they retire before the light.[34]

Qumran thus attests to the availability of the type of liturgical material out of which emerged the first two blessings. There is an early text that assumes the Amidah succeeds the Shema without any intervening blessing on redemption.[35] Subsequent versions of the text were made to conform to the later thesis that the blessing for redemption should be adjoined to the Amidah.[36]

The Rabbinic Shema Liturgy was not composed *ex nihilo*. Much of it has antecedents in Qumran and Temple liturgies. What lacks any antecedent is its generative theme of divine sovereignty. The chiastic

---

[33] Similarly, the opening chapter there is redolent of the first section especially of Deuteronomy 6:5; see Moshe Weinfeld, *Early Jewish Liturgy: From Psalms to the Prayers in Qumran and Rabbinic Literature* [Hebrew] (Jerusalem: The Hebrew University Magnes Press, 2004), 161–62.

[34] *1QS* 10:1–2; see Nitzan, Bilhah, "The Idea of Creation and Its Implications in Qumran Literature," ed. H. Reventlow and Y. Hoffman, *Creation in Jewish and Christian Tradition*, JSOT Supplement Series 319 (Sheffield: Sheffield Academic Press, 2002), 240–64, esp. 258–59.

[35] תפלה (ק"ש) כדי שיהא סומך לה (*Tosefta Berakhot* 1:4, ed. Lieberman, 1955, p. 1, l.12); see Louis Finkelstein, *New Light from the Prophets* (New York: Basic Books, 1969), 122–23.

[36] See previous note; and Kimelman, *RL*, ch. 7, "The Amidah," Epilogue.

structure underscores the theme of divine sovereignty by showing how both creation and redemption can be adduced as evidence. Indeed, it is through the realization of divine sovereignty in the present that the past and future become creation and redemption. In the spirit of Martin Buber's comment, "both creation and redemption are true only on the premise that revelation is a present experience,"[37] it can be said that both creation and redemption are perceived as true by virtue of the acceptance of divine sovereignty in the present. The liturgy hence presents a scenario of beginnings perceived as creation and endings perceived as redemption by virtue of Israel's response to revelation. By construing the Sinaitic revelation as an act of realization of divine sovereignty, creation and redemption become construable as acts that attest to divine sovereignty.

It is thus misleading both historically and conceptually to present the Shema Liturgy as organized around the three axes of creation, revelation, and redemption.[38] Only the theme of divine sovereignty possesses the explanatory power to account for the whole liturgical narrative. It alone is the master narrative. Only it explains the presence of acclamation rites in the first and third blessing, whether angelic or Israelite; only it explains the supplanting of the role of the Decalogue by the Rabbinic Shema; only it explains the applicability of the term *poreis* to the Shema as dividing it in two in emulation of Greco-Roman acclamation rites;[39] and only it explains the insertion of "Blessed be the name of His glorious kingship for ever and ever" after the Shema verse. The motifs of creation and redemption are enlisted in its service, not vice versa. In other words, God is not sovereign because He creates and redeems, rather because God is sovereign He creates and redeems.[40] The centrality of the theme of divine sovereignty accounts for its permeation of the whole Shema Liturgy, whereas the creation motif is limited to the first blessing as the redemption motif is limited to the third, except for the accretions in the first two blessings.

---

[37] See Marin Buber, "The Man of Today and the Jewish Bible," in *Israel and the World* (New York: Schocken, 1963), 96. Buber goes on to observe: "But if I did not feel creation as well as redemption happening to myself, I could never understand what creation and redemption are." This experiential understanding permeates Rosenzweig's *Star of Redemption*.

[38] See Kimelman, *RL*, ch. 6, "The Shema Liturgy," Excursus C.

[39] See ibid., Excursus B.

[40] Accordingly, the order of divine epithets in the acknowledgement clause of the third blessing is first king, then redeemer and creator.

The Shema verse becomes in the liturgy the covenantal substitute for the Decalogue as well as the theological and literary center of a symphonic composition on the acceptance of divine sovereignty. It became the verse for the mention of the acceptance of divine kingship despite the absence of any explicit mention of kingship. This is due to the perception of Zechariah 14:9, "Adonai shall be king over all the earth. In that day, shall Adonai be one and His name One," as an extension of the Shema verse. Three of the six words of the Shema verse, namely, "Adonai" twice and "One" once are recycled in Zechariah 14:9. The rest of Zechariah 14:9 focuses on the worldwide extension of divine kingship. Thus, just as Zechariah 14:9 was perceived as adding the explicit mention of kingship to the Shema verse, so the Shema verse came to be perceived in terms of the kingship reference of Zechariah 14:9. The joining of Zechariah 14:9 to Zephaniah 3:9 with its hope that all will invoke God by the same name led to the understanding of the Zechariah verse as implicit in the Shema verse. Thus the "one" of the Shema verse came also to mean "one for all," or "all for the One."[41] The liturgical Shema is the eschatological Shema.

In the case of the Shema Liturgy, the focus on when, where, and how it came into being enables the grasping of the Shema Liturgy as a coronation ceremony within the cultural context of the Roman Empire. It also enables the understanding of the Amidah as a post-Temple configuration of redemptive hopes. The Aleinu is also to be comprehended through the lens of the poetic and liturgical world of Byzantine, Palestinian Judaism, just as Adon Olam is to be deciphered in the context of medieval poetry and philosophy.[42]

THE THEOLOGICAL PATTERN OF THE DAILY LITURGY

The remaining question is whether theological patterning characterizes the whole daily liturgy. This is not a simple matter as the bulk of the liturgy was put together over time by various people or institutions. Just as individual units are the result of composition by juxtaposition, such

---

[41] See above, n. 30.
[42] See Kimelman, *RL*, ch. 2, "Adon Olam," and ch. 8, "The Aleinu." This follows the approach of my book, *The Mystical Meaning of "Lekhah Dodi" and "Kabbalat Shabbat,"* [Hebrew] (Jerusalem: The Hebrew University Magnes Press; Los Angeles: Cherub Press, 2003), in explicating Lekhah Dodi in terms of sixteenth-century Safdean, Alkabetzian-Cordoverean Kabbalah, as Moses Cordovero was the colleague and brother-in-law of the author, Solomon Alkabetz.

as the synagogue entrance prayer, Mah Tovu,[43] the preliminary blessings, Pesuqei DeZimra, the Shema Liturgy, the Amidah, even the final version of the Aleinu, so is the whole Shaḥarit. The project of making sense of any one unit is thus like the making sense of the whole Shaḥarit. In both cases, historical context and location in the service turn out to be consequential.

Illustrative examples of the significance of location are those of the Aleinu and Adon Olam. The change in venue transformed their role in the service. The Aleinu now assumes an additional role and meaning as a closing prayer independent of its earlier function in the Musaf of Rosh Hashanah. Adon Olam has also moved from serving primarily as a bedtime prayer or as a Day of Atonement post-Arvit piyyut to serving primarily as an opening Shaḥarit prayer. The Aleinu now consummates, as it were, the Shema-Amidah-centered liturgy and rounds off the service initiated with Adon Olam.

Just as Adon Olam emerged as the theological introduction to the Shema-Amidah-centered liturgy, so the Aleinu emerged as its theological conclusion. The first parts of the Aleinu and Adon Olam converge on the affirmation of universal divine sovereignty and exclusive monotheism. Although both affirmations are anchored in Creation, the prayers diverge on the theological implications. The ten verses of Adon Olam divide neatly into two sections. The first six verses make the case for God's transcendence as reflected through the notions of eternity, sovereignty, dominion, and uniqueness. The last four verses make the case for God's immanence as reflected through the notions of providence, protection, reliability, and faithfulness. Together they form a matrix of transcendent immanence and immanent transcendence. For Adon Olam, God's sovereignty, universality, eternity, and dominion make possible the divine solicitude that renders the pray-er the object of divine concern, where God becomes "my redeemer" (verse 6). The strategic placement of Adon Olam at the start of the service sustains faith in God, the eternal king, as one's protecting redeemer in the face of trial and tribulation. The rhetorical strategy consists in persuading the worshiper of God's capacity and concern, so that prayer will prove to be neither futile nor frustrating. If God controls

---

[43] See "Mah Tovu as a Psychological Introduction to the Liturgy," ed. S. Katz and S. Bayme, *Continuity and Change: A Festschrift in Honor of Irving (Yitz) Greenberg's 75th Birthday* (Lanham, MD: University Press of America, 2010), 189–202 (available at academia.edu).

The Theology of the Daily Liturgy 91

but does not care, prayer is frustrating; if God cares but does not control, prayer is futile.[44]

For Adon Olam, eternity and infinity no more belie intimacy than sovereignty belies solicitude. By interlocking God's grandeur and grace, a mental matrix for prayer is formed through which Adon Olam emerges as the theological introduction to the service. For the Aleinu, God's sovereignty, universality, and exclusive monotheism, in part 1, generate in part 2 (the *Al Kain* section) the expectation of the universalization of God's kingship to all humanity, where God becomes the redeemer of all. The two parts of the Aleinu lay out a two-stage vision where our praise of the Lord of *all* leads to His acknowledgement by *all*, and our praise of the Creator leads to the extension of divine rule throughout creation. In both, we, the worshipers, serve as the vanguard of the universal worship of God. This is Aleinu's doctrine of election.

Both Adon Olam and the Aleinu have two foci. Adon Olam shifts from God to me; the Aleinu shifts from us to them. What begins in Adon Olam as a God–individual relationship culminates in the Aleinu as a God–humanity relationship. They both focus on the human situation: one in all its individuality, the other in all its universality. Accordingly, Adon Olam lacks a "We"; Aleinu lacks an "I." In Adon Olam, I find myself in relation with God. In lines 7–8, "my" refers to God six times:

7. And it is He who is *my* God and *my* life's redeemer / *my* stronghold when in distress.
8. And it is He who is *my* banner and *my* bastion / the lot of *my* cup on the day I call.

In Aleinu, I find myself as part of a liturgical we. In lines 1–5, I become part of we/us/our six times:

---

[44] As in the other cases, the theological logic of Adon Olam harks back to Late Antiquity. In this case the logic of the position is spelled out by Epicurus (341–270 BCE), except he deals with the problem of evil which *mutatis mutandis* pertains to the problem of answering prayer.

> God either wishes to take away evils and is unable; or he is able and is unwilling; or he is neither willing nor able; or he is both willing and able. If he is willing but unable, he is feeble, which is not in accordance with the character of God. If he is able and unwilling, he is envious, which is equally at variance with God. If he is neither willing nor able, he is both envious and feeble, and therefore not God. If he is both willing and able, which alone is suitable for God, from what source then are evils? Or why does he not remove them?

Cited by Lactantius (ca. 250 CE–ca. 325 CE), *A Treatise on the Anger of God*, 28.

1. *We* are to praise the Lord of all, to ascribe greatness to the Creator of creation.
2. Who did not make *us* like the nations of the lands and did not set *us* like the families of the earth.
3. Who did not set *our* lot as theirs nor *our* destiny as all of them.
4. For they bow to naught and emptiness and pray to a God who does not save.
5. But *we* bend, bow, and give thanks before the King over the king of kings, the Holy One, blessed be He.

Both pivot on a form of the same term for divine glory. Adon Olam (line 4) uses *tiforah* to refer to God's reign alone in all His glory; the Aleinu (part 2, line 1) uses *tiferet* to refer to the manifestation of God's reign in His glory over all. Adon Olam and the Aleinu operate in tandem. The former begins by designating God as *adon olam* ("eternal lord"); the latter as *adon ha-kol* ("lord of all"). "There is no other," avers the Aleinu; "He has no second," avers Adon Olam. Together they affirm an exclusive monotheism of God as lord of all, sovereign from creation, master of space and time.

Besides exclusive monotheism, neither Adon Olam nor the Aleinu refer to the distinctly Jewish. "Israel" does not appear. God is not ethnically inflected. The staples of Judaism such as the Sabbath, the Temple, or Jerusalem get no mention. There is no reference to the pivotal events of classical Jewish history such as the Patriarchs, the Exodus, Sinai, the conquest of the land of Israel, the Davidic monarchy, or the advent of the Messiah. Both Adon Olam and the Aleinu are equally applicable to all worshipers of the one Creator God.

The liturgical destinies of the Aleinu and Adon Olam overlap. Besides the classical location of the Aleinu in the High Holiday Musaf, both it and Adon Olam seemed to have launched their subsequent liturgical career as addenda to the Arvit of the Day of Atonement. The Aleinu debuted outside the High Holiday liturgy in the mid-twelfth century as the finale to the Shaḥarit service; Adon Olam likely made its liturgical debut in the mid-thirteenth century. Nonetheless, both penetrated the daily liturgy throughout while migrating from the ashkenazic to the sefardic world over the course of the thirteenth to the sixteenth centuries. It is probably coincidental, but the prefacing of Adon Olam to the beginning of Shaḥarit, as the appending of the Aleinu to the end of Minḥah, spread in the late sixteenth century and became standard by the end of the seventeenth century. By the late eighteenth century, most ashkenazic and sefardic liturgies began daily prayer with Adon Olam and ended all three daily services with the Aleinu.

The two prayers, independent of each other originally, have become intertwined liturgically. Together, they serve as theological bookends to Shaḥarit. Despite the diversity of origins, there is a complementarity of function. Viewing them in tandem enables us to see that what Adon Olam spells out for the individual–divine relationship the Aleinu spells out for the community and subsequently humanity. The result is that the pattern of individual, communal, and universal redemption characteristic of so many individual prayers is now seen as characteristic of the whole Shaḥarit service (see below).

This characterization takes on special poignancy in the light of the relationship between the Aleinu and the Psalm 145-based Ashrei. The Ashrei advances in three stages from the individual's blessing of God (Psalm 145:2), to the community's (Psalm 145:10), to the aspiration of all humanity joining in the blessing of God (Psalm 145:21). The Ashrei thereby combines the "I" of Adon Olam with the "we" and the "they" of the Aleinu albeit preceding them historically. Most relevant is the intermediate directive between stages two and three: "to proclaim to humanity His mighty acts and the majestic glory of His kingship" (Psalm 145:12).[45] Since the second part of the Aleinu translates this into a vision for humanity's acceptance of the majesty of God's kingship, it reuses and reformulates the verse's phraseology. Absent from both the Ashrei and the Aleinu is anything distinctly Jewish besides the worship of God and the universalization of divine sovereignty. Coincidentally, both the Ashrei and the Aleinu appear in the daily liturgy three times, the latter in all three services, the former in the first two, twice in the first. The Ashrei always initiates its part of the service; the Aleinu always concludes the service.

Finally, as noted, the Aleinu is also linked to blessing 18 of the Amidah. Besides content and the absence of the distinctly Jewish, they are connected by choreography and by frequency. Both require standing and bowing all three times daily. They also share structure and thesis. As blessing 18 begins with our acknowledgement of God ("we acknowledge You") and concludes with a hope for all to follow suit ("and all the living shall acknowledge You"), so does the Aleinu. It is thus most fitting that every service with an Amidah concludes with the

---

[45] See Reuven Kimelman, "Psalm 145: Theme, Structure, and Impact," *The Journal of Biblical Literature* 113 (1994): 37–58 (available at academia.edu).

Aleinu. It is almost as if the liturgy had its own internal structuring mechanism to frame its theology.

THE RELATIONSHIP BETWEEN THE WHOLE AND THE PARTS

The whole of Shaḥarit is also to be understood from its parts and its parts from the whole. The overall arrangement reinforces the connectedness of the parts. Through the soldering of their edges, there emerges a thematic continuum with the requisite coherence to create a resemblance of a liturgical mural having a beginning, middle, and end, which serves also as culmination. The beginning Adon Olam is rounded off by the ending Aleinu. The Aleinu, in turn, consummates the Shema Liturgy and the Amidah, whereas Pesuqei DeZimra paves the path to both.

The centerpiece of Pesuqei DeZimra, the Ashrei, leads into all three of them. The Ashrei's central theme of divine sovereignty parallels that of the Shema Liturgy. Its advancement from self, to community, to humanity, corresponds to blessings 4–18 of the Amidah. And its concluding vision of the universal acknowledgement of God dovetails with that of the Aleinu. Little of this was planned or foreseeable, or so it seems. It is hence not to be subsumed strictly under the rubric of the history of the liturgy nor strictly under the literary analysis of its parts. It can, however, be subsumed under the rubric of the phenomenology of the liturgy from the perspective of the consciousness of the praying person. The liturgical compositional theory of inclusion, where ends revert to beginnings to indicate completion, is now found to have application to the entire Shaḥarit.[46]

The internal structuring mechanism of the liturgy also characterizes the total weekday Shaḥarit. Shaḥarit divides into five parts:

1. Preliminaries beginning with Adon Olam
2. Pesuqei DeZimra
3. the Shema Liturgy
4. the Amidah
5. the rest ending with the Aleinu.

---

[46] This is exemplified by the sefardic practice of rising near the beginning of Shaḥarit saying "God was king, God is king, and God will be king forever" along with Zechariah 14:9 and ending the service with the Aleinu while standing concluding again with Zechariah 14:9.

Both 1 and 3 have the Shema verse positioned at their center. The biblical middle of 2 and the Aleinu of 5 both end with Zechariah 14:9. In some rites, the Shema verse was appended to both. Uncanny is the interplay between the Shema verse and Zechariah 14:9 throughout. As explained, the Shema verse, "Hear O Israel, Adonai is our God, Adonai is one," was understood in terms of Zechariah 14:9, "And Adonai shall be sovereign over all the earth; on that day Adonai shall be one and His name one," which itself was understood as a fulfillment of the Shema verse. This understanding allows the whole service to reflect an ABAB pattern. The placement of the Zechariah verse (B) near the end of part 2 after the Shema verse (A) of part 1 can correspond to the placement of the Zechariah verse (B) at the end of part 5 after the Shema verse (A) of part 3 making for an ABAB arrangement.

The overall structure of Shaḥarit, especially with the Aleinu of part 5 following the Shema verse of part 3, reinforces the thesis of the Zechariah verse as a fulfillment of the Shema verse. The location of the Shema verse in the geographical center of part 3 of a five-part service further reinforces the centrality of the Shema verse for the whole. It is as if the total service pivots around the Shema verse as liturgically understood. This structure is further supported by the perception that Adon Olam and the Aleinu, with their various takes on the theme of the Shema verse, bookend a service at whose center is the Shema verse, which now emerges as the apex of a chiastically structured liturgy.[47]

Both modes of composition involve relocation either from the Bible or in the liturgy itself. Relocation often leads to recontextualization, reformulation, and reconceptualization. Salient examples are parts 2–4 (Pesuqei De-Zimra, the Shema Liturgy, and the Amidah). The relocation and juxtaposition of a wide variety of biblical materials in Pesuqei DeZimra produced the consummate introduction to the classical Shema-Amidah rabbinic liturgy. The reconceptualization of a biblical covenantal ceremony recast the Shema Liturgy into the rabbinic

---

[47] The Qabbalistic-based theology of the liturgy based on its four "worlds" (actualization, formation, creation, and emanation), first ascending and then descending, also perceives the liturgy as a seven-stage chiastic drama with the Amidah at its apex:

                      4. *Ha-Amidah*
   3. *Qedushah DeYoṣer*   5. *Qedushah DeSidra*
 2. *Pesuqei DeZimra*   6. *Shir Shel Yom*
1. *Qorbanot*   7. *Pitum HaQetoret*

In this scheme, 1 corresponds to 7, both cult-based; 2 to 6, both psalm-based; and 3 to 5, both Qedushah-based. The result is a pattern of ABCDCBA; see Kimelman, *RL*, ch. 5, "Pesukei DeZimra," n. 375.

coronation ceremony for the realization of divine sovereignty. And the reformulation and recontextualization of biblical material throughout enabled the Amidah to blossom into the consummate rabbinic prayer for redemption. In all three cases, the synthetic meaning exceeds the sum of the parts just as is the case for the whole Shaḥarit.

These three segments of the liturgy share a common literary structure in which the terminology of the opening selection is rethematized in the closing selection. The opening and closing blessings of Pesuqei DeZimra, Barukh SheAmar and Yishtabaḥ share a distinctive liturgical parlance; the opening and closing blessings of the Shema Liturgy echo each other's terms for divine acclamation; and the first and the erstwhile concluding eighteenth blessing of the Amidah share body language, a redemptive agenda, and divine nomenclature.

THE CENTRALITY OF DIVINE SOVEREIGNTY

What most account for the theological cohesiveness of the liturgy are the pervasive references to divine kingship. This sovereignization of the liturgy starts in the tannaitic period and increases as time goes on. Not only do all rabbinic formulated blessings, many of which are clustered in part one (Preliminaries), highlight divine kingship, every segment of the liturgy, from the daily to that of the High Holidays,[48] underwent a process of sovereignization by acquiring references to divine kingship as did the blessing formulary itself.[49]

The center of sovereignization is, of course, the Shema verse, dubbed "the acceptance of the authority of divine sovereignty,"[50] a thesis buttressed by the rabbinic insertion of "Blessed be the name of His glorious *kingship* for ever and ever" immediately following. Once the Shema was understood in terms of divine sovereignty, its rays radiated throughout the liturgy forward and backward beginning with the preceding angelic coronation of God in heaven of the first blessing and ending with the ancient Israel coronation of God at the Song at the Sea excerpted in the third blessing.

---

[48] See Kimelman, *RL*, ch. 7, n. 387.
[49] See Kimelman, "Blessing Formulae and Divine Sovereignty in Rabbinic Liturgy," 1–39. Regarding the absence of mention of kingship in the original covenantal ceremony, see Kimelman, *RL*, ch. 6, text to nn. 386–89.
[50] See ibid., n. 15.

The motif of kingship increasingly insinuated itself forward into subsequent versions of the succeeding Amidah[51] as it increasingly insinuated itself backwards into the preceding Pesuqei DeZimra, especially the opening and closing blessings.[52] In addition, kingship looms prominently in the second unit of verses of Yehie Khevod and in the last verse.[53] Indeed, to underscore the theme a synthetic verse was constructed from three verse fragments to make the point that it is Adonai who is king in the present, past, and future, saying: "Adonai is king" (Psalm 10:16), "Adonai was king" (Psalm 93:1, 97:1, 99:1; 1 Chronicles 15:31), and "Adonai will be king forever more" (Exodus 5:18). This "new verse" was deemed so effective in getting over the idea of God's eternal reign that it merited multiple repetitions in the liturgy[54] including Yehie Khevod of the Pesuqei DeZimra, and in the coronation verses of the ceremony for the taking out of the Torah. It even weaved its way into the opening lines of Adon Olam. In sefardic synagogues, before the recitation of Barukh SheAmar, it has become customary to rise at its twofold recitation as if it were a performative proclamation.[55] There was even a liturgical practice of responding to the opening verse of the Decalogue with the liturgical synthetic verse, "God is king, God was king, God will be king forever."[56] This fits the idea that both the Sinaitic revelation and the recitation of the Shema are cases of the acceptance of divine sovereignty.[57]

The kingship motif dominates much of the rest of Pesuqei DeZimra. It constitutes the theme of the pivotal verses of Psalm 145:11–13 of the Ashrei as well as the conclusion of Psalm 146 and the virtual beginning of Psalm 149. It is also the climax of the Song at the Sea (Exodus 15:18) and accounts for the inclusion of the appended verses from Psalm 22:29, Obadiah 1:21, and Zechariah

---

[51] See Kimelman, *RL*, ch. 7, nn. 229, 294. This characterizes the Babylonian version more than the Palestinian version, which did not add the motif ("The holy king") to the third blessing even on the High Holidays.

[52] See Kimelman, *RL*, ch. 5, sections 2 and 15.   [53] See ibid., section 6.

[54] See ibid., nn. 151–53.

[55] See above, n. 46. The practice is already mentioned by Abraham b. Nathan (of Lunel), *Sefer Ha-Manhig*, ed. Y. Raphael, 2 vols. (Jerusalem: Mossad Harav Kook, 1978), I, 153, lines 19–20 (ca. 1155–1215, Provence-Spain).

[56] See Ezra Fleischer, *Eretz-Israel Prayer and Prayer Rituals as Portrayed in the Geniza Documents* [Hebrew] (Jerusalem: The Hebrew University Magnes Press, 1988), after p. 320.

[57] See Kimelman, *RL*, ch. 6, parts III and IV.

14:9. The verse "Adonai, save us. May the king answer us when we call" (Psalm 20:10) occurs some five times starting with the Hodu's appendix of psalm verses and Yehie Khevod.[58] The kingship motif, as noted, is prominent in the opening verses of the only piyyut to achieve universal daily acceptance, Adon Olam, as it permeates the only classical prayer to conclude every communal service— weekday, Sabbath, and holiday—namely, the Aleinu. Indeed, the whole Aleinu revolves around the shift from our to everyone's acceptance of divine sovereignty. Lastly, the most oft-recited prayer of the daily liturgy, the Qaddish, seeks the establishment of God's kingship speedily in our days.

The liturgy advances from our acknowledgement of divine sovereignty to everyone's. The motif of the universalization of divine worship also holds the whole service together: beginning, middle, and end. It appears in the Preliminaries, in the section after the miniature Shema, *Attah Hu*, stating: "Let all humanity recognize and know that You are God, You alone, over, all the kingdoms of the world." It is pervasive in Pesuqei DeZimra beginning with the *Hodu* and its opening, "Thank Adonai; call on His name, proclaim His deeds amongst the peoples" (I Chronicles 16:8). It continues with the opening of *Mizmor Le-Todah*: "Shout out for Adonai, all [people of] the earth. Worship Adonai in joy" (Psalm 100:1b–a). It then moves onto the Ashrei and its verse "to proclaim to humanity His mighty acts and the majestic glory of His kingship" (Psalm 145:12). This process is consummated in Psalm 148 where all the dwellers of heaven and earth praise God. The universal acknowledgement of God also consummates the Amidah with its hope, in the penultimate blessing, that "all the living will acknowledge You," as it concludes the Aleinu with its final verse "And Adonai shall be sovereign over all the earth; on that day Adonai shall be one and His name one" (Zechariah 14:9).

This last verse on the universalization of divine worship goes with another on divine eternity at the beginning and the end of some versions of the liturgy. In those cases, preceding Barukh SheAmar is the synthetic verse composed of three verse fragments to make the point that God's reign lasts forever followed by Zechariah 14:9.[59] The end, in the

---

[58] See Kimelman, *RL*, ch. 5, n. 154, and text thereto.
[59] See Jacob Verdiger, *Siddur Ṣelutah De-Avraham* (Jerusalem: Mossad Harav Kook, 2016), 154, 156–57.

Aleinu, is the last of those fragments, "Adonai will reign for ever and ever" (Exodus 15:18), also followed by Zechariah 14:9.

FROM INDIVIDUAL TO COMMUNITY TO HUMANITY

In addition to the leitmotif of divine kingship, there is the thematic development from individual to community to humanity permeating much of the liturgy. This includes its best-known parts: the blessing formulary, the Ashrei, and the Shema verse.

The following charts the three-staged blessing and the three-staged Psalm 145 of the Ashrei:

"Blessed are You"—prelude (Psalm 145:1) = self—God
"Adonai our God"—(Psalm 145:10) = community—God
"King of the universe"—postlude (Psalm 145:21) = humanity—God

The six-word, tripartite structure of the blessing also corresponds to the six-word tripartite structure of the Shema:[60]

שְׁמַע יִשְׂרָאֵל \ ה' אֱלֹהֵינוּ \ ה' אֶחָד
בָּרוּךְ אַתָּה \ ה' אֱלֹהֵינוּ \ מֶלֶךְ הָעוֹלָם

The middle phrases are identical, "Adonai our God." The last phrases are theological equivalents, for the Rabbis understood the affirmation "God is one" as affirming the hope that God's reign will become one for all, thereby making Him "king of the universe."[61] The first phrases are reciprocal: the Shema (in the liturgy) opens with God addressing Israel in the second person singular ("Hear O Israel"); the blessing opens with Israel addressing God in the second person singular ("Blessed are You"). By formulating the blessing in the second person, it becomes a response to God's direct address.[62] We pray to God directly just as we were addressed by God directly. This three-fold development from self to community to humanity also characterizes the opening verses of Psalms 146–48 and blessings 4–18 of the Amidah.[63]

---

[60] The parsing of which is supported by the cantillation.
[61] See above, n. 30; and José Faur, "*Ribbono shel 'Olam* / God, *Dominus*: What Does It Mean? ed. J. Roth, M. Schmelzer, Y. Francus, *Tiferet Le-Yisrael: Jubilee Volume in Honor of Israel Francus* (New York: The Jewish Theological Seminary, 2010), 1–17.
[62] For this development, see Kimelman, "Blessing Formulae and Divine Sovereignty in Rabbinic Liturgy," 1–39.
[63] See Kimelman, *RL*, ch. 7, n. 337, and text thereto.

The shift from the community to humanity alone is also the fulcrum of the Aleinu.

A PECULIAR POST-TEMPLE LITURGY

Conspicuous by their absence for a post-Temple liturgy are traces of its destruction. The expectation for the rebuilding of the Temple and Jerusalem, for the restoration of the sacrificial cult, and for the purging of sin hardly materializes. In the light of the repeated emphasis on penance in post-First Temple liturgy,[64] this is flabbergasting. In the whole three units of the rabbinic-geonic liturgy—Pesuqei DeZimra, the Shema Liturgy, the Amidah—there is only one blessing each for the return of God to Zion, the restoration of the cult, the rebuilding of Jerusalem, and the forgiveness of sin, all in the Amidah. The other two units are totally unburdened by such concerns.[65]

Compared with the two other biblically informed liturgies of the time, Qumran and Christianity, the rabbinic daily liturgy is remarkably free of cultic imagery, penitential elements,[66] and self-deprecatory or obsequious gestures and expressions.[67] Indeed, the most repeated prayer, the Amidah, is recited in a dignified upright posture with limitations on bowings.[68] Only later did the penitential element come to dominate the post-Amidah Taḥanun.[69] Even the late-thirteenth century effort to introduce a penitential abecedary from the liturgy of the Day of Atonement into the Preliminaries failed to catch on.[70] Contrary to lachrymose and lugubrious expectations, the daily liturgy is remarkably upbeat, and theologically affirmative.

---

[64] See Ezra 9:5–15; Nehemiah 1:4–11; 9:4–10:40; Daniel 9:3–19; *Baruch* 1:15–3:8; *Prayer of Azariah, Tobith* 3:1–6; and *3 Maccabees* 2:1–10; 9:4–10:40.

[65] The exception may be Psalm 100 at the beginning of Pesuqei DeZimra, but even there the so-called cultic terms have been transferred to a noncultic venue; see Kimelman, *RL*, ch. 5, "Pesuqei DeZimra," section 5.

[66] See Richard Sarason, "The Persistence and Trajectories of Penitential Prayer in Rabbinic Judaism," ed. M. Boda, D. Falk, and R. Werline, *Seeking the Favor of God: The Impact of Penitential Prayer Beyond Second Temple Judaism*, 3 vols. (Atlanta: Society of Biblical Literature, 2008), vol. 3, 1–38; and Esther Chazon, "The *Words of the Luminaries* and Penitential Prayer in Second Temple Times," ibid., vol. 2, 177–86.

[67] See Joseph Heinemann, *Prayer in the Period of the Tannaim and Amora'im* [Hebrew], (Jerusalem: The Hebrew University Magnes Press, 1964), 153–54.

[68] See Kimelman, *RL*, ch. 7, n. 3.

[69] See Ruth Langer, "We Do Not Even Know What To Do!': A Foray into the Early History of Tahanun," *Seeking the Favor of God*, vol. 3, 39–69.

[70] See Jacob b. Jehuda, *Eṣ Ḥayyim* (Jerusalem: Mossad Harav Kook, 1962), 64.

Selected Further Reading

Blank, Deborah, ed. *The Experience of Jewish Liturgy*. Leiden: Brill, 2011.

Boda, Mark, et al., eds. *Seeking the Favor of God (Penitential Prayer in Second Temple Judaism)*, 3 vols. Atlanta: Society of Biblical Literature, 2006–2008.

Chazon, Esther, ed. *Liturgical Perspectives: Prayer and Poetry in Light of the Dead Sea Scrolls*. Leiden: Brill, 2003.

Ehrlich, Uri. *The Nonverbal Language of Prayer: A New Approach to Jewish Liturgy*. Tübingen: Mohr-Siebeck, 2004.

Elbogen, Ismar. *Jewish Liturgy: A Comprehensive History*. Philadelphia: Jewish Publication Society, 1993.

Heinemann, Joseph. *Literature of the Synagogue*. New York: Behrman House, 1975.

Hoffman, Lawrence, ed. *My People's Prayer Book*, 10 vols. Woodstock, VT: Jewish Lights Publishing, 1997–2005, and *Prayers of Awe*: 4 vols. Woodstock, VT: Jewish Lights Publishing, 2010–2013.

Kimelman, Reuven. "Rabbinic Prayer in Late Antiquity" and "The Rabbinic Theology of the Physical: Blessings, Body and Soul, Resurrection, Covenant and Election." In *The Cambridge History of Judaism, Volume 4: The Late Roman-Rabbinic Period*, 573–611, 946–97. Edited by S. Katz. Cambridge: Cambridge University Press, 2006.

Kimelman, Reuven. *The Mystical Meaning of Lekhah Dodi and Kabbalat Shabbat* [Hebrew and English]. Jerusalem: The Hebrew University Magnes Press and Cherub Press, 2003.

Kimelman, Reuven. *The Rhetoric of the Liturgy: A Historical and Literary Commentary to the Jewish Prayer Book*. Liverpool University Press, Littman Library of Jewish Civilization, 2020.

Langer, Ruth. *Jewish Liturgy: A Guide to Research*. New York: Rowman & Littlefield, 2015.

Langer, Ruth and Fine, Steven, eds. *Liturgy in the Life of the Synagogue: Studies in the History of Jewish Prayer*. Winona Lake, IN: Eisenbrauns, 2005.

Levine, Lee. *The Ancient Synagogue: The First Thousand Years*. New Haven, CT: Yale University Press, 2005.

Mack, Hananel, ed. *Studies in Jewish Liturgy: A Reader, Likkutei Tarbiz VI* [Hebrew]. Jerusalem: The Hebrew University Magnes Press, 2003.

Nulman, Macy. *The Encyclopedia of Jewish Prayer: Ashkenazic and Sephardic Rites*. Northvale, NJ: Jason Aronson, 1993.

Penner, Jeremy. *Patterns of Daily Prayer in Second Temple Period Judaism*. Leiden: Brill, 2012.

Reif, Stefan. *Judaism and Hebrew Prayer: New Perspectives on Jewish Liturgical History*, Cambridge: Cambridge University Press, 1993.

Schwartz, Dov. *Rabbi Joseph Dov Soloveitchik on the Experience of Prayer*. Boston, MA: Academic Studies Press, 2019.

PART II

MEDIEVAL

6 Maimonides' Theology
DANIEL RYNHOLD[*]

The time-honored account of the genesis of medieval Jewish philosophy proceeds as follows. By the ninth century, the then established texts of Judaism, the Tanak and the Talmud—though the Tanak in particular when it comes to Jewish philosophy—could be seen as presenting a worldview involving accounts of, among other things, God, humanity, and the world, together with the manner in which they relate to each other. The account of God in particular, while complex and nuanced, appears to be a personalist, or at least quasi-personalist account, presenting God on the model of a person—clearly far more powerful and knowledgeable than any mere human, but an account that is recognizably personal nonetheless. God relates actively to the world and to the people in it—and to one people in particular. This God speaks to individuals and to groups, oftentimes decides on their fate, and maintains those relationships through their highs and lows portrayed throughout the biblical books.

And then, among others, along came Aristotle—or for Jewish medievals, the version of Aristotle mediated through the Arabic translation movement, beginning in the latter half of the eighth century and lasting well into the tenth.[1] His God was an unmoved mover who was simply not the type of being who converses with lesser creatures, or indeed any creatures at all. The Aristotelian God was a necessary being who was the cause of the universe though not its creator, and an incorporeal unity who simply cannot have taken the Israelites out of Egypt with his outstretched arm for lack of said limb. And so begins the project of medieval Jewish philosophy. For what is one to do, asks Moses Maimonides (1138–1204) if

---

[*] I would like to thank David Shatz and Menachem Kellner for comments on earlier drafts of this chapter.

[1] While al-Ma'mūn, who reigned from 813–833, is often cited as the caliph responsible for initiating the translation movement, in truth it began rather earlier with the second Abbasid caliph al-Mansur (r. 754–775). For a thorough account, see Gutas, *Greek Thought, Arabic Culture*.

one is "a religious man for whom the validity of our Law has become established in his soul and has become actual in his belief" and yet one is also philosophically engaged? Writes Maimonides:

> The human intellect having drawn him on and led him to dwell within its province, he must have felt distressed by the externals of the Law ... [and] would remain in a state of perplexity and confusion as to whether he should follow his intellect, renounce what he knew concerning the terms in question, and consequently consider that he has renounced the foundations of the Law. Or should he hold fast to his understanding of these terms and not let himself be drawn on together with his intellect, rather turning his back on it and moving away from it while at the same time perceiving that he had brought loss to himself and harm to his religion?[2]

While it goes without saying that there is a large element of simplification in this picture, the essentials are basically sound. Jewish philosophy in the medieval era was primarily an attempt by philosophically inclined Jews to reconcile, to the extent possible, the worldview of the classical Jewish texts with the worldview of the dominant Greek philosophical accounts of reality to which they now had access, as mediated by Arabic translations and commentators.

By far the most influential Jewish philosopher to emerge out of this encounter was the aforementioned Moses Maimonides, or as he is known in many circles, Rambam (the acronym of Rabbi Moses ben Maimon), and it is to his theology, particularly his conception of God, that this chapter is devoted. A product of Muslim Spain forced to wander from one place to another with each Islamic conquest, Maimonides landed in Egypt in 1166, and soon after settled in Fustat (old Cairo), from where he would go on to serve as a court physician to Saladin.[3] It was here in Egypt that he would compose his philosophical masterpiece, *Dalālat al-Ḥā'irīn*, the *Guide of the Perplexed*, a work that still occasions lively controversy over 800 years after his death. Indeed,

---

[2] Moses Maimonides, *The Guide of the Perplexed* [henceforth *Guide*], Introduction, 5–6. References will be to part, chapter, and page number in this translation.

[3] For recent, detailed accounts of his life and work, see Herbert A. Davidson, *Moses Maimonides: The Man and His Works* (Oxford: Oxford University Press, 2005); Joel L. Kraemer, *Maimonides: The Life and World of One of Civilization's Greatest Minds* (New York: Doubleday, 2008); and Sarah Stroumsa, *Maimonides in His World: Portrait of a Mediterranean Thinker* (Princeton: Princeton University Press, 2009).

it is probably the most hotly contested work in the history of Jewish philosophy, with the precise extent of Maimonides' Aristotelianism one such matter of intense scholarly dispute, which, it should go without saying, will significantly impact his conception of God, given the divergences between the traditional Jewish and the Aristotelian views outlined above.

With the *Guide*, these disputes are exacerbated by its style, which is, in part, intended to obscure its meaning. This is a result, first, of rabbinic restrictions on disseminating its subject matter, which is among the "secret" or esoteric teachings of Judaism that not only cannot be fully comprehended, but that ought not even to be expounded in public, as made explicit in the Mishnah:

> Forbidden relations are not expounded before three, nor the *Account of the Beginning* before two, nor the *Account of the Chariot* before a single person, unless he is a sage who understands from his own knowledge. (*Mishnah Hagigah* 2:1)

Second, Maimonides, for whom these "Accounts"—and the subject matter of the *Guide*—are to be identified with natural science and metaphysics, observes the rabbinic prohibition by using artful literary methods in the *Guide*'s construction that has yielded 800 years of intense debate regarding the extent to which the book does or does not obscure his true intent. As a result, Maimonidean scholarship is replete with contradictory accounts of his opinion on all manner of topics. While the interpretation offered here is far from idiosyncratic in Maimonidean scholarship, these controversies cannot go unmentioned as we delve into Maimonides' conception of God. To slightly misquote the tannaitic sage Ben Bag Bag from *Mishnah Avot* 5, 22 "turn it and turn it for anything might be in it."[4]

---

[4] There is a voluminous literature on the whole question of Maimonidean esotericism, going all the way back to his thirteenth-century interpreters. See Aviezer Ravitzky, "The Secrets of the Guide to the Perplexed: Between the Thirteenth and the Twentieth Centuries," in *Studies in Maimonides*, ed. Isadore Twersky (Cambridge, MA: Harvard University Press, 1990), 159–207. For the modern debate, the starting point is Leo Strauss, *Persecution and the Art of Writing* (Glencoe, IL: Free Press, 1952), 38–94. A more recent approach can be found in Yair Lorberbaum, "On Contradictions, Rationality, Dialectics, and Esotericism," *Review of Metaphysics* 55, no. 4 (2002): 711–50. For a good general introduction to the various approaches and issues, including something of an anticipation of Lorberbaum's view, see Part I of Marvin Fox, *Interpreting Maimonides* (Chicago: University of Chicago Press, 1990).

FIVE PRINCIPLES OF FAITH

Given the complex structure of the *Guide*, a good way of framing the discussion initially is through Maimonides' own attempt at providing a systematic theology found in his first major work, the *Commentary on the Mishnah*, initially completed in 1168, but subjected to revision throughout his life.[5] In his lengthy and oft-studied philosophical introduction to the tenth chapter of Tractate *Sanhedrin* (known as *Pereq Heleq*), Maimonides formulates his thirteen "principles" or "foundations" (he variously uses the Arabic terms *qa'ida* and *aṣl*) of faith, which would go on to be summarized and systematized in liturgical form, and used by some as a form of exclusionary Jewish dogmatics (which, in fairness, is arguably how Maimonides himself first presented them).[6]

The first five of the principles deal directly with the nature of God, and according to some are the only subset of the thirteen beliefs in which are both necessary and sufficient for attainment of a place in *Olam Haba* (the world to come). Indeed, the idea of those who do and do not gain a portion—*heleq*—in the world to come is what provokes Maimonides' theological digression in the first place. We here paraphrase these principles so that they can act as a template for our discussion:

1. The existence of God, whose is "the most perfect type of existence ... [and] the cause of the existence of all other beings,"[7] with God's own existence being "self-sufficient."[8]
2. The unity of God, such that He is "one with a oneness for which there is no comparison at all."[9]
3. The incorporeality of God: "that this One is neither a body nor a force within a body [and] none of the characteristics of a body appertains to Him."[10]
4. The "precedence" of God, who is "He Who precedes (everything) absolutely."[11]

---

[5] As is clear both from letters he wrote later in life and annotations to what many take to be an autograph copy housed in Oxford's Bodleian Library. See Samuel M. Stern and S. D. Sassoon, "The Autograph Manuscript of Maimonides' Commentary on the Mishna," [Hebrew] *Tarbiz* 29 (1960): 261–67.

[6] For further discussion, see Menachem Kellner, *Dogma in Medieval Jewish Thought: From Maimonides to Abravanel* (Oxford: Oxford University Press, 1986).

[7] Maimonides' principles as reproduced in Kellner, *Dogma*, 11. The translation Kellner reproduces is that of David R. Blumenthal in his *The Commentary of R. Hoter ben Shelomoh to the Thirteen Principles of Maimonides* (Leiden: Brill, 1974).

[8] Ibid.   [9] Ibid.   [10] Ibid.   [11] Ibid., 12.

5. God alone is the proper object of worship and praise, and one must not "seize upon intermediaries in order to reach Him" such as, for example, angels, or the spheres that played a major part in medieval cosmology. Effectively, therefore, as Maimonides informs us: "This fifth foundation is the prohibition against idolatry."[12]

In what follows we will often refer back to these principles as we analyze each of these ideas in detail in order to expand further upon Maimonides' conception of God.

EXISTENCE, UNITY, AND INCORPOREALITY

Maimonides presents four arguments for the existence of God in the opening chapter of Book 2 of the *Guide*, though he establishes some important context toward the end of the first part, where he discusses a disjunctive method in a manner that Hasdai Crescas (ca. 1340–1410/11) counts as a further and distinct "disjunctive" argument for God's existence (that Maimonides details fully in *Guide* 2.2).[13] Regarding this disjunctive argument, Maimonides begins by stating that since nothing can create itself, if the world was "created in time, it undoubtedly has a creator who created it in time" (*Guide* 1.71, 181–82). What, though, if the world is eternal? The question of whether Maimonides believed that the world was created *ex nihilo* or was co-eternal with God as Aristotle contended is one of the most fraught questions in Maimonidean scholarship. Since Maimonides believes that there is no demonstration either way,[14] but knows that one of the opposing propositions is true, he must seek arguments for the existence of God that begin from the premise that the world is eternal, just in case that premise is the true one. Only in this way "the demonstration will be perfect, both if the world is eternal and if it is created in time" (*Guide* 1.71, 182). The four (non-disjunctive) arguments that Maimonides presents at the beginning of Book 2 are therefore based on twenty-five premises of Aristotelian science

---

[12] Ibid.
[13] Crescas actually identifies six arguments, five in *Guide* 2.1, and this disjunctive argument, first noted in 1.71 and detailed in 2.2. See Hasdai Crescas, *Or HaShem* [The Light of the Lord] [Hebrew], ed. Shlomo Fisher (Ramot Books: Jerusalem, 1990), Book I, Part 1, chs. 27–32.
[14] For a thorough account of this particular debate, see Kenneth Seeskin, *Maimonides on the Origin of the World* (Cambridge: Cambridge University Press, 2006).

(detailed in Maimonides' introduction to Book 2), with Aristotelian eternity added as a twenty-sixth.

The arguments themselves are all versions of the cosmological argument, based in large part on the arguments of his Muslim predecessors, and subsequently developed in Christian scholasticism, and we need not detain ourselves here with their details.[15] It is, however, worth saying something further about Maimonides' methodology that emerges from this discussion.

First, the insistence on starting from Aristotelian premises, even including the eternity of the world, belief in which—leaving aside for the moment debates regarding esotericism—Maimonides elsewhere remarks "destroys the Law in its principle, necessarily gives the lie to every miracle, and reduces to inanity all the hopes and threats that the Law has held out" (Guide 2.25, 328), tells us much about his commitment to the philosophy and science of his day. The significance of this cannot be overstated, given that it leads him to seek out "naturalistic" accounts for biblical events to the extent that he can. In a letter which, unlike the Guide, most certainly *was* intended for a wider public, Maimonides explicitly criticizes those who:

> like nothing better, and, in their silliness, enjoy nothing more, than to set the Law and reason at opposite ends, and to move everything far from the explicable. So they claim it to be a miracle, and they shrink from identifying it as a natural incident ... But I try to reconcile the Law and reason, and wherever possible consider all things as of the natural order. Only when something is explicitly identified as a miracle, and reinterpretation of it cannot be accommodated, only then I feel forced to grant that this is a miracle.[16]

There are good philosophical reasons for this approach in his eyes. But they are reasons that, as we will see, yield an approach that will strip God of his "personality."

---

[15] For a thorough philosophical contextualization of Maimonides' arguments, including sections on Crescas' analysis, see Herbert Davidson, *Proofs for Eternity, Creation and the Existence of God in Medieval Islamic and Jewish Philosophy* (Oxford: Oxford University Press, 1987), chs. 8–12. A detailed conceptual approach is taken in Josef Stern, "Maimonides' Demonstrations: Principles and Practice," *Medieval Philosophy and Theology* 10 (2001): 47–84.

[16] Moses Maimonides, "The Essay on Resurrection," trans. A. Halkin, in A. Halkin, and D. Hartman, *Crisis and Leadership* (Philadelphia: Jewish Publication Society, 1985), 209–245. Quotation from 223.

More generally, this places Maimonides as a *falasifa* within the tradition of *falsafa*, or Islamic philosophy, rather than in the more theological camp of the *Kalām*, whose practitioners, the *mutakallimūn*, are the butt of much Maimonidean invective throughout the *Guide*. It is important to understand this distinction with care. There are those who would argue that what differentiates these kalamic "theologians" from the *falasifa* is that the former use dialectical methods to prove conclusions upon which they are already decided, unlike the philosophers who are open inquirers. While this way of putting the distinction might sound acceptable to our modern ears, if Maimonides is attempting to *reconcile* philosophy and Torah, then given the way we have just parsed the distinction he would surely fall within the camp of the *Kalām* with their more apologetic aims. Thus, we should note that his issue with the *Kalām* has less to do with their apologetic endpoints than with their methods of attaining them. The *mutakallimūn* begin from theologically loaded premises "that would be useful to them with regard to their belief"(*Guide* 1.71, 177), and, more to the point, that do not conform either to the empirical evidence nor to the prevailing, and to Maimonides' mind, demonstrated truth of Aristotelian science, commitment to which, as Warren Zev Harvey writes, is "not merely one among several points of dispute between the philosophers and the *mutakallimūn*, but ... the essential point of dispute between them."[17] Maimonides' arguments for the existence of God therefore, and his insistence on their being founded on Aristotelian "scientific" premises, to the point of even including the problematic premise of the eternity of the world, indicate his commitment to the power of reason and his refusal to countenance alternative and unscientific worldviews, however "useful" they might prove for his presumed ends.

The approach through rational argument, though, is significant for more than simply rendering religion compatible with reason. Such arguments for the existence of God can be attacked from two different directions, one being whether they are valid arguments, the other—accepting for the sake of argument that they are—concerning what

---

[17] Warren Zev Harvey, "Why Maimonides was not a Mutakallim," in *Perspectives on Maimonides: Philosophical and Historical Studies*, ed. Joel L. Kraemer (Oxford: Oxford University Press, 1991), 105–14. Quotation from 109, emphasis in the original. Harvey also brings further support in his piece for the general view expressed in this paragraph.

they prove. And in Maimonides' case, what we prove is the existence of "an existent that is necessary of existence and is so necessarily with respect to its own essence, and that this existent has no cause for its existence and has no composition in itself, and for this reason is neither a body nor a force in a body" (Guide 2.1, 248).

This is the conclusion of the third of the four "speculations" or arguments that Maimonides presents in this chapter of the Guide—the others do not use the language of necessity, and instead demonstrate the existence of a first cause, an unmoved mover, or a being that is "perpetually existent in one and the same state, and in which there is no potentiality at all" (ibid., 249); in each of these iterations, though, God is of course an incorporeal unity.

Working again with Maimonides' third speculation, although one can—and he does—run parallel arguments for each of the others, the twenty-first Aristotelian premise that Maimonides lists tells us that if something is "composed of two notions" then this composition is "the cause of its existence as it really is, and consequently [it] is not necessarily existent ... for it exists only in virtue of the existence of its two parts" (Guide, Introduction to the Second Part, 238). So we move straight from the idea of a necessary existent to the idea that this existent cannot be composed of parts and is thus a unity. God's "oneness" for Maimonides is less a numerical statement than a claim regarding the uniqueness of God in being beyond any form of multiplicity. He exists in "simplicity" inasmuch as He is not composed of parts, which are ruled out since they would in some sense be the "cause" of His existence, when He is, of course, uncaused. And this, in turn, means that God is also incorporeal, since according to the twenty-second Aristotelian premise "Every body is necessarily composed of two things" (ibid.), so a unity without composition cannot be a body, not to mention the further point that for Maimonides a necessary being cannot be subject to "generation and corruption" so it once more cannot be corporeal. All corporeal beings, given that they are composite, can simply be "decomposed"; God cannot. We end up, therefore, with our necessary, incorporeal, simple Being, of whom Maimonides writes: "It is He who is the deity, may His name be sublime" (Guide 2.1, 248). And yet these bare characterizations, while sufficient to explain the characteristics of the world that first prompted Maimonides et al. to propose the classic arguments for God's existence, are still very far from the God of the Torah who converses with human beings and exerts providential control over history. This should not surprise us, given that the arguments are all broadly Aristotelian, and Aristotle's God is also very far away from the biblical picture. Having demonstrated to his rational satisfaction the existence of this Being then, Maimonides still has much to do if he wishes to present a robust theology.

INCORPOREALITY, SCRIPTURE, AND REVELATION

Despite the minimal positive commitments he has made so far, even at this point Maimonides' picture of God requires a thoroughgoing reinterpretation of the language of Scripture, and for reasons that will become clear, it is worth spending some time at this juncture describing his approach to biblical anthropomorphisms.

For Maimonides, the need to distance readers from the anthropomorphic conception of God that a literal reading of the Tanak might seem to imply is of the greatest importance, and for all the (often justified) talk of esotericism, Maimonides maintains that belief in divine unity and incorporeality is to be "inculcated in virtue of traditional authority" (*Guide* 1.35, 81) in everyone, including children. The ascription of corporeality is an offense against God such that you are considered "*an enemy, and an adversary* of God, much more so than *an idolater*" (*Guide* 1.36, 84).

Following on from this, that God's incorporeality rules out his having, for example, any of the limbs attributed to him in all manner of biblical contexts is clear. But other than the obvious denial of actual bodily parts to God, Maimonides also has to deal with terms that *imply* corporeality. As the third principle cited earlier states, "none of the characteristics of a body appertains to Him," so, for instance, how can an incorporeal being sit, or stand, or for that matter approach his creations or withdraw from them? Or how can a being without an eye see? The opening 49 chapters of the *Guide* are largely taken up with these sorts of issues, and Maimonides offers us interpretations of all such offending terms in a manner that allows them to be used without fear of imputing gross corporeality to God.

So, to take just one example, at *Guide* 13 Maimonides tells us that the term "to stand," besides its literal meaning, is also often used figuratively in the Tanak to mean "to abstain and desist" and at others "to be stable and durable" as in "so that they may stand forever" (Jeremiah 32:14) in reference to documents that were sealed in order to preserve them, or in other words, render them "stable and durable." "Standing" therefore, Maimonides tells us, is always to be understood in this latter sense when used in reference to God, such as when it states that "His righteousness stands forever" (Psalms, 111:3) where clearly the reference is to the permanence of his righteousness. Similar methods are applied throughout the early exegetical discussions.

Certainly there are limits on the terms that Scripture will use in describing God, consideration of which introduces the marked pragmatic element that runs through Maimonides' account of divine attributes. The use of corporeal terms, or terms that entail corporeality, serves in the first place to bring people to believe in the very existence of God "inasmuch as the multitude cannot at first conceive of any existence save that of a body alone" (*Guide* 1.26, 56). Thus Maimonides, citing (and reinterpreting) the talmudic dictum "The Torah speaks in the language of the sons of man" (*Babylonian Talmud*, Yevamot 71a), maintains that even the language that *was* allowed was only a concession to human intellectual frailty. But the very same frailties might lead people to denigrate a God described in terms that we see as human imperfections, such as drinking or being ill. These are therefore ruled out as designations that can be applied to God. To invoke (and rework) a well-worn literary quote, it turns out that even if *logically* speaking all terms indicating corporeality are equal, some are more equal than others.

Given that God is unique and utterly transcendent, we ought to expect that our language, as a human invention formed in the crucible of human needs and interests, could not be readily applied to God. Maimonides' method here is highly conservative, often appealing, as above, to terms that are used figuratively throughout the Tanak, and not just in relation to God. Yet, while it was hardly unique to Maimonides— Saadia Gaon before him had already noted that reinterpretation is needed whenever a description of God "stands in contradiction to the requirement of sound reason,"[18]—the comments of Maimonides' critics show that such rejection of corporeal descriptions of God could not be taken for granted. In a well-known critical gloss to Maimonides' claim that those who attribute corporeality to God are heretics, Rabbi Abraham ben David of Posquierres, known by the acronym Rabad, refers to those "greater and better" than Maimonides who had believed in God's corporeality as a result of the language used in Scripture and

---

[18] Saadia Gaon, The Book of Beliefs and Opinions, trans. S. Rosenblatt (New Haven: Yale University Press, 1984), II:3, 100. Maimonides' approach in the exegetical chapters is often substantially anticipated by Saadia, albeit less thoroughly and systematically.

further midrashic passages.[19] Note that Rabad himself did not take such corporeal descriptions any more literally than Maimonides. What he did object to, however, was Maimonides' description of such people as heretics.

It turns out that the critics might have had a point. While few worry overmuch about God literally being able to sit, or see, and can happily accept the necessary exegetical moves cited above, attributing speech to God falls foul of the same stricture of having "none of the characteristics of a body [appertain] to Him." Yet the denial of speech goes to the very heart of both Judaism and Maimonides' theological picture.

Speech is a physical phenomenon, inasmuch as it requires a certain physical structure in the speaker, and the setting in motion of all manner of physical interactions in order that these physically initiated movements be heard as sounds by the human ear. So how an incorporeal being could speak, such as at Sinai, becomes an issue. Even Judah Halevi, in many ways Maimonides' nemesis conceptually speaking, acknowledges the problem, but since these events clearly happened according to Halevi,[20] God must have found a way around the "limitations" of incorporeality. While "we do not know how the spiritual intention became corporealized into speech which struck our ear," clearly, as an omnipotent being, God "does not lack the power to do so" (*Kuzari* I: 89, 62–3), though Halevi is quick to point out that he cannot know "that things occurred exactly in this manner" (ibid., I: 91, 63) and appeals to a notion of "Created Speech"[21] to get around the immediate problem of God not having the physical apparatus necessary for straightforward speech. Nonetheless, it seems as if Halevi wishes to assert that God spoke directly to the entire Israelite nation at Sinai.

---

[19] See Rabad's *hasagah* (gloss) included in all standard Hebrew editions of Maimonides' *Mishneh Torah* (henceforth *MT*) at "Laws of Repentance," 3: 7. R. Joseph Caro, in his *Kesef Mishneh* commentary there, cites approvingly a source containing a more polite version of the gloss.

[20] "The testimony to this grand and lofty spectacle cannot be denied," he writes (Judah Halevi, *Kuzari*, trans. H. Hirschfeld (New York: Schocken Books, 1964), Book 1, paragraph 88, page 62 (further references in text and to this translation are cited by book, paragraph, and page number)). Halevi's general philosophical method, built upon more empirical and historical foundations, are anathema to Maimonides' more rationalist sensibility. See Daniel Rynhold, *An Introduction to Medieval Jewish Philosophy* (London: I. B. Tauris, 2009), ch. 1, for further discussion.

[21] An idea found in predecessors such as Saadia who uses the idea in a number of contexts, in particular in relation to revelation where he notes that "God created speech, which He conveyed through the medium of air to the hearing of the prophet" (Saadia, *Emunot*, II: 12, 128).

Maimonides is unwilling to make such concessions. While it is not much of a stretch to imagine that the biblical God can get around the restrictions that the laws of nature impose given that He, after all, created them in the first place, the methodological parameters we set out previously prevent this from being Maimonides' first port of call. Maimonides privileges the philosophical over the "historical" and, given the "scientific" impossibility of an incorporeal Being speaking, Maimonides has a far simpler response to the question of how God could have spoken to the people at Sinai—which is that He did not.

Specifically with respect to speech, Maimonides states that the Tanak sometimes uses "speech-words" to signify thought rather than speech, or as he puts it to denote "notions represented to the intellect without being uttered—as when it says "Then I said in my heart" (Ecclesiastes 2: 15)"—or even to denote acts of will rather than actual speech acts (though the examples he uses in this regard seem a little less convincing than those he uses for the "standing" example cited earlier). Nonetheless, this enables Maimonides to make the following statement:

> Now in all cases in which the words saying and speaking are applied to God ... they are used to denote either will or volition or a notion that has been grasped by the understanding having come from God.... *The terms in question never signify that He, may He be exalted, spoke using the sounds of letters and a voice.* (Guide 1.65, 158–9, emphasis added)

This raises the question of what, according to Maimonides, *did* happen at Sinai. The traditional conception of the revelation at Sinai is as the fundamental moment of Jewish revelation where the mitsvot that eternally bind the Jewish people (according to rabbinic Judaism) were given. And while Maimonides initially states that "speech was addressed to Moses alone," while the rest of the people "heard the great voice, but not the articulations of speech" (*Guide* 2.33, 363), this clearly contradicts the previously cited statement which tells us that such terms in the Tanak never signify actual speech. Whether or not one wishes to deem this a contradiction of the sort Maimonides has warned us of earlier, once one pieces together the various parts of the jigsaw there is an extremely strong, many would say unassailable, case to be made for denying that God literally spoke to Moses, both in reference to the details of the discussion and more generally, given that speech is a corporeal notion and God is to be distanced from any intimation of corporeality. Suddenly the attitude to reinterpreting all references to God's corporeality taken by many traditional religious believers, unruffled when it came to physical limbs or comportment, becomes somewhat less sanguine.

How, then, can Maimonides maintain that God is the lawgiver who gave the Torah? In order to understand this, one needs to study the context in which the Sinai chapter appears, which is in the lengthy section on prophecy, and following immediately upon his discussion of definitions of prophecy in Book 2, chapter 32. According to Maimonides' view, prophecy is not a supernatural endowment that God bestows on the chosen few. It is, rather, an intellectual achievement attained naturally by those elite individuals who are able to reach the necessary and exalted intellectual level, and one that is founded on prior moral and physical perfection (in particular pertaining to their imaginative faculty). One who is prepared in this way "will necessarily become a prophet, inasmuch as this is a perfection that belongs to us by nature" (*Guide* 2.32, 361). If you study hard enough for your finals, you will pass—not because God literally told you the answers, but because you knew them as a result of the work you had put in. Similarly, if you have passed the intellectual threshold for human perfection, you will, as a result, have the capacity for prophecy through your ability to see clearly the consequences of particular courses of action given your almost perfect knowledge of the laws of nature, both natural and human.

It is important that none of this is intended to eliminate God from the picture for Maimonides—far from it. But what it is clearly intended to do is force us to reconsider what we—and the Torah for that matter—mean when we ascribe acts to God. On this, Maimonides informs us toward the very end of the chapters discussing prophecy:

> It is very clear that everything that is produced in time must necessarily have a proximate cause, which has produced it. In its turn that cause has a cause and so forth till finally one comes to the First Cause of all things, I mean God's will and free choice. For this reason all those intermediate causes are sometimes omitted in the dicta of the prophets, and an individual act produced in time is ascribed to God, it being said that he, may He be exalted, has done it. All this is known. We and other men from among those who study true reality have spoken about it, and this is the opinion of all the people adhering to our Law. (*Guide* 2.48, 409–10)

Maimonides clearly states here that when the Torah speaks of acts of divine will it does not mean to indicate that God suddenly made a decision to do something. Rather, it is shorthand for saying that God is the first cause of everything that occurs. In effect, everything is an act of divine will inasmuch as it flows from the initial state and subsequent causal history of the world in accordance with all of the laws that govern it, all of which issued from God. So God is most certainly responsible for prophecy, just not in the simplistic manner that we might have assumed. Maimonides' naturalistic account of prophecy, detailed discussion of which would take us too far afield,[22] allows him to maintain that Moses did indeed receive an objective form of divine communication from God, without God having to actually do anything other than what God always does for Maimonides, which is to eternally emanate all the truths of which He is the source.

The precise mechanics of Maimonides' account of divine prophetic communication appeal to the then regnant, if unstable, hybrid of Aristotelian and Neoplatonic cosmology, which has prophecy as "an overflow overflowing from God ... through the intermediation of the Active Intellect, toward the rational faculty in the first place and thereafter toward the imaginative faculty" (Guide 2.36, 369).[23] And so, to return to Sinai, as Maimonides puts it when discussing the term "speech," the commandments were notions that Moses "grasped by the understanding having come from God." But God did not literally speak them. They are notions that someone equipped with the superior faculties of Moses is able to pick up from the intellectual "emanations" of the Active Intellect.

It should by now be clear that Maimonides is willing to take the implications of divine incorporeality much further than his predecessors—and, as it turns out, many of his successors too. His incorporeal God does not speak, and not because He chooses not to, but because He is not the type of being that speaks. More broadly, and of greater moment, we find Maimonides very clearly stating that his view of prophecy does not require a personal interventionist type God at all. It is true that he is highly critical—at least in his explicit

[22] For detailed discussion, see Howard Kreisel, *Prophecy: The History of an Idea in Medieval Jewish Philosophy* (Dordrecht: Kluwer Academic Publishers), ch. 3.
[23] Though notably for Moses the imagination has no role to play. Even in the thirteen principles of faith, Maimonides makes it clear that Moses prophesied "without angelic mediation," "Introduction to Perek Heleq," trans. I. Twersky in *A Maimonides Reader*, ed. I. Twersky (New York: Behrman House, 1972), 419, and in the *Guide*, this lack of angelic mediation is equated to his prophesying "without action on the part of the imaginative faculty" (Guide 2.45, 403). The absence of the involvement of the imagination is the reason that Mosaic prophecy comes out as *law* rather than as parables.

pronouncements—of the conception of God entailed by the Aristotelian view of the eternity of the world who "if He wished to lengthen a fly's wing or to shorten a worm's foot, He would not be able to do it" since "it is impossible for Him to will something different from what it is" (*Guide* 2.22, 319). This he contrasts with a creator God who has genuine will and volition such that He can "particularize" things as He sees fit. And yet, despite this, in a remarkable yet apparently often overlooked remark (that appears in the context of his use of eternity in proving the existence of God discussed earlier), Maimonides writes: "And you should not ask how prophecy can be true if the world is eternal, before you have heard our discourse concerning prophecy; however, at present we are not dealing with this notion" (*Guide* 1.71, 181). Regardless therefore of the controversies surrounding Maimonides' true views on creation, he here clearly implies that his views on prophecy are indeed compatible with the eternity of the world and thus, by implication, with the impersonal God of Aristotle.

The fourth principle regarding God's precedence itself obliquely references the creation question, though the idea of precedence can of course be understood causally, in a way that is compatible with Aristotelian eternity, or temporally, so as to indicate that God is the creator, though the word "temporally" here needs to be understood in a qualified fashion, since following Aristotle Maimonides maintains that time did not exist prior to the creation of the world (similarly, the word "prior" now ceases to make sense in this sentence—one begins to see the issues here). It should be mentioned, therefore, that in what is, according to many scholars, an autograph copy of the *Commentary on the Mishnah*, Maimonides amends the original principle in a marginal note to explicitly state that God is the creator—though, as Kellner notes, one can legitimately ask whether or not this statement is itself there as a sop to the masses.[24] Either way, the implications that Maimonides has drawn from his first three principles to this point have certainly led him to a theology that is thus far compatible with the eternity of the world, and has begun to denude God of his biblical personality to a point where one could easily mistake Him for the more rarefied and abstract God of Aristotle.

---

[24] See the discussion in Kellner, *Dogma*, 54–61.

DIVINE ATTRIBUTES AND NEGATIVE THEOLOGY

The discussion to this point has noted a number of significant elements of Maimonides' theology, both material and formal. But what really drives Maimonides to go to such lengths in rejecting corporeality are neither the "scientific" difficulties involved in explaining how speech can emerge from an incorporeal Being, or even semantic issues of meaning. Instead, Maimonides is compelled to take these views for far more deeply rooted metaphysical reasons that emerge when he turns to the more philosophical discussion of divine attributes that immediately follow the exegetical chapters of the *Guide*, consideration of which will round out the picture of Maimonides' conception of God

As we noted earlier, the notion of divine incorporeality is bound up with that of divine unity, which equates to the idea of simplicity, such that for Maimonides, God cannot be a composite being. But for Maimonides, the problems of composition are not simply physical. While physical composition is ruled out since it was thought to render God susceptible to "generation and corruption" such that He could therefore cease to exist like anything else, which clearly cannot be the case, in Maimonides' eyes any form of conceptual composition is just as threatening.

Taking the example cited earlier of "standing," we noted how Maimonides always interprets the term to remove the implication that God could literally stand, which would clearly require his having a body. Yet the verse Maimonides used as his example, where the term is taken to refer to permanence, speaks of the permanence of God's righteousness. So the question that remains is what we are to make of God's righteousness. And while the initial question might be prompted by purely semantic concerns—can the term "righteous" really mean the same in reference to God and humans? —Maimonides soon steers the discussion in another direction altogether.

Initially, Maimonides makes the classic scholastic distinction between essential and accidental attributes. Beginning with the former—those attributes which define the thing in question, and without which it would not be that thing—if we were, for example, to define man as "a rational animal" in good Aristotelian fashion, we would have given an explanation of what a man is. But for Maimonides, any analogous definition of God, while clearly not imputing physical parts to him, nonetheless introduces a level of multiplicity into God that is unacceptable:

For there is no oneness at all except in believing that there is one simple essence in which there is no complexity or multiplication of notions, but one notion only; so that from whatever angle you regard it and from whatever point of view you consider it, you will find that it is one, not divided in any way and by any cause into two notions; and you will not find therein any multiplicity either in the thing as it is outside of the mind or as it is in the mind ... (Guide 1.51, 113)

God for Maimonides cannot therefore, be defined even essentially, since to do so introduces a level of multiplicity that impugns his unity, and thus his incorporeality. Additionally, accidental attributes, such as the moral attribute of righteousness with which we began, or emotional affects such as anger, clearly add something to God's essence that, since they need not be there—that being the very definition of "accidental"—renders them separable qualities such that God's simplicity has been compromised.

Maimonides takes this even further, denying the legitimacy of applying predicates of relation to God, despite their not introducing multiplicity into God's essence. One could, for example, become an uncle without knowing it, which would change the relational predicates that can now truly be applied to that person without introducing any change in the person whatsoever. Nonetheless, such relations cannot be imputed to God. The issue here is that of divine transcendence, for:

How ... can a relation be represented between Him and what is other than he when there is no notion comprising any respect of the two, inasmuch as existence is, in our opinion, affirmed of Him, may he be exalted, and of what is other than He merely by way of absolute equivocation. There is, in truth, no relation in any respect between Him and any of his creatures. (Guide 1.52, 117–118)

This denial of relation is of the utmost importance. To take our earlier example, it turns out that it is not that God could speak, but chooses to remain silent. Rather, God is an impassive being who is neither affected by human behavior, nor an intentional actor in world history. He simply is not the type of being that relates to humans or indeed the world in this manner. God's utter uniqueness, therefore, or His absolute transcendence, gives us a picture of an impassive God, which leads, in turn, to an inability to apply predicates to God that we apply to any other existent. That is why we cannot insert God into the physical process of speech, or assume any semantic relation between words as applied to God and those same words in a non-divine context.

This obviously requires a level of reinterpretation of biblical terminology which would appear to rule out Maimonides' earlier appeal to the permanence of God's righteousness. While that level of reinterpretation managed to rid us of the problem term "standing," we now see that "righteousness" is no less problematic.

Maimonides does make one helpful concession in *Guide* 52, for he is willing to allow attributes of action to be predicated of God since they are "remote from the essence of the thing of which it is predicated" (*Guide* 1.52, 119). So we can speak of God's acts without passing comment on God Himself, as long as we are careful to draw a line between speaking of the acts, which is legitimate, and speaking of the qualities of the actor who performs them, which would return us to the illegitimate attribution of qualities to God. This is how Maimonides deals with such terms as "righteousness," for such moral qualities can now be understood as "attributes of action"; that is, as a shorthand for speaking of the sorts of acts that ordinarily issue from the quality of righteousness. To speak of divine righteousness is actually to speak of acts that are usually evidence of that characteristic, without going on to attribute the characteristic to God. But once again, these divine acts are not "acts" in the personal sense for Maimonides, in the manner of being intentionally chosen at a particular time as a course of action suited to the situation in which one finds oneself, or as Maimonides puts it "not because of a passion or change" (*Guide* 1.54, 125). Rather, as becomes clear from the examples Maimonides uses, these divine acts are to be equated with the laws of nature—when God promises to show Moses His "ways" by making His "goodness" pass before him, Maimonides writes that this refers to "the display ... of all existing things," and this display is of "their nature and the way they are mutually connected" (*Guide* 1.54, 124).

Clearly Maimonides is unwilling even to attribute righteousness to God in anything approaching the usual sense. That God's righteousness "stands forever," believed after the exegetical chapters to refer to the permanence of his righteousness, is now seen in fact to be some form of description of the permanence of laws of natural causality. At this point, we have a God who did not "speak" His revelation to the Israelites, and whose moral attributes become attributes of action, which in turn actually describe the laws of nature.

Yet Maimonides' work is not yet done, for even the attributes of existence, unity, and incorporeality that we have summarily used to this point cannot be understood "as is." For Maimonides, any word that we apply to God is to be understood as absolutely equivocal relative to our ordinary usage such that they have "nothing in common in any respect or in any mode; these attributions have in common only the name and nothing else" (*Guide* 1.56, 131). This famously leads Maimonides to the conclusion that "the description of God, may He be cherished and exalted, by means of negation is the correct description" (*Guide* 1.58, 134). So when we say that God is One, that is to be understood as "the denial of multiplicity" (*Guide* 1.59, 136).

It is important, however, to specify the precise nature of the negation to which Maimonides refers, for clearly an ordinary negation would simply lead us back to the positive attribute that we had intended to avoid—denying multiplicity ordinarily would lead us back to oneness. But Maimonides wishes to use these negations to indicate for their subject something "that cannot fittingly exist in it. Thus we say of a wall that it is not endowed with sight" (*Guide* 1.58, 136). The idea here is that we would not say that a wall was blind, for that would imply that ordinarily walls can see and unfortunately this one has been denied that pleasure. Instead, we would speak of a wall as not-seeing to indicate that it is not in the class of things that have the capacity of sight at all. When we speak of God, therefore, we are to take any attribution of an essential attribute as a negation in this sense. To say that God is not-dead is not to positively describe Him as having "life" but to eliminate him from the category of things that can be living or dead.

When taken to its logical conclusion this means that human language is simply inadequate for representing God since his utter transcendence means that he cannot be sensibly described in such terms at all: "Such matters as this cannot be considered through the instrumentality of the customary words, which are the greatest among the causes leading unto error ... so that we cannot represent this notion to ourselves except through a certain looseness of expression" (*Guide* 1.57, 132–3).

This is why negation is the best way to speak of God since "negation does not give knowledge in any respect of the true reality of the thing with regard to which the particular matter in question has been negated" (*Guide* 1.59, 139). Negation is therefore the best way for us to express in language the infinite distance between God and his creation. Ultimately, Maimonides quotes approvingly *Psalms* 65: 2— "Silence is praise to Thee," and advises that in place of linguistic representation "silence and limiting oneself to the apprehension of the intellects are more appropriate" (*Guide* 1.59, 139–40).

Concessions to human intellectual frailty, together with the understanding that most people are not philosophers, mean that the Torah and indeed our liturgy cannot counsel silence, though only the language sanctioned by those texts can be used for Maimonides—woe betide the poetic soul who attempts to wax lyrical about God in any other terms: "the utterances of some of them constitute an absolute denial of faith, while other utterances contain such rubbish and such perverse imaginings as to make men laugh when they hear them" (*Guide* 1.59,141). More importantly, if we wish to use these texts as the basis for an understanding of the nature of God, we will have to follow Maimonides' interpretive handbook if we are to avoid imputing multiplicity, and hence corporeality to God, however unwittingly. And following that handbook will leave us with an abstraction about which we can only ultimately say that it is absolutely nothing like anything that we actually know.

UNITY AND INCORPOREALITY REVISITED

Focusing on the nature of God, Maimonides has left us at this point with an extremely, if not radically, bare theology. His is a God who we cannot literally describe as being happy or merciful any more than we can as having a hand. For Maimonides, all linguistic representation of God problematizes divine unity and thus implies corporeality as much as literal physical designations. The concept of idolatry forbidden by the Torah suddenly has a far larger catchment area than it had previously. We are no longer simply concerned with physical images or sculpted idols, nor even with the worship of angels mentioned in the fifth of Maimonides' principles or superstitious attempts to ward off imaginary demons, for which Maimonides also clearly has nothing but contempt.[25] As Moshe Halbertal notes: "It is entirely possible for a person praying in a synagogue where no statue or other image is present nevertheless to commit idolatry by having a mental image of

---

[25] For a comprehensive examination of Maimonides' attitude to such "mystical" obfuscations, see Menachem Kellner, *Maimonides' Confrontation with Mysticism* (Oxford: The Littman Library of Jewish Civilization, 2006).

the divinity that is corrupted by anthropomorphism."[26] Maimonides has effected a shift whereby "the focus of the concept of idolatry was ... transferred from the performance of alien rituals to the harboring of alien beliefs ... from the sexual sin of idolatry to the sin of the great error."[27]

Still, the idea that any attribute, including every passion and emotion, implies plurality appears to be a strange claim. While we clearly understand how our material nature implies physical composition, many people would hesitate to say the same is implied by the use of any and all linguistic predicates. This hesitation was formulated in conceptual form by one of Maimonides' greatest philosophical "descendants" Levi Gersonides, who questioned the idea that contingent facts about the syntactical structure of our language have any such metaphysical connotations. As Gersonides writes:

> not every proposition about the essence of something implies a plurality in that thing. It does imply a plurality in the thing if one part of [the proposition] serves as a real subject [i.e., genus] for the other part [of the proposition]. But if [the former part] is not a real subject, although it is a linguistic subject, the proposition does not imply a plurality. For example, when we say "this redness is a red color," it does not follow from this assertion that the redness is composed of color and red, for the color is not a thing existing [by itself and serving as] a [real] subject for red. It is only a linguistic subject.... Accordingly, it is evident that when God (may He be blessed) is described by any attribute or by many attributes, these attributes do not imply in Him any plurality, for He has no subject [i.e., genus]. Hence, all of these attributes denote only one simple thing.[28]

Gersonides is questioning why the vagaries of our syntax should be thought to have implications for our ontology. The linguistic structures with which we are saddled mean that we often express ourselves by

---

[26] Moshe Halbertal, *Maimonides: Life and Thought* (Princeton: Princeton University Press, 2014), 290.
[27] Moshe Halbertal and Avishai Margalit, *Idolatry* trans. Naomi Goldblum (Cambridge, MA: Harvard University Press, 1992), 109. This quote appears in ch. 4 of the book, which contains a detailed account of how Maimonides understands the notion of idolatry, and how his understanding differs from earlier views.
[28] Levi Gersonides, The *Wars of the Lord*, trans. Seymour Feldman (Philadelphia: Jewish Publication Society, 1987), Book III, ch. 3, 112–14.

combining a linguistic subject with a linguistic predicate. But why would we think that the same structure is necessarily found in the mind-independent reality to which our language attempts to refer? That certain words can be used to explicate the nature of something to our own human version of conceptual satisfaction says nothing about how those things are essentially structured. For Gersonides, there is no more reason to think of God as having a separable attribute of knowledge just because our language separates "God" and "knowledge" than there is to think that the color red is composed of two ontologically separable elements—"color" and "redness."

For Maimonides, giving an account of God's nature renders God somehow "explainable" when God is supposed instead to be the ultimate explanation. This idea, which can be expressed more generally in terms of divine self-sufficiency, is precisely what allows God to be the conclusion of the different versions of the cosmological argument through his "ability" to halt the various infinite regresses that were thought to threaten the intelligibility of the universe. God cannot be defined in any way, for doing so would prevent him acting as the self-sufficient being who explains everything precisely by not Himself being subject to explanation or analysis. So the claim is that predicating any attribute of God introduces an unacceptable level of complexity into Him, making him a hostage to those elements of which He is composed. Gersonides, on the other hand, argues that this need not be the case ontologically speaking just because it is the case linguistically speaking. For Maimonides, linguistic multiplicity implies ontological multiplicity. Gersonides, who is no less insistent of divine incorporeality than Maimonides, questions this slide from one to the other.

Maimonides, in his concern to radically distinguish God from every other existent, would presumably claim that the idea that one can describe God at all would at the very least place God within a class—the class of things that can be defined. As such, God is being categorized with other existents, and thus as one of a "kind"—a "genus"—even if he is the only representative of his particular genus with no subordinate species, and this impugns his absolute transcendence. When matters are put that way, it is difficult to dispute Maimonides' conclusion. Gersonides' critique, on the other hand, raises genuine questions as to whether such bare formal commonalities genuinely threaten the necessary distance that God must maintain from his creatures in order to be deemed uniquely transcendent and worthy of worship.

THEOLOGY AND RELIGIOUS WORSHIP

The fifth principle concerns God as the only appropriate object of worship. At this point of the discussion, having stripped God of all of his personal attributes, one might wonder what is left of God *to* worship. One might even ask—who exactly is the God of Maimonides? In truth, it is rather difficult to say. As Maimonides himself advises:

> The most apt phrase concerning this subject is the dictum occurring in the Psalms [65:2] "Silence is praise to Thee." ... This is a most perfectly put phrase regarding this matter. For of whatever we say intending to magnify and exalt, on the one hand we find that it can have some application to Him, may He be exalted, and on the other we perceive in it some deficiency. Accordingly, silence and limiting oneself to the apprehension of the intellects are more appropriate. (*Guide* 1.59, 139–40)

The austere theology with which Maimonides presents us allows certain descriptions of God to pass for pragmatic reasons, but advises the sophisticated philosopher-theologian to avoid linguistic representation altogether. Again, it is important to stress that Maimonides is not claiming that God is a rather quieter or more self-contained version of the biblical God. It is not that God could intervene but chooses not to do so. Maimonides presents us with an impassive God who is just not that type of quasi-person at all. Indeed, the very notion of God as a "type" is anathema to Maimonides.

Maimonides is concerned that anything we say about God can only damn him with faint praise. As we have seen, we can understand this colloquially if we recognize that to say that He is, for example, all-powerful is simply to make a comparative assessment in relation to ourselves—which hardly renders him particularly God-like. It just makes him a better version of us. At a more abstract level, the problems arise when we attempt any sort of comparison between God and ourselves, which any language that we use to engage Him is inevitably going to do. As soon as we say that "exists" is one of God's predicates, we are saying that He is a thing that exists, as do all other existent things, and thus He shares this attribute with us and falls within a class that includes us among its members. And so his uniqueness and transcendence are constricted. Any attempt to understand God has to place Him within the straitjacket of human conceptualizations, which is clearly to limit God to terms that *we* can use and understand. And that, to Maimonides, is the beginning of the temptation to anthropomorphism, which, with its erroneous beliefs about God, means that what we are worshiping is a false God. Anthropomorphism is, for Maimonides, but a step away from the ultimate sin of idolatry, at least as he understands it.

This strand in Maimonidean thought actually takes us beyond the God of Aristotle, the First Cause or Prime Mover, and leads us to a God who owes more to Neoplatonic influences—one who is "beyond being" and therefore cannot be characterized or conceptualized at all.[29] These competing Aristotelian and Neoplatonic strands in Maimonides' thought often make for a rather unstable hybrid. But either way, we are quite some distance from the God who is understood to relate to the world on the personalist model that so entirely dominates the Tanak or the Talmud, or indeed the thought of Maimonides' near contemporaries such as Judah Halevi for whom God's calling card is that he is "the God who brought you out of the Land of Egypt," a mode of introduction that expresses the most fundamental way in which God relates to his people—personally and historically. Adhering to strict Aristotelian or Neoplatonic schemas in this instance is clearly too great a price to pay for Halevi, both philosophically and religiously. But for Maimonides, such views are at worst the first step on the slippery slope to idolatry, at best a concession to human frailty, or beliefs that are necessary for some, but are not to be taken as reflecting truth. They are among those truths that are "necessary for the sake of political welfare. Such, for instance, is our belief that He, may He be exalted, is violently angry with those who disobey Him and that it is therefore necessary to fear Him and dread Him and to take care not to disobey" (*Guide* 3.28, 512).

But in the absence of anything even approaching such a belief, one is returned to the question of how Maimonides' theology as expressed through our explication of principles 1–4 yields the God whom one ought to worship of principle 5.

---

[29] While the reading given here has generally followed the skeptical reading according to which Maimonides denies the possibility of positive metaphysical knowledge (see Shlomo Pines, "The Limitations of Human Knowledge, According to al-Farabi, ibn Bajja, and Maimonides," in *Studies in Medieval Jewish History and Literature*, ed. I Twersky (Cambridge, MA: Harvard University Press, 1979), 82–109), it should be noted that there is an alternate mystical reading according to which, while our knowledge of God might outstrip our linguistic abilities, that does not rule out the possibility of some other form of mystical cognition; see David Blumenthal, "Maimonides' Philosophic Mysticism," *Da'at: A Journal of Jewish Philosophy and Kabbalah*, 64 66 (2009): V XXV.

Here, Maimonides' general religious sensibility is of crucial importance. There are those who believe in a personal God who intervenes and controls the world in some engaged manner. The belief in that type of God is their reason for engaging in their religious practices, and, in the absence of that theological foundation, they would view their religion as baseless, and it is not difficult to see why. If God is not viewed personalistically, we have all manner of problems with notions such as miracles, providence, and petitionary prayer, not to mention God's direct communication of the mitsvot to Moses, as we have had cause to discuss. Yet there are those for whom that notion of God is deeply problematic. It might even *undermine* religious practice. How, for example, can such a God avoid being impeached by the problem of evil? Why, it might be asked, would an *interventionist* God choose not to intervene to prevent some of the greatest acts of destruction, both natural and moral, in human history? Maimonides' issue with such worship is more that it is self-interested "worship out of fear" (*MT*, "Laws of Repentance," 9: 1), or worship that is *shelo lishmah*, or "not for its own sake" (ibid., 9: 5). As the neo-Maimonidean Yeshayahu Leibowitz puts it: "Its end is man, and God offers his services to man."[30] Such views of worship in turn are often found in combination with an overemphasis on the value of the pleasures of one's this-worldly individual existence, which are to be continued in some heightened manner even after death. This outlook is contrasted by Maimonides with "worship out of love" (ibid., 9: 2) or worship *lishmah* (ibid., 9: 5), in which one is not holding out for some form of self-serving reward, but "does what is true (sic.) because it is true" (ibid.), serving God "because He is worthy of worship,"[31] through dedication to the ultimate "spiritual," or better, intellectual value of eternal truths, a pleasure to which physical pleasures cannot compare "for how could that which is eternal and endless be compared with anything transient and terminable?"[32] For Maimonides, God is the source

---

[30] Yeshayahu Leibowitz, "Religious Praxis," *Judaism, Human Values, and the Jewish State*, ed. Eliezer Goldman, trans. Eliezer Goldman, Yoram Navon, Zvi Jacobson, Gershon Levi, and Raphael Levy (Cambridge, MA: Harvard University Press, 1995), 14.

[31] Ibid.

[32] Maimonides, *Introduction to Perek Heleq*, 412. Maimonides here actually speaks of knowledge of God as the highest pleasure enjoyed in the afterlife. Since I have spent much of this piece questioning the possibility of knowledge of God according to Maimonides, this clearly raises difficult questions for Maimonides scholars. In part, the debate in the literature cited in note 29 above deals with this issue. A further

of eternal truth, and such truth is the ultimate value, not the satisfaction of our self-interested desires, tethered as they are to the fleeting temporal occupation of our material bodies. Whether God has the capacity to intervene in the world to further those interests should be of no concern to an individual who recognizes the true intellectual perfection for which humans ought to strive.

While the proponents of each view have ready responses to the challenges posed by their opponents, we see that even under the slightest critical pressure, the question of which God is more "conducive" to religious belief becomes deeply complex. People have different religious sensibilities, for want of a better term, and those sensibilities render very different views of God convincing.[33] For many the abstract God of Aristotelian philosophy cannot possibly be the God who spoke to Abraham, Isaac, and Jacob, or gave the Torah to Moses. Maimonides would agree. *That* God cannot be the God of philosophy, for the God of philosophy could never have *spoken* to the forefathers, nor physically *given* or *dictated* the Torah to Moses. But then for Maimonides, neither did the God of the Torah.

Selected Further Reading

Buijs, J. ed., *Maimonides: A Collection of Critical Essays*. Notre Dame, IN: University of Notre Dame Press, 1988.

Burrell, D. *Knowing the Unknowable God: Ibn-Sina, Maimonides, Aquinas*. Notre Dame, IN: University of Notre Dame Press, 1986.

Davidson, H. *Proofs for Eternity, Creation and the Existence of God in Medieval Islamic and Jewish Philosophy*. Oxford: Oxford University Press, 1987.

Halbertal, M. *Maimonides: Life and Thought*. Princeton: Princeton University Press, 2014.

Gutas, D. *Greek Thought, Arabic Culture: The Graeco-Arabic Translation Movement in Baghdad and Early Society (2nd–4th/8th–10th centuries)*. New York: Routledge, 1998.

Jospe, R. *Jewish Philosophy in the Middle Ages*. Brighton, MA: Academic Studies Press, 2009.

Kellner, M. *Maimonides' Confrontation with Mysticism*. Oxford: The Littman Library of Jewish Civilization, 2006.

---

approach can be found in Josef Stern, *The Matter and Form of Maimonides' Guide* (Cambridge, MA: Harvard University Press, 2013).

[33] For discussion of these issues, see David Shatz, "Divine Intervention and Religious Sensibilities," reprinted in his *Jewish Thought in Dialogue: Essays on Thinkers, Theologies, and Moral Theories* (Boston, MA: Academic Studies Press, 2009), 179–208.

Maimonides, M. *The Guide of the Perplexed*. Translated by Shlomo Pines, 2 vols. Chicago: University of Chicago Press, 1963.

Pines, S. "The Limitations of Human Knowledge, According to al-Farabi, ibn Bajja, and Maimonides." In *Studies in Medieval Jewish History and Literature*, 82–109. Edited by I. Twersky. Cambridge, MA: Harvard University Press, 1979.

Pines, S. and Y. Yovel, eds., *Maimonides and Philosophy*. Dordrecht: Martinus Nijhoff, 1985.

Rynhold, D. *An Introduction to Medieval Jewish Philosophy*. London: I. B. Tauris, 2009.

Seeskin, K. *Searching for a Distant God: The Legacy of Maimonides*. New York: Oxford University Press, 2000.

Shatz, D. "Divine Intervention and Religious Sensibilities," 179–208. Reprinted in his *Jewish Thought in Dialogue: Essays on Thinkers, Theologies, and Moral Theories*. Boston, MA: Academic Studies Press, 2009.

Stern, J. *The Matter and Form of Maimonides' Guide*. Cambridge, MA: Harvard University Press, 2013.

Twersky, I., ed. *A Maimonides Reader*. New York: Behrman House, 1972.

7 Law and Order: The Birth of a Nation and the Creation of the World
DANIEL FRANK

"... it is by law that justice herself lives."
Robert Penn Warren, *All the King's Men*

This chapter presents an episode in the medieval theology of law. For theologian-philosophers such as Saadia and Maimonides, discussions of law are embedded in broader theological discussions of the divine nature, creation, revelation, prophecy, and the human good. A quick inspection of the contents of Saadia's *Book of Beliefs and Opinions* (*Emunot ve-De'ot*, 933) makes clear its kalamic province, entailing canonical discussions of *inter alia* the nature of God, creation, law, and justice. Saadia's discussions are part of a general curriculum to lead the reader from (mere) belief in the various subjects to knowledge, and his discussion of the commandments in treatise III nests it in the context of revelation, prophecy, and tradition. Though deeply critical of Saadia at points, Maimonides' *Guide of the Perplexed* (*Moreh Nevukhim*, 1190) likewise has a pedagogical function. In leading a student from perplexity to understanding, the *Guide* moves over the course of its three parts through discussions of the nature of God, creation, prophecy, law, and human excellence, and his own explicit discussion of the laws in the third part of the *Guide* depends on previous discussion of providence and prophecy. In the spirit of such broad systematizing, this chapter will weave together some strands of those overlapping discussions, particularly Maimonidean discussions of divine nature, creation, prophecy, and law and justice.

But our story really begins "in the beginning."

The Pentateuch commences with the creation of the world and very quickly moves from a cosmic perspective to a human one. Thence it proceeds from an idyllic paradise to a fall and human corruption. Shortly thereafter, the focus is on an émigré and the travails of his family and descendants. And finally we learn of a period of servitude, followed by

The Birth of a Nation and the Creation of the World 133

freedom and the birth of a nation. So, the arc of the narrative is from the creation of the world to the genesis of a nation, a holy people. The arc is a twofold pivot from disorder to order.

This chapter will attempt to tie together very closely the arc and the bookends of the narrative, the cosmic perspective and the national one. I shall do so by means of an analogy presented by the Rabbis. I take as my starting point a remark found in the Babylonian Talmud (BT Shabbat 10a):

> כל דיין שדן דין אמת לאמיתו אפילו שעה אחת – מעלה עליו הכתוב כאילו נעשה שותף להקדוש ברוך הוא במעשה בראשית.

> Every judge who judges with complete fairness even for a single hour, the Writ gives him credit as though he had become a partner to the Holy One, blessed be He, in the creation.

In acting and judging with fairness—in applying the law in an impartial and equitable way—a judge models himself on divine creation. What does this mean? What can this mean? What has judging fairly to do with the creation of the world? In this chapter, I shall interpret this rabbinic dictum along Maimonidean lines, drawing in part on some of Maimonides' own views on creation and Mosaic prophecy. In the second part of the *Guide* Maimonides draws close connections between the two topics, and I will help myself to that in presenting my own discussion of the aforementioned rabbinic dictum. The chapter will proceed in three sections, over the course of which I shall be concerned with teasing out the juridical analogy in a variety of ways: morphologically/structurally, psychologically, and finally teleologically.

Before we get down to work, we should consider briefly the immediate context in which we find the rabbinic dictum in BT Shabbat 10a. *In situ*:

> R. Ammi and R. Assi were sitting and studying between the pillars, and every now and then they knocked at the side of the door and announced: "If anyone has a lawsuit, let him enter and come." R. Hisda and Rabbah son of R. Huna were sitting all day [engaged] in judgments, and their hearts grew faint, [whereat] R. Hiyya b. Rab of Difti recited to them: "and the people stood about Moses from the morning into the evening" [Exodus 18:13]. Now, can you really think that Moses sat and judged all day? When was his learning done? But it is to teach you that *every judge who judges with complete fairness even for a single hour, the Writ gives him credit*

as though he had become a partner to the Holy One, blessed be He, in the creation. [For] here it is written: "and the people stood about Moses from the morning into the evening", whilst elsewhere it is written: "and there was morning, and there was evening, one day" [Genesis 1:5]. [trans. H. Freedman; emphasis added]

The immediate context signals the overarching importance of judging, even over learning and study. A fair judge is credited with "creative" powers not less than those exercised in the divine creation of the world. Indeed, Moses himself is a judge, "and the people stood about Moses from the morning into the evening." The community depended upon Moses for his judgments, and, like the divine, his judgments were "creative," as God created the "day." They sustained the community. But Moses was more than a religious decisor. As prophet and the founder of the nation, Moses' unique prophecy is the promulgation of (the) law, and it is to an understanding of Mosaic prophecy as analogous to divine creation of the world that we now turn.

THE APPLICATION OF LAW

Justice and the application of law is the ordering principle of social and political life. In a very real way it "creates" (and constitutes and sustains) social and political life. Without it, there is no political order, no social or political community, as we learn early on from Glaucon in *Republic* 2 (358e–359b). Formally, judging fairly and impartially is the human analogue to divine creation, as the rabbinic dictum indicates. In acting justly and judging fairly, one is like a divine being who creates the world—both actions bring order out of chaos, and sustain such order. In acting justly and judging fairly one is, according to the Rabbis, participating optimally in the divine plan for the world.

The Sinaitic revelation is a revelation of (the) law, and Moses, a philosophical prophet according to Maimonides, is the lawgiver. In giving the law (and of course having it finally accepted), he is *de facto* the "creator" of the community, the Israelite nation. He brings a community into being and provides for its continuing sustenance on the basis of the divine legislation. I want to press an analogy between law-giving and divine creation to the limit. What Moses does in the political arena is analogous to what God does in creating the world. What Moses does at the micro level, and in historical time, is like what God does at the macro level "in the beginning." The divine plan for the world has two applications, in the natural and in the political spheres, and Mosaic legislation—the creation of a political community from/out of what we may think of as a formless mass—must be seen as quite analogous to what God does in creating the world from formless matter. Both bring order out of disorder, and order their respective creations for all time, eternally. Both nature and the state are governed by divine, eternal laws. Even though Mosaic law is binding for a *particular* community, *as law* it is inviolate, eternal, and exceptionless, and as part of the overall divine plan for *creation* it is a *natural* law, in accordance with human nature. Mosaic law, the law of Moses, is divine law applied in a particular historical context, as we shall see.

Mosaic prophecy is unique. As Maimonides understands it, Moses imitates divine actions in his political legislation (*Guide* 1.54). As God governs the natural world, so Moses legislates, and provides guidance, in the political realm. Mosaic prophecy is special insofar as it, unlike other prophecy, is grounded in an intellectual cognition unmediated by imagination (*Guide* 2.35). In demanding to know God's nature, his essence, Moses is shown directly and without mediation divine "ways," divine governance of the natural world. And in imitation of this, Moses "translates" this cosmic insight to the human realm via a particular legislation that, like creation, is of divine origin. In effect, Moses collaborates with God in bringing order out of chaos.

Moses' collaboration with God is problematic, and there has been considerable discussion in the literature as to the "authorship" of the divine law, the legislation that creates and binds the Israelite community forevermore. How shall one understand Moses' role in all this?[1] In what way, if any, is Moses the "author" of the law? How can a human, even Moses, be the author of a *divine* law? Or is he merely a scribe, a kind-of stenographer taking dictation and passing it on brainlessly? Moses' legislative prophecy, his giving of the law, is in imitation of (and analogous to) divine creation and cosmic governance of the natural

---

[1] L. Kaplan, "Maimonides on Mosaic Revelation," https://kavvanah.wordpress.com/2013/07/25/maimonides-on-mosaic-revelation-prof-lawrence-j-kaplan/ (July 2013); H. Kreisel, *Maimonides' Political Thought: Studies in Ethics, Law, and the Human Ideal* (Albany: SUNY Press, 1999), 15; S. Fleischacker, "Making Sense of the Revelation at Sinai: Revisiting Maimonides' Eighth Principle of Faith," https://thetorah.com/making-sense-of-the-revelation-at-sinai/ (March 2014); A. Ivry, *Maimonides' Guide of the Perplexed: A Philosophical Commentary* (Chicago: University of Chicago Press, 2016), 232; and most recently, C. Manekin, "Maimonides on the Divine Authorship of the Law," in C. Manekin and D. Davies (eds.), *Interpreting Maimonides* (Cambridge: Cambridge University Press, 2019), 133–51.

world. As God rules and orders the cosmos, so Moses gives the law and through it provides political governance. But the promulgation of the law is of course compatible with (non-Mosaic) divine *authorship* of it, and again the question remains concerning Moses' role. Perhaps we can say this: God is the author of the law, and the law is divine in origin in the sense that it is part of creation and the divine plan for the natural world and humankind, but it is human (Mosaic) law on account of its relevance for (and applicability to) a particular historical situation. This latter is Moses' genius—his capacity to translate, articulate, and apply that part of the cosmic divine plan in appropriate ways for a specific human political situation.[2] In *Guide* 2.33 Maimonides is clear that Moses is key to conveying the divine will to the assembled masses. He mediates between God and the assembled masses at the foot of the mountain.[3] Only Moses comprehends the divine message at Sinai, and upon this comprehension is able to translate the divine will into language that the assembled masses understand.[4] So conceived, Mosaic legislation—his prophecy—is the articulation and application of the divine plan for the world to a particular human situation. Moses is not the author of the law, it is of divine origin, but he is no mere stenographer. His legislation follows on his prudential understanding of how divine law, the law governing the created order, can be established for humankind, at least that portion of it recently liberated from Egypt.

---

[2] In an important passage that clarifies the connection between the ruler (Moses) and the divine law he applies, Maimonides writes: "Seeing that the nature of man brings with it such enormous differences between individuals and at the same time requires life in society, it would be impossible for any society to come about except through a leader who co-ordinates their actions, supplements what is imperfect and restrains exaggerations, and lays down standards for their activities and behavior so that they can always act according to the same standard. Thus the natural differences will be masked by the large degree of conventional co-ordination and the community will be well-ordered. *For this reason I say that the Law, though it is not part of nature, yet is closely interwoven with nature.* It is part of the wisdom of God in maintaining this human species—since He willed its existence—that He made it part of their nature that some individuals possess the faculty of leadership" (*Guide* 2.40 [trans. Rabin], emphasis added). Pines renders the italicized section, "[t]herefore I say that the Law, although it is not natural, enters into what is natural." The law is of divine origin, but it would come to naught, were it not for Moses and his political leadership, his ability to apply that part of the divine plan in appropriate ways for a specific human situation. In this sense the divine law "enters into what is natural."

[3] Deuteronomy 5:5: "I stood between the Lord and you at that time to declare unto you the word of the Lord."

[4] Ivry, *Maimonides' Guide of the Perplexed*, 124.

Moses' legislation is creative, taking into account the particular historical context and a particular audience, and prescribing a law adequate to the situation.

Even more, from the rabbinic side, Moses is not just the lawgiver, the founder of the Israelite nation, but he is also understood as the *interpreter*, the judge and adjudicator of the law, the first in the line of rabbis who "discussed" (interpreted) the Oral Law. The very beginning of *Pirkei Avot* pronounces the descent of the Torah from Sinai to Moses to Joshua, etc. In Moses, the legislative and judicial branches meet. While Moses is the author of neither the Written nor the Oral law, his prudential and imaginative capacities, coupled with keen exegetical skills, are key to the successful implementation of the divine law. In this context, we should recall the initial rabbinic dictum in BT Shabbat 10a that frames our discussion. There we read that as Moses judged, "... the people stood about Moses from the morning into the evening." Rabbi Moses (Moshe Rabbeinu) adjudicated and explicated the law for the community; they hung on his every word and judgment. In this way, Moses, like the author of the divine law, sustains the community.

In sustaining the community, we should say a little more about that particular community and the specific historical context in which the law was promulgated. Moses is legislating specifically to a rabble of idolatrous ex-slaves. In fact, the liberated Israelites are in a very real way still slaves, slaves to their past. This is why, at least according to Maimonides, they wander in the desert, never to reach the Promised Land (*Guide* 3.32).[5] The Promised Land, the future, is not for them, but for their non-idolatrous successors. But it will not be available for those descendants, until, and unless, the present generation accepts the yoke of the law, and thereby constitutes itself into a nation, a "holy people," by virtue of acceptance of commandments of divine origin, whose primary intention is the ultimate extirpation of idolatrous worship (*Guide* 3.29). Mosaic legislation takes on the particular deontic form it has because of the servile audience to whom it is delivered. In sum, Mosaic legislation is a particular law, legislated in a particular way, for a particular people, and constitutive of its being.

---

[5] And this is why some of the laws, such as the laws pertaining to sacrifice (*korbanot*), are indexed with specific reference to their past (*Guide* 3.32). Maimonides makes the general point: "It is impossible to pass all at once from one extreme to another; it is not in keeping with human nature for man to abandon suddenly all he has been used to."

Forever binding, in its eternality and exceptionless-ness, it mimics the laws of nature.

One final point, a point of scholarly controversy, may be raised in this section. Divine creation of the world is generally understood as creation *ex nihilo*, creation from absolute non-existence, without a material substrate. God is understood as bringing everything into existence, including matter. This is also the normal construal of Maimonides' own view on the issue (*Guide* 2.13, 2.25). He describes such creationism as "the [view] held by those who believe in the law of Moses" (*Guide* 2.13), and as "fundamental to our entire law" (*Guide* 2.27). But in pressing the analogy between divine cosmic governance and human, Mosaic legislation, we may perhaps come to view divine creation in a somewhat different way. As noted previously, Moses creates a nation from out of a rabble of slaves. If you will, he creates a nation from (pre-existent) formless matter. If such a construal of the birth of the nation is analogized to the divine creation of the world, we are led to revise the standard view, and Maimonides' own presumed view, of creation, creation *ex nihilo*. Pressing the analogy, the understanding of the birth of the nation from a (pre-existent) formless rabble would tend to support what Maimonides takes to be the "Platonic" view of creation, creation *de novo*, from pre-existent (formless) matter (*Guide* 2.13). *Ex hypothesi*, Moses, like the Platonic demiourgos of the *Timaeus*, imposes form (law, structure) on formless matter, chaos. Now I suppose the nature of "chaos" runs the gamut from formless matter to not-being, but even if we tilt toward the latter gloss, I think we might understand not-being as unformed being, rather than as absolute non-existence. So, our divine/human analogy with respect to creation and legislation may pay dividends in understanding Maimonides' own preferred view on the mechanics of creation. This is just a suggestion, and I shall say no more on this highly contested issue.[6]

---

[6] Along these lines, see further: H. Davidson, "Maimonides' Secret Position on Creation," in I. Twersky (ed.), *Studies in Medieval Jewish History and Literature* (Cambridge, MA: Harvard University Press, 1979), 16–40; N. Samuelson, "Maimonides' Doctrine of Creation," *Harvard Theological Review* 84.3 (1991): 249–71; T. M. Rudavsky, *Maimonides* (Malden, MA: Wiley-Blackwell, 2010), 73–4. I might just add that some further corroboration of this "Platonic" view of creation comes from his analogous position on prophecy, outlined in *Guide* 2.32. There Maimonides presents three views of prophecy and the one he declares as "the ... view of our faith, and a principle of our religion" is the one that presupposes substantial *preconditions* for prophecy to be operative. Maimonides quotes BT Shabbat 92a: "Prophecy only dwells upon him who is wise, strong, and rich."

IMITATIO DEI AND THE PROMULGATION OF LAW

Now I turn to some psychological features that the analogy impresses upon us. In legislating the law as he does, in imitation of divine creation and governance of the natural world, Moses acts as God acts. In imitating God, in acting as God acts ("As he is gracious, so you be gracious; as He is merciful, so you be merciful"—*Siphre* on Deuteronomy 10:12 re Leviticus 19:2), Moses legislates *dispassionately*, given the very *incorporeal* nature of divinity. At the very end of *Guide* 1.54 Maimonides writes:

> The highest virtue to which man can aspire is to become similar to God as far as this is possible, [and] that means we must imitate His actions by our own, as has been indicated by our Rabbis in their comment on the words, *Ye shall be holy* [Leviticus 19.2]: "As He is gracious, so be thou gracious; as He is merciful, so be thou merciful" [*Siphre* on Deuteronomy 10:12]. The outcome of our discussion [Maimonides concludes] is thus that the attributes which are applied to Him are attributes of His actions, but He himself has no attributes. [trans. C. Rabin][7]

This passage, nested within Maimonides' celebrated discussion of divine attributes, is full of interest for us in the present context. In becoming God-like, in imitating divine "ways," Moses legislates in a manner analogous to the beneficent divine governance over nature. For Maimonides, *imitatio Dei* is to imitate divine activity. Once again, as the Rabbis commented on Deuteronomy: "As He is gracious, so be thou gracious; as He is merciful, so be thou merciful" (*Siphre* on Deuteronomy 10:12). It is crucial that we understand this aright. To imitate divine activity, to act as God acts, is not just to do certain actions, but to do them *just as* God performs them.[8] And how does God perform acts of mercy, etc.? In a word, "dispassionately," without affection. On pain of idolatrous anthropomorphism, God must be understood as incorporeal, and

---

[7] Moses Maimonides, *The Guide of the Perplexed* (trans. C. Rabin) (Indianapolis: Hackett, 1995).

[8] One may compare Aristotle: "Actions are called just and temperate when they are such as the just or the temperate man would do; but it is not the man who does these that is just and temperate, but the man who also does them *as* just and temperate men do them." (*Nicomachean Ethics* 2.4 [1105b5–9]). Aristotle and Maimonides may be seen to differ fundamentally on the foundation for paradigmatic moral agency. The foundational role that Aristotle gives to the prudentially wise, virtuous person (the just person, the temperate person) is assumed by God in Maimonides.

a corollary to this is a complete absence of any (corporeal) feeling or emotion as God acts. Maimonides writes in 1.54:

> ... God is called jealous, vengeful, wrathful, and furious. This means that such actions as with us would spring from psychological states like jealousy, revenge, hatred, or anger, emanate from God because those that are punished thereby have deserved them, not in consequence of any affection—far be it from us to impute to Him such lack of perfection. In the same manner all divine acts are actions that resemble human actions springing from certain affections and psychological states, but with God they do not spring from anything that is in any way superadded to his essence.

And he continues:

> A ruler—if he is a prophet—must model his conduct on these [divine] attributes. Acts of this kind should with him spring from mature reflection and be commensurate with the crime, rather than from mere affection. He should never give rein to his anger or allow his affections to get the better of him, for all affection is evil, but he must keep aloof from them as far as that is possible for man. If he does so, he will on some occasions be "gracious and merciful" [Exodus 34: 6–7] to some men, not out of tenderness and sympathy, but because such a course is indicated. To others he will be "jealous, revengeful, and angry" [Nahum 1: 2] because they deserve it, not out of mere annoyance. This will go as far that he may give orders to burn a man alive without being annoyed or angry or ill-disposed towards him, only because he considers that he has deserved such treatment, and realizes the great benefit that is likely to accrue from such an action to many others.

We may here discern retributive, utilitarian, and desert features in prophetic actions. However, of greater importance for us now is the *way* in which justice is meted out. Maimonides is clear that to act as one ought, if one is to model one's actions on the divine, is to act dispassionately, without anger, mercy, or any affection. Herbert Davidson puts the point this way: "Maimonides is exhorting the man who attains knowledge of God to imitate Him in the manner in which he interpreted imitation of God earlier in the [*Guide*]. God possesses no qualities, characteristics, or moral virtues; acts of loving-kindness, justice, and righteousness flow not from qualities in the soul but dispassionately, from human reason."⁹ God, an incorporeal being, cannot act from any kind of habituated disposition, so the legislative prophet (Moses), in imitation of God's ways, must act dispassionately, rationally if you will. The analogy that obtains between divine cosmic governance and human Mosaic legislation requires dispassion as the legislator acts.

The very end of the *Guide* (3.54) articulates and finalizes Maimonides' view on the issue. The discussion there concerns the *summum bonum*. With reference to Jeremiah 9.22–23,[10] Maimonides outlines a four-fold hierarchy of human goods (material, bodily, moral, and intellectual goods). At the highest (intellectual) level one is commanded to imitate God and his governance over nature. One should exercise loving-kindness, justice, and righteousness, in imitation of divine governance. Maimonides writes:

> The perfection of man in which he can truly glory is that achieved by him who has attained comprehension of God to the extent of his powers, and knows in what manner God provides for His creatures in creating them and governing them; and who after comprehending this, aims in his own conduct at loving-kindness, justice, and righteousness, so as to imitate God's actions, as we have repeatedly explained in this treatise.

The Maimonidean intellectual and moral paradigm is Moses, a veritable Platonic philosopher-king,[11] and Mosaic prophecy, the legislation of the law, must be understood as analogous to, in imitation of, divine cosmic governance. Lawrence Kaplan puts the point well: "In a word, Moses' political governance of Israel was an imitation of the divine cosmic governance of mankind ... Moses' act of Imitatio Dei was the formulation, the legislation, of the revealed Law."[12] As God governs the world, so humans are enjoined to act. I emphasize again the

---

[9] H. Davidson, *Maimonides the Rationalist* (Oxford: Littman Library of Jewish Civilization, 2011), 265–6; see also J. Stern, *The Matter and Form of Maimonides' Guide* (Cambridge, MA: Harvard University Press, 2013), 340–9; D. Frank, "Anger as a Vice: A Maimonidean Critique of Aristotle's Ethics," *History of Philosophy Quarterly* 7 (1990): 269–81.

[10] "Thus said the Lord: Let not the wise man glory in his wisdom; let not the strong man glory in his strength; let not the rich man glory in his riches. But only in this should one glory: that he understands and knows Me. For I the Lord act with loving-kindness, justice, and righteousness in the world; for in these I delight."

[11] For this construal, see L. V. Berman, "Maimonides, the Disciple of Alfarabi," *Israel Oriental Studies* 4 (1974): 154–78.

[12] Kaplan, "Maimonides on Mosaic Revelation," online.

psychological implications of acting *as* God acts. God is incorporeal and his actions cannot be expressive of any affection. His loving-kindness, justice, and righteousness flow from a "rational dispassion." In imitation of this, we should act similarly dispassionately. In judging fairly, impartially, and dispassionately, one brings order out of disorder, and, so construed, the judge acts as God acts in creating a world from pre-existent chaos.

THE FOUNDATIONS OF THE LAW

So far, then, we have discerned some structural and psychological features of a rabbinic analogy between judging fairly and divine creation. Finally, I turn to some teleological features that the analogy between creation and divine cosmic governance on the one side, and justice and Mosaic legislation on the other supports. God creates intelligently and for a purpose, whose ultimate purpose we humans may never fully know, given our finite intellect, but whose local purposes we may ascertain through science and the study of nature. Inasmuch as the divine law and its Mosaic legislation are parts of the overall divine plan, we may assume purposiveness in its content and its promulgation.[13] (God, like nature, does nothing in vain.[14]) For his part, Maimonides understands the law as supporting both social and political ends for all, as well as supra-political goals for some (*Guide* 2.40, 3.27). As noted, the revealed law is given at a certain time, to a certain people. It is purposed to human material nature and the historical moment of its legislation, and is meant to wean the recipients of the legislation from a servile and idolatrous mentality (*Guide* 3.29, 3.32). As God creates a world from unformed matter, so Moses creates a people and a nation from a formless rabble of ex-slaves, and as the natural world functions in accordance with universal laws, so the political realm is governed and constituted by a rational law aiming at specific ends. Indeed, both the natural world and the political realm (continue to) exist only as long as they are law-governed.

---

[13] J. Stern, *Problems and Parables of Law: Maimonides and Nahmanides on Reasons for the Commandments (Ta'amei Ha-Mitzvot)* (Albany: SUNY Press, 1998), 16–20; D. Rynhold, *Two Models of Jewish Philosophy: Justifying One's Practices* (Oxford: Oxford University Press, 2005), 6–12, 18–26.

[14] *Guide* 3.25. For Aristotle (as for Spinoza), it is *nature* that does nothing in vain (*de Anima* 434a31; *de Incessu Animalium* 704b15).

The purposiveness of law and the order it supports carries with it a divine prescription. Incumbent upon those who follow the law in precisely the purposive and rational manner in which it was divinely revealed to Moses and legislated by him is to act with a keen sense of the trajectory and arc of the law. Following the law is optimally done if done with an understanding of the purpose(s) for which it was given.[15] In effect, this is a call for ascertaining *ta'amei ha-mitzvot*, an etiological project that the medieval philosophers, such as Saadia and Maimonides, took as commanded for those able to engage in it.[16] In its own way, this is a "scientific" endeavor, analogous to the study of nature. Josef Stern writes: "Just as knowledge of God's attributes of action, His governance of nature, is attained through study of natural science, so one understands the *ta'amei ha-mitzvot*, why and how the Mosaic commandments came to be legislated, by studying their *natural* causes. Maimonides' presentation of *ta'amei ha-mitzvot* in Part 3 of the *Guide* might, in short, be described as the natural science of the law, on a par with Aristotelian natural science of the physical world."[17] Stern discerns an analogy between the Aristotelian and the Maimonidean projects. Both are meant to unearth the reasons (the "why and how") that explain the relevant data. In fact, the two projects are but two applications of a single overarching one. As the divine law is part of the overall divine plan for creation, the study of it is subsumed under the study of the created order, the order of nature.

The project of *ta'amei ha-mitzvot* is one that understands the law, and acting in accordance with the law, in terms of its telic import, both political and supra-political. From this angle, acting in accordance with the law is at its highest level not the result of a divine command, so much as from an understanding and appreciation of its goals and the ends it is meant to subserve. As the study of nature, its causes and foundations, leads one to an appreciation, even love, for the creator and its ways, so the study of the law given to Moses—the project of ascertaining the purpose and reasons for the law, its natural and historical causes and foundations—leads one to act less out of fear than out of a sense of gratitude for the beneficence of a structure that creates a true

---

[15] That practice is optimally motivated by insight and understanding is captured by Maimonides' oft-quoted dictum: "Love is proportionate to apprehension." (*Guide* 1.39, 3.28, 3.51).

[16] For Saadia, *Emunot ve De'ot*, treatise III (on Commands and Prohibitions); for Maimonides, *Guide* 3.25–49.

[17] Stern, *Problems and Parallels of Law*, 20 (emphasis in original).

political community and the possibility of transcendence.[18] Here the analogy between cosmic governance and Mosaic legislation underwrites a "duty to philosophize," a demand on those who are capable to move beyond the "given," to scrutinize the divine plan for the world and for humankind.[19] It should be noted that such scrutiny is not so much "theoretical" as it is practical, for the inquiry into causes enhances practice. Imitation of God, acting as God acts, with an understanding of the aims and purposes of divine law, is motivational and action-guiding.

The duty to philosophize, to understand the aims and purposes of the law, and to act accordingly must be more fully fleshed out. The entire discussion concerning the reasons and purposes for the laws strives not only to elicit the general intelligibility of the laws, but to maintain some sort of distinction between the *mishpatim* and the *hukkim*. Further, and importantly, as much as countering the Ash'arite claim that all the laws are the product of divine will and Saadia's view that only *some* of the laws (the *hukkim*) are the product of divine will, Maimonides, in his quest to display the purposiveness of all the laws, is *also* concerned to forestall hyperrationalism, the philosopher's attempt to discover reasons for absolutely every particular in the law. It is quite pointless, according to Maimonides, to search for a reason why a lamb rather than a ram was used for a certain sacrifice or why a certain number of lambs were sacrificed.[20]

Searching for a reason for every particular proves to be vain, for there never was a reason for God's choice in the first place. While Maimonides is clear that historical knowledge is certainly helpful in gaining an understanding of the reasons for the law—the laws concerning sacrifice (*korbanot*[21]) are a case in point—he is equally insistent that "no cause will ever be found for the fact that one particular sacrifice consists in a lamb and another in a ram and that the number of the victims should be one particular number."[22] Given this, Solomon's traditional wisdom concerning the grounds for the commandments (*ta'amei ha-mitzvot*) is confirmed: it rightly extends to "the utility of a given commandment in a general way, not an examination of its particulars."[23]

---

[18] See note 15.
[19] H. Davidson, "Philosophy as a Religious Obligation," in S. D. Goitein (ed.), *Religion in a Religious Age* (Cambridge, MA: Association for Jewish Studies, 1974), 53–68; D. Frank, "The Duty to Philosophize: Socrates and Maimonides," *Judaism* 42.3 (1993): 289–97.
[20] *Guide* 3.26.   [21] See note 5.   [22] *Guide* 3.26.   [23] Ibid.

A question arises just here: In a section where Maimonides devotes great effort in ascertaining the intelligibility of the laws, and counters Saadia on just this point, why should he wish *also* to emphasize a residual lack of a demonstrable reason? One reason is, as noted, to forestall hyperrationalism, the (mad) attempt to find reasons for every particular. Another reason, a corollary to the foregoing, is Maimonides' desire to forestall antinomianism, non-performance of the laws.[24] Although there is a deep need and even duty for those able to inquire into the reasons and purposes of the commandments to do so, there is apparently an equal need, Maimonides seems to suggest, to recognize *limits* to the inquiry. Not to recognize limits is to court antinomianism. In the case of the non-philosophical masses, an unbounded inquiry could lead to confusion and hence to a failure of belief and a disregard of the commandments. For the philosophical elite, too, the inquiry into causes could well culminate in antinomianism; in *not* discovering a reason for some particular, the intellectual might well query God's wisdom and, as a result, withhold his assent to the commandment. For these reasons, then, there is a need for Maimonides to state explicitly that the law is in part inscrutable.

However, in addition to hyperrationalism and its correlative antinomianism, there is, I believe, another reason for Maimonides' desire to emphasize that some of the laws are in their particulars without reason, although still the consequence of divine wisdom. I suggest that the residual non-teleological[25] aspects of details of particular laws, their *matter* as it were, are highlighted by Maimonides as emblematic of our corporeality, that part of human life that is "natural" and enmattered, and, in the end, cannot finally be brought under the rule of reason. The particulars of the commandments, in their indeterminacy and recalcitrance to the otherwise teleological nature of the law, are emblematic of our (finite and material) nature. We have noted previously that the revealed law, supportive of both social and political ends, as well as supra-political goals for some, are given at a certain time, to a certain people. Indexed to human material nature and a particular historical time and circumstance, the law is meant, overall, to wean its recipients

---

[24] For a full discussion of this point, see J. Stern, "The Idea of a *Hoq* in Maimonides' Explanation of the Law," in S. Pines and Y. Yovel (eds.), *Maimonides and Philosophy* (Dordrecht: Martinus Nijhoff, 1986), 113ff.

[25] Twersky describes these non-teleological features as "contingent," in I. Twersky, *Introduction to the Code of Maimonides* (Mishneh Torah) (New Haven: Yale University Press, 1980), 398.

from a servile and idolatrous mentality. But as we learn from the biblical narrative, "[i]t is impossible to pass all at once from one extreme to another; it is not in keeping with human nature for man to abandon suddenly all he has been used to" (*Guide* 3.32). Furthermore, "[m]atter is a strong veil preventing the apprehension of that which is separate from matter as it truly is ... whenever our intellect aspires to apprehend the deity or one of the intellects, there subsists this great veil interposed between the two" (*Guide* 3.9).[26] The divine project to extirpate idolatry, to instruct humankind in the ways of God, is monumental. It is on-going, and backsliding is to be expected. This recalcitrance of humankind to law and order, the very nature of matter to constrain form, necessitates a nuance in the analogy that has governed our study. The application of divine law, the imitation of divine governance over nature, and the etiological project of *ta'amei ha-mitzvot* must all be understood as constrained by human nature and its very materiality. From this limitation, it will follow that divine creation and governance must be appreciated as projects that are forever unfinished, works-in-progress.

So, we discern here in this discussion of the teleological aspects of the law, a deep realization of human limitations. These limitations are not so much epistemological, as they are ontological. They are brute facts. Matter constrains form. As Maimonides notes, human beings need law to achieve certain political as well as spiritual and intellectual ends.[27] The law provides the framework for the good life, but a good *human* life, one in accord with human nature *as it is*. For all we have noted about the transformation of unformed matter, and the creation of a nation from a formless rabble of ex-slaves, there is a limit to possibility. We are what we are, and the law, in its very fullness and particularity, signals this.

The analogy we have been focusing on in this chapter between the birth of a nation and the creation of the world depends upon parallels between natural and human law, between creation and justice, and between divine governance and Mosaic legislation. In the end, the parallels converge.[28] "The Law enters into what is natural." The divine and

---

[26] For discussion of the constraints of matter and the limits of human transformation, see Stern (2013), 387–88.
[27] *Guide* 2.40.
[28] Stern (1998) writes, "... the parallel Maimonides constantly emphasizes between the Law and divine (i.e., natural) acts is not a parallel between two *different* domains but within *one* domain." (20; emphasis in original); see also Rynhold, *Two Models of Jewish Philosophy*, 7–8.

the human intersect. This is not a Christian moment, but in the Semitic monotheistic traditions, this intersection catalyzes the emergence of an eternal law that creates human community. As the Rabbis see it, human beings, through acts of justice and fair dealing, are partners in the divine plan for the world, in an ongoing divine creation, making the created realm a better place. In acting justly, we imitate God.[29]

Selected Further Reading

Berman, L. V. "Maimonides, the Disciple of Alfarabi." *Israel Oriental Studies* 4 (1974): 154–78.

Bland, K. "Moses and the Law According to Maimonides." In *Mystics, Philosophers and Politicians: Essays in Jewish Intellectual History in Honor of Alexander Altmann*, 49–66. Edited by J. Reinharz, and D. Swetschinski. Durham, NC: Duke University Press, 1982.

Davidson, H. "Maimonides' Secret Position on Creation." In *Studies in Medieval Jewish History and Literature*, 16–40. Edited by I. Twersky. Cambridge, MA: Harvard University Press, 1979.

Davidson, H. *Maimonides the Rationalist*. Oxford: Littman Library of Jewish Civilization, 2011.

Davidson, H. "Philosophy as a Religious Obligation." In *Religion in a Religious Age*, 53–68. Edited by S. D. Goitein. Cambridge, MA: Association for Jewish Studies, 1974.

Fleischacker, S. "Making Sense of the Revelation at Sinai: Revisiting Maimonides' Eighth Principle of Faith," https://thetorah.com/making-sense-of-the-revelation-at-sinai/ (March 2014).

Frank, D. "Anger as a Vice: A Maimonidean Critique of Aristotle's Ethics." *History of Philosophy Quarterly* 7 (1990): 269–81.

Frank, D. "The Duty to Philosophize: Socrates and Maimonides." *Judaism* 42.3 (1993): 289–97.

Ivry, A. *Maimonides' Guide of the Perplexed: A Philosophical Commentary*. Chicago: University of Chicago Press, 2016.

Kaplan, L. "I Sleep but My Heart Waketh: Maimonides' Conception of Human Perfection." In *The Thought of Moses Maimonides: Philosophical and Legal Studies*, 130–66. Edited by I. Robinson, L. Kaplan, and J. Bauer. Lewiston, NY: Edwin Mellen Press, 1990.

---

[29] I cannot resist drawing a parallel here between such partnership with the divine, and the point I take Socrates to be getting at in the *Euthyphro*. At 13d ff., Socrates is keen to discover what "service" humans provide the gods, which the latter cannot provide for themselves. No answer is forthcoming, but the subtext seems clear. The "divine" service that humans can provide is psychic improvement through the practice of philosophy. The gods cannot make human beings better (only we can); likewise, in acting justly and judging fairly *we* collaborate with the divine in making the world a better place.

Kaplan, L. "Maimonides on Mosaic Revelation," https://kavvanah.wordpress.c om/2013/07/25/maimonides-on-mosaic-revelation-prof-lawrence-j-kapla n/ (July 2013).

Kreisel, H. *Maimonides' Political Thought: Studies in Ethics, Law, and the Human Ideal.* Albany: SUNY Press, 1999.

Kreisel, H. *Prophecy: The History of an Idea in Medieval Jewish Philosophy.* Dordrecht: Kluwer, 2001.

Manekin, C. "Maimonides on the Divine Authorship of the Law." In *Interpreting Maimonides*, 133–52. Edited by C. Manekin and D. Davies. Cambridge: Cambridge University Press, 2019.

Reines, A. "Maimonides' Concept of Mosaic Prophecy." *Hebrew Union College Annual* 40/41 (1969–70): 325–61.

Rudavsky, T. M. *Maimonides*. Malden, MA: Wiley-Blackwell, 2010.

Rynhold, D. *Two Models of Jewish Philosophy: Justifying One's Practices.* Oxford: Oxford University Press, 2005.

Samuelson, N. "Maimonides' Doctrine of Creation." *Harvard Theological Review* 84.3 (1991): 249–71.

Stern, J. "The Idea of a *Hoq* in Maimonides' Explanation of the Law." In *Maimonides and Philosophy*, 92–130. Edited by S. Pines and Y. Yovel. Dordrecht: Martinus Nijhoff, 1986.

Stern, J. *The Matter and Form of Maimonides' Guide.* Cambridge, MA: Harvard University Press, 2013.

Stern, J. *Problems and Parables of Law: Maimonides and Nahmanides on Reasons for the Commandments (Ta'amei Ha-Mitzvot).* Albany: SUNY Press, 1998.

Twersky, I. *Introduction to the Code of Maimonides (Mishneh Torah).* New Haven, CT: Yale University Press, 1980.

8 The Mystical Theology of Kabbalah: From God to Godhead

ADAM AFTERMAN

INTRODUCTION

Kabbalah (lit. tradition) is the central and most important medieval trend of Jewish mysticism. Surfacing at the end of the twelfth century in southern France in the study halls of two prominent Jewish rabbinic dynasties, it continued to flourish and develop in Germany, Spain, and Italy,[1] amounting to a major form of Jewish mysticism and spirituality. In the following pages I will discuss the conceptualization of the Godhead in classic Kabbalah. In order to clarify and elucidate its many aspects and elements, I will utilize the analytical terms (albeit foreign to Kabbalah): theosophy, theurgy, and mysticism.[2]

The heart of kabbalistic theology lies in its rich conceptualization of the Godhead, spanning from the infinite supernal realm to the human material realm. The mapping of the divine emanation and multiple channels connecting its various elements within itself and with man was derived through mystical tradition and insight. Owing to its divine nature, the study of this esoteric knowledge is termed "theosophy." This knowledge may be divided into two central traditions, the first divine names and the second *sefirot* or emanative entities comprising the dynamic Godhead. Gershom Scholem wrote regarding these traditions:

> The process which the Kabbalists described as the emanation of divine energy and divine light was also characterized as the unfolding of divine *language*. This gave rise to a deep-seated parallelism between the two most important kinds of symbolism used by the

---

[1] For more on the beginning of the Kabbalah tradition, see Gershom Scholem, *Origins of the Kabbalah*, ed. R. J. Zwi Werblowsky and trans. Allan Arkush (Princeton: Princeton University Press, 1987).

[2] I would like to thank my student Eugene D. Matanky for his generous help in preparing this chapter for publication.

Kabbalists to communicate their ideas. They speak of attributes and of spheres of light; but in the same context they speak also of divine names and the letters of which they are composed.[3]

These disparate traditions developed separately and in concordance with one another. Both emanation traditions are founded upon, but ultimately diverge from, the classic rabbinic-mythical homilies and the medieval philosophical conceptualizations of the divine. Kabbalah reworked the ancient sources found in the Bible and midrash, with certain philosophical tendencies, transforming them into a systematic theosophy. Through this innovative and complex matrix of texts and ideas, medieval kabbalists forged a unique Jewish theology on a par with the more rationalistic programmatic attempts by contemporary Jewish philosophers and theologians. The dynamic Godhead proposed by these personalities allowed for the Jewish people, due to their intimate connection to this dynamism and their ability to affect it, to take center stage within both lower and supernal realms. This affected dimension of divinity presumes that God is in relation with other beings, both in a positive empowered manner, as well as in a negative weakened manner. The religious daily life of the Jew is hyper-accentuated, involving theurgic elements hitherto unbeknown in Jewish thought. While one may find certain rabbinic statements that suggest that God is empowered by the religious actions of the Jewish people, nothing can be found that truly compares to the theurgic role that the Jew comes to play in the kabbalistic conceptualization of the Godhead. This theurgic element, which focuses on the dynamics of the supernal Godhead, is complemented by a mystical element, which focuses on the different manners in which the divine and man interact, whether it be through human ascension throughout the heavenly realms or through the divine overflow descending upon and even embodied by man. Furthermore, these elements are interwoven with mythical and symbolic imagery, such as marriage and covenant.

This notion of God stands in stark contrast to the "unmoved mover" of the philosophical tradition. A God who is in need of man is a vulnerable God, an imperfect God. While this connotation may appear to compromise the stature of the divine, for whom any lack may be

---

[3] Gershom Scholem, *On the Kabbalah and Its Symbolism*, trans. Ralph Manheim (New York: Schocken Books, 1965), 35–36.

configured as "imperfection," it was precisely this conceptualization that brought the divine into greater presence within the daily life of the Jewish people. Unlike the philosophical God, for whom commandments are at most a path for man to reach true philosophical principles and at least folk traditions that hold no true philosophical purpose and are only there for political purposes, the God of the kabbalists needs the Jewish people to fulfill the commandments for ontological purposes, in order to bring harmony to the Godhead and supernal and lower realms. In other words, commandments, through their theurgical understanding, are of both personal mystical importance and cosmic significance.

This active partaking in the life of God blurs the ontological gap, propagated by philosophical traditions incorporated within Judaism, between the divine and man not only in regard to the supernal realm, but also concerning man's ability to transcend his mundane existence and subsequently, achieve mystical union with the divine.[4]

Since these terms do not appear in kabbalistic literature, rather they are utilized as academic tools to better clarify specific aspects of the Jewish mystical tradition, in many sources it is nigh impossible to fully distinguish between these different elements. Therefore, in the following section I will primarily discuss the major principles and characteristics of *kabbalistic theosophy*, from the thirteenth and fourteenth centuries (commonly referred to as Spanish or Early Kabbalah), followed by a presentation of key themes and dynamics found within the texts that map out the divine emanation that also touch upon the *theurgic* element, and lastly return to the mystical elements in the final part of this essay.[5]

---

[4] See at length Adam Afterman, *"And They Shall Be One Flesh": On the Language of Mystical Union in Judaism* (Leiden: Brill, 2016) and the discussion below.

[5] For several key discussions of thirteenth-century kabbalistic theosophies, see Gershom Scholem, *Major Trends in Jewish Mysticism* (New York: Schocken Books, 1941), 205–43; Gershom Scholem, *Kabbalah* (Jerusalem: Keter, 1974), 105–16; Gershom Scholem, *On the Mystical Shape of the Godhead: Basic Concepts in the Kabbalah*, ed. Jonathan Chipman and trans. Joachim Neugroschel (New York: Schocken Books, 1991), 15–55; Isaiah Tishby, *The Wisdom of the Zohar*, trans. David Goldstein (Oxford: The Littman Library of Jewish Civilization, 1989), 1: 229–443; Arthur Green, *A Guide to the Zohar* (Stanford: Stanford University Press, 2003), 28–59, 101–08; Moshe Hallamish, *An Introduction to the Kabbalah.*, trans. Ruth Bar-Ilan and Ora Wiskind-Elper (Albany: SUNY Press, 1999), 121–65; Elliot K. Ginsburg, *The Sabbath in the Classic Kabbalah* (Albany: SUNY Press, 1989), 24–58.

THE HISTORICAL DEVELOPMENT OF THE KABBALISTIC GODHEAD

As has been discussed by numerous scholars, Kabbalah incorporated many different elements, both from within traditional rabbinic literature, as well as a plethora of medieval philosophical and hermetic positions. Kabbalah surfaced at the end of the twelfth century in the rabbinic study hall of a prominent rabbinic family.[6] The imagery and characteristics ascribed to the divine within this tradition drew heavily upon the mythical, anthropomorphic, and anthropopathic divine entity presented in biblical and rabbinic literature. For example, in the Bible we find God "moving about in the garden [of Eden]" (Genesis 3:8), regretting his decision to make man and becoming "saddened" (ibid., 6:6) and descending "to look at the city and tower that man had built" (ibid., 11:5). This mythic trend is continued and modified within rabbinic literature, in which God is removed to some extent, no longer strolling in the garden; however his connection to man is amplified to the point that man is understood to be an icon of God, meaning not only a representation, but also sharing essential qualities.[7] The Sages had no qualms regarding the portrayal of God in liturgy and *piyyutim*, as the king of the universe, fulfilling commandments, a warrior and future avenger, an elderly judge, and other figures. Other classic rabbinic sources elaborate upon God's *Sophia* (Wisdom), spirit, and *Shekhinah* (indwelling), whose theological and ontological statuses were never fully articulated in a systematic fashion. Additional texts present God's attributes, stature, and limbs as hypostatic entities, at times acting quasi-independently, even "arguing" with God, whereas other passages concentrate on God's divine names, such as the Tetragrammaton, which functions and operates through other divine names. All of these images, mythopoetic renderings, and diverse elements strewn throughout the vast rabbinic corpus did not amount to a systematic theology or coherent account of a "Godhead." One may even postulate that situated at the core of these aforementioned rabbinic sources is the rejection of the idea of systemization regarding the

---

[6] See Scholem, *Origins*, 108–09.

[7] See Yair Lorberbaum, *In God's Image: Myth, Theology, and Law in Classical Judaism* (New York: Cambridge University Press, 2015). Also, see Dov Weiss, *Pious Irreverence: Confronting God in Rabbinic Judaism* (Philadelphia: Pennsylvania University Press, 2016), 149–55, for a summary of scholars who have explored the humanization of God in rabbinic context.

divine persona, as well as his attributes, and therefore they utilized numerous and contradicting conceptualizations to depict God's interaction vis-à-vis the world.[8] These images formed a fecund ground from which to harvest fruitful mythical and mystical understandings of the divine in the medieval transformation of Jewish thought, which we will now discuss.

With the introduction of Neoplatonic, Neoaristotelian, and Hermetic traditions into Judaism,[9] Jewish thinkers began to incorporate these new schemata into classical rabbinic thought. Certain aspects of these traditions presented new issues for Jewish thought, primarily the philosophical understanding of God's unchanging nature and non-corporeal features. As mentioned, the biblical and rabbinic God is not systematically sketched out; furthermore, he does not abide by these philosophical considerations. Much effort was made by Jewish medieval philosophers to rid the Jewish God of these mythical features, while others focused more on squaring the relation between the Jewish God and the world, via astrological and emanational speculations. In the kabbalistic tradition, the entities that were once hypostatic in relation to God, either in rabbinic or philosophic literature, were now dialectically imbibed into the dynamic flow of the Godhead. By undergoing this systematization, these elements, hitherto not well defined or delineated, became significant aspects of the newly stipulated Godhead. For instance, the crown discussed in numerous

---

[8] For classic accounts of rabbinic theology, see Abraham J. Heschel, *Heavenly Torah: As Refracted Through the Generations*, ed. and trans. Gordon Tucker with Leonard Levine (New York: Continuum, 2005); Max Kadushin, *The Rabbinic Mind* (New York: Blaisdell, 1965); Arthur Marmorstein, *Studies in Jewish Theology* (London: Oxford University Press, 1950); Efraim E. Urbach, *The Sages: Their Concepts and Beliefs* (Jerusalem: The Hebrew University Magnes Press, 1975).

[9] See Daniel H. Frank and Oliver Leaman, eds., *The Cambridge Companion to Medieval Jewish Philosophy* (New York: Cambridge University Press, 2003); Moshe Idel, "Hermeticism and Kabbalah," in *Hermetism from Late Antiquity to Humanism*, ed. Paolo Lucentini, Ilaria Parri, and Vittoria Perrone Compagni (Turnhout: Brepols, 2003), 385–428; Moshe Idel, "Jewish Kabbalah and Platonism in the Middle Ages and Renaissance," in *Neo-Platonism and Jewish Thought*, ed. Lenn E. Goodman (Albany: SUNY Press, 1992), 319–31. For the later manifestations of these systems of thought in Kabbalah, see ibid., 331–44; Moshe Idel, "The Magical and Neoplatonic Interpretations of the Kabbalah in the Renaissance," in *Jewish Thought in the Sixteenth Century*, ed. Bernard Dov Cooperman (Cambridge: Harvard University Press, 1983), 186–242; Moshe Idel, "Hermeticism and Judaism," in *Hermeticism and the Renaissance: Intellectual History and the Occult in Early Modern Europe*, ed. Ingrid Merkel and Allen G. Debus (Washington, DC: Folger Shakespeare Library, 1988), 59–76.

rabbinic texts was transformed into the highest *sefirah* of the Godhead, likewise, *Shekhinah*, God's indwelling or presence, became the lowest *sefirah* of the Godhead. Furthermore, a fundamental principle found in kabbalistic theology is the connection between the supernal and lower realms. This connection underlies all of material reality, creating chords, channels, and continuum, which span human and metaphysical existence, creating a vast network joining "branch to root," man to the divine.

CLASSIC RABBINIC SOURCES

As discussed above, the rabbinic tradition includes extensive midrashim (homilies) and talmudic discussions concerning God's being, personality, relationship with the people of Israel, as well as roles, such as king, lover, judge, and warrior. All of these depictions can be found either explicitly or implicitly within the Hebrew Bible. These portrayals share an anthropomorphic and anthropopathic conception of the divine.[10] The primary sources utilized by the Jewish mystical tradition discussed in rabbinic texts are the "Account of Creation,"[11] the "Account of the Chariot,"[12] associated with the first chapter of Ezekiel, and the fifth chapter of the Song of Songs, considered to be an esoteric description of God's appearance. The interpretation of these sources was left relatively open within rabbinic tradition. An additional source for the kabbalistic conception of the Godhead and its internal dynamic forces is the discussion of God's *middot* or characteristics, specifically those of mercy and judgment.[13] These two capacities are also associated with his right and left "hands" and with the two primary divine names, *adonai* (judgment) and *YHWH* (mercy). It is unclear if these *middot* are purely functional or hypostatical. Within kabbalistic literature these *middot* are developed further and are in addition associated with ten names and ten limbs.[14] This decadic system eventually constitutes the

---

[10] See Michael Fishbane, *Biblical Myth and Rabbinic Mythmaking* (Oxford: Oxford University Press, 2004), 31–92.

[11] Daniel Abrams, "Some Phenomenological Considerations on the "Account of Creation" in Jewish Mystical Literature," *Kabbalah* 10 (2004): 7–19.

[12] See Adam Afterman, *"Ma'aseh Merkava* in Rabbinic Literature: Prayer and Envisioning the Chariot," *Kabbalah* 13 (2005): 249–70 [Hebrew].

[13] See Moshe Idel, *Absorbing Perfections: Kabbalah and Interpretation* (New Haven, CT: Yale University Press, 2002), 226–34; Moshe Idel, *Kabbalah: New Perspectives* (New Haven, CT: Yale University Press, 1988), 128–34.

[14] Moshe Idel traces this decad structure in conjunction with the human body to rabbinic literature, ibid., 113–22.

primary element of the Godhead. These "psychological" aspects of divinity reflected the rabbinic attempt to discern the mind of God. Furthermore, these elements allowed for the portrayal of an affected God, one who suffers with his children in exile and rejoices in their observance of commandments.

Alongside these classic rabbinic sources, which were generally concerned with the hermeneutical and legal aspects of the Bible and halakhah, existed a more mystical tradition, whose exact relation to rabbinic literature and to the Rabbis is unclear, referred to as Merkavah or Hekhalot mysticism.[15] Although its relation to rabbinic literature is a matter of scholarly dispute, nevertheless, it was viewed by most Jews, both in the East and West, as an authentic and esoteric part of "rabbinic" Judaism. This literature is characterized by a focus on heavenly ascent, the architectural design of the heavens, and the different categories of angels, as well as the deity himself. This literature, specifically *Shiur Qomah* ("Divine Stature"),[16] is significantly more explicit than corresponding midrashic and talmudic literature regarding God's appearance, corporeal dimensions, and "throne." These traditions were transmitted to and disseminated throughout Europe in the early medieval period and presented plentiful mythopoetic imagery for philosophical exploration and innovation.

THE MEDIEVAL THEOLOGICAL REVOLUTION: NEOARISTOTELIANISM AND NEOPLATONISM

The introduction of philosophical categories into Jewish rabbinic thinking caused a substantial shift regarding the understanding of the boundary between the supernal and mundane realms. As mentioned above, in the Bible it is questionable if such a boundary exists, while in rabbinic literature it would appear that it is quite a permeable one at best. In the medieval period this border became more fixed due to Neoplatonic and Neoaristotelian thought, which posited a more absolute divide between the heavens and the earth, yet still did not rid itself of a point of contact, which ultimately led to the development of a metaphysical ladder

---

[15] See Ithamar Gruenwald, *Apocalyptic and Merkavah Mysticism* (Leiden: Brill, 1980).
[16] Martin S. Cohen, *Shiur Qomah: Liturgy and Theurgy in Pre-Kabbalistic Jewish Mysticism* (Tübingen: Mohr Siebeck, 1985); Scholem, *On the Mystical Shape of the Godhead*, 15–55.

connecting the two realms.[17] While God is still placed beyond the physical world, there are entities that connect the realms, either separate intellects within the Neoaristotelian system or the *nous* within the Neoplatonic.

The physical realm is characterized by multiplicity, whereas the divine realm is of a simple unity, popularized through and known within Islamic thought as *tawhid*. A major focus of medieval spirituality was the bridging of this gap, from the corporeal to the non-corporeal—man's integration within the divine. The intensity and extent of integration was largely dependent on the philosophical system being employed. A central theme developed in these systems is a type of "spiritual energy," conveyed as light, air, spirit, water, and the like, which flows through the different levels of emanation or spheres, depending on the system, until it reaches the lowest realm—the physical realm. This bond between these realms helped the development of the understanding of man as a microcosm, paralleling that which occurs within the divine.[18]

The other important philosophical strand is Jewish Neoplatonism, which was the major philosophical source and context for the development of early kabbalistic theology.[19] The emanational ontology proposed by neoplatonists is clearly situated at the foundation of the kabbalistic Godhead. The conceptions of overflow and ascent are indebted to this worldview in which the human soul was understood as being able to "climb" the metaphysical ladder and ultimately unite with the One. However, an important distinction should be made, whereas the *nous* (intellect) and "world-soul" described in Neoplatonic thought were considered separate entities (not divine), for the kabbalists these elements are understood as being an integral part of the divine. Within this medieval theological revolution, the idea of "metaphysical overflow" was translated into Jewish terms, such as the talmudic extra soul bestowed upon the Jewish people on the Sabbath, as well as God's holy spirit, referred to in biblical and rabbinic literature, which is now

---

[17] See Alexander Altmann, "The Ladder of Ascension," in *Studies in Mysticism and Religion Presented to Gershom G. Scholem on his Seventieth Birthday by Pupils, Colleagues, and Friends*, eds. Ephraim. E. Urbach, R. J. Zwi Werblowsky, and Ch. Wirszubski (Jerusalem: The Hebrew University Magnes Press, 1967), 1–32.

[18] See Elliot R. Wolfson, "Bifurcating the Androgyne and Engendering Sin: A Zoharic Reading of Genesis 1–3," in *Hidden Truths from Eden: Esoteric Readings of Genesis 1–3*, ed. S. Scholz and C. Vander Stichele (Atlanta, GA: SBL Publications, 2014), 84–91.

[19] See n. 9.

understood to be a divine energy that man may embody under correct conditions.[20]

With this in mind, it would be incorrect to state that kabbalists were crude corporealists. In fact, many studied and were influenced by Maimonides' argument for the incorporeality of the divine. However, unlike Maimonides, they were unwilling to forego the biblical anthropomorphic language for allegorical-philosophical interpretation, in which God's "image" (ṣelem) merely refers to the intellectual faculty; rather they placed the biblical terminology into a theosophical-symbolic order, creating a complex conceptualization of the material and spiritual. For example, R. Joseph Gikatilla, a thirteenth-century kabbalist who was highly influenced by Maimonidean philosophy, wrote that the purpose of anthropomorphic language was to convey the deepest essence of the divine:

> Just because we were created in His own image and likeness, don't think that the eye which is written in the Torah is really a human eye, or that the hand is truly a human hand. These terms reflect the deepest essence of the blessed creator. They are the sources of that which emanates to all those under the dominion of His blessed Name.[21]

This difference between philosophical-allegorical and kabbalistic-symbolic readings may be exemplified by the biblical verses that depict God's organs. Maimonides, the preeminent medieval Jewish philosopher, wrote:

> God, may He be exalted above every deficiency, has had bodily organs figuratively ascribed to Him in order that His acts should be indicated by this means ... Accordingly He has no organs; I mean to say by this that He is not a body and that His acts are performed through His essence and not through an organ ... Thereby I mean that there does not exist in Him anything other than His essence in virtue of which object He might act, know, or will.[22]

The utilization of anthropomorphic language is to convey items of a metaphysical nature to man, who would not understand otherwise;

---

[20] See: Adam Afterman, "From Prophetic Inspiration to Mystical Integration: The Holy Spirit in Medieval Jewish Thought," Heiko Schulz (ed.), *Prophecy and Reason in Judaism, Christianity and Islam*, Tübingen: J. C. B. Mohr (forthcoming); Adam Afterman, "On the Rise of the Holy Spirit in Sixteenth-Century Kabbalah" (forthcoming).

[21] Joseph Gikatilla, *Gate of Light: Sha'are Orah*, trans. Avi Weinstein (San Francisco: HarperCollins, 1994), 7.

[22] Maimonides, *Guide of the Perplexed*, 1.46, §§1:100–02.

however in truth, God has no organs or limbs. God's "outstretched arm" is merely one of the many possible terms to denote divine action, which in itself is nothing other than human perception, for in actuality God is only his simple essence. In contrast, R. Meir ibn Gabbai writes, "man is structured according to the design of the supernal edifice, is made in the likeness of the glory, and his structure corresponds to the structure of the supernal chariot and all its parts."[23] Furthermore, Ibn Gabbai articulates that: "Everything is in the supernal image and model and things materialize below which reflect and testify to their causes above, that were made and structured according to the design of the chariot of the supernal lights which are contained within each other."[24] Employing the kabbalistic locution of "limb strengthens limb," Ibn Gabbai, as well as the majority of kabbalists, place much emphasis on which body part is being used for which action. God's use of his "arm" is important for it teaches us how man is to use his own arm, and man's use of his arm to fulfill the commandments strengthen God's own "arm." This understanding is positive in nature and not negative like that of Maimonides.

A further difference between philosophers and kabbalists may be demonstrated by analyzing their respective understandings of God's unity, which is intricately connected to the topic discussed above. Whereas philosophers ascribed to a "simple unity," kabbalists understood unity in a more complex manner—a unity that allows for multiplicity. On this point the kabbalists were repeatedly attacked. In an infamous letter, R. Meir ben Simeon of Narbonne wrote against the doctrine of the emanated *sefirot*, "one should not associate anything with Him, for it is not right to associate the Creator with that which He has created, or matter with its Maker, or the emanated with the Emanator";[25] others, including kabbalists such as Abraham Abulafia, asserted that the decad proposed by the kabbalists was worse than the trinity developed in Christianity.[26] We will touch upon this topic again in our discussion of the apophatic and kataphatic understandings of the Godhead.

---

[23] See Meir Ibn Gabbai, *Avodat ha-Qodesh* (Jerusalem: Shivlei Orchot Hachaim, 1992), 2: 16. Translation from James A. Diamond, *Maimonides and the Shaping of the Jewish Canon* (New York: Cambridge University Press, 2014), 149, as well as his discussion of Ibn Gabbai and Maimonides, ibid., 137–62.
[24] Ibn Gabbai, *Avodat ha-Qodesh*, 3: 25. Translation from Diamond, *Maimonides*, 150.
[25] See Tishby, *Wisdom*, 1: 239.
[26] See Marc B. Shapiro, *The Limits of Orthodox Theology: Maimonides' Thirteen Principles Reappraised* (Oxford: The Littman Library of Jewish Civilization, 2011), 40.

SEFER YEṢIRAH

Sefer Yeṣirah is a short enigmatic treatise written in Hebrew that surfaced in the Jewish world in the tenth century and was seemingly composed some time between the sixth and seventh centuries.[27] The following source appears to have many different and variegated influences, including but not limited to astrological material.[28] Its content differs from all other extant rabbinic literature. Its anonymous author describes the manner in which God created the cosmos with and through His Wisdom yet without referring to or quoting biblical verses or rabbinic traditions. The work's greatest contribution to Jewish mystical thought is the quasi-scientific manner in which it depicts creation as occurring through the utilization of the Hebrew language—transforming Hebrew into the underlying ontological stratum of existence.

This composition served both Jewish philosophers and kabbalists for the purpose of appropriating the Jewish God of the Bible and Talmud for their contemporary scientific and philosophic schema. However, it should be noted that a fundamental difference existed between their respective conceptualizations. On the one hand, philosophers, such as Saadia Gaon (ninth–tenth centuries), understood this text as illustrating the manner in which the transcendent God interacted with the immanent world through his created entities and linguistic components. For these thinkers the composition does not discuss a dynamic God, but rather only refers to the genesis of the world and man. In this manner it was incorporated into Jewish thought under the guise of "The Account of Creation," an esoteric rabbinic doctrine referenced in *Mishnah Ḥagigah* 2: 1, famously defined as sub-lunar physics by Maimonides. On the other hand, early kabbalists viewed the first chapter of this book as discussing the very unfolding of the sefirotic dimension of the Godhead, which discusses at length the number of *sefirot* and their structure: "Their end is fixed in their beginning, and their beginning in their end."[29] For them, the descriptions are not of created entities, but

---

[27] Tzahi Weiss, "Sefer Yeṣirah" and Its Contexts: Other Jewish Voices (Philadelphia: University of Pennsylvania Press, 2018).

[28] See A. Peter Hayman, *Sefer Yeṣirah: Edition, Translation and Text-Critical Commentary* (Tübingen: Mohr Siebeck, 2004), 36–37.

[29] Ibid., 74. Also, see Marla Segol, *Word and Image in Medieval Kabbalah: The Texts, Commentaries, and Diagrams of the Sefer Yetsirah* (New York: Palgrave Macmillan, 2012), 65–87, regarding the frequency of both the linear anthropoid and tree-like structure, as well as the ring-like structure in this work, and the consequential fluidity of the kabbalists' conceptualization of the Godhead.

of the emanation of the divine itself, from the linguistic cornerstones of the divine, manifested as the Tetragrammaton, to the underlying linguistic ontology of existence itself.[30] Thereby man is understood to be not only a microcosm of the divine macrocosm, a common idea in medieval Jewish philosophy, but also a projection and a theomorphic extension of the divine itself.

The emergence of the kabbalistic Godhead was a result of the unique combination and synthesis of a spectrum of Jewish sources with external, mainly philosophical and hermetical, sources. The medieval shift that brought about the movement from God to a Godhead was principally achieved through the absorption of biblical and midrashic content into structures absorbed from medieval theology and *Sefer Yeṣirah*. The transformation of the biblical and rabbinical God into the kabbalistic Godhead was done by "stretching" God into an organism of potencies and qualities. All the biblical and midrashic elements that only vaguely related to God and were of questionable hypostatic status were now all absorbed into the divine mechanism, arranged as to correlate to specific qualities of his being and not merely his "ways of functioning" or relating to the Creation. The combination of these distinct and to some extent contradictory models and cosmological schemata, together with earlier content, produced complex theories of the Godhead and its inner life and its relationship to the Jewish people. It is important to note that from the beginning the kabbalist presented different and often contradicting theosophies, and, consequently, it is impossible to relate to one fundamental kabbalistic theosophy. Let us now discuss the *sefirot* that make up this Godhead.

THE SEFIROT

The early kabbalists adopted the structure of ten *sefirot* from *Sefer Yeṣirah* and filled it up with biblical and midrashic terms referring to specific aspects or element in the dynamic mentality of God. In other words, the kabbalists identified the rabbinical informal and undefined list of God's *middot*—his mental and psychological faculties and qualities that function, at the same time as instruments with which he creates and interacts with the world—with the *sefirot*.

---

[30] Gershom Scholem, "The Name of God and the Linguistic Theory of the Kabbala," *Diogenes* 20, no. 80 (1972): 164 94.

The most common order and names of the ten *sefirot*, often arranged as an anthropos or tree,[31] is as follows: *keter* (crown), *ḥokhmah* (wisdom), *binah* (understanding), *ḥesed* (grace), *gevurah/din* (power/judgment), *tif'eret* (beauty), *hod* (splendor), *neṣaḥ* (endurance), *yesod* (foundation), *malkhut/shekhinah* (kingdom/presence). These *sefirot* emanate from one another in an organic flowing from the head through the torso to the phallus and lastly, to *Shekhinah*, represented by both the corona of the phallus as well as the mouth, both corporeal images alluding to the materializing power that *Shekhinah* possesses when the emanation process has been completed and the physical world created.

Following the layout in *Sefer Yeṣirah*, the *sefirot* are arranged along three parallel columns in the following manner:

	keter	
binah		ḥokhmah
gevurah		ḥesed
	tif'eret	
hod		neṣaḥ
	yesod	
	malkhut	

Owing to their correlation with both God's mental faculties and attributes, the *sefirot* are ranked accordingly, with the highest three *sefirot* correlating to God's mind, which when compared to the Neoplatonic emanation schema correlate to the metaphysical *nous*. The following seven *sefirot* are correlated with God's lower faculties, such as his emotions and psychological faculties, which are correlated to God's soul. These *sefirot* are, when compared to the aforementioned *sefirot*, more visible and extroverted in their function. The more esoteric functions that begin in the higher *sefirot* are actualized gradually as they flow through the Godhead.[32]

---

[31] On diagrammatic portrayals of the *sefirot*, see J. H. Chajes, "Kabbalistic Diagrams in the British Library's Margoliouth Catalogue," in *The Polonsky Foundation Catalogue of Digitised Hebrew Manuscripts* (2016): 1–8, and "Kabbalah and the Diagrammatic Phase of the Scientific Revolution," in *Jewish Culture in Early Modern Europe: Essays in Honor of David B. Ruderman*, ed. Richard I. Cohen, Natalie B. Dohrmann, Adam Shear, and Elchanan Reiner (Cincinnati: Hebrew Union College Press, 2014), 109–23.

[32] However, before we discuss this, one important note must be made. The theosophical-theurgical strand of Kabbalah is not the only type of Kabbalah that was developed. Alongside it and from within it arose a different branch that has been referred

I would be remiss if I did not discuss another tradition within the *Zohar* regarding the configuration of the Godhead—the doctrine of countenances (*parṣufin*). Although its greater importance lies in its interpretation within Lurianic Kabbalah, no discussion of the kabbalistic Godhead can ignore it. This tradition is found in a unique section of the *Zohar* referred to as the *Idrot* (Assembly).[33] In this section we find a slightly different configuration of the Godhead, one based on persona, specifically: "The Ancient of Days" (*Atiq Yomin*), described as a countenance radiating pure white light and compassion, this same countenance is referred to as "The Large Countenance" (*Arikh Anpin*) and "Ancient Holy One" (*Attiqa Qadisha*). Following this countenance, in the *Idra Zuṭa* (Lesser Assembly), are those of "Father" (*Abba*) and "Mother" (*Imma*). Next and situated beneath the highest entity is the "Small Countenance" (*Ze'ir Anpin*) and with him the "Female" (*Nuqvah*). These countenances roughly correlate to the ten *sefirot* described above, with *Ze'ir Anpin* correlating to the six *sefirot* of ḥesed, gevurah, tif'eret, hod, neṣaḥ, and yesod. Much of the language for this section may be found in the Book of Daniel and the *Shi'ur Qomah*, referenced above.

The *sefirot* were described by the kabbalists through the employment of a rich and diverse vocabulary, much of it taken from earlier layers of rabbinic Judaism in particular from the midrash, for describing the *sefirot*.[34] For example, the usage of the image of the crown—not only

---

to by Scholem, and extensively analyzed by Idel, as Prophetic or Ecstatic Kabbalah; see Moshe Idel, *The Mystical Experience in Abraham Abulafia*, trans. Jonathan Chipman (Albany: SUNY Press, 1988); Moshe Idel, *Studies in Ecstatic Kabbalah* (Albany: SUNY Press, 1988); Moshe Idel, *Language, Torah, and Hermeneutics in Abraham Abulafia*, trans. Menahem Kallus (Albany: SUNY Press, 1989). For a contrasting view, see Elliot R. Wolfson, *Abraham Abulafia – Kabbalist and Prophet: Hermeneutics, Theosophy, and Theurgy* (Los Angeles: Cherub Press, 2000). This school was founded by Abraham Abulafia in the late thirteenth century and differs from the primary kabbalistic tradition, specifically in its understanding of *sefirot*. Whereas in theosophical Kabbalah the *sefirot* are parts of the Godhead, the Abulafian God is conceptualized as closer to that of Maimonides, meaning that its simple unity is preserved. The *sefirot* are therefore conceptualized as inner human potencies. On this point, see Idel, *Kabbalah: New Perspectives*, 146–53. Also, see Wolfson, *Abraham Abulafia*, 94–177. Because of this factor, the prophetic-ecstatic kabbalistic tradition is much more mystical in nature and not very theosophical or theurgical. See Afterman, *"And They Shall Be One Flesh"*, 151–88.

[33] See Pinchas Giller, *Reading the Zohar: The Sacred Text of the Kabbalah* (Oxford: Oxford University Press, 2001), 89–157, regarding this section and its reception and importance in later Kabbalah, especially that of Luria.

[34] See the partial list in Green, *A Guide to the Zohar*, ix.

as to refer to the first and "highest" *sefirah*, the crown on the head of the king, but in some discussions each of the *sefirot* is referred to as a crown, and in particular the last *sefirah* is described as a diadem.[35] Other imagery was introduced through the philosophication, specifically Neoplatonic, of biblical terms, investing new semantic meanings into ancient words. Strong Neoplatonic thematic images such as light and water entered the Jewish philosophical lexicon and were then adapted to pre-existing concepts, which were further developed within the kabbalistic Godhead.[36] In addition to the images, whether biblical or philosophical, the *sefirot* were also visualized as an array of colors, with each *sefirah* receiving its own shade.[37] This imagery of colors functioned as an apt metaphor for the understanding of the *sefirot* as refracting the infinite divine light into a spectrum of variegated colors, representing the various manners in which the divine functions in this world, while remaining concealed.

This imagery is related to a fundamental dispute in regard to the nature of the kabbalistic Godhead, namely: are the *sefirot* divine, that is, one with God's essence? Or rather are they vessels in which the divine essence resides and functions? Those kabbalists who viewed the *sefirot* merely as "vessels" or "crowns" describe how the transcendent essence of God sits on a specific "throne" or adorns a specific "crown," meaning it functions specifically through that *sefirah*. In contrast, those who viewed the *sefirot* as the "essence of God" did not usually envision a divine power (such as *Ein Sof*) beyond and above the *sefirot*. This

---

[35] See Scholem, *Major Trends*, 213; Arthur Green, *Keter: The Crown of God in Early Jewish Mysticism* (Princeton: Princeton University Press, 1997), 154; ibid., 151–65 regarding the image of the crown in the *Zohar*. Also, see Elliot R. Wolfson's numerous discussions of the gender ramifications of this imagery, see *Language, Eros, Being*, 73, 365, 369, 375, 377, 389; Elliot R. Wolfson, "Coronation of the Sabbath Bride: Kabbalistic Myth and the Ritual of Androgynisation," *Journal of Jewish Thought and Philosophy* 6 (1997): 335–39; Elliot R. Wolfson, "Occultation of the Feminine and the Body of Secrecy in Medieval Kabbalah," in *Rending the Veil: Concealment of Revelation of Secrets in the History of Religion* (New York and London: Seven Bridges Press, 1999), 113–54.

[36] See my recent discussion of the rationalization and scientifation of biblical language, "From Prophetic Inspiration to Mystical Integration: The Holy Spirit in Medieval Jewish Thought," Heiko Schulz (ed.), *Prophecy and Reason in Judaism, Christianity and Islam*, Tübingen: J. C. B. Mohr (forthcoming).

[37] Regarding the role of colors in the visualization of *sefirot*, see Gershom Scholem, "Colours and Their Symbolism in Jewish Tradition and Mysticism," *Diogenes* 27 (108): 84–111; 28(109): 64–76; Idel, *New Perspectives*, 103–11; Moshe Idel, "Visualization of Colors: David ben Yehudah he-Ḥasid's Kabbalistic Diagram," pts. 1 and 2, *Ars Judaica* 11 (2015): 31–54; 12 (2016): 1–13.

leads us to the question of transcendence and immanence, as well as kataphatic and apophatic conceptualizations, regarding the Godhead.

DIVINE ESSENCE AND HYPOSTATIC ENTITIES

In the kabbalistic tradition regarding the Godhead, alongside the teachings regarding the *sefirot*, there are a number of entities that are identified with the divine. These entities are already to be found in biblical and rabbinic literature, such as God's name, through such biblical verses as, "God and his name will be one" (Zechariah. 14:9) or midrashic segments such as, "Before the world was created, the Holy One, blessed be He, with His Name alone existed, and the thought arose in Him to create the world."[38] These type of statements are further developed within the mystical tradition and kabbalistic systemizers, such as the anonymous author of *Ma'arekhet Elohut*, Meir ibn Gabbai, Cordovero, and those who followed their lead. Many of these thinkers attempted to square the diverse and even contradictory positions found within biblical, rabbinic, and kabbalistic literature. In this following section we will briefly explore a number of such entities, namely, God as Name, God as Torah, God as His Glory, God as married to the Jewish people, and lastly God as his Indwelling (*Shekhinah*), and their development within kabbalistic thought.

GOD AS THE TETRAGRAMMATON

Of special significance in kabbalistic literature is the Tetragrammaton, YHWH. This divine name, commonly referred to as the *shem ha-meforash* (the explicit name), is traditionally unutterable, except for on the Day of Atonement during the High Priest's service. According to Jewish tradition, following the Temple's destruction, the tradition surrounding this name's pronunciation was lost, thereby transforming it into an extremely esoteric matter. As Elliot R. Wolfson has discussed in his many studies regarding the nature of secrecy in kabbalistic literature, the secret is that which fundamentally cannot be revealed. Meaning, within Jewish mystical literature the unutterable name is no longer due to lost tradition, but rather its very esoteric nature

---

[38] *Pirqei de-Rabbi Eli'ezer*, ch. 3. Translation from Gerald Friedlander, *Pirke de Rabbi Eliezer, Translated and Annotated with Introduction and Indices* (London: Kegan Paul, Trench, Trübner & Co, 1916), 10.

makes it unutterable—no matter the pronunciation, the ineffable name can never be truly announced for paradoxically "the ineffable name cannot be pronounced except through its epithet."[39]

This name is considered God's personal name, the name used specifically for his relationship with the Jewish people. Within the mystical tradition it is portrayed as the root word that simultaneously lies beyond existence. The Hebrew alphabet is conceptualized as flowing forth from this primordial name. The Godhead as well is wrapped up in this textual emanation, envisioned as a dynamic process that interweaves all of existence through a linguistic stratum.[40] Among the sefirotic emanation it was correlated with *tif'eret*, situated at the heart of the Godhead, with a path to every other *sefirah*.

These conceptualizations are developed from within the rabbinic tradition. Sources such as those cited above, which depict God and his name as predating the creation of the world, lend credence to the hypostatic qualities associated with this name. The qualities were further developed by mapping it onto the kabbalistic Godhead and configuring it as the substratum of existence.

Additionally found within ancient Jewish traditions are other permutations of divine names, such as the 42- and 72-letter names, all based upon this original 4-letter name, alluded to both in classic rabbinic literature as well as in Hekhalot literature. Such traditions were advanced primarily within German Pietistic literature and thought.[41] These teachings were continued by certain Spanish kabbalists and were incorporated into their understanding of the Godhead.

The divine names are also simultaneously identified with the Torah. As Nahmanides wrote: "The entire Torah is replete with the names of the Holy One, blessed be He, and in each and every pericope there is the name by which a certain thing has been formed or made or sustained by it."[42] This tradition is found throughout a wide range of kabbalists who envisioned the Torah as being entirely made up of the

---

[39] See Wolfson, *Language*, 123.   [40] See Gikatilla, *Gates of Light*, 159–60.
[41] Currently Moshe Idel has written extensively regarding these various traditions, the transmission of these traditions, as well as the different schools; for example, see Moshe Idel, "Some Forlorn Writings of a Forgotten Ashkenazi Prophet: R. Nehemiah Ben Shlomo ha-Navi," *Jewish Quarterly Review* 95 (2005): 183–96; Moshe Idel, "From Italy to Ashkenaz and Back: On the Circulation of Jewish Mystical Traditions," *Kabbalah* 14 (2006): 47–94.
[42] Moses Naḥmanides, "Torat ha-Shem Temimah," in *Kitvei ha-Ramban*, ed. C. D. Chavel (Jerusalem: Mosad Harav Kook, 1961), 2: 167. Translation from Idel, *Absorbing Perfections*, 321. Also, see ibid., 314–89.

divine name, whose root is the Tetragrammaton. Thus the Torah, as a sequence of letters, is the fullest articulation of the Godhead. The Torah as divine name is the garment, a text in which, "the tetragrammaton is woven in a hidden way and sometimes even directly; and, in any event, the tetragram refers back to it in every possible kind of metamorphosis and variation."[43] This development was also founded upon the aforementioned midrash regarding God and his name pre-creation, in conjunction with the rabbinic traditions that espoused the existence of the Torah before creation as well.[44] I will now discuss the identification of God with the hypostatic Torah.

GOD AS THE TORAH AND THE COMMANDMENTS

God as Torah is another of the important hypostatic themes. Its strongest expression may be found in the writings of R. Menaḥem Recanati. He wrote: "For the Torah is not something outside him and he is not outside the Torah, therefore the Sages of the Kabbalah said that the Holy One, blessed be he, is the Torah."[45] He further wrote regarding the commandments that "whoever performs one commandment causes that power to descend upon the same commandment above, out of the 'Annihilation of Thought,' and he is considered as if he literally maintained one part of the Holy One, blessed be He."[46] These conceptualizations can be found within other kabbalistic literature as well. The identification between the divine and the Torah is quite strong.

This identification is mapped out as well on the sefirotic realm, which correlated the written Torah with *tif'eret* (also correlated with the divine name *YHWH*, as discussed above) and the oral Torah with *malkhut*. The Torah as a whole is also correlated with the *sefirah* of ḥokhmah, due to the connection made between Torah and wisdom in

---

[43] Scholem, "The Name of God," 179.
[44] See for example, Genesis Rabbah, 1:1; Pirqei de-Rabbi Eliezer 11; Leviticus Rabbah 19:1.
[45] Menaḥem Recanati, *Sefer Ṭa'amei ha-Miṣvot ha-Shalem*, ed. S. H. Liebermann (London: Maḥon Oṣar Ḥokhmah, 1962), 2b. See Scholem, *On the Kabbalah and Its Symbolism*, trans. Ralph Manheim (New York: Schocken Books, 1965), 44, regarding this tradition, as well as ibid., 32–86. Also, see Moshe Idel, "The Concept of the Torah in the Hekhalot Literature and Its Metamorphoses in Kabbalah," *Jerusalem Studies in Jewish Thought* 1 (1981): 49–84 [Hebrew].
[46] Recanati, *Sefer Ṭa'amei ha-Miṣvot ha-Shalem*, 3c. Translation from Moshe Idel, *Kabbalah in Italy 1280–1510: A Survey* (New Haven, CT: Yale University Press, 2011), 126–27. For more on this kabbalist, see ibid., 89–138.

classic rabbinic literature. Consequently, the identification of the Torah and the Godhead also means that the Godhead incorporates the commandments and Jewish rituals in their spiritual or metaphysical form.[47] The rabbinic homilies describing God performing Jewish ritual were transformed into an understanding of the nature of the divine—the divine is liturgical, he is made out of the commandments, concomitantly the rituals are divine.[48] This leads to the primary manner through which one may reach, cleave to impact, and affect the Godhead. By fulfilling the earthly commandments, one causes the Godhead to fulfill that same supernal commandment.[49] With this we have completed two-thirds of the famous kabbalistic statement, "God, His Torah, and Israel are one."[50]

GOD AS THE FEMININE ELEMENT

A major theme found in kabbalistic literature is the role of the feminine.[51] This feature distinguishes this literature from other Jewish genres. Much of the imagery and themes developed can be found within biblical and rabbinic texts. In the Bible, God and the Jewish people are bound by a covenant. This relationship is explored in various rabbinic texts, utilizing numerous types of relationships. One of the most celebrated relationships is that of God as husband and Israel as wife. This relationship is developed and explored within rabbinic literature, which placed a special importance on the "marriage ceremony" at Sinai and the lover and beloved referenced in Song of Songs.[52] When describing this relationship the Rabbis generally referred to God

---

[47] See the discussion by Moshe Idel, *Enchanted Chains: Techniques and Rituals in Jewish Mysticism* (Los Angeles: Cherub Press, 2005), 122–64.
[48] See ibid., 165–204.
[49] See Adam Afterman, "The Phylactery Knot: The History of a Jewish Icon," *Te'udah* 26 (2014): 441–80.
[50] For more on this phrase, see Isaiah Tishby, *Messianic Mysticism: Moses Hayim Luzzatto and the Padua School*, trans. Morris Hoffman (Oxford: The Littman Library of Jewish Civilization, 2008), 454–85.
[51] See Hava Tirosh-Samuelson, "Gender in Jewish Mysticism," in *Jewish Mysticism and Kabbalah: New Insights and Scholarship*, ed. Frederick E. Greenspahn (New York: New York University Press, 2011), 191–230 and the research discussed therein.
[52] See Yochanan Muffs, "Joy and Love as Metaphorical Expressions of Willingness and Spontaneity in Cuneiform, Ancient Hebrew, and Related Literatures," in *Christianity, Judaism and Other Greco-Roman Cults, for Morton Smith at Sixty*, ed. Jacob Neusner (Leiden: Brill, 1975) 3: 1–36.

as the Holy Blessed One (*ha-qadosh barukh hu*) and his hypostatic mate as The Assembly of Israel (*kenesset yisra'el*),[53] as well as *Shekhinah*, which is additionally understood as God's presence. In numerous talmudic and midrashic texts the Rabbis imagine and describe *kenesset yisra'el* speaking with God or being contrasted with him.[54] In these cases, although it is possible that it is referring to a mythical amalgamate of the Jewish people, there is reason to believe that the early kabbalists did not merely read their theosophical systems back into these sources, but rather these sources, in their original context, already reflect a hypostatic understanding of this entity.

Shekhinah undergoes the most radical transformation within Kabbalah. From its rabbinic origins as designating the divine presence and only sometimes a hypostatic entity, it is transformed within Jewish philosophical literature to be synonymous with the *Kavod* (Glory), *Sofia* (Wisdom), and other entities, and in the same fashion is understood as a created entity, through which God bridges the metaphysical divide. This move is crucial for its further development within kabbalistic literature. As part of its philosophical makeover, *Shekhinah* is stripped of her mythical content and is absorbed within the reigning medieval schemata becoming identified with the Active Intellect. As we have seen with other aspects of the Godhead, the kabbalists took a different approach. Instead of depriving God of the mythical and anthropomorphic elements, they enhanced them and began to coordinate and systematize them, thereby forming the Godhead. The *Shekhinah* within this reformation became the tenth and last *sefirah*, the opening onto the material world.[55]

This liminal placement of this entity was crucial for the dynamics involved within theurgic and mystical activities, of the descent of the

---

[53] On this term in particular in rabbinic literature and its development in Kabbalah, see Moshe Idel, *Kabbalah and Eros* (New Haven, CT: Yale University Press, 2005), 26–30; Moshe Idel, "The Triangle Family: Sources for the Feminine Concept of God in Early Kabbala," in *Tov Elem: Memory, Community and Gender in Early Medieval and Early Modern Jewish Societies – Essays in Honor of Robert Bonfil*, eds. Elisheva Baumgarten, Amnon Raz-Krakotzkin, and Roni Weinstein (Jerusalem: Bialik Institute, 2011), 92–100 [Hebrew].

[54] See for example, Mekhilta de-Rabbi Yishmael 15: 2: 2; Exodus Rabbah 33: 3; b. Sanhedrin 102a.

[55] It should be noted that the term *Shekhinah* was used far less frequently than that of *malkhut*; see Daniel Abrams, *Kabbalistic Manuscripts and Textual Theory: Methodologies of Textual Scholarship and Editorial Practice in the Study of Jewish Mysticism* (Jerusalem: The Hebrew University Magnes Press, 2010), 119.

divine powers and the ascent of the kabbalist. This was also a natural development of its previous role as a sub-divine entity. Furthermore, its strong identification with the holy spirit, which also underwent a philosophication, allowed it to be readily available for this precise position. The greater feminine features,[56] attributed to *Shekhinah*, are believed by some scholars to have developed in tandem with theological developments within the Christian world.[57] The feminization of this *sefirah* led to important consequences.

The incorporation of the feminine within the Godhead is one of the major expressions of the dynamic fluid nature of the divine; simultaneously it reintroduced certain mythic-erotic elements into the divine persona. Furthermore, the raising of this entity into the Godhead, after it had already been identified with the Jewish collective, was a major force behind the kabbalistic ontological understanding of the Jewish people.[58] With this transformation we arrive at the completion of the kabbalistic statement, "God, Torah, and the Jewish people are one."

COMPLEX DIVINE UNITY

These hypostatic entities discussed above complicated the monotheistic picture presented by Jewish philosophers. God's unity as understood by the philosophers differs tremendously from that which can be found in the Bible (such as Deuteronomy 6:4: "The Lord is one") or in rabbinic literature. Whereas rabbinic literature is more focused on God being the only true and *singular* God, Jewish philosophers were focused on the understanding of the divine *simple* unity. While the Rabbis described God in semi-corporealistic form, the Jewish philosophers viewed this as potentially undermining God's simple unity and therefore considered this form of expression as allegorical. It is on this issue that the kabbalists offer a very complex and dialectical understanding of unity which allows for a dynamic Godhead that nonetheless remains monotheistic

---

[56] Urbach holds that *Shekhinah* within rabbinic literature is not feminine or hypostatic, *Sages*, 63–65; for a contrasting view, see Idel, "Family," 99–100.

[57] See Arthur Green, "Shekhinah, The Virgin Mary, and the Song of Songs: Reflections on a Kabbalistic Symbol in Historical Context," *AJS Review* 26 (2002): 1–52; Peter Schaefer, "Daughter, Sister, Bride, and Mother: Images of the Femininity of God in the Early Kabbala," *Journal of the American Academy of Religion* 68 (2000): 221–42. Cf. Wolfson, *Language*, 455–56 n. 224, 486 n. 191, 499–500 n. 111.

[58] On this point, see Elliot R. Wolfson, *Venturing Beyond: Law and Morality in Kabbalistic Mysticism* (Oxford: Oxford University Press, 2006), 17–185.

God. This matter is heavily related to the previously discussed issue of God's apophatic and kataphatic nature.

ONE GOD, THE DIVINE FAMILY, AND HIS LIVING PERSONALITIES

One of the most important features of the kabbalistic Godhead is the fact that, despite its apparent dynamic diversity, it is in fact united, organic, and is to be considered as "one." All kabbalistic discussions of the Godhead stress this ontological unity, especially in light of accusations to the contrary. The polytheistic charges against the kabbalistic conception are primarily based on the (mis)understanding of the kabbalist's goal of harmonistically unifying the Godhead. As we will discuss below, the Godhead is conceived as generally being in a disharmonious state, due to God's and Israel's exilic condition; it is upon the kabbalist to perform the commandments and thereby redeem God. Following the incorporation of the gendered mythopoetic rendering of the Godhead, these states of exile and redemption were primarily represented through this symbolism of sexual union and abandonment.[59]

The dynamic state of the Godhead is affected by diurnal and nocturnal cycles, the rhyme and rhythm of the week and annual holidays. Unlike the perfect unknowable God of the philosophers, the Godhead ebbs and flows together with the national-historical narrative of the Jewish people and the personal-temporal current of the individual Jew as they traverse the cyclic course of the seasons. Examples are generally found regarding the *Shekhinah*, the feminine entity separated from the Godhead when in a state of disharmony. For instance in the *Zohar* and *Tiqqunei Zohar*, the *Shekhinah* is in exile at night, searching for her mate to conjoin with her and raise her from the dust; she unites with her husband, the Holy One, blessed be He, on Sabbath Eve, through the corporeal intercourse of the kabbalist with his wife at the same time;[60] she is found in a state of uncleanliness before the holiday of *Shavu'ot*, the seven weeks after *Pesaḥ*, paralleling the seven days of uncleanliness during which a wife is not permitted to her husband; and consequently, when the Jewish people are redeemed from exile, she is redeemed as well and the Godhead is forever united. All of the actions comprise different rituals

---

[59] See n. 52, regarding gender and Kabbalah studies.
[60] See Wolfson, *Language*, 296–332.

performed by the kabbalist, but it is important that each ritual is performed at the correct time in the correct fashion, thereby bringing harmony to the supernal realm, as well as mystical experience induced by the kabbalist himself, expressed through such terms as the overflow of the holy spirit, integration into the Godhead, the reception of an additional soul, and the like.[61]

Alongside the symbolic sexual relationship of *Shekhinah* and other *sefirot*, there exists a further dynamism, that of divine family, generally portrayed through a tetrad of *sefirot*.[62] The father, ḥokhmah, the mother, *binah*, the son *tif'eret*, and the daughter *malkhut*. The relations that accompany these *sefirot* are somewhat troubling, as ultimately the daughter and the son are sexually paired. Because of the incestuous nature of this familial relationship, the kabbalists stated, "that which is forbidden below, is permitted above."[63] These personas are paralleled by other structures, such as that of the patriarchs, Abraham (ḥesed), Isaac (gevurah), and Jacob (tif'eret), who are joined by *Shekhinah* to create a "chariot" for God to sit upon and act through. The multiple and complex symbolic systems that exist within the sefirotic realm create the variegated and rich mythopoetic landscape within which the Godhead operates. These correlations also allow for the adaptation of pre-existing biblical and rabbinical literature to have semantically new meanings within this new setting. Stories concerning the patriarchs are no longer just about the flesh and blood biblical characters, but rather are describing supernal actions and dynamics. Classic midrashic allegories that referenced kings, sons, wives, and daughters, were able to be reformatted within the sefirotic pleroma, bringing to light hitherto unexplored implications and conceptualizations. Furthermore, these relations are fluid: while the daughter may be the lowest in the hierarchy, when paired with the son, she ascends up the chain, eventually being reunited with the father from whom she came. As Scholem wrote:

> The Sefiroth of Jewish theosophy have an existence of their own; they form combinations, they illuminate each other, they ascend

---

[61] See n. 20.
[62] See Wolfson, *Language*, 155–57, 326, regarding the tetrad and triad structure concerning the divine family.
[63] See Ruth Kara Ivanov Kaniel, *Holiness and Transgression*, trans. Eugene D. Matanky (Boston, MA: Academic Studies Press, 2016), 49, 124–45.

and descend. They are far from being static. Although each has its ideal place in the hierarchy, the lowest can under a certain aspect appear as the highest. In other words, what we have here is something like a real process of life in God.[64]

THE DARK SIDE: THE "OTHER SIDE" (SIṬRA AḤRA)

No discussion of the kabbalistic Godhead is complete without discussing the problem of evil. A popular medieval theological conception of God is that he is omnibenevolent, and thus evil is fictitious at best, lacking all true ontological status.[65] This conception was shared by the kabbalists to some extent; however, their own understandings of God were more complex. As we have seen, the emanation of the *sefirot* from their ultimate source within the *Ein Sof* eventually leads to the formation of the terrestrial dimension. Yet, within this dimension evil is pervasive. The question then becomes if everything emanates from the Godhead, how does evil come to be? It must be that evil is within the Godhead itself!

The kabbalists possess a range of opinions regarding the specifics of demonic emanation,[66] but importantly this emanation also consists of ten "*sefirot*" in triune form; in other words, a parallelism is created between the two configurations by the zoharic authors.[67] Another common feature among the kabbalists' conceptions is that the "left side" of the sefirotic tree, specifically the *sefirah* of *din*, is associated with evil, as well as the feminine.[68] Lastly, the demonic forces are often understood as swaying the *Shekhinah* toward them, or even taking her hostage. These demonic forces are related to previous traditions concerning demons that plague the Jewish people, specifically, Samael and Lilith.[69]

---

[64] Scholem, *Major Trends*, 224–25.
[65] Scholem, *On the Mystical Shape of the Godhead*, 58.
[66] See Elliot R. Wolfson, *Luminal Darkness: Imaginal Gleanings from Zoharic Literature* (Oxford: Oneworld Publications, 2007), 2.
[67] The most explicit accounting of this emanation is that found in the Cohen Brothers' Kabbalah, see Gershom Scholem, *Qabbalot R. Ya'aqov ve-R. Yiṣḥaq benei R. Ya'aqov ha-Qohen* (Jerusalem: Ha-Madpis, 1927) [Hebrew]. In the *Zohar*, see Tishby, *Wisdom*, 2:447–546.
[68] See the many studies of Elliot Wolfson regarding this phenomenon, Wolfson, *Luminal Darkness*, 1–55.
[69] See Joseph Dan, "Samael, Lilith, and the Concept of Evil in Early Kabbalah," in *Essential Papers on Kabbalah*, ed. Lawrence Fine (New York: New York University Press, 1995), 154–78; Wolfson, *Venturing Beyond*, 93, 107, 148–50. On demons in

If Samael is conjoined with *Shekhinah* instead of the Holy One, blessed be He, then the demonic forces suction off the divine powers and channel them toward evil. This imagery is connected to the previously discussed sexual symbolism, in which *Shekhinah* is portrayed as a wayward wife, just as Israel is depicted within classic prophetic literature, such as the Book of Hosea. The terrestrial correlation to the wayward *Shekhinah* is Jewish promiscuity with non-Jewish or menstruating women. The kabbalist must direct his energies toward rescuing the "damsel in distress." Ultimately, evil is shown to lack ontological character and is reincorporated within the Infinite.

Now that we have discussed the complex inner workings of the Godhead, we can raise the question of "what is the relationship between the infinite and the *sefirot*?" This question is referred to within kabbalistic literature as the relation between "the essence and the vessels." Is the relationship between them one of identification, in which the Infinite is entirely materialized through and identified with the *sefirot*, thereby creating a positive understanding of the Infinite, or is it beyond the vessels, never fully identified with them, and rather only acts through them, thereby allowing it to remain transcendent and completely unknowable? This question is never fully answered within kabbalistic literature, the most famous discussion being that of Moses Cordovero in *Pardes Rimonim*; however, multiple scholars have mapped out the implications and different understandings of this relationship, which we will now dsicuss.

KATAPHATIC-IMMANENT AND APOPHATIC-TRANSCENDENT CONCEPTIONS OF THE GODHEAD

A fundamental issue within kabbalistic literature regarding the Godhead is the relation between the Infinite (*Ein Sof*) and *sefirot*. This issue is complicated, as different strands of kabbalistic thought formulate this issue in contradictive, or at the very least, complex terms.[70] An early scholar of Kabbalah, Joshua Abelson, wrote:

---

general, see Esther Liebes, ed., *Devils, Demons and Souls: Essays on Demonology by Gershom Scholem* (Jerusalem: Yad Izhak Ben-Zvi and the Hebrew University of Jerusalem, 2004) [Hebrew].

[70] The famed systematic-kabbalist, R. Moses Cordovero, dedicated much of his writing, both in *Pardes Rimonim* and *Sefer Elimah*, to this matter. See Joseph Ben Shlomo, *The Mystical Theology of Moses Cordovero* (Jerusalem: Bialik Institute, 1965), 87–169 [Hebrew].

God, in the Zohar, is the great Unknowable, the Supreme Incomprehensible. God is exalted above human understanding; the depths of the Divine wisdom are beyond human penetration ... . Here we have the doctrine of the Divine Transcendency *par excellence*. Nevertheless, God in the Zohar is very knowable, very fathomable. The universe as well as man's heart reveal His infinite power and infinite love. Nay, even the human organs and limbs reflect certain static and dynamic characteristics of Deity. The world is an image of the Divine. There is constant and conscious interaction between "the above" [the celestial kingdom] and "the below" [the mundane kingdom]. Here we have the doctrine of the Divine immanence *par excellence*. It is the ceaseless interweaving of these two doctrines in the pages of the Zohar that supplies the book with its uncompromisingly spiritual atmosphere.[71]

Gershom Scholem in his analysis of *Ein Sof* traces its apophatic character to the thought of R. Isaac the Blind, in his commentary on *Sefer Yetzirah*,[72] in which philosophical conceptualizations of the divine are combined with the sefirotic system,[73] thereby granting the Infinite an apophatic character as is commonly found among medieval Jewish rational philosophy. Scholem's conception of *Ein Sof* as apophatic and transcendent was also heavily influenced by his understanding of Jewish mysticism as incapable of attaining the highest mystical function, *unio mystica*,[74] since a pure transcendent being cannot be united with in any manner. Scholem's studies of *Ein Sof* were not monolithic and he distinguished between different kabbalistic doctrines, as he acknowledged differences between its conceptualization in different strata of the *Zohar*,[75] as well as its extremely transcendent nature in Lurianic Kabbalah, in which *Ein Sof* takes on a much more

---

[71] Joshua Abelson, "Introduction," in *The Zohar*, trans. Maurice Simon. (London: Soncino Press, 1931–1934), xvi.

[72] See Scholem: *Origins of the Kabbalah*, 261–89; *Kabbalah*, 88–105; *Major Trends*, 207–43.

[73] For more on this shift and a re-analysis, which demonstrates the kataphatic nature of *Ein Sof* in this context, see Sandra Valabregue-Perry, "The Concept of Infinity (*Eyn-sof*) and the Rise of Theosophical Kabbalah," *Jewish Quarterly Review* 102, no. 3 (2012): 405–30.

[74] On this, see Moshe Idel, *Kabbalah: New Perspectives*, 59–73. See also my own discussion of mystical union in Jewish mysticism, "*And They Shall be as One Flesh*".

[75] See Tishby, *The Wisdom of the Zohar*, 246–51.

transcendent character.[76] This apophatic character is well characterized by Azriel of Gerona's statement in *Bi'ur Eser Sefirot*: "Know that *En-Sof* cannot be an object of thought, let alone of speech, even though there is an indication of it in every thing, for there is nothing beyond it. Consequently, there is no letter, no name, no writing, and no word that can comprise it."[77] Although Scholem and his students recognized that *Ein Sof* may have more positive formulations, nonetheless they either resorted to dogmatic statements of an apophatic nature,[78] or portrayed those as exceptions and minority views.[79]

Scholem's characterization of *Ein Sof* as *deus absconditus* did not go unchallenged. The next generation of scholars, notably Moshe Idel and Elliot R. Wolfson, re-examined the primary material, both through phenomenological and textual lenses. Whereas Scholem placed an emphasis on the conceptualization of an "apophatic" *Ein Sof* transcending the sefirotic realm,[80] which he believed to be common to all kabbalists, Idel, in a number of studies, has problematized this statement. He

---

[76] Scholem's conceptualization of *Ein Sof* was followed by his student Isaiah Tishby in *The Wisdom of the Zohar*, 232–55, as well as Tishby's student Moshe Hallamish in *An Introduction to the Kabbalah*, trans. Ruth Bar-Ilan and Ora Wiskind-Elper (Albany: SUNY Press, 1999), 121–25.

[77] See Azriel of Gerona, *Bi'ur Eser Sefirot*, ed. Moshe Shatz (Jerusalem: Mahon Pithi Megadim, 1997), 35. As translated in Tishby, *Wisdom of the Zohar*, 234.

[78] See Scholem, *Major Trends*, 215: "For, to repeat, the Divine Being Himself cannot be expressed. All that can be expressed are His symbols."

[79] See Tishby, *Wisdom of the Zohar*, 245.

[80] See Scholem, *Kabbalah*, 88: "God in Himself, the absolute Essence, lies beyond any speculative or even ecstatic comprehension. The attitude of the Kabbalah toward God may be defined as a mystical agnosticism ... In order to express this unknowable aspect of the Divine the early kabbalists of Provence and Spain coined the term *Ein-Sof* ("Infinite")"; Scholem, *Origins of the Kabbalah*, 267–68: "['en sof] does not present itself so much as a negative attribute of the deity within the framework of an intellectual knowledge of God, but rather as a symbol of the absolute impossibility of such knowledge"; Scholem, *On the Mystical Shape of the Godhead*, 38: "The underlying principle might be formulated as follows: 'Ein-Sof, the Infinite—that is, the concealed Godhead—dwells unknowable in the depth of its own being, without form or shape. It is beyond all cognitive statements, and can only be described through negation—indeed, as the negation of all negations. No images can depict it, nor can it be named by any name. By contrast, the Active Divinity has a mystical shape which can be conveyed by images and names." Summarized by his student Isaiah Tishby, *The Wisdom of the Zohar*, 237: "At the very beginning of the new speculative kabbalah, *En-Sof*, which represented the God of Plotinus and his followers, was joined to the system of the *sefirot*, which was the Jewish version of the Gnostic *pleroma*, and so the kabbalistic mystery of the divine, comprising the hidden God and the revealed God, came into being."

has demonstrated that the realm of *Ein Sof* was understood by some kabbalists as consisting of an anthropomorphic sefirotic realm itself![81] Through the examination of early kabbalistic material Idel provided a polyphonic view of this concept.

The understanding of *Ein Sof* as an apophatic entity has been challenged as well by Wolfson on phenomenological grounds. He has come to term his conception of *Ein Sof* as a "meontological" being(-not),[82] which is to be differentiated from the nothingness of non-being. Through his understanding of the divine pleroma as the site of the *mundus imaginalis*, in which "the formless may assume form in the form that has been rendered formless,"[83] Wolfson comes to a paradoxical conceptualization of *Ein Sof*, stating that it "both is what it is not and is not what it is because it neither is what it is not nor is not what it is."[84] Meaning, that *Ein Sof* is a chasm in which "abiding and nonabiding are one and the same."[85] In other words, *Ein Sof* is the essence which refuses to be reified or essentialized, transcending the dichotomy of being and non-being. Owing to its utter unity, it transcends conventional understandings of unity, for unity denotes duality, whereas this unity is one that does not and therefore is even beyond unity. By transcending even transcendence, *Ein Sof* is rendered agnostically immanent.[86] Exemplifying this type of understanding is an anonymous text on the nature of the *sefirot*: "One who says that *ein sof* is [encompassed] with the *sefirot* or remains outside the *sefirot*; it is all heresy. Know this."[87]

---

[81] See Moshe Idel, "The Image of the Man Above the *Sefirot*: R. David ben Yehuda he-Ḥasid's Theosophy of Ten Supernal *Ṣaḥṣaḥot* and Its Reverberations," *Kabbalah: Journal for the Study of Jewish Mystical Texts* 20 (2009): 181–212. For Idel's more pointed criticism of Scholem's position, see Idel, "On Binary 'Beginnings' in Kabbalah Scholarship," *Jewish History* 18 (2004): 319–26.

[82] See Elliot R. Wolfson, *Open Secret: Postmessianic Messianism and the Mystical Revision of Menaḥem Mendel Schneerson* (New York: Columbia University Press, 2009), 66–129; Elliot R. Wolfson, "Nihilating Nonground and the Temporal Sway of Becoming," *Angelaki: Journal of Theoretical Humanities* 17, no. 3 (2012): 31–45. Although he only began using this term to characterize *Ein Sof* in his book *Open Secret*, the conceptualization is already present in his earlier works: Elliot R. Wolfson, "Negative Theology and Positive Assertion in the Early Kabbalah," *Da'at* 32–33 (1994): v–xxii; Wolfson, *Language*, 100–05. Lastly, see his discussion regarding *Ein Sof* and temporality, Elliot R. Wolfson, *Alef, Mem, Tau: Kabbalistic Musings on Time, Truth, and Death* (Berkeley: University of California Press, 2006), 61–117.

[83] Wolfson, *Language*, 538, n. 352.   [84] Wolfson, "Nihilating Nonground," 39.

[85] Wolfson, *Open Secret*, 114.   [86] Ibid., 47, 50.

[87] Oxford Opp. 487, 57a; JTS 1896, 69a. As cited in Hartley Lachter, *Kabbalistic Revolution: Reimagining Judaism in Medieval Spain* (New Brunswick: Rutgers University Press, 2014), 53.

MAN AND THE GODHEAD: MYSTICAL UNION

As I have alluded to above, man is a microcosm and living organic extension of the Godhead. We have repeatedly seen the important theurgic role that man plays within the structure of the Godhead, whether it be through his elevating the *Shekhinah*, the corporeal performance of specific commandments that strengthen the corresponding "divine limbs," or the general unification of the *sefirot* through prayer and Torah study. However, I have not thoroughly explored the corresponding dynamic, that of mystical union. Man's contact with the divine realm does not only affect the Godhead, but also causes a transformation within man's being. This is due to the kabbalistic conception, explicitly described in sixteenth-century Kabbalah, of continua and channels that connect man and God in an ontological fashion. These channels may be clogged depending on man's transgression, or freely flowing depending on his merits; however, they are always metaphysically present. I will now discuss the different ways in which mystical union has been conceived in academic scholarship.

The divergent conceptions of the Godhead, discussed above, spawned different opinions and conceptualizations of mystical union. A common schema for all kabbalists is that the divine essence is encapsulated in the ineffable 4-letter name, which is revealed through the 22 letters of the Hebrew alphabet embodied in the text of the Torah and which act as the substratum of the spatiotemporal world. Furthermore, the human body is understood as a microcosm of the divine macrocosm, in which the *sefirot* correlate with the limbs of the corporeal body. In my own studies, I have traced the evolution and development of integrative mystical language, from Philo through classic Kabbalah.[88] However, the possibility of mystical union and its phenomenological representation is a point of dispute among scholars.

As mentioned above, Scholem categorically stated that Jewish mysticism did not contain a state of mystical union.[89] This view is heavily influenced by Hermann Cohen, the leading Jewish intellectual of Germany, who designated Judaism as the religion that demarcated between the realm of transcendence and immanence, thereby fulfilling the ethical call, allowing for what "is" to strive to

---

[88] See Adam Afterman, *Devequt: Mystical Intimacy in Medieval Jewish Thought* (Los Angeles: Cherub Press, 2011) [Hebrew]; Afterman, *"And They Shall Be One Flesh"*.

[89] For Idel's criticism of this stance, see *Kabbalah: New Perspectives*, 59; Idel, *Enchanted Chains*, 31–75; Idel, *Studies in Ecstatic Kabbalah*, 1–33.

be what "ought."⁹⁰ Scholem claimed that the highest mystical experience allowed by the theological constraints of Judaism is one of communion, or *devequt*, and not *unio mystica*.⁹¹

This opinion was first challenged to some degree by Scholem's student Isaiah Tishby.⁹² The true challenge came from Moshe Idel in his path-breaking work *Kabbalah: New Perspectives*. Idel challenged Scholem's entire edifice by calling attention to "peripheral" figures and kabbalistic systems, namely Abraham Abulafia's school of prophetic-ecstatic Kabbalah. He demonstrated that within this school there are clear cases of mystical union.⁹³ In this regard Idel was followed by both Elliot Wolfson and Haviva Pedaya regarding the significance of ecstatic unitive experiences in Kabbalah, both in Geronese Kabbalah,⁹⁴ as well as classic "theosophic" texts, such as the *Zohar*.⁹⁵ Idel's conceptualization of mystical union in ecstatic kabbalistic literature is, as a whole, a kataphatic one. Abulafia understood mystical union as the integration of the human intellect with the divine or Active Intellect, rather than a form of unknowing and unbecoming, mystical union attained through conscious mystical techniques and knowing. The state of union brings about visualizations and states of prophecy, positive phenomena, rather than states of nullification.⁹⁶

In my own work, I have demonstrated that mystical union originated in the mystical theology of the Jewish Hellenistic philosopher of the first century Philo of Alexandria,⁹⁷ and I have analyzed the linguistic development of diverse and varied locutions concerning this concept that were utilized by Jewish mystics for the evolution of their unique

---

⁹⁰ See Afterman, *"And They Shall Be One Flesh"*, 6–16; Ron Margolin, *The Human Temple: Religious Interiorization and the Structuring of Inner Life in Early Hasidism* (Jerusalem: The Hebrew University Magnes Press, 2005), 6–33 [Hebrew].

⁹¹ Scholem, *Major Trends*, 55; Gershom Scholem, *The Messianic Idea in Judaism and Other Essays on Jewish Spirituality* (New York: Schocken Books, 1971), 203–27.

⁹² Tishby, *Wisdom of the Zohar*, 985–87.

⁹³ See Idel, *Kabbalah: New Perspective*, 59–64; Afterman, *"And They Shall be as One Flesh"*, 151–70.

⁹⁴ Haviva Pedaya, *Vision and Speech: Models of Revelatory Experience in Jewish Mysticism* (Los Angeles: Cherub Press, 2002), 150 [Hebrew].

⁹⁵ See Wolfson, *Through a Speculum That Shines: Vision and Imagination in Medieval Jewish Mysticism* (Princeton: Princeton University Press, 1994), 374; Wolfson, *Language*, 246.

⁹⁶ See Idel, *The Mystical Experience in Abraham Abulafia*, 8, 64, 83, 124–32.

⁹⁷ Adam Afterman, "From Philo to Plotinus: The Emergence of Mystical Union," *Journal of Religion* 93, no. 2 (2013): 177–96.

forms of unitive mysticism. Much of my studies have discussed the complex and intricate ways in which man and God are found in a dynamic organic system, which allows for the ascent of the mystic and the descent of the divine overflow. The mechanics involved in different stages and states of mystical union have varied across the history of Jewish mysticism and, through their investigation, we are better able to understand key philosophical and theological turns within this tradition.[98]

Elliot Wolfson's emphasis on the hyperlinguistic manifestation of the world and God allows for the conceptualization of all acts of Torah study as sites for mystical union, in which the corporeal body undergoes a process of textualization and the divine becomes embodied within. However, due to his meontological understanding of *Ein Sof*, mystical union is phenomenologically different. What is union with "the nothing that is not even [nothing] and therefore more than nothing"?[99] Wolfson discusses, albeit regarding the identification (and differentiation) of God and the world, a state of "reciprocal transcendence" in which "God and world abide in the difference of their belonging-together, indeed they belong together precisely in virtue of their difference."[100] Following Wolfson, I would like to suggest that *the moment of mystical union* with the absolute nothingness, which is more than nothing and therefore less than nothing, is to transcend the binary model of union and communion, in which one's essence is transformed into its always already state of nothingness. However, this is not as a "final" state, not as a singular moment of absolute illumination, but rather as a perpetual dynamism and therefore is never fully realized, except as that which can never be fully realized, for the moment it is realized it begins again, but anew, the running and returning of *ratso va-shov*, which **is itself** the state of union, a union beyond union.

CONCLUDING REMARKS: PHILOSOPHICAL LANGUAGE AND MYSTICAL INTERPRETATION

The development of kabbalistic theosophy should be understood in light of the medieval theological and philosophical revolution. The

---

[98] Afterman, *Devequt*; Afterman, *"And They Shall Be One Flesh"*; Adam Afterman, "'As in Water, Face Reflects Face: Mystical Union in *Sefer Reshit Chochmah*," *Da'at* 84 (2017): 155–82 [Hebrew].

[99] Wolfson, *Open Secret*, 75.   [100] Ibid., 91.

move from the biblical God to the kabbalistic Godhead runs through the prism of medieval philosophy. The philosophical transformation of biblical and rabbinic Judaism, which emptied certain terms of their original meaning and semantically charted them along new trajectories, allowed for these terms to be further developed along diverse lines of thought. While philosophical thought aligned the God of the Bible with the God of the Philosophers, kabbalistic thought further explored the midrashic mode of interpretation, which was able to take more liberty than it previously had, due to the allegoric interpretation of the philosophers. In other words, the kabbalists built upon the allegorical model, adding a distinctive symbolic-theosophic structure to their interpretations. For example, the Shekinah's identification with the Active Intellect in medieval Jewish philosophy is further developed with her role as the "mouthpiece" of the Godhead. For in the kabbalistic conception she is not only the allegorical opening point of influx, she is also symbolically related to other openings found throughout biblical literature, thereby enhancing the theosophical understanding of the Bible.[101]

Once God as a theological idea was introduced into Jewish thought, the path toward the emergence of the Godhead—a synthesis of the philosophical God, the metaphysical structures of emanation and overflow, and the biblical and midrashic content—was opened. Without the theological and philosophical radical shift toward the idea of God as a being of simple unity, the kabbalistic reaction, which was simultaneously a creative hermeneutical shift of its own, would not have been possible. Yet, since this theosophical conceptualization of the Godhead within Judaism occurred following the canonization of biblical and classic rabbinic texts, as well as decisive Jewish philosophers, it was never able to take an absolute authoritative role within Jewish thought and represents only one of the various understandings of the Jewish God.

---

[101] Regarding the allegorical interpretation, see Warren Zev Harvey "On Maimonides' Allegorical Readings of Scripture" in *Interpretation and Allegory: Antiquity to the Modern Period*, ed., Jon Whitman (Leiden: Brill, 2000), 181–88. Regarding the symbolic interpretation, see Oded Yisraeli, *Temple Portals: Studies in Aggadah and Midrash in the Zohar*, trans. Liat Keren (Berlin: De Gruyter and Magnes, 2016). See also Idel, *Absorbing Perfections*, 272–351.

Selected Further Reading

Afterman, Adam. *"And They Shall Be One Flesh": On the Language of Mystical Union in Judaism*. Leiden: Brill, 2016.

Afterman, Adam. "From Philo to Plotinus: The Emergence of Mystical Union." *Journal of Religion* 93.2 (2013): 177–96.

Ginsburg, Elliot K, *The Sabbath in the Classic Kabbalah*. Albany: SUNY Press, 1989.

Green, Arthur. *Keter: The Crown of God in Early Jewish Mysticism*. Princeton: Princeton University Press, 1997.

Hallamish, Moshe. *An Introduction to the Kabbalah*. Translated by Ruth Bar-Ilan and Ora Wiskind-Elper. Albany: SUNY Press, 1999.

Idel, Moshe. *Enchanted Chains: Techniques and Rituals in Jewish Mysticism*. Los Angeles: Cherub Press, 2005.

Idel, Moshe. *Kabbalah: New Perspectives*. New Haven, CT: Yale University Press, 1988.

Scholem, Gershom. *On the Kabbalah and Its Symbolism*. Translated by Ralph Manheim. New York: Schocken Books, 1965.

Scholem, Gershom. *On the Mystical Shape of the Godhead: Basic Concepts in the Kabbalah*. Translated by Joachim Neugroschel. New York: Schocken Books, 1991.

Tishby, Isaiah. *The Wisdom of the Zohar*. Translated by David Goldstein. Oxford: The Littman Library of Jewish Civilization, 1989.

Weiss, Tzahi. *"Sefer Yeṣirah" and Its Contexts: Other Jewish Voices*. Philadelphia: University of Pennsylvania Press, 2018

Wolfson, Elliot R. *Abraham Abulafia – Kabbalist and Prophet: Hermeneutics, Theosophy, and Theurgy*. Los Angeles: Cherub Press, 2000.

Wolfson, Elliot R. *Alef, Mem, Tau: Kabbalistic Musings on Time, Truth, and Death*. Berkeley: University of California Press, 2006.

Wolfson, Elliot R. "Negative Theology and Positive Assertion in the Early Kabbalah." *Da'at* 32–33 (1994): v–xxii.

Wolfson, Elliot R. *Through a Speculum That Shines: Vision and Imagination in Medieval Jewish Mysticism*. Princeton: Princeton University Press, 1994.

PART III
MODERN

9 R. Kook: A This-Worldly Mystic

TAMAR ROSS

INTRODUCTION

Rabbi Abraham Isaac Kook [R. Kook] (1865–1935) is arguably the most audacious, original, and profound thinker emerging from the ranks of Orthodox Judaism in the modern period.[1] His personal charisma, gentle piety, and intellectual prowess already achieved acclaim during his youth and the earlier years of his rabbinic career in Lithuania. During this time, he composed several legal and moral treatises, commentaries, and sermons, and contributed articles to rabbinic journals that occasionally engaged in the confrontation between traditionalism, influences of the Enlightenment, and nascent Zionist efforts toward national revival. However, the catalyst for the unique body of thought with which he is now predominantly associated was his decision to immigrate to Palestine in 1904, first accepting the position of religious authority of Jaffa and the surrounding Jewish settlements, and subsequently serving as Chief Ashkenazi Rabbi of Jerusalem and of all of British mandatory Palestine. These years were marked by an extraordinary flourishing of the spirit as evidenced in his spiritual diaries, which bear witness to an intensely rich inner life, suffused with a palpable sense of holiness and occasional mystic/prophetic experience, intensified even further during an intermittent period of exile in Europe where he was unexpectedly stranded due to the eruption of World War I.

The paradox confronting R. Kook with full force upon his arrival in Jaffa was that the chief facilitators of what appeared to be first steps toward fulfillment of the traditional messianic dream (settlement of the land, ingathering of the Exiles, and release from the yoke of foreign rule)

---

[1] For an incisive personal and intellectual biography, see Yehudah Mirsky, *Mystic in a Time of Revolution* (New Haven, CT, and London: Yale University Press, 2014)

were avowed atheists, consciously rejecting the religious legacy of their forefathers. R. Kook found it difficult to dismiss the passionate idealism and moral fervor of young secular pioneers struggling to ensure the physical welfare of the Jewish people, and to create a social order predicated upon the ideals of justice, equality, and political independence. His solution to the dilemma, first explicated in one of the earliest articles he wrote after settling in Palestine,[2] was to reinterpret the talmudic statement that the Messiah will arrive in a generation that is *kulo hayav* or *kulo zakkai* (completely guilty or completely innocent)[3] to mean that the generation will not be either *hayav* or *zakkai*, but both at the same time.

On the surface, R. Kook argues, the current generation of Zionists is totally wanting; its professed stance is overt brazenness toward Heaven. But this is so only because the perpetrators of this militantly antireligious view do not recognize the subconsciously religious nature of their motives. Discrepancy between their high moral standards and organized religion as popularly conceived leads them to chafe against a diaspora mentality that devalues immersion in the practical affairs of everyday life and regards universal considerations of social and physical well-being, as well as the creative urge for self-expression, as irrelevant to the divine. Their rebellion against halakhah is likewise merely the flip side of a contemporary yearning for the breadth of prophetic vision.[4] Viewed from the vantage point of eternity, such a generation is *kulo zakkai*, reflecting an intuitive desire to extend their spiritual horizons beyond concern for personal reward and punishment and narrow observance of mitsvot to collective expression in all facets of life. R. Kook was convinced that responding to this desire would inevitably lead to a more satisfactory formulation of what faith in God really means—a knowledge previously held by rare individuals, but now demanded by the Jewish masses and eventually by the nations of the world at large. Once leaders of the professedly religious camp would face the challenge of secularism, and reformulate their expression of faith in less narrowly clerical terms, the antireligious trappings of Jewish nationalism would fall away, revealing its redemptive message to all.

---

[2] Rav Kook "Hador,"*Ikkevei ha-Tzon* (1985): 107–16.   [3] TB, Sanhedrin 98a.
[4] "The Sage is More Important than the Prophet," *Orot* (1969): 120–21; English translation in *Abraham Isaac Kook – The Lights of Penitence, the Moral Principles, Lights of Holiness, Essays, Letters, and Poems*, ed. Ben Zion Bokser (New York/ Ramsey/ Toronto: Paulist Press, 1978), 253–55.

In the interim, appreciating their essentially God-oriented character justified tolerance, cooperation, and even loving embrace of the secularists, regarding their rebellion as a spiritual blessing in disguise.

R. Kook's conciliatory message and sense that his generation was witnessing "the footsteps of the Messiah" were attuned to the spiritual and sociological needs of his time. Addressing a community riddled with tensions between the pioneering spirit of an emerging nationalism and the weight of 2,000 years of exilic Judaism, his celebration of the fullness of life engaged with an earthy romantic spirit fueling the rebellion of Zionist pioneers against the cerebral ascetic nature of diaspora Judaism with idealization of the "new Hebrew" living the life of the land. Identifying the Zionist project with traditional messianic visions encouraged interaction between diverse factions and opinions,[5] seeking and discovering holiness even in the mundane.[6] It also allowed for a positive attitude to liberal ideas of autonomy, individual expression, self-fulfillment, and a qualified degree of pluralism within a communitarian ethos.[7] But while R. Kook's utopian vision, and the special role of the Jewish people in this process of its fulfillment, serves as the chief interest and cause for celebration of his thought to the present day, the truth is that his worldview harbors more radical theological implications whose precise roots, import, and significance often get lost in its popular renditions. These implications demand more careful scrutiny.

The project of crafting a fully coherent account of R. Kook's theology is admittedly daunting. As asserted by many of his admirers, the attempt to stereotype R. Kook by fitting him into any prefabricated intellectual box does him an injustice. His supreme mastery of the wealth of Jewish tradition, alongside the unconventionally broad sweep of his interests, defy neat categorization. Efforts at reconstructing the eclectic conceptual baggage informing R. Kook's worldview are further aggravated by the many stylistic difficulties of its literary expression—a phenomenon of which he was painfully aware. For starters, R. Kook consciously favored a literary style that is associative and freewheeling rather than closely analytic, so that attempts to

---

[5] See Tamar Ross, "Between Metaphysical and Liberal Pluralism: A Reappraisal of R. A. I. Kook's Espousal of Toleration", in *AJS Review – The Journal of the Association for Jewish Studies* 21.1 (Spring 1996): 61–110.

[6] *Shmoneh kevatzim* (henceforth: SK)3, file 8, section 85.

[7] Ross, "Between Metaphysical."

formulate systematic and logical summaries of his thought invite artificial imposition of alien categories that inevitably reflect the subjective lens, particular interests, or areas of expertise of the writer. Beyond impossibly long-winded sentences and the ponderous style characterizing the traditional rabbinic format of his earlier essays and monographs, R. Kook's more personal and poetic diaries employ a unique and esoteric terminology that requires deciphering. The fact that this terminology refers more to abstract concepts than to concrete data, or at times to both planes at once, compounds the difficulty. It also explains why the overwhelming bulk of his voluminous literary legacy still remains inaccessible to non-Hebrew readers.

Owing to these obstacles, much scholarly ink has been spilt in debating whether R. Kook should be viewed as an old-time traditionalist seeking to transmit the richness of this legacy to a new generation of secularists unschooled in its vocabulary, or as a modernist bent on translating and addressing contemporary issues and values in traditional terms. Others query the extent to which he was affected by contemporary philosophical trends, and whether his allusions even to well-rooted concepts of Jewish thought, and Kabbalah in particular, should be taken as precise references to their original connotations, or rather as loose, flowery metaphors for expressing his own unique brand of spirituality. All these alternatives undoubtedly contain some measure of truth. They also reflect various stages of the spiritual odyssey that R. Kook himself underwent, initially peppering his immersion in classical rabbinic sources after the fashion of Lithuanian Talmudism with an interest in the themes of medieval Jewish rationalism and pietist literature, then opening himself out to the world of Jewish mysticism, and eventually melding it with the rise of nationalism and a novel appreciation of modernity at large. Nonetheless, I believe that unraveling R. Kook's highly idiosyncratic terminology by first reading it in the context of Lurianic Kabbalah and viewing its distinctive contours as his initial frame of reference[8] is an indispensable tool for those seeking to reveal the deeper meaning of R. Kook's theological enterprise. More specifically, I refer to a particular group of Luria's disciples originating in Lithuania, who have only recently come to be recognized as an independent school of Kabbalah charting a distinct

---

[8] As per R. Kook's own testimony that all of his thoughts have their source in the writings of R. Isaac Luria; see *Hareayah Kook: Lasheloshah be-Elul* I (Jerusalem: Machon Harav Tzvi Yehuda, 2003), 46.

path of its own,[9] partially in reaction to their Hasidic protagonists. In order to substantiate this claim, I would like to digress momentarily and review some of the steps that led to this development.

LITHUANIAN KABBALAH AND THE HASIDIC/ MITNAGDIC DIVIDE

In the popular imagination Judaism is usually regarded as the classical paradigm for theistic religious belief. As such, God is pictured in personalist terms as a superior Other who stands over and above the world, manipulating it from without. An overview of Jewish theology over the ages yields a more nuanced picture, beginning with biblical images of God dwelling within the world, and rabbinic references to the fullness of God's presence and vulnerability to the effects of His creation. The pendulum swung further when Aristotelian influences and Maimonides' negative theology confronted the distinctive amalgam of gnostic elements and Neoplatonic ideas characterizing medieval Kabbalah. According to the latter, the *Ein Sof* (or Infinite One) as He is in Himself, is so utterly beyond grasp that He is not even mentioned in the Torah. God in His manifestations, by contrast, is the God of religion who created the world by emitting a series of increasingly material and particularized extensions of His essence, in a process similar to birth.[10]

A significant twist to this vacillation occurred in the sixteenth century, with the innovations of Rabbi Isaac Luria. In contrast to his predecessors who carefully avoided any reference to activity within the *Ein Sof*, Luria suggested that the emanative process depicted by classical Kabbalah was necessarily preceded by an act of contraction (*tsimtsum*) in order to make room for a finite worldly reality.[11] While the substance of creation emanates—as in classical Kabbalah—in the form of

---

[9] Raphael Shuchat, "Lithuanian Kabbalah as an Independent Stream in Kabbalah Literature" [Hebrew], *Journal for Study of Jewish Mystical Literature* 10 (2004): 181–206.

[10] For further explication of the kabbalistic concept of God, see Isaiah Tishby, *The Wisdom of the Zohar: An Anthology of Texts*, trans. David Goldstein (Oxford: Littman Library of Jewish Civilization, 1989), part I, ch. 2; Gershom G. Scholem, *Major Trends in Jewish Mysticism* (New York: Schocken, 1941), Sixth Lecture.

[11] For a fuller account of Lurianic Kabbalah, see Scholem, ibid., Seventh Lecture. For sources in earlier Kabbalah qualifying attribution of *tsimtsum* exclusively to Luria, see Moshe Idel, "On the Concept of Tzimzum in Kabbalah and its Research", in *Proceedings of the Fourth International Conference on the History of Jewish Mysticism: Lurianic Kabbalah* (2002), 59–112.

a gradually diminishing ray of light stemming from the *Ein Sof*, indicating a panentheistic picture of God–world relations, the fact that this ray of light was now clearly demarcated from its source by the circle of empty space into which it descends, signified a partial return toward theism.[12] Challenges to these implications were raised by several of Luria's more philosophically inclined disciples, who questioned the viability of a literal understanding of *tsimtsum*.[13] Their qualms regarding the legitimacy of attributing change to a timeless infinity, or emptying any "space" (even when understood spiritually) of God's infinite and all-pervading presence, led to the development of what eventually became known in modern scholarship as "the allegorical interpretation of the doctrine of *Tzimtzum*" (or, as kabbalists themselves termed it: *tsimtsum shelo kepshuto*).

According to the original expositors of this school of thought, Luria's doctrine of *tsimtsum* did not refer to the creation of an actual void within *Ein Sof*, but rather to a covering over or concealment of some aspect of God's absolute existence. Such concealment engenders an illusory realm of appearance, allowing various elements of God's infinity to view themselves as separate, despite the fact that ontologically they remain merged with the whole. While this metaphoric interpretation resolved difficulties of a theoretical nature, its acosmic implications did not sit well with one of the essential corollaries of Jewish monotheism: submission to divine command. Moral responsibility and observance of mitsvot involve confronting a diversified world, differentiating between holy and profane, good and evil, and recognizing a hierarchy of clearly demarcated entities and values.

Responding to this threat, Lithuanian Jewry of the eighteenth and nineteenth centuries produced two new varieties of Lurianic mysticism, both of which embraced *tsimtsum shelo kepshuto* but strove to stem its anti-nomistic potential. I refer here to the Hasidic movement, particularly as developed by R. Shneur Zalman of Lyadi (Rashaz),

---

[12] Even within this more circumscribed stance, greater fine-tuning of the pantheistic-theistic spectrum was generated by Luria's students, who exhibited varying degrees of interest in preserving substantive differences between the *Ein Sof* and the finite world of creation which emerged out of the void. For a more detailed description, see: *Encyclopedia Judaica, Kabbalah*, 590; Isaiah Tishby, *The Doctrine of Evil and the Kelippah in Lurianic Kabbalism* [Hebrew] (Jerusalem: The Hebrew University Magnes Press, 1965), 24–28.

[13] For an initial formulation of this interpretation, see Joseph Ergas, *Shomer Emunim* [Hebrew], second polemic, 34, 39.

founder of Habad, and to the ideology of the Mitnagdim, as explicated by R. Hayim of Volozhin, a prominent disciple of their fiercest opponent, the illustrious R. Elijah of Vilna.[14] Despite bitter exchanges between the two movements, both drew upon a theology that distinguishes between three levels of awareness, which virtually represent three levels of being. The first, or highest level, which I will dub Stage One, refers to all that there is. As such, it transcends and defies definition. Even the attribute "God" as applied to this all-encompassing entity is inadequate, as this would imply comparison with something outside the realm of infinite being. From the vantage point of creation, however, two other levels can be spoken of. Stage Two signifies how we, stretching our imagination beyond the limits of our illusory sense of separate existence, might envision God's relationship to the world from His point of view (*metzido*). Stage Three defines how we, as perceiving creatures, experience God's relationship to the world from our point of view (*metzideinu*).

Rashaz and R. Hayim agreed regarding the ineffability of Stage One, which for our purposes I shall term, somewhat misleadingly, "pan-cosmism."[15] They also agreed (with a few

---

[14] For further discussion of their respective views and reference to primary sources see Tamar Ross, "Two Interpretations of the Doctrine of Tzimtzum: Hayim of Volozhin and Shneur Zalman of Lyadi", *Mehkarei Yerushalayim B'machshevet Yisrael* [Hebrew] 2, (Jerusalem: Hebrew University, Machon le madaei ha-yahdurt, 1981), 153–69; For English language discussion of each, see Rachel Elior, *The Paradoxical Ascent to God: The Kabbalistic Theosophy of Habad Hasidism*, trans. Jeffrey M. Green (Albany: SUNY Press, 1993), 79–91 and Norman Lamm, *Torah for Torah's Sake in the Works of Rabbi Hayyim of Volozhin and His Contemporaries* (New York: KTAV, 1989).

[15] The ontological status of the world *vis-à-vis* God is generally defined as cosmic or acosmic. According to the first approach, the world and God exist ontologically, whereas the second, acosmic, approach affirms only the existence of God. An acosmist might view the world as totally illusory, or as illusory only to the extent that it is accorded reality outside the context of the divine. But at this point it should be noted that even the term "world" in such discussions is not sufficiently clear. In a secular framework, although the term "world" bears many connotations, generally it refers to "all that there is." In a religious framework, by contrast, the term "world" is usually brought in opposition to the term "God" (i.e., "all that is not God"), operating under the assumption that only in this last sense is there any point in discussing the relationship between God and the world, and the ontological status of the world as opposed to God's. As against this, however, account should be taken of the approach of some religious mystics, who—due to absolute refusal to define God—will contend that even a God who nullifies the "world" (in the limited sense of this term in a religious context) does not exist ontologically, because there is no ontological status to anything beyond "all that there is." Therefore, even in a religious framework, one can hold the

differences)[16] regarding the acosmic nature of Stage Two: from God's "point of view" His existence is absolute, so that there *is* no point of view, no differentiation, and no reality other than God. Their main point of difference concerned Stage Three: how we perceive God's relationship to the world from our point of view. To the extent that this perspective defines the texture of normative religious worship and its ultimate objective (which we may term, for our purposes, as Stage Four), one may readily understand why this difference provoked great acrimony between the two movements.

According to Rashaz, although the light of the Ein Sof fills all worlds so that nothing is void of God's presence, the very delineation of our world (in contradistinction to God) renders the derivative ray of light which sustains it as qualitatively different from its monolithic source. Precisely for this reason, the supreme religious goal is to pierce our illusory sense of separate existence and merge—to whatever extent possible—with God's undifferentiated unity. This is accomplished by creating a "dwelling place" for the highest reflection of that unity in this world (*yetzirat dirah ba-tahtonim*), negating the "reality" of separation (*bittul ha-yesh*) by eradicating our false sense of independent selfhood. Combining spirit and matter in the study of Torah and performance of mitsvot is an important tool in this endeavor, but the ultimate arena is the world at large. R. Hayim, by contrast, contended that although God's aura (originating in His primordial Torah) appears to us as a ray of descending gradations so that its final and lowest point is so far removed from its source that it appears qualitatively different, ontologically our world and God's remain one and the same. Hence, there is no reason to strive for dramatic shifts of consciousness on the earthly plane.[17] The task of the faithful is to relate to reality as it appears to us, confident that through study of Torah for its own sake (rather than as

---

view that only the world (in the sense that is generally attributed to this term in secular contexts) has ontological status, whereas a God that nullifies the "world" (in the narrower sense of "all that is not God") is no less illusory than "world" in its limited sense. What exists is only "all that there is," which transcends linguistic definition, and cannot be referred to even as Being.

[16] Including some confusing discrepancies in their use of classical kabbalistic terminology for designating divine immanence and transcendence, and Rashaz's introduction of a distinction between the light of *Ein Sof* (referring to Stage 2) and its source (Stage 1) as an additional barrier between the substance of infinity and its worldly reflection; see Ross, "Two Interpretations," 158–64.

[17] As R. Hayim puts it, perceiving the essence of God's undifferentiated unity is both "forbidden and impossible"—*Nefesh ha-Hayim* (Bnei Brak, 1989), Gate 3, ch. 6.

a vehicle for spiritual rapture) and normative halakhic practice, we enhance God's unity and fortify the connection between God's relative transcendence from our point of view and God as He is in Himself.

R. KOOK AND THE NOTION OF PERFECTIBLE PERFECTION

When introducing all this mystic baggage as preamble to the thought of R. Kook, I do not mean to imply that R. Kook's worldview can or should be reduced to the filter of the R. Hayim/Rashaz polemic. Apart from the fact that R. Kook, in consonance with the general tradition of Lithuanian Kabbalah, drew upon a vast array of kabbalistic and non-kabbalistic sources, no less important is the role that his subsequent exposure to currents of modern European thought and to the rise of secular Zionism played in informing his unique adaptation of this legacy.[18] Nevertheless, despite the fact that R. Kook's transposition of the Hasidic/Mitnagdic controversy to contemporary issues began to emerge clearly only after his move to the Holy Land, the bare bones and distinctiveness of his religious temper first developed against the background of this particular divide[19] and an explicit interest on his part in preserving the relative advantages of each worldview, while avoiding their respective drawbacks.[20]

In a notable passage written during his early years in Palestine, Kook expresses appreciation for a "monotheistic view that tends to Spinozist explication"[21] which he attributes to the intellectual element of modern Hasidism," obviously referring to Habad.[22] He nonetheless rejects

---

[18] Regarding R. Kook's exposure to contemporary European philosophy, see Eliezer Goldman, "The Consolidation of R. Kook's Ideas: The Writings between 1906–1909" [Hebrew] *Bar Ilan Yearbook* 22–23 (Ramat Gan: Bar-Ilan University,1988), 87–120; regarding the Zionist influence, see Rivka Shatz-Oppenheimer, "Utopia and Messianism in Rav Kook's Teachings" [Hebrew], *Kivvunim* 1 (1978): 15–27.

[19] According to family tradition, his mother (of Habad descent) and his father (an alumnus of R. Hayim's famed Yeshiva of Volozhin) argued between themselves whether their child prodigy was destined to become a Hasidic master or a Mitnagdic rabbi. Portraits of Rashaz and R. Elijah of Vilna subsequently featured side by side on the walls of his study in Jerusalem.

[20] For references, see Reuven Raz, *Rabbi Kook between Hasidim and Mitnagdim* [Hebrew] (Jerusalem: Mosad Harav Kook, 2016), 11–14.

[21] In an earlier publication of this passage (*Orot hakodesh* II, pp. 399–400), edited by Kook's close disciple, R. David Hacohen, the term "Spinozist" was substituted with "pantheistic," reflecting Hacohen's wariness of Kook's Spinozist leanings.

[22] SK1 (Jerusalem, 1997), file 1, sections 95–96. In an earlier passage, R. Kook appropriates Habad terminology (*dilug*) in critiquing Spinozist determinism; see "rishon

striving to live in accordance with its acosmic implications in light of several more practical considerations. First, "release from the prison of our imagination is often more difficult than escape from physical walls"; in other words, such a view is not really feasible given our conceptual limitations.[23] Second, despite the spiritual comfort it affords, awareness of God's all-embracing unity does not satisfy another requisite for human flourishing—namely, our innate urge for progress and freedom of choice.[24] And third, "the world of practical affairs will not run properly unless we lower our sights,"[25] and prevent abandoning the field to the wicked and morally negligent. Thus, although ordinary monotheism is not true in and of itself, when it draws upon the more comprehensive view it is worthy of serving as its "vessel," or "garment."[26]

In expressly rejecting the Habad ideal, R. Kook seems to be aligning with R. Hayim's cautionary anti-spiritualist stance, according to which awareness of God's reality from His point of view should be treated as "burning embers" —approached momentarily in order to fuel our worship, but not too closely for fear of being consumed.[27] However, even a cursory view of R. Kook's writings *in toto* indicates that for all his defense of traditional theistic practice, his spiritualist vision extends beyond Mitnagdism and Hasidism alike.

In abstract philosophical terms, R. Kook's theology begins with the paradox of an infinite, perfect God, who—precisely because of His infinite perfection—lacks the quality of lack, and hence the capacity for growth, and improvement.[28] Appropriating Mitnagdic "realism" in acknowledging that finite beings can never totally abolish an intrinsic sense of independent selfhood on the one hand, yet are unwilling to forgo the Hasidic yearning to achieve some measure of identity with God's infinite perfection on the other, R. Kook presents an understanding of the latter as necessarily wanting. This antinomy, it would appear, exists only in the mind of finite beings, for it is only in a world of lack that perfection (*shlemut*) and perfectibility (*hishtalmut*) can be distinguished, and the impetus for growth considered a virtue.[29] Nonetheless,

---

leYaffo," in *Kevatzim Meketav Yad Kodsho*, ed. Boaz Ofan (Jerusalem: Machon le-hotzaat Ginzei ha-Reayah, 2006), section 112, p. 144.

[23] SK1, ibid., section 96.   [24] SK1, ibid., section 393.   [25] SK1, ibid., section 97.

[26] SK 1, ibid., section 96. See also SK1, ibid., section 65, where R. Kook recommends enveloping the inspiring thought that "there is nothing other than He" (as popularly articulated by Habad) with the "clipped wing" conception of cosmic realism.

[27] *Nefesh Ha-hayim* [Hebrew], Gate 3, ch. 1.   [28] SK3, file 7, section 58, p. 151.

[29] Ibid.

while we may never achieve total identification with that infinite perfection that constitutes ultimate reality, we can improve upon what appears in our eyes as its intrinsic flaw by applying the dynamic will for improvement to the multitude of its seemingly finite reflections. In this manner, God's undifferentiated unity is infinitely expanded via the perpetual striving of the world of appearances, to a degree that from our point of view exceeds that of infinite perfection on its own.[30]

In addition to passages that present R. Kook's view of God–world relations in the form of direct philosophical argument, it is more often left for the reader to glean from the added connotations he heaps upon traditional kabbalistic imagery, when overlaying it with another level of his own terminology, or applying it to new contexts that broaden its significance.[31] Scholars have long noted the shift in post-Lurianic Kabbalah from a predominantly theosophic interest in the *sefirot* (the ten emanations that classical Kabbalah established as primordial divine manifestations emerging within the Godhead) to a broader interest in developing their symbolic implications.[32] As a first step, conflicting descriptions in earlier sources that portrayed the process of emanation as descending either in concentric circles (as exhibited in the vessels of the *sefirot*) or in linear fashion (as represented in the expanding ray of light they contained) were no longer taken as mere geometric differences. Beginning with *tsimtsum*, these were now understood metaphorically as representing the source of all expansion and movement and that of passive containment, or more broadly as two distinct forms of God's management of the world—the general and the particular. Mitnagdic representatives of the Lithuanian school of Kabbalah developed this notion further, associating the circular principle with the fixed and morally indifferent laws of nature and the linear with individual providence and the intervention of miracles, as exemplified in the differing destinies of Gentiles and Jews. Hasidim, and to a certain extent even R. Hayim, pursued another track, applying the symbolism of Luria's graphic and intricate

---

[30] Ibid.
[31] For a monumental effort to provide a comprehensive list of R. Kook's kabbalistic terms, their sources, and the precise meanings that he attached to these, see Yosef Avivi, *The Kabbalah of R. Kook*, 4 volumes [Hebrew] (Jerusalem: Yad Ben Zvi, 2018).
[32] For a broader survey, see Mordechai Pachter, "Circles and Straightness – A History of an Idea" [Hebrew], *Daat* 18 (Winter 1987): 59–90

theosophic and cosmological descriptions to the inner psychology and spiritual experience of man.

In R. Kook's hands, the intertwining of theosophy, history, divine providence, and human psychology reaches its peak, when the contrary principles of circle and line, vessels and light now appear as derivative reflections of perfection and perfectibility, necessity and freedom of choice, generality and individuation that operate on all levels of being. At times the various modes of interaction between them can be understood conceptually as alternative responses to the logical conundrum of limited, static perfection into which we, as imperfect beings, are thrust.[33] Elsewhere, they function more concretely as elements of a divine trajectory that prefigures relationships between male and female, intellect and intuition, science and religion, particularity and universalism, war and peace, spirit and matter, miracle and nature, intelligentsia and the masses, and virtually any other worldly duality that can be identified and addressed.

When delineating stages of this trajectory, R. Kook often alludes to Luria's detailed account of the dramatic events within the Godhead that followed upon *tsimtsum:* the cosmic mishap of the breaking of the vessels of the last seven *sefirot* whose differentiated character proved too fragile to contain the intensity of the lights for which they were originally intended, and the process of repair (*tikkun*) which entails rebuilding these vessels after separating the sparks of light still clinging to and nurturing their shattered remnants that now constitute the evil of this world, and returning them to their source. Luria's dense descriptions provided R. Kook with a rich storehouse of metaphysical precedent to be transferred from the realm of the divine to this-worldly interests. If Luria's visions portrayed *tikkun* as a reconfiguration of God's primordial manifestations into more robust constellations (*partzufim*) that move from stable complementary relations to more sporadic and hierarchical relations before achieving fruitful harmony, these modes of interaction now function as archetypal patterns that pervade all aspects of the world, as we know it, in the struggle to improve upon the original unity of infinite perfection in finite terms.

---

[33] See Benjamin Ish Shalom, *Rav Avraham Itzhak HaCohen Kook – Between Rationalism and Mysticism*, trans. from Hebrew by Ora Wisking-Elper (Albany: SUNY Press, 1993), 43–46.

In this context, the souls of the secular Zionists are understood as fallen sparks of light stemming from the highest level of being, that initial sea of chaos that preceded the delineation of constricting vessels, definitions, and rules.[34] The task of the righteous is to rescue these powerful anarchic sparks now crying out for salvation,[35] uniting them with their more individuated and cultivated counterparts in one all-inclusive vessel. This vessel is identified with the last *sefirah*— the feminine aspect of the Godhead, and the metaphysical source of the concrete land and nation of Israel, which is now charged with the task of fulfilling the same unifying function here on earth. By bringing together the sparks of holiness gathered from the nations of the world during exile, the Jewish people are destined to display the idea of God's unity on a national scale, embodying a model of collective harmony that will eventually be emulated by the world at large. Universal readiness to absorb this new vision was confirmed in R. Kook's eyes by new approaches to the scientific study of anthropology and cosmology, and particularly in the growing acceptance of the theory of evolution, all of which have begun to replace atomistic views of reality with greater appreciation of the vastness of the universe, alongside the inter-connectedness between different levels of being.[36]

R. KOOK AND GERMAN IDEALISM

Aside from its grounding in traditional kabbalistic motifs, R. Kook's focus on the relationship between static perfection and dynamic perfectibility incorporates some of the tropes of German philosophy regnant in his day. Building upon Kant's distinction between the noumenal and the phenomenal, and the concomitant claim that the objects of human cognition are appearances and not things in themselves, exponents of this school of thought developed a more radically idealistic view, claiming that *all* that exists is necessarily preceded by a single unconditional non-material first principle (be it mind, spirit, reason, or will), of which the material world is to be understood as a partial manifestation. All subsequent principles are then conditioned by the difference between one principle and another.

---

[34] "Souls of Chaos," *Orot*, 121–22, English translation in Bokser, *Abraham Isaac*, 256–58.
[35] SK1, file 2, section 14.   [36] SK2, file 1, sections 117–23.

The resurfacing of deliberations regarding the relationship between an all-inclusive unembodied infinity and its diverse and finite manifestations, so central to the development of the allegorical interpretation of the doctrine of *tsimtsum*, suggests that the traffic between German idealism and kabbalistic eschatology was not a one-way affair.[37] This affinity did not escape R. Kook, who engaged with this modern permutation and integrated some of its more philosophical formulations with his kabbalistic worldview. While explicitly rejecting Schopenhauer's one-sided view of blind will, as well as French philosopher Henri Bergson's view of eternal movement, as the metaphysical core of our phenomenal reality,[38] he shared their rejection of Spinoza's materialist approach to metaphysics and its determinist implications. R. Kook's implementation of the Lurianic narrative as the model for more complicated interplay between static perfection and dynamic perfectibility appears to sit more comfortably with the more nuanced formulations of the relationship between an underlying metaphysical unity and its substantiation developed by Schelling and Hegel. At different moments, R. Kook's view of the relationship between the one and the many appears to draw both on Schelling's early reliance on intellectual intuition as a means of grasping the ultimate "unity of opposites" and on Hegel's more dialectic understanding of history as the unfolding of transcendent Spirit in time and its objectification in human institutions.[39] Indeed, Schelling's intuitive and Hegel's dialectical formulations might simply have represented for R. Kook reference to different stages of differentiation and concretization depicted by Luria in the interaction of the *partzufim*.

Another offshoot of German idealism inviting comparison was the neo-Kantian project initiated by the Jewish philosopher Hermann Cohen who sought, in a manner of demonstration which he called

---

[37] For discussion of this double-edged relationship, see Paul Franks, "Inner Anti-Semitism or Kabbalistic Legacy? German Idealism's Relationship to Judaism," in *Yearbook of German Idealism*, volume VII: *Faith and Reason*, eds. Fred Rush, Jürgen Stolzenberg and Paul Franks (Berlin: Walter de Gruyter, 2010), 254–79.

[38] SK1, file 1, section 435; SK2, file 4, section 68.

[39] Concerning Schelling, see Avinoam Rosenak, *The Prophetic Halakha: Rabbi A.I.H. Kook's Philosophy of the Halakhah* [Hebrew] (Jerusalem: The Hebrew University Magnes Press, 2007), 44–57. Concerning Hegel, see Elchanan Shilo, *Kabbalistic Dimensions in the Thought of Harav Kok – Their Relationship to Hegel and the Zeitgeist* [Hebrew] (MA thesis, Bar Ilan University, 2000); Aviad Bieler, "R. Kook and Hegel" [Hebrew], *Alon Shvut: Bogrim* 7 (1995): 133–75.

"transcendental method,"[40] to base assumptions regarding the existence of God and moral duty on firmer grounding than the speculative inferences allowed for by Kant's critique of pure reason. On what appears to be R. Kook's own testimony, the main points of two seminal essays that he published in 1906, with an eye to familiarizing a younger generation of Jews with traditional Jewish ideas, accord with a lecture of Cohen's that appeared in a Hebrew periodical two years earlier.[41] In this lecture, Cohen contended that the only religion that liberated itself from the charms of mythology was the ethical monotheism of Judaism established by the prophets, and continued by the Sages and Maimonides, all of whom understood the idea of God to have a fundamentally moral meaning and purpose for human beings. It is by emulating the moral attributes linked to the divine idea and applying them to the spiritual yearning for social justice, and not by striving mystically for union, according to Cohen, that we achieve a proper correlation to the divine.

Kook's above-mentioned essays echo Cohen's hostility to Spinoza's alleged equation of God with nature,[42] asserting that the latter's idolatrous presumption that it is possible to approach the divine, bereft of its phenomenal manifestations, is childish in its obliviousness to the gap between the perceiver and the object of his perception. Like Cohen, R. Kook nonetheless finds Kant's distinction between "the thing in itself" and its manifestations theologically wanting. In a long epistle to religious anarchist, Shmuel Alexandrov, regarding the distinctiveness of Jewish belief, he first stoutly declares that "we (i.e., the Jewish people, who were always privy to the secrets of Kabbalah) did not need Kant to reveal this secret to us—that all human cognitions are relative and subjective." This, however, is immediately followed by the contention that only a descendant of pagans [e.g., Kant] who "were able to divert their minds from the God of Israel, 'whom they [the Jews] called the God of gods', could divert his mind from that which is inevitably higher than everything, even though for us [also] He is as if without

---

[40] For a brief synopsis, see *The Encyclopedia of Philosophy* II, ed. Paul Edwards (NewYork and London: Pearson, 1967), 126–27.

[41] For details, see Avivi, *The Kabbalah*, vol. 1, 146–47. The reference is to "Knowledge of God" and "The Service of God", the last two chapters in A. I Kook, *Ikkevei ha-Tzon*. For an abbreviated version of the last chapter in English, see *The Essential Writings of Abraham Isaac Kook*, ed. Ben Zion Bokser (Teaneck: Amity House, 1988), 49–52.

[42] For a vehement critique of Cohen's pantheistic reading of Spinoza, see Yitzhak Y. Melamed, "Cohen, Spinoza and the Nature of Pantheism," *JSQ* 25 (2018): 1–10.

existence, and bears no intellectual or metaphysical form."⁴³ In other words, by failing to recognize the full implication of infinity, Gentile versions of monotheism conceive of God as an object amongst others (or, in R. Kook's words, "perceivable infinity"—a contradiction in terms).⁴⁴ According to R. Kook, it is this lapse that enabled Kant to maintain his agnostic stance regarding metaphysics. As against this, he asserts: "It is necessary to show how one may enter the palace: by way of the gate. The gate is the divine dimension disclosed in the world, in all its phenomena of beauty and grandeur ... The highest domain of divinity toward which we aspire ... descends for us into the world, and we encounter it and delight in its love and find peace in its tranquility."⁴⁵

IMPLICATIONS FOR TRADITIONAL JEWISH BELIEF AND PRACTICE

R. Kook's appreciation of the futility of approaching divinity without the mediation of its manifestations leads him to relate to classical Jewish beliefs and practices in a manner that, like Cohen, divests them of personalist visions of God and infuses them with moral significance. Contrary to the usual understanding of God as an all-powerful, unapproachable figure standing over and above His creation, R. Kook's spiritual diaries generally refer to the object of religious life in abstract terms, such as "divinity" (elohut), "the divine perfection" (ha-shlemut ha-elohit), or "the highest holiness" (ha-kodesh ha-elyon), Unlike Cohen's "religion of reason," however, R. Kook portrays the relationship between impersonal divinity and its moral attributes in the emanative terms of classical Kabbalah, as a continuum between higher and lower levels of being, rather than conceptually as the relationship between an a priori postulate and its logical derivatives. Thus the moral urge for perfection, terminologically associated with the linear principle of expansion and freedom of will (haratzon hahofshi),⁴⁶ is depicted in the broadest sense possible, as an intrinsic yearning for divine plenitude that *ipso facto* animates the soul of all that exists.⁴⁷

---

[43] *Iggerot ha-Reayah* I (Jerusalem: Mosad Harav Kook, 1985), Letter 44, pp. 47–48; For an annotated English translation of the complete letter, see *Rav A.Y. Kook – Selected Letters*, trans. and ed. Tzvi Feldman (Ma-aleh Adumim: Ma'aliot Publications, 1986), 80–107.
[44] Ibid., 48. [45] "A Thirst for the Living God", Bokser, *Abraham Isaac*, 251.
[46] SK1, file 1, section 364, p. 124. [47] SK1, file 1, section 102, p. 34.

In humans, this yearning assumes the form of a natural intuitive morality, which is ideally guided and supplemented by the ethical standards of Torah, but also bears independent value as a reflection of the divine.[48] In other words, while appropriating the Kantian distinction between morality that flows naturally from a "holy will" (if it exists) and a deontological system that grounds moral behavior on compliance with a categorical imperative out of a sense of duty that overcomes self-love, R. Kook denies that only the latter is viable for humans.[49] Implicitly acknowledging Nietzsche's influential critique of religion as an oppressive belief system that induces a slave mentality and a depressing "jealousy of God" that squelches vitality, creativity, and any healthy sense of self,[50] R. Kook retaliates with an image of "the God of Israel who is the infinite unperceivable root of all existence," who "brings joy to all and gives life to everything," and is "revealed through the subjective revelation of all hearts who seek and comprehend him."[51] In this spirit, R. Kook suggests that, beyond the likelihood that future conditions will undoubtedly render some commandments redundant, talmudic mention of the possibility that mitsvot will be revoked in "the ends of days"[52] comes to teach that in ideal circumstances those mitsvot that remain will flow naturally as expression of our innermost wishes.[53]

In a similar vein, R. Kook predicates the ultimate authority of the Torah itself on the willingness of its recipients to accept it,[54] its

[48] SK1, file 1, section 74, 75. For more extensive discussion of the relationship between natural morality and the Torah, see Naama Bindiger, *The Moral Conception of Rav Kook: Meta-Ethics, Normative Ethics and Application* [Hebrew] (Ph.D. diss., Ben Gurion University, 2016).

[49] SK1, file 1, section 132, 133, pp. 49–50; see Elchanan Shilo, "R. Kook's Interpretation of Lurianic Kabbalah: The Appearance of New Souls and Worldly Repair", *Iyyunim be-Tekumat Yisrael* 18 (2008): 56, n. 6.

[50] SK1, file 1, section 129.

[51] *Iggerot ha-Reayah* I, Letter 44, p. 48; Feldman, *Selected Letters*, p. 94. For amplification, see Jason Rappoport, "Rabbi Kook and Nietzsche – a Preliminary Comparison of their Ideas on Religions, Christianity, Buddhism and Atheism," *The Torah u-Madda Journal* 12 (2004): 99–129.

[52] Inferred by R. Yosef in BT 61: 2, from the ruling that it is permissible to bury the dead in shrouds in the normally forbidden mix of linen and cotton (*kilayim*).

[53] *Iggerot ha-Reayah* II (Jerusalem, 1956), Letter 630, pp. 250–51. For exemplification of this attitude in R. Kook's understanding of the nature of Abraham's trial in the binding of Isaac, see Jerome I. Gellman, *The Fear, the Trembling, and the Fire – Kierkegaard and Hasidic Masters on the Binding of Isaac* (Lanham, MD, London, NewYork: University Press of Amrica, 1994), 99–120.

[54] *Eder ha-Yakar* (Jerusalem 1982), 39.

resonance with their most exalted sensibilities,[55] and its benign influence on the welfare of the Jewish people,[56] rather than on the transmission of heteronomous dictates in a one-time, never-to-be-superseded revelation, imposed from without. This implies that the full meaning of the Torah's original message is never exhausted at any particular point in time. Rather, it evolves in accordance with the healthy instincts of the Jewish people[57] or the ability of its established authorities to re-interpret it in light of new historical circumstances.[58] The convening of such forces is another form of revelation that reflects and responds to the constantly evolving spiritual needs of the Jewish people and of humanity at large.[59] At times, R. Kook portrays the orchestration of historical events and their attunement to the rate of human progress in traditional terms, evoking the image of deliberate manipulation on the part of an external super-power in heaven,[60] but even in such instances individual providence hardly figures. More often, his rendition of divine influence is reminiscent of process theology and its view of God as an impersonal sacred force that unfolds progressively from age to age, thereby blurring the distinction between heaven-sent messages and human discovery.

One of the most striking implications of this naturalistic variation on the medieval theme of divine accommodationism[61] is the positive role that doubt plays in the religious life.[62] If the object of our innermost passion is infinity, heresy also has its place. Despite his fierce objection to what he perceives as the idolatrous nature of Spinoza's metaphysics, R. Kook discerns even in this equation of God with nature (which, he suggests, could hardly have arisen were it not for strength of the "lights of divine unity" embedded in Spinoza's Jewish soul) a legitimate inner core, regarding which Maimonides and then the Besht (founder of

---

[55] SK1, file 1, section 633, p. 201.   [56] *Iggerot ha-Reayah* I, 48–49.
[57] SK1, file 2, section 30, p. 304.
[58] *Iggerot ha-Reayah* I, Letter 90, pp. 103–04, in response to a query regarding the Torah's attitude toward slavery.
[59] Ibid.
[60] See, for example, *Iggerot ha-Reayah* I, Letter 20, p. 20, regarding contemporary inability to perform the commandment of chastising sinners (*Tokheha*), or ibid., Letter 91, pp. 105–07, regarding correlation between certain scientific discoveries and our spiritual needs.
[61] For elaboration on accommodationism in general, see Stephen D. Benin, *The Footprints of God – Divine Accommodation in Jewish and Christian Thought* (Albany: SUNY Press, 1993).
[62] See, for example, SK1, file 1, section 155.

Hasidism) initiated a historical process of purifying it from its dross.[63] Just as *tsimtsum* is necessary for overcoming the lack of lack in infinite perfection, historical circumstances prompting the shattering of a current formulation of faith should be understood as response to spiritual growth which requires reconstruction in a new and improved version.[64]

R. Kook's broad implementation of Lurianic doctrine provided him with the raw materials for his distinctive "theodicy of modernity."[65] Just as the secularism of Zionist *halutzim* returning to the land is sublimated expression of the gap between the limited spiritual interests of diaspora Judaism and the yearning for a more comprehensive spirituality, so the challenges of the Enlightenment and new scientific discoveries function similarly as a necessary and welcome response to antiquated religious models that have outlived their day. Because holiness does not lie in that which is exalted and separate, the more inclusive the nature of any belief, the more authentic its reflection of God's infinite unity. Thus the value of religious doctrine is not reflected in the degree of its correspondence to a fixed and objective metaphysical truth lying "out there," but rather in the measure of its ability to absorb and amplify upon more limited or even rival manifestations of the universal urge for perfection.[66]

The importance R. Kook places on inclusivism extends to religious practice as well. Rather than traditional images of inter-personal conversations with an omnipotent God that petition Him directly to comply with our requests, theurgic techniques that seek to achieve this objective indirectly by increasing the flow of bounty within the Godhead, or rationalist explanations that point to its salutary contemplative or psychological effects, R. Kook grounds the power of prayer on

---

[63] *Kevatzim me-Ketav Yad Kodsho,* section 117. For fuller analysis of this passage and its implications, see Lilach Bar-Bettelheim, "The Concept of Zimzum and Pantheism in the Unedited Texts of Rabbi Abraham Isaac Hacohen Kook" [Hebrew] *Daat* 83 (2017): 323–25.

[64] *Iggerot ha-Re-ayah* I, Letter 134, pp. 163–64; English translation in Bokser, *Essential Writings,* 77–80.

[65] A term coined by Mirsky, see n. 1.

[66] For further amplification, see Tamar Ross, "The Cognitive Value of Religious Truth Claims: Rabbi A. I. Kook and Postmodernism", *Hazon Nahum: Jubilee Volume in Honor of Norman Lamm,* eds. Yaakov Elman and Jeffrey S. Gurock (New York: Yeshiva University Press, 1997), 479–527. When accorded its proper place, the particular character of each belief is not nullified, but its significance is transformed within the context of the ever-expanding whole.

more holistic assumptions regarding the inherent connection between man, the phenomenal world, and being at large.[67] In this spirit, he explains the halakhic injunction to build synagogues with windows in light of his understanding that acknowledging the value of the external world is a necessary condition of worship[68]. When an individual expresses natural yearning for the divine, he unites with the fundamental ideal of all that exists.[69] To the extent that this collective awareness functions in his prayer, its significance is not merely contemplative and limited to his individual psyche. Rather, it tangibly affects and uplifts the state of the cosmos at large.[70] The same applies to the concepts of sin and repentance. These too do not signify the solitary acts of an individual confronting his Creator, but rather varying degrees of estrangement or identification with a vast and interconnected scheme, whereby the relationship between the various parts and their degree of attachment to the whole bear tangible effects.

THE SPECTER OF PANTHEISM AND MYSTIC ASCENT

R. Kook's holistic view of reality undoubtedly reflected and shaped his own personal experience but the urgency he felt in disseminating this understanding of the "secrets of the kabbalah" was also driven, as indicated above, by his conviction (accompanied occasionally with trepidation and doubt) that the world at large was progressing toward a more inclusive vision that heralded redemption. The messianic aspect of his vision morphed into a powerful movement, exerting formidable influence on the cultural and political destiny of the state of Israel to the present day. While some of R. Kook's more substantive applications of this vision to Jewish belief and practice were absorbed by the rank and file of religious Zionism, reviving an interest in Jewish theology and an emphasis upon divine immanence in history that contrasted sharply with the relative indifference to such issues typifying non-Zionist ultra-Orthodoxy,[71] his propensity for blurring distinctions between the divine

---

[67] Yuval Kahan, "Divine Faith: The Metaphysical Orientation of Rav Kook – Metaphysics, Theology, Mysticism" [Hebrew] (MA thesis, Hebrew University, 2004), 54–58.
[68] Rav Kook, 'Olat ha-Reayah I (Jerusalem: The Hebrew University of Jerusalem, 1962): 25.
[69] Ibid., I, 13. [70] Kahan, "Divine Faith," 54–58.
[71] For a full-blown analysis of this phenomenon, see Dov Schwartz, The Theology of the Religious Zionist Movement [Hebrew], (Tel Aviv: Am Oved, 1996).

and the human bore features whose similarity to pantheism appeared at times too close for comfort in the eyes of some of his closest disciples. This concern was a primary consideration in their efforts to prevent complete and uncensored publication of his writings for many years.[72] The fact that this battle has recently been lost to some extent, with much of the old material republished in in its original form and chronological order, and several new works released, has encouraged revisiting this issue.[73] Several factors, however, still obscure the clarity of this discussion.

One complication is debate amongst scholars, no less than traditionalists, regarding the extent to which normative Judaism has harbored pantheism in the past, provoking strong desires to either appropriate or reject the label.[74] To the extent that an all-embracing understanding of the term "God" refers to the sum total of every individual and contingent "thing" that exists in the natural world, some also find difficulty in regarding the particular set of emotive reactions (reverence, awe, love) which this sense of identity with the world evokes in its adherents as anything other than masked atheism.[75] Over and above these biases, terminological imprecision confuses matters further: If, rather than deification of a this-worldly aggregate of individual parts, "pantheism" refers to a grab-bag that throws every particular "thing" into an abyss of annihilation (as per Hegel's disparaging characterization of Spinoza's monism), it seems to be a misnomer for acosmism, its direct opposite in its annulment of distinctions. But to the extent that acosmism involves merely a disparity between what *is* (Stage Two) and what we *know* of it (Stage Three), it more accurately qualifies as panentheism (i.e., that the world is contained within God, but that God is more than the world). This still leaves room for important differences when characterizing the nature of the world as currently perceived (Stage Three), and that toward which we strive (Stage Four). When viewed on their own, each of these stages may entail varying

---

[72] For an account of the editing process and its motives, see Avinoam Rosenak, "Hidden Diaries and New Discoveries: The Life and Thought of Rabbi A. I. Kook," *Shofar: An Interdisciplinary Journal of Jewish Studies*, 25.3 (Spring 2007): 111–47.

[73] See, for example, Kahan, "Divine Faith"; Bar-Bettelheim, "The Concept."

[74] For references and explication of the rival views, see Bar-Bettelheim, ibid., 308–9, n. 47.

[75] As per Schopenhauer's complaint that "to call the world God is not to explain it; it is only to enrich our language with a superfluous synonym for the word 'world'" (Schopenhauer, 1851), II: 99.

degrees of divine transcendence of immanence, or—in the case of Stage Four—even acosmism or pantheism as the teleological ideal.

Recently, Yosef Avivi[76] has suggested that we coin a new term, "pan-emanationism," in order to faithfully capture R. Kook's distinctive contribution to Jewish theology.[77] In light of his seeming opposition to the possibility of ever encountering "the thing as it is in itself," this comes to substantiate the claim that R. Kook consistently, and as a matter of principle, related awareness of the comprehensive unity of all that exists to divine emanation rather than to divinity itself, in a deliberate effort that distances him not only from pantheism, but also from panentheism.[78] The suggestion is interesting and supported, as we have seen, by some of R. Kook's own declarations.[79] Nonetheless, the effectiveness of this theological "safety net" in shielding his worldview from its perceived threats is questionable.

If *every* thing in our world (including the assumption of God's infinity) is merely a phenomenon of God, this nevertheless indicates that God is the source of all that flows from Him. This makes the world wholly dependent on God and not really an autonomous entity, the very type of charge that theists seek to avoid. In a similar vein, the disparity between saying that God's emanations are everywhere and saying that God's absolute infinity is completely beyond access is difficult to explain without some appeal to the limits of human perception, further undermining the ontological basis of theistic distinctions. Moreover, when the peak of religious consciousness is portrayed as merging with the divine, such a theology certainly bears an existential "feel" of *unio mystica*, irrespective of whether this union takes place within *Ein Sof*, or within the world of emanations. Thus, for example, when—in amplifying the critique of Kant quoted above[80]—R. Kook contends that Israel's "majestic idea" is evidenced in the very nomenclature of the *sefirot*, whereby "Nothingness (Ayin, an appellation of *keter*, the highest *sefirah*) and "I" (Ani, an appellation of Malkhut, the lowest *sefirah*)

---

[76] Avivi is an independent scholar whose technical proficiency in the classical kabbalistic literature that, to his mind, served as the basic raw material for R. Kook's thought has earned the qualified respect of some academicians as well as that of avowed disciples of R. Kook.

[77] Avivi, *The Kabbalah*, vol. 4, 1378–80.   [78] Avivi, ibid.

[79] See also SK2, file 3, section 353, where the human inability to ever know anything except via its manifestations is stated quite baldly.

[80] See n. 38.

are composed of the same letters,"[81] the fact that this identity is attributed to the world of emanations rather than its source is of little consequence in mitigating a pantheistic sense of identity with the divine. And when R. Kook elsewhere states that only when adopting humility (another appellation of *keter*) that transcends Wisdom (an appellation of the second *sefirah*), and understanding that "every being in the world is to be comprehended only on the basis of attributes and one's relationship to them ... will it be made clear that a person's own existence is to be defined in terms of a relationship to attributes, and that the relationship of the divine to him is the essence of his life and the truth of his existence,"[82] one is again hard put to distinguish this mind-set on an experiential level from the Hasidic ideal of *bittul ha-yesh*— that is, annihilation of our illusory sense of self within the divine totality.[83]

Restricting R. Kook's theology to an exclusively emanationist context also fails to remove the problematic aspect of some of the non-normative or even anti-nomistic sentiments now exposed in the uncensored version of R. Kook's personal diaries. These attest to the anguish of *Tzadikim* (i.e., individuals endowed with rare spiritual capacities) when forced to confine their spiritual life to prescribed rules, communal responsibilities, conventional societal norms, and even to exoteric Torah study and engagement with the legalistic minutiae of halakhah.[84] In various passages, R. Kook encourages such individuals (obviously including himself, in all humility, in this category) to recognize the gift of their uniqueness and flow with their inclinations, ignoring the constraints of this-worldly distinctions for the sake of ecstatic glimmers of that which lies beyond; other passages express disappointment with his inability to immerse himself in the "real" world and its practical concerns. Such disparities can be taken as symptomatic of ambivalence or fluctuations in R. Kook's own stance, or of

---

[81] *Iggerot ha-Reayah*, I, Letter 44, translated in Feldman, *Selected Letters*, 93.

[82] Kook, "The Service of God", 146; trans. Bokser, *The Essential Writings*, 51.

[83] In this connection, the fact that R. Kook appropriates the terminological distinction between *Ein Sof* and its light (*Or Einsof*), originally employed by Habad as a means of differentiating between the ineffability of Stage One and Two (see n. 14) but used more often in order to distinguish between Stage Two and Three [see Tamar Ross, "The Concept of God in the Thought of Harav Kook – Part I," *Daat* 8 [Hebrew] (Winter 1982): 118–19; Dov Schwartz, "From 'Ein Sof' to the 'Light of Ein Sof' in Rabbi Kook's Thought" [Hebrew], *A New Spirit in the Palace of Torah – Jubilee volume in Honor of Professor Tamar Ross* (Ramat Gan: Bar-Ilan University Press, 2018), 119–64], is noteworthy theologically, but does not obviate the difficulty.

[84] For a few samples of such passages in English translation, see Rosenak, "Hidden Diaries."

wariness in exposing it to the masses.[85] Their full theological import, however, is best understood in light of his perception of the enhanced role and responsibility of the *Tzadik* in a messianic age.

As opposed to spiritual giants of previous generations, who sought merely to extract "holy sparks" from the profane (*berur berurim*) and return them to their source, R. Kook understood the more unified view of reality that he associated with redemption to be reflected in a heightened power of the *Tzadik* to elevate the discrete elements of the universe *in toto* (*haalaat olamot*), relating to them all with indiscriminate love as divinity proper.[86] Such an individual does not eat *in order* to be able to pray, or set *particular times* for the study of Torah or performance of mitsvot; his every wish is prayer, and his every movement a spontaneous expression of the divine.[87] Closer examination of R. Kook's personal accounts, however, reveals that he viewed this ascent from the level of "spark gatherers" to that of "uplifters of worlds" as comprised of two stages.[88] The first indeed involves flight from materialistic worldly distractions, which allows the *Tzadik* to quench his thirst for "that reservoir that is above all that is and is not,"[89] and to experience the feeling of non-being when encountering the expansiveness of God's undifferentiated infinity.[90] While the very presence of saintly individuals capable of achieving such heights exerts a measure of beneficial influence on their surroundings, this experience ideally leads to another stage, in which the *Tzadik* combines his experience of God's absolute unity with practical involvement in the nitty-gritty and

---

[85] As per Bar-Bettleheim's suggested explanation ("The Concept", 324–25) for a similar disparity between R. Kook's evaluation of Spinoza when formulated for public consumption and his more personal writing. In the former, the spiritual inability of the masses to distinguish between pantheism and atheism in an age of secularism warranted vehement denigration of Spinozism, but in the latter, R. Kook's attraction to the pantheistic nuances of Spinoza's thought comes through more clearly.

[86] For further discussion of R. Kook's distinction between *berur berurim* and *haalaat olamot*, see Ross, "The Concept – Part II" *Daat* 9 [Hebrew] (Summer 1982): 54–61; Kahan, "Divine Faith," 46–52.

[87] SK I, file 2, section 34.

[88] For a more exhaustive analysis of R. Kook's typology of these two stages, see Tomer Persico, "R. A. I. Kook: on Great Tzadikim and the Straight of Heart: At the Peak of Mystic Achievement," *Moreshet Yisrael* 5 (2008): 106–38.

[89] "Shall I Abandon the Source of Love", Bokser, *Abraham Isaac*, 383. This poem, as well as the entire section of poems in which it appears (371–86), exhibits R. Kook's ambivalence with regard to this stance.

[90] *Hadarav: Personal Episodes*, ed. Ran Sarid (Ramat Gan: Reut, 1998), 43; SK2, file 3, section 291, pp. 105–06.

moral responsibilities of everyday life. In this second state of consciousness, distinctions between the holy and the profane are not obliterated, nor is the profane regarded merely as an instrument or means to the holy. Rather, both participate in a higher form of holiness (*kodesh elyon*), whereby each and every particular is sanctified *as such*; mercy is balanced with judgment, spirit with matter, and necessity with freedom of choice. Only when the *Tzadik*'s brush with boundless infinity is followed by return to the reality of a diversified universe and accompanied by clear vision of the all-embracing unity of its manifold particulars and distinctions can his redemptive mission be achieved in full. Such an amalgam was personified, according to R. Kook, in the image of Moses. As both prophet and law-giver, he serves as a paradigmatic model for messianic times.[91]

Does this vision of the *Tzadik* and his spiritual trajectory comport with pan-emanationism, that is, the understanding that our experiences of the divine are forever blocked from "the thing as it is in itself"? R. Kook indeed associates all three levels of mystic ascent with specific sefirotic manifestations as depicted by the Kabbalah: the first with *Gevura*, the *sefirah* of judgment and constraint; the second with *Hessed*, the *sefirah* of unconstrained mercy; and the third with the more expansive and all-pervasive linear movement of *keter*. Nevertheless, an implicit parallel between R. Kook's tri-partite typology of the *Tzadik* and the differing conceptual stages of God–world relations alluded to in allegorical interpretations of the doctrine of *tsimtsum*,[92] and R. Kook's own view of the relationship between "the language of esoterics" (i.e., Kabbalah) and "absolute truth"[93] suggests a more ambivalent response.

The "spark gathering" *Tzadik* of pre-messianic times functions within an admixture of good and evil that supports Stage Three views of the cosmos as an independent and imperfect reality that, in accordance with Rashaz or R. Hayim, is distinct to one degree or another from the divine. The lure and the danger of unmitigated Hessed, as experienced by the first category of "world uplifters," indicate that the boundary between the world of emanations and their undifferentiated source, while desirable, can be porous, enabling a fleeting experience of Stage Two acosmism, according to which God is all. The spiritual state of the

---

[91] See "The Sage is More Important than the Prophet", *Orot*, 120; trans. in Bokser, *Abraham Isaac*, 253–55.
[92] Persico, "On Great Tzadikim," 9–11.   [93] SK1, file 1, section 876; file 5, section 237.

Tzadik who nevertheless returns to the divisions of this world, but includes them all as part and parcel of an ultimate unity, is reminiscent of the pan-cosmism of Stage One, which demolishes the God–world binary completely. Under such conditions, the ontological status of "God" or "not God" are equally illusory, and there is no need to flee from the secular in order to reach the holy, which is identified simply with "all that there is." But while the ineffability of Stage One defies definition, the ultimate goal of this-worldly existence (Stage Four) is not to obliterate particulars, but rather to vivify and facilitate their infinite proliferation.[94] R. Kook envisions perpetuation of this dynamic state of affairs even under messianic conditions, when awareness of the all-inclusive unity of finite beings will no longer be limited to rare individuals, and perfection and perfectibility will conflate. The ability of this conflation to still accommodate infinite expansion is rationalized in mythic terms: the very "memory" of primordial lack will suffice to insure a ceaseless urge for perfectibility and growth extending beyond that which has already been achieved.[95] "When the world will be uplifted, nature will resemble miracle in its revelation of ideal desire ... [but] even then a hidden light will appear as a higher miracle, whose light will radiate and enliven the light of the ordinary miracle, which will then resemble the content of that which is now [regarded as] nature."[96] Holiness does not harbor exaggeration; all that is imaginable truly exists.[97] Even when human perception of infinity is bound to the limits of this-worldly manifestations, there is a dialectical relationship between what is and what can be. Thus, in direct opposition to Maimonides' negative theology, the best avenue for approaching the divine is by discovering supernal holiness in the plenitude of infinite striving, whose upward spiraling produces tangible effects.[98]

The bottom line of all these considerations suggests that the distinctiveness of R. Kook's theology is best characterized not by its allegiance to emanationism, but rather by its final ideal, which can be summarized as panentheism turned on its head: when enveloping God's infinite and undifferentiated unity with a unity of parts we enhance divine perfection *from our point of view* by endowing it with

---

[94] Kook, *'Olat ha-Reayah* I, 50–51. [95] SK1, file 2, section 318, pp. 392–93.
[96] SK1, file 2, section 8. [97] Ibid., sections 9–11.
[98] See Tamar Ross, "Immortality, Law, and Human Perception," *Rabbi Abraham Isaac Kook and Jewish Spirituality*, eds. Lawrence J. Kaplan and David Shatz (New York and London: New York University Press, 1995), 237–53.

the capacity for infinite growth. Attaching ultimate value to a unity of parts in our (illusory) cosmic reality trumps self-annihilation in God as He is in Himself.

SOME CONCLUDING REMARKS

While responding to the needs of his times, there are many strands in R. Kook's thought that comport remarkably with current sensibilities. His assumption of the influence of consciousness on experience accords with new age spirituality and a rising sense that our scientific models have not yet scratched the surface of mind–matter relations, or the role of consciousness in nature. His readiness to forgo correspondence theories of truth meshes well with a postmodern inclination to view scientific as well as metaphysical models of reality as reality-producing constructs constantly open to revision in the wake of their ongoing brush with the dynamics of human experience. The same may be said for R. Kook's softening of boundaries between God and the world, which extends to other binaries as well,[99] and appears uncannily prescient in anticipating the present cultural tendency to view all discrete entities as elements of a spectrum. His expansive appeal to kabbalistic imagery, rather than reliance upon the formulation of precise theological statements, suggesting that knowledge of the unseen necessitates anatomical and objective imaging via a process in which intuition, imagination, will, and a sense of identity are central, is likewise congenial to a contemporary rejection of modernist positivism and its reliance upon reason as the ultimate key to advancement. Nonetheless, commitment to the core essentialism embedded in this imagery regarding the privileged status of the Jewish people in bringing about the redemption and to a concrete timetable that presumes to identify the state of human progress in this regard, limits the pliability of this model, and clashes with some of the problematic aspects of ethnocentric nationalism in an age of globalization. When undergoing the test of time, it may well be that the experiential and constructivist aspects of R. Kook's theology will outlive the political and collectivist themes for which he is best known today.

---

[99] See Ross, "Feminist Aspects in the Theology of R. Kook" [Hebrew], in *Derekh Haruach*, a volume honoring Eliezer Schweid, eds. Aviezer Ravitzky and Yehoyada Amir (Jerusalem: Hebrew University, 2005), 717–52.

Selected Further Reading

Agus, Jacob. *Banner of Jerusalem: The Life and Times of Abraham Isaac Kook.* New York: Bloch Publishing, 1946.

Ben-Shlomo, Yosef. *Poetry of Being: Lectures on the Philosophy of Rabbi Kook.* Tel Aviv: Mod Books, 1990.

Bokser, Ben Zion, editor and translator. *Abraham Isaac Kook – The Lights of Penitence, the Moral Principles, Lights of Holiness, Essays, Letters, and Poems.* New York, Ramsey, NJ, Toronto: Paulist Press, 1978.

Bokser, Ben Zion, editor and translator. *The Essential Writings of Abraham Isaac Kook.* Teaneck: Amity House, 1988.

Feldman, Tzvi, editor and translator. *Rav A. Y. Kook – Selected Letters.* Ma-aleh Adumim: Ma'aliot Publications of Yeshivat Birkat Moshe, 1986.

Gellman, Jerome I. *The Fear, the Trembling, and the Fire – Kierkegaard and Hasidic Masters on the Binding of Isaac*, chapter 5: The Passion. Lanham, MD, London, NewYork: University Press of America, 1994,

Mirsky, Yehudah. *Mystic in a Time of Revolution.* New Haven, CT, and London: Yale University Press, 2014.

Rappoport, Jason. "Rabbi Kook and Nietzsche – a Preliminary Comparison of their Ideas on Religions, Christianity, Buddhism and Atheism." *The Torah u-Madda Journal* 12 (2004): 99–129.

Rosenak, Avinoam. "Hidden Diaries and New Discoveries: The Life and Thought of Rabbi A. I. Kook." *Shofar: An Interdisciplinary Journal of Jewish Studies* 25.3 (Spring 2007): 111–47.

Ross, Tamar. "Between Metaphysical and Liberal Pluralism: A Reappraisal of R. A. I. Kook's Espousal of Toleration." *AJS Review* 21.1 (Spring 1996): 61–110.

Ross, Tamar. "The Cognitive Value of Religious Truth Claims: Rabbi A. I. Kook and Postmodernism." In *Hazon Nahum: Jubilee Volume in Honor of Norman Lamm*, 479–527. Edited by Yaakov Elman and Jeffrey S. Gurock. New York: Michael Sharf Publication Trust of the Yeshiva University Press, 1997.

Ross, Tamar. "Immortality, Law, and Human Perception." In *Rabbi Abraham Isaac Kook and Jewish Spirituality*, 237–53. Edited by Lawrence J. Kaplan and David Shatz, New York: NYU Press, 1994.

Shalom, Benjamin Ish. *Rav Avraham Itzhak HaCohen Kook – Between Rationalism and Mysticism.* Translated by Ora Wisking-Elper. Albany: SUNY Press, 1993.

Schwartz, Ari Ze-ev, ed. *The Spiritual Revolution of Rav Kook: The Writings of a Jewish Mystic.* Translated by Ari Ze'ev Schwartz. Jerusalem: Gefen Publishing House, 2018.

Yaron, Zvi. *The Philosophy of Rabbi Kook.* Translated by Avner Tamschoff. Jerusalem: Eliner Library, 1991.

10 Rosenzweig's *Midrashic* Speech-Acts: From Hegel and German Nationalism to a Modern-day *Ba'al Teshuvah*

JULES SIMON

Modern Jewish theology has been deeply enriched through the contributions of the German-Jewish philosopher and teacher, Franz Rosenzweig, although his contributions have only begun to be more fully recognized at the end of the twentieth century and the beginning of the twenty-first century.[1] In 2004, the International Rosenzweig Gesellschaft was formed along with the *Rosenzweig Jahrbuch/Yearbook* in order to stimulate and disseminate the burgeoning field of research related to and inspired by his writings and life. However, as is evident from the other chapters in this volume, the development of Jewish theology has been forming for several millennia from the time that the Hebrew Bible first began to take shape, an historical heritage recognized by Rosenzweig and one for which his contributions are significant and potentially transformative.[2]

---

[1] With respect to Rosenzweig's "standing" in the Jewish tradition and, specifically in modernity, the editor of this volume, Steven Kepnes, has claimed that Franz Rosenzweig is "The greatest modern Jewish theologian" because of how he insisted on God as an "independent reality." Kepnes defended that claim, in his talk "Jewish liturgy as Jewish theology" presented at the Albert and Vera List Fund for Jewish Studies Lecture at the Harvard Divinity School in 2015 (retrieved 11/11/2018 https://www.youtube.com/watch?v=ENquVPVppEk), which he had first introduced in his book *Liturgical Time:* Franz Rosenzweig's *Star of Redemption* (Oxford: Oxford University Press, 2007), 79–130. Building on his understanding of Rosenzweig, Kepnes extends what he learned from Rosenzweig's works by explicating Jewish theology through the Jewish prayer-book, the Siddur.

[2] The list of contemporary modern Jewish philosophers and theologians who have been deeply influenced by Rosenzweig's thought is far too extensive for a footnote, but a very few of those who have been influenced by Rosenzweig's philosophical theology, and whose works have directly influenced my own, include: Walter Benjamin, Emmanuel Levinas, Emil Fackenheim, Norbert Samuelson, Wolfdietrich Schmied-Kowarzik, Myriam Bienenstock, Barbara Gali, and Robert Gibbs. With the exception of Barbara Gali and perhaps Norbert Samuelson, each of those figures considered

Rosenzweig was born into an assimilated Jewish family in Kassell, Germany, where he became deeply engaged in confronting the pressures to "convert" to Christianity by friends and Jewish relatives who had already adopted a Christian way of life. As a young man, he embraced German culture and *Bildung*, eventually writing his dissertation on G. W. F. Hegel's political philosophy that was published in 1920 as *Hegel and the State*, one year before *The Star of Redemption* was published, the work for which he is most well known and which includes the clearest articulation of his theology. Moreover, if we want to identify the proximal impetus of Rosenzweig's contributions to Jewish theology, it is unavoidable that we start by recognizing the relationship of these two primary works. His work on Hegel epitomizes the scholarly depth and breadth of Rosenzweig's engagement in the dominant political and Christian-oriented '"historicist" ethos of his day. Interestingly, that work also represents one of Rosenzweig's principal counterpoints in engaging with his contemporary socio-political conditions, an engagement that further exemplifies Rosenzweig's full embrace of one of the most important elements of the Jewish theological tradition, namely, the way in which Jews living in exile have historically interpreted the Torah as an engaged, dialectical response from the dual perspectives of the living scriptural authority of their respective communities of faith and the non-Jewish contexts in which they found themselves. In an attitude of belief in the Jewish faith tradition into which he was born and educated, Rosenzweig followed the precedent of that living faith community which consisted in teaching guiding ways of thought based on interpreting passages of the Hebrew Bible by means of both the normative traditions of Jewish Law—the Torah—along with the philosophical and scientific practices of one's own particular and contemporary socio-historical context of experiencing the world. Such a twofold approach results in a better understanding of one's current world situation—in the form of a descriptive understanding of history and prescriptive norms for action aimed at a messianically transformed future—as well as a better, evolved understanding of the biblical scriptures. Indeed, Rosenzweig's work can and should be considered to be a modern addition to the hallowed living tradition of relating oral to written Torah that is known as midrash.

himself or herself to be a philosopher, and yet each in their own way has informed my interpretation of Rosenzweig's *theology* that is the subject of this chapter.

But Rosenzweig's complex theological position challenges conventional apologetic approaches because of his commitment to a dialogical variation on what has become known as dual-covenant theology. In fact, his approach reverses standard patterns of supercessionist and triumphalist forms of theological posturing that have historically characterized the relationships of the three great monotheisitic faith traditions of Judaism, Christianity, and Islam. In Rosenzweig's construction, Judaism constitutes the flaming core of a creatively reconstructed, faith-based model that validates the deep and rich historical, scriptural, and liturgical traditions of both Judaism and Christianity. The complementary relationship of Judaism and Christianity is architectonically modeled after an image of the Star of David, with Judaism constituting the center and originary power of the Star and Christianity constituting the "missionary" rays of the Star. The three-fold expression of historical Christianity—Roman Catholicism, Protestantism, and Eastern Orthodoxy—extend and engage the theological roots within Judaism while simultaneously confronting the socio-political epochs in the course of history with ethical face-to-face relationships, transforming unenlightened and reified pagans in the world with revelatory experiences of being loved. Controversially, Rosenzweig situates Islam as the theological foil to both faith communities of Jews and Christians since the Islamic form of faith, with its roots in the philosophical Atomism of the *mutakallimūn*, retains a theocratic and dictatorial hierarchical political structure. From Rosenzweig's perspective, Islam is not based on the experience of revelatory and redeeming love and thus does not allow for the creation of ever-new forms of midrashic-based, enlivening experiences of faith, hope, and love in the world.

Rosenzweig's midrashic-based reconstruction of Jewish theology is founded on traditional Jewish text-centered teachings and practices, which Rosenzweig realigns and thus renews by affirming the long-held Jewish form of Messianism that is politically and historically engaged in the world. Various forms of Messianism have been embodied for several millennia through interrelated expressions of speech-acts, textual-narrative traditions, and ritual embodiments of the Law of Ethics.[3] My overarching claim in this chapter is that Rosenzweig has

---

[3] As I spell out in the rest of the chapter, it seems to me that Rosenzweig set a compelling path for rethinking, reimagining, and recreating the traditional understanding of the revelation of Torah with his speech-thinking approach to understanding Messianism that is based on enlivening an authentic sense for *Jewish* responsibility, not only with respect for what is at stake politically and ethically for

been able to establish an authoritative place in the Jewish theological tradition precisely because of how he sets out his midrashic interpretation of a distinctively Jewish Messianic tradition.

The key elements of Rosenzweig's Jewish theology are set out in *The Star of Redemption* with the specifically "theological" dimension expressed through his construction of a philosophy of language that he calls Speech-Thinking (*Sprachdenken*) which leads to a theory of truth, by the end of the book, that he identifies as a "messianic theory of knowledge" that testifies to the "God of truth."[4] Thus, the thesis I present in this chapter is that, for Rosenzweig, the main issue for Jewish theology in the modern period is not idolatry, not Kabbalah, not science, and not systematic theology or systematic philosophy, and not even the nature of covenant;[5] rather, it is all of those in the

---

the modern nation state of Israel, but also and especially for those Jews who find themselves living in exile.

[4] Four years after publishing *The Star of Redemption* Rosenzweig published an article, "The New Thinking" (1925) which provides a rethinking of the purpose and intent of his magnum opus, *The Star of Redemption*, recasting it as both a peculiar kind of system of philosophy and, theologically, as primarily and "essentially," a book for Jews. It is also where he at first characterizes his way of philosophizing as *"erfahrende Philosophie"* (117) or "experiencing philosophy," as opposed to that kind of philosophy that reduces everything to either the "I" or "the world" or "God." But then he goes on to describe his way of philosophizing as *"erzählende Philosophia"* (121) or "narrating philosophy" which, I argue, is another way of preparing us for the peculiarly Jewish midrashic form of speech-act philosophy that is tied up not only with temporal ways of thinking, with "timely" thinking, but with retelling the theological "story" of creation, revelation, and redemption which captures, for Rosenzweig, the narration of the past (creation), the living dialogue of the present (revelation), and the prediction of belief in a messianic future of global peace and understanding (redemption). For the quote, "messianic theory of knowledge," see Franz Rosenzweig, "The New Thinking" in *Franz Rosenzweig: Philosophical and Theological Writings*, translated and edited, with notes and commentary, by Paul W. Franks and Michael L. Morgan (Indianapolis and Cambridge, MA: Hackett Publishing Company, 2000), 136.

[5] For an argument identifying Rosenzweig's thinking with the traditional Jewish rejection of idolatry, see Leora Batnitzky, *Idolatry and Representation: The Philosophy of Franz Rosenzweig Reconsidered* (Princeton:Princeton University Press, 2009); for an argument defending Rosenzweig's work as systematic philosophy, see Benjamin Pollock, *Franz Rosenzweig and the Systematic Task of Philosophy* (Cambridge and New York: Cambridge University Press, 2009); for an argument that Rosenzweig's work should be read as aligned and allied with an existentialist reading of Martin Heidegger's, see Peter Gordon, *Rosenzweig and Heidegger: Between Judaism and German Philosophy* (Berkeley: University of California Press, 2003); and for a reading of Rosenzweig from a perspective of Jewish mysticism, see Elliot Wolfson, *Giving Beyone the Gift: Apophasis and Overcoming Theomania* (New York: Fordham University Press, 2014); and Dana Hollander on covenant and

form of what I call Messianic Aesthetics.[6] What I mean by Messianic Aesthetics refers to the "embodied" ways in which Rosenzweig's commitment to the ethical norms inherent in the teachings and life practices of Jewish faith traditions and communities assume their distinctively lived world expressions. For Rosenzweig, such teachings and practices are experienced and expressed aesthetically on the body, on one's arms and head, in the home, on the street, and lived in one's communities in order to "demonstrate" the truth of Jewish commitment to sharing the light of their messianic way of life. Those expressions embody an ethical normativity "located" in what Jews traditionally understand as "the Law" that is carried out in the written and oral teachings that "correlate" a practicing and observant Jew's concern for his/her own community with concomitant concern and service for others who are not directly part of the Jewish community—the widow, orphan, and stranger. This, by any other description, is the basic meaning of Messianism, that is, a Messianism that is based on a set of theological beliefs that puts into socio-political practice the ethical command of a Jew (and thereby the Jewish community) to love and to serve thy neighbor as commanded by the love of God. Rosenzweig sets out this teaching-as-a-practice throughout the entirety of *The Star of Redemption*, using a powerful speech-act philosophy in order to bring the structures of the interrelated processes of creation, revelation, and redemption into functional and dynamic relations. For example, he sets out the foundations of his speech-acts already in the transition section from Part I to Part II of *The Star* where he deals specifically with the changing historical relations of the disciplines of philosophy and theology. His argument is that philosophy and theology need each other for their respective strengths: accentuating objectivity, in the case of philosophy, and

---

chosenness in "The Significance of Franz Rosenzweig's Retrieval of Chosenness," in *Jewish Studies Quarterly* 16(1) (2009): 146–62.

[6] For my first publication that dealt with Rosenzweig's "messianic aesthetics," see: Jules Simon, "Rosenzweig's Messianic Aesthetics" in *Franz Rosenzweigs Neues Denken*, edited by Wolfdietrich Schmied-Kowarzik (Freiburg: Verlag Karl Alber GmbH, 2006), 407–17. For a detailed and full account of this approach, see my presentation of Rosenzweig's "The Messianic Aesthetic" in Jules Simon, *Art and Responsibility: A Phenomenology of the Diverging Paths of Rosenzweig and Heidegger* (New York: Bloomsbury, 2011), ch. 4, 111–52. In the analysis of Rosenzweig's use of midrash that follows I draw extensively on how I explicate that historical phenomenon more fully in my text and in the context of the argument that I make about the difference between Rosenzweig's midrash and Heidegger's methodological hermeneutic phenomenology.

subjectivity, in the case of theology. By joining forces, so to speak, philosophy and theology create the best possible life of faith for the Jewish community and thus, by extension, for the rest of the world. The entirety of Part I of *The Star* can fruitfully be understood as Rosenzweig's laying down of the philosophical foundations, with phenomenological expositions of the elements God-World-Human, for the speech-acts that constitute the specifically theological books of Part II, Creation-Revelation-Redemption, which prepares the reader for the specifically socio-historical community formations of Part III, The Fire-The Rays-The Star or Eternal Truth.

In brief, the heart of Rosenzweig's theological contribution can be said to consist of a revision of what constitutes "revelation" for the Jewish community of believers. One of his central tasks is to present "Revelation as Aesthetic Category" but in the sense of inspiring us to grasp the ethicality of the speech-act of love that calls us to express our full humanity by accepting the love of God which plays out in loving my neighbor as my self. Indeed, in Book 3 of Part II of *The Star*, Rosenzweig describes the process whereby one who is singled out in love by God is commanded to love one's neighbor "as oneself." As I articulate in what follows, Rosenzweig works out his engagement with Messianism in the modern world with a speech-thinking approach to Messianic Aesthetics that includes such acts of love and thereby renews the traditional Jewish practice of midrashic commentary.[7]

---

[7] For a related demonstration of Rosenzweig's speech-act approach to philosophy of language, as a foundation for his theological stance, see Robert Gibbs, *Correlations in Rosenzweig and Levinas* (Princeton: Princeton University Press). See especially chs. 3 and 4, 57–104: ch. 3 "Speech as Performance (I): The Grammar of Revelation" which ends with the section "The Moods of Theology"; ch. 4 "Speech as Performance (II): Logic, Reading, Questions" which ends with "The Question of Theology." Gibbs convincingly demonstrates how Rosenzweig, unlike Hermann Cohen, correlates philosophy and theology *through speech*. The core of Gibbs' argument that he presents in Chapter 1 has to do with his comparative analysis of the function of *correlation* in Cohen's work with the way that Gibbs argues correlation works in Rosenzweig's *The Star of Redemption*. He claims that "the bridge of reason [from Cohen] was abandoned in favor of a bridge of speech" for Rosenzweig. According to Gibbs, unlike Cohen, Rosenzweig does not augment his philosophical work by way of religious experience, as Cohen does, but with theological concepts. Rosenzweig "abandons the bridge of reason ... in favor of a bridge of speech" in order to employ the theological categories of Creation, Revelation, and Redemption as a way to *correlate* the elements of God-World-Human—partly discussed in this chapter beginning on page 224. See Gibbs, *Correlations in Rosenzweig and Levinas*, p. 20. What

Before I introduce and elaborate on Rosenzweig's Messianic Aesthetics and its connection with his use of midrash, I present a brief description of midrash. In *Understanding Rabbinic Midrash: Texts and Commentary*, Gary Porton provides the following definition of midrash:

> Midrash is "a type of literature, oral or written, which has its starting point in a fixed, canonical text, considered the revealed word of God by the Midrashist and his audience, and in which this original verse is explicitly cited or clearly alluded to, ... For something to be considered Midrash it must have a clear relationship to the accepted canonical text of Revelation. Midrash is a term given to a Jewish activity which finds its locus in the religious life of the Jewish community. While others exegete their revelatory canons and while Jews exegete other texts, only Jews who explicitly tie their comments to the Bible engage in Midrash."[8]

This definition highlights the "clear relationship" that every form of Jewish midrash has to the Bible, as a "revealed" set of scriptures and thus as a source of authority for teaching and practice.

In *Back to the Sources*, Barry Holtz further defines midrash by distinguishing between aggadic and halakhic forms:

> Midrash—the act and process of interpretation—works in both the halakhic and aggadic realms. That is, sacred texts, most notably the Bible, are carefully interpreted, both to derive points of law and to give occasion for theological statements and parables. [And] ... both halakhic and aggadic sorts of Midrash seem to develop out of the same set of forces. Primarily we can see the central issue behind the emergence of Midrash as the need to deal with the presence of cultural or religious tension and discontinuity. Where there are questions that demand answers, and where there are new cultural and intellectual pressures that must be addressed, Midrash comes into play as a way of resolving crisis and reaffirming continuity with the traditions of the past.[9]

Gibbs accomplishes with this reference in his text is to contextualize how Rosenzweig rejects the approaches of both dogmatic and apologetic theology.

[8] Gary Proton, *Understanding Rabbinic Midrash: Texts and Commentary* (New York: KTAV, 1985), 6–8. See Jacob Neusner, *What is Midrash?* (Minneapolis, MN: Fortress Press, 1987).

[9] See Barry W. Holtz, *Back to the Sources: Reading the Classic Jewish Texts* (New York: Simon and Schuster, 1986), 178.

Holtz explains that since the Bible is the primary source, looking to the forces and peculiar tensions of the Bible becomes the first step not only in attempts to understand the function of midrash but in order to practice it. Rabbis in the Middle Ages, when the body of midrashim developed, roughly 400–1200 CE, began this practice of exploring the textual resonance of biblical narratives and passages in order to determine the ways in which what was written in those passages could speak to issues of their day. Conversely, the very traditions of evolving interpretive practices that emerged from the lived communities of Jews faced with preserving and cultivating their Jewish ways of life and beliefs in their exilic conditions, began to be accumulated, at first orally for hundreds of years and then in written form, also for hundreds of years. This dialectical process of relating textual traditions with the ongoing practices of Jewish religious identity as a communal, exilic, and messianic community is what is known today as midrash.

In a short but informative book, *What is Midrash?*, Jacob Neusner provides a typology of midrash—as "Paraphrase, Prophecy, Parable"—together with a functional description, namely, midrash as "Exegesis, Document, Process," all of which can be said to have their origin in the condition of what he calls the inauguration of the process of routine and ubiquitous self-interpretation of the scriptures by the writers of the Hebrew Bible itself.[10]

And in his study, Holtz adds that in the twentieth century, actively practicing midrash in the Jewish community seems to have been reborn. He notes how Arthur Green's "The Children in Egypt and the Theophany at the Sea," published in 1975, explores issues of theology and belief with an exposition of midrashim about children at the sea and the relevance of that story for today. "We have to reread [the stories of the Bible] to realize that they are surprisingly topical. Job is our contemporary."[11] He also points to Elie Wiesel's *Messengers of God* as

---

[10] For this position, he draws on Michael Fishbane's hermeneutics and his argument that the Hebrew Scriptures already contain the antecedents for later Jewish biblical exegesis: "... the broad range of stylistic patterns from many periods, together with their corresponding technical terms, strategies or procedures, suggest that exegetical techniques and traditions developed locally and cumulatively in ancient Israel from monarchic times and continued into the Graeco-Roman period, where they served as a major reservoir for the Jewish schools and techniques of exegesis then developing ..." from Michael Fishbane, *Biblical Interpretation in Ancient Israel* (Oxford: Clarendon Press, 1983), 525.

[11] See Arthur Green, "The Children in Egypt and the Theophany at the Sea," in *Judaism* 24.3 (Fall 1975), 446–56.

a midrashic commentary on the atrocities of the Shoah.[12] Mara Benjamin develops a similar theme about the renewal of midrash and focuses directly on the singular role of Rosenzweig in that process with her book, *Rosenzweig's Bible: Reinventing Scripture for Jewish Modernity*, and sets herself the task to investigate "... some of the strategies a modern religious thinker might employ when confronting the challenges modern thought poses to the traditional claims of a religious tradition ... [in order to understand how one might claim] ... a privileged place for the Bible within a community of faith"[13] in the face of modern secular challenges to revelation. In doing so, she clearly situates Rosenzweig's work in that process of renewal, especially in how she focuses on his efforts to apply his renewal of the interpretive methods in the Jewish tradition to his later translations of Judah Halevi's poems and the Bible with Martin Buber.

However, Benjamin does not reach deeply enough into what constitutes the radical nature of Rosenzweig's renewal of the midrashic tradition, supported as it is by a powerful logic of speech-act analyses and Rosenzweig's thoroughgoing immersion in the history of philosophy, especially Hegel's philosophy of history. Rosenzweig's position goes well beyond being merely a dialectical response to the secular challenges of modernity, although it is that. Benjamin proposes that Rosenzweig took up the self-appointed task to reformulate "the concept of revelation" for "skeptical modern readers"[14] and observes how " ... Rosenzweig demonstrated a serious engagement with the ways in which the modern intellectual situation precludes the simple reappropriation of the Bible as Scripture."[15] Her point is that Rosenzweig recognized that modern historicism seriously and successfully undermined the uniquely authoritative meaning of the Bible and, from her perspective, Rosenzweig played an essential role in renewing the place of Scripture in the religious life of the modern individual and community. However, she modulates that judgment by describing Rosenzweig's commitment as a kind of biblical absolutism, which meant, in her words, that "he avoided an honest reckoning with the modern critique of Biblical

---

[12] See Elie Wiesel, *Messengers of God: Biblical Portraits and Legends* (New York: Random House, 1976). For example, the chapter "Cain and Abel: The First Genocide" exemplifies Wiesel's midrashic effort to "make sense of" contemporary acts of genocide, such as the Shoah, 37 ff.

[13] See Mara Benjamin, *Rosenzweig's Bible: Reinventing Scripture for Jewish Modernity* (Cambridge and New York: Cambridge University Press, 2009), 4.

[14] Ibid., 5.   [15] Ibid., 175.

authority."[16] The key to her claim is that with *The Star of Redemption*, Rosenzweig had waged a war to "compel recognition of the power of revelation ..."[17] that was set in the context of the conflict between the modern world of secularism and theological belief of Europe. However, Benjamin's interpretation, that Rosenzweig's theology was a matter of "strategizing" in the face of the challenges of modern historicism, shifts attention away from the deep roots of how Rosenzweig's New Thinking contributes to the "modern" renewal of midrash as a Jewish interpretive tradition. Secondly, while her insight about the centrality of the concept of revelation in *The Star of Redemption* is true to Rosenzweig's project, her subsequent claims that the theological stringency of the position in *The Star* is displaced in Rosenzweig's later writings—specifically with his translations of the Hymns of Judah Ha Levi and the Bible translation with Martin Buber—does not fully account for the philosophical and ethical importance of his "theological" renewal of midrash in *The Star of Redemption*.

The transformative potential of Rosenzweig's work has to do, rather, with the renewal of a living *theological* response which entails evaluating Rosenzweig's contribution in the face of the deeper challenges of modern epistemology, science, and politics. And in every case, those contributions need to be measured for their ethically normative foundations. That is what makes Rosenzweig's contribution an especially Jewish one.

From this perspective, we can follow the lead of Norbert Samuelson who has argued that Rosenzweig's work is a modern-day *Guide of the Perplexed* but a special kind of guide, namely, one for those—both Jews and other humans in general—who are perplexed by the complex issues of modernity, such as philosophy, science, language, culture, and the nation-state. Most importantly, and unlike Benjamin's "strategizing" position, Samuelson contends that one of the fundamental "constructive" elements in Rosenzweig's work, that is directly relevant for the *constructive* function of his theology, is that he presents a way to develop a modern Jewish practice that is meaningfully responsive to traditional teachings on Jewish mitsvot and halakhah.[18] For Samuelson, that has to do with

---

[16] Ibid., 173.   [17] Ibid.
[18] See Norbert Samuelson *A User's Guide to Franz Rosenzweig's Star of Redemption* (Abingdon: Routledge, 2010). In this thorough and authoritative comprehensive explication of Rosenzweig's work, Samuelson explicitly states: "... I intend my

the ways in which Jews, specifically, but other believing humans, in general, can make sense of authoritative scriptural and oral teaching traditions while still making sense of the challenges that philosophy and modern science present to traditional faith communities.

As I explicate in what follows, Rosenzweig's renewal of midrash in the twentieth century is twofold in that, first, he makes sense of an historically existing Jewish community whose very constitution as a coherent and identifiable community has been bound up with interpreting the Bible—as Scripture. This he does in order to make sense of contemporary *theological* concerns of how to address specific questions of human ethical relations in the world in the context of the phenomenon of communities of belief. That very community of interpreters, however, has historically weighed these concerns against the traditional teaching that God "historically" revealed the Torah—the Law—in a particular speech-act at a distinct place and in a distinct time to the entire People of Israel on Mount Sinai. There are two related sub-issues here which have to do with the second "fold" of his renewal. The first is Rosenzweig's theological contribution to renewing the tradition of midrash in a way that engages specific issues of modernity, such as the nature of what constitutes "authentic" Jewish belief and, secondly, the role that a "believing community" plays in the larger, historical context of a non-believing, secular humanism.[19] The second sub-issue is what to make of Rosenzweig's

commentary to be simple and not complex – either philosophically or historically. In traditional Jewish terms, the concern of the commentary is to present the PASHAT (simple meaning) of the text and not REMES (what the text alludes to), DeRASH, how the text can be applied to contemporary situations [what I am referring to as MIDRASH in this chapter], or SOD, what the text may mean at a deeper conceptual or spiritual level]" (from the Preface, xxxiii). I was one of a handful of his students who sat with Samuelson over the course of a *havurah* style of close reading of the text in weekly session over the course of several years. Independent of my readings of Rosenzweig that have been influenced by Samuelson, I have argued that Rosenzweig clearly sets out an alternative to the powerful philosophical inspirations of Heidegger and the tradition of neo-Hegelian phenomenology on the one hand, and Cassirer and neo-Kantian post-Enlightenment rationalism, with its turn to epistemological formalism and symbolic forms of logic, on the other. See my book, *Art and Responsibility: A Phenomenology of the Diverging Paths of Rosenzweig and Heidegger* (New York: Bloomsbury Publishing, 2011). Much of my interpretation of Rosenzweig's theology in this chapter is informed by that earlier, extensive engagement with his work.

[19] Rosenzweig already addressed this issue in straightforward fashion with his essay "Atheistic Theology." However, his treatment there is cursory and limited to a confrontation with Buber's position, which he identified as not critical enough of

theological assertion, played out in *The Star*, that revelation is, at its core, better understood as a communicative speech-act that, while resting on the *content* of the transmission of the *ethical law* at Sinai, is constantly renewed through *revelatory* acts of love such as those expressed in *Shir ha Shirim*.

Addressing these related concerns is at the heart of understanding Rosenzweig's radical renewal of traditional Jewish theological teaching because, for Rosenzweig, all midrashim address two similar questions: What is the *right response* to understanding this or that contemporary situation that solicits the intention to turn to midrash in the first place? And relatedly, what is the *right way to act* in this or that situation, guided by midrash? The former falls into the traditional category of aggadic midrashic literature—that which refers to narrative literature, parables, theological literature, or homilies—while the latter falls into the traditional category of halakhic midrashic literature—that which is concerned with laws and codes of behavior. And this distinction is the key to understanding Rosenzweig's realignment of *Torah min Ha Shamayim*. What I propose in this chapter is that Rosenzweig's radical realignment happens through the messianic aesthetic of revelatory speech-acts that take shape as an expression of the ethical normativity of the mitsvot of the Torah, traditionally associated narrowly with the "giving of the Law" at Mt. Sinai. In effect, the entire expression of Rosenzweig's *The Star* is a midrashic speech-act. However, for the sake of simplifying an explanation of that judgment, we can restrict our attention to the central, explicitly theological part of the text, that is, all of Part II of *The Star* and its character as logical sets of syntactically ordered and semantically interdependent analyses of language with theological connotations.

In Book 1 of Part II, Rosenzweig analyzes the opening verses of the first book of Bereshit by analyzing the narratives of creation, with their temporally past and spatially fixed coordinates, and the place in that narrative of the self-exclusivity of the elements and of human beings. The peculiar aesthetic form of that narrative is epic, its grammar is indicative, its key words are *knowledge and faith*, and its culminating thesis is the phenomenon of death. Ethically, such a domain deals with

---

the repetition of philosophical approaches that discounted the very nature and empirical character of belief and the ethical enactment of love for others in the world, based on that belief. Cf. Franks and Morgan, "Atheistic Theology", 10–24.

the formation of individual identity, namely, with the monological "I."

He analyzes the biblical *Shir Ha Shirim* in Book 2 of Part II in order to re-narrate the event of revelation, with its focus on the temporal present, temporality as such, and the relational and non-relational aspects of reality that specifically determine the foundations of human ethics. Its peculiar aesthetic form is the lyrical poem-song, its grammar is imperative, and its key words are *faith and love* and it is ordered around the phenomenon of relationship as such. Ethically, this domain presents the reader with various structures of dynamic relations that take the dialogical form of an "I and you."

The final domain is highlighted by considering the hymns of praise in the Psalms (תהילים), especially Psalm 115, and has to do with redemption, the future, eternity, social structures, and activities of communities. Its peculiar aesthetic forms are drama and song, its grammar is dative, and its key word is *hope*. Ethically, this level deals with broader social structures represented by the challenge of the stranger as neighbor, namely, that one who stands outside the circle of family and loved ones but who is nonetheless called to join in and become a member of a community. Addressing the anonymous neighbor is a further response to the demands of *justice*, namely, that each and every human being should—by being personally attended to—have the opportunity to live a more vital and meaningful life. As an ethical task, commanded as a biblically grounded mitsvot, loving an *other* and providing her or him with the opportunity to respond and to thus "come alive" as a unique, particularized individual, dissolves the homogenizing and reifying hold that the world has on an individual and is therefore an act of redemption, an "attending" form of justice.

But how are we to conceive that moment when a third is sought to join in with an initial community of two? What are the concrete steps that must be taken? For Rosenzweig, the way to answer these questions requires a theological orientation, and thus embraces one's lived world condition of finding oneself living in a "faith" community of those who believe in each other and in a God variously understood as Creator, Revealer, and Redeemer. The first steps of the philosophico-theological process takes the form of engaging in midrashic analysis, which enables one to interpretively address such questions. As noted, Rosenzweig exemplifies these sorts of speech-acts for us by constructing a particular midrash that responds to the concrete, historical challenges of his place and time, namely, how to express a *living and meaningful faith* in the face of the challenge of the erosion of traditional forms of belief. His constructive midrash is based on the ancient biblical text *Shir ha Shirim* because of his judgment that that text itself expresses an interpretive self-reflective act that explores revelation, as such, as a speech-act of a love relation that can only be expressed through present-tense forms of face-to-face imperative commands of love and response to love.

In Rosenzweig's hands, midrash does not begin with a traditional form of "theological" conceptual analysis, that is, analysis that proceeds by theoretical or logical stipulations. Rather, midrash begins with a direct embrace of one's empirically embodied experience out of which we wrestle, or induce, conceptual meaning. The beginning of Rosenzweig's formal consideration of the term we use to describe the "experience of" (that is, the "wrestled-out of") lived meaning is a particular sentence that, according to Rosenzweig, has universal application, namely: *Love is as strong as death*. Found in one of the oldest and one of the most pagan of biblical texts, *Shir ha Shirim*, Rosenzweig takes up this biblical text as he received it, "embodied" in the living, historical Jewish-community-in-exile, and demonstrates for us, with this scriptural text in hand, how to become situated in a defined, particular socio-historical context. What I mean by this is that *from* a context in which a community of humans found liberation from enforced slavery through speech-acts of love and proclamations of faith in each other, as in God, can and should also be understood as *similar to* the context of contemporary secular human conditions—what Rosenzweig refers to as the world of unbelief or what can also be understood as modern secular humanism that emerged from eighteenth-century Enlightenment. By taking up the biblical text in the way that he does, he calls forth the living rhythms of the cultural language-world of the Bible—what he refers to as the world of belief—and weds them via midrash into the world of modern, secular unbelief.

This pairing of the resonance of biblical text with the speech-acts in play in one's contemporary socio-historical condition is what Rosenzweig understands as midrash. It is also the work of translation. However, it is not the form of biblical interpretation referred to by Mara Benjamin nor the formal techniques that Jacob Neusner analyzes in his short, informative text. By identifying such a grammatical or linguistic point to express the work of midrash as the work of revelation, Rosenzweig invites us to accept the condition that humans enliven the very spirit of being human in their lived-world experiences in the actual, relational world of particular non-denominational human communities, an anarchic condition of a primordial faithlessness that has been taken up and interpreted by a variety of faith communities.[20] But without any direct reference to historical faith communities, such as Jewish or Christian communities, Rosenzweig situates at the heart of his midrash on the "nature" of revelation the sentence from *Shir ha Shirim* that is embedded in the heart of the Bible, *Love is as strong as death*, with the intention of demonstrating, through a particularly Jewish midrashic activity, that this archetypal, secular love song is the quintessential text to which Jews and other living beings can turn in order to best understand the dynamics of the *experience of loving* and *of being loved*. What this means is that a love relationship—as it occurs in itself—is not merely referred to by the midrashic speech-act, but is itself an expression of revelation, of love. To readers of Rosenzweig, this makes theological sense since the dynamics of human-to-human love relationships best serve to *actually reveal* what Rosenzweig presents as the essential function of a God–human relation for any understanding of the actuality of any other human-to-human love relations in general.[21] In order to grasp the significance of that demonstration for his theology, it is necessary to walk through some additional details of Rosenzweig's renewal of the practice of midrash with *The Star*.

THE ANALOGY OF LOVE AS ETHICAL DIALOGUE

As is clear from the statement, "Love is *as* strong *as* death," Rosenzweig initially begins his midrashic task by comparing two concepts on the level of analogy, namely, the concepts of love and death. There are two respects in which Rosenzweig uses analogy as an analytical tool to disclose the similar and dissimilar structures of the two experiences of love and death in reference to the experience of the earth-bound souls of

---

[20] This is how Rosenzweig begins *The Star* with his existential reflection on death and the deconstruction of the perennial claims of Idealist philosophy to know the All and thus to be able to do away with the tensions involved in "actual" belief. See Franz Rosenzweig, *Der Stern der Erlösung: Franz Rosenzweig: Der Mensch und sein Werk: Gessamelte Schriften* 2 (Hague: Martinus Nijhof, 1977; originally published 1921), 3 ff.; and *The Star of Redemption*, translated by William W. Hallo (Notre Dame and London: University of Notre Dame Press, 1975), 3 ff. All citations in the following refer to these two editions of Rosenzweig's text.

[21] He is also able to highlight the relation of pagan and believer because of the situatedness of this secular love poem in a collection of "divine" texts.

a man and woman: (a) as a paradigmatic analogy to the love relationship of God with the human; and (b) as applied to the aesthetic/theological categories of creation, revelation, and redemption and their respective temporal horizons of past, present, and future. For the midrashic interpretation, the aesthetic continuum of creation-revelation-redemption is analogously equivalent to the temporal complex past-present-future, and we are encouraged to bridge the gap between concept and reality, that is, the gap from speech-thinking to speech-acts. But to complicate matters, the very artificiality of Rosenzweig's preferred aesthetic form—his midrashic model with its theological vocabulary—is the interpretive device used to engage and transform other humans in their secularly insulated realities. One way to begin to think about it is as an act of embodied, enlivening, and revelatory love. Rosenzweig's theological performance in the central books of *The Star* correlates directly with an enactment of an aesthetic performance that intertwines with the theory in which we have already been educated (Part I and Book 1 of Part II) and anticipates that which is to come (Part III and Book 3 of Part II).

The analogies of the relations God => human to human ⇔ human and to woman ⇔ man are just as important as the continuum because, as Rosenzweig claims, the event of love with which the revelatory love of *Shir ha Shirim* resounds is more than analogy. As a speech-act, the revelatory event that occurs in a relationship of love expressed by *Shir ha Shirim* expresses that transformative process by which humans convert themselves into other than what they are: "Revelation is to the soul the lived experience of a present which although it rests on the existence of the past, it does not dwell therein, rather it walks [changes, converts, turns—*wandeln*] in the light of the divine countenance."[22] The point of using a term such as *"wandeln"* signifies that an empirical effectiveness holds in the kind of transformative experience of love that happens as the dialogical relationship that Rosenzweig depicts in his theological construal of this particular, historically situated and originated speech-act.

What I mean by "historically situated and originated" calls for further explication, keeping in mind the tensions between the two kinds of love at stake in this midrash—human to human and God to human//human to God. It is not the case that just any love poem could adequately serve for Rosenzweig's midrashic demonstration as does *Shir ha Shirim*. Rosenzweig notes that in order to authentically and expressively communicate love from one to another, one has to

---

[22] Rosenzweig, *Der Stern*, 174; *The Star*, 156.

speak from one's heart to the heart of another. Such a speech-act, in order to be authentically heart-to-heart, has to come from the roots of one's historically embedded and culturally situated life, that is, from one's actual place in an existing "lived world" community of believers. This limiting condition restricts the possibility of such an expressive speech-act "counting" as authentic if it is reducible to a randomly stipulated, generalizable, or universalizable variable. In other words, a genuinely authentic speech-act of love has to express the uniquely personal history of this or that particular human individual. This means that, from Rosenzweig's theological perspective, to love is to love in particular. In a love relationship, the lover calls the beloved by her or his name and only answers when the beloved, for her or his part, calls the lover by her or his name in turn.

However, at the same time, Rosenzweig insists that love can only happen entirely in the moment of proximity and with the very expression of desirable presence. And as presence, love transforms the particular individual from a metaethical self, blind and mute to others, to relational and thus ethically sensitive soul—all ears and mouth openly receptive to and expressive toward the other.

The transformation accomplished in the relation, a transformation called revelation, transforms the individual involved by impelling her, as if by command, to turn to her neighbor in love simply because she is there, now. Rosenzweig again refers to this text at the very end of *The Star* after the reader has learned more about how Rosenzweig understands the communal ramifications of the ethical imperative to love one's neighbor. In the central parts of his text where he is theoretically concerned with theologically informed aesthetics, he makes a bold claim for the medium of art to initiate such a transformation, although it takes an actual speech-act beyond art, beyond constructs of theology—from one actually living and embodied human to another actually and socially embodied human—to ultimately accomplish change in the world.[23] And because

[23] The importance of the work of art—in this case, the work of theology for Rosenzweig's Messianic Aesthetics—is to mediate the initial encounter of the mediation of an object, where the possibility of doing violence to the other, by laying one's hands on the other, is obviated. The work of art—here, the theological saying—is used to initiate the contact which, after establishing familiarity, can become a tender "relation-building" caress as an expression of human desire for the sake of the metaphysical Other in a Levinasian sense. See "Phenomenology and Eros" in Emmanuel Levinas, *Totality and Infinity* (Pittsburgh: Duquesne University Press, 1969), 256–66.

Rosenzweig's theological formulations are just as much aesthetic formulations, he can say that just as each of the individual details of a work of art is *ensouled* with life by an artist, each individual human being in the community of all humans is "analogously" *ensouled* through various speech-acts of love of a human who has already been loved to the next human who happens along in her life.

One of the consequences of Rosenzweig's theological commitment is the possibility for enacting ethical dialogue in the sense that it is only in the authentic demand to love that one encounters the "I" of one's dialogue-partner. In fact, the other is only able to emerge as distinctly and absolutely other in the mutual interchange of denying oneself in being-open to desiring this particular other standing over against me, a denial that—paradoxically—is only made possible through recognizing the tragic isolation that was the case in having rejected, or negated, just this very other in their radical otherness. The result of such a voluntary self-denial—a negation of the rejection of that other—is an affirmative process of entering into a "growing" relationship based on increasing the level of mutual trust between the two who stand in dialogue. This relationship of mutual trust should then lead to the process of *Steigerung*, through affirmatively sustaining the growth of one another as a qualified means for helping each other achieve more complete and fulfilling lives. The mediation is qualified for the sake of resisting an ethics of crassly exploiting the other as merely the means of self-serving or self-aggrandizing ends. Rosenzweig notes that this process of voluntary self-denial and *Steigerung* is finalized in his midrashic retelling of the narrative of *Shir ha Shirim* by categorizing the enunciation as a "saying of the Eternal" (*Spruch des Ewigen*), which crystallizes his speech-thinking/speech-act treatment of revelation into a receptive focus. Midrashically, Rosenzweig interprets the verbal enunciations by the biblical prophets' "saying of the Eternal" as the "saying of God,"[24] a saying that prepares the believing and receptive listener by leading her to receive a specific kind of speech-claim—a speech-judgment—by an other whose applied validity is unlimited because this judgment is a judgment of the *Eternal*. However, it is not entirely clear why such speech-claims should be applicable to "all," as Rosenzweig claims, merely based on their originary reception from the "eternal." It might be clearer if the origin were the "universal"

---

[24] A common phrase in German, *"Spruch"* means a "saying."

(*Allgemein*), which would encompass every one in its universality. But then that would be a return to a Hegelian ontology of ethics.

One construal of Rosenzweig's ambiguous use of the oracular phrase "speech of the eternal" is to make it universally applicable as a once-and-for-all revelatory event. However, this would make it a tyrannical form of fatalistic necessity and align it with Rosenzweig's assessments of Islamic theology, that is, a dictatorial and tyrannical once-and-for-all-time necessary love of Allah, to which the believing Muslim is commanded to submit. Rather, the necessity and universality of the claim should be based on the condition that in order for that which occurs within the relation to be effective, it has to be made known or be made public. In other words, it is not a logically necessary relationship of entailment but is, instead, a kind of pragmatic working out of the trust relationship by way of testifying and witnessing to the validity of the actual experience of having been loved. Indeed, the actual spokenness of the speaking is emphasized such that in order for any love relation to be designated as a revelatory one—one that opens something to the world in a creatively new and effective way—everything that occurs within the limits of that relation must be sounded word and must thereby "demonstrate" or prove itself by empirical effectiveness. Said otherwise, the occurrences must be empirically and sensually sounded because, otherwise, like any other expression that cannot be sounded, it would fall into the category of pre-world, that is, into the algebraic-symbolic language of the proto-cosmos (of Part I of *The Star*), or into the post-world—the geometrically structured, figurative-ritual language of the hypercosmos (of Part III of *The Star*).

Accordingly, in the mutual interchange of a love relationship, the beloved soul answers the love-demand of the lover with a love-confession, in German, a *Liebesgeständnis*. Literally, the loved one *stands* by her love in a durative speech-act, which is an act of signifying as testifying to the presence of the other, as other. For Rosenzweig, the ultimate significance of conditioning the relationship on the unpredictability of sounded word in an *actual uncertainty of human-to-human dialogue* is that it enables us to incorporate the limited aesthetic categories of theological language into what can be considered the larger domain of truth or reality which occurs in the broad range of our inter-human and lived-world activities.

SPREADING THE LOVE AS THE WORK OF "MESSIANIC" AESTHETICS OR THE WORK OF MIDRASH AS A THEOLOGY OF SOCIAL JUSTICE

Consequently, by standing up to the actual effects of her responsibility to and with the other in the present, the soul transforms the ephemeral present into an experience of temporality that will endure; it will endure because it is already directed toward the future with the promise of effectiveness-to-come. As opposed to the dark and gloomy coveredness of the past, the future—with its promise of a continuing *Steigerung* relationship, the presently experienced event of revelatory love—appears bright and light. Hence, the beloved *wants* to continue in the light of her present condition, namely, as the one who is *singled out and attended to*, desired, and beloved in a love relationship. Moreover, because she wants to, she wills to continue, igniting a desire that triggers volition. With hope in her heart inflamed by desire for the other, the beloved's love assumes the characteristic structure of "faithfulness to constancy," and thus only occurs with "reference to the future."[25] The beloved soul desires to remain faithful to the other who loves her—to God and, thus in effect, to his or her human lover. She desires to remain faithful because, by assuming responsibility for the constancy of her witnessing the validity of the love of her lover, she experiences temporal and spatial orientation through being attended to (as *attending justice*) by the lover. This dialogue continues through how she then carries on by directing her own attention to the other, in her turn, with her desire that thereby informs her ability to respond to that other.

Rosenzweig's midrash explores just this phenomenon of "attending to" by exposing the turning point where the soul turns from a state of detached self-concern to one of engaging other-concern. Having been attentively addressed by one who loves her, the soul becomes consciously aware that standing in the light of a love relationship is much better than her previous state. Rosenzweig's theological model of the soul includes this "evaluating" ability of the human soul to make comparisons because of the soul's prior philosophical "mathematical" education in the realm of the protocosmos. What this means is that being educated as a non-believing self is neither negated nor forgotten but, instead, provides the instrumental tools that enable the soul to

---

[25] See 2 Samuel 12:13 and Psalms 51:6.

make judgments as such. This is only possible because humans have historically developed various knowledge "systems" of categorization.

And indeed, the freely orienting transformation is such that the soul now loves, and *acts*, by *speaking* in another way than she had done in the past. She now loves in the way she has experienced love, namely, with the determined and determining certainty of a speech-act, impelled by an other and with a transcendence of concern for her own self-centeredness. She is now free to love her neighbor in this turn from self-concern to other-concern, in the way God—or another human lover —loves her, namely, as an other. No longer merely concerned with one's own self, the soul can now immediately relate with an *other*. Her twofold confession/acknowledgment of her past/present status is none other than the soul's own admission of love. Such is the process which the soul enacts in order to liberate herself from the imprisoning "chains of shame," which results in complete, trustful submission to the openness of a love relationship. This peculiar kind of submission initially takes form on a cognitive level by way of an interior dialogue but, as submission becomes conversion, this is then translated into a freedom to act, that is, a freedom to openly turn to the face of the other. That turning is a turn toward *speaking*.

This movement of turning is from the isolation of speech-thinking to the social engagement of speech-acting and, theologically, represents Rosenzweig's original contribution to understanding and promoting a *phenomenological-ethics* account of the experience and significance of revelation—as midrash.[26]

Rosenzweig's midrash on *Shir ha Shirim* exemplifies the kind of textual interpretation where the sensual and over-sensual sense of the embodied-in-ritual poem coincides in such a way that reality is transformed through a particular enactment of just this "biblical" work of art. In the case of this specific poem, the utterly pagan-become-

---

[26] I introduce the term "phenomenological ethics" in my book, *Art and Responsibility: A Phenomenology of the Diverging Paths of Rosenzweig and Heidegger*, and am developing that as a methodological alternative to the standard normative ethical theories of virtue ethics, deontological ethics, and utilitarian ethics in a book-length treatment. For a sample of previous applications of this theory, and as it relates to Rosenzweig's midrashic form of phenomenological ethics, see Jules Simon, "Making Ethical Sense of *Useless Suffering* with Levinas," in *The Double Binds of Ethics after the Holocaust: Salvaging the Fragments*, edited by Jennifer Geddes, John Roth, and Jules Simon (New York: Palgrave Macmillan, 2009), 133–54; and Jules Simon, "Urban Desertification and a Phenomenology of Sustainability: the Case of El Paso, Texas" in *Interdisciplinary Environmental Review* 15, no. 2/3 (2014): 160–82.

sanctified *Shir ha Sharim*, Rosenzweig interprets how the bridegroom referred to in the poem is in reality a shepherd, imagining to himself what it feels like to be a king. In his interpretation, the bridegroom-shepherd-king embodies the process of our own over-sensual and over-lapping and thus aesthetically altering process of the sensual texture of our reading. Reading is not only a bodily sensual activity but it is also precisely effective "super-sensually" in so far as the midrashic speech-act effects change on extant reality, *on us and our extant realities*, just as the midrash that is Rosenzweig's text itself does. Indeed, what we learn is that this more-than-human dimension of the love dialogue in *Shir ha Shirim* depends on the very phenomenon of a speech-act as a fusion of sensual utterance with supersensual communication of meaning:

> Since she [love] speaks – and she must speak, because there really is no other speaking-out-from-itself than the speech of love – therefore, since she speaks, she already becomes more-than-human; because the sensuality of the word is full to the brim with its divine super-sense; love is, as speech itself, sensual-supersensual.[27]

In other words, in the actual, physically sensual uttering of the words of speech occurs an experience of how we reference a *beyond* of the presently occurring experience of reality—we *experience* the "divine super-sense." In the dialogue of love in *Shir ha Sharim*, a limit is encountered which separates the one and the other— the man from the woman, the beloved from the lover—indicated by referring to the model presenting the absolute transcendence of God from the human. It is the limit, margin, or "border" (*Rand*), where the connection and division of the one from the other takes place. It is an absolute division because there is no identification of the one with the other, as there would be in an Hegelian dialectic.

In Rosenzweig's midrash, the beloved initiates another love-action in the way that she has learned to love from the lover, namely, through remembrance as a unique way of putting together again that which originally transpired in the earlier experience of revelatory love. For Rosenzweig, the remembrances are themselves part of the traditional heritage of how Oral and Written forms of Torah mutually influence each other through the process of embodying midrashic renewal. Acting on such remembrances enables the beloved, in her participation as a dialogue partner with God and other humans, to break through the

---

[27] Rosenzweig, *Der Stern*, 224; *The Star*, 201.

limits of ego-centrism and xenophobic politics, to transform the public domain into one of interdependent, love-endowed speech-actors empowered with the dictum: "As he loves you, so [should] you love."[28] For Rosenzweig, this particular speech-act, as an actually expressed and textually embedded utterance, has the double value of being able to provide the initial occasion for comparative recall that then becomes an imperative for prescriptive action. On Rosenzweig's reading, the analogical *"Wie"* (translated "as" or "how") opens the sentence and evokes the memory of an objective experience, indicated by the use of the third person objective pronoun "he." With the use of the present form of the verb, "he loves" (*Er liebt*), however, the sentence also evokes the present nature of the comparative experience. Moreover, the form of the sentence fragment is highly individualized, and thus is flexible enough to apply to the unique way in which each reader addressed through the text may have experienced a love relationship. Finally, the resolution of the sentence carries the prescriptive form, "so you should" with the present verb form of "love," coupled with the outward, public-facing, word for the familiar "you" (*Du*) occupying the sentence conclusion, thus encouraging an ongoing concern for the next "you." Such an imperative command is an ethical prescription that holds universally, but only in the sense that the demand to love another is a demand to love that other who is not identical to me, in the similar but not identical way as I have been loved by one who has not "appropriated" me for his ownmost (Heideggarian) ethos.[29] In other words, I love another in such a non-possessive way that the other is liberated to love the next tragically isolated one who comes along with their particular desires and sufferings, and who expresses a need and/or a desire to be loved.

Rosenzweig's midrashic "speech-act" oriented philosophical theology is a modern variant of constructive theology, and continues to develop as it has become part of the New Midrashim of postmodernity. Given the increasing significance of the socio-political role that new and ongoing interpretations of his philosophical theology are producing, actual developments of renewed ethical relations, stemming from renewed practices of demonstrations of faith commitments by

---

[28] Ibid., *Der Stern*, 228; *The Star*, 204.
[29] Martin Heidegger provides a normative, phenomenological treatment of "authenticity" and "inauthenticity" and one's "ownmost ethos" in his groundbreaking work, *Being and Time*, trans. Joan Stambaugh (New York: SUNY Press, 2010; originally published by Max Niemeyer Verlag, Tübingen, 1953).

members of Jewish communities in the world, are beginning to appear as the kind of Messianic Aesthetics envisioned by Rosenzweig. The indications of such an "actualizing" renewal can be seen in the ways that members of those communities demonstrate the lineaments of his philosophical theology.

The conceptual process laid out by Rosenzweig happens when the beloved moves from out of the closed circle of two-aloneness and revelatory love, from the closed circle of Jewish family that produces autonomous individuals, normatively educated to the ethical nature of the Law promulgated at Sinai and midrashically interpreted through the revelatory language of love exemplified in *Shir ha Shirim*, to incrementally build communities step by loving step in the world.[30] This gradual, incremental process occurs when modern individuals are liberated from their identity-forming self-reflexivity that is necessarily self-defiant and results in ontological seclusion from that very world. Such is the case with cities where most people in the modern world now live, increasingly isolated and out of touch with each other, struggling to survive and thus on the edge of violent conflicts or desperate suicides. Building on his presentation of the multi-layered dimensions of this dialogical experience that constitutes love relationships, Rosenzweig turns our attention, in Book 3 of Part II and the entirety of Part III of *The Star*, to the very significance of these kinds of love relations for broader social relations and community formations. Again, this is what I am calling his Messianic Aesthetics and which is at the core of his renewal of midrash in the Jewish theological tradition that includes the many and varied traditional forms of liturgical and ritual practices of modern Jewish communities. It is midrash because of how that particular practice is grounded in interpretations of biblical Scripture as have I laid out

---

[30] Robert Gibbs has similarly argued for this interpretation of this part of Rosenzweig's speech-acts being open and accessible to all peoples: "Rosenzweig's use of theological concepts depends on the universally accessible, human experience of speech. Perhaps the most important reinterpretation in my book is intended to free Rosenzweig from the constraints of Jewish sectarianism. The theological concepts in a deep sense derive from Judaism, but their application is not exclusive and their validity does not derive from 'Jewish religious experience.' Revelation, and indeed creation and redemption, are accessible to all peoples of all cultures in all places, but they are not themselves the product of pure reason; rather, they emerge from speech. The shifts toward experience, theology, and speech are the bases of Rosenzweig's claim to be moving away from philosophy, but he still retains the desire for a thought which is not exclusive, but open universally." Gibbs, *Correlations in Rosenzweig and Levinas*, p. 20, n. 7. For me, this is simply another expression of Rosenzweig's "Messianic Aesthetics."

in this chapter. It is a Messianic Aesthetic precisely because of how the ethical "command" as content is built into the specifically aesthetic forms of grammatical speech-act analyses that make up the components of the work of the midrash.

In closing, I would be remiss if I did not briefly articulate how a significant facet of Rosenzweig's renewal of traditional midrashic practices is in how he understands liturgical ritual as itself a performative kind of speech-act.[31] He takes us from the phenomenon of textual interpretations as an aesthetic activity called midrash to other aesthetic performances like community-forming rituals such as Passover (*Pesach*) and the Festival of Booths (*Sukkot*). These latter Jewish festivals commemorate the ongoing condition of exile as the time of wandering over the space of the earth, directed to the ideal of eventual rest when the fullness of communication and the Eros of love relations will take place. These are none other than expressions of a Messianic Aesthetics to which I have been referring to throughout this chapter. For Rosenzweig, humans remain essentially restless, with the work of transforming the others of our common world into loving ones who are still outstanding. To be "outstanding" means to have experienced revelation, which further means to understand the meaning of creation and which finally also entails the imperative—the command—to become part of helping to redeem the world by loving others, each in his or her turn. Having been loved, which for Rosenzweig is commanded by the Torah, those loved ones are directed, by way of the resounding normative implications of their revelatory experiences, to also love by testifying to the rest of the world about the empirically verifiable effects of love that they themselves have experienced. Those effects have to do with inspiring phenomena such as the empirically verifiable dialogue of speech-acts, the historical formation of communities based on forming new kinds of love relationships (for example, Jewish–Christian relations), and enlivening the passion to love one's neighbor, one neighbor at a time and one midrashically influenced speech-act at a time. For Rosenzweig, the underlying dynamic that motivates all of these works of love is the traditional ideal of those communities that the one God of love alone is God.[32]

---

[31] See Steven Kepnes for Rosenzweig and "revelation" as Liturgy, *Liturgical Time*; see n. 1.

[32] Rosenzweig, *Der Stern*, 364; *The Star*, 327.

Selected Further Reading

Batnitzky, Leora. *Idolatry and Representation: The Philosophy of Franz Rosenzweig Reconsidered*. Princeton: Princeton University Press, 2009.

Benjamin, Mara. *Rosenzweig's Bible: Reinventing Scripture for Jewish Modernity*. Cambridge and New York: Cambridge University Press, 2009.

Fishbane, Michael. *Biblical Interpretation in Ancient Israel*. Oxford: Clarendon Press, 1983.

Franks, Paul W. and Michael L. Morgan, eds. *Philosophical and Theological Writings*. Indianapolis and Cambridge, MA: Hackett Publishing Company, 2000.

Gibb, Robert. *Correlations in Rosenzweig and Levinas*. Princeton: Princeton University Press, 1992.

Gordon, Peter. *Rosenzweig and Heidegger: Between Judaism and German Philosophy*. Berkeley: University of California Press, 2003.

Green, Arthur. "The Children in Egypt and the Theophany at the Sea." *Judaism* 24.3 (Fall 1975): 446–56.

Holtz, Barry W. *Back to the Sources: Reading the Classic Jewish Texts*. New York: Simon and Schuster, 1986.

Kepnes, Steven. *Liturgical Time: Franz Rosenzweig's Star of Redemption*. Oxford: Oxford University Press, 2007.

Kepnes, Steven. "Liturgical Time: Franz Rosenzweig's Star of Redemption." In *Jewish Liturgical Reasoning*, 79–130. Oxford: Oxford University Press, 2007.

Levinas, Emmanuel. *Totality and Infinity*. Pittsburgh: Duquesne University Press, 1969.

Neusner, Jacob. *What is Midrash? And Understanding Rabbinic Midrash: Texts and Commentary*. New York: KTAV, 1985.

Rosenzweig, Franz. *The Star of Redemption*. Translated by William W. Hallo. Notre Dame, IN, and London: University of Notre Dame Press, 1975.

Samuelson, Norbert. *A User's Guide to Franz Rosenzweig's Star of Redemption*. Abingdon: Routledge, 2010.

Simon, Jules. *Art and Responsibility: A Phenomenology of the Diverging Paths of Rosenzweig and Heidegger*. New York: Bloomsbury Publishing, 2011.

Wiesel, Elie. *Messengers of God: Biblical Portraits and Legends*. New York: Random House, 1976.

11 Levinas' Theological Ethics

RICHARD A. COHEN

THE PRIMACY OF ETHICS

For Emmanuel Levinas the central and driving inspiration of Judaism, its root meaning and highest mission, its very holiness lies in *ethical command*.[1] Without diminishing the exigency of this claim or the singularity of Judaism, indeed quite the reverse, he argues no less for the primacy of ethics for all religions and for all human endeavors, because the responsibilities of ethical transcendence, the heights of goodness, and the aspirations for justice lie at the source of intelligibility itself, including science, art, sociality, economics, politics, culture, and everything else that matters. By the push and pull and the orientation of its vectors—good and evil, justice and injustice, responsibility and irresponsibility—ethics is the Archimedean point of all that is significant, meaningful, and worthy.

Levinas does not limit ethics to utilitarian calculation or the pursuit of happiness. Its keynote is responsibility as caring for the other person, which resounds also in caring for all others. It begins and ends in the elevation of human sociality, not in the self but starting from the other person, that is to say, in the moral responsibility one always already has for the neighbor, to alleviate the other's suffering, to respond to the vulnerability and needs of each, and thus also for all, through the difficult risks of creating a just world. Ethics begins in the commanding "face of the other"—soliciting my responsibility. Contrary to Buber, Levinas does not interpret encounter or meeting as an ontological event, a matter of being or becoming whole. Ethics is first obligation: incumbent on me, originating in the other's suffering. It arises beyond and disturbing my natural care for myself, my place in the sun, my self-interest, and my

---

[1] The term "theology" is already problematic; see, "Against Theology: 'The Devotion to a Theology Without Theodicy'," in Richard A. Cohen, *Levinasian Meditations* (Pittsburgh: Duquesne University Press, 2010), 296–313.

convenience. Ethics tears apart the complacency of identity, whether of self or world, shatters the smug veneers of good conscience for what is *better than being*: helping the other and providing for all others. Indeed, nothing takes precedence over care for the neighbor. Nothing is more important, more precious, more pressing, or of greater consequence. Nothing is more meaningful. For Levinas the incomparable priorities of morality and justice, putting the other first, constitute the vocation of Judaism, the transcendence of the Holy as non-indifference to suffering. "God rises to his supreme and ultimate presence as correlative to the justice rendered unto men."[2] In "religious" terms: "Height is heaven. The kingdom of heaven is ethical."[3] In "philosophical" terms: "Ethics is not simply the corollary of the religious but is, of itself, the element in which religious transcendence receives its original meaning."[4]

Accordingly, ethics is not a bonus, luxury or treat, to take or to leave. It is the very source of meaning, of significance and signification. "To be or not to be," Levinas observes, alluding to Hamlet, but also suggesting Parmenides, Hegel, Heidegger, and Sartre, among others, "is not the question where transcendence is concerned."[5] Not what *is*, but what *ought* to be, that is the question. From it all prioritizing, all emphasis, all *importance*, all better and worse, derives. To be, the being of beings, is not first a given or a gift, but a responsibility, a challenge. The first question, the question before all questions is "Do I have the right to be?"[6] Humans are not atoms, cogs, or herd animals, parts of a system, network, or bacchanal. Humanity is precious in each person, a dignity sharper than self-consciousness, a vigilance or wakefulness responsive, alert, a generosity toward the other person. The first transcendence, cutting deepest, rising highest, and the paradigm of all transcendence, all the way to "the Name," "God," is the alterity of the other person as a vulnerability soliciting and obligating me as responsibility. "The ethical order does not prepare us for the Divinity;

---

[2] Emmanuel Levinas, *Totality and Infinity*, trans. A. Lingis (Pittsburgh: Duquesne University Press, 1969), 78.
[3] Emmanuel Levinas, *Otherwise than Being or Beyond Essence*, trans. A. Lingis (Pittsburgh: Duquesne University Press, 1998), 183.
[4] Emmanuel Levinas, *Beyond the Verse*, trans. G. D. Mole (Bloomington: Indiana University Press, 1994), 107.
[5] Levinas, *Otherwise than Being*, 3.
[6] Emmanuel Levinas, *Ethics and Infinity*, trans. R. A. Cohen (Pittsburgh: Duquesne University Press, 1985), 121.

it is the very accession to the Divinity."[7] Transcendence arises not in myth, story or faith, not in dogma, catechism or theology, which at best are its postscripts. The first imperative, the imperative of all imperatives, is to love the neighbor, to alleviate suffering. "This seems to me fundamental to the Judaic faith," Levinas writes, "in which the relation to God is inseparable from the Torah; that is, inseparable from the recognition of the other person. The relation to God is already ethics; or, as *Isaiah 58* would have it, the proximity to God, devotion itself, is devotion to the other man."[8] "The face to face remains an ultimate situation."[9]

Thus Levinas rejects for their immaturity and irresponsibility religions' mythic and dogmatic poses, however perennially popular they be. Blind faith, after all, is not the overturning but the dialectical partner of the knowledge it pretends to disdain. Science adheres to the evidence dogma stubbornly disdains, but both make *knowing* primary, for or against. For Levinas, contrary to the hegemonic claims of self-consciousness and knowledge, natural or supernatural, genuine religion arises in conscientiousness, in ethical responsibility. Prayers, rituals, sacred texts, beliefs, stories, holidays, and all the richness of particular living traditions are important, indeed essential, but not in or by themselves, but rather and precisely because and insofar as they spur morality and justice. Such is what Levinas, borrowing an expression from Buber, calls "biblical humanism."[10] It is to hold highest not handles, parchment, and ink, which are indispensable, certainly, but the *teachings* of the Torah, its emphatic and challenging *holiness*. To raise the Torah high is to obey its ethical imperatives, in or out of synagogue, with or without synagogue, Jew or non-Jew. Nor for Levinas are Torah or ethics reducible to free choice, autonomy, the freedom of the market, but rather arise as a prior obedience, *always already obligated* to and for the other, Jew or stranger, daughter or orphan, wife or widow, near and far. The holy is infinite because ethical demands are infinite. Ethics—Judaism as care for each and all others—goes against the grain. Morality and justice are not easy but difficult, demanding, and challenging,

---

[7] Emmanuel Levinas, *Difficult Freedom*, trans. Sean Hand (Baltimore: Johns Hopkins University Press, 1990), 102.
[8] Emmanuel Levinas, *In the Time of the Nations*, trans. M. B. Smith (Bloomington: Indiana University Press, 1994), 171.
[9] Levinas, *Totality and Infinity*, 81.
[10] Emmanuel Levinas, *New Talmudic Readings*, trans. R. A. Cohen (Pittsburgh: Duquesne University Press, 1999), 117.

requiring sacrifices, of oneself for-the-other. Levinas has no illusions about this: "No one is good voluntarily."[11] Neither does he offer excuses or escapist consolations. Nothing is better, higher or more holy—or more difficult.

One of the most distinctive features of Levinas' account of ethics, and hence of Judaism, is that it does not begin with the self or end in personal salvation. The other person, the neighbor, "the widow, the orphan, the stranger," the one in need, comes first, sets the first imperative. Personal salvation would require social redemption. The true or higher self does not arise by itself, whether by self-annihilation or ecstatic union with the Godhead, but in its responsibilities, above all to provide for and never abandon the other. The veritable image of holiness is maternal. The other is mortal, vulnerable, subject to pains, illness, wounds, in need of food, clothing, shelter, love, medicine, education, culture, companionship, and so on. The true self arises in and through its concrete responses, its uniqueness manifest as ethical investiture, that is, not as a thing, according to specific spatial-temporal differences, like a fingerprint or snowflake, but as non-substitutable by its shouldering of responsibilities, by its non-indifference to the other and to all others, by its self-sacrifice and generosity. Here I am, ready to help you—such is the higher self. Such a self arises in the simplest gestures, saying "hello," or opening the door for another, "After you," as Levinas has said. Not freedom, but not slavery either—service. The Bible calls Moses "God's servant" in this sense. Of the bound freedom of responsibility Levinas points out that "no one is enslaved to the Good. ... All my inwardness is invested in the form of a despite-me, for-another. Despite-me, for-another, is signification par excellence."[12] "I am obliged without this obligation having begun in me."[13] "Beyond egoism and altruism it is the religiosity of the self."[14] Ethics, religion, Judaism arise as the priority of the other person, the demand to alleviate suffering, as my supreme responsibility, myself despite-myself as responsibilities—to and for the other, morality, and to and for all others, justice.

Certainly such an account of responsibility gives concrete meaning to the claim of *Genesis Rabbah* (12:15, 21:8) by which the world and

---

[11] Levinas, *Otherwise than Being*, 11.   [12] Ibid.   [13] Ibid., 13.   [14] Ibid., 117.

humanity are said to have been created and to endure "with both attributes, mercy and justice."

BEYOND KANT

Of all philosophers Levinas is closest to Kant. To compare and contrast their thought thus highlights Levinas' filiations and originality. Four similarities stand out. First, Levinas accepts Kant's refutation of all possible rational proofs for God's existence. Rational theology is over. Second, Levinas accepts Kant's epistemological limitation of speculative metaphysics. Mythic religion is over. Third, Levinas agrees with Kant's thesis that science, owing to its *interest* in truth, is grounded in the primacy of ethics. And fourth, Levinas agrees with the central thesis of Kant's *Religion Within the Limits of Reason Alone* (1793) that religion is grounded in ethics and its highest vocation is ethical.

Regarding this fourth point, one sees that the significant distinction Levinas makes between "religion for adults," that is, ethical religion, and "primitive" religion, the exaltation of faith, mystery, orthodoxy, sacrament or participatory ecstasy, parallels Kant's distinction in Part III of *Religion Within the Limits of Reason Alone* between "true religion," which promotes ethical aims, and "ecclesiastical faith," which worships worship instead. "It does not enter their heads," Kant writes—as could Levinas—of the divagations of the latter, "that when they fulfill their duties to men (themselves and others) they are, by these very acts, performing God's commands and are therefore in all their actions and abstentions, so far as these concern morality, perpetually in the service of God, and that it is absolutely impossible to serve God more directly in any other way."[15] So too, in the name of adult religion, could Levinas endorse Kant's claim that for true religion "there exists absolutely no salvation for man apart from the sincerest adoption of genuine moral principles into his disposition."[16] For both thinkers, in Kant's words, "the moral improvement of men constitutes the real end of all religion,"[17] and "the final purpose even of reading these Holy Scriptures, or of investigating their content, is to make men better."[18] To be sure, ethical religion, as Dostoyevsky's Grand Inquisitor reminds us, for all its truth and worthiness, and in some measure because of

---

[15] Immanuel Kant, *Religion Within the Limits of Reason Alone*, trans. T. M. Greene and H. H. Hudson (New York: Harper & Row, 1960), 94.
[16] Ibid., 78.   [17] Ibid., 102.   [18] Ibid., 102.

them, has yet to achieve the popularity of mythic and authoritarian religion. But the seductions of the latter, its overconfidence, its cowardice, its miscarriages and violence, come as part of the price of human freedom, of the ongoing and undecided struggle between "ought" and "is," and serve to remind even the most religiously committed souls that within organized religion itself the elevated and elevating ethical demands of transcendence remain unfulfilled and pressing.

Yet for all their closeness, and despite their shared advocacy of ethics, Levinas represents a radical improvement over Kant. And this is because between Kant's rationalism and Levinas' ethics lies Edmund Husserl's phenomenology. Kant's greatness is at the same time his limitation. He is great because his *rationalism* represents the conclusion and culmination of the original Western conception of Reason, that is, reason conceived since ancient Greece as the conformity of being to demonstrative *logos*. He is limited, however, because this entire conception of Reason, discerning and powerful as it was, turns out to be prejudiced and hamstrung by its inner adherence to erroneous and unresolvable metaphysical dualisms inherited by the ancient Greeks from Persia and India. The truths of science, Husserl showed, are true not because they conform to the standards of non-contradiction and excluded middle, that is, the standards of propositional logic, or because their objects can be measured, quantified, and mathematically formalized, but because they are backed by *evidence*, repeatable evidence available to all unprejudiced inquirers. Husserl saw, then, that the true object of science is whatever appears to the rigorously honest inquirer, that is, phenomena—hence the name "phenomenology." The scientist, then, is the inquirer open "to the things themselves," which includes not only quantifiable objects but the wider variegated world of significations and significance, including all the incalculable events and happenings studied by the so-called *human sciences*. Here is not the place to elaborate Husserl's insights and method. The point is that Kant missed out, and replicated unexamined metaphysical dualisms, but Levinas did not. For all its unequaled brilliance, Kant's philosophy remains captive to a world metaphysically divided between mind and matter, spirit and letter, soul and body, freedom and necessity. So despite his genius and however ethical his intention, he could not—because no one can—put Humpty Dumpty back together again. Begin with two worlds, and you end with two worlds—Kant himself knew this, but he knew of no other form of rationality, no alternative conception of science. Levinas, in contrast, was an early and outstanding student of phenomenology, and became one of its masters in his own right. So even though he moved beyond the phenomena of phenomenology for the transcendence of ethics, nowhere is his thought haunted or hampered, as was Kant's, by an inheritance of metaphysical dualisms. Thus in the Preface to *Totality and Infinity* Levinas openly declares that "the presentation and the development of the notions employed owe everything to the phenomenological method," and then immediately qualifies this methodological adherence, "but phenomenology ... does not constitute the ultimate event of being itself."[19] The ultimate event is of course ethical, the responsibility of the I for the other. But the world in which such responsibility arises is not the counterfeit dualist universe of Kant, despite its "logic" (and even less is it the multitudes of more simplistic dualist worlds propagated by lesser thinkers, theologians, and outright spiritual charlatans). The world as Levinas grasps it is the world described by the science of Husserlian phenomenology, the real world, one lived concretely by flesh and blood beings, a world of meaning, embodiment, temporality, historical change, one—such is Levinas' claim—whose ultimate sense derives not from phenomenality, however, but from the transcendence of ethics.

The upshot, then, is that while Kant and Levinas equally esteem science and argue for the primacy of ethics, Kant's conception of science and ethics are both skewed and distorted by artificial dualisms, whereas Levinas' conceptions are not. To be sure, Levinas' phenomenological descriptions are subject, as are all scientific hypotheses, to revision and improvement. But this is one of the benefits of science. The more accurate his account of the world, the more precise is Levinas' account of the irruption of the ethical. In any case, Levinas does not reduce the irruption of ethical significance to worldly significations, and, leaving that aside, articulating the surplus of ethical proximity in a language always prone to congealing into its own self-relating differential network of significations accounts for a good deal of the difficulty of his writings. Thus, against the grain, as it were, breaking with the tendency of knowing to self-enclosure, Levinas strives to articulate "intelligibility as proximity,"[20] "proximity and not truth about proximity,"[21] the primacy of the "wisdom of love" over philosophy's traditional "love of wisdom."[22] The primacy of the

---

[19] Levinas, *Totality and Infinity*, 28.   [20] Levinas, *Otherwise than Being*, 167.
[21] Ibid., 120.   [22] Ibid., 162.

other, the "face to face" or proximity, is not easy existentially or, as Levinas' writings bear witness, grammatically.

CONTEMPORARY THOUGHT

The contemporaneity of thought, whether oriented by science, aesthetics, or in the exceptional case of Levinas by ethics, in each instance is manifest as a radical break with the more or less violent artifices—against body, language, time, politics, and so on—which pretended to assuage what was really the self-inflicted self-alienation produced by the West's venerable but untenable commitments to metaphysical dualism. Or, to express this breakthrough positively, contemporary thought takes seriously *language, time, embodiment, worldliness, sociality*, and the *political*. Instead of castigating *this world* as deception, fall and sin, as illusion, "veil," "garment" or "shell," as obstruction and obstacle to another ethereal but allegedly truer more spiritual world, it recognizes in precisely these same phenomena, seen without the distortion of metaphysical lenses, the very means and manner of all that is meaningful, important, precious, without conflating the trivial and the inspirational, all the way to the holy. Along these lines, we should perhaps underscore the fact that of all major figures of twentieth-century *Jewish* thought, from Buber to Soloveitchik, only Levinas mastered and fully utilized the new methods and resources of Husserlian phenomenology. For these reasons, as faithful Jewish reader and creative phenomenological scientist, but above all and consistent with both as an original ethical thinker, Levinas is now acknowledged as one of the very few philosophers, and fewer Jews, who have entered the small pantheon of great Western thinkers. His first book, *The Theory of Intuition in Husserl's Phenomenology* (1930), published when he was 24, and his subsequent expository articles, along with the writings of Paul Ricoeur, introduced phenomenology to the French-speaking world.[23] The profound and rigorous proposals of his two major works, *Totality and Infinity* (1961) and *Otherwise than Being or Beyond Essence* (1974), and all of his own philosophy have been recognized as a major contribution to Western and now global philosophy, distinctively renewing with the greatest rigor the claims of ethics as first

---

[23] See Richard A. Cohen, "Emmanuel Levinas," in *The Routledge Companion to Phenomenology*, eds. S. Luft and S. Overgaard (New York: Routledge, 2012), 71–81.

philosophy, and at the same time remaining faithful to the heritage of Judaism.

We have seen that Levinas adopts phenomenology while rejecting its ultimacy. He rejects the Western heritage of metaphysical dualism, and even more profoundly rejects the Western heritage of giving primacy to knowledge and being. For Levinas the true and the good cannot be divorced, but not because one must know the good, as Socrates thought, but rather because ethical responsibility is the root condition of all intelligibility, including scientific knowledge. Ethics not only has philosophical dignity, its dignity is foundational, and permeates all registers of meaning. Here we can see another good reason why Levinas endorses and engages in talmudic discourse (in his case aggadic), not only because of the talmudic rabbis' keen attentiveness to the plenitude of the real, to the concrete and particular, to persons and places, to the specific rather than the general, which Levinas greatly values, but also and more profoundly because their clarion sobriety is thereby able to be all the more rigorously attentive and more nuanced with regard to the morality and justice—the holiness—their discussions always serve. Levinas praises and engages in what he calls the "paradigmatic modality of talmudic reflection,"[24] not only because like phenomenology its "paradigmatic conceptualism is a theoretical procedure for comprehending the Real,"[25] that is, because it "watches over the general in the light of the particular,"[26] but even more importantly, and in this closer to the drama of Plato's dialogues than to pure contemplation or knowledge, even phenomenological knowledge, because of its refined attention to the transcendence of the ethical, to the moral and the just: "from the Torah it extracts *ethical meaning as the ultimate intelligibility of the human* and even of the cosmic."[27] Far from the dry nitpicking or legal formalism of which it has sometimes been accused, talmudic reasoning is paradigmatic as an instance, a very great instance, of knowledge in the service of ethics.

Let us turn from Levinas' place in Western philosophical history, from his relations to Kant, his phenomenology and talmudic reasoning, to exhibit his contemporaneity and originality more specifically and directly in terms of language, time, body, politics, and Zionism.

---

[24] Levinas, *Beyond the Verse*, 103.
[25] Emmanuel Levinas, *Nine Talmudic Readings*, trans. A. Aronowicz (Bloomington: Indiana University Press, 1990), 93.
[26] Levinas, *Beyond the Verse*, 79.   [27] Levinas, *Nine Talmudic Readings*, 93.

LANGUAGE AND MEANING: PROPHECY

We turn first to language, truth, and meaning. "True thought," Levinas writes, "is not a 'silent dialogue of the soul with itself' but the discussion between thinkers."[28] Such an understanding of thinking stands opposed to classical thought, whose ideal was ideation ideating ideas and nothing else, as, for instance, we find in the following claim by the modern rationalist Spinoza: "For it is when a thing is perceived by pure thought, without words or images, that it is understood."[29] From this idealist-dualist perspective Spinoza compares and condemns Moses, the greatest of the Jewish prophets, for his ignorance. Moses spoke to God merely face to face, mired thereby in body and imagination, in contrast to what Spinoza affirms to be the perfect intelligence of Christ: "If Moses spoke with God face to face as a man may do with his fellow (that is, through the medium of their two bodies), then Christ communed with God mind to mind."[30] Indeed, Spinoza condemns all the Hebrew prophets and all the talmudic rabbis for the ignorance of their carnal thinking, whereas Christ and true philosophers (not surprisingly including Spinoza), by their minds alone—and indeed each one alone—know the truth.

Levinas radically rejects all such arrogant impunities and the metaphysical dualisms by which they are motored, no matter how venerated. Examining language and meaning anew and more closely, without prejudice, he discovers that the "face to face"—conversation, communication, speaking—is precisely their real source. Conversation is not a ladder to be climbed and thrown away in the name of an impossibly pure immaterial truth, but the access to and means of truth. It is no accident, then, that inter-human interchange, ultimately ordered by ethics, is traced even in the most rarified regions of truth, in science and knowledge. Scientific hypotheses to be true must be verified, by other scientists. Accordingly, and regarding all registers of signification, from science to humor, Levinas supplements the two leading theories of truth in the West, namely *correspondence* and *coherence* models, with a third, a *communicative-ethical* paradigm. "The relation between the same and the other, metaphysics, is primordially enacted as

---

[28] Levinas, *Beyond the Verse*, 49.
[29] Baruch Spinoza, *Theological-Political Treatise*, 2nd ed., trans. S. Shirley (Indianapolis: Hackett, 2001), 54.
[30] Spinoza, *Theological-Political Treatise*, 14.

conversation."³¹ (Yes, Levinas' philosophy is metaphysical, but not dualist.) Conversation, communication, speaking and listening, here lies the ultimate source point of signification. And—most important—conversation begins in hearing the other, respecting the other's singularity and alterity, hence as an *ethical* relation. Levinas: "Speech belongs to the order of morality before belonging to that of theory."³² Again: "The banal fact of conversation, in one sense, quits the order of violence. This banal fact is the marvel of marvels."³³

Thus in the responsibility elicited by the face of the other person, and not first on tablets of stone, Levinas first discovers the "Thou shalt not kill." To not murder is the condition of ethical proximity. Ethical proximity arises in the demand to not murder. Such is this prohibition's concrete sense, its imperative significance, its original order, before it is reordered by representation. And this imperative, again conceived concretely, is the very condition of conversation, and hence of truth as well. One must quit the order of violence, beginning with my own violence, my animal vitality, spontaneity, and egoism. Across conversation, starting with the other—not in self-assertion, or shouting down, or already knowing, in a word, not in monologue, meditation, or the so-called "inner dialogue" of self with itself—does meaning arise. For Levinas, then, contra Spinoza, intelligibility begins in and as "prophecy," broadly understood as moral exigency, in the saying of the other which is always already a call, an imperative, a demand for peace, for respect, for aid, as well as it being a call to justice for all for those not present. Levinas: "That is the resonance of every language 'in the name of God', the inspiration or prophecy of all language."³⁴ To be sure, *one can refuse the other*, deny shelter, deny medical attention, deny education, shut them up and shut them in; humans are free— but whatever the evil or injustice of my response the other's solicitation remains the primary event. Like everything else in Judaism and in his philosophy Levinas finds the root inter-human sense, in this case for the idea of prophecy. An interviewer once asked him to predict something, to which Levinas responded with his usual modest humor and penetrating seriousness: "It is true that all men are prophets. Did not Moses say in the words of Numbers 11:29, 'That

---

³¹ Levinas, *Totality and Infinity*, 39.   ³² Levinas, *Difficult Freedom*, 9.   ³³ Ibid., 7.
³⁴ Levinas, *Otherwise than Being*, 152.

all the people of God be prophets,' and does not Amos go still further, to all of humanity: 'The Eternal God has spoken, who shall not prophecy' (Amos 3:8)."[35] Discourse, language, whether English, Chinese, Spanish, Hebrew, another, including literature, poems, songs, scientific treatises, jokes, sacred texts, and their translations, all these are not obstacles to spiritual life but its medium. Hebrew is special for certain Jews; Arabic for certain Muslims; Tibetan for certain Tibetans—but everyone speaks, reads, converses in a specific language, or in several languages; Solomon and St. Francis apparently also in animal languages. There is no pure language, contra Spinoza. Spirit and letter are inseparable. Language is "prophetic" because the other's speaking is from the first elevated and elevating, morally demanding, and crying out for justice.

The first word, before everything said, the word which launches all that is said, the original intelligibility of what is intelligible, arises in the emphasis of command, an imperative, to serve the other: "the other does not appear in the nominative, but in the vocative." Language, prophecy, religion, these are interchangeable terms for Levinas: what counts is not what is said, but the manner of saying, the uprightness of radical transcendence as ethical imperative. Thus what is first is not this or that word said, but the *saying* of the said. This is original prophecy, a solicitation which cannot be captured in what is said, in theses or dogmas or credos, but brings these and all spoken words to life by lending them *importance*. Which explains why after having completed *Totality and Infinity*, Levinas reminds his readers in the Preface that they must read it again, and again, because "it belongs to the very essence of language, which consists in continually undoing its phrase by the foreword or the exegesis, in unsaying the said, in attempting to restate without ceremonies what has already been ill understood in the inevitable ceremonial in which the said delights."[36] One is reminded of the annual rereading of the Torah in the synagogue, a rereading that never ends, and yet in some sense is in each instance a first reading, one never heard before. The "inevitable ceremonial" must be shattered by a renewed saying, saying what cannot be said, beginning with *Shema*, "hear," "listen," repeated morning and night, keeping Judaism alert, a vigilance, its Torah a Torah of life, "a foreword preceding languages, it is the proximity of one to the other."[37] Levinas

---

[35] *Is it Righteous to Be? Interviews with Emmanuel Levinas*, ed. J. Robbins (Stanford: Stanford University Press, 2001), 226.
[36] Levinas, *Totality and Infinity*, 3.   [37] Levinas, *Otherwise than Being*, 5.

hears this ethical vigilance most especially in the biblical Hebrew *hineni*, "here I am," *at the ready*, which appears even in his philosophical writings, as for instance in one passage without any reference to the Bible or Hebrew he describes the true self, the responsible self, as follows: "The word *I* means *here I am*, answering for everything and for everyone."[38] In sum, "communication of truth is not an addendum to truth but belongs to the reading itself."[39] So, too, with truth: "Responsibility for the others or communication is the adventure that bears all the discourse of science and philosophy."[40]

TIME AND ETERNITY: MESSIANISM

The dualist rejection of time for eternity, despite the noise of its self-applause, is purchased only by forsaking reality, reason, and morality. To degrade the changing temporal world as evil, sinful, and demonic at the same time calls into question the God who created and called it good. Furthermore, divinity limited to miracles, which is the only way for eternity to gain entrance to the world of time, does not glorify God or the world but destroys all possible sense, because from miracles anything, everything, and nothing follows: loaves, toads, brooms, plagues, blessings, devastation, or whatever. Logic and causality go out the window. Nor does burying one's head in sand or filling one's head with it—which is the role of religion for some people—resolve these imponderables, because intelligence is not to blame for them and stupidity is not their answer.

Levinas will have none of it. Not only because it is false, and because the consequence of such a contrived metaphysics is a disordered and nonsensical world, as clear thinkers have repeatedly shown, but no less because to adopt such dualism and its compensatory myths is *unworthy* of Judaism, a betrayal of its higher, more exalted, more sober, and demanding notion of holiness. "If purely thaumaturgical miracles seem spiritually suspect to us and acceptable as simple figures of the Epiphany," Levinas will say, "it is not because they alter the order but because they do not alter it enough, because they are not miraculous enough, because the Other awakening the Same is not yet other enough through them."[41] Transcendence is not adequately grasped, not

---

[38] Ibid., 114.   [39] Levinas, *In the Time of the Nations*, 66.
[40] Levinas, *Otherwise than Being*, 160.
[41] Levinas, *Beyond the Verse*, 211 (note 12) and *New Talmudic Readings*, 70.

sufficiently appreciated by dualist knowing, or by any knowing, for that matter, and all the less by the obverse of knowing, blind faith. The harm done to the demands of genuine transcendence is perhaps nowhere more egregiously evident than in the deprecating pretentions of ecclesiastical exaltations of eternity over time.

Taking time seriously, probably more than anything else, is the defining characteristic of contemporary thought. Dualism was not only the cause but also the effect of what had been the longest outstanding unsolved problem, for more than 2,000 years, of philosophy, and theology, namely, the unanswered paradoxes of Zeno. An understanding of time constrained by the propositional logic of affirmation and negation, of being and non-being, meant interpreting the past as what *is no* longer, what *is not*, and the future as what has *not* yet come into being, hence also *is not*, so that only the present *is*, but in such a way that even the present as instantaneous "now" also lacks being because it is infinitely compressed or squeezed, as it were, between the non-being of the past and the non-being of the future. Thus even the present becomes specious. All this was strikingly mocked by Zeno's clever paradoxes which showed that by adhering strictly to such a conception of time the fleet-footed Achilles would never pass the slowest tortoise in a race, the swiftly flying arrow could never reach its target, and so on. More clever and more stubborn theologians, instead of revising or yielding their dualism, insisted—against all sense, common or scientific—that God not only created the world in the beginning but that He constantly created it anew from one instant to the next, giving humans the illusion of a temporal continuity which had, as Zeno saw all too well, no real being, or rather has only miraculous being.

Finally, in the late nineteenth century, the philosopher Henri Bergson in France solved Zeno's paradoxes by cutting the Gordian knot. The problem never was with time but with its reduction to propositional logic. Time, Bergson realized, is not found in discontinuous stops, in dyadic being and non-being, zero and one, but rather in an indissoluble flowing, an interpenetration of past-present-future, what he called "duration." Time cognitively represented—clock time—is practical, useful, able to measure, but all the same it is derivative. The truth of time, its duration, is only discoverable through intuition, by entering into it, experiencing it, an approach which already intimates the phenomenology Husserl would later rigorously elaborate.

Bergson's discovery was an intellectual breakthrough of the first order, the beginning of making sense of time as time, time no longer forced to fit the Procrustean bed of metaphysical dualism. After Bergson, Husserl's phenomenological investigations uncovered in more precise detail the rich and complex structures of time as duration, and then building on these studies his student, Martin Heidegger, in his aptly entitled master work, *Being and Time*, showed their existential and historical significance. Levinas reaped profoundly the considerable intellectual discoveries of Bergson, Husserl, and Heidegger on time, as few philosophers and as no other contemporary Jewish thinker did, so it seems to me.

But he also made a most profound and original contribution to the contemporary rethinking of time. After Bergson instead of one theory of time plagued with unanswered paradox, there were now two: abstract, represented, or clock time, time as measurement; and time as duration, temporal flow or interpenetrating synthesis of past-present-future. The former would be grounded in the latter, as ideation is grounded in existence. Levinas, unique in contemporary thought, boldly proposed a third conception, and proposed it as the ground of duration (and hence also as the ground of clock time): intersubjective or ethical time. Time would thus not be sufficiently grasped by cognitive representation or by existential intuition, but would arise through ethical transcendence, in the face to face and in human sociality. Such is perhaps Levinas' most original, radical, and consequential conception. If it holds up, aside from everything else it would alone justify his exalted stature as a thinker. Of course it does not stand alone but permeates all his thought. Here we can only sketch some of its features.

Regarding duration, Levinas realized that while Bergson solved the problem of intellectualist atomization, the existential and enduring synthesis of past, present, and future would itself collapse into an extended self-presence if the transcendence of these same dimensions were not also guaranteed. Sociality or intersubjectivity ethically understood answers to this requirement because the I and Other bound ethically, the one responsible to and for the other, means that the I and Other are at once *in relation and out of relation.* Or more precisely, and putting time into this equation or into this disequilibrium, it means that they—I and Other, I me responsible for-the-other—are not "at once," not at the same time, that the irreducible *in and out of relation* is not a simultaneity or a synchrony but more fundamentally a *diachrony*. Time too is structured ethically, inter-subjectively, shattered by transcendence.

The future is not just my projection, the past not just my retention, memory or history; rather these syntheses, which would otherwise become my very self-presence, are shattered by a past and a future *not my own but the Other's*. Only a past that is "immemorial," that was *never present* and never will be present is truly past. And only a future always outstanding, *always yet to come*, is truly future, irreducible to presence. But where and how do we find such a past and such a future? Levinas' answer: from the Other, but from the Other as ethical imperatives. How so? The self arises in responsibility to and for the Other, yes, but this means that the self in its responsibility is always too late, that the other has already suffered, already is in need. Responsibility is always trying to catch up, to repair the irreparable. It has never done enough because it could not fix problems before encountering them; or could only fix some problems, but others unaccountably also arise. The past—its deepest sense, its genuine sense as transcending the present in its pastness—is thus constituted by the inadequacy of my moral obligations and responsibilities, my always being too late. Similarly, but in its own specific way, does the transcendence of the future, the futurity of the future, arise as an ethical imperative, not of morality, however, or not immediately from morality, but from justice, or more exactly from the absence of justice. Because the world is comprised of many persons morality is not enough; no matter what I do for the other who faces, there is more to be done and there are others to take account of, others who are other to the other, and other to others as well. We are born into a society of many, not only of two. To alleviate the suffering of the neighbor I must therefore labor to create a world of justice for all, a world where everyone can be moral without harm. But that justice, which is morally required, has not yet been established, it remains future; and that is the deepest sense of the future, the justice not yet achieved, the justice required by and for everyone and yet outstanding, to which I must dedicate myself in my responsibility.

Thus the primacy of ethics calls for a new understanding of time, as ethical, as imperative, as transcendent. Accordingly, we are better able to grasp what Levinas means by the following: "Judaism is a non-coincidence with its time, within coincidence: in the radical sense of the term it is an *anachronism*.... Monotheism and its moral revelation constitute the concrete fulfillment, beyond all mythology, of the primordial anachronism of the human."[42] Time's dimensionality as well as its directionality, the very possibility of progress or regress, are functions not of being, existence, or reason, but of deeper, more compelling ethical exigencies, kindness toward the other and justice for all, in a world not yet but coming in "time bearing a promise,"[43] *messianic time*. We will return shortly to the political aspect of the messianic. Here let us only add that in treating time as a function of intersubjectivity, and the future in terms of the justice yet to be established, Levinas conceives futurity generationally, across fecundity, from "generation to generation," the future as care for tomorrow's generation and for generations unborn, in a word, time as living tradition, past and future.

Conjoining time and ethics—the past as obligation, the future as justice—also means that time breaks with the order of nature, with natural and calculated continuities, with the recuperations and self-defenses of egoism, in a rupture, reversal, or inversion Levinas describes in *Totality and Infinity* as "the posteriority of the anterior."[44] Nature, the said, the represented, identity, present themselves as origins, as self-sufficient, as absolute, but they are anything but. Despite their counter-tendencies, their significance derives from a prior responsibility, from moral response to the face, which launches discourse and meaning in the first place. Hence what proposes itself to knowing as first is already second, already deposed, inverted, however it disguises its insufficiency in whatever modest or grandiose garbs. To say this otherwise: the egoist subject, choosing and self-interested, seemingly the source or arbiter of meaning, is before all else already chosen, *elected*, responsible—too late and too early, as we saw above. Such an inversion is indeed difficult to articulate, even though every articulation depends upon it. One difficulty is the congealing of meaning, its tendency toward self-sufficiency, what Levinas has called its "ceremonial," which in its most powerful form, as scientific knowledge, enlists the powerful support of epistemological theories of coherence and correspondence. Yet being-for-the-other, responsibility, the imperative, conditions the self-nomination of the nominative. Ethics is uncontainable, a rupture or surplus, or as Levinas also says, "trauma." To be responsible is to be "hostage" to the other, even "maternal," the other in oneself. The priority of the posterior, ethical time underlies Levinas' exegesis of the peculiar and much commented upon declaration of the

---

[42] Levinas, *Difficult Freedom*, 212–13.   [43] Levinas, *Is it Righteous to Be?*, 185.
[44] Levinas, *Totality and Infinity*, 54.

Jewish people at Mount Sinai (Exodus 24:7): *"naasey v'nishma,"* "we will do and we will hear":[45] ethical obedience and covenant *preceding* knowledge, contract, self-interest, choosing. "The antecedence of responsibility to freedom would signify the Goodness of the Good: the necessity that the Good choose me first before I can be in a position to choose, that is, welcome its choice."[46]

Such an election, the "already past" of responsibility, the "not yet future" of justice, investing selfhood as obligation and work, is higher and holier than an allegedly unbound and unregulated free choice.[47] Freedom is more difficult. Each person is already guilty. Each person has too much to rectify. Bad conscience is higher than good. In these ruptures and surpluses, in the responsibilities they call forth, life is meaningful. Such is the holiness of temporality. Or as Levinas once put the matter most succinctly: "Time is better than eternity"[48] – no doubt also recalling the rabbinic prohibition based on Proverbs 17:5 and codified in the *Shulchan Aruch* that the dead are "poor" and should not be mocked because they, unlike the living, are no longer able to fulfill mitsvot.

BODY AND SUFFERING: GENEROSITY

Contemporary thought begins with the integral unity of soul and body, mind and matter, spirit and letter, and so on. Such integrity is hardly alien to Judaism, which for ages has suffered attacks for being "carnal" rather than spiritual. Surely much of the Talmud, as much of Jewish daily life, is devoted to the body, to food, to property, to time schedules, and in ancient Israel to agriculture and sacrifices, never separating mind from matter, spirit from letter. These are the concerns and tasks of revelation, redemption, and holiness conceived by the Jewish prophets and rabbis as the imperatives of morality and justice. As contemporary philosophy so too does Levinas, utilizing the phenomenological method, remain close to the concrete, to the structures and significance of embodiment, dwelling, worldliness, and labor. His first two philosophical books, *Existence and Existents* and *Time and the Other*, published in 1947, and Part 2 of *Totality and Infinity*, elaborate careful and groundbreaking descriptions of the concatenated layers of constitutive

---

[45] Levinas, *Beyond the Verse*, 146.   [46] Levinas, *Otherwise than Being*, 122.
[47] See, "Choosing and the Chosen: Levinas and Sartre," in Cohen, *Levinasian Meditations*, 128–49, 337–40.
[48] Levinas, *Is it Righteous to Be?*, 176.

sense in human sensibility: its sensing, desires, worldliness, labor, vulnerability, suffering, mortality, and the like. Far from being despised or discounted, the body is recognized as the very site and means of spiritual discipline. Arms, hands: they work, they type, they beg, they give, they caress, they hug ... what would spirituality be without them? The Torah for humans is not the Torah of angels.

Accordingly, the deepest layer—the highest imperative—of Levinas' ethics transpires across the integrally *visceral and moral significance of suffering*. Ethics, humanity, religion begin not with a theosophical or theological God, the "omni" divinity. Nor do they begin with the self, in purification, meditation, or ecstasy. What comes first, what awakens spirituality, is the other person in his or her vulnerability, mortality, suffering. Divine and holy command, mitsvah, first appears not carved on stone but on the face of the other: Help me! Feed me! Protect me! Do not abandon me! Levinas often quotes Rabbi Israel Salanter: "The other's material needs are my spiritual needs." Spirituality arises not by escape from the world but by healing it (*tikkun olam*), starting with the neighbor. The deepest covenant is indeed written in flesh as my heart, the other's suffering soliciting my compassion. Levinas: "To be human is to suffer for the other."[49] The suffering of the other awakens my responsibility, and this awakening—never awake enough—is religious consciousness. In a major essay aptly called "God and Philosophy," Levinas writes: "The recurrence in awakening is something one can describe as a shudder of incarnation through which a subject becomes a heart, a sensibility, and hands which give."[50] More briefly, "The fear of God is the fear for others."[51]

"'Face' ... is nakedness, helplessness, perhaps an exposure to death."[52] All humans are mortal. But the mortality *most important, most compelling* is not my own, as Heidegger would have us believe, but the other's. Thus Levinas' arresting claim: "The doctor is an a priori principle of human mortality."[53] But even further, *extremis*, the ultimate structure of election, of moral obligation, occurs as a "dying for ..." the other. Transcendence can demand that much, that far. Such is the ethical significance of *"kiddush HaShem,"* "sanctification of God's name." Levinas recalls Queen Esther: "Rather than accept the death of others, abandon the others to their death, perish from spiritual loss,

---

[49] Levinas, *Nine Talmudic Readings*, 188.
[50] *The Levinas Reader*, ed. S. Hand (Oxford: Basil Blackwood, 1989), 182.
[51] Levinas, *Is it Righteous to Be?*, 162. [52] Ibid., 145.
[53] Levinas, *Totality and Infinity*, 234.

Esther prefers her death. Esther will answer (Esther 4:16): 'And then I will present myself to the king, and if I must perish, I shall perish.'" And continues his ethical exegesis: "There is a significant repetition of the identical verb 'perish' in this dialogue to which too little emphasis is given. An ethical advent: the death of the other takes precedence in my concern over my own."[54]

Humans are embodied, are sensible, suffering cuts deepest and cannot be rationalized or spiritualized away. We all eat and drink. Because I need and enjoy food, the other's hunger makes all the more sense; viscerally, is all the more compelling. But ethics comes first. "The sensibility has meaning only as a 'taking care of the other's need,' of his misfortunes and his faults, that is, as a giving. But giving has meaning only as a tearing from oneself despite oneself ... Only a subject that eats can be for-the-other."[55] Sociality is not contemplative, ethereal, or angelic; it begins in shared sensibility, across imperatives arising from a community of flesh. Levinas writes: "It is not a gift of the heart, but of the bread from one's mouth, of one's own mouthful of bread. It is the openness, not only of one's pocketbook, but of the doors of one's home, a 'sharing of your bread with the famished', a 'welcoming of the wretched into your house' (Isaiah 58). The immediacy of the sensibility is the for-the-other of one's own materiality; it is the immediacy or the proximity of the other."[56] And more radically still, or more delicately, or more responsibly: "even within one's own suffering, to suffer for the suffering my suffering imposes on the other."[57]

Thus is the body metaphysical without dualism, via ethical imperative: "all the gravity of the body"[58] arising from the face of the other, reaching to my heart and hands, my money, my home, "denuding beyond the skin,"[59] "exposure without assumption,"[60] all the way to "denuding to death,"[61] "dying for ... " the other.

POLITICS AND JUSTICE: ZIONISM

Two contending political orientations traverse Western political theory and practice: ethical politics versus *realpolitik*, justice versus power. For the one, politics is an extension of ethics into the public sphere,

---

[54] Levinas, *In the Time of the Nations*, 31.   [55] Levinas, *Otherwise than Being*, 74.
[56] Levinas, *Otherwise than Being*, 74.   [57] Levinas, *Nine Talmudic Readings*, 188.
[58] Levinas, *Otherwise than Being*, 149.   [59] Ibid., 49.   [60] Ibid., 180.   [61] Ibid., 49.

power regulated by the striving for justice; for the other, politics is exclusively a matter of power, of "might makes right." Plato, Aristotle, Bible and Talmud, and Levinas, belong to the first; Machiavelli, Hobbes, and Carl Schmitt, Nazi jurist and apologist, to the second. For *realpolitik*, ethics is not only extraneous to politics, it is positively harmful. So, for instance, Spinoza, disciple of Hobbes, in *Theological-Political Treatise* argued that one cause of the collapse of the ancient Jewish Commonwealth was of all things prophets upbraiding kings![62] Nothing could be more opposed to Levinas' ethical-political thought than unbridled power politics.

Realpolitik sees humans as beasts in need of restraint. Only the brute power of sovereign government stands between civilization and barbarism. For Levinas, in contrast, along with long Jewish tradition, politics and governance serve justice. The standard of law is not its dictate but fairness. In a profound insight, Levinas understands justice to regulate not beastliness but the infinity of morality, to rectify and provide measure for what would otherwise be unlimited obligations and responsibilities to the neighbor. Yes, subjectivity arises as infinite responsibility to and for the other, all the way to "dying for" the other, but the other is not alone. There are other others, near and far. The infinity of goodness must account for everyone, must rise also to justice, a justice that limits its infinite generosity. If I give my food to the hungry neighbor, as I should, what prevents others from going hungry? Levinas will see the origin of justice as the limitation not of beastliness but of goodness in the Talmud's injunction to set the worker's wages before the work is begun; otherwise the employer's financial obligation may well become exorbitant, all the way to bankruptcy.[63] Without a contract who can say how much the employer owes the worker? So the infinite obligations of morality must be limited—by justice. Limits are just when they attempt to maximize morality for all, providing the maximum material and spiritual conditions for each and every person to flourish, providing for their needs and respecting their dignity. These are not noble but hollow words. Justice is the driving force of politics and, as we have seen, the very futurity of the future, the hope of and for all humanity.

For Levinas, then, justice, ethical politics, must both rectify morality and remain guided by it. Justice is the effort to create a world in

---

[62] See Spinoza, *Theological-Political Treatise*, ch. 18, 207.
[63] See Levinas, *Nine Talmudic Readings*, 94–119.

which each person can be moral without harm to anyone else, which is to say, a world in which each person and all persons are cared for and respected. Morality without justice is mere sentimentality. But justice without morality becomes tyrannical, anonymous, inhuman, indifferent, without end or exit, Kafkaesque.

No doubt, and Levinas is fully aware, that such a politics is "utopian"—or he calls it "messianic"—in the sense that no actual state has ever been fully just, enabling a fully moral citizenry. Just as morality arises as infinite responsibility, just politics is also ongoing, a progress, a making the world just without rest. The "ought" never "is," which is why bad conscience is higher than good, and why for justice "like goodness – aiming at the Desired does not fulfill it, but deepens it."[64] For Levinas aiming for a political state whose power is regulated and guided by justice is the distinctive, highest, holiest sense of "Zionism," the true "State of David" or "State of Israel." Zionism for Levinas thus describes neither state sovereignty nor pious yearning apart. Truly pious yearning demands political action, ethical politics. Zionism is precisely that, the highest ethical task of politics, the always utopian labor of creating a just state. "Is not the ultimate finality of Zionism," Levinas asks rhetorically, "to create upon Israeli soil the concrete conditions for political invention, and to make or remake a state in which prophetic morality shall be incarnate, along with its message of peace?"[65] Or in even bolder formulations, again in a Talmudic Reading, beginning with an exegesis on the Temple showbread: "The table on which the bread is exposed before the Lord symbolizes the permanent thought that political power – that is to say, the king, that is, David, that is, his descendant, that is, the Messiah – is vowed to men's hunger .... Not to the end of times, to the hunger of hungry men; kingship in Israel is always Joseph feeding the people. To think of men's hunger is the first function of politics."[66]

Joining morality and justice, Levinas supports democracy, at once liberal and social. Liberal in acknowledging the uniqueness of each individual, ensuring human rights, enabling free association, discussion and debate, and the public deliberation essential to establishing just laws and peacefully changing leaders, aiming for justice for all. So too, then, the liberal freedoms must be fleshed out concretely, augmented by positive freedoms, by public provision for humanity's material

---

[64] Levinas, *Totality and Infinity*, 34.   [65] Levinas, *Is it Righteous to Be?*, 198.
[66] Levinas, *Beyond the Verse*, 18.

conditions such as health care, public education, social security, housing, culture, a sustainable and healthy environment, and the like—a *"democratic socialism,"* as Levinas declares in one of his Talmudic Readings, that "should be dear to us."[67] "Personal perfection and personal salvation," Levinas writes in another Talmudic Reading, "are, despite their nobility, still selfishness."[68] Or more concretely: "Authentic humanism, materialistic humanism. Hearts open very easily to the working class, wallets with more difficulty." And even more viscerally and radically: "To be able to eat and drink is a possibility as extraordinary, as miraculous, as the crossing of the Red Sea."[69] Justice requires far more than human rights; it requires a humane society, the care of each for each and of each for all. Such is Levinas' demand for the world, and his demand for the concrete political utopianism of an ethical messianic Zionism.

Let us conclude with an exegesis: "The traumatic experience of my slavery in Egypt constitutes my very humanity, a fact that immediately allies me to the workers, the wretched, and the persecuted peoples of the world.... Man ... can master the hostile forces of history by helping to bring about a messianic reign, a reign of justice foretold by the prophets. The waiting of the Messiah marks the very duration of time."[70] Thus "waiting for the Messiah" becomes political activism in the name of a just society, one always more just than the present one which is always never just enough. Such is Levinas' equation of "biblical humanism" and "Zionism" and the "State of Israel," not as power or being but as the better than being, the justice always in the process of becoming more just. Of which in his penultimate Talmudic Reading he says: "democracy ... a State open to what is better, always on the alert, always renovating,"[71] "that the acceptable political order can only come to humanity by way of the Torah, its justice, its judges, and its learned teachers. Messianic politics,"[72] "the democratic State as being precisely an exception to the tyrannical rule of political power which, according to the elders of the Negev, would merit only hatred."[73]

"To be conscious of being a nation implies being conscious of an exceptional destiny. Every nation worthy of the name is chosen."[74] Chosen: such is Levinas' distinctive teaching, not for power, or wealth,

---

[67] Levinas, *Nine Talmudic Readings*, 196.   [68] Ibid., 97.   [69] Ibid., 132.
[70] Levinas, *Difficult Freedom*, 26.   [71] Levinas, *New Talmudic Readings*, 96.
[72] Ibid., 95.   [73] Ibid., 96.   [74] Levinas, *Difficult Freedom*, 224.

SHORT BIBLIOGRAPHICAL ADDENDUM

or fame, but for what is better, for morality and justice; chosen for the highest vocation, for ethical responsibilities to and for the other, for each other and for all others.

Levinas' most important philosophical books are two: *Totality and Infinity* (1961) and *Otherwise than Being or Beyond Essence* (1974). Selected key philosophical articles appear in *Collected Philosophical Papers*, edited by Alphonso Lingis. Levinas' "Talmudic Readings" and other Jewish writings appear in five collections: *Difficult Freedom* (1963; 2nd ed. 1976); *Beyond the Verse* (1982); *Nine Talmudic Readings* (1968 and 1977); *In the Time of the Nations* (1988); and *New Talmudic Readings* (1996). (Dates are for original French editions.) *The Levinas Reader*, edited by Sean Hand, contains a representative sample of both philosophical and Jewish writings. In all his writings Levinas teaches the same ethics; therefore classifications of his writings as "philosophical" or "Jewish" at best reflect a difference in their idiom and audience, but not their substance.

Selected Further Reading

Cohen, Richard A. "Emmanuel Levinas." In *The Routledge Companion to Phenomenology*, 71–81. Edited by S. Luft and S. Overgaard. New York: Routledge, 2012.

Cohen, Richard A. *Levinasian Meditations*. Pittsburgh: Duquesne University Press, 2010.

Hand, S. ed. *The Levinas Reader*. Oxford: Basil Blackwood, 1989.

Kant, Immanuel. *Religion Within the Limits of Reason Alone*. Translated by T. M. Greene and H. H. Hudson. New York: Harper & Row, 1960.

Levinas, Emmanuel. *Beyond the Verse*. Translated by G. D. Mole. Bloomington: Indiana University Press, 1994.

Levinas, Emmanuel. *Difficult Freedom*. Translated by Sean Hand. Baltimore: Johns Hopkins University Press, 1990.

Levinas, Emmanuel. *Ethics and Infinity*. Translated by R. A. Cohen. Pittsburgh: Duquesne University Press, 1985.

Levinas, Emmanuel. "God and Philosophy." In *Collected Philosophical Papers: Emmanuel Levinas*, Translated by Alphonso Lingis. Dordrecht: Martinus Nijhoff Publishers, 1987.

Levinas, Emmanuel. *In the Time of the Nations*. Translated by M. B. Smith. Bloomington: Indiana University Press, 1994.

Levinas, Emmanuel. *New Talmudic Readings*. Translated by R. A. Cohen. Pittsburgh: Duquesne University Press, 1999.

Levinas, Emmanuel. *Nine Talmudic Readings*. Translated by A. Aronowicz. Bloomington: Indiana University Press, 1990.
Levinas, Emmanuel. *Otherwise than Being or Beyond Essence*. Translated by A. Lingis. Pittsburgh: Duquesne University Press, 1998.
Levinas, Emmanuel. *Totality and Infinity*. Translated by A. Lingis. Pittsburgh: Duquesne University Press, 1969.
Robbins, J. ed. *Is it Righteous to Be? Interviews with Emmanuel Levinas*. Stanford: Stanford University Press, 2001.
Spinoza, Baruch. *Theological-Political Treatise*, 2nd ed. Translated by S. Shirley. Indianapolis: Hackett, 2001.

PART IV
CONTEMPORARY ISSUES

12 The Holocaust and Jewish Theology
MICHAEL L. MORGAN

In 1966 Richard Rubenstein wrote that the central problem for Jewish theology was the question of God and the death camps; he also observed that at the time, in his view, the question had been by and large neglected or ignored by Jewish theologians. There is good reason to agree with Rubenstein on both counts—about the theological situation in 1966. If Rubenstein had been asked in, say, 1986, two decades later, whether he could say the same things, he would no doubt have denied that he could. Rubenstein might not have been satisfied by what had been written and said by Jewish theologians in the interim, but he surely would not have denied that there were those who took the question of God and the death camps to be central to Jewish self-understanding and that the issue and others akin to it had not been ignored. And finally, if Rubenstein had been asked, even a decade later, in 1996, if that were still true, he surely would have said that it was not and that any sense of theological urgency had seemed to have passed. What Jewish theology there was in 1996 and what Jewish theology there might still be, neither takes the Nazi atrocities, the death camps, and the horrors of the assault on Jews, Judaism, and all humanity to be central to Jewish self-understanding. Times change but not always in tune with our deepest concerns or our most profound sense of urgency. Or, in other terms, what we take to be the deepest and most urgent concerns facing us is something that changes as the times do.

RICHARD RUBENSTEIN: AUSCHWITZ AND THE "DEATH OF GOD"

In an essay published in 1962, Rubenstein reported on an interview he had conducted in August 1961 in Berlin with Heinrich Grüber, Dean of the Evangelical Church of East and West Berlin. In the essay Rubenstein described the way that Grüber had employed the framework of the traditional problem of evil or theodicy in order to explain the historical plight of the Jewish people. Positioning himself on the biblical portrayal of a providential God, Dean Grüber had pointed to other cases where the sufferings of the Jewish people ought to be understood as manifestations of God's anger. In his brief introduction to the reprint of the essay in *After Auschwitz* Rubenstein described his response to the Dean's use of the framework of theodicy and of a providential God this way: "After my interview, I reached a theological point of no return – If I believed in God as the omnipotent author of the historical drama and Israel as His Chosen People, I had to accept Dean Grüber's conclusion that it was God's will that Hitler committed six million Jews to slaughter. I could not possibly believe in such a God nor could I believe in Israel as the chosen people of God after Auschwitz."[1] A few years later, in 1965 and 1966, Rubenstein formulated these same doubts. In 1965, in an autobiographical piece, he would proclaim, "God really died at Auschwitz."[2] And a year later, in 1966, although he would write that "no man can really say that God is dead," he would go on to clarify: "I am compelled to say that we live in the time of the 'death of God'" and "when I say we live in the time of the death of God, I mean that the thread uniting God and man, heaven and earth, has been broken. We stand in a cold, silent, unfeeling cosmos, unaided by any purposeful power beyond our own resources. After Auschwitz, what else can a Jew say about God?"[3]

In North America, among the Jewish theologians working in the postwar period, Rubenstein was probably the earliest voice to address the theological impact of the Nazi death camps and the Holocaust, and in particular what those events mean for the belief in God and the relation between God and the Jewish people. Emerging around 1960, his views had crystallized by 1966. In order to understand precisely what Rubenstein's views were, we need to ask how he moves from Dean Grüber's interpretation of Jewish life within a biblical, providential framework to the rejection of that framework. Then we need to clarify the implications of that rejection. And finally we should ask what role Auschwitz and the Holocaust seem to have played in Rubenstein's conclusions about God and the Jewish people.

First, the interview with Dean Grüber had impressed Rubenstein—and provoked him—insofar as it exemplified one way that traditional

---

[1] Richard Rubenstein, *After Auschwitz*: History, Theology and Contemporary Judaism, first edition, (Basingstoke: Macmillan, 1966), 46; see also 52–55.
[2] Ibid., 224. [3] Ibid., 151–52.

theological thought, Christian and also Jewish, would have approached the sufferings and horrors of the death camps. The framework involved treating God as a historical agent and as "omnipotent and beneficent," treating the Jewish people as God's chosen and "treasured" people. Moreover, although Rubenstein took Dean Grüber and "traditional Jewish theology" to be applying the framework of the problem of theodicy or evil to the events of the Holocaust and the suffering of the Jewish people, in order to seek a solution to that problem and hence to provide an "explanation" for the suffering and atrocities, Rubenstein's response is not to reject one solution in favor of another. What he does, which he makes most clear in his contribution to the "Symposium on Jewish Belief" in 1966, is to identify what applying the framework of a providential God of history to Auschwitz requires and then, by rejecting this implication, he goes on to reject the framework conception itself. That is, he claims that "traditional Jewish theology ... has interpreted every major catastrophe in Jewish history as God's punishment of a sinful Israel" and that he "fail[s] to see how this position can be maintained without regarding Hitler and the SS as instruments of God's will." This would mean that "the traditional believer is forced to regard the most demonic, antihuman explosion in all history as a meaningful expression of God's purposes." Surely Rubenstein was aware that the problem of evil could be and has been solved or "negotiated" in a variety of ways. There have been solutions that focus on suffering as punishment or as educational in some way or as "apparent" when viewed in a larger frame of reference; there is the widely employed free-will response that focuses on moral evil and divine interest in human beings being responsible for the choices between right and wrong, good and evil. There may be one or more solutions to the problem that can avoid Rubenstein's charge that employing the theistic and providential framework, as we might call it, always leads to treating Hitler as God's historical agent. But Rubenstein's point is that for the "traditional Jewish believer and theologian" such a God must be involved and the events must ultimately be God's responsibility. Some may, and indeed have, found this acceptable. Of course they may have found it disturbing or enigmatic or even very hard to accept and yet nonetheless have accepted it and sought to cope in various ways. But Rubenstein's response was different. To him, as he put it, "the idea is simply too obscene for me to accept."[4] By using the word "obscene," which one

[4] Ibid., 153.

associates with something being disgusting or repulsive and hence impossible to live with, Rubenstein is showing that the issue here for him is not narrowly logical or even epistemic. Rather it is deeply visceral and indeed existential. If the result of living Jewishly within the framework of a providential God is to be required to employ the schema of theodicy, then, Rubenstein argues, he and perhaps many others would find such a way of taking Judaism and of being Jewish to be impossible to live with. This is the first step in his theological reasoning about Judaism, God, and the death camps. The providential God of history and Judaism as a religion of history are no longer acceptable.

What does Rubenstein take the implications of such a rejection to be? What does it mean for Jewish life, Jewish belief, and in particular Jewish beliefs about God? The first thing that Rubenstein says is: "Although I believe that a void stands where once we experienced God's presence, I do not think Judaism has lost its meaning or power. I do not believe that a theistic God is necessary for Jewish religious life."[5] That is, without confidence in the providential care and protection of God as a historical agent, the Jewish people and all individual Jews nonetheless need to cope with the challenges and trials of everyday life and of history. This is what Judaism, through its practices, its beliefs, and its communal system of support, provides. For Rubenstein, religion and religious communal life serve a variety of psychological and social purposes, and he even notes that the "forces within the psyche" that contribute to the formation of communal practices and communal life "have little to do with rational argument." For many people, religious life contributes a great deal to the shape of their identities, and religious practices help participants to celebrate and cope with moments of joy and sorrow, fear and sadness. Rubenstein speaks of "myth and ritual [as] the domains in which we express and project our unconscious feelings concerning the dilemmas of existence."[6] In short, for Rubenstein and those who accept his scruples about a continued commitment to a God of history and to Judaism as a religion of history, life still poses a host of challenges, psychological,

---

[5] Ibid., 153. See also 225: "What then of Judaism? It is the way we Jews share our lives in an unfeeling and silent cosmos. It is the flickering candle we have lighted in the dark to enlighten and to warm us."

[6] Ibid., 221, 222. On 222: "I cannot dispense with the institution through which I can dramatize, make meaningful, and share the decisive moments of my life. For me, that institution is the synagogue."

social, and existential, and religious practices and beliefs, "myth and ritual," serve as an organized set of ways of coping with those challenges.

Furthermore, dismissing the conception of God as a God of history does not require that all other conceptions of God also be set aside. Rubenstein, we should recall, said that "we live in the time of the 'death of God'" and that this is a "cultural fact." It is not, in other words, a metaphysical claim or an ontological one about the existence of God.[7] Rather it is a claim about how the concept of God is understood or how the symbol "God" is interpreted or what the word "God" is taken to mean. This, I take it, is what Rubenstein means when he says that "the time of the death of God does not mean the end of all gods. It means the demise of the God who was the ultimate actor in history."[8] What has come to an end is the plausibility of a certain conception or interpretation of God and no doubt also any confidence it such a conception. The "demise" of such a historical God is the decline of this conception as a cultural icon. Moreover, Rubenstein offers, as a replacement for this conception of a God of history, an alternative. "I believe," he says in 1966, "in God, the Holy Nothingness known to mystics of all ages, out of which we have come and to which we shall ultimately return.... In the final analysis, omnipotent Nothingness is Lord of all creation."[9] His reinterpretation of Judaism from a religion of history to one of nature and the God of Judaism from a God of history to a God of nature was inspired by his reading of Mircea Eliade and by Rubenstein's appropriation of themes from the Lurianic and other kabbalistic traditions. In

---

[7] Ibid., 151. [8] Ibid., 154.
[9] Ibid., 154. Rubenstein's sources for such a conception of God along kabbalistic lines are Isaac Luria and Schneur Zalman of Ladi. See 230–31 and 219–220. He also refers to Zalman Schachter, who was popularizing a kind of pop-Kabbalah in the sixties among college students and others. Most likely, Rubenstein learned a good deal about Kabbalah from Gershom Scholem's *Major Trends in Jewish Mysticism*, originally published in 1941 (Jerusalem: Hebrew University) and after two further editions in hardback appearing in paperback in 1960. The book was wildly popular among rabbis, college students, and rabbinic students in the sixties. For many liberal American Jews, their first introduction to the Jewish mystical or kabbalistic tradition may have come with *Nine and a Half Mystics*, written by Herbert Weiner, rabbi in South Orange, New Jersey, and published in 1969. Later in 1970, in the last chapter of *Morality and Eros*, "God after the Death of God" (New York: McGraw Hill) Rubenstein explores this notion of God as the Holy Nothingness, drawing upon Hegel, Tillich, the Lurianic Kabbalah, and other sources. There as elsewhere he uses the expression the "ground of Being" frequently and with somewhat pantheistic overtones.

short, Rubenstein argues that the conception of the God of traditional Jewish theism is now subject to doubt and dismissal, and in its place he recommends what he calls a "mystical paganism," with a God of nature or creation, out of which nature arises and into which it will decline.[10] As long as history goes on and nature exists, all resources for human life and fulfillment are finite and limited.

Finally, we might ask whether for Rubenstein it was the death camps and the Holocaust that led to his revised conceptions of Judaism and of Jewish theological beliefs. And even further, was it the Holocaust that led Rubenstein to take theological beliefs to be historically constituted and revised or rejected on the basis of their historical context? Did he take theological thought to be historically determined, and if so, did he think that such determination applied to all such thought and in every way? Answers to these questions are hard to give and harder to support. In the first edition of *After Auschwitz* Rubenstein included an essay originally written when he was a graduate student at Harvard and given as a talk at a conference in 1955. In it we can see many themes that came to characterize his thinking in the mid-sixties, once he had come to be associated with the "death of God" movement in Christian theology and its central figures, among them William Hamilton, Thomas Altizer, and Paul Van Buren. All of the themes that we have reviewed can also be found in the early essay, including the erosion of traditional Jewish justifications for authority and for the meaningfulness of Jewish rituals, symbols, and beliefs. As Rubenstein admits, his thinking about religion and culture is influenced by Paul Tillich whose lectures he attended at Harvard and whose work he no doubt studied. As he puts it in the essay: "As Tillich has suggested, we live in an age of 'broken symbols.' The problem of the symbolic content of Judaism in our time is to find a viable basis for continuing to maintain Jewish religious practice after its traditional validations have become altogether transparent to us .... It is no longer possible to accept the traditional justifications of the authority of Judaism ...."[11] And indeed the challenges to Jewish ritual practice, to the institution of the synagogue, and to much of liturgical practice also apply to the problem of the

---

[10] See Rubenstein, "The Symbols of Judaism and the Death of God," 240.

[11] Ibid., 229. See also, 233: "The fact that myth and religious symbol no longer are regarded as true at the manifest level is entirely irrelevant to their central function, which is to give profound expression to our feelings at the decisive times and crises of life."

The Holocaust and Jewish Theology 273

meaning of God in Judaism, and these led Rubenstein to reject "a theistic, creator God" for God as the "ground of being and the *focus of ultimate concern.*"[12] On the one hand, then, Rubenstein's critique of traditional Jewish theological concepts, including his critique of the conception of God as a providential, historical agent, comes in part from his Tillich-inspired interpretation of the challenges of modernity and the Nietzschean slogan, the "death of God." But, on the other hand, even in this early essay, Rubenstein makes clear that he appreciates, if only in inchoate form, the challenge to Jewish belief that arises with the death camps. Early in the essay, he remarks: "For many, the problem of finding a new rationale [for their theological commitments] has been aggravated by the death of their personal God. After Auschwitz many Jews did not need Nietzsche to tell them that the old God of Jewish patriarchal monotheism was dead beyond all hope of resurrection."[13] In 1955, then, before Rubenstein had interviewed Dean Grüber and before he had come to employ the traditional problem of evil and the framework of a religion of history that it expresses in order to reject the God of traditional Jewish theism in favor of some other conception of God, he both drew on critiques of religion in the modern world and yet also had an "intuition" that interpretations of traditional Jewish "myths, symbols, and practices" would have to be revised. Auschwitz and the death camps appear to be an important contributory reason for Rubenstein and Jews like him, he believed, to revise and possibly jettison Jewish theological ideas but not at all the exclusive reason. Furthermore, Rubenstein seems to have drawn on contemporary intellectual resources, such as the thinking of Paul Tillich, for the view of religion and culture as constituted by symbols and practices that are interpreted and reinterpreted in diverse historical contexts in order to enable them to be used to cope with continuing and unique psychological and historical crises. Auschwitz itself was not the primary reason for Rubenstein to accept such a view of thought, culture, and history, and perhaps not a reason at all, although as a case in point its resistance to a kind of theological explanation and comprehension, as he later would argue, certainly confirmed such a view.[14]

---

[12] Ibid., 237–40 and especially 238.
[13] Ibid., 227 and also 238: "For those who face these issues, the Father-God is a dead God. Even the existentialist leap of faith cannot resurrect this dead God after Auschwitz."
[14] In the second edition of *After Auschwitz*, published in 1992, Rubenstein eliminates some of this earlier material and, at the same time, includes several somewhat later

TWO TRADITIONAL VOICES

During the years of the Nazi assault on the Jewish people many traditional, Ultra-Orthodox rabbis, most frequently East European, delivered sermons that sought to make sense of the persecutions and suffering which their congregants were undergoing. In diaries, response, and other writings too we find stories of rabbis who spoke out against the atrocities and urged piety and fidelity to God in the midst of the horrors. We now have accounts of many such sermons and episodes, and some have even been translated and anthologized.[15] In general, rabbinic responses are couched in thick theological terms and call upon traditional teachings about God's providential care for the Jewish people and the coming of the Messiah, even when they express puzzlement and even admit ignorance of how the suffering and the atrocities fit into God's plan. Rarely does this literature express theological innovation. With regard to traditional Jewish theology, for such innovation we need to turn to the two Orthodox thinkers most commonly associated with post-Holocaust Jewish thought, Eliezer Berkovits and Irving Greenberg.

Eliezer Berkovits

Berkovits was a student of R. Yechiel Weinberg at the Hildesheimer Rabbinical Seminary in Berlin and a halakhic scholar, rabbi, theologian, and philosopher. He received his degree in philosophy from the University of Berlin in 1933 with a dissertation on David Hume,

---

essays that focus on central Jewish theological concepts, several other theological responses, and the theological impact of the Holocaust in general. See Richard L. Rubenstein, *After Auschwitz: History, Theology, and Contemporary Judaism*, 2nd ed. (Baltimore: The Johns Hopkins University Press, 1992), especially chs. 8, 9, and 16. Chs. 8 and 9 derive from "The Silence of God: Philosophical and Religious Reflection on the Holocaust," ch. 10 in Richard L. Rubenstein and John K. Roth, *Approaches to Auschwitz* (Louidville, KY: Westminster John Knox Press, 1987), which itself derives from earlier material from the 1970s and 1980s. Chapter 10 is a revised version of the last essay in Rubenstein, *Morality and Eros* (New York: McGraw-Hill, 1970), 183–96. By and large, these later essays elaborate his earlier views, at least concerning the role of religious "myth and ritual," the treatment of the "death of God" as a cultural event involving an assessment of human experience and the way God as a symbol is interpreted, and finally concerning the rejection in Judaism of the paternal, historical biblical God.

[15] The most useful collection can be found in Steven T. Katz, Shlomo Biderman, and Gershon Greenberg, eds. *Wrestling with God: Jewish Theological Responses during and after the Holocaust* (Oxford: Oxford University Press, 2007), especially Part I, "Ultra-Orthodox Responses During and Following the War," 11–201.

deism, and natural religion. After serving congregations in Berlin, Leeds, Sydney, and Boston, Berkovits moved to Skokie, IL, where in 1958 he became chair of the philosophy department at the Hebrew Theological College. His major work dealing with Judaism and the Holocaust, published in 1973, was entitled *Faith after the Holocaust*. Several of his early books deal with central themes in Jewish theology and philosophy, and while he had begun to write about the implications of Nazism and the Holocaust for Jewish belief around the time of the Six Day War in 1967, the 1973 book is his most comprehensive and developed formulation.

Berkovits represents a sophisticated version of the Modern Orthodox movement of *Torah im Derekh-Eretz* associated with Esriel Hildesheimer and passed down to Berkovits' teacher and mentor, R. Yechiel Weinberg. Berkovits was a trained philosopher, whose critiques of figures such as Martin Buber, Mordecai Kaplan, and others are philosophically astute and penetrating. To the question of the theological implications of the Holocaust for understanding Judaism and the historic task of the Jewish people, Berkovits brings both a traditional sensibility and philosophical sophistication. His traditional theological scruples provide him with his conception of divine providence and history and also with his conviction that the core truths of Jewish faith are applicable to historical experience. But centrally, for Berkovits, Judaism is grounded in the biblical text and its authority and in the halakhic tradition. The biblical text articulates the truths about creation, revelation, and redemption, and the conception of divine providence and history that is expressed biblically and then refined and interpreted in the Talmud and rabbinic literature, once formulated, holds for all subsequent history. Hence, as Berkovits puts it, "the Holocaust does not preempt all of Jewish history." Rather its meaning is disclosed by locating it within the Jewish philosophy of history, and this means appreciating that "the Holocaust poses no greater challenge to Jewish belief than the death of one innocent child."[16] In short, the Jewish theological solution to the problem of evil and innocent suffering was confronted biblically and refined in rabbinic literature. Confronting the Holocaust theologically, according to Berkovits, one must find its meaning within the traditional framework. But what is that framework?

[16] Eliezer Berkovits, *Faith after the Holocaust* (New York: KTAV, 1973).

According to Berkovits, God created the natural order, placed humankind within it, and then gave a special mandate to the Jewish people to realize the moral ideals of justice and peace within history. He takes this divine mandate to involve distinguishing between the natural forces that drive history according to principles of power and its imposition and, on the other hand, the moral forces that can elevate human history by bringing about a humane and just society. The former he calls "power history" and the latter "faith history." The responsibility of the Jewish people is to live "faith history." But this philosophy of history requires what Berkovits calls a theory of divine providence, a view about how God is related to humankind in such a way that human beings have responsibility for engaging in faith history and controlling power history. In short, God must be related to human will in such a way that human beings can act voluntarily in behalf of history's moral purposes. As a solution to the traditional problem of theodicy, Berkovits' conception takes the shape of a "free-will" response.

For Berkovits, then, creation is a two-stage process. First, God created the natural or "secular" world, which is imperfect on its own but which at the same time can be "sanctified" or "redeemed." In Judaism, this secular or natural world is "not-yet holy," and it is the creation of the human being, the second stage of creation, whereby history is born and the temporal continuous process of redemption ... begins. "From the very beginning man has been placed into this world ... that he may sanctify the secular, *l'taken olam b'malkut Shaddai*, and establish the city of man as the Kingdom of God .... Man, according to his own strength, continues the work of creation and becomes, urged on by God's call, a humble associate of the Creator."[17] Only with the second stage of creation, then, does history arise, and hence "history is man's responsibility .... Here, within the God-given task of sanctification, is the source of man's freedom as well as of his responsibility. The God who calls man to responsibility is the guarantor of his freedom to act responsibly."[18] Berkovits points to a rabbinic text in which this "God-given" task or heritage, the law, study and observance of it, and this freedom are associated. As he says, "Freedom – on the Tablets."[19] That is, Berkovits cites the famous midrash from *Pirke Avot* 6:2 on Exodus 32:16, which tells us that the tablets were God's work and the writing God's writing, "carved (*charut*) on the tablets." And the Rabbis say, "do not read *charut* (engraved); read

---

[17] Berkovits, *Faith after the Holocaust*, 60.   [18] Ibid., 61.   [19] Ibid.

cherut (freedom)." For Berkovits, then, creation and redemption or sanctification are mediated by human responsibility and freedom, on the one hand, and the law, on the other. The law requires human freedom; moreover, human freedom is expressed through the law. Although he does not mention Kant here, Berkovits' association of freedom with law is very Kantian in spirit; if freedom is a form of causality, it must be law-governed, which is why the freedom that is at the core of moral reason is autonomy, the law that reason makes for itself. But, he goes on to argue, the reality of that freedom requires a very precise divine action, a form of divine hiding, absence, or self-limitation.

Berkovits puts this divine self-limitation this way: "The hiding God (El Mistater) is present; though man is unaware of him, He is present in his hiddenness. Therefore, God can only hide in this world. But if this world were altogether and radically profane, there would be no place in it for Him to hide. He can only hide in history.... God hides in human responsibility and human freedom."[20] The hiding God, then, is also the saving God, but He saves in his hiddenness, in his presence in human freedom and responsibility.[21] Moreover, Berkovits prefers to emphasize the seeming paradox of God's presence as absence, of his hidden presence, or of his unconvincing absence. All of these formulations are intended, it would seem, to focus on a tension or even a dialectic, between a divine retreat or withdrawal and a divine presence or involvement.[22] It is this tension or dialectic that is the centerpiece of what Berkovits calls a "Jewish philosophy of history" and an account of "divine providence."

Berkovits presents this account in chapter 4 of *Faith after the Holocaust*.[23] The precise setting is the problem of theodicy and "undeserved suffering in history," and in the case of the Holocaust "injustice absolute." In order to clarify the biblical and talmudic ways of dealing with these phenomena, Berkovits turns once again to the notion of God's hiding His face, *hester panim*. The expression in the Bible has two meanings: one concerns "divine judgment and punishment," while the other refers to human suffering that results, not from divine judgment, but rather from "the evil perpetrated by man." The

---

[20] Berkovits, *Faith after the Holocaust*, 64.
[21] Ibid., 65. That God both hides His face and yet is the savior of Israel, Berkovits derives from Isaiah 45:15.
[22] Ibid., 99, where Berkovits takes the Rabbis to have joined together God's silence with His presence: "The one who is silent may be so called only because he is present."
[23] Berkovits, *Faith after the Holocaust*, 94–113.

latter is the result, Berkovits notes, from "indifference – God seems to be unconcernedly asleep during the tribulations inflicted by man on his fellow." Berkovits calls upon Psalm 44 and then turns to the Talmud for further confirmation of this second meaning, which is the one that we have seen him call upon in order to clarify the human role in creation, history, and redemption. There God's hiding His face made possible human freedom and responsibility in the service of the law and sanctification of the natural world; here that same divine process of withdrawal makes possible injustice and suffering.[24]

Once again Berkovits turns to Isaiah 45:15 and the notion of a hiding God who is also a saving God, but he now exploits various talmudic texts to show that this means that God creates humankind with the freedom to choose between good and evil, with the responsibility for becoming righteous and avoiding wickedness. These are options or possibilities that God Himself must respect, if he is to respect what is essential to human existence:

> Man cannot be bludgeoned into goodness. If God did not respect man's freedom to choose his course in personal responsibility, not only would the moral good and evil be abolished from the earth, but man himself would go with them. For freedom and responsibility are of the very essence of man. Without them man is not human. If there is to be man, he must be allowed to make his choices in freedom. If he has such freedom, he will use it. Using it, he will often use it wrongly; he will decide for the wrong alternative. As he does so, there will be suffering for the innocent.[25]

What we have here, then, is a version of a synthesis of several strategies that have been used to justify divine omnipotence and goodness when confronted with innocent suffering. In particular, Berkovits here employs one version of the so-called "Free-Will Defense." He draws on talmudic texts in order to formulate it, and he concludes by calling it a "divine dilemma," for it does not shrink from praising God for being "long-suffering" and "patient," both with the righteous and the sinful, and for being a God who hides His face. God risks a great deal on man, but in creating him, God nonetheless cannot abandon him:

---

[24] Ibid., 94–96. Berkovits cites Psalms 44:24–27; 13:2.   [25] Ibid., 105.

> But man left to his freedom is capable of greatness in both – in creative goodness and destructive evil. Though man cannot be man without freedom, his performance in history gives little reassurance that he can survive in history .... If man is not to perish at the hand of man, if the ultimate destiny of man is not to be left to the chance that man will never make the fatal decision, God must not withdraw his providence from his creation. He must be present in history. That man may be, God must absent himself; that man may not perish in the tragic absurdity of his own making, God must remain present. The God of history must be absent and present concurrently. He hides his presence. He is present without being indubitably manifest; he is absent without being hopelessly inaccessible .... Because of the necessity of his absence, there is the "Hiding of the Face" and suffering of the innocent; because of the necessity of his presence, evil will not ultimately triumph; because of it, there is hope for man.[26]

Earlier, the dialectic or tension between God's presence and absence seemed to focus on the reality of human freedom and the task of redemption, indeed in the conjunction of freedom with law. Here, the dialectic or what Berkovits calls a dilemma concerns God's hiding of His face and His patience, which requires His providence. Exactly what this means is not clear, although it might mean that while God absents Himself in order to make freedom possible, He reserves the possibility of miraculous intervention when it is needed to save humankind from tragic self-destruction.[27] For our purposes, however, we can ignore this qualification and pay exclusive attention to the central motif, that of the hiding of God's face and the way in which it makes "room" for human freedom.

Berkovits refers to this divine withdrawal or self-limitation in a variety of ways. As we have seen, the primary image he employs is that of God's hiding His face (*hester panim*). He also speaks of this act as "God's renunciation of his power on man," "divine self-restraint,"

---

[26] Ibid., 107.
[27] Berkovits makes this distinction between divine agency via withdrawal and divine agency through miraculous intervention at *Faith after the Holocaust*, 109, where he claims that the first occurs within history but the latter "outside of history." His example is the Exodus, which is an expression of divine might and hence cannot be within history.

and the "shackling of his omnipotence."[28] Nowhere in *Faith after the Holocaust*, however, does Berkovits so much as suggest that this motif of divine self-limitation should be associated with or interpreted in terms of the kabbalistic or specifically Lurianic notion of *tzimtzum*. For such a hint, we need to turn to an earlier work of Berkovits, his more systematic and metaphysical work, *God, Man and History*, published first in 1959 and then in a second edition in 1965.

The argument of *Faith after the Holocaust* is a particular application of the conception of God and the Jewish philosophy of history articulated in this earlier work. In the later work, divine self-limitation or God's hiding His face occurs as a structural feature of creation in general and in particular of the dimension of creation that involves humankind, freedom, and history. In the earlier work, in his discussion of creation, Berkovits identifies this same feature broadly as a "presupposition" of creation itself:

> God's involvement with the realm of finite reality is imaginable only as an act of divine "self-limitation," as it were. God, notwithstanding His transcendence, bends down to the world of finitude. He "humbles" Himself, as it were, in order to relate Himself. He "reduces" Himself so that He may enter into the narrow straits of a relationship with finite existence. But the fundamental act of divine involvement is creation itself; we shall, therefore, have to look at it as the basic deed of divine self-limitation. God creates the world of finite being by curbing the full manifestation of His essence and power. In order to create, He must restrain His infinite potency to such a degree that nothing may issue from the work of His hand which surpasses the boundaries of a finite universe. Creation is only conceivable as an act of divine "self-abnegation." God is involved in the destiny of finite being as the result of an act of "self-denial."
>
> This is, perhaps, the fuller meaning of the concept of the "hiding" God. God not only veils His presence, so that it may be endured by man; He "denies" His essence so that the world of finitude may come to be and He Himself remain[s] involved in it. An act of self-limitation is the premise of creation, as well as of God's involvement in the destinies of the world of man.[29]

---

[28] Ibid., 109.
[29] Eliezer Berkovits, *God, Man and History: A Jewish Interpretation* (Middle Village: Jonathan David Publishers, 1959), 64.

Fundamentally, then, divine self-limitation and the imagery of God's hiding His face characterize creation itself. They also, however, apply to the account of evil and human responsibility that we saw formulated in Berkovits' later book and is already developed in the more systematic, earlier one:

> ... God, in creating the universe, has delegated a measure of responsibility for its own history to creation. We do not find ourselves in a universe of puppets, dangling from the strings of the Almighty and automatically obeying every one of His commands, but in a universe in which freedom makes the deed possible. No doubt, God took a risk with creation by granting it consciousness and free decision. The freedom may be misused at any time or it would not deserve its name.[30]

In a previous chapter Berkovits describes this creation of humankind as a matter of granting a measure of independence to a being who is largely dependent. "He is free to be himself because God cares for him. Without that freedom the relationship would become valueless, for man would cease being a person .... It is a moral necessity ... that [God] should be 'hiding,' so as to preserve the personal identity of man .... Man may confront the Divine Presence only because God curbs and constrains—as it were—His transcendence. God 'denies' Himself in order to affirm man. By an act of divine self-denial man is made free to deny Him .... The act of divine self-denial is the precondition of the fundamental religious experience."[31] In short, then, what Berkovits calls "divine self-denial" or "God's hiding His face" or divine self-limitation is a presupposition of both creation in general and the creation of human beings as free and responsible in particular.

As he does later in *Faith after the Holocaust*, Berkovits cites, as a proof-text for the biblical provenance of the notion of the hiding God, Isaiah 45:15: "Indeed, Thou art a God that hidest Thyself, O God of Israel, the Saviour." But in *God, Man and History* the context differs, and Berkovits makes an important distinction. The context is the more general one of the very possibility of revelation or the divine–human encounter. In the moment of revelation, man is both threatened by God and His transcendence and also sustained by God. This is where Berkovits describes God's self-denial as a precondition of the encounter between man and God, and he takes it to be a reading of Isaiah 45:15. In

---

[30] Ibid., 80. [31] Ibid., 34–35.

a helpful note, however, this reading leads Berkovits to distinguish between "God's hiding Himself" and "God's hiding His face." In the encounter or in revelation, God does "face" man; "it is the divine essence which is veiled or hidden, so that man may 'face' God." That is, in revelation, God's essence is hidden, which is required for human freedom, but not His face. On the other hand, there can be a moment when God withdraws his concern altogether and hence when revelation does not occur at all. This is "God's hiding His face." It is a "breakdown in the relationship." But if this distinction applies, then there are two forms of divine self-limitation. God can withhold His essence but not his manifestation, or He can withhold His face or His manifestation as well as His essence. In the latter case, there is no revelation at all; in the former, there is revelation but only because man is free to receive it. In short, there is a sense in which the hiding God is a precondition of human freedom, but there is another sense in which it is not.[32]

In a footnote to the account of creation and divine self-limitation, which we cited earlier, Berkovits provides his sole reference to the Lurianic notion of *tsimtsum*.[33] Clearly, he is reticent about identifying his notion of the hiding God or of divine self-limitation with the Lurianic concept of *tsimtsum*. What are his reasons? Basically, Berkovits takes his conception and that of the kabbalists to involve a categorical difference. Citing Gershom Scholem's discussion in *Major Trends in Jewish Mysticism* (260 ff.), Berkovits argues that whereas his own conception of divine self-limitation is a "logical requirement for God's involvement in a finite reality," the kabbalistic notion is "almost a 'spatial' concept" according to which "*Tsimtsum* applies to the withdrawal of divine substance into God, in order to make 'room' for creation," that is, "in preparation for creation."[34] That is, as he goes on to point out, the issue concerns the very concept of creation. For him, divine withdrawal is constitutive of creation—of its very essence, as he puts it. For the kabbalists —especially Luria—*tsimtsum* is preparatory; creation follows. Berkovits takes this distinction to turn on the very logic of the notion of creation; as he puts it: "the act of creation demands self-limitation and self-abnegation; otherwise

---

[32] Ibid., 34–35 and especially n. 9, 165.   [33] Ibid., 173–74, n. 14.
[34] See Gershom Scholem, *Major Trends in Jewish Mysticism* (New York: Schocken, 1941 and 1954), 260–64. For a later treatment by Scholem, see *Kabbalah* (Jerusalem: Keter Publishing, 1974), 129–35 and *passim*, reprinted from the *Encyclopedia Judaica*.

creation would not be finite. But if it were not finite, it could not be apart from God; in other words, it could not be creation." That is, for Berkovits, creation and then humanity, freedom, and so forth—all must be finite and hence separate from God, which is Absolute and infinite. Creation is about dependency, and it requires a dualism of the finite and the infinite, the worldly and the transcendent. Berkovits never says that one could not reinterpret *tsimtsum* to fit such a dualism, but he does suggest that if Scholem is to be believed, that dualism is not found in Luria and the Kabbalah. What is found there is the need for room or a spatial location in which creation, itself a matter of divine presence, can take place. To use Platonic categories, for the kabbalists, if the divine is pure form, then creation requires a material substrate, originally separate from form, on which form imposes itself or on which form is imposed by an independent divine agency. For Berkovits, the representative or delegate of the divine in the world and in history is free human agency; for the Kabbalists, as he reads them, one might surmise, the world is already divinely formed or organized. For Berkovits, redemption or sanctification, which he takes to be the rabbinic ideal, is the human task of transforming what is already formed but not completed or perfected. On his reading, redemption for the Kabbalist is freeing the divine form to reunite with the Godhead and hence to leave behind the material substrate. That is, Berkovits has a greater appreciation of the value of redeeming the world than the Kabbalists, whose ideal is redemption from and not of the world. And, if this is right, he associates this difference with the difference between his own conception of divine self-limitation and the kabbalistic notion of *tsimtsum*.

Given this background picture of a traditional Jewish philosophy of history and conception of divine providence, what impact does the Holocaust have? Here, Berkovits' answer is psychological rather than theological. As he puts it, with regard to the Holocaust, the central question is not "where was God?" but rather "where was man?" That is, if history is a human responsibility, then the Holocaust was the outcome of human decisions and human actions. Furthermore, responding to the Holocaust, on the part of the Jewish people, is also a human responsibility. And, Berkovits argues, the upshot of the Nazi destruction and the demise of European Jewry is its psychological effect on the Jewish will to follow God's commands and to realize the moral purposes of "faith history." In short, the impact of the Holocaust is primarily on Jewish will and not on Jewish ideas; it is, as I have put it, psychological and not theological. As we have seen, the armature of

Berkovits' traditional Jewish theology was developed by him long before the late 1960s, when intellectual encounters with the death camps became prominent features of Jewish life. What distinguishes his view, then, is Berkovits' sensitivity to the challenges on Jewish life, that is, Jewish will and Jewish commitment, which the Holocaust and the memory of the Holocaust presented. At the same time that for him the Holocaust required no alteration in the content of Jewish faith, as it were, it did require historical and psychological changes in order to revive Jewish commitment to moral purposes and hence to prevent the lapse into total despair.

Irving Greenberg

Irving Greenberg's writings in Jewish theology, especially those of the late 1960s and early 1970s, reflect a more radical response to the horrors of Auschwitz, theologically speaking. If Berkovits' thinking exhibited a serious sense of honesty and respect for the victims of the death camps, Greenberg's thinking is at least as sensitive and indeed more radical, given his starting point. Greenberg was trained as an orthodox rabbi at the Beth Yosef Seminary, studied with R. Joseph Soloveitchik, served as a rabbi, received a doctorate in history from Harvard with a dissertation on Theodore Roosevelt and labor in the early decades of the twentieth century, taught at Yeshiva University and City College in New York, and went on to establish and direct a number of prominent national Jewish organizations. Within the orbit of Orthodox Judaism in America, Greenberg stands as a very progressive member, both intellectually and in terms of the themes of his leadership, which circled around a strong commitment to pluralism, to Jewish unity, and to interpreting Orthodoxy in a very liberal and progressive fashion. When, in his widely cited essay, "Cloud of Smoke, Pillar of Fire,"[35] he claims that Judaism is a religion of history, he means that Judaism originated in founding historical experiences, always responded to and was altered by ongoing historical events, and looks forward to the future resolution of historical problems. In particular, he argues, the Holocaust is so momentous an event that no Jewish concepts and principles can continue to be affirmed today or simply be recovered uncritically and without an initial skepticism and concern. Although Greenberg affirms this

---

[35] Irving Greenberg, "Cloud of Smoke, Pillar of Fire." *Auschwitz: Beginning of a New Era? Reflections on the Holocaust*, ed. Eva Fleischner (New York: KTAV, 1977).

radically historicist conviction about the continuity of Jewish ideas and principles after Auschwitz, he nonetheless clings to some concepts and themes as prima facie undeniable and somehow mandatory for ongoing Jewish life and belief. But this tension may be more psychological than theoretical. In principle, Greenberg appears to hold at least that no element of Jewish belief can be endorsed after those events without acknowledging and accepting its ambiguous and even paradoxical character, its instability, and our uncertainty about it. In short, Berkovits' traditionalism may be mitigated by his openness to the modern world and to modern thinking, but it is indeed much less compromised than is Greenberg's, which to some may not seem traditionalist at all. For him, even the core theological commitments of Judaism are susceptible to continued rethinking after the Holocaust and are likely to be less secure and less precise than one might have hoped.

In the early essay mentioned above, Greenberg states explicitly that all theological claims must be exposed to the challenge of the death camps and their atrocities. That is, both the meaning and the truth of such claims—about the dignity of humankind, God's providential care for human beings in general and the Jewish people in particular, hopes for the messianic coming, and even about how to understand and cope with suffering and catastrophe—must be reconsidered in the light of the horrors and evil of Auschwitz and all it stands for. Moreover, he claims that once such a process of exposure has been carried out, the concepts and beliefs that remain must all be "dialectical." By this term, Greenberg makes it clear that he means that all central Jewish concepts and principles, for example, the concept of the covenant, must be interpreted as involving internal complexity, ambiguity, uncertainty, and even a paradoxical or conflicting character. Hence, he argues that even faith in God must involve both confidence in some ways and at some moments, alternating with doubt and skepticism in other ways and at other times. He calls this a situation of "moment or dialectical faith." And in the essay, Greenberg also explores critically any contemporary, post-Holocaust retrieval of traditional Jewish models for confronting and coping with suffering, for example, the response of Job, the model of the suffering servant, and the consolations of *Lamentations*.

Greenberg's account never pushes for revisions in the very conception of God in Judaism, but he does argue that a new conception of the covenant between God and the Jewish people is required. Greenberg takes the biblical notion of the covenant to involve divine purpose, the human role in perfecting creation, divine restraint, human freedom, and a commitment to redemption. As a divine relationship with people in history, it is subject to change. In its classical form, then, it is both voluntary and involuntary to different degrees, albeit with an emphasis on God's rule and His plan. The revised and post-Holocaust covenant modifies how the covenant is taken by its human participants. Greenberg calls this recovered albeit revised concept of covenant an "open covenant" or a "voluntary covenant." It involves a relationship of mutual concern between God and the Jewish people, divine responsibility, and certainly expectations for the life of the Jewish people and for Jews. But, at the same time, it also makes expanded room for and indeed calls for a great degree of human freedom to reinterpret and understand in new circumstances what it is that God demands of the Jew and what traditional commands can no longer be justified or at least not in the way they have been in the past. Such openness to new circumstances, to ongoing restrictions to a sense of human dignity and worth, and to assaults on the very notion of human dignity calls for novel expressions of human deliberation, reflection, interpretation, and decision, concerning, for example, the roles and responsibilities of women in Jewish life. Substantively, there are issues that arise out of the Holocaust and its assault on human dignity and worth that demand resistance and even opposition, Greenberg argues, and among them is the dehumanizing assault on human spontaneity itself, that is, on human freedom and will. In short, for Greenberg, some form of voluntarism in a post-Holocaust world is itself an opposition to Nazi purposes, and employing that voluntarism in behalf of revising traditional commandments can often take shape as a mode of opposition as well.

In fact, as a devastating assault on humankind, on the Jewish people, and on the covenant, the Holocaust, as Greenberg suggests, "exposed a divine absence that left the covenant with no justifiable authority."[36] But the fact that Jewish life continued during the Holocaust and has continued thereafter indicates that the covenant is still an ongoing relationship, although the only explanation for its continuity is that Jews took it upon themselves voluntarily and not because it had been commanded. What was once a "commanded" relationship is now a "voluntary" one. In Greenberg's words, "[the covenant's] authority was broken, but the Jewish people, released from its obligations, chose voluntarily to take it on

---

[36] See Michael L. Morgan, *Beyond Auschwitz: Post-Holocaust Jewish Thought in America* (Oxford: Oxford University Press, 2001), 136, citing Irving Greenberg, "Voluntary Covenant," 15.

again ... God was no longer in a position to command, but the Jewish people was so in love with the dream of redemption that it volunteered to carry on its mission."[37] In short, the Holocaust was "the shock that almost destroy[ed] the covenant" but did not.[38]

Greenberg, then, in some ways shares with Rubenstein the belief that religious beliefs and rituals in general, and Jewish ones in particular, undergo historical change, with regard to their meaning and their truth, how compelling they are, and how firmly practiced. Unlike Berkovits, Greenberg takes the Holocaust then to be theologically as well as psychologically and historically influential. Indeed, he even learns from the Jewish people's continued commitments and allegiance an important lesson about the voluntary authority for the post-Holocaust covenant. In several respects, then, Greenberg is most similar to Emil L. Fackenheim, who also took the Holocaust to be historically and theologically momentous and who focused on the way a continued sense of solidarity with Judaism and the Jewish people would require a hermeneutical recovery of the Jewish past.[39]

RADICAL THEOLOGICAL REVISION

In one case, Auschwitz did indeed lead to radical theological revision, that is, even to a revised conception of God or divinity. The thinker I have in mind is Hans Jonas, once a student of Heidegger and Rudolf Bultmann, among others, and a significant philosopher in his own right. Known for his influential early book on Gnosticism and his later work on moral responsibility and ecology, Jonas' earliest contribution to post-Holocaust Jewish thought came in 1961, and some have claimed that since the 1960s—or at least since the 1980s—he should have been considered as a philosopher who made an original contribution to Jewish theology after Auschwitz.[40] The question of how to understand

---

[37] Ibid., 16.
[38] See Morgan, *Beyond Auschwitz*, 136–39, for a discussion of this stage of Greenberg's thinking and the challenges it makes to traditional notions of authority in Judaism.
[39] See Emil L. Fackenheim, "The 614th Commandment" and "Jewish Faith and the Holocaust" in *The Jewish Return into History* (New York: Schocken, 1978); *God's Presence in History* (New York: New York University Press, 1970), ch. 3; and *To Mend the World* (New York: Schocken, 1982). For discussion, see Morgan, *Beyond Auschwitz*, and Fackenheim's *Jewish Philosophy: An Introduction* (Toronto: University of Toronto Press, 2013).
[40] The fullest expression of Jonas' theological views after the Holocaust can be found in the essay "The Concept of God after Auschwitz: A Jewish Voice," *The Journal of*

Jonas' contribution, however, whether to take it as original theological or even as largely moral-political, may only be academically interesting. Clearly, his two or three essays that deal with God after Auschwitz reveal themes that can be compared with what we find in figures such as Rubenstein, Fackenheim, Berkovits, and even Emmanuel Levinas. But it may be that what is most interesting in Jonas' thinking is what is distinctive of his overall approach and its motivations and not its details.

Jonas' essay has three parts. First, he makes some introductory comments about the problem and how he proposes to deal with it. Second, drawing on his 1961 lecture on immortality, Jonas narrates a cosmological story about God and the natural order, what he calls a "myth." Third and finally, he examines several implications of the myth for his question about how one ought to conceptualize God after Auschwitz and the death camps. In his introductory comments, Jonas says that his proposal will be an example of a "speculative theology" (131), and since he is also a philosopher and reflective about how one might approach a problem such as this one, about the concept of God appropriate for Judaism in a post-Holocaust world, we should look at what he says about this "speculative theology" and why proposing a myth or set of images is an appropriate way to approach the question.

Jonas notes, for example, that while we might, after Kant, agree that we have no way of knowing about God's existence, the importance of God encourages us to look for other ways, other than inquiry about God's existence, to grasp the role God plays and how we might understand the very concept of God. As he puts it, "bowing to the decree that 'knowledge' eludes us here, nay, even waiving this very goal from the outset, one may yet meditate on things of this nature in terms of sense and meaning" (132). In other words, addressing the question about God and the death camps ought to lead us to consider what, after Auschwitz, we might take the concept of God to mean, and of course there are

---

Religion 67.1 (Spring 1987): 1–13, delivered in German as a lecture at Tübingen University. It is an expanded and revised version of an essay of the same title, published in *Out of the Whirlwind*, ed. A. H. Friedlander (New York: Union of American Hebrew Congregations, 1968), which drew on the 1961 essay, "Immortality and the Modern Temper." For convenience I refer by and large to the 1987 version, as it is reprinted in Hans Jonas, *Mortality and Morality: A Search for the Good after Auschwitz*, ed. Lawrence Vogel (Evanston, IL: Northwestern University Press, 1996), 131–43, 207–8. All references here are to the reprinted version in this volume.

various ways we can inquire into what a concept means. Furthermore, Jonas is explicit that this is a historical question as well as a hermeneutical one. As he puts it, "what did Auschwitz add to that which one could always have known about humans and from times immemorial have done? And what has it added in particular to what is familiar to us Jews from a millennial history of suffering and forms so essential a part of our collective memory?" (132) Human beings in general, and Jews in particular. have always had to deal with suffering, often suffering of the innocent that is the result of despicable and horrific acts. In the case of Jews and Judaism, the problem of Job as the problem of theodicy has been the traditional framework or structure for confronting, seeking to understand, and responding to such suffering. Here, like Rubenstein, Greenberg, and Fackenheim, Jonas takes as his starting point the problem of theodicy and proceeds to raise doubts that traditional solutions—such as divine punishment for sin and Jewish unfaithfulness to the covenant or self-sacrifice and martyrdom as expressions of supreme faith—are any longer, after Auschwitz, at all acceptable. "Nothing of this," he says, "is still of use in dealing with the event for which 'Auschwitz' has become the symbol" (133).[41]

On the one hand, then, as Jonas turns to the "concept of God" and how, after Auschwitz, it can still be "thinkable," it looks like he is recommending that we abandon the framework of the problem of theodicy and nonetheless go on as Jews by considering a new way of understanding the traditional vocabulary of "God" and various expressions associated with it. That is, one might take Jonas to be following the path taken by Rubenstein, Fackenheim, and Greenberg that involves a radical revision in the recovery of traditional Jewish concepts. At one point, for example, he says, "[Auschwitz] has, indeed, ... added to the Jewish historical experience something unprecedented and of a nature no longer assimilable by the old theological categories" (133). However, on the other hand, there are times when Jonas seems to accept

---

[41] Jonas quickly but incisively lists some objections to various traditional responses within the framework of the traditional problem of theodicy; see "The Concept of God after Auschwitz," 133. How could Auschwitz be a venue for heroism or defiance or witness, for example, "since it also devoured the infants and babes" (133). Nor did the victims die as persons, since the deprivation and dehumanization left them with little sense of dignity. Jonas' point is not simply that specific solutions to the problem of theodicy do not work when applied to Auschwitz; rather the model itself is deeply flawed in some way. This brings him closer to Rubenstein, Greenberg, and Fackenheim than to others.

the continuing relevance of the model of the problem of theodicy and the challenge that Job faced or at least its terms, so that what he seems to be suggesting is a new "solution" to the old problem. This way of understanding Jonas' approach is suggested, for example, by his remark that "to the Jew, who sees in 'this' world the locus of divine creation, justice, and redemption, God is eminently the Lord of *history*, and in this respect 'Auschwitz' calls, even for the believer, the whole traditional concept of God into question .... Accordingly, one who will not thereupon just give up the concept of God altogether ... must rethink it so that it still remains thinkable; and that means seeking a new answer to the old question of (and about) Job. The Lord of history, we suspect, will have to go by the board in this quest" (133). Or, as he also puts it, "what God could let it happen?" on the assumption, of course, that Auschwitz does not obliterate or wipe away the concept of God but rather leads to its reinterpretation.

This, then, appears to be the challenge Jonas faces: to rethink the concept of God as a God somehow related to the world and *history* and yet not simply as an agent whose absence is left inexplicable. Jonas' method for responding to this task, moreover, is to propose a myth—one that he had earlier used in 1961 to clarify what the concept of "immortality" might mean today—in order to present and illuminate this new understanding of the concept of God, that is, a post-Holocaust understanding of what "God" might be taken to mean. As Jonas points out, using myth to deal with profound subjects otherwise unknowable is a strategy that he—following various German readers—found in Plato's use of myth in the dialogues.[42]

Jonas' myth, which draws on various sources, including kabbalistic and especially Lurianic sources as well as evolutionary biology, portrays a creator God and the relative independence of the created world, as a site of suffering and pain, to which God responds. The concept of God, as he goes on to show, by interpreting the myth, includes a God that is suffering, becoming, caring, and limited in power.[43] It is a concept that

---

[42] The role of myth in Plato's dialogues and especially whether such myths, Plato's inventions, have any cognitive role to play at all, are matters of ongoing controversy. For a helpful, recent interpretation, see Daniel S. Werner, *Myth and Philosophy in Plato's Phaedrus* (Cambridge: Cambridge University Press, 2012), ch. 1.

[43] In describing God as caring, Jonas also claims that He is "an endangered God, a God who runs a risk" (138). Invested in what happens in nature and history, God has given human beings freedom to act and hence He is running a risk with regard to God's hopes and desires for humankind and the future of life in the world.

breaks with traditional Jewish theological categories in various ways, seems supported by the Bible and traditional themes in some ways, and yet does still cling to the idea of an ongoing relation between God and the world and history. But how, then, might Jonas' project best be understood: as breaking with the framework of theodicy and with traditional Jewish categories and recovering Jewish ideas and themes with a new interpretation of them; or, in contrast, as accepting a host of traditional Jewish ideas, including the framework of the problem of theodicy, and solving the latter problem in a different way? One could, I think, tell both stories and conclude them in the same way, with the conception of a suffering, caring, changing, and finite God. Does it matter, then, which view we take of Jonas' project? Does it tell us something significant about how he understands the Holocaust and its impact on the continuity of history and of Jewish thought and its relation to history? We should keep these questions in mind as we probe further into Jonas' account.

Of the four features that characterize this "new" concept of God, the one that is most significant for Jonas, and that he takes the most time to explain and elaborate, is divine finitude, the limitation on divine power, and the denial of omnipotence. Perhaps looking at what he says here will help us to understand better whether he takes this concept of God to be a break with the whole framework of theodicy or rather a solution within its parameters. Jonas first turns to what he refers to as an ontological and logical "paradox in the idea of absolute power" (138). As he puts it, "from the very concept of power, it follows that omnipotence is a self-contradictory, self-destructive, indeed, senseless concept" (138). Jonas does not refer here to what is called the "paradox of omnipotence," that God could not be all-powerful, for He cannot create a stone that He cannot lift or make a law that He cannot break. Rather his argument is that power must be limited or resisted, for if not, then it cannot be power, but if so, then the concept of unlimited power is incoherent.[44] Alternatively, as he formulates it, power is relational and must be divided; the very idea of a comprehensive and unlimited power is incoherent.[45] Such an argument, of course, which has medieval roots, does not derive in any way from the historicity of the Holocaust and in fact is a conceptual and not an empirical one.

---

[44] Jonas, "The Concept of God after Auschwitz," 138–39.
[45] Ibid., 139: "In short, it cannot be that all power is on the side of one agent only. Power must be divided so that there be any power at all."

After proposing these doubts about the very idea of unlimited power, Jonas turns to the problem of theodicy in its traditional form. Here his argument, which he admits is a theological one against this notion of absolute, unlimited divine power, is that committing ourselves to divine goodness and the existence of evil makes it unavoidable that God's power must be limited. One might seek to avoid this conclusion by taking God to be completely or wholly "inscrutable" and "beyond our understanding," but since, in Judaism, this conclusion is unacceptable, given the facts of revelation and Torah, we must conclude that God is limited in divine power. In fact, Jonas does not simply list this argument as another argument alongside the earlier one he rehearsed. Putting it more precisely, what he contends is that the earlier logical argument indicts the very concept of a being of unlimited power; this makes the concept of omnipotence "dubious," as he puts it; and since it is, this recommends that when we face the problem of theodicy, it is the premise about divine omnipotence that is most likely to be dismissable. Indeed, to summarize, Jonas argues that: (1) since the evidence of Auschwitz shows us that either God is not good or His ways are inscrutable or He is not omnipotent; and (2) since Judaism rejects an inscrutable God; and (3) since he has already shown the concept of omnipotence to be incoherent on logical grounds; and (4) since one does not want to abandon divine goodness, what is left is to admit to God's limited power.[46]

Jonas' argument is not yet complete. He claims that his conclusion is conditional: after Auschwitz, only a conception of God as limited in power is compatible with "any acceptable theology continuous with the Jewish heritage" (140). In fact, Jonas goes further: divine power can be seen to be limited only "by something whose being in its own right and whose power to act on its own authority he himself acknowledges" (140). That is, Jonas argues that the forces that limit divine power must have a kind of independence, albeit one that is "acknowledged" or "recognized" by God. At the same time, he makes clear that during the Holocaust, when the suffering and the atrocity was at such an extraordinary level, God did not intervene; He was silent. But how can we understand this silence? Jonas notes that his myth explains that the silence was "not because he chose not to [intervene], but because he *could* not intervene" (140). During history and as long as the world exists, God "has divested himself of any power to interfere with the

---

[46] This is the gist of Jonas' argument on pp. 139–40.

physical course of things" and yet whose call to divine purposes can still be heard. This is a result similar to Berkovits' claim that during history, divine absence makes possible the capacity for human voluntary actions, while the "command" to act in behalf of humane and just ideals continues to be heard, with the option to follow that command resting in human hands. It is also reminiscent of Fackenheim's proposal that during the Holocaust, while no saving divine presence was felt, a divine commanding presence was indeed heard. But Jonas is not satisfied to leave things with this claim. He continues to push further the question of how this limitation on divine power is compatible with "traditional Jewish ideas."

How do we understand the relation between God and the natural, historical process in such a way that God remains the God of creation and yet cannot interfere in the world process? Jonas proposes that "the elimination of divine omnipotence leaves the theoretical choice between the alternatives of either some preexistent – theological or ontological – *dualism*, or of God's *self*-limitation through the creation from nothing" (141). The former alternative will not do, for a two-god theology is incompatible with traditional Jewish belief and a Platonic view, drawn from the *Timaeus*, does not apply to "positive evil, which implies a freedom empowered by its own authority" if it is going to apply, Jonas suggests, to the "fateful hour" of the Holocaust (141). Only the second alternative does not conflict with the oneness of God and the traditional Jewish notion of creation out of nothing, which it can endorse by supplementing such creation with the idea of divine self-contraction and self-limitation. It is this kind of view that Jonas' myth seeks to express, and in so doing, he claims, the myth actually articulates a theme already found in the Lurianic Kabbalah. Calling on the work of Gershom Scholem, Jonas cites "the idea of *tsimtsum*, that cosmogonic counterconcept of the Lurianic Kabbalah ... [which] means contraction, withdrawal, self-limitation" (142). *Tsimtsum*, as is well-known, in the Lurianic myth of creation, is the divine act which makes room for the subsequent creation, for "without this retreat into himself, [the act of the *Ein-Sof*], there could be no 'other' outside God, and only his continued holding-himself-in preserves the finite things from losing their separate being again into the divine 'all in all'" (142). Indeed, Jonas' myth goes further, he points out, insofar as the divine power has wholly and totally ceded control in the space vacated for creation to finite beings and to the finite, natural world. Having given itself wholly to the world and to humankind, it becomes the turn of humanity to return or give back to God (142). During history and in nature, it is the human task to do what can be done to prevent any divine regret for having created the world, and this means to oppose, mitigate, and perhaps even prevent human evil.

If we step back, then, and reflect upon Jonas' attempt to rethink Jewish theological commitments after Auschwitz, we can see that the horrors and evil of the Holocaust enter into his mythic response and its philosophical articulation and interpretation at certain key points. Jonas seems willing to reappropriate or recover several central traditional Jewish theological ideas, regarding God and God's relation to the Jewish people, to humankind, and to the natural order. His attention is on one central Jewish idea, that of God and how God can now be understood. His view is that the concept we have of God now ought to be of a changing, suffering, and caring God who nonetheless is limited in power with respect to natural events and human conduct in history. Human beings and not God are responsible in history for satisfying God's interests and goodness; during history, God withholds himself and in creation establishes what is not God as independent in being and power or capacity. The concept of such a limited God is not only compatible with other Jewish beliefs, Jonas claims; it is itself an extension of a concept of God found within Judaism itself, in particular in the kabbalistic cosmogony of Isaac Luria.

CONCLUSIONS

Unlike Rubenstein, then, Jonas does not "use" the framework of the problem of theodicy to reject the God of history and a conception of Judaism as a religion of history. And unlike Berkovits, Jonas does not assimilate a theological understanding of a Jewish conception of history and divine providence to a view of such matters already present in rabbinic Judaism. For Berkovits, the Holocaust has no theological implications; for Rubenstein, Auschwitz in principle could render any and every Jewish belief false or at least subject them to revision. Jonas takes Auschwitz to be unprecedented and of momentous importance to any attempt to rethink Jewish theological beliefs today, but substantively he finds more of traditional Jewish understanding congenial than does Rubenstein, but with regard to the concept of God in particular, he is more radical than Berkovits in what he finds recoverable from the Jewish past.

Jonas takes theological reflection to be of continuing importance, so that he is unwilling to set it aside in favor of confronting now, directly and in opposition, the Holocaust's continuing legacy of suffering, evil, hatred, and atrocity. That is, while Jonas does find an important place for human conduct in taking responsibility for making society and the world better places in which to live, he takes it to be central to Judaism and perhaps even prior in importance, to understand theologically where such responsible conduct fits into a Jewish *Weltanschauung*. This is a distinctive position. For many, the central question for post-Holocaust Jewish life is the practical one, that of resistance and response. Theological and philosophical reflection may have ongoing roles to play for some, especially for those who are moved to seek strong justifications for what they do and who take public debate about the direction and substance of Jewish obligations and responsibilities to require theoretical support and defense. But for many, Auschwitz itself challenges the coherence and comprehensiveness and even the possibility of Jewish theology, as it challenges all of our ways of understanding ourselves, human society, history, and more. With regard to the Holocaust, thought reaches an impasse, and to go on means to go on in life, in our actions and in our lives, independent of any philosophical and theological thinking in which we may be tempted to indulge. But this is not Jonas' position, nor does he seem to take Auschwitz to be as momentous a rupture in our lives and in our thinking as do Greenberg and Fackenheim, for example. But this modesty may have its benefits. It certainly challenges him, and yet it enables him to come to more theologically novel results than we found in Rubenstein, Berkovits, and Greenberg.

In this essay I have focused on how a small number of Jewish thinkers sought to grapple with the implications of the Holocaust for a central question of Jewish belief. That question concerns how to conceive of God and God's relation to individuals and to the Jewish people. Rubenstein established this question as central, and yet arguably post-Holocaust Jewish theology did not give radical answers to that question. Unlike other Jewish intellectuals and leaders, the figures I have discussed all took Nazi totalitarianism, the assault on Judaism and the Jewish people, and the death camps to be events of momentous historical significance. Central concepts and beliefs of Judaism had to be exposed to those events and to be reconsidered. For these thinkers, it was important that the Holocaust was an evil event, whose features as a whole were unlike any previous event with regard to the horrific nature of its methods and procedures, to its policies and programs, and to the constellation of forms of conduct that were responsible for its realization. They frequently called it "unprecedented," emphasizing its historical and temporal role, and took it to be transformative. It was a constellation that left us and our world changed. To be sure, subsequent events have included atrocities and horrors of momentous significance as well, but there is reason to think that our responses to them are and ought to be understood in terms of the event in whose shadow they have occurred. In this sense, the Jewish theological responses to the Holocaust are not the last word by any means, but they are an important and unavoidable word and one that now constitutes a crucial stage in the tradition of Jewish theology.

Selected Further Reading

Berkovits, Eliezer. *Faith after the Holocaust*. New York: KTAV, 1973.
Berkovits, Eliezer. *God, Man and History: A Jewish Interpretation*. Middle Village: Jonathan David Publishers, 1959.
Fackenheim, Emil L. *Fackenheim's Jewish Philosophy: An Introduction*. Toronto: University of Toronto Press, 2013.
Fackenheim, Emil L. *God's Presence in History*. New York: New York University Press, 1970.
Fackenheim, Emil L. *The Jewish Return into History*, New York: Schocken, 1978.
Fackenheim, Emil L. *To Mend the World*. New York: Schocken, 1982.
Greenberg, Irving. "Cloud of Smoke, Pillar of Fire." In *Auschwitz: Beginning of a New Era? Reflections on the Holocaust*, 26–55. Edited by Eva Fleischner. New York: KTAV, 1977.
Jonas, Hans. "The Concept of God after Auschwitz: A Jewish Voice." *The Journal of Religion* 67.1 (1987): 1–13.
Jonas, Hans. *Mortality and Morality: A Search for the Good after Auschwitz*. Edited by Lawrence Vogel. Evanston, IL: Northwestern University Press, 1996.
Katz, Steven T., Shlomo Biderman, and Gershon Greenberg, eds. *Wrestling with God: Jewish Theological Responses during and after the Holocaust*. Oxford: Oxford University Press, 2007.
Morgan, Michael L. *Beyond Auschwitz: Post-Holocaust Jewish Thought in America*. Oxford: Oxford University Press, 2001.
Rubenstein, Richard L. *After Auschwitz: History, Theology, and Contemporary Judaism, Second Edition*. Baltimore: The Johns Hopkins University Press, 1992.
Rubenstein, Richard L. *Morality and Eros*. New York: McGraw-Hill, 1970.
Rubenstein, Richard L. and John K. Roth. *Approaches to Auschwitz*. Louisville, KY: Westminster John Knox Press, 1987.

13 Theology and Halakhah in Jewish Feminisms
RONIT IRSHAI

INTRODUCTION

In "The Jew Who Wasn't There,"[1] Rachel Adler asserted that not only does Jewish tradition discriminate against women halakhically, it also classifies them as "others" and relegates them to the margins of Jewish life. Her article was the catalyst for seminal discussions of the possibility of a Jewish feminist theology and of halakhah's place and importance for Jewish feminism. Although "theology" was taken as referring to an overarching ideological framework, which also includes an engagement with halakhah, halakhah was seen, at least in the first generation of Jewish feminist thought, as a problematic field that could not be made compatible with the new feminist aspirations.

Although Adler herself offered a broad treatment of the halakhic problem (which I consider below), she understands that from the feminist perspective it is logical to argue that there is little sense to engaging in halakhic analysis. Halakhah does not affirm gender equality; moreover, harsh injustices can be perpetrated (and, in practice, are perpetrated) against women under its auspices, primarily with respect to marriage and divorce, and against gays and lesbians. As Adler has written:

> Whether gender justice is possible within *halakhah* and whether a feminist Judaism requires a *halakhah* at all are foundational questions for feminist Jewish theology that have no parallel in Christian feminist theology. [...] Appropriating the terms and

---

[1] Rachel Adler, "The Jew Who Wasn't There," *Davka* (Summer 1971): 7–11. See also Mara Benjamin, "Tracing the Contours of a Half Century of Jewish Feminist Theology," *Journal of Feminist Studies in Religion* 36.1 (2020): 11–31. Benjamin discusses Jewish feminist theology by adding new dimensions such as: activism, embodiment, immanence and Jewish trans theology as well.

method of *halakhah* itself, many feminists concluded, drew them into a game they could not win. [...] *Halakhah* became the feminists' elephant in the living room. Everyone agreed it was in the way, and no one knew how to get rid of it.[2]

In fact, when Ellen Umansky wrote her article about the creation of a Jewish feminist theology, halakhah was not part of the project she envisioned.[3] In her opinion, one of the impediments to the creation of a Jewish feminist theology is the fact that it is not always possible to bridge the gap between human experience and the tradition, because symbols of divinity prescribed by the tradition are not necessarily products of women's imagination and are not necessarily meaningful for women. Hence Jewish feminist theology must be a "responsive theology" that responds to the traditional theology. It would express an a priori commitment to the traditions' basic sources and categories of God, Torah, and the People Israel, but not necessarily to its norms (194).

Judith Plaskow focused the bulk of her attention on forging a new Jewish feminist theology; she questioned whether "halakhah" can be a feminine medium in any sense and whether Jewish feminists should even deal with it.[4] In the very interesting debate between Plaskow[5] and Cynthia Ozick[6] in the early 1980s, Plaskow asserted that women's inferior status in halakhah is only a symptom of a broader ideological system rooted in the deep theological structures of Judaism; this means that women cannot expect justice with just making changes in halakhah. She holds that women's otherness is linked to the masculine aspect of the deity and received dramatic expression in the terms we use about God. Although women do participate in religious rituals, religious language broadcasts a different message. It denies their humanity and ignores their experience. And because that language is

---

[2] Rachel Adler, *Engendering Judaism: An Inclusive Theology and Ethics.* (Philadelphia: Jewish Publication Society, 1998).

[3] Ellen M. Umansky "Creating a Jewish Feminist Theology: Problems and Possibilities," in *Weaving the Visions: New Patterns in Feminist Spirituality*, ed. Judith Plaskow and Carol Christ (San Francisco: Harper & Row, 1989), 187–98.

[4] Judith Plaskow, *Standing Again at Sinai: Judaism from a Feminist Perspective* (San Francisco: Harper & Row, 1990).

[5] Judith Plaskow, "The Right Question is Theological," in *On Being a Jewish Feminist: A Reader*, ed. Susanna Heschel (New York: Schocken, 1983), 223–34.

[6] Ibid., Cynthia Ozick, "Notes Toward Finding the Right Question." 120–151.

not subject to halakhic amendment, the situation cannot be altered through halakhah. Plaskow published her theological doctrine in *Standing Again at Sinai* (1990), which became part of the canon of Jewish feminist theology. Ozick, by contrast, believed that the problem of women in Judaism is a sociological fact. In other words, it is not bound to the deep theological structures but is a result of mutable social influences that can be remedied through halakhic means. Although Ozick issued a harsh indictment of the patriarchal Jewish tradition that silenced women and thus effectively eliminated their voice and potential contribution to the tradition, she still believed that a remedy could be found on the strictly halakhic dimension.

One might think that it is natural for feminists affiliated with the liberal Jewish streams to avoid engagement with halakhah, given its already problematic status in those streams, and to focus their efforts to reconstruct Judaism, in light of the feminist critique, on the theological level. But Orthodox Jewish feminists could be expected to take up the task wholeheartedly. Somewhat surprisingly, though, this has not been the case.

Tamar Ross, the leading theologian of Orthodox feminism, has argued that though the tools for remedying halakhah are to be found within halakhah itself, the precondition for renewal does not lie exclusively in the hands of the halakhic decisors but also entails a remedial theology that she proposes Jewish feminism adopt.[7] In any case, most of Ross's efforts are in the theological realm, not the halakhic. This choice means that she effectively accepted the position of the feminist theologians of the non-Orthodox streams, despite the major difference in their descriptions of the problem as well as the theological solutions they propose.

Meanwhile, Tova Hartman, another Orthodox feminist thinker, did not treat the halakhic problem at all, because, in her view, "the challenge of feminism to Modern Orthodoxy is far deeper than a challenge to specific aspects of *halakha*, or even to the halakhic process as a whole. [...] What I propose, then, is not a halakhic debate".[8]

But as long ago as 1981 Blu Greenberg, one of the pioneers of Orthodox feminism, published *On Women and Judaism*, in which

---

[7] Tamar Ross, *Expanding the Palace of Torah: Orthodoxy and Feminism* (Waltham, MA: Brandeis University Press, 2004).

[8] Tova Hartman, *Feminism Encounters Traditional Judaism* (Waltham, MA: Brandeis University Press, 2007), 16.

she called for a reshaping of halakhah.[9] Although this was the first time such a call had been sounded in the Orthodox world, it was actually the Reform Adler who provided a detailed account of what this reshaping entailed. She held from the outset that an overhaul of halakhah is a significant element of the theological project of Jewish feminism, because, taking her cue from Robert Cover, she believes that the forms of Jewish life cannot survive without the normative demand. She expressed this feminist-theological approach to halakhah in *Engendering Judaism* (1998).[10] There she formulates the ways in which Judaism in general, and halakhah in particular, must be developed in the spirit of justice and gender equality.

As Orthodox feminism developed, however, it followed several lines of thought about the options for confronting the halakhic challenge in greater detail. I myself attempted to integrate ideas about the significance of the assertions about the gender bias of halakhah, along with a practical demonstration of its effects, drawn from the halakhic literature,[11] with a suggestion, from the field of the philosophy of halakhah, to overcome these biases.[12] I did not abandon the theological dimension, however. Admittedly I did not consolidate a positive theology for Jewish feminism, as Plaskow, Adler, and Ross did, but a "negative" theology. I am not referring here to the doctrine of "negative attributes," but rather to the simple question of whether the theological concepts that ground traditional halakhah, which prevent the implementation of halakhic ideas that are more respectful of women, can be identified. I designated this "negative" theology "Akedah Theology."[13] If the conservative theological foundations that are incompatible with feminist ideas can be identified, not only will we be more aware of the theological obstacles to the development of feminist halakhah, we will also be able

---

[9] Blu Greenberg, *On Women and Judaism: A View from Tradition* (Philadelphia: Jewish Publication Society, 1981).

[10] Adler, Rachel. *Engendering Judaism: An Inclusive Theology and Ethics* (Philadelphia: Jewish Publication Society, 1998).

[11] Ronit Irshai, *Fertility and Jewish Law: Feminist Perspectives on Orthodox Responsa Literature* (Waltham, MA: Brandeis University Press, 2012).

[12] Ronit Irshai, "Toward A Gender Critical Approach to the Philosophy of Jewish Law (Halakhah)," *Journal of Feminist Studies in Religion* 26.2 (2010): 55–77.

[13] Ronit Irshai, "Religion and Morality: Akedah Theology and Cumulative Revelation as Contradictory Theologies in Jewish Modern-Orthodox Feminism," *Journal of Modern Jewish Studies* 16.2 (2017a): 219–35.

to devise a feminist theology that deals with these deep-rooted concepts.

FEMINIST THEOLOGIES

Tamar Ross and Judith Plaskow agree that the main challenge that feminism poses to Judaism is theological, related to the belief in revelation and the conceptualization of God.[14] Nonetheless, Ross and Plaskow differ greatly in their analysis of the feminist challenge and in their responses to this challenge. For Plaskow, the main theological challenge is the masculine imagery associated with God and its problematic ramifications, which permeate the entire Jewish tradition. That imagery has led to the definition of women as the Other and their marginalization or exclusion from public communal life. Put differently, because Jewish monotheism posits a hierarchical relationship between God and humanity, and God is conceptualized exclusively in masculine terms and humanity in feminine terms, there is a causal connection between the conception of God and the patriarchal social structure. The inevitable result is injustice to women, because only men are deemed to be like God, whereas women are in some way less than the human standard. Although Plaskow highlights this injustice and severely critiques this masculine conception of God, she is not willing to give up the monotheistic idea of revelation. Instead, she addresses injustice to women by adding feminine imagery to the God talk. For Plaskow, feminine imagery does not jeopardize monotheism, given that all anthropomorphic language merely expresses the inevitable limits of human cognition; in this regard, there is no difference between masculine and feminine imagery. It is false to argue that masculine imagery does not undermine monotheism, but feminine imagery does.[15] Feminism, in her opinion, demands a new understanding of the Torah, God, and the Jewish people, an understanding that reflects a renewed definition of Jewish humanness. This can be achieved by renovating the Jews' historical memory, revising the language of prayer, and creating new women's ceremonies and liturgy, as well as

---

[14] The comparison between Plaskow and Ross is taken from Ronit Irshai, "Tamar Ross: An Intellectual Portrait," *Library of Contemporary Jewish Philosophers: Tamar Ross – Constructing Faith*, eds. Hava Tirosh-Samuelson and Aaron W. Hughes (Leiden and Boston, MA: Brill Academic Publishers, 2016).

[15] This is the gist of Plaskow's response to Ozick. See Plaskow, "The Right Question is Theological," 1983.

by writing feminist midrashim. Taken together, all these can provide the basis for a theology that makes it possible to annul women's otherness in Jewish tradition.

Like Plaskow, Ross does not necessarily reject the feminist critique that the masculine conception of God generates a notion of reality that is hierarchically gendered. But as an Orthodox Jew she does reject the practical conclusions that Plaskow, as a liberal Jew, draws from this. In other words, Ross shares Plaskow's description of the problem, but differs regarding its solution. The key differences between these two leading feminist theologians can be summarized as follows: First, Ross's main theological effort focuses on how to salvage the belief in the divine origin of the Torah while fully acknowledging that revelation is subject to the limits of human biases. Recognizing the deep masculine bias that permeates Scripture throughout, including the Pentateuch, she agrees that skepticism about divine revelation forces us to ask whether *any* verbal message, even one that claims revelatory status, can truly be regarded as divine.[16] At this juncture Ross develops her theory of "cumulative revelation," which is based on several assumptions:

1. Revelation is an ongoing and cumulative process—a gradual and dynamic development of the original Torah, such that the Torah's ultimate meaning is revealed only over the course of time.
2. The divine voice does not speak through vocal cords (or via a created voice), but rather through rabbinic interpretation and the mouthpiece of history, which serves as its trigger.
3. Although the sequence of "hearings" sometimes appears to contradict the original message, that message is never replaced. It always remains as the cultural-linguistic filter through which new messages are to be understood. Even when we absorb new insights, they do not abrogate the privileged status of the original tradition.
4. If a particular idea or social form takes root and is accepted by the Torah-committed community, this acceptance may be understood to confirm its divine source[17] (Ross and Gellman 1998; Ross 2004).[18]

---

[16] Ross, *Expanding the Palace of Torah*.
[17] Tamar Ross and Yehuda Gellman, "The Implications of Feminism for Orthodox Jewish Theology," in *Multi-Culturalism in a Democratic Jewish State: Prof. Ariel Rosen-Zvi Memorial Volume*, eds. Menachem Mautner, Avi Sagi, and Ronen Shamir (Tel Aviv: Tel Aviv University Press), 443–74.
[18] Ross, *Expanding the Palace of Torah*, 197–200.

This model is both postmodern in essence and Orthodox in spirit. It is postmodern in that it offers an extremely relativist conception both of the divine word and of prevailing social perceptions. If it is the community of the committed that retroactively determines whether new ideas are to be regarded as "the word of God," then any idea—moral and noble, or racist and vile—can in principle be accepted as the word of God. But this model is also Orthodox at its root, because each new layer does not nullify the preceding revelation to which it accrues. On the contrary, all preceding layers necessarily serve as the filter through which the new perception is perceived. Such an approach frees one of the need to justify the essentially masculine language of prayer via acrobatic forms of apologetics or radical revision. The foundational language of the original text is accepted as such, but is infused with new meaning in accordance with the additional insights afforded by a new divine message. In the event that feminist insights become part of the common consensus, innovation at the narrative level can lead to the radical understanding that these too are an aspect of God's original word, although heretofore hidden, so long as they remain accountable to the layers preceding them. Despite the new historical context that gives rise to new meanings, the antecedent core may never be abrogated. Applying the concept of cumulative revelation to the challenges of our day, including that of feminism, allows believers to view these challenges as merely another tool or vehicle for discovering the full implications of God's eternal word. Such a view does not condone violating or replacing the original patriarchal message. Rather, it understands the rise of feminism as a clear indication that we have outgrown patriarchy's previous configuration and are duty-bound to carry it to a higher and more refined stage, one that generates new spiritual connotations.

Appreciating the fact that meaning is context-dependent encourages a movement away from the limited theistic view of God as standing over and above the world and controlling it from without, and favors a more substantive and intimate understanding of the relationship between the two. This view is congenial to feminism due to its ability to refine the hierarchical model typifying monotheism and to depict the relationship between God and humanity in a more "feminine" fashion. In addition, however, it also allows the religiously committed to understand how the Torah can be completely human and completely divine at one and the same time.

Plaskow does not go as far as to suggest that the biases of human language can cast doubt on the divine source of the Torah. She seeks a fundamental revision of Jewish historical memory, because it does not take women into account. Ross, by contrast, does not believe that such a revision is legitimate and justified, because it undermines an entire world of Jewish identity constituted by Jewish historical memory. Indeed, given that human conceptions are always bound to history, the patriarchal historical memory of Jewish monotheism should remain unchanged, because it reflects a foundational human conception of divine revelation in the past. Furthermore, even if we witness a new understanding of God's message, we are not required to erase all previous ideas. Rather, a new concept always builds on older layers, which function as filters through which the new revelation is perceived and applied. Ross then draws a sharp distinction between form and content. Radical innovation is possible on the level of content, if we admit that feminist insights (to the extent that they are endorsed by the community of Jewish believers) are truly divine. On the formal (i.e., halakhic) level, however, every innovation must take account of the existing tradition.[19] In other words, as an Orthodox Jew Ross highlights continuity with previous revelations, and in turn with the entire line of Jewish tradition, even though she endorses radical theological insights of feminism; thus, form and content are in tension with each other. By contrast, the liberal Plaskow seeks greater coherence between form and content: the forms of religious language must express the egalitarian content.

A second difference between Ross and Plaskow concerns the concept of revelation. For Plaskow, the feminist critique does not alter the concept of revelation: God remains transcendent to the world and in a hierarchical relationship with humanity. Ross's notion of revelation revises this notion because she emphasizes that cognition is context-dependent. Accordingly, she proposes a more intimate understanding of the relationship between the divine and the human (as explained above), which softens the typical hierarchical view of monotheism and presents the relationship between God and humanity in a more "feminine" or feminist manner.

Third, despite her more feminist understanding of revelation, Ross preserves the traditional concept of Jewish law as the product of divine

---

[19] Tamar Ross, "Modern Orthodoxy and the Challenge of Feminism," in *Jewish Orthodoxy: New Perspectives*, eds. Joseph Salmon, Aviezer Ravitzky, and Adam Ferziger (Jerusalem: The Hebrew University Magnes University Press, 2007), 255–94.

revelation. Plaskow is indebted to Buber's view of the law (Tirosh-Samuelson, 163).[20] For Buber, law belongs to the realm of instrumental I–It relations; hence the relationship between human beings and God, the I–Thou relation, cannot be based on law. Like Buber, who doubted the importance of law, Plaskow too questions whether women can express their feminine spiritual identity and relationship with God through halakhah. By contrast, Ross takes her inspiration not from Buber but from Rabbi Abraham Isaac Hakohen Kook and his peculiar blend of Kabbalah, Hasidism, and philosophy. Theologically, Rabbi Kook's thought was extremely radical, but his halakhic project was traditional and conservative. Again we see that Plaskow the liberal theologian has no difficulty arguing for radical changes in halakhah, to the point of rewriting historical memory; whereas Ross wants to circumvent the problem by means of an idea that, although quite radical theologically and providing a metaphysical justification for halakhic changes derived from feminist insights, in practice requires taking account of all previous revelations, as the halakhic tradition has done for centuries.

FEMINIST JEWISH MIDRASH AS THE WELLSPRING OF A NEW THEOLOGY

Plaskow's programmatic call for a new religious language and for basing Jewish theology on feminine foundations provided an impetus to the new phenomenon of the last four decades in which women compose feminist midrashim as part of a new Jewish feminist theology.

This adoption of midrash for theological objectives is motivated by the idea that although the sacred texts are fixed and canonized, their interpretation is not.[21] In reaction to the absence of half the population from the

---

[20] Hava Tirosh-Samuelson, "Feminism and Gender," in *The Cambridge History of Jewish Philosophy, vol. 2: The Modern Age*, eds. Martin Kavka, Zachary Braiterman, and David Novak (New York: Cambridge University Press, 2012), 154–89.

[21] For a comprehensive survey of Jewish feminist midrash and of the literature on the topics, see: Jody Myers, "The Midrashic Enterprise of Contemporary Jewish Women," in *Jews and Gender—The Challenge to Hierarchy, Studies in Contemporary Jewry, Volume 16*, ed. Jonathan Frankel, 119–41 (New York: Oxford University Press, 2000); Ellen Umansky and Dianne Ashton, eds. *Four Centuries of Jewish Women's Spirituality—A Sourcebook*. (Waltham, MA: Brandeis University Press, 2009); Naomi Graetz, *Unlocking the Garden: A Feminist Jewish Look at the Bible, Midrash, and God* (Piscataway, NJ: Gorgias, 2005); Ronit Irshai, "'And I Find a Wife More Bitter Than Death' (Ecclesiastes 7:26): Feminist Hermeneutics,

official record of the Jewish people, these feminists set out to fill this lacuna by creating midrashim in which they retold biblical stories from the perspectives of their female characters. To quote Judith Plaskow:

> The open-ended process of writing midrash—simultaneously serious and playful, imaginative, metaphoric—has easily lent itself to feminist use. Feminist midrash shares the uncomfortable self-consciousness of modern religious experimentation: elaborating on the stories of Eve and Dina, we know that the text is partly an occasion for our own projections, that our imaginative reconstructions are a reflection of our own beliefs and experiences. But if its self-consciousness is modern, the root conviction of feminist midrash is utterly traditional. It stands on the rabbinic insistence that the Bible can be made to speak to the present day. If it is our text, it can and must answer our questions and share our values; if we wrestle with it, it will yield up meaning.[22]

So, the various streams of Jewish feminism turned to midrash as a tool for expression, in order to add the woman's voice that is generally absent from the biblical and other traditional texts, but also to erect a bridge between their religious or intellectual commitment and the androcentric and patriarchal text.[23] Orthodox women, as Jody Myers has shown, were also involved in this enterprise.[24] But as she notes, Orthodox writing was marked by apologetics, an essentialist approach to womanhood and motherhood, and acceptance of theological constraints (ibid. 124–28). However, Modern Orthodox feminist midrash has changed since then. It has become less apologetic and essentialist and less inhibited by theological barriers, and now dares to advance trenchant criticism of the portrayal of women in the Bible and Talmud.[25]

In recent years, the writing of feminist midrashim has become popular in Israel, too, as attested by the publication of the two volumes of *Dirshuni* (Interpret Me).[26]

Women's Midrashim, and the Boundaries of Acceptance in Modern Orthodox Judaism," *Feminist Studies in Religion* 33.1 (2017b): 69–86.

[22] Plaskow, *Standing Again at Sinai*, 53–54.

[23] Charlotte Fonrobert, "The Handmaid, the Trickster and the Birth of the Messiah: A Critical Appraisal of the Feminist Valorization of the Midrash Aggada," in *Current Trends in the Study of Midrash*, ed. Carol Bakhos (Leiden: Brill), 245–75.

[24] Myers, "The Midrashic Enterprise of Contemporary Jewish Women."

[25] Irshai, "'And I Find a Wife More Bitter Than Death'."

[26] Nehama Weingarten-Mintz and Tamar Biala, eds. *Dirshuni: Israeli Women Writing Midrash* (Tel Aviv: Yedioth Ahronoth [Hebrew], 2009); Biala, Tamar, ed. *Dirshuni: Israeli Women Writing Midrash*, vol. 2. Tel Aviv: Yedioth Ahronoth [Hebrew]. 2018.

These volumes collect hundreds of midrashim written by women affiliated with various religious denominations (Orthodox, Conservative, Reform) or with none. However, because most of them come from the Modern Orthodox community in Israel, I believe it is justified to view this as a new phenomenon in this stream. What is special about those volumes, beyond being the first collections of feminist midrashim written and published in Hebrew, is that they are among the first fruits of the women's Torah study revolution taking place in the Modern Orthodox sector in both Israel and North America. It is not only that this revolution has led to less apologetic writing, with fewer inhibitions. It is also that as women become more familiar with and expert in the rabbinic literature, they feel free to employ the style and tools of traditional midrash to create a feminist alternative, informed by intense criticism of the image of women in the Bible and Talmud. The impression is that, despite their declared commitment to halakhah, they are not limited by theological inhibitions. On the contrary, for Rivka Lubitch, one of the leading creators of these midrashim, acceptance of the text's sanctity and timelessness produces the certainty that we can and must produce insights that allow us to extract the story of women from the normative male narrative and from between its lines. Viewing discrimination against women as directly related to their irrelevance in religious life, she considers feminist midrash to offer a solution in two senses: First, it produces heroines with whom readers can identify; second, it shows us that the speaker's voice may be a woman's. Her writing illustrates how ideas first advanced by liberal Jewish feminism in the 1970s have now trickled into Orthodox feminism as well.[27]

FEMINIST THEOLOGY AND HALAKHAH

Blu Greenberg's *On Women and Judaism* was a pioneering presentation of the barriers halakhah erects to gender-egalitarian ideas that are not hierarchical. She expressed her strong conviction that Jewish ideals and values and the halakhic lifestyle itself can effect the desired change, and coined the phrase, "Where there was a Rabbinic will, there was a halakhic way" which many rabbis saw and still see as a threat to Orthodox Judaism.[28]

---

[27] The resemblance to Umansky's criteria for feminist midrash is telling. See Umansky, "Creating a Jewish Feminist Theology," 193–96.
[28] Greenberg, *On Women and Judaism*, 44.

By contrast, Rachel Adler called for a major remake of halakhah from a broader theological perspective. Asserting that halakhah is the core of the Jewish world and that no Jewish form can survive without it, she opted for a jurisprudential approach that could respond to the call to create what she calls "proactive halakhah".[29] In this she drew on the legal philosopher Robert Cover and his influential "Nomos and Narrative."[30]

Cover suggested that law and culture are intertwined. He built a model of law that could preserve a coherent legal system while also allowing for interpretive pluralism. In Cover's terms, "nomos" is the world of normative law as expressed in the principles of justice, legal institutions, systems of formal rules, and social conventions. By contrast, "narrative" is an amalgam of language, discourse, myth, and values; in other words, the human story is expressed in history and literature, as well as in the actual lived experience of a concrete group of people, the community. The two concepts are interdependent. Nomos exists and derives its meaning only from within the context of a narrative that sets it in the time, space, society, and culture in which the drama of the actual human experience occurs; this is what lends the nomos its meaning. Conversely, narrative requires the moral perspective of nomos; in other words, the element that is embodied and shaped by norms and the law. On the surface, it would seem that narratives can bear multiple and possibly even contradictory meanings, both obvious and hidden, both conservative and subversive, whereas nomos allows for only one binding configuration and interpretation, which is "frozen" in the existing law. But when nomos is viewed as embedded within a narrative, it becomes clear that the potential for legal change is already there as well. Taking nomos in the context of narrative opens law up to a variety of interpretations that may, over time, produce a situation in which the law itself changes, pulling the present reality closer to an alternative future. In this sense, and taking a long-term view, one might imagine law as a bridge that links one vision (of the past) to another (future, desirable, possible). In every such instance, certain threads that are interwoven into (present, existing) law are plucked out of the complex and variegated fabric of the narrative. Law is therefore the

---

[29] Adler, *Engendering Judaism*.
[30] Robert Cover, "Nomos and Narrative," *Harvard Law Review* 97.4 (November 1983): 4–68.

expression of a current worldview as depicted by a narrative that joins reality and vision and connects past, present, and future.

Taking her theoretical framework from Cover, Adler began developing the idea of "proactive halakhah" that initiates rather than reacts, as part of her general vision of "engendering Judaism." She criticized liberal halakhah as merely reacting to classical halakhah, in an attempt to adapt itself to modernity, while leaving the basic system untouched. Instead, she held that Cover's idea of the essence of the law could be used to explain the aim of religious feminism. The model in which law is a bridge supported by a commitment to a particular praxis that is based on our narrative is not possible without the concept of halakhah, because it is only through halakhah that Jews can embody their sanctified values and stories in a communal praxis. At the same time, however, it is possible to create a new nomos and advance toward it. Accordingly, narrative will be central to any project for a new Jewish nomos, because Judaism is based on narrative. Hence the creation of proactive rather than reactive halakhah requires a new understanding of Jewish narratives and values. It is on this point that feminism, thanks to the new methodologies it developed, can make a decisive contribution to understanding and employing narratives in order to devise a new halakhah. It was in this spirit that, in the last chapter of her book, she introduced the "Lovers' Covenant *(B'rit Ahuvim),*" a marriage ceremony based on the laws of partnership rather than on those of acquisition, as a marriage contract between two independent and equal subjects.

In Adler's position we can see the integration of the halakhic vision with theology. Theology is the narrative dimension, which ultimately provides the constitutive foundation of Jewish praxis. Despite her Orthodox commitment, Ross's view of halakhah does not seem too far from Adler's.

However, Ross herself devotes significant effort to explicating where her thinking diverges from Adler's. Whereas Adler identifies completely with Cover's model when it comes to the influence of narrative on the establishment of nomos, Ross adds an additional step and makes retention of a metaphysical dimension an essential component of her philosophy of halakhah. She also believes that in order for halakhic changes to be accepted and absorbed by the religious world, two additional constraints that Adler ignores must be taken into account: solidarity with the larger community of the halakhically committed and an "appeal to the ruling body of experts"—in other words, not sidestepping rabbinic authority.

HALAKHAH AND "AKEDAH THEOLOGY"

As we have seen, theology and halakhah are not necessarily dichotomous categories of Jewish feminist thought. I too have endeavored to understand the mechanisms of halakhah and their possible incorporation of feminist ideas[31] and posed questions about the connection between halakhah and theology. The first stage of this project is a comprehensive consideration of the meaning of gender-based biases in halakhah. Tracing the various streams of feminism, I offered three main categories: biases based on different ways of thinking; biases based on different life experience; and biases based on men's control over women. Even though they all exist in the halakhic tradition to various degrees, they have not yet been the subject of a full discussion in connection with various halakhic issues.[32]

In the second stage of my project, building on new insights borrowed from the philosophy of halakhah, I developed the idea of creating "alternative halakhic stories" as a new halakhic narrative that stands in contrast to the classical and hegemonic halakhah.[33]

The development of an "alternative halakhic story" has two elements:

1. Creating a halakhic genealogy (in each different area of halakhah) with the goal of uncovering the hidden values or moral paradigms on which halakhic rulings related to women are based and the exegetical tactics and rhetoric that have been used to generate the prevailing hegemonic story. This can pave the way to creating a different halakhic genealogy, based on the same sources but with different predispositions.
2. Proposing a preference for halakhic principles that can overcome halakhic rules that fail to produce gender justice for women.

After I applied this methodology to two domains of halakhah—those pertaining to abortion and to contraception[34]—and I homed in on the gender notions at the basis of halakhic jurisprudence, my conclusion, unsurprisingly, was that the interpretive options of halakhah (even Orthodox halakhah) are open to ideas that are more respectful of women and more egalitarian; what prevents their general application is not the mechanisms of halakhah but broader theological obstacles

---

[31] Irshai, *Fertility and Jewish Law*.   [32] Ibid.
[33] Irshai, "Toward a Gender Critical Approach."
[34] Irshai, *Fertility and Jewish Law*.

that cannot be separated from the world of halakhah. I then inquired what species of theology is blocking the way to a more egalitarian halakhah that is more respectful of women. My answer was that one of the major obstacles is what I call "Akedah Theology," clearly formulated by Rabbi Joseph D. Soloveitchik and Prof. Yeshayahu Leibowitz.[35]

Akedah Theology associates obedience to the divine imperative embodied in halakhah with the binding up (Hebrew *akedah*, referring to the Binding of Isaac) of all our specifically human inclinations, desires, and needs, *including our moral principles*. Although not all divine injunctions are necessarily at odds with morality, the ultimate test of believers' faith and commitment to God, when they do face such a dilemma, is manifested by their willingness to bind up their moral ideas and submit to the divine injunction.[36] Not surprisingly, some rabbis believe that this theology must be adopted with regard to certain halakhic issues pertaining primarily to women. This even becomes the litmus test for women's observance and religious commitment, allowing people to discredit religious feminism on the grounds that it has a theological flaw that reflects a weakness of faith.

There is clearly an unavoidable collision between Akedah Theology and any idea that demands religious recognition of human moral insights. In the present generation, religious feminism is the most salient example of moral criticism of patriarchal religious ideas,[37] with its stubborn demand, in the name of modern values such as human dignity and equality, for changes in theology and halakhah.

The effort to understand which theological approaches block the spread of feminist ideas in the Orthodox world is part of the feminists' growing realization that the theological dimension should not be ignored. I believe it is possible to attribute this change partly to disappointment with the rabbinic establishment, which, as Greenberg famously wrote, can be creative and lenient and practice exegetical gymnastics if it wishes to but which, when it comes to gender issues, has generally taken an unyielding stand against every

---

[35] Joseph Soloveitchik, *The Secret of the Individual and the Collective: A Selection of Hebrew Writings*. Jerusalem: Orot [Hebrew]. 1975.; Yeshayahu Leibowitz, *Faith, History, and Values* (Jerusalem: The Hebrew University Magnes Press 1981/82) and Judaism, Human Values and the Jewish State (Cambridge, MA: Harvard University Press, 1992).

[36] Irshai, "Religion and Morality."

[37] Adler makes it plain that the task of Jewish feminism is a moral one stemming from the demand for gender justice. See Adler, *Engendering Judaism*.

attempt to demonstrate that flexible interpretation is possible here, too.

CONCLUSION

The theological journey of Jewish feminism began with a call for a comprehensive gender-sensitive overhaul of the three primary categories of Jewish theology: God, the Torah, and the Jewish people. Plaskow called for reshaping Jewish historical memory, the community, the language employed about God, and rituals. Halakhah was left out of the picture. Ross believed that the most urgent theological problem is reconciling the candid recognition that the divine text itself has suffered from the limits of human condition and is biased from a gender perspective with the belief in the eternity of the Torah and in the God-given "Torah from Heaven." In her view, the problem of halakhah can be resolved only after the emergence of a theology that can deal adequately with this problem.

Robert Cover's "Nomos and Narrative" opens the way to a deeper understanding of how law functions and the extent to which it is anchored in communal narratives that provide its meaning. As we have seen, Rachel Adler was the first to draw on Cover in order to devise a theology that could help Judaism move toward gender justice. Cover's idea that narrative is the soil from which law springs and which gives law its meaning led to an increasing realization that even were it possible to delineate halakhic mechanisms that could create a more just and egalitarian halakhah, as long as the story that religious society tells itself about men and women, and about femininity and masculinity and the relations between them, is a patriarchal account, and as long as the interpretation of the canonic texts does not take women's perspectives into account, the desired change in halakhah cannot take place. Moreover, even if halakhic changes in the spirit of gender equality and justice are introduced, they will be on a weak footing as long as the formal justification underlying them depends on problematic theological approaches. The identification of these problematic theological approaches and the description of the problematic gender biases on which the halakhic world rests, along with the development of an alternative "halakhic story," are my own modest contribution to the discussion.

In other words, we have returned to the starting point, but, I believe, with deeper and more complex insights. The theological debates within Jewish feminism focused on identifying the core theological problem, on clarifying the relationship between halakhah and theology, and on inquiring about the importance of halakhah for Jewish feminist life and the possibility of modifying it by means of the traditional formal tools. Quite interestingly, and although the Orthodox tendency was and remains to emphasize halakhah and minimize theology, fifty years into the process it can be said that all currents of Jewish feminism accept the primacy of theology over halakhah. Even those who believe that halakhah has a place in Jewish feminism understand that halakhic change that stands alone and is not anchored in a complete theological doctrine is impossible. Changing the narrative is, indeed, the key to gender justice in the Jewish world.

Selected Further Reading

Adler, Rachel. *Engendering Judaism: An Inclusive Theology and Ethics*. Philadelphia: Jewish Publication Society, 1998.

Adler, Rachel. "I've Had Nothing Yet, So I Can't Take More." *Moment* 8 (1983): 22–26.

Adler, Rachel. "The Jew Who Wasn't There: Halakhah and the Jewish Woman." *Davka* (Summer 1971.): 6–11. Reprinted in Susanna Heschel, *On Being a Jewish Feminist*, 12–18.

Benjamin, Mara. "Tracing the Contours of a Half Century of Jewish Feminist Theology." *Journal of Feminist Studies in Religion* 36.1 (2020): 11–31.

Biala, Tamar, ed. *Dirshuni: Israeli Women Writing Midrash*, vol. 2. Tel Aviv: Yedioth Ahronoth [Hebrew], 2018.

Cover, M. Robert. "The Supreme Court, 1982 Term—Foreword: Nomos and Narrative," *Harvard Law Review* 97.4(1983): 4–68.

Fonrobert, Charlotte Elisheva."The Handmaid, the Trickster and the Birth of the Messiah: A Critical Appraisal of the Feminist Valorization of Midrash Aggada." In *Current Trends in the Study of Midrash*, 245–75. Edited by Carol Bakhos. Leiden: Brill, 2006.

Graetz, Naomi. *Unlocking the Garden: A Feminist Jewish Look at the Bible, Midrash, and God*. Piscataway, NJ: Gorgias, 2005.

Greenberg, Blu. *On Women and Judaism: A View From Tradition*. Philadelphia: Jewish Publication Society, 1981.

Hartman, Tova. *Feminism Encounters Traditional Judaism*. Waltham, MA: Brandeis University Press, 2007.

Heschel, Susanna, ed. *On Being a Jewish Feminist: A Reader*. New York: Schocken, 1983.

Irshai, Ronit. "'And I Find a Wife More Bitter Than Death' (Ecclesiastes 7:26): Feminist Hermeneutics, Women's Midrashim, and the Boundaries of Acceptance in Modern Orthodox Judaism." *Feminist Studies in Religion* 33.1(2017b): 69–86.

Irshai, Ronit. *Fertility and Jewish Law: Feminist Perspectives on Orthodox Responsa Literature*. Waltham, MA: Brandeis University Press, 2012.

Irshai, Ronit. "Religion and Morality: Akedah Theology and Cumulative Revelation as Contradictory Theologies in Jewish Modern-Orthodox Feminism." *Journal of Modern Jewish Studies* 16.2(2017a): 219–35.

Irshai, Ronit. "Tamar Ross: An Intellectual Portrait", *Library of Contemporary Jewish Philosophers: Tamar Ross – Constructing Faith*, 1–40. Edited by Hava Tirosh-Samuelson and Aaron W. Hughes. Leiden and Boston, MA: Brill Academic Publishers, 2016.

Irshai, Ronit. "Toward A Gender Critical Approach to the Philosophy of Jewish Law (Halakhah)." *Journal of Feminist Studies in Religion* 26.2 (2010): 55–77.

Leibowitz, Yeshayahu. *Faith, History, and Values*. Jerusalem: The Hebrew University Magnes Press, 1981/1982.

Leibowitz, Yeshayahu. *Judaism, Human Values, and the Jewish State*. Cambridge, MA: Harvard University Press, 1992.

Myers, Jody. "The Midrashic Enterprise of Contemporary Jewish Women." In *Jews and Gender—The Challenge to Hierarchy, Studies in Contemporary Jewry, Volume 16*, 119–41. Edited by Jonathan Frankel. Oxford: Oxford University Press, 2000.

Ozick, Cynthia. "Notes Toward Finding the Right Question." In *On Being a Jewish Feminist*, 120–51. Edited by Susanna Heschel. New York: Schocken, 1983.

Plaskow, Judith. "Jewish Theology in Feminist Perspective." In *Feminist Perspectives on Jewish Studies*, 62–81. Edited by Lynn Davidman and Shelly Tenenbaum. New Haven, CT: Yale University Press, 1994.

Plaskow, Judith. "The Right Question is Theological." In *On Being a Jewish Feminist*, 223–34. Edited by Susanna Heschel. New York: Schocken. 1983.

Plaskow, Judith. *Standing Again at Sinai: Judaism from a Feminist Perspective*. San Francisco: Harper & Row, 1990.

Ross, Tamar. *Expanding the Palace of Torah: Orthodoxy and Feminism*. Waltham, MA: Brandeis University Press, 2004.

Ross, Tamar. "Modern Orthodoxy and the Challenge of Feminism." In *Jewish Orthodoxy: New Perspectives*, 255–94. Edited by Joseph Salmon, Aviezer Ravitzky, and Adam Ferziger. Jerusalem: The Hebrew University Magnes Press, 2007 [Hebrew].

Ross, Tamar and Yehuda Gellman. "The Implications of Feminism for Orthodox Jewish Theology." In *Multi-Culturalism in a Democratic Jewish State: Prof. Ariel Rosen-Zvi Memorial Volume*, 443–74. Edited by Menachem Mautner, Avi Sagi, and Ronen Shamir. Tel Aviv: Tel Aviv University Press [Hebrew], 1998.

Soloveitchik, Joseph Dov. *Halakhic Man*. Philadelphia: Jewish Publication Society, 1983.

Soloveitchik, Joseph Dov. *The Secret of the Individual and the Collective: A Selection of Hebrew Writings*. Jerusalem: Orot [Hebrew], 1975.

Tirosh-Samuelson, Hava. "Feminism and Gender." In *The Cambridge History of Jewish Philosophy, Vol. 2: The Modern Age*, 154–89. Edited by Martin

Kavka, Zachary Braiterman, and David Novak. New York: Cambridge University Press, 2012.

Umansky, Ellen, M."Creating a Jewish Feminist Theology: Problems and Possibilities." In *Weaving the Visions: New Patterns in Feminist Spirituality*, 187–98. Edited by Judith Plaskow and Carol Christ. San Francisco: Harper & Row, 1989.

Umansky Ellen M. and Dianne Ashton, eds. *Four Centuries of Jewish Women's Spirituality—A Sourcebook* (revised edition). Waltham, MA: Brandeis University Press, 2009.

Weingarten-Mintz, Nehama and Tamar Biala, eds. *Dirshuni: Israeli Women Writing Midrash*. Tel Aviv: Yedioth Ahronoth [Hebrew, 2009]

14 Jewish Models of Revelation
ALAN BRILL

The concept of revelation is a principal focus of Jewish theology. In this chapter, I present a range of contemporary Jewish theological approaches to revelation with the aim of highlighting an array of opinions for beginning a discussion of a Jewish theology of revelation. I want to move the discussion from the historical problem of biblical authorship to a theological rubric. The question of what we can say about history is not the same as the question of what a person gives assent to as theology.[1]

METHOD

The theological formulations of Judaism are diverse and historically situated. Judaism is not limited to biblical Scripture but runs through the whole gamut of rabbinic literature, along with the medieval and modern formulations, as well as contemporary understandings. I present a wide scope of opinions as a textual basis for what to work with; however, it is without concern for the philosophic question of epistemology, of whether there can be a possibility of a revelation. To formulate a Jewish theology of revelation, one must have some prior acceptance of the canon. Channeling Paul Ricœur, revelation precedes faith because before anyone believes, there must be prior knowledge of symbols, texts, and ideas.[2] In turn, these symbols only yield their

---

[1] In my approach toward revelation, I follow the method in my book on *Judaism and Other Religions: Models of Understanding* (New York: Palgrave Macmillan, 2010) where I used theological models in order to move beyond denominational and historical approaches to a typological approach of inclusive, exclusive, universal, pluralistic, and halakhic. I moved the discussion from the historic rubric of "disputation to dialogue" to one of theological rubrics. The book was an outgrowth of a 2004 chapter similar to this one. My degree in Catholic theology, combined with Orthodox training and erudition, colors what I see.

[2] Paul Ricoeur, "Toward a Hermeneutic of the Idea of Revelation," *The Harvard Theological Review*, vol. 70, No. 1/2 (Jan.–Apr., 1977), 1–37.

meaning to someone who has some implicit faith, in the Jewish case, as implicit acceptance of Torah in whatever definition. God is known through the Torah or as it states in the *Zohar*, "The Holy One blessed be He and the Torah are One" (I:24a). My approach is a faith seeking understanding, a hermeneutics of trust (or at least agonic struggle), not suspicion or doubt, and ending with a constructive purpose. In a Catholic theological context, this approach is part of systematic theology, not apologetic theology.

I use models in theology because a "models approach" helps one place the thinkers into conceptual rubrics and allows a theologian to discuss where one aligns oneself. This approach provides an effective way to introduce the theological diversity within Judaism about revelation and demonstrates to the reader that they themselves can develop their own theology by standing on the shoulders of the great theologians of the past and present. Prior reflections provide real resources for thinking.

There are many essays on Jewish philosophic thinking about revelation that survey the modern philosophic classics in historic order—Cohen, Buber, Rosenzweig, and Heschel, usually only for historical or historicist interest. On the other hand, the most popular presentations of Jewish theology usually divide thinkers by the non-theological category of twentieth-century denominations: Reform, Conservative, and Orthodox.

The theological question of revelation is not the same question as the origin of Scripture. The problem of authorship of the biblical text is usually conflated with the philosophic problem of a divine revelation; the question of biblical authorship is an empirical question, the nature of revelation a theological one. Usually, Jewish articles place all thinkers who are not the bookends of the naturalistic and supernatural verbal plenary in one undifferentiated group, thereby placing Heschel, Jacobs, Rosenzweig, Levinas, Leibowitz, and Levenson into one muddled middle group.

Instead, this chapter will follow the general rubrics and models of the Catholic theologian Avery Dulles in his *Models of Revelation* as modified by postliberal Evangelical mainline theologian Gabriel Fackre in his *Doctrine of Revelation: A Narrative Approach*. I will also use the discussions of the last twenty-five years on these thinkers.[3]

---

[3] Avery Dulles, *Models of Revelation*, (Maryknoll, NY: Orbis Books, 2001). Gabriel Fackre, *The Doctrine of Revelation: A Narrative Interpretation*, (Grand

Dulles offers five models of revelation: (1) Revelation as doctrine—as proposition statements; (2) Revelation as history—God reveals in great deeds or events, Scripture bears witness to God's actions. Dulles finds this a minority Christian position, but it is actually the largest Jewish category; (3) Revelation as inner experience—God is known through religious experience and mystical experience; (4) Revelation as dialectic presence—God cannot be known in nature or history or experience, but is known in transcendence or transcendent moral order; and (5) Revelation as inner awareness—revelation as a creative, expanded consciousness, and insight. Dulles argues that all five models have the same referent and are not looking at different objects.

In this chapter, I will add two more models useful for a Jewish theology: a sixth model of those who believe humanistic positions that do not have a revelation of content and a seventh model that demonstrates a postliberal emphasis on the acceptance of the textual tradition.

Gabriel Fackre makes two important amendments to Dulles' models theory. First, that a single thinker will use different models for different purposes. Second, he asserts that the models can be metaphorically arranged as opaque sheets layered on a model. As an evangelical, he stresses the need to not marginalize the narrative and verbal aspects of revelation and instead uses the other models to explain it. Fackre notes that a theologian may choose to combine several of the models to make a workable theology in the same way a contemporary philosophic argument may be built of several combined classic elements. Fackre begins his exposition of revelation by pointing out that the model of revelation is not isolated; rather there is interdependence of authority, doctrine, and hermeneutics. I will also add that all of these models are themselves capacious and subject to interpretation in different hermeneutic contexts, both historical and theological. Theological positions remain open to their hermeneutical horizons, events of dialogue, and socio-political applications.

Rapids, MI: W. B. Eerdmans Publishing Company, 1997). There were many articles and critiques of Dulles in Lindbeck, Tracy, Frei, Moran, Fackre, and others in which they each responded to the claims and commented on Dulles. On the interfaith aspects, see Keith Ward, *Religion and Revelation: A Theology of Revelation in the World's Religions* (Oxford: Clarendon Press, 1994). Recent works include Mats Wahlberg, *Revelation as Testimony: A Philosophical-Theological Study* (Grand Rapids, MI: Eerdmans, 2014); Matthew Levering, *Engaging the Doctrine of Revelation: The Mediation of the Gospel through Church and Scripture* (Ada, MI: Baker Academic, 2014).

JEWISH REVELATION AS OPPOSED TO CHRISTIAN REVELATION

In order to make use of the aforementioned Christian theologians, I must note that for Christian theology, (my primary referent is Catholic thought) revelation is not the same as Jewish revelation. This was already clearly articulated by Moses Mendelssohn in his classic work *Jerusalem*.[4] In most Catholic thought, revelation means God's self-disclosure of Himself after the Fall of Adam allowing the possibility of grace and salvation. Those who have not heard of revelation cannot, and will not, be saved. The covenant of salvific grace starts with its expression in God's covenant with Abraham (see Genesis 12:1–3, 17:1–14). For Christians, God did not do away with the covenant of grace when he gave the law at Sinai. God did not intend that thenceforth man was to be saved by keeping the law: "By the works of the law shall no flesh be justified" (Galatians 2:16). For many Christian thinkers, even the availability of knowing a theistic God requires a special revelation.[5]

In contrast, Jewish concepts of revelation focus on Torah, as a way of life, as an object to study, and most importantly as a covenant. Exodus describes the giving of the Torah at Sinai, midrash portrays the patriarchs as already studying Torah, and many Jewish texts consider the innovations during the course of studying Torah. For Jewish thinkers, revelation is not the making of God available to the world, but rather a teaching and rule of life. In Judaism, knowledge of God for all people does not need a special revelation nor is salvation a major Jewish theological point. For some Jewish models of revelation, revelation at Sinai is a continuous process, personal experience, and individual engagement. The rabbinic literature portrays the giving of the Torah to Israel as God wedding the Jewish people or, alternately, as Torah itself wedding the Jewish people.[6]

---

[4] *Moses Mendelssohn, Jerusalem, Or, On Religious Power and Judaism*, Alexander Altmann, intro., Allan Arkush, trans. (Hanover and London: Brandeis University Press, 1983), 90–94, 97–98, 123–24. Comparisons with Islamic thinkers on the concepts of *wahy*, *ilham*, and *tanzil* which define Muslim concepts of revelation also deserve to be considered. However, I am working based on Christian language and books.

[5] *Classical Christianity and Rabbinic Judaism: Comparing Theologies* by Jacob Neusner & Bruce D. Chilton (Ada, MI: Baker Academic, 2004).

[6] Solomon Schechter, *Aspects of Rabbinic Theology* (New York: Schocken Books, 1961).

For both faiths, revelation is logos; however, for Christian theology this generally means incarnation and the direct availability of God through Christ. Christian theology focuses on Jesus, the Christ, as the direct revelation through faith and relationship: "No longer will a man teach his neighbor, or a man his brother, saying, 'Know the Lord,' because they will all know me, from the least of them to the greatest" (Hebrews 8:11; also John 6:45). Christ does not save by words but by his body. Some Protestant thinkers place the majority of their interest in faith and soteriology and therefore place even less weight on revelation.[7]

In Jewish thought, Torah as words is always a text to be studied. Various thinkers portray this wisdom as ranging from divine wisdom and will, light of the divine, rational universal "ethical monotheism," to a halakhic guide, to a gnostic knowledge of divine secrets. The outcome of Jewish revelation is Torah in words, ideas, and texts. An image of the Jewish view is contained in *Tractate Avot*, which describes an educating scholarly tradition of sages handing down an oral tradition, raising up students, adjudicating law in the name of revelation, and earning merit by the study of Torah.[8]

REVELATION AS A THEOLOGICAL PROBLEM

Revelation as a modern theological problem grew out of the problems generated by the eighteenth-century Enlightenment view in which autonomous reason was contrasted with supernatural revelation amidst an era of anti-clericalism. In the nineteenth century, revelation was less of an issue because most European religious thinkers believed in "spirit" that guides humanity. In the twentieth century, the problem returned as a major issue before the onslaught of secularism, modernism, and science.[9]

Medieval thought did not have the modern category of revelation because they accepted prophecy and tradition as valid sources of

---

[7] Bruce D. Chilton and Jacob Neusner, *Classical Christianity and Rabbinic Judaism* (Grand Rapids, MI: Baker Academic, 2004).

[8] Pre-modern approaches to Jewish revelation also focused on the words and graphic images of the words of revelation as having power beyond the meaning of the text. This placed the Jewish approach closer to Vedic approaches than Christian ones. On this, see Barbara A. Holdrege, *Veda and Torah: Transcending the Textuality of Scripture* (Albany: SUNY Press, 1996).

[9] Dulles, *Models of Revelation*, 3–18.

knowledge. For them, human knowledge and divine knowledge are comingled. They have various forms of intuitionism, meta-consciousness, prophecy, and contemplation. Their philosophic context of a Platonic-Aristotelian framework supported such discussions. Their theological issue was the tension between prophetic-religious knowledge vs reason, not the very possibility of a revelation.[10] Prophecy, according to medieval thinkers such as Saadiah, Halevi, and Maimonides among others, while certainly contributing to the contemporary discussion, has its own concerns beyond the scope of this chapter on contemporary thought. Similarly, the interpretation and renewal of Sinai, along with the tension between concealment and revealment of the Torah in medieval and early modern Kabbalah, has its own trajectory.[11]

Jewish revelation shifted in its relation to the ongoing rabbinic tradition as part of revelation. In the late nineteenth and early twentieth centuries, many Reform thinkers excluded rabbinics, the Oral Law, and Kabbalah from revelation focusing solely on Scripture revelation.[12] In contrast, the recent late twentieth- and early twenty-first-century conceptualizations of Judaism consider the Jewish religion as an unfolding textual tradition; hence, contemporary theologians place greater emphasis on rabbinics and Kabbalah. Many Jewish thinkers now include and encourage a culture of talmudic debate and multiple opinions as part of their very definition of Judaism. In addition, there has been an influence from academic Jewish studies' use of literary theory emphasizing intertextuality, plurality of meanings, hermeneutics, and knowing a text through tradition. It is important to note that because one views the unfolding of revelation over the centuries as exegesis, plurality and hermeneutics does not mean that the initial revelation is hermeneutical.[13]

---

[10] See Ibn Kammuna, *Examination of the Three Faiths*, trans. Moshe Perlmann (Berkeley and Los Angeles: University of California Press, 1971) who lays out the dynamic of medieval prophecy in its most direct forms.

[11] Howard Kriesel, *Prophecy: The History of an Idea in Medieval Jewish Philosophy* (Dordrecht: Kluwer Academic Publishers, 2001); Gershom Scholem, *On the Kabbalah and Its Symbolism* (New York: Schocken Books, 1960), especially ch. 2, "The Meaning of the Torah in Jewish Mysticism"; Moshe Idel, *Absorbing Perfections: Kabbalah and Interpretation* (New Haven, CT: Yale University Press, 2002).

[12] Christian Wiese, *Challenging Colonial Discourse: Jewish Studies and Protestant Theology in Wilhelmine Germany* (Leiden: Brill, 2005).

[13] For some of this change from seeking an essence of Torah to enjoyment of rabbinic plurality, see Geoffrey H. Hartman and Sandford Budick, eds., *Midrash, and Literature* (New Haven, CT: Yale University Press, 1986); Daniel Boyarin, *Intertextuality and the Reading of Midrash* (Bloomington: Indiana University Press, 1990).

Returning to my discussion of the five models, many of the thinkers I will refer to below had long careers with several books. I picked out from their works formulations that illustrated the categories or models I am using. I have chosen these texts and thinkers because each of them predominantly focuses on a single model of revelation. I did not attempt to contextualize the ideas of each thinker within the broader narrative arc of their writings. Those thinkers whose thought is woven tightly of several models were not included, but this is not to imply they are less important; rather they may be more important but not useful for illustration.[14] These thinkers would offer insight into the priorities of Jewish theology when balancing multiple goals. Finally, each of these texts is capacious and open to a wide range of hermeneutic interpretation.

MODEL 1: HISTORIC EVENT

I will not be following the same order as Dulles, and I am placing the historic model first because the historical approach plays a larger role in Judaism.[15] In this approach, revelation consists of a transformative event within sacred history. In this event, God communicates His will. The emphasis is on God's transcendence and His freedom, the mighty deeds of God, and the intense separation of the infinite transcendent and finite humanity. There was a moment of meeting God that is greater than the record of revelation recorded in the text of Torah itself.

The "Historic Event Model" is most common in Jewish thought and includes a diverse group of thinkers from different points on the spectrum. The clearest version of this approach in the twenty-first century is the concept of a covenant theology, which posits that God, in an event, gives a covenant to the children of Israel as part of His plan for that people.

---

[14] Most notably, I am thinking of Benjamin D. Sommer, *Revelation and Authority: Sinai in Jewish Scripture and Tradition* (The Anchor Yale Bible Reference Library, New Haven, CT: Yale University Press, 2015), who was more complex in four ways: he combined the historic question with the theological question, a goal I am trying to avoid; he uses several of the models; he places much of revelation in the unfolding of the Oral Law; and he acts a secondary commentary on several of the thinkers discussed here.

[15] My order is slightly different from that of Dulles because his evaluation of the role of each model in Christian thought is not exactly the same as in Jewish thought. So too, I have slightly modified the names of the models to better reflect the Jewish formulations.

Jon Levenson presents a biblical covenant theology. The Sinai revelation is the event where God's covenantal love for Israel is revealed, an event that discloses not only the meaning of Judaism, but also where Israel becomes God's vassal. It is not an ordinary historical event. Levenson writes: "We know nothing about Sinai, but an immense amount about the traditions concerning Sinai."[16] Rather, "History is the arena in which Israel has met and comes to know the deity who has become her suzerain."[17] At this event in history Israel accepted the covenant: "Covenant-love is mutual; it distinguishes a relationship of reciprocity ... Israel for her part, is to realize her love in the form of observance of her master's stipulations, the mitzvoth, for they are the words of the language of love." Love is expressed "in loyalty, in service, and in unqualified obedience to the demands of the Law. The lesser king (or vassal) "loves" his lord by showing him exclusive loyalty and observing the norms of the treaty."[18]

The second version of this model, the Existential revelation (which was quite common in the twentieth century) is an encounter of the infinite divine and the finite human that in turn creates a written account. In the nineteenth century, Hegel critiqued Spinoza's theory of immanence for precluding the possibility of revelation from a transcendent God outside of nature. Instead, Hegel argued for the immanence of the transcendent within religion and the state. In the twentieth century, this approach is formulated among certain Jewish thinkers as an Existential event rupturing human finite existences, the idea of the infinite confronting the finite being in place of covenant. The encounter generates a Torah to study and mizvot to follow.

I have chosen to look at both Eleizer Berkovits and Emil Fackenheim in order to emphasize that we can find both an Orthodox and Reform rabbi sharing a conceptual model with similar language, even if they differ on the text of the Torah and the Oral Law created at that encounter. One thinker draws Reform conclusions and the other Orthodox conclusions from the same event. I have selected them to underscore the idea that the theologies do not need to be based on denominations.

---

[16] Jon D. Levenson, *Sinai and Zion* (San Francisco: Harper Collins, 1985), 17.
[17] Levenson, *Sinai and Zion*, 38.
[18] Jon D. Levenson, *The Love of God: Divine Gift, Human Gratitude, and Mutual Faithfulness in Judaism* (Princeton: Princeton University Press, 2015), 77.

Rabbi Eliezer Berkovits presents a paradoxical event with the divine in which finite humanity gains dignity through the encounter with the infinite divine at Sinai. Humanity is then sent forth into history with the mitsvot as a guide. The important part of the encounter is the paradox of meeting the infinite. Moses' encounter transforms history:

> God's presence seems to be threatening; it imperils the life of the person to whom it wishes to communicate itself ... Standing at the mountain of Sinai, the children of Israel trembled with fear at the voice of God, which yet was conferring on them their greatest distinction ... Thus we are faced with a strange paradox ... there can be no religion without some active relationship between man and God; in the relationship, however, man cannot survive.
>
> The paradox is resolved by God, when He "shows" Himself to man. God, who reveals His "unbearable" Presence to the helpless creature, also sustains man in the act of revelation ... Through the peril that confronts him, he is bound to recognize his nothingness before God; yet, in the divine affirmation, the highest conceivable dignity is bestowed upon him: he is allowed into fellowship with God ... I find it impossible to visualize how an infinite, incorporeal Being speaks to a man "face to face ... God spoke to Moses" is an impenetrable mystery. The divine revelation of the Bible is the mysterious contact between God and man by which God communicated His truth and His law to Israel through Moses in a manner that excluded every possibility of doubt in the mind and conscience of the recipient of the revelation. Only a Moses could have described the actual event and only for Moses himself.[19]

Berkovits, himself, does not claim these experiences for himself or the contemporary age (unlike the experiential model below); rather, we live in an age of the hiddenness of God, still guided by this original encounter. For Berkovits: "The meaning of the revealed word or commandment is given in the oral tradition, the *Torah she-be'al peh* alone ... because of the oral tradition, the Torah is for man." This corollary of understanding the Sinai revelation via the Oral Law defines his Orthodoxy. Berkovits thinks that we do not accept revelation based on the strength of its contents since "Revelation is not a rational, but a supra-rational category." (This is in contrast to the human awareness model that stresses the identity of revelation with its content.)

---

[19] Eliezer Berkovits, *God, Man and History* (New York: Jonathan David, 1965), 32–33.

Emil L. Fackenheim offers a similar approach from a Reform perspective. Fackenheim, as professional philosopher, reflects more technical Kantian limits on human knowledge and presents a more precise use of Buber's ideas of encounter. Fackenheim is similar to Berkovits in that he holds: "The Torah reflects *actual events* of divine revelation, or incursions into human history, not a mistaken human belief in such incursions." As noted, his difference as a Reform thinker is that he considers the Torah as "a *human* reflection of these events of incursion; the reception is shot through with appropriation and interpretation. Even a human listening to a human voice is inevitably an interpreting; this is *a fortiori* inevitable when the human 'listening' is in faith and the 'voice' heard is of divine." Fackenheim, therefore, does not consider "all 613 commandments are equally binding" and the "oral Torah inescapably reflect[s] the ages of their composition." Unlike the human awareness model below, Fackenheim rejects "any liberal dissipation of the event of divine incursion into 'creative' human 'insight,' mistaken for revelation by those who achieved it."[20]

MODEL 2: HIGHER DIVINE WISDOM: DIALECTIC

The next position, which Dulles calls the dialectic model, assumes that revelation rises above the natural realm into the transcendence of the divine; there is a gap between the human and the divine. In all versions of this approach, the emphasis is on divine decree, divine will, and divine wisdom, which creates norms that humans cannot know through reason alone.[21] Sinai is a basic postulate of the Jewish faith when the divine will is accepted.

One version of this, the Neo-Scholastic, acknowledges that there are limits to reason and, as a result, we require a revelation because there are truths about our world that cannot be known by natural reason or there is knowledge about God that is not available to natural reason. Another version of this, the dialectic theology version, focuses on the need for a divine norm to elevate human existence from the natural to the level of a confronted being with a higher norm that transcends the self.

Rabbi Aharon Lichtenstein (1933–2015), Rosh Yeshiva of Yeshivat Har Etzion, in some of his early writings, presents an argument highly

---

[20] Emil Fackenheim, *Commentary: Condition of Jewish Belief* (New York: Macmillan, 1966), 251–52.
[21] Dulles, *Models of Revelation*, 41–45, 84–97.

reminiscent of the Catholic Neo-Scholastic Étienne Gilson. In his discussion of revelation, Lichtenstein distinguishes between aspects of revelation that we need divine revelation to know and those that could have been known without revelation:

> First, revelation reveals about God and his will, part of the knowledge only able to be known through revelation and some of the knowledge available through natural means: "(a) The revelatum, to use a Thomistic term, whose truths inherently lie beyond the range of human reason and which therefore had to be revealed if they were to be known at all (b) The revelabile ... whose truths could have been discovered by man in any event."[22]

Second, Lichtenstein asserts that the textual aspect of revelation is composed by God and not just a message from God: "in as much as it is not merely a document delivered (salve reverentia) by God but composed by HIM, it constitutes in its normative essence an expression of His will. As such, it affords us an indirect insight into what is otherwise wholly inscrutable." Accordingly, as a divine document it "presents direct statements about divine attributes" and "Torah study connects one to God's presence and it is a religious experience."

Third, and finally:

> Lichtenstein describes the text of the Torah as a "dialectal encounter with the living God ... it is repeated recurrently through genuine response to God's message, which ushers us into his presence." The focus is on the event of study of the Torah text as divine will and wisdom; we know about God through the text and not through historical events.[23]

Rabbi Joseph Dov Solovetichik (1904–1993) has strong elements of the dialectic theology of Karl Barth and Emil Brunner. He echoes the need for a higher norm that transcends the self to give us moral norms. His essay *Confrontation* offers a clear presentation of this view; however, his other essays have varying formulations of this dialectic theology. Natural man discovers his limits and loses his primal immediacy with nature, which in turn leads to his discovery of the singularity of

---

[22] Fackenheim, *Commentary: Symposium on Jewish Belief*, 132–34. This distinction between truths known only via revelation and those that could have been known by reason goes back to the medieval rational tradition.

[23] Fackenheim, *Commentary: Symposium on Jewish Belief*, 132–34.

human existence. Revelation is the divine moral challenge directing man to his destiny as a free creative being able to engage in moral commitment, which in his case is halakhah, the divine norm:

> [N]atural man, moving straight forwards, comes suddenly to a stop, turns around, and casts, as an outsider, a contemplative gaze upon his environment ... and finds himself encountering something wholly other than his own self, an outside that defies and challenges him. At this very moment, the separation of man from cosmic immediacy, from the uniformity and simplicity which he had shared with nature, takes place. He discovers an awesome and mysterious domain of things and events which is independent of and disobedient to him, an objective order limiting the exercise of his power and offering opposition to him.
>
> In the wake of this discovery, he discovers himself. Once self-discovery is accomplished, and a new I-awareness of an existence which is limited and opposed by a non-I outside emerges, something new is born – namely, the divine norm. "And the Lord God commanded the man." With the birth of the norm, man becomes aware of his singularly human existence which expresses itself in the dichotomous experience of being unfree, restricted, imperfect and unredeemed, and, at the same time, being potentially powerful, great, and exalted, uniquely endowed, capable of rising far above his environment in response to the divine moral challenge. Man attains his unique identity when, after having been enlightened by God that he is not only a committed but also a free person, endowed with power to implement his commitment, he grasps the incommensurability of what he is and what he is destined to be.[24]

In this model of revelation, one should also situate the view of Yeshayahu Leibowitz who rejected any historical or empirical element to revelation and instead focused entirely on faith as "an evaluative decision that one makes, and, like all evaluations, it does not result from any information one has acquired, but is a commitment to which one binds himself." Jewish faith, therefore, rather than consisting of propositional beliefs concerning God upon which foundation halakhic

---

[24] Joseph B. Soloveitchik, "Confrontation" from *Tradition: A Journal of Orthodox Thought* 6. 2 (1964): 5–29.

328   Alan Brill

observance is based, is instead founded upon the evaluative decision to commit to that very system of observance.[25]

Leibowitz holds that faith demands him to recognize revelation as ontologically real. He grounds the ultimate authority of the Torah as God's word exclusively on the decision of the rabbinic Sages to accept it as such, rather than on any objective historical occurrence. Any historical event has little bearing on the Jewish commitment to follow God's will. Leibowitz thinks that any talk of divinity should not be understood cognitively but in terms of the normative demands it imposes."[26]

Whereas Lichtenstein thinks that the act of faith allows us to treat the text of the Torah as giving wisdom beyond the natural realm and as allowing us to attain a knowledge of God, Leibowitz, by contrast, posits that the meaning of revelation is normative demand alone.

MODEL 3: PROPOSITIONAL

This position assumes that the verbal propositional record of revelation is the revelation; it is what Dulles calls the doctrinal. Verbal means that every word of the five books of Moses is God-given as a doctrinal statement. The idea is that every single word in the Bible is there because God wanted it there and that Moses served as a stenographer. Propositional means that revelation is not a general manifestation of a divine message; rather, even if a statement is symbolic or parabolic, the believer is to translate the statement into a proposition. It is the one usually associated, many times as a stereotype, with Orthodoxy.

In addition, some versions of this approach also claim inerrancy of the text of revelation: either, a mild form that allows for mistakes in transmission and other inaccuracies of an inconsequential nature, or a near complete inerrancy of original autographs and divine protection of manuscripts.[27]

One of the most articulate and informed presentations of this approach is by R. Yaakov Weinberg (1923–1999), Rosh Yeshiva of Ner Yisrael Rabbinic College. He clearly presented the verbal propositional approach in which "every letter of the Written and Oral Torah

---

[25] *Judaism, Human Values, and the Jewish State*, ed. Eliezer Goldman (Cambridge, MA: Harvard University Press, 1995), 25, 37.
[26] Yeshayahu Leibowitz, *Emunah, Historiah, ve-Arakhim* [Faith, History, and Values], (Jerusalem: Academon, 1982), 154.
[27] Dulles, *Models of Revelation*, 36–52.

transmitted through Moshe Rabbeinu was of Divine origin." For Weinberg, "Moshe Rabbeinu merely served as a conduit for communicating it, or as a 'scribe.'" The record of revelation is to be considered "absolute and not open to change" because "any ambiguity in the laws of the Torah would render it non-absolute and therefore non-binding." The message of the revelation focuses on producing a binding set of rules. For him, "if the Torah is subject to choice, it has no meaning."[28] For him, Moses did not have free will nor did he inflect any of his personality into the text. He was a vessel for receiving and transmitting the clear word of God. This revelation included the Oral Law and all debate in understanding the Oral Law was solely the result of mistakes that occur in transmission.

Weinberg, based on explicit rabbinic sources, rejects textual inerrancy as well as the concept that the current text is the same as the one given at Sinai because Tractate Sofrim 6:4 unambiguously states that Ezra compared various Torah scrolls to create a uniform text. He notes that "as long as the Temple stood and the Torah scroll which Moshe Rabbeinu wrote was kept there, the Jewish People had a standard to which to compare all new Torah scrolls that were written" but "after the destruction of the Temple, when Ezra returned to Israel, he found three Torah scrolls which were all considered valid." He notes that "these were very minor variances—changes which did not seem to affect the meaning significantly." Maimonides' statement that "the entire Torah in our possession today" is the same as that given to Moses "must not be taken literally, implying that all the letters of the present Torah are the exact letters given to Moshe Rabbeinu. Rather, it should be understood in the general sense that the Torah we learn and live by is for all intents and purposes the same Torah that was given to Moshe Rabbeinu."

More in line with Christian Fundamentalist approaches is the Jewish outreach program Discovery Seminar, which teaches a strong version of textual inerrancy. Conveniently skipping over the traditional rabbinic statements of textual variants in the time of Ezra or the medieval discussions of variant texts, they assert that: "Following the destruction of the Second Temple in 70 CE, the Sages would periodically perform global checks to weed out any scribal errors." The Seminar claims that only "nine letter-differences are found in their scrolls. These

---

[28] Yaakov Weinberg, *Fundamentals and Faith: Insights into the Rambam's 13 Principles*, ed. Mordechai Blumenfeld (Brooklyn: Targum Press, 1991).

are all spelling differences. In no case do they change the meaning of the word."[29]

MODEL 4: EXPERIENTIAL MYSTICAL

This model treats revelation as a religious experience in the William James sense of a mystical or experiential sense of God. For James, religious doctrines are verbalizations of the experience, which can be feeling, the intuitive sense of the radical contingency of all things, or a higher state of consciousness. This experience of the mystical realm, described by Everlyn Underhill, Rudolf Otto, or William Alston, is the ability of humans to have a mystical experience of God.

I reiterate this to differentiate this experiential position from the experiences of the historical event or the higher consciousness. This approach generally starts with sources from Kabbalah and Hasidic thought, then explains them in modern terms.[30]

Abraham Joshua Heschel's *Torah From Heaven* best exemplifies this experiential approach. Heschel encourages us to directly feel God in the Torah: "You cannot grasp the matter of the 'Torah from Heaven' unless you feel the heaven in the Torah. All temporal questions are in the context of eternity ... But whoever denies the wondrous has no share in this world; how much more so can such a person have no dealing with heavenly matters."[31] He assumes that the prophets, the visionaries, the mystics, and even the rabbi of the Oral Law all had experiences of God. The prophets hear words from the Almighty and learn what is on the mind of the Holy and Blessed One at that moment.[32]

---

[29] "Accuracy of Torah Text May 14, 2002 | by Aish HaTorah's Discovery Seminar" online www.aish.com/h/sh/tat/48969731.html (accessed August 14, 2018). The nine differences are those shown comparing the twentieth-century texts of Yemenite and standard Torah scrolls. They ignored the rabbinic material cited by Rabbi Weinberg showing the hundreds of differences, including Sofrim 6:4, the work of the Masoretes (seventh–tenth centuries), and the work of Rabbi Meir Halevi Abulafia (thirteenth century). On the topic, see B. Barry Levy, *Fixing God's Torah: The Accuracy of the Hebrew Bible Text in Jewish Law* (Oxford: Oxford University Press, 2001).

[30] Dulles, *Models of Revelation*, 68–83.

[31] Abraham Joshua Heschel, *Heavenly Torah: As Refracted Through the Generations* (London: Continuum, 2006), 668.

[32] Ibid., 293.

Heschel famously distinguished between Torah from Heaven and Torah from Sinai, giving precedent to the former.[33] "We call our Torah 'Torah from heaven,' because the original Torah is even now in heaven."[34] He attempts to explain this supernal idea to a skeptical reader who thinks that the idea "of a Torah literally existing in heaven may seem at first like a strange growth, the chaff and straw of our religious imagination" and far from our terrestrial world; however, "the supernal realm contains the secret and origin of everything terrestrial." I must reiterate that as a thinker who oscillates between the persona of Rabbi Akiva and Rabbi Yishmael, Heschel also has aspects of the dialectic and new awareness models. At many points, Heschel uses the medieval prophetic idea of conjunction and prophecy, which are similar in many respects to the modern ideas of mysticism or union with the divine.[35]

Aryeh Kaplan would also fall into this model, even though some of his writings have verbal and historic event elements. Rejecting those who treat revelation as a mere human psychological awareness, Kaplan who creatively reinterprets medieval material, thinks that prophets are the "instrument through which God exerts His power ... They [have] ... experiences that are as real as physical sensation, leaving absolutely no doubt as to their authenticity." For Kaplan, the source of these prophetic experiences is a "deep meditative state." In contrast, Moses' experience was a nullification of the self, making himself "completely nonexistent before God" where "his physical nature no longer acted as a barrier between him and God. Moses' revelation was therefore, of a direct nature ... The revelation of Moses was not prophecy, but a totally different, higher spiritual experience."[36]

The writings of Rabbi Abraham Isaac HaKohen Kook also have many passages that fit this experiential model: "For the Jews who stood at Mount Sinai, it was not only Torah and mitzvot that were

---

[33] Ibid., 321.   [34] Ibid., 264.
[35] Ibid., 265. It is important to note that Neil Gillman presented Heschel as closer to model number 5's new awareness, focusing on the Bible as midrash and as human interpretation. He avoids Heschel's strong Rabbi Akiva, kabbalistic, and Hasidic elements as well as the dialectic elements. While Gillman acknowledges that for Heschel "the theological sin is literal-mindedness"—*Sacred Fragments* (Philadelphia: Jewish Publication Society, 1990), 24—Gillman does not develop or use the pervasive experiential element in Heschel's theory of revelation.
[36] Aryeh Kaplan, *The Handbook of Jewish Thought*, vol. 2 (Brooklyn: Moznaim Publishing, 1983) and *Inner Space: Introduction to Kabbalah, Meditation and Prophecy* (Brooklyn: Moznaim Publishing Corporation, 2nd ed., 1991), vii, 5, 132.

revealed. They also discovered their own true, inner essence. They attained a sublime level of natural purity." The experience allowed them to "follow their natural essence, unhindered by any spurious, artificial conventions." For Kook, the giving of the Torah and the revelatory experience was the point when the supernal light was brought down to this world. While Kook sees this as an event that took place, he views the lights as ever flowing from the divine. This source of life and the light of the Torah is seen through and manifested through time.[37]

MODEL 5: HUMAN INNER AWARENESS

The fifth model is the New Awareness model in which revelation is about human insight and creativity, as a breakthrough in content which is in turn labeled as a revelation. This approach usually treats religion as symbols of human creation and does not necessarily require a personal God. In many ways, the anthropocentrism of this model is the opposite of the theocentrism of the dialectic position. Even when a theologian grants that God may cause the insight, nevertheless, the emphasis remains on the human insight. Dulles finds that this model does not take Scripture seriously nor does it have a serious encounter with the divine. Human insight, creativity, and naturalistic causes play the major role in revelation. This approach is generally associated with liberal Jewish theologies. Paradoxically, this approach and the experiential models open up the potential for revelation in other faiths.

Gabriel Fackre, as a Protestant theologian, is more appreciative of this category, but places it under the realm of natural theology and the human inclination to seek God. Fackre also distinguishes between the universalism of Paul Tillich in which the awareness is a natural awareness and the doctrinal position of Karl Rahner where the awareness is a given from God in the form of the supernatural existential. Through Tillich's perspective, one can clearly distinguish between his systematic theology and his universal human concern. This chapter will follow Fackre by separating the new awareness model from the next contentless model, yet the lines may still be porous at points.

Rabbi Jacob B. Agus, one of the leading theologians of the mid twentieth-century Conservative movement, treated revelation as

---

[37] *Mo'adei HaRe'iyah*, p. 486, as translated in *Silver From the Land of Israel* from the writings of Rabbi Abraham Isaac HaKohen Kook, ed. Rabbi Chanan Morrison (Jerusalem: Urim, 2010).

a creative self-revelation: "The word of God in the heart of man is not an auditory hallucination, but a power, a deposit of energy, a momentary upsurge toward a higher level of being. So, all of Scripture speaks of the divine word as the power of creation in the universe." He credits a diverse number of thinkers as having influenced his thought, including Mendelssohn's natural theology, Tagore's religious virtuosity, Emerson's transcendentalism, and especially Mordecai Kaplan's transcendental naturalism.

For Agus, revelation is tied to its evolutionary content in which we recognize "freedom as the vertical dimension of evolution from the amoeba to the human, and from the primitive to the prophet or the philosopher." For Agus, "the divine word is articulated in a new vision of freedom, the import of the first commandment ... freedom is the 'divine image' in man." Agus thinks we still find this freedom in our contemporary lives "in the quest of the intellect, or in the judgment of conscience, or in the aesthetic drive of productivity ... asserting an identity between his own spirit and the universal laws of being."[38]

Agus connects this contemporary exhortation to creative freedom and Sinai. He asserts that the "account of the divine revelation at Sinai" does not represent "a historical event, but a paradigmatic image of the perennial course of revelation." Whatever "actually happened in the wilderness of Sinai is of great historical interest. But historical events should be studied by the appropriate methods of inquiry." However, "the scientific reconstruction of the steps whereby the primitive religion of the Semitic nomads became the Jewish religion is not directly relevant to my understanding of the character of divine revelation."[39]

In a similar vein, Bernard Bamberger presents a completely universal approach that focuses on the human ability for religious genius. Bamberger affirms belief in God and that Israel experienced "His revelation." Yet, he treats the revelation as a universal phenomenon: "I cannot believe that He has revealed Himself only in Israel; and I do not see how any revelation can come to man except through man." There are "great insights attained by the philosophers, scientists, poets, and prophets of many peoples; it applies also to Hebrew Scripture and tradition." He acknowledges both divine inspiration and human fallibility in the doctrine, not because of historical criticism, but

---

[38] Jacob Agus, *The Condition of Jewish Belief*, 1st ed. (New York: Macmillan, 1966), 9–11.
[39] Ibid.

rather because for Bamberger "the Torah contains some elements which are intellectually untenable and some that are morally indefensible."[40] For him, revelation is not self-evident; instead, it requires scrutiny of its content.

Another approach focuses on national spirit. Harold M. Schulweis, reminiscent of nineteenth-century views in which the divine spirit inheres in nations, views revelation as grounded in the collective peoplehood of Israel. He rejects both an eternal revelation as well as revelation as human insight: "The origin of Torah lies not in an extramundane source which has cast down absolute truths upon a receiving people, nor is it the arbitrary projection of human inventiveness flung upward." For him, the third option is to treat "Torah as revelation" where it is "the product of Israel's creative transaction with history." Schulweis strongly affirms that revelation requires "commitment to follow *what* revelation demands" as well as the need to offer "grounds for distinguishing true from false revelation." For him, the ascription of "revelatory disclosures" are "wrought out of the wrestlings of our people with idolatry, superstition, and enslavement and out of their acknowledgement of such values as compassion, justice, peace, and freedom."[41]

A famous holder of this position is Rabbi Louis Jacobs who considers revelation as a human awareness. Jacobs is usually presented as an Orthodox rabbi who accepted biblical criticism. Alternatively, he is also presented together with Conservative thinkers who accept a divine Torah but also accept biblical criticism. He is an exemplar of the purpose of this essay, which is to move the discussion away from the historic question of the text and toward questions of theological formulation.

Unlike Heschel, or even Fackenheim, Jacobs considers it "increasingly difficult to believe that the Torah is the result of a direct divine communication." The Bible "can no longer be seen as revelation itself. But it is the record of revelation."[42] He is willing to consider the source of Torah in primitive custom but to be followed anyway: "Our modern Jewish believer may become convinced that these had their origin in primitive taboos yet it is not their origin that matters but what they have become. These laws have served the cause of self-discipline by

---

[40] Ibid., 17–22.   [41] Fackenheim, *Commentary: Symposium on Jewish Belief*, 216–20.
[42] Louis Jacobs, *'Beyond Reasonable Doubt'. A Sequel to We Have Reason to Believe*, (Oxford: Littman Library of Jewish Civilization, 1999), 44.

making the Jew conscious of his religion even when indulging his natural physical appetites." We can accept the values of Torah, even when it does not have roots in revelation.

Commenting on those Jewish thinkers who see Torah as from heaven, Jacobs saw that, in the modern age, it is really a metaphor for a divine naturalism:

> Religious modernists believe in "Heaven"—in this context, the rabbinic synonym for God—and they believe in the Torah (the Jewish religion) as much as their ancestors did. But in light of modern knowledge, it is the "from" in the doctrine—"the Torah is from Heaven"—that has to be understood in terms of divine-human co-operation. In much the same way, the benediction, *hamotzi lechem min ha'aretz*—"who bringeth forth bread from the earth"—does not mean that God brings bread, ready made from the ground.[43]

Jacobs notes in some of his mature works the influence of the theology of Jakob J. Petuchowski on his own work on revelation, which he states is about treating the Torah as heavenly and less about the mechanism.[44]

MODEL 6: REVELATION WITHOUT CONTENT

This category of revelation may or may not be a category of revelation, depending on who is counting. These forms of revelation use the word loosely for our quest for the transcendent or meaning in life without necessarily requiring a specific revelation of content like the other six models. For example, Paul Tillich's ultimate concern is the concept of the "'courage to be' in the face of non-being," which underscores revelation as "the *mystery* of the ground and the abyss of being."[45] This form of revelation is usually—although not always—theocentric, but it is not necessarily theological revelation. One might term this form as theo-religious[46] but not theology. They are philosophical and psychological

---

[43] Louis Jacobs, "Human Element in Divine Revelation," *The Jewish Chronicle* (24 May, 1996).
[44] Jakob J. Petuchowski, *Ever Since Sinai: A Modern View of the Torah* (New York: Scribe Publications, 1961).
[45] Paul Tillich, *The Courage To Be* (New Haven, CN: Yale University Press, 1952).
[46] See Cass Fisher Chapter 17 in this Companion where he uses the related notion of "theo-realism."

senses of the divine, highly influential modern religious thought and the spiritual life; nevertheless, without the content of theological revelation, Dulles excluded these theistic thinkers entirely. In contrast, Fackre includes them as forms of man's natural search for God, which in twentieth-century Protestant theology is referred to as natural revelation (not to be confused with natural theology of the eighteenth century.)[47]

Martin Buber's view of revelation as presence without any content is an ideal example of this theo-religious approach that does not have theological content. There is a moment of meeting, an in-between, in which revelation is of sheer presence, "an ineffable, pure form that carries not an iota of determinate or object-like conceptual or linguistic content."[48] For Buber, "every religion is a human truth" where a "particular human community" relates to the Absolute.[49] Yet, his thought was highly influential on many of our other models and thinkers including Berkovits, Fackenheim, Fishbane, and Levinas. Many Jews not sensitive to or concerned with our models may consider Buber another example of the fifth model. For Buber, the "purpose of revelation is the relation itself-touching the You."[50] A pure moment of being without content: "That which reveals is that which reveals. That which has being is there, nothing more."[51] Buber starts from the human experience of faith, which makes him think of revelation in these terms: "that which reveals is that which reveals. That which is is, and nothing more. The eternal source of strength streams, the eternal contact persists, the eternal voice sounds forth." From a reception of revelation, one receives a presence as power. Revelation is an incomprehensible event.[52]

In addition, there is also the revelation of negative theology in which revelation plays the role of placeholder, as a trace that does not vanish but continues to haunt, or a nothingness in the center of reality. In contemporary Christian theology, the minimal theology thinker Gianni

---

[47] Gabriel Fackre, *The Doctrine of Revelation: A Narrative Interpretation* (Edinburgh: University of Edinburgh Press and Grand Rapids, MI: W. B. Eerdmans, 1997).

[48] Michael Zank and Zachary Braiterman, "Martin Buber", *The Stanford Encyclopedia of Philosophy*, ed. Edward N. Zalta (Winter 2014): <https://plato.stanford.edu/archives/win2014/entries/buber/>.

[49] Martin Buber, *A Believing Humanism: Credo Perspectives* (New York: Simon and Schuster, 1969), 113–15.

[50] Martin Buber, *I-Thou* (New York: Charles Scribner's Sons, 1958), 112.   [51] Ibid., 160.

[52] Ibid., 112.

Vattimo holds this position and there are many readings of Derrida in contemporary theology that emphasize his negative theology.[53]

A perfect Jewish version of this approach is Gershom Scholem's nothingness of revelation without meaning and without significance but which does not disappear: "You ask what I understand by the 'nothingness of revelation'? I understand by it a state in which revelation appears to be without meaning, in which it still asserts itself, in which it has validity but no significance." For Scholem, meaning is lost, but "still does not disappear, even though it is reduced to the zero point of its own content, so to speak."[54]

MODEL 7: HERMENEUTICAL REVELATION

The seventh model, which was not yet fully articulated when Dulles formulated his categories, treats revelation not as experience, history, or even a human awareness, but rather as an intensification of understanding giving significance; there are disclosures of divine meaning in the study of Torah. The major shift in this twenty-first-century model is that there is little interest in justifying beliefs. Rather, as the Christian thinker Ronald Thiemann formulated it, it is about commitment and coherence. For Jews, it would be about commitment to Torah, textually, and its interpretation. According to Dulles, this theory of revelation "has the great value of pointing out that religious knowledge is never a matter of mere information. The believer is not a mere spectator but a participant in the reality that is believed." Revelation is "comprehensible only from within."[55]

The French Jewish thinker Emmanuel Levinas delivered many lectures and wrote many essays for the Jewish community on the Bible, revelation, and exegesis. The presentation below is based on his Jewish-

---

[53] Michael Fagenblat, ed. *Negative Theology as Jewish Modernity* (Bloomington: Indiana University Press, 2017).

[54] Gershom Scholem, letter to Walter Benjamin, September 20, 1934, quoted in Eric L. Santner, *On the Psychotheology of Everyday Life: Reflections on Freud and Rosenzweig*. (Chicago: University of Chicago Press, 2001), 38.

[55] Dulles considered some aspects of postliberal approaches as part of the verbal-dogmatic approach and found it not rich enough in possibility. George Lindbeck, "Dulles on Method," *Pro Ecclesia* 1 (1993): 53–60; with "Rejoinder to George Lindbeck," 61–62; Avery Cardinal Dulles, "Postmodernist Ecumenism. Book review of *The Church in a Postliberal Age*, George Lindbeck," *First Things* 136 (October/2003): 57–61; "George Lindbeck replies to Avery Cardinal Dulles," *First Things* 139 (January/2004): 13–15.

theological not his philosophic writings, and it does not attempt to harmonize the differences between the two. For Levinas, exegesis is greater than genesis of a text in that the act of reading the text awakens us to the living God: "Surely we should think of Revelation, not in terms of received wisdom, but as this awakening."[56]

For him, the vast texts of Torah along with the subsequent commitment to Torah study serves as "a system of signs to be interpreted."[57] Levinas believes that Revelation is a call to exegesis, which is the reader's ability to re-connect to the Saying, to re-enter the domain of inspiration that permeates the text.[58] This understanding of exegesis is based upon an essential belief that the Torah contains more than it contains—a surplus of meaning, perhaps inexhaustible. Giving priority to the Oral Law over the written Torah, in this act of study, we seek God. Rather than a fixed new insight, revelation is ongoing and personal.

Levinas claims that "absolute truth" can only be expressed through the full spectrum of multiple voices of multiple people. Seeking itself is essential for the actualization of the full voice of the text responsive to the fullness and uniqueness of each person: "These and those are the words of the living God."[59] The dialectic of meaning is ever continuous; we can never give absolute closure to one voice for no one meaning can bind the infinite within itself. Levinas, in multiple places, gives more importance to a text's exegesis than to its genesis.[60]

Echoing elements of Franz Rosenzweig, Levinas writes about revelation as an ongoing love relationship that makes demands in the here and now:

> God's first word to the soul that is united with him is "love me"; so, everything that he could still reveal to it otherwise under the form of law, is transformed without further ado into words which he commands it "today" ... All Revelation is placed under the great sign of the today; it is "today" that God commands and it is "today" that his voice is to be heard. It is the "today" in which the love of the lover lives – this imperative today of the commandment.

---

[56] Emmanuel Levinas, "Revelation in the Jewish Tradition," *The Levinas Reader*, ed. Sean Hand (Oxford: Basil Blackwell, 1989), 209.
[57] Ibid., 204. [58] Ibid., 194–95.
[59] Emanuel Levinas, "The Jewish Understanding of Scripture," *Cross Currents* 44.4 (Winter 94/95), available at: www.crosscurrents.org/levinas.htm
[60] Ibid.

In some of his ethical essays, he treats revelation as the demand of the ethical. "The invisible of the Bible is the Good beyond being. To be obliged to responsibility has no beginning ... that is, responsibility for others. It is the trace of a past that refuses itself to the present, the trace of an immemorial past."[61] The biblical responsibility is a trace to remind us of our obligation, which in his Jewish writings means the study of Torah.

Brian Klug, philosopher at Oxford University, ventures into theology to offer a Wittgenstein-influenced theory of revelation based on commitment to a system without asking for evidence:

> Then what makes a belief religious? "It appears to me," wrote Wittgenstein in 1947, "as though a religious belief could only be something like passionately committing oneself to a system of coordinates. Hence, although it's belief, it is really a way of living, or a way of judging life." ... In light of Wittgenstein, we can say that the doctrine of Torah from heaven makes the following demand on us: embrace the idea with a passion – 'believe, through thick & thin' – or leave it be, but don't ask for the evidence. It is not a hypothesis or theory.

In contrast, Klug finds Louis Jacobs' idea of "divine-human cooperation" as entirely lacking the needed theological power for a theology of revelation. Jacobs' belief may be a "reasonable belief" but it is not a "belief that possesses the grandeur, the vigour and the power required for 'a basic article of Jewish faith'".[62] Klug finds Jacobs' parallel with *hamotzi*, the blessing over bread, which God "brings forth from the earth," inadequate and prefers "a parallel with manna, the mysterious substance that sustained the Israelites in their wanderings through the wilderness, the food that fell from the skies." The emphasis is on the fact that even though it was from God, people had to gather it. So too Torah has "no end to gathering its meaning." For Klug, this is "the weight of the doctrine of *Torah min HaShamayim* (Words from

---

[61] Levinas, *Humanism of the Other*, trans. Nidra Poller (Champaign, IL: University of Illinois Press, 2003), 54.

[62] Brian Klug, "Grammar from Heaven: The Language of Revelation in Light of Wittgenstein," St Benet's Hall Oxford, June 2013, a version of which appeared without the discussion of Jacobs as Brian Klug, "Speaking of God: Ludwig Wittgenstein and the Paradox of Religious Experience," in *Religious Experience Revisited: Expressing the Inexpressible?* eds. Thomas Hardtke, Ulrich Schmiedel, and Tobias Tan (Leiden and Boston, MA: Brill, 2016).

heaven never settle on the page)." Therefore, "no thoughtful believer – no one who embraces the 'traditional picture' in all its majesty – could possibly be a fundamentalist."

Another similar recent view, this time by the Rosh Yeshiva of Siah Yitzhak, Rabbi Shagar-Shimon Gavriel Rosenberg (d. 2007). Shagar starts with the Kook concept mentioned above that in "encountering the truth of existence grants a believer his own existence," but quickly moves to a more postliberal approach by stating that: "Even if the source of revelation is in man's soul and innerness, it is still experienced as transcending him and his concepts."[63]

Following a cohesion theory of truth in which one accepts the Torah narrative without any foundations, he considers the "revelation of the Torah, like the creation of the world, is not evaluated based on an external fact. The Torah is speech that creates, rather than depicting or representing." The revelation of Torah is the means by which we construct our lives; we live "in spoken words, in the open book, in understanding." Hence, "words construct their meaning, which is not evaluated based on exacting adherence to existence but rather based on internal coherence, on being substantive and not artificial." Torah is the linguistic world we accept upon ourselves and live within, an entire created world, which Shagar compares to the worlds of the movie, *The Matrix*.

Connecting these ideas to Chabad Hasidic thought, Shagar considers the supernal knowledge (*Da'at Elyon*) as creating its own inner reality while lesser knowledge (Da'at Tahton) deals with matching reality and facts. Revelation is the constructive higher knowledge that constructs our reality. Questions of history or logic are the lower perspective; an inner reality is the higher perspective: "The revelation of the Torah" for Shagar, "is not tied to any special insight or deep understanding"; rather, it is available to "every Jew that is involved in Torah for its own sake, conscious of the divine command."[64]

I conclude with the approach of Michael Fishbane, who posits that "exegesis is a vehicle of divine revelation." According to Fishbane, we

---

[63] Rabbi Shimon Gavriel Rosenberg, "Face to Face: From Rav Shagar's teachings for Shavuot 2007," edited by Eitan Abramowitz in advance of the conference organized for the sake of Rav Shagar's recovery. Accessed online August 15, 2018, in Hebrew at: https://siach.org.il/%D7%A4%D7%A0%D7%99%D7%9D-%D7%91%D7%A4%D7%A0%D7%99%D7%9D/ and in English at https://kavvanah.wordpress.com/2017/05/24/shavuot-rav-shagar-face-to-face

[64] Ibid.

are always already in a hermeneutical situation, inasmuch as we are constantly interpreting the plenitude of presence. Fishbane develops the concept of the "Torah kelulah," the fullness of the moment, which is in itself the "Torah of God," inseparable from the divine source itself. Revelation in the broadest sense is a profoundly attuned act of interpretation, wherein one faces mindfully the fullness of the moment, receives the commands and meanings that issue therefrom, and responds actively and relationally with her whole being. For Fishbane, we lead a textualized life in which the text and its interpretation shape our life.[65]

Moses' revelation on Sinai represents, for Fishbane, an archetypal moment of this process. The Rabbis refracted this written Torah into the oral Torah, and we continue to expand this oral Torah today through our own hermeneutical understanding, which are revelatory engagements with texts and life. Fishbane's concept of revelation owes much to his deep historical and theological readings of midrash, Kabbalah, and Hasidut, where he examines how those texts treat revelation as a weave of interpretation, and yet echoes of Martin Heidegger, Martin Buber, Paul Ricœur, and Emmanuel Levinas are ever present. Fishbane works with a direct and personal experience of attunement to God and a greater literary sense of the mythical imagination; hence, unlike the other postliberal approaches, this position, with elements of the experiential and human awareness models, presents a greater attentiveness to the role of human involvement with the hermeneutical project.

TOWARD EVALUATION

As a concluding point, we must begin to ask about the usefulness of each model, what is good and bad in each of them. For a theology of revelation, one can interrogate each model and ask of it philosophic, theological, and pastoral questions. Does a given model correlate with the Bible? With rabbinic literature? With prior Jewish thinkers? With logic or philosophic analysis? With our lived experience? Is a given model useful or meaningful in our decade or with our given presuppositions?

---

[65] Sam Berrin Shonkoff, "Michael Fishbane: An Intellectual Portrait" in Michael Fishbane, *Jewish Hermeneutical Theology* (Leiden and Boston, MA: Brill, 2015), 23; Michael Fishbane, *Sacred Attunement: A Jewish Theology* (Chicago and London: The University of Chicago Press, 2008).

Dulles uses seven criteria to evaluate each model: (1) Faithfulness to Bible and subsequent tradition; (2) Internal coherence; (3) Plausibility in light of other fields; (4) Does it correlate with experience?; (5) Practical fruitfulness in pastoral and social contexts; (6) Theoretical fruitfulness for embracing philosophy and theology; and (7) Value for dialogue.

A position can fail plausibility or fruitfulness in pastoral settings but can still be a valid philosophic position and vice versa. For examples, I may evaluate them for their contemporary theological usefulness for creativity in reading prior texts, for reaching millennials in a congregation, or for their usefulness in an interfaith encounter. But one theory generally does not fulfill more than a few criteria. A fuller exploration, and the next step in the discussion, would develop the strengths and weaknesses of each position and conduct evaluations.

I assume that some of these positions will be reformulated in our current era of anatheism, new materialism, and inclusionary theologies. There will also likely be new twenty-first-century approaches; nevertheless, Levinas expressed well the goal of this chapter: "The ontological status or regime of the Revelation is therefore a primordial concern for Jewish thought, posing a problem, which should take precedence over any attempt to present the contents of that Revelation."[66]

Selected Further Reading

Berkovits, Eliezer. *God, Man and History*. New York: Jonathan David, 1965.
Dulles, Avery. *Models of Revelation*. Maryknoll: Orbis Books, 2001.
Fackre, Gabriel. *The Doctrine of Revelation: A Narrative Interpretation*. Grand Rapids, MI: W. B. Eerdmans Publishing Company, 1997.
Fishbane, Michael. *Sacred Attunement: A Jewish Theology*. Chicago and London: The University of Chicago Press, 2008.
Heschel, Abraham Joshua. *Heavenly Torah: As Refracted Through the Generations*. London: Continuum, 2006.
Jacobs, Louis. "Human Element in Divine Revelation." *The Jewish Chronicle*, May 24, 1996.
Kaplan, Aryeh. *Inner Space: Introduction to Kabbalah, Meditation and Prophecy*. Brooklyn: Moznaim Publishing Corporation, 1991.
Klug, Brian. "Speaking of God: Ludwig Wittgenstein and the Paradox of Religious Experience." In *Religious Experience Revisited: Expressing the*

---

[66] Levinas, *Levinas Reader*, 192–93.

Inexpressible?, 243–61. Edited by Thomas Hardtke, Ulrich Schmiedel, and Tobias Tan. Leiden and Boston, MA: Brill, 2016.

Leibowitz, Yeshayahu. *Emunah, Historiah, ve-Arakhim*. Jerusalem: Academon, 1982.

Levenson, Jon D. *Sinai and Zion*. San Francisco: Harper Collins, 1985.

Levinas, Emmanuel. "The Jewish Understanding of Scripture." *Cross Currents* 44.4 (Winter 94/95): 488–504.

Levinas, Emmanuel. "Revelation in the Jewish Tradition." In *Levinas Reader*, 192–93. Edited by Sean Hand. Hoboken: Blackwell Publishers, 1989.

Mendelssohn, Moses. *Jerusalem, Or, On Religious Power and Judaism*. Translated by Allan Arkush. Hanover and London: Brandeis University Press, 1983.

Shonkoff, Sam Berrin. "Michael Fishbane: An Intellectual Portrait." In *Michael Fishbane: Jewish Hermeneutical Theology*, 1–2. Edited by Hava Tirosh-Samuelson and Philip S. Bernstein. Boston, MA: Brill, 2015.

Soloveitchik, Joseph B. "Confrontation." *Tradition: A Journal of Orthodox Thought* 6.2 (1964): 5–29.

15 Jewish Theology of Religions
ALON GOSHEN-GOTTSTEIN

THEOLOGY OF RELIGIONS: THE PRACTICE AND THE DISCIPLINE

Jewish Theology of Religions is as old as Judaism itself. And yet, it is the newest of reflective disciplines, one that has barely taken hold in a Jewish context. In the most basic way, Jewish Theology of Religions is a reflection carried out from within Judaism in relation to other faiths, their beliefs, their validity, and what value, if any, Judaism finds in them. Such reflection is a fundamental correlate of Judaism's taking a stance over and against other religions of the day, affirming its particularity, calling for a different approach to God and His service. Jewish rejection of the idolatry of other faiths of the Ancient Near East is the most ancient expression of a Jewish Theology of Religions. But it is neither systematic nor consistent. Within the Bible itself we already find multiple voices with regard to other gods and other faiths. We need only recall Yehezkel Kaufmann's description of the Book of Genesis as lacking any reference to idolatry and its accommodation of other approaches to faith to realize that from its earliest foundations Judaism maintains multiple, at times conflicting, voices in relation to other gods, faiths, and religions.

Jews in all generations have taken a stand in relation to neighboring religions. Whereas rabbinic religion represents across-the-board rejection of contemporary religions —on moral, theological and historical (persecution of Israel) grounds—perspectives become more complex in the Middle Ages as Judaism engages with Christianity and Islam, and even more so in modernity, when the range of religions to which Judaism responds is broader. The past half century has seen a change in cultural atmosphere, where contemporary social needs, stemming from the legacy of war and destruction (including the Holocaust) and the need for co-existence in an increasingly globalized world, push most religious traditions toward good neighborly relations and the quest for tolerance, respect, and deeper acceptance of the religious other. One of the expressions of this drive has been the increasing involvement of Jews in interreligious dialogue and also in systematic reflection on other faiths, reconsidering past heritage and attempting to state a contemporary Jewish vision of other religions, in line with contemporary needs and sensibilities.

The contemporary pursuit of a systematic view of other religions is where present-day Jewish Theology of Religions differs from thousands of years of speculation. Rather than the *ad hoc* response to a god, a belief, an alternative religious reality, it seeks to articulate a systematic view not only of one religion but of all religions in relation to Judaism. It is thus a form of taking stock of Israel's particularity and positioning in relation to the very reality of religious difference, carried out against the particular historical background of the day. Such reflection is typically carried out in an academic/theological context, in line and as part of similar reflective exercises undertaken by thinkers and theologians of other faiths. Thus, the discipline of Theology of Religions, as distinct from practices that we may in retrospect describe by such a term, is part of broader practices carried out in academic and theological circles.

As will become evident in the following discussion, one of the major factors shaping a Jewish view of other religions is Jewish law, the halakhah. Because attitudes to other religions have been shaped by halakhah or contributed to its shaping, the greatest challenge in terms of a contemporary Jewish theology of religions relates to Jewish Orthodox thinkers, whose views are shaped by the halakhah more than other streams of contemporary Judaism. Also in sociological terms, the Orthodox community provides the greatest challenge in formulating a position toward other religions that would impact contemporary relations between different faith groups. The present essay will therefore draw on resources of the halakhah and of classical Jewish thinkers who would be classified today as Orthodox.[1]

---

[1] There is a long tradition of engaging other religions, running from the beginning of the Enlightenment up to present times, that is non-Orthodox. Much of it developed in nineteenth- and early twentieth-century Reform thought and a significant part of it was written in German. This trajectory of theological reflection is carried out independently of halakhic thinking. Significantly, it deals with religions in their abstraction, but does not engage their ritual reality, which is one of the main concerns of halakhic tradition. This philosophical tradition would not be recognized, in substance as well as in terms of authority, by more traditionally minded Jews. As these constitute the group most in need of a contemporary articulation of a Jewish view of

CHRISTIAN AND JEWISH THEOLOGY OF RELIGIONS

Recognizing how the discipline of Jewish Theology of Religions is situated within a broader framework goes a long way to accounting for its formation and achievements to date. Theology of Religions, like much of theology, develops in a Christian philosophical/theological milieu. Strictly speaking, one should speak of "Christian Theology of Religions," just as the present analysis is being carried out in relation to "Jewish" Theology of Religions. Yet, discussion in Christian circles usually fails to include that qualification, much as internet domain names in the US are exempt from adding the country name as a suffix to addresses. The default of "Theology of Religions", then, is Christian.

The broader Christian framework of the discipline has quantitative and qualitative implications for engagement in reflection on other religions from a Jewish perspective. Quantitatively, one notes a disproportion in the scope of Christian engagement in Theology of Religions, compared with similar Jewish attempts. A random perusal of Google Books shows hundreds of titles that qualify as (Christian) Theology of Religions. On the Jewish side, no more than five or six titles qualify. A similar picture emerges from a consultation of library catalogues and the index of articles in Jewish studies (Rambi). Jews are clearly less engaged and less interested in Theology of Religions than are their Christian counterparts. Before considering how this fact corresponds to the qualitative, substantive dimensions of the respective theologies of religion, let us consider why Jews would show lesser interest in the field. Several factors are to be considered.

A. The discipline is young and it may take a while till it takes hold among Jewish thinkers.
B. Jews on the whole show far less interest in theology. Theology is explored by a very narrow elite of thinkers who are trained in dialogue with broader conventions that are, once again, shaped by Christian practices. Jewish approaches to other religions are heavily conditioned by halakhah. While there is extensive reflection on other religions, in their generality and in relation to individual religions, the most dominant factor in shaping attitudes is the

other traditions, I will be developing my thoughts in ways that speak to this community.

halakhah. If theoretical reflection is seen as subservient to halakhah (even if in reality the relations are the reverse), this provides a disincentive to systematic theological reflection on other religions.
C. More significantly, Jews show much less interest in other religions. The primary Jewish concern is survival, whether survival of the people or the maintaining of fidelity to the religious path. Within that, interest in the other is much narrower, often marginal.
D. For those Jews who do care about a Jewish view of other religions, existing precedent developed over millennia of Jewish reference to other religions provides adequate resources for shaping approaches to other faiths. Among Orthodox Jews, such precedent is all too often a limiting or rejecting view of other faiths, which once stated does not invite further reflection.

As a result of these considerations one may generalize that Jewish scholars who engage in a Jewish Theology of Religions do so not only because of a felt need to articulate a view of other faiths for practical purposes of coexistence but also out of deep concern for Judaism, its mission, and its ideals. Articulating a Jewish view of other faiths is more than prescribing guidelines for good neighborly relations. It goes to the heart of Judaism's continuing relevance, its enduring message on humanity's stage, expressed in how it relates to other religions. A Jewish Theology of Religions is at its core as much a statement about Judaism as it is a view of other faiths. Consequently, it is practiced by a fairly narrow class of scholars who feel the need to revisit this question, against the backdrop of humanity's religions.

Because Jews enter the field of Theology of Religions, which has been defined in light of predominantly Christian concerns, many of them pick up the conversation where their Christian colleagues have left it off, adapting and applying categories developed within the Christian context and more significantly—viewing the enterprise of Theology of Religions along the same lines that Christian thinkers have developed. To date, the question has not been posed whether the challenges and tasks of a Jewish Theology of Religions are the same or different from those of a Christian Theology of Religions. That *Christian* Theology of Religions is presented as "Theology of Religions," without this specific qualification, readily contributes to the integration of Christian discourse within a Jewish milieu, without due consideration of what might be the specific task of a Jewish Theology of Religions.

THEOLOGY OF RELIGIONS AND RELATED CONCERNS

A complicating factor in the development of a Jewish Theology of Religions is that its concerns are closely associated with and impacted by related areas. These feed into Theology of Religions and overlap with it, thereby obscuring its particularity. Three such areas can be mentioned:

A. Interreligious dialogue. The practices of encounter and dialogue on the ground require justification and often statements relating to the need for dialogue function as though they were contributions to Theology of Religions.

B. The special heritage of Jewish–Christian relations. Of all reciprocal relations that have fed reflection and publications, Jewish–Christian relations is the field most toiled. In large part, Christian interest in theology and dialogue has led to Jewish response and engagement with an agenda that is often set by Christian concerns. This includes understanding Christianity in its Jewish context, reading the Bible and cognate literatures, the long history of Jewish–Christian relations that includes persecution, dealing with anti-semitism and holocaust and, in a different register, dealing with joint service to society at large. These and other concerns lend a dimension of theoretical reflection to Jewish–Christian relations and in the process contribute to a Jewish Theology of Religions. However, the tradition of Jewish–Christian relations also obscures the concerns that should lie at the heart of a more strictly defined Jewish Theology of Religions. There is a need to develop a Jewish Theology of Religions as a discipline that is broader than the scope and interest of Jewish–Christian relations.

C. One of the leading notions of a Christian Theology of Religions is pluralism. Pluralism is also a concern of many contemporary Jewish theologians. Interest in pluralism on the Jewish side is fed by multiple interests. These include liberal social theories, concerns for handling internal Jewish diversity, the need for providing theoretical justification for Jewish singularity in a minority context, and the appeal to pluralism as a safeguard of identity. These and other concerns have fed into a stance of several Jewish thinkers who consider pluralism a positive social virtue and who seek to provide religious rationale for its practice.

A look at the handful of book-length publications that could be considered under the rubric of Theology of Religions reveals how much they owe to the three factors noted above and often to a combination of all three. The work of Michael Kogan is representative. His *Opening the Covenant*[2] is explicitly cast as a theology of Christianity and in many ways the designation is justified, inasmuch as it seeks to offer a Jewish theological appreciation of Christianity. However, the discussion shifts between all areas described above. The same may be said of Dan Cohn Sherbok's *Judaism and Other Faiths*.[3] Though it supposedly deals with "religions," all the data is taken from Judaism's engagement with Christianity, presented historically, rather than theologically. A theologically pluralist agenda (in the sense to be discussed below) is plonked upon a future vision, without any attempt to justify why pluralism is the way of the future and without any visible relationship with the body of the discussion. Pluralism seems to be a self-evident ideology and it interacts with attempts at positive appreciation of Christianity, as well as other religions (not discussed by him).

David Hartman, a great champion of pluralism, internal to Judaism as well in relation to other faiths, approaches other religions with an openness that stems from such a pluralist orientation. Hartman applies the canons of internal Jewish pluralism to relations with other faiths, but he does not engage any other religion in its specificity, nor does he ask the hard questions that have defined Jewish attitudes to other religions for millennia and that I shall present below.[4] Jonathan Sacks' *The Dignity of Difference* falls into the same category. In its first edition it sought to offer a pluralist Jewish view of other religions.[5] The view of other religions was a statement in principle of Jewish pluralism and did not engage any topics that a more detailed and studied Jewish Theology of Religions should undertake.

---

[2] Michael Kogan, *Opening the Covenant: A Jewish Theology of Christianity* (Oxford: Oxford University Press, 2008).

[3] See Dan Cohn Sherbok, *Judaism and Other Faiths* (Basingstoke: Macmillan, 1994).

[4] Hartman is a popular champion for interreligious pluralism. While he did not write a sustained book-length argument, parts of his book *Conflicting Visions: Spiritual Possibilities of Modern Israel* (New York: Schocken, 1990) are devoted to the theme.

[5] Jonathan Sacks, *The Dignity of Difference: How to Avoid the Clash of Civilizations*, (London: Continuum, 2002, 2nd ed. 2003).

THE CONCERNS OF A JEWISH THEOLOGY OF RELIGIONS

Theology of Religions is driven by multiple concerns that represent the theological interest of the reflecting tradition. These give expression to the deep structure of the religion, how it is organized, what drives it, and therefore what it considers most important as it reflects on the place and value of other religions. It stands to reason, a priori, that each religious tradition will undertake the task of reflecting upon other religions from within its own particular parameters, expressing the concerns that are dear to it and that reflect its particular structure. If so, one cannot assume that the concerns of one religion's Theology of Religions will be the same as those of another. Owing to the confusion between Theology of Religions as an area of philosophical and theological reflection and its particular Christian form, attempts at developing a Jewish Theology of Religions have followed the contours established within the Christian context, without due consideration of where the particularity of each religion's vision comes to expression.

Christian Theology of Religions brings together several concerns, grouped around one central concern. The central concern is salvation. Can other religions lead to salvation or is salvation the exclusive lot and promise of Christianity? This question readily leads to a consideration of other religions in terms of truth. The assumption is that if they are true they have the power to save and if they have the power to save they are true. The move from one theoretical concern to the other relates to religions in their generality, and typically does not engage the particularity of religious teaching. A third concern grows out of these. If only Christianity can deliver salvation, this raises the problem of justice. It is unjust that the only gateway to salvation should be provided by a religion that is not available to all, and has not always been there as a means of saving humanity. The drive for justice thus complements the drive for truth and both are organized around a soteriological focus.

This construct is totally foreign to Judaism. The very notion of salvation is not self-evident in a Jewish context and certainly does not occupy the defining place it does in Christianity. Judaism has no interest in looking at other religions in terms of soteriology. Consequently, the problem of justice would never arise. The issue of truth is relevant. However, it alone does not sustain the concerns of a Jewish Theology of Religions. These are organized differently.

The primary concern of a Jewish Theology of Religions is the validity of other religions. The question then is not whether they are effective in delivering their promise of salvation but whether they are legitimate, acceptable as religious configurations, acceptable to God, and in line with any number of guiding principles in light of which their validity and legitimacy may be defined. The problem of religious truth does, of course, play into this concern. If the religion is false, it is likely not valid. However, this assumes a very simple notion of truth, either in light of a correspondence theory wherein religious statements correspond to reality out there (historical or metaphysical) or as otherwise correct in terms that could translate to a God's-eye approach to the religion. Because much of Jewish tradition does not privilege truth as the primary lens for viewing other religions, the concern for truth may be of significantly less importance than it is within a Christian context. What it means for a religion to be true could be equivalent to it being valid or legitimate, and this could be established by criteria that are not cognitive or that do not draw on factuality or philosophical veracity of claims. While truth is certainly one dimension of a Jewish Theology of Religions, its application can be subject to other criteria of validity, thereby reducing the difficulty in recognizing other religions as valid despite disagreeing with many of their faith claims, pitched as truth claims.[6] That legitimacy of a religion or its validity should be the primary concern of a Jewish Theology of Religions makes the entire approach very judgmental. But it is no less judgmental than the Christian's declaration of the efficacy or inefficacy of another religion.

PLURALISM, INCLUSIVISM, EXCLUSIVISM

Probably the single most common working tool in the analysis undertaken as part of Christian Theology of Religions is the threefold distinction—pluralism, inclusivism, exclusivism—introduced by Alan Race and made popular by John Hick.[7] The distinction refers, in its original context, to views of other religions that consider them to have no saving power (exclusivism), that have value in and of themselves, regardless of Christianity (pluralism), and those whose salvific power is owed, in some way, to Christianity, while nevertheless operating autonomously within another religious framework. The edge around which most of

---

[6] The subject is examined at length in *Religious Truth: Towards a Jewish Theology of Religions*, ed. Alon Goshen-Gottstein (Oxford: Littman Library of Jewish Civilization, 2020).

[7] John Hick, *God Has Many Names* (London: Macmillan, 1980).

Christian Theology of Religions revolves is the distinction between inclusivism and pluralism—how far can Christian faith legitimate other faiths on grounds that accept those faiths on their own merit, rather than as an expression of some Christian principle.

Jews entering the field of Theology of Religions have applied these categories to a Jewish view of other religions.[8] Alan Brill has assembled a treasure of Jewish attitudes to other faiths, as resources for contemporary approaches, and analyzed them in light of this categorization.[9] His discussion goes beyond this threefold division in two ways. First, he introduces a fourth category—universalism, the recognition of one God, common to different faiths. Second, in light of Jewish sources, he offers various ways in which each of these categories can be applied on different grounds—historical, moral, metaphysical etc. This adds significant nuance to the discussion and allows the particularity of specific Jewish views to come across. However, the underlying assumption must be queried. Brill's application of these categories profiles the notion of truth and its presence in other religions.[10] If one recognizes that the quest for truth is not what lies at the heart of a Jewish Theology of Religions, then approaching Jewish sources through this threefold (fourfold, if truth is the heart of the matter) prism may miss the mark in terms of what matters most. Brill's important collection presents snippets of texts and contemporary academic insights. These may provide building blocks for the construction of a Jewish Theology of Religions, but they are not integrated into larger wholes. Brill shows us that all these options exist in Judaism. He also shows us that certain individuals can hold positions variously classified. The classification may in that case be useful as a heuristic device for reading sources, but it obscures the fact that the individual texts and the diversity of theoretical perspectives under which they may be grouped, do not reflect the broader concerns of the tradition or even of individual thinkers. The need for appreciating the complexities in the thought of individual thinkers informs the second part of the present essay that focuses on case studies of leading authorities, profiling complexities in their thinking, complexities that in turn

---

[8] See Cohn Sherbok, *Judaism and Other Faiths*.
[9] Alan Brill, *Judaism and Other Religions: Models of Understanding* (New York: Palgrave Macmillan, 2010).
[10] It is important to recognize that truth is not the organizing principle in Brill's own theology of religions as he himself points out in *Judaism and Other Religions*, 26–28, and as his later publications demonstrate.

suggest the complexity of the enterprise of developing a Jewish Theology of Religions.

Let us consider an instance that demonstrates the difference between truth and validity. Brill presents us with positions that recognize multiple revelations in history, with different religions being revealed to their respective intended audiences and peoples.[11] Such a notion of multiple revelation also informs the work of several contemporary pluralist thinkers: David Hartman, Kogan, Irving Greenberg.[12] If salvation were the concern, multiple revelations would certainly resolve that problem. But if truth is the concern, what does it mean that there are multiple revelations? I do not think that any of the thinkers associated with such a notion, neither medieval nor modern, would be willing to ascribe to the *details* of belief, law, and practice of another religion the same status of "truth" that they would claim for their own faith, unless they totally renounce any claim for real truth value to their own faith.[13] My point is that if we use the criterion of validity we can say that recognition of other religions as having a basis in parallel revelation make these traditions *valid* for their practitioners, based on the notion that controls the Jewish quest for validity—revelation. Nevertheless, this does not make all the details of these religions— law, particular beliefs, customs etc. — true. With regard to these even authorities who recognize multiple revelations would have to take a position of rejection. Jews do not believe in Mary's immaculate birth or Jesus' messianic status, they do not believe in Muhammad being the seal of the prophets, and they do not believe that Krishna is an incarnation of God. Applying a theory of pluralism, especially one couched in terms of revelation, is meant to afford *legitimacy* to these religions, in a language by means of which Jews afford such legitimacy. It does not mean that everything the religion teaches is true.

With reference to truth, Jewish thinkers inadvertently are forced to one of two positions. Either they must become agnostic with regard to truth, in either metaphysical or historical terms,[14] or they must adopt different approaches to different parts of the religion under review.

---

[11] Ibid., 111.
[12] See Hartman, *Conflicting Visions*, 246; Kogan, *Opening the Covenant*, 170; Irving Greenberg, *For the Sake of Heaven and Earth: The New Encounter Between Judaism and Christianity* (Philadelphia: Jewish Publication Society, 2004), 49.
[13] As Cohn Sherbok, *Judaism and Other Faiths*, is willing to do.
[14] Ibid., and Kogan, *Opening the Covenant*, 161.

According to this latter view, in some way the religion is true, and criteria for that must be established. In other ways it is false or it has teachings that are partially true, pending interpretation provided by Jews.[15] Assessing other religions in terms of truth gets one into the inevitable entanglement of the limits of truth and just what one means by it. This is also where pluralism reaches its limits, as it pushes us to cognitive relativism or agnosticism, or alternatively ends up manifesting traits that are less than pluralist, in the full theoretical sense.

A strong pluralist ethos would like to proffer equal status on all religions. One is as good as the other and no religion can claim superiority or precedence of any kind. Pluralists have a hard time with a view of other religions still maintaining some dimension of superiority. For example, Kogan criticizes Greenberg for not being fully pluralistic and for insisting on some ways in which Judaism is superior.[16] In terms of the present discussion, at certain points in his thinking the pluralist Greenberg turns inclusivist.[17] I would argue that this is inevitable, once another religion is viewed in its particularity, in relation to specific truth or faith statements, rather than in the abstraction of defining it in terms of truth. The upshot is that religions are viewed as simultaneously exclusivist, inclusivist, and pluralist, depending on the aspect of the religion under discussion. The taxonomy loses much of its efficacy when it is transported to Jewish soil.

If we concede the limited usefulness of existing categories, we may be able to see more clearly the dynamics of pluralism and inclusivism. In constructing a Jewish pluralist view, thinkers appeal to Jewish ideas and constructs. These must have some continuity with tradition. The notion of a "Noachide covenant" is one category that has been put in the service of a pluralist view. According to this view, Judaism has a message for the world, that of the seven Noachide commandments, fundamental moral laws, that are binding upon all of humanity.

---

[15] Irving Yitz Greenberg is a champion of this approach, as he seeks to make sense of key Christian faith tenets from a Jewish perspective. See Alon Goshen-Gottstein, "Genius Theologian, Lonely Theologian: Yitz Greenberg on Christianity," in *A Torah Giant: The Intellectual Legacy of Rabbi Dr. Irving (Yitz) Greenberg*, ed. Shmuly Yanklowitz (Jerusalem: Urim, 2018), 71–92.

[16] Kogan, *Opening the Covenant*, 161.

[17] Greenberg's notion of a failed Messiah, by means of which he describes Jesus, is an attempt to understand what kind of Messiah Jesus was in terms of Judaism's understanding of a Messiah. A truly pluralist approach might have allowed for multiple messiahs for multiple communities.

Accordingly, Judaism's view of universal moral obligation is cast by some as a covenant that applies to all of humanity and as such is Judaism's way of affirming value in others. The problem is that the category is an internal one, extended to others in an inclusivist move, and therefore falls short of true pluralism. The same would apply even to the frequent appeal to the notion of man, or humanity, being created in God's image (Genesis 1:26) and to any validation of other religious systems in light of this principle. These categories are very appropriate in providing a framework for viewing other religions. Trouble begins when we seek to construct a pluralist edifice upon categories drawn from one's own tradition. There is no way of engaging in such an exercise without it being inclusivist. Noachide commandments are an internal Jewish category and the construct that expands these commandments into a full-blown view of other religions is not pluralist. It relies on Jewish language and Jewish categories to interpret the reality of the other. The image of God is a high point of Jewish religious thought. But applying it is still a means of understanding the other from within one's own theoretical framework. If a Jewish Theology of Religions seeks to understand the other, it must do so in terms drawn from the Jewish tradition. The very act of doing so moves the argument to the domain of the inclusivist. While it may express a pluralist sensibility, in the common sense, it is often an inclusivist project, in the technical sense used in Theology of Religions.

ELEMENTS OF A JEWISH THEOLOGY OF RELIGIONS

We are now at a point where we can consider how to go about developing a Theology of Religions. The following points should inform a systematic approach to other religions:

A. A theory or a perspective should be as broad as possible and cover as many religions as possible. A good Theology of Religions will offer perspectives on all religions. To date, no one has attempted a thorough analysis of the stakes and possibilities involved in a Jewish view of all religions. The broader the scope, the greater the value of a Theology of Religions. The theology of one religious tradition is of value, but risks operating along idiosyncratic parameters that are relevant to one specific religion. It will therefore easily move from a theological perspective to a historical review of relations, as have some of the works surveyed above.

B. A Jewish Theology of Religions has to stand in continuity with tradition and its concerns. There is a constructive tension between drawing from the tradition and seeking to advance it in certain ways. Luckily, as I shall illustrate in what follows and as Alan Brill has demonstrated in his work, tradition is rich in precedents and it is not as if we must now correct fundamental flaws that have hampered Jewish tradition since its inception. A careful balance must be sought between drawing from the past and staking a vision for the future. The optimal scenario is that the core of that vision draws from tradition and a theologian's constructive work is to help align details of tradition to such a preexisting vision. All this is in contradistinction to an attitude that simply affirms that we must change or change orientation because it conforms to the writer's spiritual intuitions, without accounting for them from within or in dialogue with Jewish tradition.[18]

C. The scope of issues a Theology of Religions will tackle must be expansive. The problem with some of the existing discourse is that it is too closely focused on one particular issue only, typically the issue of truth. Instead, we must consider multiple perspectives, all of which contribute to philosophical perspectives as well as emotional and existential attitudes toward other religions.

Relevant perspectives include:

1. Idolatry, Avodah Zarah. There is no doubt that this is the most fundamental category by means of which Judaism, halakhic Judaism, considers the legitimacy and validity of other religions. Religions that are deemed idolatrous would seem, at first sight, to be devoid of value, illegitimate. The pronouncement on Avodah Zarah is halakhic, and may rely on what is seen rather than what is understood of the other's faith. This is the single greatest problem in the practice of halakhah and a Jewish Theology of Religions—considering the other faith only after proper understanding has been attained. As a broad, and necessarily inaccurate generalization, one may say that for most of Jewish history, views of other religions were formed without engaging in the practices of dialogue, study, and understanding

---

[18] The final part of Cohn-Sherbok's work, *Judaism and Other Faiths*, illustrates this approach.

that we would consider essential to pronouncing judgment on another faith. This shocking claim is borne out by evidence spanning prophetic mockery of idol worship to contemporary halakhic perspectives on Hinduism.[19] What Theology of Religions has to offer to the practices of halakha, which it must take seriously in constructing an authentic Jewish perspective on other religions, is the call to serious study and understanding. Inasmuch as Avodah Zarah is also a form of othering, mockery, and distancing, drawing in part from social needs, we must purify its very use, and get to the core of what is essential to a Jewish view of God and how that relates to other religions. Here we realize how Jewish Theology of Religions ultimately points to core concerns of Jewish theology and self-understanding.

2. Legitimation of other religions. If Judaism's concern is validation of a religion, mechanisms for validation of other religions as theoretical constructs and concrete realities must be affirmed. The issue of the very validity of other religions is itself the subject of difference of opinion between two of the voices we will be studying below. Consider Maimonides' prohibition upon a non-Jew to form a new religion as an extreme instance of undermining recognition.[20] Contrast this with Meiri's views permitting the development of other religions by non-Jews.[21] The question of legitimacy of other religions is thus at the heart of a Jewish Theology of Religions.

3. Israel's particularity. Judaism is the particular story of one people's faith. That faith, however, is of universal significance, expressed in the blessing to Abraham, the vision of the prophets, and ultimately in the very purpose of Judaism. A Jewish Theology of Religions must account for what it is that makes Israel unique and how its special mission finds expression in a world populated by multiple religions with which it seeks to have harmonious relations, rather than a world full of foreign gods. That other religions challenge Israel's particularity or its endurance adds a layer of complexity to Judaism's relationship with and view of those religions. A Jewish Theology of Religions is not only about viewing other religions. It is

---

[19] See Alon Goshen-Gottstein, *Same God, Other God: Judaism, Hinduism and the Problem of Idolatry* (New York: Palgrave Macmillan, 2015), 27–39.

[20] Maimonides, MT *Laws of Kings*, 10:9.

[21] See Gerald Blidstein, Maimonides and Meiri on the Legitimacy of Non-Judaic Religions, *Scholars and Scholarship: The Interaction between Judaism and Other Cultures*, ed. Leo Landman (New York: Yeshiva University Press, 1990), 27–35.

also about affirming, identifying, and pointing to Israel's enduring mission today, especially in relation to other religions.
4. Religious truth defines for many people the core challenge of Theology of Religions. While I take exception to such a view, one must nonetheless work through the meaning of truth on multiple levels. These include understanding the concept in its abstract sense, as it applies to other religions as broad entities, the criteria for its application, as well as how it relates to particular teachings. While idolatry constitutes the biggest block for the halakhic mind, religious truth is viewed by the common man as the biggest challenge for religions, marshaling competing truth claims.

Because truth can be applied on the macro-level to the testimony of a religion as a whole, and on the micro-level in relation to individual teachings, when considering the value and validity of another religion we must focus our attention on different dimensions of the religious life of each religion. As we shall see below, Maimonides' different attitude when it comes to the core of Christian faith contrasted with Christian respect for Scripture suggests that we should be open to viewing another religion from multiple angles. Ideally, the more comprehensive the view, the more dimensions are included in the approach to the religion.[22]

Three dimensions seem central to a view of another religion:

A. Teachings. These include theoretical teachings on the nature of God, the world, revelation, and particular teachings that relate to the particularity of the religion and various beliefs that are specific to it. These have been handled in the past in the context of polemics and disputations. A view informed by a Theology of Religions seeks to understand, stake differences, and arrive at a balanced appreciation, without the polemical and oppositional orientation that was characteristic of the past.

B. Morality. One of the key areas for evaluating another religion is the quality of its moral life and the way in which it forms the human character and broader society. While this may be considered

[22] The work of David Novak deserves mention in this context. Over the course of several monographs he has explored in depth various aspects of a Jewish view of others and other religions. These include *The Election of Israel* (Cambridge: Cambridge University Press, 1995); *The Image of the non-Jew in Judaism* (New York: Edwin Mellen, 1983); *Jewish-Christian Dialogue* (Oxford: Oxford University Press, 1989); *Jewish-Christian Relations in a Secular Age* (San Francisco: Swig Judaic Studies Program, 1998).

a component of truth, this is also a self-standing dimension of evaluating a religion by its fruits, rather than by its theological teachings. For some Jewish authorities, this has served as the single most important criterion for validating other religions, over and against concerns over teaching and even of idolatrous worship practices. We shall see this shortly when we consider the views of R. Menachem Hameiri.

C. The mystical life. All too often we consider religions from their public, visible, and political side. Given that Jews have encountered other religions largely under situations of political dominion, tension, and conflict, one need not be surprised by the lack of appeal to the interior spiritual life. A balanced assessment of a religion should consider what its finest fruit is, what it is capable of producing. Appreciating the testimony of mystics opens the door not only to appreciation of the depth of spiritual experience but also to comparative appreciation across traditions, based on the theoretical possibility of common experience.[23]

D. Advancing this line of thought, religion should be appreciated by its finest exemplars. As a complement to the study of ideas, both philosophical and moral, we can turn to the lives of great individuals across traditions. What does the testimony of saints, of outstanding individuals, those to whom I refer as religious geniuses, do to our evaluation of another religion?[24] A study of religion through its finest exemplars opens an entirely new perspective of appreciation. If one is willing to admit such testimony, then one gains entry to the life of prayer, miracles, and living in God, as these find expression in different religions. Rather than dismissing these as magic or superstition and similar strategies for ignoring these testimonies, we must incorporate these dimensions into our consideration of another religion and of other religions as a whole. To drive the point home: if a great figure of another religion enjoys obvious intimacy with God and has an outstanding religious life, interior and exterior, as determined by literary and contemporary testimony, how could that change our assessment of the religion that

---

[23] I am currently coordinating the work of an interreligious think tank on the subject of mysticism and identity. Papers prepared by the think tank point to such common experience. The work will be published in the Interreligious Reflections series, presently housed at Wipf and Stock.

[24] See Alon Goshen-Gottstein, *Religious Genius – Appreciating Outstanding Individuals Across Religions* (New York: Palgrave Macmillan), 2017.

person practices? Does the existence of righteous individuals who rise to great spiritual heights in religions that some deem idolatrous (Christianity, Hinduism) say something about our verdict concerning these religions as idolatrous? Does it require of us to introduce further nuance into our view of other faiths?

The promise of a Jewish Theology of Religions is that of applying systematic and complex criteria and perspectives by means of which we can move beyond facile characterizations and the disparaging perspective they engender. A Jewish Theology of Religions is an invitation to learn, understand, reconsider, and eventually take a stand *vis-à-vis* another religion or other religions as a whole. The stand that will be taken, factoring in all that has been described above, is bound to be richer than what has preceded us, shedding new light not only on the religions upon which it reflects but also upon Israel, its faith and mission. Ultimately, Jewish Theology of Religions is an essential part of the spiritual growth and fulfillment of Judaism itself.

Having laid down these theoretical principles, I would like to move in the second part of the essay to three case studies. These case studies illustrate a methodological approach that tackles the challenges of a Jewish Theology of Religions by appeal to precedents of notable teachers and individuals. Focusing attention on individual teachers allows us to explore the methodological problems as they pertain to each of the individuals and therefore to evaluate the contribution and the challenges posed by the contribution of each individual teacher in a more systematic manner. I suggest that the systematic study of the positions of teachers and religious authorities allows us to work through issues, problems, limits, and challenges in a way that is more constructive and engaged than what we all too often encounter, which are random quotes from tradition, using a pick-and-choose methodology that suits the theological preference of whoever is citing these authorities. Jewish Theology of Religions is a field that is in its infancy. Rather than rushing to conclusions we would wish to reach, and relying in the process on the "best of" our tradition, it requires the patient study and struggle with a rich tradition and what it has to offer us today. Such struggle, I suggest, is best carried out in dialogue with the thought of notable individuals. Hence, I move now to a sketch of three such notable individuals.

CASE STUDY A: MAIMONIDES

Maimonides is one of the most influential of Jewish thinkers when it comes to philosophy, theology, and halakhah. And his influence is also seen when it comes to the Jewish attitude to other religions. His influence owes largely to his halakhic rulings in relation to the halakhic status of Islam and Christianity. Maimonides rules the former is not considered idolatrous; Avodah Zarah and various restrictions that would apply to transactions with idolaters do not apply to Muslims. By contrast, Christianity is deemed by him to be idolatrous. Maimonides' views on Christianity are the norm today in Israel and in most of the Orthodox and Ultra-Orthodox world. A long tradition that existed in Europe during the Middle Ages and into modernity, according to which Christianity is not considered idol worship for non-Jews, though it is forbidden for Jews, has been largely sidelined in recent decades. This is in and of itself a worrying phenomenon. It represents a flattening of the richness of halakhic discourse. It also demonstrates the degree to which halakhah determines views of the other. Maimonides' diverse statements are an invitation for further consideration and reflection on the educational and theological levels. The increasing prominence of his position has negative public consequences in terms of attitudes to Christians in situations ranging from chance encounters to questions of distribution of public funds in Israel. The ruling that Christianity is idolatrous informs an exclusionary discourse that is often at odds with fundamentals of democracy and of various Jewish values relating to the other and the stranger.

In terms of the classification of positions, following the threefold categorization discussed above, Maimonides' ruling would most readily qualify as exclusivist, in the sense that it affords no positive value to Christianity. It is therefore surprising to find him offering the following reflection on the purpose of Christianity in God's plan:

> The human mind has no power to reach the thoughts of the Creator, "for His thoughts and ways are unlike ours" (Isaiah 55:8). All these matters of Jesus of Nazareth and of the Ishmaelite who stood up after him are only intended to pave the way for the Anointed King, and to mend the entire world to worship God together, thus: "For then I shall turn a clear tongue to the nations to call all in the Name of the Lord and to worship him with one shoulder" (Zephaniah 3:9).

Thus the messianic hope, the Torah, and the commandments have become familiar topics of conversation among the inhabitants of the far isles and many peoples, uncircumcised of heart and flesh. (*Laws of Kings* 11:3)

Valueless from a halakhic perspective, Christianity nevertheless plays its part in a divine plan. Islam's halakhic advantage over Christianity does not improve its view in terms of a philosophy of history. This famous passage provides a counterpoint in terms of positive appreciation of Christianity. Clearly, it is inclusivist, offering a limited appreciation of Christianity, based on Jewish criteria. Though limited in its appreciation, it could still condition a different attitude to Christians than the exclusivist rejection.

The picture of Maimonides on Christianity is further complicated when we consider a responsum of Maimonides in which he permits teaching Torah to Christians and not to Muslims, because the former have a respectful attitude to the Scripture common to Judaism and Christianity.[25] David Novak has gone as far as suggesting that this ruling constitutes a reversal of his ruling on Christianity's idolatrous status.[26] While I would not go that far, for present purposes we could find in it a limited pluralism, that recognizes Christians in some specific capacity as equals, following a parallel path. Maimonides' view of Christianity is thus highly contextual. It shifts from topic to topic. This suggests that negative attitudinal consequences are not inevitable, even if one follows Maimonides' legal ruling on Christianity.

We must thus reconcile the complexities in Maimonides' writings *vis-à-vis* Christianity. We must also consider how these views cohere with Christian self-understanding and whether they do it justice. We must consider what options and choices a contemporary Jewish Theology of Religions faces and how to negotiate the increasing popularity of Maimonides' ruling in Orthodox Jewish circles, especially in Israel, with a rich tradition that sees Christianity in other terms. At a more fundamental level, we must consider what is the sin of idolatry and how much weight we wish to assign to it. All these options must be explored in the framework of a Jewish Theology of Religions. Choices

---

[25] Maimonides, *Teshuvot Harambam*, vol. 1, ed. J. Blau (Jerusalem: Mekitze Nirdamim, 1960), 284–85.
[26] David Novak, "Maimonides' Treatment of Christianity and its Normative Implications," in *Jewish Theology and World Religions*, 217–33.

have to be made using Judaism's internal criteria, precedents, and values. The categories of pluralism, inclusivism, and exclusivism contribute little to this process. Rather than import categories of a Christian theology of religion, we will be better off identifying categories that are internal to Jewish discourse and allowing those to enrich the broader global conversation of Theology of Religions.[27]

CASE STUDY B: R. MENAHEM HAMEIRI

The second case study profiles the question of validation of other religions as the core of a Jewish approach to other religions. In the process of establishing means of validation, the question of religious truth is revisited and recast in terms that are broad and expansive, thereby largely sidestepping the question of truth as a point of division and competition between religions.

The fourteenth-century Catalan rabbi, Menahem Hameiri (henceforth: Meiri), authored an encyclopedic commentary on the entire Talmud. This work establishes him as a leading halakhic voice, though his prominence is somewhat muted by the manuscript's loss and eventual rediscovery only in the twentieth century, by which time other halakhic positions established prominence. Meiri is well known as a champion of Jewish tolerance in relation to other religions.[28] In his talmudic commentary, he systematically rejects application of laws that were intended for idolaters to contemporary faiths, that is Christianity and Islam. The formal reasoning is that these faiths have an ordered moral life and that morally ordered society trumps idolatry or more likely is proof of belief in a true God.[29] Moshe Halbertal has shown that at the core of Meiri's views is not simply the replacement of theological criteria for assessing other faiths by moral criteria. Meiri's views are based on a principled view of what makes a faith system a valid religion.[30] His entire discourse is shaped by the concern for

---

[27] I am grateful to Francis Clooney who, in reviewing my work, suggested that Christians need not feel the burden of doing all the lifting in the domain of theology of religions and that they can benefit from the work of scholars in other religions. See his review of my *Same God, Other God: Judaism, Hinduism and the Problem of Idolatry* in *Religious Studies* 78.2 (2017): 505–6.
[28] Jacob Katz, *Exclusiveness and Tolerance* (Oxford: Oxford University Press, 1961).
[29] See my discussion in ch. 10 of *Same God, Other God*.
[30] Moshe Halbertal, "Ones Possessed of Religion: Religious Tolerance in the Teachings of the Me'iri," *The Edah Journal* 1.1 (2000): 1–25.

validity of religion and the mere designation of a religion, in the colloquial sense, as a "religion", in the sense of a valid religious system that is therefore recognized by Judaism, holds the key to understanding his radical tolerance. A religion (read: a valid religion) is known by the fact that it teaches an ordered moral life for the individual and society. At its core is relevant belief in fundamental theological principles that uphold such teaching. These include God's existence, the creation of the world, and continuing providence and retribution. These minimal theological foundations ensure upholding of the moral order. This sums up the core of Meiri's Theology of Religions.

The view is startling in its simplicity and is as significant for its omissions as it is for its emphases. In viewing another religion, details of faith and variations in understanding God do not affect the fundamental legitimacy of another religion. Similarly, ritual seems to matter little. The very concerns that, though not spelled out, likely led to Maimonides' designation of Christianity as Avodah Zarah, are done away with by this new definition. Meiri's views may be considered in light of the "same God" question. Rather than debating whether another religion is Avodah Zarah, and examining, to that end, its doctrines and rituals, Meiri goes to the heart of what matters most in religion and how it relates to God. The purpose of religion, in this reading, is the ordering of society and the moral advancement of the individual. These, in turn, provide indication of the nature of God who informs the religious system, ascertaining it is really God, and thereby legitimating the religion.

As noted above, in line with this thinking, and contrary to Maimonides' position, Meiri takes the stand that non-Jews may invent or develop their own religions. One assumes that rituals and various supporting beliefs are necessary religious needs and they provide the filling to the skeleton of faith, comprised by the moral life. What matters most is not the filling, but that moral skeleton.

Meiri is a champion of religious pluralism. As soon as criteria are established for defining what is a valid religion, all religions, and for Meiri these are all the religions of his time, qualify as equally valid.

Meiri's pluralism is based on applying minimal standards to the definition of a valid religion. All the complexity that I presented above as part of a comprehensive approach to a Jewish Theology of Religions is absent here. Instead, Meiri goes to the theological-moral core of religion and emerges with a contemporary pluralistic vision that effectively eliminates the concern for idolatry and potentially opens the path to engagement across religions.

Meiri's model is important in establishing how a traditional Jewish pluralistic Theology of Religions could be constructed. But it comes at a cost. Meiri has stripped religion of what matters most to its believers. Religion, we realize today more than ever, is about particularity. This is true also for the universal faiths that nevertheless uphold the particularity of revelation, practice, theology, deity, method of worship etc. Differently put: there is at work in every religion an interplay between its universal components and its particular identity. The tension between particularity and universality, all too familiar in the case of Judaism, takes on different expressions when considered in the context of universal religious principles and the particularity that makes each religion what it is.

Meiri's work is vital for aiding those who engage with contemporary religions to find a way that takes them beyond the relational, theological, and practical constraints of systems such as that of Maimonides, constraints that may not provide adequate foundations for advancing contemporary pluralist sensibilities. While acknowledging this debt and while holding on to Meiri's teachings as foundations for a theoretical and practical approach to other religions, one must also consider whether the moves he makes are not too broad to satisfy all the needs and challenges that a Jewish Theology of Religions must address. The particularity of Israel does not feature in Meiri's system. What is Israel's mission if all religions are valid? The meaning of ritual, for Jews and for non-Jews, is not adequately addressed. Are all religious systems valid and equal? Is there some priority and advantage to Judaism over other religions? It is likely that Meiri held there was. His position was articulated as talmudic glosses on texts that applied to a religious world that was already foreign to him and from which he needed to maintain his distance. But they lack the systematic consideration that a Theology of Religions must develop.

Meiri opens the way for us to undertake the task of Theology of Religions in an open and accommodating spirit. He allows us to recognize God as one in all religions. With that path cleared, we can then ask some of the questions that he did not, likely because social circumstances at the time did not require them. These questions do justice to the enduring concerns of a Jewish Theology of Religions as it has found continuing expression in various references to other religions. Meiri remains in a minority position, certainly as far as his broader theoretical approach is concerned. His insights must be integrated with the ongoing concerns of Jewish Theology of Religions. These require us to consider what he cast aside in his quest for legitimation of other religions. Reintegrating these concerns will likely be done in a manner that goes beyond the concern for legitimation or delegitimation. Rather, once legitimation and validity have been affirmed, other issues relating to understanding, spiritual growth, truth, purpose, historical vision, and more come to the fore. These provide the fullness for the discussion of a Jewish Theology of Religions, much as religion itself provides a vital plenitude to the moral foundations upon which it is built.

CASE STUDY C: RABBI ABRAHAM ISAAC KOOK

The third case study is an example of a thinker who tackles multiple dimensions of a Jewish Theology of Religions and whose lifelong engagement with the subject is an example of the challenges and struggles that are part and parcel of any attempt to tackle the challenge of a Jewish view of other religions. This thinker's comprehensive and extensive engagement with the subject of other faiths provides the alternative model to the single-focus pluralism made possible by Meiri's recognition of contemporary religions. While his work is not definitive, and certainly not the final word on the subject, it provides a model for struggling on multiple fronts, taking into account the riches of the different aspects of Jewish tradition —halakhic, philosophical, mystical, and more. It also provides an opportunity to introduce the reader to newly discovered materials of a foremost Jewish thinker, one whose voice can stand up to some of the negative currents that characterize contemporary Jewish attitudes to members of other faiths.[31]

Rabbi Abraham Isaac Kook (1865–1935) was the Chief Ashkenasik Rabbi of Mandatory Palestine, and a philosopher, kabbalist, and theologian of the first order. Rav Kook is at one and the same time a point of intellectual and spiritual synthesis of all the theoretical and theological streams and philosophies that preceded him and an original innovator drawing from his first-hand cognitions of the spiritual life. Concern with other religions is a life-long interest of Rav Kook's. In one way or another, he returns to different facets of his view of other religions throughout his oeuvre. It is telling that a comprehensive

---

[31] On these trends, see my *Luther the Antisemite: A Contemporary Jewish Perspective*, (Minneapolis, MN: Fortress Press, 2018).

thinker[32] would devote extensive attention to idolatry, the status of other religions, and issues that distinguish Judaism from other religions. Clearly, within a theological worldview properly constructed around the larger picture—Judaism's role and God's purpose for all—issues of Theology of Religion will occupy a place of honor.

The study of Rav Kook's attitudes to religions has received a huge boost by the recent publication of *Linevuchei Hador*, a previously unknown work of Rav Kook's that dates back to his time in Bauska, Latvia, prior to his immigration to Israel, and is thus a window into his early thought.[33] The book is written as a kind of contemporary *Guide of the Perplexed*, and Rav Kook seeks to confront various theoretical challenges facing the generation. In this, it is one of his few systematic writings written as a whole literary unit, rather than as a commentary or as diary entries. Within this work, several chapters are devoted to the status of other religions.[34] This suggests how central the concerns of a Jewish Theology of Religions are to Rav Kook's views of what constitute contemporary theological challenges.

These chapters contain some of the most startling statements regarding a Jewish view of other religions, and are a great treasure for the "pluralist" approach. Once we recognize the dominant concern of a Jewish Theology of Religions to establish the validity of other religions, we realize that this is indeed the heart of Rav Kook's project in these chapters. Like Meiri, and unlike Maimonides, he recognizes the validity of other religions as such, extending such validity even to idolatrous religions, following the principle that individuals are found who can receive the inspiration of the holy spirit, the lowest level of prophecy. These offer a moral teaching suitable to those religions. This includes religions that have no relationship to Judaism and that are classified as Avodah Zarah. The moral teaching is grounded in the dual perspectives of outstanding individuals and a form of divine guidance. These are adapted to the particularity of different peoples, each of

---

[32] I use the term as an alternative to systematic thinker. One may debate how systematic his thinking is, but it is certainly comprehensive in its scope and offers a view of what he considers most vital to a thriving Jewish outlook. Students, followers, and scholars have been engaged in the task of systematizing or working through the systematic implications of his vast corpus.

[33] Abraham Kook, *Linevuchei Hador* (Tel Aviv: Miskal Books, 2014).

[34] Ibid., chs. 8, 14(1), 39, 46, 52. That the discussion is not consecutive points to the fact that even this comprehensive discussion is not developed as a continuous unit of thought, but rather tackled from various perspectives that have to be brought together in order to construct his complete view.

which receives a teaching appropriate to its mentality and conditions. Foundational morality is supported by religious practices and doctrines that are relativized in relation to the receiving peoples. The concern of reducing religion to morality is overcome by the realization that those moral teachings are actually forms of revelation. Significantly, Rav Kook does not appeal to the classical notion of the Noachide commandments, stemming from one common revelation, itself a teaching of Judaism. In so doing, Rav Kook opens up a genuinely pluralist approach to other religions, based on notions of multiple revelations, righteous individuals, wisdom, the recognition that all is under God's guidance, and, finally, the divine love and concern for all.

Religions that spring forth from Judaism are higher as far as the purity of divine knowledge is concerned. Here Rav Kook makes an "inclusivist" move, considering their light to be received from the light of the Torah. That his view of idolatrous religions is pluralist and his view of Islam and Christianity is inclusivist and that these moves are made in close sequence suggests that, while it is interesting to use the classifications, inclusive and pluralist, in terms of his own thinking they would have little traction. Religions are ranked in line with the degree of light and truth they possess. Rav Kook's task is to establish mechanisms for recognizing their respective validity and to develop an ethos of respect and appreciation for all forms of the religious life. As he states, there is no need to hold other faiths as lacking in value in order for Judaism to have value. Rav Kook is painfully aware of the negative attitudes Jews apply to idolaters and seeks to replace these attitudes with respect through multiple strategies. His willingness to accommodate other religions extends to the recognition of the validity of miracles performed by great teachers, as necessary instruments for acceptance of their teachings as well as the accommodation of views that divinize teachers or see them as incarnations, as necessary adaptations to the theological condition of the receiving peoples. His approach is instrumentalist. He is willing to accept much that should be considered false in these religions, as it serves a good end: that of providing fundamental religious and moral teaching. Like Meiri, he is willing to accept religions including their particular beliefs and religious practices. However, while Meiri ignores these, focusing on the core principle of validation, Rav Kook articulates how the particularities of the religious life contribute to its core drive: advancement of the moral life and guidance toward fuller knowledge of God. Because Meiri's theory grows out of an attempt to contain talmudic legislation regarding the idolatrous non-

Jew, he never develops a fully fledged theory of how other religions relate to Judaism. Rav Kook does just that, and here a clear hierarchy emerges. Israel is at the top of the pyramid. Rav Kook's pluralism is designed to enhance respect and to offer fundamental validation. It does not proffer equal status. There is clear path of evolution toward the fullness of religious life, found only in the collectivity of Israel.

In this early work, Rav Kook considers the anti-Judaism of Judaism's daughter-religions as the dark side of their immature religious personality and is forgiving of it, seen in the larger context. This issue, however, will continue to capture his attention throughout his reflective career. The irenic views expressed by the early Rav Kook give way to a much more complex relationship to other religions, in his later works. The ingredients remain the same: a positive view of other religions, seen within a broader evolutionary perspective; appreciation of outstanding individuals; recognition of fundamental value in light of moral standards. However, these undergo significant complexification as Rav Kook considers Israel's spiritual reality and how it relates to other religions. Over and against the harmonious and irenic Rav Kook emerges a body of statements that elevates the metaphysical status of Israel. As this rises, so the value of other religions potentially decreases. Antisemitism and anti-Judaism, primarily of Christianity, feed into a highly critical view of Christianity, and undermine its moral authenticity, thereby pulling the rug from under the principle of validation that served Rav Kook in the first instance. An irenic tone is replaced by powerful polemics, couched in a unique spiritual and mystical language.

These changes occur even as the irenic tone and universal perspective are maintained. This leads to serious hermeneutical challenges in reconstructing the fuller views of Rav Kook's Theology of Religions, as expressed throughout his career. Are the later views a consequence of his increasing engagement in Kabbalah? Are they a result of encounter with Christianity over the years of World War I, when he was exiled in Europe? Do they reflect his moral stance as it developed in response to the reality of war? And should Rav Kook's thought be analysed by means of an attempt to describe a linear progression, or by identifying theoretical focal points and exploring each in its own right? The size of the corpus and its complexities, questions of development, and weighing the impact of external historical influences all make the task of reconstructing Rav Kook's lifelong project of engaging other religions a complex task. This task has never been undertaken systematically.

Contemporary theological needs as well as the recent publication of *Linevuchei Hador* make the task that much more urgent and exciting. In many ways Rav Kook encapsulates the challenges of a Jewish Theology of Religions and issues an invitation to serious and consistent attention to this area of study. While most of his students will content themselves with *ad hoc* citations of passages, taken out of context, Rav Kook himself is an example of a near-contemporary religious thinker, rooted in tradition in its full expanse, open to all with almost unprecedented universal love, and grounded in a direct experience and profound relationship with God. From this special position he reminds us that the task is timely and urgent. The challenges and complexities found in his oeuvre reflect the difficulty of the task at hand.

Bringing to light Rav Kook's previously unpublished early thought is a great boost to the field. Unpacking his full Theology of Religions over a lifetime of work will be a major contribution.[35] But above all, the person and precedent of Rav Kook are a reminder not only of how complex the field is but also of how vital it is. Rav Kook is testimony to the fact that Jewish spiritual and theological regeneration must include careful consideration of other religions. Rav Kook has been a prophetic figure for many aspects of contemporary Jewish rejuvenation. Here, then, is one other dimension of this great figure's prophetic role, extending to Judaism and world religions.

CONCLUSION

Jewish Theology of Religions is a field that very much exists and is yet in its infancy. Positions regarding other faiths abound in Jewish writings over three millennia. Yet, the task of reflecting on other religions in a systematic fashion from the vantage point of present-day relations between religions has only begun. For purposes of co-existence and advancing harmonious relations between religions, we possess the necessary tools and resources that allow Judaism to take its place in a constructive manner alongside other world religions on the global stage. However, the task of a Jewish Theology of Religions is more complex and goes to the core of Judaism's own vocation and mission. Accordingly, like Jewish theology and indeed Judaism itself, it is still work in progress. Recognizing this amounts to an invitation to engage

---

[35] I pray God will enable me to complete this task one day.

with the field in a thoughtful and considered manner. The essay presented herewith offers parameters for how such considered reflection may be undertaken.

Selected Further Reading

Blidstein, Gerald. "Maimonides and Meiri on the Legitimacy of Non-Judaic Religions." In *Scholars and Scholaship: The Interaction between Judaism and Other Cultures*, 27–35. Edited by Leo Landman. New York: Yeshiva University Press, 1990.

Brill, Alan. *Judaism and Other Religions: Models of Understanding*. New York: Palgrave Macmillan, 2010.

Goshen-Gottstein, Alon. "Genius Theologian, Lonely Theologian: Yitz Greenberg on Christianity." In *A Torah Giant: The Intellectual Legacy of Rabbi Dr. Irving (Yitz) Greenberg*, 71–92. Edited by Shmuly Yanklowitz. Jerusalem: Urim, 2018.

Goshen-Gottstein, Alon. *Luther the Antisemite: A Contemporary Jewish Perspective*. Minneapolis, MN: Fortress Press, 2018.

Goshen-Gottstein, Alon. *Religious Genius – Appreciating Outstanding Individuals Across Religions*. New York: Palgrave Macmillan, 2017.

Goshen-Gottstein, Alon, ed. *Religious Truth: Towards a Jewish Theology of Religions*. Oxford: Littman Library of Jewish Civilization, 2020.

Goshen-Gottstein, Alon. *Same God, Other God: Judaism, Hinduism and the Problem of Idolatry*. New York: Palgrave Macmillan, 2015.

Greenberg, Irving. *For the Sake of Heaven and Earth: The New Encounter Between Judaism and Christianity*. Philadelphia: Jewish Publication Society, 2004.

Halbertal, Moshe. "Ones Possessed of Religion: Religious Tolerance in the Teachings of the Me'iri." *The Edah Journal* 1.1 (2000).

Hartman, David. *Conflicting Visions: Spiritual Possibilities of Modern Israel*. New York: Schocken, 1990.

Katz, Jacob. *Exclusiveness and Tolerance*. Oxford: Oxford University Press, 1961.

Kogan, Michael. *Opening the Covenant: A Jewish Theology of Christianity*. Oxford: Oxford University Press, 2008.

Novak, David. *Jewish-Christian Dialogue*. Oxford: Oxford University Press, 1989.

Sacks, Jonathan. *The Dignity of Difference: How to Avoid the Clash of Civilizations*. London: Continuum, 2002.

Sherbok, Dan Cohn. *Judaism and Other Faiths*. Basingstoke: Macmillan, 1994.

PART V
ANALYTIC PHILOSOPHY AND THEOLOGY

16 Can There Be a Positive Theology?
KENNETH SEESKIN

One way to establish a positive theology is to argue that personhood is so central to our understanding of divinity that any theology which denies that God is a person cannot be valid. This is the issue at stake in the age-old controversy between the God of the philosophers and the God of Abraham, Isaac, and Jacob. The problem with this approach is that *personhood* is a loaded term. For human beings, being a person has to do with how one deals with fear, pain, insecurity, limited knowledge, disappointment, and relations with other people. Clearly God does not experience anything like this. For the purpose of this discussion, I will limit divine personhood to two faculties: knowledge and will. If God possesses these faculties, then he is capable of choosing between alternatives, which means that he can approve of some things and disapprove of others.

Instead of looking at the claims of people who argue for a stronger conception of divine personhood, I propose to examine the possibility of a positive theology by focusing on three thinkers generally associated with the opposite position: Maimonides, Kant, and Cohen. Contrary to what some may think, we will see that they all make contributions to positive theology in their own way.

MAIMONIDES: FROM THE VIA NEGATIVA TO THE VIA POSITIVA

We can begin by going to the heart of the enemy camp and examine Judaism's most distinguished practitioner of negative theology. For Maimonides the crux of negative theology is the claim that no attribute can be literally true of God. There are two reasons for this, one religious, one philosophic. The religious reason involves the desire to block the tendency to think of God as a bigger, better, stronger version of something else. Maimonides therefore maintains that "in every case in which you affirm of Him an additional thing [i.e., an attribute], you become one who likens Him to other things ..."[1] To liken God to other things—to find a common measure of comparison—is either to deify those things or to mundanize God. The religious term for either is idolatry.

As a bulwark against idolatry, Maimonides maintains throughout the *Guide of the Perplexed* that terms that apply to God and humans such as *knows*, *lives*, or *exists* are completely equivocal so that there is nothing in common between God's knowledge, life, or existence and ours. In fact, he is so insistent on this point that he maintains it must be taught to everyone, not just the educated few.[2]

The philosophic motive has to do with divine simplicity, a subject on which Maimonides is equally insistent:[3]

> For there is no oneness at all except in believing that there is one simple essence in which there is no complexity or multiplicity of notions, but one notion only; so that from whatever angle you regard it and from whatever point of view you consider it, you will find that it is one, not divided in any way and by any cause into two notions; and you will not find therein any multiplicity either in the thing as it is outside of the mind or as it is in the mind ...

Obviously the two motives are related for nothing else in the universe is simple in this way.

Equally obvious is the fact that the philosophic motive has more serious consequences than the religious. Equivocal predication is still a form of predication. Even if we say that God's knowledge has nothing in common with ours, the statement "God is wise" makes God the bearer of an attribute. By contrast, radical simplicity does not allow for any predication at all because to predicate one thing of another is to have two things before one's mind and therefore to admit complexity.

The problem with complexity is that in Maimonides' universe, nothing complex can be preeminent. Again there are two reasons for this. The first holds that if something falls under a larger category, it is a species of a genus. But, Maimonides replies, a genus (animal) is logically prior to its species (rational animal), from which it follows that if

---

[1] Moses Maimonides, *The Guide of the Perplexed*, trans. Shlomo Pines (Chicago: University of Chicago Press, 1963) 1.59, 139 [hereafter, *Guide*].
[2] *Guide* 1.35, 80.   [3] *Guide* 1.51, 113.

God belonged to a genus, something would be logically prior to God, which is absurd.[4] The second holds that anything that admits complexity in the form of two or more attributes must have a prior cause responsible for bringing the two together.[5] Thus a God who possessed multiple attributes would be dependent on something outside himself, which is equally absurd.

It follows that divine simplicity is incompatible with predication in any form. In keeping with the *via negativa*, Maimonides says that negations like "is not powerless" or "does not lack knowledge," are preferable to their positive counterparts because they do not purport to give us essential attributes. But, once again he replies, they are still objectionable because while they characterize God by way of exclusion, they do seek to characterize him, which means to make him the bearer of a property, albeit a negative one.[6]

It goes without saying that Maimonides has to pay a price for such an extreme position because everything the philosophic tradition regards as a metaphysical truth about God involves predication. For example:

God exists.
God is logically simple.
God is immutable.
God knows the form and structure of everything that exists.
God is responsible for everything that exists.
God performs actions that resemble actions in us that proceed from moral qualities.

Maimonides certainly allows us to say such things; in fact, he himself says them or things very much like them.[7] He offers multiple proofs for the existence and simplicity of God, and says that God's knowledge is perfect. Although he does not claim to know exactly *how* God is responsible for the existence of other things, he leaves no doubt *that* he is. That God performs actions that resemble moral actions

---

[4] *Guide* 1.52, 114–15. [5] *Guide* 2, Introduction, 238, Premise 21.
[6] See *Guide* 1.58, 134: "Thus the attributes of negation have in this respect something in common with the attributes of affirmation, for the former undoubtedly bring about some particularization even if the particularization due to them only exists in the exclusion of what has been negated ..."
[7] On this point, see Hilary Putnam, "On Negative Theology," *Faith and Philosophy*, 14 (1997): 407–13. Note that Putnam calls "God performs actions ..." the familiar antinomy of negative theology.

in us is part and parcel of his analysis of attributes of action.[8] So Maimonides cannot claim that these statements are meaningless. He can claim, however, that they are not true of God in the way that normal predicates are true of their subjects.

To take a simple example, consider "God exists." On the surface it may appear that "God exists" and "John exists" are parallel. But closer analysis shows that this cannot be true. For everything other than God, existence must be added to the subject in order to indicate that it has been realized. For God it is otherwise. Existence cannot be added to God without compromising divine simplicity.[9] Put otherwise, "God exists" cannot be about two things. It follows that for God and God alone, existence and essence must be identical. If so, then "exists" cannot be true of God in the way that it is true of everything else. Nor can "God exists" be taken as a literal truth without a great deal of explanation. The gist of that explanation is that "exists" is an equivocal term whose application to God exceeds the limits of human understanding.

The fact that these statements are not literally true raises an important question: Why should we hold that literal truth is the only legitimate form of assertion? Why can we not admit that something can be both meaningful and true because it is part of an educational process that leads the mind to the ultimate intellectual achievement: recognition of the ineffability of God? Along these lines, Maimonides says that while negative predicates are not literally true of God, they do serve a heuristic function to the degree that they "conduct the mind toward the utmost reach that man may attain in the apprehension of Him."[10]

If we admit that a statement can acquire its meaning by being part of a learning process, then metaphysical truths like those above have an important role to play. They form the basis of a positive theology of sorts, with the qualification that positive theology is a stepping stone to something higher rather than the last word on the subject. The last word is, in fact, no word at all as Maimonides makes clear when he quotes Psalm 65 ("Silence is praise to Thee").[11]

The standard objection to negative theology is that when we say "God is good" or "God is the cause of everything that exists" we think we are committing ourselves to more than a necessary step on the road

---

[8] I will have more to say about attributes of action below. [9] See *Guide* 1.57 and 1.63.
[10] *Guide* 1.58, 135. [11] *Guide* 1.59, 139.

to silence.[12] If silence is the highest praise, why do we have three prayer services a day? At a more technical level, Gersonides objected that Maimonides has committed himself to a pernicious form of metaphysical realism.[13]

According to Gersonides, predication implies plurality if one part of a proposition attributing something to God is a real subject or genus for the other part; it does not imply plurality if one part is only a linguistic subject. To see his point, consider a simple example. "This redness is a red color" does not imply that redness is composed of two things—redness and color—because color does not exist as a separate entity. In Gersonides' words, it is only a linguistic subject and thus the proposition in question is a nominal as opposed to a real definition. This means that the proposition is an account of how a name is used rather than an account of a thing. As applied to God, Gersonides argues that attributes like goodness, knowledge, or power are not real subjects that inhere in God but just names that we apply to God. As such, they do not imply that God is complex any more than Gersonides' example of redness implies that it is complex.

Plausible as this objection may seem, Maimonides could reply as follows. I can regard redness as a single thing if I look at a color patch in isolation from everything else. But if I am painting my kitchen and considering red as opposed to green or yellow, then redness does share something with other colors beyond a linguistic name or *flatus vocis*. There is a reason why red, green, or yellow are grouped together and it is not just that we happen to talk that way. As Harry Wolfson put it in characterizing Maimonides' position: "Universals ... exist in the mind, but the human mind does not *invent* them out of nothing. What the mind does is only *discover* them in the multifarious individuals."[14]

---

[12] Students of medieval philosophy will note that this objection was voiced by Thomas Aquinas in *Summa Theologica* 13.2.
[13] See Gersonides (Levi ben Gershon), *Wars of the Lord*, Vol. 2, Book 3, trans. Seymour Feldman (Philadelphia: Jewish Publication Society, 1987), 112–14.
[14] Harry A. Wolfson, "Crescas on Divine Attributes," *Jewish Quarterly Review* 8 (1916): 12–13. Note, as Wolfson does in n. 12, that Maimonides' remark at *Guide* 3.18, 474 ("I say that it is known that no species exists outside the mind, but that the species and the other universals, are, as you know, mental notions and that every existent outside the mind is an individual or a group of individuals") should not be taken to mean that Maimonides was a nominalist in a strict sense. All it means is that he did not believe, as Plato did, that species or universals exist separately from the things that embody them. While Maimonides was not a Platonist, it does not follow that he thought species and universals were simply verbal expressions.

Unless this were true, why do we not say that red, green, and, say, sweetness are all colors?

Needless to say, the debate between realists and nominalists will not be resolved in this essay. My point is that Gersonides' objection to negative theology simply assumes that nominalism is true. If it is not, if when thinking about how to paint my kitchen I have two things before my mind—a specific color and the property it shares with other colors—then the objection falls apart. As we saw, Maimonides argued that there cannot be any multiplicity in God *either* as he is outside the mind *or* as he is in the mind. Given a claim like "God is good," we cannot help but hold two things before our mind, in which case we are thinking of God as complex.

Behind Maimonides' view is what one might call his gut feeling that once we make God the subject of predication and apply a litany of predicates, we compromise God's uniqueness no matter what our position on the realism/nominalism debate. Better to say that our final approach to God is to give up predication in any form and be content with a studied silence.

That silence is characterized as follows:[15]

> Glory then to Him who is such that when the intellects contemplate His essence, their apprehension turns into incapacity; and when they contemplate the proceeding of His actions from His will, their knowledge turns into ignorance; and when the tongues aspire to magnify Him by means of attributive qualifications, all eloquence turns into weariness and incapacity!

As indicated above, Maimonides pays a high price for this view. If our apprehension turns into incapacity and our knowledge into ignorance, then strictly speaking, theology, which is to say a *logos* or account of God, is impossible.

Loosely speaking, it is not. As we saw, positive statements about God are permissible *given the appropriate qualifications*. Those statements comprise a theology according to which God exists, is active, and is neither a body nor a force in a body. But there is another reason to say things about God: our sense that God is the source of morality. Unless God is merciful, gracious, and willing to forgive sin, it would be hard to explain what we are doing when we offer praise to God.

---

[15] *Guide* 1.58, 137.

To stay with Maimonides, God's moral qualities are explained with reference to the aforementioned attributes of action. Maimonides' exact wording on such attributes reads as follows:[16]

> The meaning here is not that He possesses moral qualities, but that He performs actions resembling the actions that in us proceed from moral qualities – I mean from aptitudes of the soul; the meaning is not that He ... possesses aptitudes of the soul.

The biblical text in question is Exodus 33, where God tells Moses that while he cannot see God's face, God will reveal his goodness or back side. The goodness of God revealed to Moses is then described as follows (Exodus 34:6–7):

> A God compassionate and gracious, slow to anger, abounding in kindness and faithfulness, extending kindness to the thousandth generation, forgiving iniquity, transgression and sin; yet he does not remit all punishment ...

Not only are these attributes predicative in nature but, according to tradition, there are thirteen of them. Maimonides responds by saying that the moral attributes are not properties of God himself but properties of the world God has created—everything about which God said "Behold, it is very good" at Genesis 1:31.[17]

To use his examples, God is said to be merciful when one observes the extent to which animals in the natural order are given the necessary means to protect themselves and forage for food. God is called gracious because he has given the gift of existence to things that have no right to claim it. What is noteworthy about these claims is the qualification with which they are expressed: not that God *is* merciful or gracious but that he is *said to be* merciful and *called* gracious.

Let us grant that Maimonides has provided an analysis that makes praise of God meaningful even if it is not the meaning most people understand. Again the question is whether his analysis captures everything we want to say. If Maimonides is right, our praise of God is indirect, hence the reference to God's back side at Exodus 33. Instead of praising what God *is*, we are praising what God has *made* or *done*.

To this one could object that the writings of the prophets contain no such distinction: God detests injustice, religious hypocrisy, promise-breaking, and anything else that involves one person taking advantage

---

[16] *Guide* 1.54, 124. [17] Ibid.

of another. Maimonides can account for this too. Cruel or antisocial behavior creates an environment in which it is difficult for people to perfect their nature as human beings.[18] That is what is meant by saying that God is angry. But the fact remains that the Bible leaves us with a much stronger impression: that God *himself* is merciful and gracious and that God *himself* detests injustice, religious hypocrisy, promise-breaking, etc.

THE PRACTICAL TURN

Having rejected much of traditional metaphysics, Immanuel Kant argued that it was moral ideas, not metaphysical ones, that gave rise to the correct conception of God.[19] In the same vein, Hermann Cohen pointed out that among the various qualities revealed to Moses at Exodus 34, metaphysical ones such as omniscience or omnipotence are nowhere mentioned.[20] The upshot is that Moses is not invited to think about God as he is in himself but (for Maimonides) God in relation to the world or (for Cohen) God in relation to human beings.

No doubt Cohen overstates his case by claiming that for Maimonides the place of being is taken by action.[21] Still it is hard not think that he is on to something. It is as if God has said to Moses: "Don't focus on me as I am in myself but to me as I relate to you." Cohen took this to mean that it is not God's causal activity that should concern us but his status as an agent who acts for a purpose. The problem is that to conceive of God as an agent, we have to ascribe to him the two faculties mentioned at the beginning of this essay: knowledge and will. The problem is that doing so resurrects the issue of complexity. If God possesses both, then in addition to understanding the alternatives before him, he must choose one over all the others.

Maimonides agrees that God always acts with a purpose in mind.[22] Once we get beyond the negative theology chapters and move into the practical chapters, he allows himself considerable license in saying how God's knowledge and will are related. Sometimes he suggests that they are distinct—as when he says that God does not will everything that is

---

[18] *Guide* 3.27, 511; 3.54, 635.   [19] Kant, *Critique of Pure Reason*, A816/B844 ff.
[20] Hermann Cohen, *Religion of Reason out of the Sources of Judaism*, trans. Simon Kapan (New York: Frederick Ungar, 1972), 94.
[21] Note that when it comes to the Tetragrammaton (*Guide* 1.61, 148; 1.63, 156), Maimonides is quite happy to talk about simple or necessary existence.
[22] *Guide* 3.25, 503–05; 3.31, 523–4.

possible but only what his wisdom requires.[23] This implies that God wills only a subset of all the possibilities that he understands, namely those that make rational sense. If this is the case, then the object of his knowledge must be greater (perhaps infinitely greater) than the object of his will, from which it follows that his knowledge and his will are different.

At other times, he suggests that knowledge and will are the same—as when he says that one can refer to either God's will or his wisdom in seeking an explanation.[24] The best example of this occurs at *Guide* 3.14, 456, where he claims that when we give up the need to seek the final end of everything, our soul becomes calm because we accept the fact that some things depend for their existence on the divine will or, "if you prefer you can also say: on the divine wisdom." Sometimes, as in the passage quoted above, he suggests that will is consequent on wisdom, and sometimes that wisdom has the power to choose between alternatives.[25]

In keeping with Aristotle, Maimonides might have distinguished theoretical wisdom, which grasps everything that is logically possible, from practical wisdom, which focuses on things that fulfill a noble purpose. Unfortunately, there is no term in the *Guide* that is the equivalent of Aristotle's *phronesis*. Moreover, a distinction between two types of divine knowledge would imply even more complexity in God. Recall that it is not just that God as he is outside the mind who cannot admit complexity but that our conception of God in the mind cannot admit it either.

Rather than accuse Maimonides of inconsistency, or of trying to address two different audiences, it would be better to say that he came up against an intractable problem. If we maintain strict adherence to divine simplicity, we end up with silence. If we let in basic metaphysical claims about God, we end up with deism, by which I mean a God who serves as the unconditioned ground of existence but nothing more. If we want to talk about God as an agent who exercises will and discretion, then we have to make compromises with divine simplicity. God must know the difference between good and evil, desire the former and reject the latter. According to Kant, this move represents the transition from conceiving of God as the cause of the world to conceiving of him as the author of the world.[26]

---

[23] Ibid., 504.   [24] *Guide* 1.69, 202; 2.27, 332–33.
[25] Also see *Guide* 2.19, 302; 3.26, 509.
[26] Immanuel Kant, *Lectures on Philosophical Theology*, trans. Allen W. Wood and Gertrude M. Clark (Ithaca, NY: Cornell University Press, 1978), 29.

In contrast to Maimonides, Spinoza bit the bullet. If God cannot admit complexity in any form, then God's knowledge and will must be identical. This means that God must know everything he wills and will everything he knows. Because God's knowledge is both necessary and eternal, God's will must be necessary and eternal as well.[27] If so, then God cannot do anything different from what he has always done, in which case it makes no sense to say that God chooses a noble purpose over an ignoble one.[28] By the same token, if God is not affected by anything, he cannot love or hate anyone.[29] By identifying God with nature (*deus sive natura*), Spinoza sought to eliminate any sense of personality in God.[30]

Maimonides too said that nothing that exists necessarily serves a purpose.[31] But unlike Spinoza, he parts company with causal determinism. While the existence of God is eternal and necessary, the same is not true of the world for which God is responsible. On the contrary: "What exists, it causes, and its effects, could be different from what they are."[32] So while God's existence does not serve a purpose, the things God has made do. Accordingly:[33]

> For we say that in virtue of His will He has brought into existence all the parts of the world, some of which have been intended for their own sakes, whereas others have been intended for the sake of some other thing that has been intended for its own sake.

This does not mean that we can always determine which things are which. Nor does it mean that all things exist for the sake of humans. What it means is that "All that exists was intended by Him ... according to His volition."[34] The same is true when it comes to the law, where Maimonides continues to talk about God's intention.[35]

It follows that, despite the austerity of his negative theology, when it comes to practical matters, Maimonides was willing to make the transition from God as cause to God as author. This allowed him to put forward what could be regarded as a positive theology in another sense. God is not only the creator of the world but a governor who rules over it. That world is one in which every species is generously provided

---

[27] Benedict Spinoza, *Ethics*, trans. Edwin Curley (London: Penguin Classics), 1.17, scholium and 1.33.
[28] Ibid., 1. Appendix.   [29] Ibid., 5. 17c.   [30] Ibid., 4. Preface.   [31] *Guide* 3.13, 448–49.
[32] Ibid., 452.   [33] Ibid.   [34] Ibid., 3.13, 454.   [35] Ibid., 3.13, 530.

for. The human species has been given a law which shows it how to achieve the highest level of perfection.

We can dispute whether God revealed his intention to Moses or whether Moses was wise enough to understand what God wants. Either way, human beings are in possession of a list of the things God likes and hates. Those who study the list and endeavor to live by it will come to forgo bodily pleasures, love God above all else, and in so doing inherit eternal life. Although Maimonides allows for the possibility of miracles, when push comes to shove, they are temporary occurrences and do not contribute much to the overall picture.[36] In the end, all that matters is study, reflection, and obedience to the commandments.

Reasonable as this theology is, by encouraging us to think of God as an author or governor, it runs the risk of anthropomorphism. Both would be objectionable to Spinoza, whose God neither creates nor oversees the natural order. Maimonides' way of answering the charge of anthropomorphism would be to treat these terms as attributes of action. Even though it is legitimate to think of God as an author or a governor, it does not follow that these are properties of God in the normal way. God's internal nature is as mysterious as ever. All we are saying is that the world for which God is responsible exhibits qualities that resemble a well-constructed book or a well-governed city. Asked *how* God is responsible for such a world, once again we would have to plead ignorance. As Maimonides admits in his discussion of the Book of Job: "Our intellects do not reach the point of apprehending how these natural things that exist in the world of generation and corruption are produced in time..."[37]

It is clear that in order to say something positive about God, Maimonides has to leave us with a great deal of unknowing. Although intellect and will must combine to form a unity in God, we cannot say how. Nor can we say how God comes to produce a world that exhibits order and purpose. From Maimonides' perspective, confessions of ignorance are the price we pay for trying to imbue our understanding of God with moral significance. While those who are unwilling to pay this price may achieve logical consistency, they will have to pay another price which is even more egregious: A God who, contrary to Exodus 34, is indifferent to mercy, justice, or forgiveness of sin.

---

[36] *Guide* 2.25, 329. [37] *Guide* 3.23, 496.

THE PRACTICAL TURN IN KANT

By the time we get to Kant and Cohen, metaphysics no longer takes center stage. According to Kant, the deistic conception of God "is wholly idle and useless and makes no impression on me if I assume it alone."[38] As a result, he opts for a conception of God that brings together creator of the world and author of our moral laws—better yet an author who serves as an ideal of perfect morality and therefore a model for us to emulate. As Kant saw it, the value of metaphysics (or what he calls *ontotheology*) is that it allows us to purify our conception of God of anything connected with empirical principles or the realm of sense.[39] Such is his defense against the charge of anthropomorphism. But in purifying our conception of God, we must still make room for life, intelligence, and will if it is to have any influence over our behavior.

More precisely, God influences our behavior in the following way. Reason compels us to pursue the highest good, which consists of a state in which people achieve happiness in proportion to their virtue. This is only possible if the realm of nature can be brought into harmony with the realm of freedom. Since there is no a priori connection between nature and freedom, the only thing that can insure their compatibility is an author who brought nature into existence with a moral purpose in mind. Therefore, morality demands a supreme being who possesses life, intelligence, and will in superlative fashion.

At this point we face a familiar problem: How can we know what life, intelligence, and will are in God without basing our understanding on what they are in us? As Kant points out "many of our concepts are associated with determinations which have some deficiency in them."[40] Again he turns to the *via negativa* for help, hoping to root out anything that smacks of sensibility. But as he himself comes to see, there is a question of what will be left once the *via negativa* does its work. According to him, what we find will be "quite insignificant and small in degree."[41]

As a second solution, Kant turns to the *via eminentiae* which provides a limited but positive conception of God. Whatever properties God has must be compatible with an infinite degree of perfection, thus infinite knowledge and an infinitely pure will. This would rule out anything connected with space or time. A lesser thinker would now be satisfied that he had cleared the ground for a positive conception of

---

[38] Kant, *Lectures*, 30.   [39] Ibid., 32, 79–81.   [40] Ibid., 52.   [41] Ibid., 53.

God and thus for a positive theology. God has all perfections to an infinite degree.

For better or worse, Kant still expresses doubts. In humans, intelligence and purity of will do not always go hand in hand. Though I cannot infer that they are incompatible in God, neither can I infer that they are compatible. To infer compatibility, I would have to know that all possible effects of one are compatible with all possible effects of the other. More fully:[42]

> Applying this to God, I must all the more admit my inability to see how a synthesis of all possible realities could be possible as regards their effects. For how can my reason presume to know how all the highest realities [perfections] operate, what effects would follow from them, and what sort of relation all these realities would have to each other? But I would have to be able to know this if I wanted to see whether or not all realities could be united together in one object. And only this would show me whether God is possible.

He concludes that while we cannot prove that God is possible, neither can we prove that God is impossible. To be sure, there are grounds for supposing that God is possible such as the need for a benevolent author of the world to ground our obligation to pursue the highest good. Near the end of the *First Critique* (A 828/B 856), he claims that nothing can shake his belief in God since if God did not exist, our moral principles would be overthrown and we would become abhorrent in our own eyes. Yet powerful as this motive is, it shows that theology rests more on hope than on knowledge.

GOD AS THE GUARANTOR OF REDEMPTION

Not surprisingly, Cohen follows Kant in arguing that it is God's moral significance that matters most. Although he accepts the principle of divine simplicity, it does not play nearly as important a role in his thought as it does in that of Maimonides. In fact, Cohen argues that simplicity is not enough because all it does is separate God from matter, which by its very nature is composite.[43] Rather monotheism requires uniqueness (*Einzigkeit*), which means that God is not only separate from but incomparable to anything else. This is what distinguishes monotheism from pantheism, which Cohen considers just as

---

[42] Ibid., 57.   [43] Cohen, *Religion of Reason*, 44.

objectionable as anthropomorphism. Instead of being that *in* which or *through* which the world exists, God transcends the world and serves as its logical ground. Cohen therefore invokes the terms *being* and *existence* (*Dasein*) to characterize this relationship. Existence presupposes being in the way that things which change presuppose something permanent. Only God has true being.

Obviously Cohen cannot leave things there because it would give us a God completely removed from the world. This would mean that God's uniqueness is entirely negative and that our understanding of God has no ethical import. As Cohen puts it: "God cannot remain without the world, without the human world."[44] To introduce ethical significance to our understanding of God, Cohen argues for two points. The first is that God is not just separate from the world, but as the ground or origin of existence, its creator. Again from Cohen: "Thus, being properly speaking, is not conceived for its own sake ..."[45] Or, more fully: "Creation is God's primary attribute; it is not only the consequence of the uniqueness of God's being; creation is simply identical with it."[46]

As a creator, God's uniqueness implies that he is related to the world and yet transcendent to it. Still the world is not an ethical concept. That brings us to Cohen's second point: God's full significance can be grasped only to the degree that he is related to the human world. It is here that we get the claim that God is the ground and eternal source of morality. Cohen characterizes the relation between God and humans as *correlation*, which means that the terms, though related, remain distinct. This eliminates any suggestion of pantheism, mystical union, or a Hegelian-like identity through difference. From Cohen's perspective, then, God is separate from the world but intimately involved with it.

This involvement reaches its highest point when a person comes to God seeking redemption. If the moral law were the only standard against which we could measure ourselves, then, Cohen insists, its abstract nature would have no ability to free us from sin.[47] To overcome sin, which is to realize our full potential as human beings, we must come before God, take responsibility for our past actions, and ask for forgiveness. As Cohen puts it: "The redemption by God leads us to the reconciliation of man with himself ... It is only the reconciliation with God which brings the individual to his maturity as the I."[48] Or better yet, it is only by taking responsibility for our past actions and exercising

---

[44] Ibid., 45, cf. 59–61.   [45] Ibid., 60.   [46] Ibid., 67.   [47] Ibid., 87.   [48] Ibid., 189.

the freedom to change our ways that we realize our freedom as moral agents.

In this way, the act of seeking redemption brings God and human into correlation with each other. Humans need God to complete the task of sanctification because without God there would be no way to liberate ourselves from the guilt and despair that comes with taking responsibility for what we have done. By the same token, unless God is capable of granting forgiveness, in Cohen's eyes, his goodness would be in doubt.[49] Cohen therefore goes so far as to say that "the entire monotheistic worship is based on forgiveness of sin."[50]

The basic claim that Kant and Cohen are making is that we need a certain conception of God to arrive at an adequate conception of ourselves. We must now ask whether this claim is justified. Is our inability to understand ourselves without God reason enough to say that we have come to the proper understanding of God? Cohen would replay that without God's goodness, our conception of God would be entirely negative, taking us back to a God who is idle and useless as far as we are concerned. This is the God whose worship consists in the studied silence that Maimonides found in Psalm 65. But, Cohen would add, this God was too restrictive for Maimonides and is certainly too restrictive for us. Other than trying to characterize God as he relates to us, what choice do we have?

The answer is that we have no real choice as long as we assume that it is the practical dimension of God that matters most. By now it should be clear that this too is problematic. Why should we assume this? Two answers suggest themselves. First there is Exodus 33, which says that God revealed all of his goodness to Moses. Second there is the prayer book which consists almost exclusively of praises of God. So Kant and Cohen do have a leg to stand on.

At a deeper level, though, Kant and Cohen are assuming that metaphysics, including proofs for the existence of God, were disposed of in *The Critique of Pure Reason*. Not everyone would agree. Though Maimonides thought that the metaphysics of his day had flaws, it is far from clear that he would have agreed with the criticisms offered by Kant. Like most medievals, he offered a variety of proofs for God's existence. Behind these proofs is the assumption that knowledge leading to the existence of a thing is different from knowledge leading to its essence.[51] Accordingly we can know *that* God is even if we cannot say

---

[49] Ibid., 209.   [50] Ibid.   [51] *Guide* 1.46, 97.

what God is. In any case, Maimonides would not have agreed that our sole reason for believing in God is that doing so allows us to arrive at an adequate understanding of ourselves.

CONCLUSION

Let us return to the central question: Is there such a thing as a positive theology? The simple answer is yes. In one way or another, all three of the thinkers we have considered have positive things to say about God. But we would be ignoring a wealth of material if we failed to add that positive theology comes at a cost. In the case of Maimonides, the cost involves tolerating a less than rigorous account of divine simplicity. In the case of Kant and Cohen, it involves approaching God from the standpoint of a human-centered world.

It is not my purpose to proclaim one or the other of these views correct. My claim is more modest: that under the circumstances, none of them can be known to be true. If theology is measured against the standard of an established science such as biology, geology, or psychology, then it will fall short due to the lack of agreement on basic principles. That raises yet another question: Is this a fair comparison? Do we expect theology to settle questions once and for all or do we expect it to offer guidance on what is by any estimation a speculative and controversial subject matter? I submit that it is the latter.

Even if we turn to Maimonides, who is often regarded as a dogmatist on these matters, we find him saying that the secrets of the Torah are not fully and completely known to anyone so that his purpose in writing the *Guide* is that the truth be glimpsed and then concealed.[52] Moreover one who has come to understand some of these secrets "will be unable to explain with complete clarity and coherence even the portion that he has apprehended, as he could do with the other sciences whose teaching is generally recognized."[53] This is another way of saying that when we are talking about God, the biggest mistake we can make is not to admit an ample amount of humility. It is not just that God is more exalted than we are but that, as beings whose knowledge is tied to experience of the earthly realm, our grasp of what is beyond it comes in bits and pieces if it comes at all.

The mention of humility takes us back to negative theology. Whatever one may think about the logic of predication, negative

[52] *Guide* 1, Introduction, 6–7.   [53] *Guide* 1, Introduction, 8.

theology has the virtue of reminding us that we cannot approach God in the way that we approach other subjects. There is nothing superior to God from which we can derive conclusions *about* him and nothing in the world comparable to God from which we can extrapolate *to* him. Anything we say about God is paradoxical in the sense that it represents a human attempt to come to grips with something that exceeds the limits of human understanding. If a studied silence is too austere to satisfy our religious needs, then we should admit that as soon as we go beyond it, we must proceed with the utmost caution recognizing that anything we say will be fraught with difficulties.

Selected Further Reading

Cohen, Hermann. *Religion of Reason out of the Sources of Judaism*. Translated by Simon Kapan. New York: Frederick Ungar, 1972.

Gershon, Levi. *Wars of the Lord*, Vol. 2, Book 3. Translated by Seymour Feldman. Philadelphia: Jewish Publication Society, 1987.

Kant, Immanuel. *Lectures on Philosophical Theology*. Translated by Allen W. Wood and Gertrude M. Clark. Ithaca, NY: Cornell University Press, 1978.

Maimonides, Moses. *The Guide of the Perplexed*. Translated by Shlomo Pines. Chicago: University of Chicago Press, 1963.

Putnam, Hilary. "On Negative Theology." *Faith and Philosophy* 14 (1997): 407–13.

Spinoza, Benedict. *Ethics*. Translated by Edwin Curley. London: Penguin Classics, 2005.

Wolfson, Harry A. "Crescas on Divine Attributes." *Jewish Quarterly Review* 8 (1916): 12–13.

17 Theological Realism and its Alternatives in Contemporary Jewish Theology

CASS FISHER

The central claim of theological realism is the belief that God exists independently of our thought about God. Understood on such terms, the most ardent proponents of natural theology and the most demure adherents of negative theology could both endorse theological realism. Theological realism is, however, much more than a claim about God's independent existence; it is an inquiry into the power and limits of theological language and our ability to acquire knowledge of God. According to John Hick, "the debate between realist and non-realist understandings of religious language exposes the most fundamental of all issues in the philosophy of religion today."[1] For Hick, the question of theological realism is principally a modern one spurred by Ludwig Feuerbach's depiction of theology as a human projection. Although one might look to earlier strata of modern philosophy, particularly Kant, as instigating concerns regarding theological realism, Hick is surely correct that interest in theological realism intensified in the modern period along with the critiques of metaphysics and theology in German idealism, logical positivism, phenomenology, and postmodern thought. While Jewish thinkers have made important contributions to the debates regarding theological realism, overall, Jewish philosophers and theologians have addressed theological realism more obliquely than their Christian counterparts. Michael Scott and Andrew Moore have averred that "the interpretation and relative importance of the various aspects of the realism problem as well as the types of antirealist opposition, differ with each philosophical setting."[2] Similarly, one must admit that discussions of theological realism have a unique constellation in Judaism where the role of theology has been far

---

[1] John Hick, "Religious Realism and Non-realism," in *Disputed Questions in Theology and the Philosophy of Religion* (New Haven, CT: Yale University Press, 1993), 3–16, p. 3.
[2] Andrew Moore and Michael Scott, eds. *Realism and Religion: Philosophical and Theological Perspectives* (Aldershot: Ashgate, 2007), 1.

less secure in the modern period than it is in Christianity. As I intend to show, Jewish scholars have reflected deeply on the question of theological realism but laying out the alternatives they have proposed resists a neat schematism that can easily distinguish realists from their opponents.

For theological realism to be more than a claim about God's independent existence an additional cognitive requirement is necessary indicating how we come to such knowledge. Although there will be reasons to qualify this term shortly, I will refer to this as theological realism's "knowledge condition." Specifying the parameters of this knowledge condition has been a central feature of discussions of theological realism throughout the twentieth century. For instance, Douglas Carver writes in the preface to the 1931 edited collection *Religious Realism*:

> Religious Realism, as the term is used in this volume, means centrally the view that a religious Object, such as may appropriately be called God, exists independently of our consciousness thereof, and is yet related to us in such a way that through reflection on experience in general and religious experience in particular, and without any dependence upon the familiar arguments of epistemological idealism, it is possible for us to gain either (as some would maintain) adequately verified knowledge or (as others would be content to affirm) a practically valuable and theoretically permissible faith not only that that religious Object exists but also, within whatever limits, as to what its nature is.[3]

While in the aftermath of logical positivism and A. J. Ayer's verificationist challenge to religious language, theological realists no longer speak of "adequately verified knowledge," the debate about what constitutes the proper knowledge condition for theological realism persists. A helpful first step in assessing alternative accounts of the knowledge condition is to look at the critics of theological realism and their claims about the cognitive support necessary to uphold a realist position. Merold Westphal, in his essay, "Theological Anti-Realism," writes:

> The crucial issue in the realism/anti-realism debate is epistemic not metaphysical. To define a realism that is incompatible with

---

[3] Douglas C. Macintosh, ed. *Religious Realism* (New York: Macmillan, 1931), Cited in William Owen, Review of *Religious Realism*, ed. D. C. Macintosh, *Review & Expositor* 30.3 (1933): 341–44.

Kantian anti-realism we will require a double thesis, first metaphysical and then epistemic. Realism is the view (a) that the real is and is what is independently of what, if anything, we may think or say about it, and (b) that we human knowers are capable of knowing it as it is in that independence, mirroring it without distortion. Theological realism, our present concern, would be the special case of this double thesis applied to God.[4]

Westphal believes realism to require perfect knowledge of God's independent existence, a criterion so demanding that the knowledge necessary to secure theological realism would be identical to God's self-knowledge. Peter Byrne rejects the idea that theological realism requires a "God's-eye view of all of the facts"[5] and instead offers a seemingly more modest knowledge condition that emphasizes the "accumulation of reliable belief."[6] Byrne argues:

> Beliefs which are the product of rational procedures are to be explained differently from those which are not. If a system of thought shows no evidence that it has been open to the truth, that is a strong indication that is not the product of genuine rational procedures. That such a system of thought has been closed to the truth, and with it real-world influences via truth-indicators, is in turn indicated by the absence of accumulation of insight and discovery in it.[7]

In Byrne's view, there is no evidence that religious beliefs are produced in such a manner that there is an increase in our knowledge of God. He says of the Christian tradition that over its entire history "the stock of reliable beliefs about the Christian God, about its attributes and plans, has not increased one iota."[8] Accordingly, Christianity, and presumably other religious traditions along with it, is not a form of realism.

Proponents of theological realism have not produced a widely accepted knowledge condition nor is there agreement that such a condition is necessary. John Hick, for instance, defends what he calls a "critical realism" modeled on Kant's philosophy. In Hick's view, all religions refer to the same ultimate reality but do so through the conceptual framework of their specific traditions. According to Hick, this

---

[4] Merold Westphal, "Theological Anti-Realism," in *Realism and Religion*, 131–45, p. 132.
[5] Peter Byrne, *God and Realism* (Aldershot: Ashgate, 2003), 70.   [6] Ibid., 162.
[7] Ibid., 159.   [8] Ibid., 162.

ultimate reality is a noumenal being that we cannot know in itself. For Hick, the truth of religious beliefs is not assessed according to their correspondence with reality but rather by their effectiveness in moving the practitioner from self-centeredness to God-centeredness.[9] As our religious language fails to capture the truth about God there is no role for a knowledge condition in Hick's account. A number of Christian proponents of theological realism are also associated with Reformed epistemology, but here, too, the term "knowledge condition" is not entirely fitting. Following Thomas Reid, Reformed epistemologists reject the internalist criterion that we should have cognitive access to that which secures our beliefs. In their view, this is not how we formulate the vast majority of our beliefs. For the reformed epistemologists, we have no alternative but to rely on our standard belief-forming practices, even within the precincts of religion. Alvin Plantinga defends Calvin's notion that we have an innate source for the formation of religious beliefs, the *sensus divinitatis*, which can produce "properly basic beliefs," that is, beliefs that have warrant and are not inferred from or dependent upon other beliefs.[10] William Alston defends the contribution that mystical perception makes to our religious beliefs and to do so he brings together Reid's commonsense philosophy with Wittgenstein's work on forms of life. For Alston, it is rational for us to rely on our "socially established" belief-forming practices, among which he includes "Christian mystical practice," so long as we have no reason to believe them to be unreliable.[11]

Westphal is correct to see theological realism as consisting of both metaphysical and epistemological issues, but some advocates of theological realism also highlight a third semantic component emphasizing our capacity to refer to and make truth-claims about God. Andrew Moore brings these points together when he defines realism along the following lines:

> The philosophical doctrine known as realism can be expressed in terms of three characteristic claims. Ontologically, the realist holds that there is a reality independent of and external to human minds

---

[9] John Hick, *An Interpretation of Religion: Human Responses to the Transcendent* (London: Macmillan, 1989), 36.
[10] Alvin Plantinga, *Warranted Christian Belief* (Oxford: Oxford University Press, 2000).
[11] William Alston, *Perceiving God: The Epistemology of Religious Experience* (Ithaca, NY: Cornell University Press, 1991).

and that its being what it is does not depend on our conceptions or sense experiences of it (as idealists hold); reality is there to be discovered as it objectively is rather than subjectively invented, constructed, or projected. Epistemologically, the realist holds that reality can be (approximately) known as it is and not just as it appears to us to be. Semantically, the realist holds that it is possible to refer successfully to reality and so make (approximately) true statements about it.[12]

Transferred to the religious context, theological realism makes three principal claims: "(1) God exists independently of our awareness of him, but that (2) despite this, we can know him, and that (3) human language is not an inadequate or inappropriate medium of truthful speech about God."[13] Including a semantic component in theological realism brings to light the significant implications realism has for how we understand theological language. For those who embrace the semantic component of realism, theological realism entails an affirmation of our theological language and our ability to know God. Indeed, it is the support realism brings to theological language that motivates many realists. Speaking of Christianity, but in terms that could easily be extended to Judaism, William Alston writes:

> The basic point is that it is fundamental to traditional Christian understanding that we interact with God in various ways, both here and hereafter. This interaction can be initiated from either side. From the divine side God is portrayed as active in human history, shaping the destiny of people and peoples in accordance with His master plan for His creation—selecting the Hebrews for a special mission and destiny, communicating His will to us through them, rescuing them from bondage in Egypt, seeking to influence them through the prophets, becoming incarnate in order to release us from sin and death and initiate a new covenant, guiding the church through its history, and so on. From our side we enter into dialogue with God in prayer, and we respond, or not, to His actions and messages. Thus God is taken to be a real presence in the world, a supreme personal being with whom we can enter into personal

---

[12] Andrew Moore, "Theological Realism and the Observability of God," *International Journal of Systematic Theology* 2.1 (2000): 79–99, p. 80.
[13] Ibid., 81.

relationships, a being Who, to understate it, enjoys a reality in His own right, independently of us and our cognitive doings.[14]

In Alston's view, the Christian religious life requires an understanding of God as an independent being about whom much is known and said. In his view, these are fundamental requirements of the divine–human relationship. Moving away from matters internal to the religious life, Roger Trigg offers an alternative defense of theological realism that takes truth seriously. When religion is construed as private and subjective it loses its claim to truth and its place in public discourse. As he says, "what is subjective merely relates to individuals. What is objective, and independent of all our conceptions, is of concern to all. Realism must in the end be a philosophy about public religion, and it must make all religion, true or false, a fit subject for public reasoning."[15]

If as Alston claims realism plays a crucial role in conceptualizing and fostering the divine–human relationship and as Trigg claims realism secures religion's place in public discourse, why have Jewish philosophers and theologians been reluctant to adopt realist approaches to Jewish theological language? This is a complicated story that could be told in different ways. I will here only sketch what I take to be the most significant factors that have made a realist approach to theological language less attractive in the Jewish context.

Beginning from the perspective of the Hebrew Bible, it is surprising that theological realism has not been more dominant in contemporary Jewish theology. As William Alston articulated above, it is, surely, a core message of the Hebrew Bible that God enters into relationship with humans, a position that requires God's independent existence and our ability to acquire knowledge about God. The seemingly natural fit between realism and Jewish theology is disrupted with rabbinic theology. The Rabbis' penchant for using parables in their theological discourse lends the impression that they are not invested in making literal truth-claims about God. This fact is amplified by the division of rabbinic discourse into halakhah and aggadah, with aggadah including folk tales and legends along with the Rabbis' theological reflections.

---

[14] William P. Alston, "Realism and the Christian Faith," *International Journal for Philosophy of Religion* 38.1 (1995): 37–60, p. 45.

[15] Roger Trigg, "Theological Realism and Antirealism," *A Companion to Philosophy of Religion*, 2nd ed., eds. Charles Taliaferro, Paul Draper, and Philip L. Quinn (Oxford: Blackwell Publishing, 2010), 651–58, p. 657.

Although scholars have argued for several decades that the homiletic midrashim are not collections of sermons, the fact that texts such as *Leviticus Rabbah* and *Pesikta de-Rav Kahana* are divided according to liturgical readings has led to the widely held view that the *Sitz im Leben* of the aggadah was the synagogue. On this view, aggadic theology is an edifying discourse directed at the religious formation of the laity and does not reflect the Rabbis' theoretical interests in trying to understand God and the divine–human relationship. This view appears to be bolstered in the medieval period by efforts to minimize the significance of aggadah at the hands of Jewish philosophers and in the religious polemics rabbinic Jews were involved in with Christians and Karaites. From the Bible forward, Judaism has always expressed concern about the limits of its theological language. Interest in this topic intensified in the medieval period as Jewish philosophers and mystics embraced apophaticism, or negative theology. Nonetheless, these theologies are all realist; they affirm the independent existence of God and our ability to know that to a greater or lesser extent.

While Hick's contention that challenges to realism are a modern phenomenon holds in the Jewish context as well, resistance to theological realism within Judaism is a complex phenomenon and not the result of thinkers endorsing any single critique of theological language. More than anything else, it is a matter of how scholars have construed the place of theology within Judaism. Although Moses Mendelssohn was a realist of the most metaphysical sort, his denial of Judaism's possession of revealed truths in *Jerusalem* precipitated the view that theology plays a negligible role in Judaism.[16] As has been well documented, with the emergence of *Wissenschaft des Judentums* in nineteenth-century Germany, Jewish scholars were motivated by the hope for political emancipation to present Judaism as a modern religion that required no irrational beliefs. As these scholars were participants in an intellectual climate dominated by German idealism and its critiques of metaphysics and theology, denuding Judaism of its theological content was little sacrifice. Antitheological approaches to Judaism persisted in the twentieth century and up to the present as many Jewish philosophers and thinkers have drawn their philosophical resources from continental and postmodern philosophy, both of which rest upon the critique of ontotheology. Contemporary Jewish philosophers and

---

[16] Moses Mendelssohn, *Jerusalem: Or On Religious Power and Judaism*, trans. Allan Arkush (Waltham, MA: Brandeis University Press, 1983), 89–90.

theologians have also emphasized the importance of apophaticism within Judaism. While one could reasonably argue that discourse about a transcendent being must end in apophaticism, strong versions of apophaticism that allow no positive claims about God are antithetical to theological realism. Adding to the antitheological and antirealist sentiments within Jewish philosophy and theology is the fact that philosophers and theologians from across the religious spectrum have appealed to Wittgenstein's philosophy to understand Jewish theology. As Wittgenstein takes religious language to be non-theoretical, his influence on Jewish thinkers has put further pressure on realist accounts of Jewish theological language that defend our capacity to make truth-claims about God.

In what follows, I will discuss the main proponents of theological realism within modern and contemporary Jewish thought and I will survey the principal alternatives to a realist account of theological language. For a variety of reasons, an essay such as this cannot endeavor to place every major contemporary Jewish thinker along a continuum stretching from realism to anti-realism. While perhaps heuristically helpful for mapping the field of contemporary Jewish thought, such an exercise would make for a tedious and lengthy read. In most cases, it requires significant analysis to identify Jewish thinkers' positions on realism as they tend to address the topic in circuitous and sometimes contradictory ways. As a result, it is not uncontroversial whether one classifies a particular thinker as a realist or as adopting an alternative position. Additionally, some Jewish thinkers are not easily classifiable, at times taking strongly realist positions while in other instances embracing poetic and apophatic approaches to Jewish theological language. I will thus look for paradigm cases and not attempt to capture the field as a whole. A final complication is that a number of Jewish thinkers are adamantly realist about God but at the same time express deep reservations about our capacity to make theological truth claims about the divine. As it would badly distort the views of these thinkers to either deny their realist sensibilities or to associate them with "theological" realism, I will refer to them as "theo-realists" and address their thought alongside theological realism.

THEOLOGICAL REALISM AND THEO-REALISM

Theological realism, as I have argued, is best understood as the claim that God exists independently of our thought about God, that we have some basis for believing this, and that we can truthfully assert as much. Eliezer Berkovits' work is a good initial example of theological realism for several reasons. First, Berkovits affirms both experience and reason as sources for our beliefs about God. Second, Berkovits articulated his realist position in the middle part of the last century at the height of logical positivism and its verificationist challenge to religious belief. This was a period when theological language was under considerable attack and Berkovits' defense of theological realism sets him apart from contemporaries such as Martin Buber and Abraham Joshua Heschel who instead sought to preserve the divine–human relationship by affirming God's reality while severely restricting theological language. Finally, Berkovits serves as a useful starting point because he clearly and powerfully distills what is at the heart of the debate around theological realism. In his 1959 work, *God, Man and History*, Berkovits says "unless God is accessible to me, unless I am able to confront him myself, unless he is concerned about the way I live and behave, however insignificant I may otherwise be, religion is not possible for me."[17] Much like the William Alston quotation above, Berkovits sees God's independent existence and our ability to know and experience God as crucial features of the divine–human relationship. Speaking of the divine–human relationship, Berkovits flatly asserts "all relationship requires two participants: man as well as God must exist."[18]

To appreciate the theological realism that sets Berkovits apart from his theo-realist contemporaries one must look to his account of the divine–human encounter, an experience he takes to be the foundation of religion. He writes:

> The God of religion, we have observed, must be a living one. And a living god is one who stands in relationship to the world— that is, a God who not only is, but is also for man, as it were, who is concerned about man. We may know of the relationship only if it is real, if the divine concern is actually revealed to man. This is what we have called the encounter, which is the fundamental religious experience.[19]

For Berkovits, the divine–human encounter has a definitively cognitive character that he directly links to the reality of God.

---

[17] Eliezer Berkovits, *God, Man and History*, ed. David Hazony (Jerusalem: Shalem Press, 2004), 43.
[18] Berkovits, *God, Man and History*, 35.   [19] Ibid., 34.

According to Berkovits, "we derive from the encounter the most relevant part of our knowledge and understanding of God."[20] The divine–human encounter is not just productive of knowledge for Berkovits; it transforms our cognitive capacities. As he says, "the unexpected event of the encounter will expand the frontiers of the possible and modify accordingly the notion of rationality."[21] One significant way in which the encounter enriches human cognition is that recognizing God in the encounter allows for a metaphysical "recognition" of God that can augment the religious life.[22] In Berkovits' view, "there is no path from the metaphysical Absolute to the God of religion, but there is one from the revealed God of religion to the Absolute of metaphysics and its incorporation into the body of religious affirmations."[23]

After the sustained attacks on ontotheology and metaphysics in the modern and postmodern periods, one might think that theological realists such as Berkovits recklessly ignore the bounds of human reason in speaking about God. It is crucial to note that theological realists often express considerable concern about the limits of our theological language. For Berkovits, independent of the divine–human encounter, the philosophical absolute remains unknowable in its perfection. Through the encounter, we acquire the ability to know God's relational attributes, but God's essence remains beyond our ken. This is a significant departure from negative theologies such as that of Maimonides that claim we only know God by asserting what God is not. According to Berkovits, "The negative attributes will never do. Religion cannot forgo the love and the mercy of God, or even his justice and anger. Such attributes have to be related to him in a positive sense, or else there is no basis for a living God of religious relevance."[24] Although Berkovits does not use the contemporary language of "theological realism," his insistence on God's independent existence along with our ability to know God through experience and reason make him a paradigm example of theological realism.

A second example of a prominent thinker whose views on theological language are best described as realist is Franz Rosenzweig. Rosenzweig's work makes a valuable contribution to the discussion because the diverse interpretations of his difficult thought illuminate what is at stake in the debate about theological realism. In fact, many contemporary interpreters have attributed to Rosenzweig philosophical

[20] Ibid., 20. [21] Ibid., 47. [22] Ibid., 47. [23] Ibid., 55. [24] Ibid., 56.

and theological views that are diametrically opposed to theological realism, identifying him as a postliberal, a postmetaphysical, or an apophatic thinker.[25] Interpretations of Rosenzweig that place severe limits on theological language undermine the possibility of theological realism by rejecting the theological reasoning necessary to affirm God's independent existence. What complicates matters is that the scholars who emphasize the limits Rosenzweig places on theological language are responding to a feature of his thought that is as crucial as his theological realism. Rosenzweig is rightly concerned with both the power and the limits of theological language and so it becomes a question of how to balance these elements of his thought.

Rosenzweig, it should be said, eschewed labels. In an introduction to his work that he withdrew prior to publication titled *Understanding the Sick and the Healthy*, he says: "Our enemy is not idealism as such; anti-idealism, irrationalism, realism, materialism, naturalism, and what not are equally harmful."[26] What justifies reading Rosenzweig against the grain of his own thought is the ongoing difficulties in coming to agreement about his basic philosophical and theological commitments. Despite his protestations, the realist orientation of Rosenzweig's theology is evident from the beginning of *The Star of Redemption* where he rejects negative theology and says that he seeks to establish the "absolute factuality" or "positivity" of God, World, and the Human Person.[27] Indeed, the central theme of Part I of the *Star* is

[25] For a presentation of Rosenzweig as a postliberal, see Leora Batnitzky, *Idolatry and Representation: The Philosophy of Franz Rosenzweig Reconsidered* (Princeton: Princeton University Press, 2000); For a presentation of Rosenzweig as a postmetaphysical thinker, see Peter Eli Gordon, *Rosenzweig and Heidegger: Between Judaism and German Philosophy* (Berkeley: University of California Press, 2003). For presentations of Rosenzweig as an apophatic thinker, see William Franke, "Franz Rosenzweig and the Emergence of a Postsecular Philosophy of the Unsayable," *International Journal for Philosophy of Religion* 58.3 (2005): 161–80; Elliot Wolfson, *Giving Beyond the Gift: Apophasis and Overcoming Theomania* (New York: Fordham University Press, 2014).

[26] Franz Rosenzweig, *Das Büchlein vom Gesunden und Kranken Menschenverstand*, ed. Nahum Glatzer (Düsseldorf: Joseph Melzer Verlag, 1964), 50, and *Understanding the Sick and the Healthy: A View of World, Man, and God*, ed. and trans. Nahum Glatzer (Cambridge, MA: Harvard University Press, 1999), 55.

[27] Franz Rosenzweig, *Der Mensch und Sein Werk: Gesammelte Schriften*, 4 vols. (The Hague: Martinus Nijhoff, 1976 [henceforth *GS*]). *The Star of Redemption* is collected in *GS* 2. I will quote from Hallo's translation of *The Star* and give German and English page numbers. Franz Rosenzweig, *The Star of Redemption*, trans. William W. Hallo (New York: Holt, Rinehart, and Winston, 1970). Rosenzweig, *Stern*, 25/ *Star*, 23.

Rosenzweig's effort to establish the irreducibility of the three elements of his system: God, World, and the Human Person. This fundamental feature of Rosenzweig's philosophical system speaks in favor of a realist reading of his theological language in that God necessarily exists independently of our thoughts about God. The issue of necessity is crucial because much of Rosenzweig's theological claims throughout the *Star*, both implicitly and explicitly, hinge on his reflections on God's perfection.[28] Giving further support to a realist reading of Rosenzweig's thought, like Berkovits, Rosenzweig affirms both reason and experience as sources for our beliefs about God. Although Jews tend to think of revelation as a historical event that occurred at Mt. Sinai, rabbinic tradition imagines that God's call continues into the present. Rosenzweig radically extends this theologoumenon by conceiving of revelation as a personal encounter with God. In line with Rosenzweig's concerns about the power and the limits of our theological language, he restricts the content of revelation to the divine command, "Love me!"[29] Rosenzweig argues that divine transcendence prevents humans from reciprocating God's love directly, which leads him to the view that the divine–human relationship is properly developed through communal prayer in the celebrations of the liturgical calendar. The culmination of the liturgical year is Yom Kippur, when the communal prayers draw God's presence into the synagogue. Rosenzweig's defense of God's independent existence and our ability to know God through reason and experience place the *Star* firmly in the camp of theological realism.

Scholars have noted a shift in Rosenzweig's thought after the publication of the *Star*. This shift is not, as some have maintained, a move away from philosophy; rather, the persistent theme throughout Rosenzweig's course notes, letters, and writings after the *Star* is the unexpected presentation of his thought as a form of common sense. Although Rosenzweig's use of the term, "common sense," is idiosyncratic, his turn to common sense lends further support to the view that

---

[28] See Cass Fisher, "Divine Perfections at the Center of the Star: Reassessing Rosenzweig's Theological Language," *Modern Judaism* 31:2 (2011): 188–212, and "Speaking Metaphysically of a Metaphysical God: Rosenzweig, Schelling, and the Metaphysical Divide," in *German-Jewish Thought Between Religion and Politics: Festschrift in Honor of Paul Mendes-Flohr on the Occasion of His Seventieth Birthday*, eds. Martina Urban and Christian Wiese (Berlin: Walter de Gruyter, 2012), 151–66.

[29] Rosenzweig, *Stern*, 197/*Star*, 176.

Rosenzweig is best viewed as a theological realist.[30] The individuation of God, World, and Human Person, for which he laboriously argues in Part I of the *Star*, is now depicted as a fact that we know intuitively as a product of common sense. Furthermore, common sense also mirrors Parts II and III of the *Star* in the belief that God, World, and the Human Person can only be known in their relations. Some of Rosenzweig's richest theological reflections come in his commentary on the poems of Jehuda Halevi, with whom he felt a great spiritual kinship. Accompanying Rosenzweig's emphasis on common sense in his post-*Star* writings is an insistence that God is both far and near. The far God, for Rosenzweig, is the one who can be known through reason while the near God is the God of experience. Affirming the validity of both forms of cognition, Rosenzweig says:

> Even in the most dreadful nearness the human can look away and then does not know in the least what has happened to him. And in the farthest distance the glance of God and of the human can burn into one another, so that the coldest abstractions become warm in the mouth of Maimonides or Hermann Cohen—more than all our distressed prattle. Near, far, it doesn't matter! What does matter is that here as there, what is spoken is spoken before His countenance—with the You of the refrain of our poem, the You that never turns away for a moment.[31]

For Rosenzweig, whether we approach God through reason or experience is irrelevant; what matters is the sincerity and directness with which we seek God. As many of Rosenzweig's interpreters are quick to note, he is as much concerned about the limits of theological language as he is about our ability to speak about God. He also offers helpful guidance on this point in his commentary on Halevi's poems:

> But just as we have to heed the limits of our knowledge, so too, and not less, the limits of our not-knowing. Beyond all our knowledge, God lives. But before our not-knowing begins, your God presents

---

[30] See Cass Fisher, "Absolute Factuality, Common Sense, and Theological Reference in the Thought of Franz Rosenzweig," *Harvard Theological Review* 109.2 (2016): 342–70.

[31] Rosenzweig, GS, 4:1, 71; Barbara Galli, *Franz Rosenzweig and Jehuda Halevi: Translating, Translations, and Translators* (Montreal: McGill-Queen's University Press, 1995), 206.

Himself to you, to your call, to your assent, to your readiness, to your glance, to your life.[32]

Rosenzweig represents a prime example of the fact that theological realism is compatible with the epistemic humility any legitimate theology must embrace.

No contemporary Jewish philosopher or theologian has done more to advance the cause of theological realism than Jerome (Yehuda) Gellman. In numerous articles on theological realism, theological reference, religious language, religious belief, two monographs on religious experience, and a recent trilogy addressing key theological issues, Gellman defends theological realism and demonstrates the crucial role it plays in Jewish religious life.[33] His many contributions to the subject are marked by highly detailed argumentation that coerces assent. While the breadth of his work prevents an adequate survey in the present context, two early articles are particularly noteworthy. In the article "Theological Realism," Gellman analyzes the merits of theological instrumentalism and theological realism. Theological instrumentalism is a non-cognitive approach to theological language that emphasizes "the emotive, conative, regulative and persuasive functions of religious language."[34] Gellman identifies several problems for the theological realist (divine predicates and anthropomorphism, sortal incoherence of divine attributes, and various other theological

---

[32] Rosenzweig, GS 4:1, 57–58; Galli, Franz Rosenzweig and Jehuda Halevi, 200.
[33] See Jerome Gellman: "The Meta-Philosophy of Religious Language," Noûs 11.2 (1977): 151–61; "Theological Realism," International Journal for Philosophy of Religion 12.1 (1981): 17–27; "God and Theoretical Entities: Their Cognitive Status," International Journal for Philosophy of Religion 13.2 (1982): 131–41; "Religion as Language," Religious Studies 21.2 (1985): 159–68; "Naming, and Naming God," Religious Studies 29.2 (1993): 193–216; "The Name of God," Noûs 29.4 (1995): 536–43. See also Jerome Gellman: Experience of God and the Rationality of Theistic Belief (Ithaca, NY: Cornell University Press, 1997); "Identifying God in Experience: On Strawson, Sounds and God's Space," in Referring to God: Jewish and Christian Philosophical and Theological Perspectives, ed. Paul Helm (New York: Routledge, 2000), 71–89; Mystical Experience of God: A Philosophical Inquiry (Aldershot: Ashgate Publishing, 2001); "Beyond Belief: On the Uses of Creedal Confession," Faith and Philosophy 23.3 (2006): 299–313; God's Kindness Has Overwhelmed Us: A Contemporary Doctrine of the Jews as the Chosen People (Boston, MA: Academic Studies Press, 2013); This Was from God: A Contemporary Theology of Torah and History (Boston, MA: Academic Studies Press, 2016); Perfect Goodness and the God of the Jews: A Contemporary Theology (Boston, MA: Academic Studies Press, 2019).
[34] Gellman, "Theological Realism," 17.

inconsistencies), which give the initial advantage to theological instrumentalism. Gellman goes on to defend theological realism by distinguishing between "basic doctrine" and "realist theory" which leads to a two-tiered account of religious language that includes a "religious object-language" and a "religious meta-language."[35] On this proposal, sentences in the "religious object-language" have no truth value and are purely instrumental. The question of truth only arises in the "religious meta-language," the content of which can be quite different from the basic doctrine expressed in the "religious object-language." Understood on these terms, theological realism regains its advantage over theological instrumentalism on the basis of "linguistic morality" in that theological instrumentalism denies the theological truth claims of religious believers.[36] Gellman's article, "God and Theoretical Entities: Their Cognitive Status," is also of considerable interest as it explores the question of theological realism in tandem with realism and instrumentalism in science. Two points from Gellman's more recent work amplify the present discussion. First, he calls into question "the very possibility of being able to state a nonrealist view of God, one that does not affirm God's real, genuine, actual, independent existence, within traditional Judaism."[37] Second, Gellman provides further evidence that one can be a theological realist while maintaining legitimate concerns about the limits of our theological language. He describes his theological orientation in the following terms:

> I do not believe that any human knows much about what God is really like, or what in our language corresponds to what God is really like. On the other hand, while I acknowledge that God is covered in mystery, I do not suffer from what William Alston once called "transcendentitis," which is the condition of people who maintain that God is absolutely unknowable (at least by any positive predicate). This condition does not do justice to the nature of the religious life, and too often is the last safe-house for those who find it difficult to believe in God at all. My view of God finds a middle path between literalism and transcendentitis.[38]

---

[35] Ibid., 22.   [36] Ibid., 27.
[37] Gellman, *This Was from God*, 16. The quotation from William Alston is from Alston, "Realism and the Christian Faith," 53.
[38] Gellman, *God's Kindness Has Overwhelmed Us*, 20.

In contrast to the theological realism defended by Berkovits, Rosenzweig, and Gellman, it is a second form of realism that I call "theo-realism" that has preoccupied many modern and contemporary Jewish thinkers. Theo-realism takes a strongly realist stance about God but expresses equally strong skepticism about our ability to make truth-claims about God. Theo-realism is best exemplified in the works of Martin Buber and Abraham Joshua Heschel produced in the 1950s, a theologically inhospitable period marked by logical positivism. Buber captures the theologically adverse intellectual climate in his 1952 work, *Eclipse of God*, where he says that the "thinking" of his time "seeks, on the one hand, to preserve the idea of the divine as the true concern of religion, and, on the other hand, to destroy the reality of the idea of God and thereby also the reality of our relation to Him. This is done in many ways, overtly and covertly, apodictically and hypothetically, in the language of metaphysics and of psychology."[39] Heschel offers a similar assessment of the profound allergy to religious thought and experience in the modern world in a book published the previous year titled *Man is not Alone*, where he writes: "Intimidated by the vigor of agnosticism that proclaims ignorance about the ultimate as the only honest attitude, modern man shies away from metaphysics and is inclined to suppress his innate sense, to crush his mind-transcending questions and to seek refuge within the confines of his finite self."[40] Both Buber and Heschel respond to the rejection of religious belief and experience by vehemently defending the reality of God but denying our ability to make truth-claims about the divine. In taking this path, Buber and Heschel seek to preserve the divine–human relationship while simultaneously defusing the critiques of religion.

Buber's theo-realism is evident throughout *The Eclipse of God*. Early in the book, he says that he seeks to defend "the simple thesis that 'faith' is not a feeling in the soul of man but an entrance into reality, an entrance into the whole reality without reduction and curtailment."[41] He amplifies this point in the second essay, "Religion and Reality," where he declares that "The relationship between religion and reality prevailing in a given epoch is the most accurate index of its

---

[39] Martin Buber, *Eclipse of God: Studies in the Relation Between Religion and Philosophy* (Atlanntic Highlands, NJ: Humanity Books, 1952), 17.
[40] Abraham Joshhua Heschel, *Man is not Alone: A Philosophy of Religion* (New York: Farrar, Straus, and Giroux, 1951), 44.
[41] Buber, *Eclipse of God*, 3.

true character."[42] Following themes from *Two Types of Faith*, published in 1951, Buber says epochs can be distinguished between those which have an immediate faith relationship ("believing-in") and those in which faith is mediated by ideas ("believing-that").[43] In essence, Buber is mapping his I–Thou and I–It relations onto history in order to critique periods in which instrumental rationality, theological or otherwise, displaces dialogical relations. The theological implications of Buber's argument are profound. God is ultimately real as is evident in Buber's comment that "I–Thou finds its highest intensity in religious reality, in which unlimited Being becomes, as absolute person, my partner."[44] At the same time, however, Buber says that God "eludes our direct contemplation."[45] God, for Buber, is "formless" and there is nothing that can be known objectively about God.[46] God "suffers" the "untrue images" we project onto the divine as they are our only means of conceiving God.[47] Buber's reasons for limiting theology are multiple. Among other things, he is clearly concerned to uphold human autonomy in the divine–human relationship. Accordingly, he says that the encounter with God "gives us something to apprehend, but it does not give us the apprehension."[48] He also distinguishes talking to God from talking about God. In a statement that captures the essence of theo-realism, Buber says "it is not necessary to know something about God in order to really believe in Him: many true believers know how to talk to God but not about Him. If one dares to turn toward the unknown God, to go to meet Him, to call to Him, Reality is present."[49]

The philosophical and theological tensions that permeate Buber's thought from the early '50s are also evident in Heschel's work from that period. In his 1951, *Man is not Alone*, Heschel also defends the reality of God. As he says, "God is one means He alone is truly real."[50] Elsewhere in the text, he further extrapolates: "The existence of God is not real because it is conceivable; it is conceivable because it is real."[51] Despite

---

[42] Ibid., 13. [43] Martin Buber, *Two Types of Faith* (New York: Macmillan, 1951).
[44] Buber, *Eclipse of God*, 44 f. [45] Ibid., 14.
[46] "The religious reality of the meeting with the Meeter, who shines through all forms and is Himself formless, knows no image of Him, nothing comprehensible as object. It knows only the presence of the Present One. Symbols of Him, whether images or ideas, always exist first when and insofar as Thou becomes He, and that means It ...." Ibid., 45.
[47] Ibid., 46. [48] Buber, *Eclipse of God*, 98f. [49] Ibid., 28.
[50] For a nuanced discussion of Heschel as a theological realist see Shai Held, *Abraham Joshua Heschel: The Call of Transcendence* (Bloomington: Indiana University Press, 2013), 106–7. Heschel, *Man is not Alone*, 117
[51] Ibid., 91.

the suggestiveness of this comment, Heschel's theology is no more positive than Buber's. Heschel repeatedly asserts that our thinking cannot contain the divine. For instance, he says that "no thing can serve as a symbol or likeness of God—not even the universe."[52] It is not simply that there is no adequate symbol for God, our language falters when it comes to the divine. Heschel asks but does not answer the following poignant question:

> We are driven to know God in order to conform to His ways. But to know Him we would have to attain the nearly impossible: to render the ineffable in positive terms. The question, then, arises: If, in order to be known, the ineffable has to be expressed, does it not follow that we know it as it is not?[53]

Heschel and Buber take such skeptical positions on theological language that one might wonder whether they are not better classified as fictionalists. To my mind, their adamance about the reality of God prevents construing them as fictionalists. For Heschel, access to ultimate reality comes through "radical amazement" regarding which he says: "Radical amazement has a wider scope than any other act of man. While any act of perception or cognition has as its object a selected segment of reality, radical amazement refers to all of reality."[54] Through opening ourselves to wonder, we experience the ineffable. This, he says, is the beginning of religion.

Heschel's designation of God as utterly ineffable sharply undercuts our theological language. According to Heschel, "we have neither an image nor a definition of God. We have only His name. And the name is ineffable."[55] "God," he says, "begins where words end."[56] Just as it is tempting to see Heschel as a fictionalist, one might also think he is a non-cognitivist or even an apophatic thinker. He does speak of religious awe generating "a certainty without knowledge."[57] Heschel identifies knowledge with logic and belief with the acceptance of propositions, both of which fall short in the religious context: divine ineffability means that God eludes human logic and the religious life cannot be reduced to the mere assent to a set of propositions. Instead, God is properly approached through understanding and faith. According to Heschel, "we know a thing, we understand a personality."[58] In

---

[52] Ibid., 34. [53] Ibid., 98. [54] Ibid., 13. [55] Ibid., 97. [56] Ibid., 98.
[57] Ibid., 22. This certainty is so absolute it "is not even surpassed by the axiomatic certainty of geometry." Ibid., 27.
[58] Heschel, *Man is not Alone*, 133.

privileging understanding over knowledge in the divine–human relationship, Heschel is not abandoning cognition. Experience of the ineffable, as he says, leads us "from an intuition of His presence to an understanding of His essence."[59] Heschel's preference for faith over belief in part stems from his now outmoded voluntarist notion of belief that he associates with "personal conviction."[60] In contrast to belief, faith represents a lived relation to God; faith, he says, "is not only the assent to a proposition, but the staking of a whole life on the truth of an invisible reality."[61] Faith for Heschel has cognitive content but is not reducible to such.

What is most commendable in the theo-realism proffered by Buber and Heschel is their creative and valiant efforts to preserve the divine–human relationship within an intellectual climate that was becoming increasingly antagonistic to theology. Nonetheless, their theo-realism is problematic for two reasons. First, defending the reality of God while at the same casting doubt on our ability to speak about the divine is a strategy that can only lead to self-referential incoherence. Indeed, Buber and Heschel make numerous claims about God that should be prohibited by the strictures they place on theological language. How, for instance, can Buber assert that God "does not despise all these similarly and necessarily untrue images, but rather suffers that one look at Him through them"?[62] Or again, how can he claim that "the religious reality of the meeting with the Meeter, who shines through all forms and is Himself formless, knows no image of Him, nothing comprehensible as object"?[63] Are there not already significant theologies behind the ideas of God as one who meets us or as the Being present in every form? Similarly with Heschel, how can he say that "every man is in need of God because God is in need of man" without transgressing his limits on theological language?[64] Would it not be better to admit that we can and must speak of God and proceed from that point? This leads to the second problem with theo-realism. Theo-realism is a conversation stopper. It seeks to convince us that everything that can be said of God has already been articulated.

Despite the significant shortcomings of theo-realism, a shared element within Buber's and Heschel's thought remains instructive for all who pursue a realist Jewish theology. Buber and Heschel both realize that, despite the challenges to religious language, a realist orientation to God requires the ability to refer to God. Buber says:

---

[59] Ibid., 67. [60] Ibid., 166. [61] Ibid., 167. [62] Buber, *Eclipse of God*, 46.
[63] Ibid., 45. [64] Heschel, *Man is not Alone*, 247 f.

> The religious communication of a content of being takes place in paradox. It is not a demonstrable assertion (theology which pretends to be this is rather a questionable type of philosophy), but a pointing toward the hidden realm of existence of the hearing man himself and that which is to be experienced there and there alone.[65]

Ironically, Buber dodges the verificationist critique of religious language by accepting it. Unlike theology, true religious language is not assertory.[66] Instead, religious language refers to God ostensively. Despite the many points that count against theological reference in Heschel's thought, he also preserves our referential capacity.[67] Similar to Buber, Heschel says "while we are unable either to define or to describe the ineffable, it is given to us to point to it. By means of indicative rather than descriptive terms, we are able to convey to others those features of our perception which are known to all men."[68] As I will discuss in the conclusion, Jewish realists have more robust resources today for defending theological reference. Nonetheless, realists can learn from Buber's and Heschel's work that theological reference plays a crucial role in any realist orientation to God.

WITTGENSTEINIAN APPROACHES TO JEWISH THEOLOGY

A surprising turn in contemporary Jewish philosophy and theology has been the wide embrace of the work of Ludwig Wittgenstein by Jewish philosophers and theologians from across the religious spectrum. The belief that Wittgenstein's philosophy can shed light on Jewish theology is surprising not just because Wittgenstein was not Jewish and at times expressed seemingly antisemitic views, but also because Jewish

---

[65] Buber, *The Eclipse of God*, 43.
[66] Heschel amplifies his claim that faith incorporates assertion, but is not reducible to it, by saying that religious language "is not a sober assertion but an exclamation." Heschel, *Man is not Alone*, 167.
[67] "Citizens of two realms, we all must sustain a dual allegiance; we sense the ineffable in one realm, we name and exploit reality in another. Between the two we set up a system of references, but we can never fill the gap. They are as far and as close to each other as time and calendar, as violin and melody, as life and what lies beyond the last breath." Heschel, *Man is not Alone*, 8.
[68] Ibid., 21. Further on in the work, Heschel offers additional resources for theological reference when he says: "We must be in possession of an a priori idea of the divine, of a quality or relation representing to us the ultimate, by which we would be able to identify it when given to us in such acts." Heschel, *Man is not Alone*, 100.

thinkers with such diverse philosophical and religious commitments find common ground arguing that Wittgenstein, who thought sporadically but deeply about religion, could be the key for understanding the troubled place of theology within Judaism. An equally peculiar fact of the rise of the Jewish Wittgensteinians is that Jewish thinkers are turning to Wittgenstein at the precise time that Christian philosophers and theologians are abandoning his philosophy.[69] What then explains this turn of events and how is it related to the problem of theological realism?

Like Buber and Heschel, Wittgenstein is rightly seen as a thinker who sought to defend religion at a time when it was coming under increasingly severe criticism. In his 1931 essay "Remarks on Frazer's *Golden Bough*," Wittgenstein adopts a strategy to defend religion by rejecting its theoretical component, a move that shapes his subsequent thought on the topic.[70] In response to Frazer's attributing a primitive rationale to magic, ritual, and religion that causes them to appear absurd from the perspective of the modern scientific worldview, Wittgenstein argues that we misunderstand religion when we take it as a mistaken explanation of reality. The purpose of religion is not to give a theoretical account of the world. As he says: "No *opinion* serves as the foundation for a religious symbol."[71] The limits that Wittgenstein places on the role of reason within religion reappear in a course he gave on belief in 1938. Wittgenstein says of the religious believer:

> ... he has what you might call an unshakeable belief. It will show, not by reasoning or by appeal to ordinary grounds for belief, but rather by regulating for in all his life. This is a very much stronger fact—foregoing pleasures, always appealing to this picture. This in one sense must be called the firmest of all beliefs, because the man risks things on account of it which he would not do on things which are by far better established for him.[72]

---

[69] See Cass Fisher "The Posthumous Conversion of Ludwig Wittgenstein and the Future of Jewish (anti-) Theology," *AJS Review* 39.2 (2015): 333–65, pp. 335–36.

[70] Ludwig Wittgenstein, "Remarks on Frazer's Golden Bough," in Ludwig Wittgenstein, *Philosophical Occasions*, ed. James C. Klagge and Alfred Nordmann (Indianapolis: Hackett Publishing, 1993).

[71] Ibid., 123.

[72] Ludwig Wittgenstein, *Lectures & Conversations on Aesthetics, Psychology and Religious Belief*, ed. Cyril Barrett (Berkeley: University of California Press, 2007), 54.

Wittgenstein is, of course, famous for insisting on the importance of how we use language and he applies a similar approach to the matter of religious belief. It is not that belief plays no role in religion but, rather, that it functions differently. Religious beliefs are like pictures that guide our lives; they do not require evidence to support them and they cannot be harmonized with science. In a discussion of religion in *Culture and Value*, Wittgenstein says: "Rules of life are dressed up in pictures. And these pictures can only serve to *describe* what we are to do, not *justify* it. Because they could provide a justification only if they held good in other respects as well."[73] For Wittgenstein, the purpose of religious belief is to transform our lives; it is not a cognitive exercise that tells us about the way things are.

To be sure, there is much else in Wittgenstein's philosophy that is valuable to the study of Jewish theology particularly his concepts of "language games" and "forms of life," but it is his account of religious belief that bears most directly on the issue of theological realism. A common theme among Jewish Wittgensteinians is that theology is not about God, a position that is in direct opposition to theological realism. Alan Mittleman, for instance, says: "The word *God* does not make a claim about the furniture of the universe. Rather, to speak of God is to underwrite a form of life that allows us to respond with love and courage and hope to the mystery out of which we come and toward which we progress."[74] Tamar Ross makes a similar claim when she says: "When an Orthodox Jew says, 'I believe in Torah from Heaven,' her primary concern is not to discuss facts or establish history, but to make a statement on an entirely different plane. It reflects her wish to establish a much stronger claim that will regulate her entire life."[75] While there are certainly good reasons to acknowledge the way in which religious beliefs shape religious lives, theological realists are also committed to the fact that we can and do speak truthfully about God. Avi Sagi takes a particularly strong stand against this position: "Truth claims about the world, about God, and about crucial events such as the Sinai theophany, are religiously irrelevant. In other words, religion is a value system that neither relies upon nor reflects metaphysical

---

[73] Ludwig Wittgenstein, *Culture and Value*, ed. G. H. Von Wright, trans. Peter Winch (Chicago: University of Chicago Press, 1980), 29.
[74] Alan Mittleman, "Asking the Wrong Question," *First Things* 189 (January 2009): 15–17, p. 17.
[75] Tamar Ross, *Expanding the Palace of Torah*, 193–94.

assumptions or factual data that could be translated into truth claims."[76]

The Jewish Wittgensteinians cited above are but a small sample of the Jewish philosophers and theologians who have been drawn to Wittgenstein's philosophy.[77] Their thought makes explicit a common Wittgensteinian response to theological realism: Jewish theology plays an important role in shaping the lives of practitioners but it does not tell us anything about God. What motivates an account of theology that has nothing to say about God? Yuval Lurie responds to this question in an insightful way:

> Although Wittgenstein aspires to eliminate instrumental beliefs from religious faith, this personal aspiration of his is not characteristic of religious faith in all cultures throughout the history of humanity. It seems to be an attitude of faith more prominent among religious believers in modern Western culture. In a way, it is also a response to the philosophical assault on religious faith that was expressed in Positivism, which explained religion as an early stage in human cultural development of explaining the nature of the world. From this perspective, Wittgenstein's attempt to disengage religious faith from instrumental explanations about the nature of the world typifies his own way of making room for religious faith alongside a scientific conception of life and world.[78]

While Lurie's assessment is helpful in understanding Wittgenstein's reasons for rejecting the theoretical function (what he calls, "instrumental beliefs") of religious language, the question that remains is why so many contemporary Jewish thinkers are eager to endorse an account of theology that provides no knowledge of God? Surely, contemporary Jewish thought is no longer in the grips of Positivism. I do not think there is a simple answer to this perplexity. Perhaps it is the unique forms of theological thinking in Judaism and the long history of reducing Jewish theology to homiletics that make Wittgenstein's approach to religious language more amenable to Jewish thinkers than to their Christian counterparts. While that may be, I suspect it is the fact that Jewish thinkers

---

[76] Avi Sagi, *Jewish Religion after Theology*, trans. Batya Stein (Boston, MA: Academic Studies Press, 2009), 27.
[77] For a partial bibliography of Jewish Wittgensteinians, see Fisher, "Posthumous Conversion," 333, n. 2.
[78] Yuval Lurie, *Wittgenstein on the Human Spirit* (Amsterdam: Rodopi, 2012), 219.

have more fully embraced the critiques of metaphysics as the result of drawing their philosophical resources from continental and postmodern philosophy. Whatever explains Wittgenstein's pronounced influence on contemporary Jewish thought, the discipline and future of Jewish theology look very different if there are no truth-claims to be made about God. While rhetorical and sociological analyses have much to contribute to the study of Jewish theology, absent a discourse about God it is difficult to see how Jewish theology can recover its former vitality and assert its relevance in contemporary Jewish religious life.

POETIC, FICTIONALIST, AND APOPHATIC APPROACHES TO JEWISH THEOLOGY

A lasting insight of the work of Buber and Heschel is that theological realism is bound up with the question of theological reference; however, both thinkers advocated for an ostensive form of reference that avoids propositional language. Poetic, fictionalist, and apophatic approaches to Jewish theology represent further explorations in non-propositional Jewish theology. On some construals of theological realism, one could adopt a poetic or fictionalist account of theological language and still be a realist. Janet Soskice, for instance, argues that religious language is metaphorical but still realist.[79] Jewish philosophers and theologians who highlight the similarities between poetry and theology do so on the basis of very different theological commitments and with greater or lesser degrees of nuance. Yochanan Muffs makes a particularly blunt identification of Jewish theology and poetry when he says:

> Those who say Judaism had no formal theology before the Middle Ages are probably right; all we have are legal statements that are binding and poetic statements about the world, that in the main, are not. Even though certain actions were made normative, the subjective reactions were not fixed: Midrash is the subjective, evocative, nondeterminate, personal reaction to the law. Theologies, on the other hand, are rational and clear— and as normative for belief as law is normative for action.[80]

---

[79] Janet Soskice, "Religious Language," in *A Companion to Philosophy of Religion*, 2nd ed., eds. Charles Taliaferro, Paul Draper, and Philip L. Quinn (Oxford: Blackwell Publishing, 2010), 348–56.
[80] Yochanan Muffs, *The Personhood of God: Biblical Theology, Human Faith and the Divine Image* (Woodstock, VT: Jewish Lights Publishing, 2005), 110.

Given his immense sensitivity to the divine–human relationship as it surfaces in classical Jewish literature, it comes as a surprising claim from Muffs that biblical and rabbinic thought about God is poetic rather than theological. In part, what motivates his view is a distorted notion of theology, pervasive in Jewish studies, that theology is necessarily systematic and dogmatic. Muffs goes on to argue for a remythologizing of God that raises the possibility that his approach is better described as fictionalist. For instance, he says that: "Fully realizing that the anthropomorphic God is to a very great degree a projection of man's understanding of his own psyche (not merely of his own intellectualized and abstracted ideals), we must turn up the mythical decibels of the old personal God."[81] He goes on to add that "if the divine projections are not quite ontology, they may be more than mere poetry."[82] Muffs appears to adopt a realist orientation, but he leaves the status of our theological language indeterminate.

Howard Wettstein's Wittgensteinian approach to Jewish theology shares Muffs' poetic view of biblical and rabbinic theology along with Muffs' understanding of theology as a rational discourse alien to biblical and rabbinic thought. According to Wettstein: "The Bible's characteristic mode of 'theology' is story telling, the stories overlaid with poetic language. Never does one find the sort of conceptually refined doctrinal propositions characteristic of a philosophical approach."[83] For Wettstein, the rational and propositional approach to theology is a medieval corruption of earlier Jewish ways of thinking and speaking about God. In contrast to Muffs, Wettstein makes the important point that: "likening biblical/rabbinic remarks to poetry certainly does not imply or even suggest that these remarks involve no beliefs, no real commitments; that they are, as one might say, 'just poetry.' For such commitment-neutrality is surely not true of poetry itself."[84]

Buber, Heschel, and Muffs suggest that our theological language fails to capture the truth about God and, so, there is a temptation to consider these thinkers as holding a fictionalist stance about theology. More recent work extends the discussion of fictionalism by emphasizing the role of the imagination in the religious life and by calling into question the centrality of belief. Nehama Verbin argues that fictional

---

[81] Ibid., 193.   [82] Ibid.
[83] Howard Wettstein, *The Significance of Religious Experience* (Oxford: Oxford University Press, 2012), 108.
[84] Ibid., 87.

works "play a transformative and constitutive role in our lives," but that they do so "primarily by eliciting imaginings rather than by prescribing beliefs."[85] Verbin distinguishes between fiction and fictitious; in contrast to the fictitious, which is simply false, fiction can address reality and speak truthfully about it. What fiction does not offer is justification for its claims and so she argues it is not a source of knowledge. Fiction opens up a world of possibility that fully involves us imaginatively in the text in a manner that can be transformative. Turning to the homiletical, she says:

> Since preachers do not ordinarily use arguments for God's existence or probable existence that prescribe beliefs, but tell stories that excite emotions and prescribe imaginings, we may conclude that coming to faith is first and foremost coming to imagine, and coming to participate fully in a game of make-believe, or in other words, coming to live in a fictional narrative.[86]

Samuel Lebens is not a fictionalist regarding theological language, but he is sympathetic to its main points that the cognitive life of the religious practitioner extends far beyond belief and that imagination has a significant role to play. For instance, he says that "even where belief is an essential ingredient for the religious life, such as the belief that God exists, it is not a sufficiently absorbing epistemic state. Whenever belief is required so too is make-belief."[87] Lebens offers as examples of such "make-belief" the idea that the world hangs in a balance awaiting our actions to tip it toward good or evil and the idea from the Haggadah that we must consider ourselves as having been liberated from Egypt. Lebens' work strengthens the view that Jewish theology can benefit from attending to the role of the imagination in the religious life without reducing it to such.

A final alternative to theological realism is apophaticism or negative theology. If apophaticism is simply the claim that God ultimately eludes our reflective capacities, then all theologies should conclude in apophaticism. In recent years, scholars of Judaism have set forth

---

[85] Nehama Verbin, "Faith and Fiction," in *Faith in the Enlightenment? The Critique of the Enlightenment Revisited*, ed. Lieven Boeve et al. (Amsterdam: Rodopi, 2006), 182–94, p. 182.
[86] Verbin, "Faith and Fiction," 193.
[87] Samuel Lebens, "The Epistemology of Religiosity: An Orthodox Jewish Perspective," *International Journal for Philosophy of Religion* 74.3 (2013): 315–32, p. 326.

stronger accounts of apophatic theology that deny the possibility of any positive knowledge of God. There is, of course, good precedent for such a position in the thought of Maimonides as Kenneth Seeskin's work attests. Seeskin presents what he takes to be a standard view of Maimonides on theological language: that divine simplicity leads to the claim that we can know God's actions but not God's essence and that God's transcendence of our cognitive categories prohibits positive assertions about God, leaving us with the negative attributes. Seeskin, however, goes further and argues that what the standard account leaves out is that "even negations introduce some degree of distortion."[88] He goes on to say:

> To say that God does not lack power or intelligence is still to put a boundary around God and view God under a description. To return to the proposition "God is wise," even the negative rendering cannot be taken at face value. To interpret it correctly, we would have to point out that while it is true that God does not lack wisdom, we should not think that we have an identifying description of God. In truth all we have is the claim that, whatever it may be, God's wisdom is unlike anything else. It could be said therefore that what the most negative predicates provide is an approximation, a set of very general directions for how to think about God. In Maimonides' opinion, they take us to the limit of what the human mind is capable of understanding but stop short of literal truth.[89]

Seeskin argues that the function of theological language "is not referential but heuristic."[90] The goal of theological language is to discover its own inadequacy and to lead us to a silent contemplation of God. If theological realism requires cognitive content and the capacity to speak truthfully about God, then strong readings of Maimonides' negative theology will fall outside its bounds.

Like Seeskin, Elliot Wolfson advocates for a strong form of apophaticism, an "apophasis of apophasis," that not only renounces all positive theological language but also critiques previous accounts of negative theology.[91] According to Wolfson, a "theolatrous impulse ... lies coiled

---

[88] Kenneth Seeskin, "Sanctity and Silence: The Religious Significance of Maimonides' Negative Theology," *American Catholic Philosophical Quarterly* 76.1 (2002), 7–24, p. 13.
[89] Seeskin, "Sanctity and Silence," 14. [90] Ibid., 9.
[91] Elliot Wolfson, *A Dream Interpreted within a Dream: Oneiropoiesis and the Prism of Imagination* (New York: Zone Books, 2011), 32.

in the crux of theism" in its insistence on cognizing the transcendent.[92] In his view, divine transcendence "cannot be enclosed within the boundaries of what may be experienced or comprehended."[93] With respect to cognition of God, Wolfson argues that "incomprehensibility" is part of the "formal definition" of God, making all assertions about the divine, positive or negative, idolatrous. Regarding experience of God, he claims that "no justification exists to postulate an experience of revelation by means of which one could chance upon a transcendent being in the phenomenal sphere of becoming."[94] Borrowing a term from Buber, Wolfson says it is "theomania" that compels thinkers to turn the transcendent into an object of thought and that this "theolatrous" tendency extends to apophatic theology. Along such lines, he argues that: "What is necessary, although by no means easy, is the termination of all modes of representation, even the representation of the nonrepresentable, a heeding of silence that outstrips the atheological as much as the theological, the saying of an unsaying that thinks transcendence as the other beyond theism and atheism." On multiple occasions, Wolfson says that this elimination of all discourse about God is the "exigency of the moment."[95] In the course of defending his position, Wolfson offers important insights about poetry, fiction, and apophaticism, and subverts the priority of the real over against what he calls the irreal, the domain of dream and imagination. While theological realists will recoil from Wolfson's indictment of religious language, they should not ignore the challenges that he or Seeskin make to a realist orientation.

CONCLUSION

Contemporary Jewish reflection on the philosophical status of Jewish theological language has been diverse and fluid. Rather than presenting a clearly delineated set of alternative approaches, Jewish philosophers and theologians have drawn widely on the resources available to them. Hybrid approaches are thus common, such as theo-realists who are adamant about the reality of God but who flirt with fictionalist accounts of theological language, or the Wittgensteinian who appreciates the poetic element within Jewish theology. Rather than

---

[92] Elliot Wolfson, *Giving Beyond the Gift: Apophasis and Overcoming Theomania* (New York: Fordham University Press, 2014), 260.
[93] Ibid., 30.   [94] Wolfson, *A Dream Interpreted within a Dream*, 32.
[95] Ibid., 30; Wolfson, *Giving Beyond the Gift*, 152 and 235.

methodological promiscuity, this hybridity is better understood as the result of highly creative responses to exceedingly difficult questions: how do we speak of God and what is the status of our theological language? It is worth pointing out that for reasons that have yet to be clearly articulated Jewish thinkers have taken these questions harder than some of their Christian counterparts. While Jewish philosophers and theologians express perpetual concern about how finite creatures can capture a transcendent being in words, William Alston and Nicholas Wolterstorff both assert that God is precisely the type of being that can be referred to using a definite description, and Alston makes the additional point that participating in communal religious practices allows us to successfully use direct reference to refer to God as well.[96] Jewish theological realists would do well to follow these thinkers and reconsider the assumptions that have guided much modern and contemporary Jewish thought.[97]

Fortunately, new resources are available to Jewish philosophers and theologians to aid this transition. As evidenced by Buber and Heschel, any meaningful form of realism depends upon our capacity for theological reference. New theories of reference developed by John Perry, Kepa Korta, Francois Recanati, and Imogen Dickie emphasize the social and communicative function of reference rather than reducing reference to the mere picking out of objects.[98] Reference, for these philosophers, is a communicative tool we deploy in order to shape the beliefs and actions of others. These are significant shifts in how to think of reference that would allow Jewish philosophers and theologians to move away from the beguiling questions surrounding divine transcendence and instead focus on the role of reference within discourse. Several of these philosophers envision reference functioning as a file system in which each file has an epistemic relation to its object that secures reference. Understanding

---

[96] William Alston, "Religious Language," in *The Oxford Handbook of Philosophy of Religion*, ed. William J. Wainwright (Oxford: Oxford University Press, 2005), 220–44, p. 229. Nicholas Wolterstorff, *Practices of Belief: Selected Essays Vol. 2*, ed. Terence Cuneo (Cambridge: Cambridge University Press, 2010), 370.

[97] The most notable exception is Jerome Gellman who has made numerous and important contributions to the subject of theological reference. For a partial list of his work on that subject, see n. 33.

[98] John Perry, *Reference and Reflexivity* (Stanford: Center for the Study of Language and Information, 2001); Kepa Korta and John Perry, *Critical Pragmatics: An Inquiry into Reference and Communication* (Cambridge: Cambridge University Press, 2011);. François Recanati, *Mental Files* (Oxford: Oxford University Press, 2012); Imogen Dickie, *Fixing Reference* (Oxford: Oxford University Press, 2015).

reference on such terms could advance our understanding of Jewish theology in multiple ways. Here are a few examples. A person using a mental file for reference does not need to know that the file refers to its object; rather, it just needs to be the case that the file has the right epistemic relation to its object. Adopting such an approach to reference preserves the capacity for non-expert users of a file (i.e., the laity) to successfully refer. A second benefit of conceiving of reference as a file system is that an active file is in a "buffering" state as it continues to collect information about its object.[99] The idea of an ever-expanding "God-file" fits well with much Jewish theology that has a more recursive form than the systematic and dogmatic character of other traditions. Finally, multiple files with their unique epistemic relations to their objects can be grouped under an "encyclopedic file" in a manner that could unify the different ways of thinking and speaking about God within Judaism and allow the epistemic credentials peculiar to each form of theological predication to combine in mutual support.[100]

Judaism has a rich theological tradition and Jewish thinkers over the millennia have utilized a multitude of ways of conceptualizing and expressing their ideas about God and the divine–human relationship. Jewish Wittgensteinians are surely correct that there are valuable insights to be gleaned from Wittgenstein's philosophy for understanding Jewish theology; those advocating poetic and fictionalist approaches make an important contribution by emphasizing the role of the imagination in the religious life; and apophaticists provide a crucial reminder about the limits of our theological language. Nonetheless, much hangs on the questions of whether God exists independently of us and whether we have the capacity to speak truthfully about God. A synthesis of all these insights that does justice to the panoply that is the Jewish theological tradition still awaits us.

Selected Further Reading

Alston, William P. "Realism and the Christian Faith." *International Journal for Philosophy of Religion* 38.1 (1995): 37–60.
Alston, William. "Religious Language." In *The Oxford Handbook of Philosophy of Religion*, 220–44. Edited by William J. Wainwright. Oxford: Oxford University Press, 2005.

---

[99] Perry, *Reference and Reflexivity*, 131.   [100] Recanati, *Mental Files*, 73.

Berkovits, Eliezer. *God, Man and History*, ed. David Hazony. Jerusalem: Shalem Press, 1965.

Byrne, Peter. *God and Realism*. Aldershot: Ashgate, 2003.

Fisher, Cass. "Absolute Factuality, Common Sense, and Theological Reference in the Thought of Franz Rosenzweig." *Harvard Theological Review* 109.2 (2016): 342–70.

Fisher, Cass. "The Posthumous Conversion of Ludwig Wittgenstein and the Future of Jewish (anti-) Theology." *AJS Review* 39.2 (2015): 333–65.

Fisher, Cass. "Religion without God? Approaches to Theological Reference in Modern and Contemporary Jewish Thought." *Religions* 10.1 (2019): 1–25.

Gellman, Jerome. "God and Theoretical Entities: Their Cognitive Status." *International Journal for Philosophy of Religion* 13.2 (1982): 131–41.

Gellman, Jerome. "The Name of God." *Noûs* 29.4 (1995): 536–43.

Gellman, Jerome. "Theological Realism." *International Journal for Philosophy of Religion* 12. 1 (1981): 17–27.

Hick, John. "Religious Realism and Non-realism." In *Disputed Questions in Theology and the Philosophy of Religion*, 3–16. Edited by John Hick. New Haven, CT: Yale University Press, 1993.

Moore, Andrew and Michael Scott, eds. *Realism and Religion: Philosophical and Theological Perspectives*. Aldershot: Ashgate, 2007.

Trigg, Roger. "Theological Realism and Antirealism." In *A Companion to Philosophy of Religion*, 2nd ed., 651–58, 657. Edited by Charles Taliaferro, Paul Draper, and Philip L. Quinn. Oxford: Blackwell Publishing, 2010.

Westphal, Merold. "Theological Anti-Realism." In *Realism and Religion*, 131–45. Edited by Andrew Moore and Michael Scott. New York: Routledge, 2007.

Wolterstorff, Nicholas. *Practices of Belief: Selected Essays Vol. 2*. Edited by Terence Cuneo. Cambridge: Cambridge University Press, 2010.

18 A Defense of Verbal Revelation
SAMUEL FLEISCHACKER

I

I have elsewhere proposed an understanding of revelation in which believers submit to the authority of a sacred text in order to break free of purely naturalistic approaches to the significance of their lives. Modern naturalistic ethical views are incapable of providing us with a view of our lives as worth living, I argue, and it makes sense, in response to that fact, to put one's faith in a non-naturalistic God and a text that purports to represent that God's will.[1] I defend submission to a text, that is, as having ethical importance: the text becomes an expression of God's presence in the world, which we recognize by submitting to it.

One feature of this view that might trouble some readers is that submission to a text amounts to heteronomy, an acknowledgment of a source of ethical wisdom beyond one's own reason. Those impressed with the Kantian idea that our ethical lives should express our freedom may find it unacceptable to suggest that we should instead submit to another's word in this way. To this objection it is worth noting that I regard submission to a text as a moment of heteronomy within a more broadly autonomous life. If persuaded of the need to receive ethical wisdom from a non-naturalistic source, we are in the first place *freely choosing* to set aside our free choice. We also need to determine how to interpret what we accept in this moment of heteronomy, however, and apply it to the rest of our lives—how to make sense of the text to which we are submitting. And in this interpretive

---

[1] Samuel Fleischacker, *Divine Teaching and the Way of the World* (Oxford: Oxford University Press, 2011); Samuel Fleischacker, *The Good and the Good Book* (Oxford: Oxford University Press, 2015). In these books, I make room for non-naturalistic belief systems that are not theistic; for the purposes of this chapter, we can set that wrinkle aside.

process, we are once again autonomous. I will not dwell on these points here, but we will see later that this notion of revelation as a moment of heteronomy nested within autonomy fits nicely into a traditional Jewish understanding of the way written Torah is nested within oral Torah.

A larger problem, to which I will devote the bulk of this essay, is whether the idea of a text as expressing God's will makes any sense in the modern world. Modern theology, in part under the impetus of modern biblical criticism, has overwhelmingly moved toward a view of God as beyond speech, and of the Torah, correspondingly, as the record of various human beings' attempts to figure out what God might want of them, rather than a divine intervention into human affairs. If any human–divine encounter lies behind the Torah, it is thought—at Sinai, or in any other aspect of Jewish history—that encounter can be conceived only as a silent, ineffable I–Thou moment which has been approximated, sometimes more adequately, sometimes less so, in the stories and laws contained in the Torah. The Torah cannot *literally* be God's word; that is at best a rough metaphor.

Take this essay as an attempt to bring out the motivations for this view and then, wholly, to upend it—from a perspective as committed to the accuracy of modern biblical criticism, and to a progressive understanding of God and halakhah, as that of those who uphold it. In the words of the later Wittgenstein: "A picture [has] held us captive."[2] And that picture, of a necessarily non-verbal God and a necessarily non-divine Torah has, I believe, prevented modern Jews from being able to maintain a view of revelation that was once central to our tradition. Maimonides says that we should see every verse and every letter of the Torah as "contain[ing] within it wisdom and wonders to whomever the Lord has granted the wisdom to discern it"—as, in a robust sense, divine.[3] I would like to recuperate that view.

If a picture has held us captive, then breaking that captivity is essential if we are to entertain a new picture. Accordingly, my project here is largely to shake up modern objections to the idea of a God Who

---

[2] Ludwig Wittgenstein, *Philosophical Investigations*, trans. G. E. M. Anscombe (Oxford: Blackwell, 1953), § 115.
[3] Moses Maimonides, "Eighth Principle of Faith," *Commentary to the Mishnah*, Sanhedrin X, 1. Note Maimonides' careful phrasing. I argue in http://thetorah.com/making-sense-of-the-revelation-at-sinai/ that Maimonides did not by any means accept the "stenographic" view of the Torah—the idea that Moses literally wrote down words spoken to him by God.

appears to us in language. However, undermining these objections will also, I hope, make clearer what I mean by saying that the Torah is the word of God, and what the advantages are of such a view. So the largely negative argument of this essay—the critique *of* critiques of verbal revelation—is meant to have a constructive upshot. It is, we might say, a *via negativa* to a positive Jewish theology.

II

Words are human, God is beyond words, and the Torah is a human attempt to grasp what the encounter with God might be like. This view, which I will call "wordless encounter theology," is held today by practically all progressive Jewish Bible scholars and theologians, even on the liberal end of Orthodoxy. It is also widely represented as characteristic of sophisticated, modern Jews, as opposed to the naïve traditionalists who treat the Torah as God's word. Staking his ground as the founder of Britain's Masorti movement, Rabbi Louis Jacobs wrote: "The believer in verbal inspiration believes that he has in the Bible ... the *ipssissima verba* of the prophets, indeed, of God Himself. The more sophisticated believer, nowadays, cannot accept this for the soundest reasons."[4] These "more sophisticated believers" instead see revelation as a non-verbal encounter with God and Scripture as a humanly composed attempt to describe that encounter.

Before Jacobs, Abraham Joshua Heschel had written, famously, that: "As a report about revelation, the Bible itself is a midrash." "The nature of revelation is ineffable," said Heschel and "human language will never be able to portray" it.[5] "Any genuine encounter with reality," so certainly any genuine encounter with God, takes place at an "immediate, preconceptual, and presymbolic" level (*GSM* 115): a level that lies below language. Similar themes appear in the work of Heschel's student, Neil Gillman.[6] And in his recent *Sacred Attunement*, Michael Fishbane also echoes Heschel, characterizing language as a human tool that "carve[s]

---

[4] Louis Jacobs, *A Jewish Theology* (London: Behrman House, 1973), 205.
[5] Abraham Joshua Heschel, *God in Search of Man* (New York: Farrar, Straus & Giroux, 1955), 184–5. Henceforth: *GSM*.
[6] See for instance Neil Gillman, *Sacred Fragments* (Philadelphia: Jewish Publication Society, 1990), 4–6, or, *The Way Into Encountering God in Judaism* (Woodstock, VT: Jewish Lights Publishing, 2000), 155. The biblical theologian Benjamin Sommer also champions a view of this sort, partly by way of Heschel, in his *Revelation and Authority* (New Haven, CT: Yale University Press, 2015).

a sphere of sense out of the limitless 'whole' [of the universe]," while God appears to us in moments that "rupture" the spheres we carve, allowing a "vastness" beyond language to break in on us. "Human speaking brings something of the ineffable divine truth to expression," says Fishbane: the Torah, and other scriptures, are a human-all-too-human attempt to capture a divinity who transcends language.[7]

At the origin of this sort of theology stands Martin Buber, whose I–You encounter—the core of all revelation, for Buber—is widely understood to be prelinguistic: "Only silence toward the You, the silence of *all* tongues, the taciturn waiting in the unformed, undifferentiated, prelinguistic word leaves the You free."[8]

All this sounds beautiful. But it is very unclear what it amounts to. And it is yet more unclear how any halakhic form of Judaism—any form of Judaism committed to the wordy Torah, and its even wordier rabbinic commentaries, as the ultimate authority over our religious lives—can be squared with such a view. That might not have been a worry for Buber, whose Judaism was mystical, anti-rabbinic, and dismissive of halakhah, but it should be a worry for Jacobs and Heschel and Gillman and Fishbane. If there is no good way of squaring wordless encounter theology with halakhic Judaism, we should also wonder whether halakhic Jews who uphold it are really so "sophisticated." As we shall see, there are moreover large doses of theological and philosophical naiveté within the view.

In any case, most of those who draw on wordless encounter theology treat it as dogma: instead of examining it, they take it to be obvious. Our intensely critical and agonistic tradition usually avoids dogma, and progressive Jews, especially, should be uncomfortable with unexamined beliefs. With that in mind, let us examine the dogma.

III

A historical note to start off with. Buber's and Heschel's views are rooted in a critique of language, and romanticization of silence, characteristic of a swathe of early twentieth-century modernists. Hugo von Hofmannsthal's 1902 "Letter of Lord Chandos," written in part to

---

[7] Michael Fishbane, *Sacred Attunement* (Chicago: University of Chicago Press, 2008), 17, 39. Henceforth: *SA*.

[8] Buber, *I and Thou*, trans. W. Kaufmann (New York: Simon & Schuster, 1970), 89. But cf. p. 141, which seems to give greater place in revelation to language, and 160, which is richly ambiguous on this subject.

A Defense of Verbal Revelation   427

explain his own abandonment of lyric poetry, exemplifies this movement. Hofmannsthal describes experiences of ordinary objects that fill him with awe or horror or excitement, then says:

> As soon ... as this strange enchantment falls from me, I find myself confused; wherein this harmony transcending me and the entire world consisted, and how it made itself known to me, I could present in sensible words as little as I could say anything precise about the inner movements of my intestines or a congestion of my blood.[9]

Hofmannsthal suggests that what is significant about the world cannot be put into words, and that what words do convey is trivial. He was shortly to change his mind about this, apparently, finding an outlet for the expression of what he cared about in theater (he became Richard Strauss's main librettist). But the idea that words and significance come radically apart was to be echoed by many other writers and artists of the 1910s and 20s. It is a theme of Wittgenstein's *Tractatus Logicus-Philosophicus* (1922), which ends by urging us to cease trying to put ethical and religious ideas into words. It is also a theme of Heidegger's *Being and Time* (1927), which presents language as based on more fundamental preconceptual and prelinguistic structures of signification, and suggests that ordinary speech inevitably involves a "fall" into inauthenticity. Much of Kafka may be read as a satire of the attempt to find meaning in life by way of language.[10] Silence is a great virtue in Herman Hesse's *Siddhartha* (1922) and Hesse often speaks of finding God, or Being, in a silent listening to water and trees. Similar themes pervade Rilke's writings; Rudolf Otto presents the "numinous" as beyond words and concepts in his *Idea of the Holy* (1917); and Arnold Schönberg devoted his *Moses und Aron* (1926–32) to exploring the difficulty of putting religious experience into words (I think this opera is indeed the deepest Jewish exploration of wordless encounter theology). Buber and Hesse were close friends, and Buber's *I and Thou* was written at the height of the movement I have been describing (1923). Heschel was steeped in it in his university training, and engaged in his writings with Buber, Otto, and Heidegger.[11]

---

[9] http://depts.washington.edu/vienna/documents/Hofmannsthal/Hofmannsthal_Chandos.htm

[10] See my "Religious Questions: Kafka and Wittgenstein on Giving Grounds," *Sophia* 21:1 (1982): 3–18.

[11] Buber and Otto appear in *The Prophets* (New York: Harper & Row, 1962), Heidegger in *Who is Man?* (Stanford: Stanford University Press, 1965). Shai Held misses a trick,

The point to note here is that the idea that deep significance must elude language was a dominant theme in *one*, very limited and peculiar, period of modern thought. The later Heidegger and the later Wittgenstein both repudiated their own early animadversions on language; I will indeed draw on Heidegger as a source for the return to language I will advocate in this chapter. I have said nothing as yet to argue for such a return, of course, but the historical point I have raised should at least suggest the possibility that progressive Jewish theologians, far from representing the height of "sophisticated" modern thought, are stuck in a moment of early twentieth-century Expressionism that modernity as a whole has long passed by. I am myself fascinated by Expressionism, and regard Kafka, Otto, Schönberg, and the early Heidegger as artists and writers of great power and continuing relevance. But we should worry if we remain caught up in their philosophical assumptions. Certainly their worldview should no longer seem *obvious* to us.

IV

Let us now consider the advantages that wordless encounter theology is supposed to bestow on modern Judaism. Two are mentioned especially often:

a) It fits with modern scholarly approaches to the Bible. If the Torah was not written by Moses, and most of the events in it never happened, and if the prophetic and wisdom writings were also not written by the people to whom they are attributed, and are filled with historical inaccuracies, then to attribute them to God would seem to make God out to be a liar. In any case, if this is how the Bible was composed, we have no historical reason to think that God *did* speak to any of its authors. Far better, then, to see it as a human attempt to capture, in words, something that its authors took to be a wordless encounter with the divine. We can even say that some or all of the Bible's authors *did* have an encounter with the divine, or

in his otherwise thoughtful book on Heschel, when he ties Heschel to the critique of technology and of "ontotheology" in Heidegger but not to the emphasis on prelinguistic and preconceptual experience in *Being and Time*: Held, *Abraham Joshua Heschel: The Call of Transcendence* (Bloomington: Indiana University Press, 2013), 46–50. Held does bring out the problems in Heschel's romanticization of the prelinguistic (ibid., 52–6, 66–9).

that the history of Israel as a people amounts to such an encounter, and that the words of the Bible reflect that experience. None of these claims can be disproven by historical evidence. So if we adopt wordless encounter theology, we can keep history and faith separate.

b) It allows for radical halakhic change. If the Torah is but a human attempt to capture what God might ask of us, to translate a wordless encounter with God into a way of life, then we modern humans are in position to translate that encounter into different terms. No religious authority need attach to commands that issue from the worldview of priests and scribes who lived many centuries ago. Of course, we are linked to these priests and scribes by historical memory —we grow up on their words and stories—and that may give us some inclination to continue in the path they laid out as long as we find it morally admirable and spiritually inspiring. But if we do not see it that way any more, if indeed we find aspects of their worldview appalling or meaningless, then we should feel free to come up with new rules and rituals; we may even have an obligation to do that. A complete overhaul of the Torah's attitudes toward women and gay people might, for instance, be required of us.

V

But in fact wordless encounter theology is neither necessary nor sufficient for either of these projects. As regards the first, if historical study sheds doubt on whether God spoke to Moses or Isaiah, or whether the documents we have record what God said to them, then it also sheds doubt on whether Moses or Isaiah encountered God wordlessly. Historical scholarship has indeed given us reason to doubt the accuracy of practically everything in the Bible, including the very existence of Moses. What would count as historical evidence of a divine–human encounter is hard to imagine, moreover, and the fact that the biblical documents never describe wordless encounters between God and humanity makes it unlikely that we could find such evidence even if we could specify it. Finally, if, as historical critics often maintain, the documents were written largely by priests and courtiers and scribes in the interest of acquiring or maintaining their own power, then it seems yet more improbable that we will be able to trace their source to extraordinary spiritual experiences. So wordless encounter theology is hardly sufficient to maintain a faith in the religious significance of the Bible, once we accept the findings of modern historical scholarship.

Wordless encounter theology is also not necessary to maintain such a faith. Suppose the Torah was written by the individuals or schools known as J, E, P, H, and D; suppose also that most or all of the prophetic writings are pseudonymous, highly redacted, and do not reflect the real proclamations of any single figure. Why should this messy process not just *be* the way that God speaks to us? Why should God not be able to express Godself even through what seem to us highly politicized processes—to use our human struggles for place and power as tools to provide us with something in which we can nevertheless locate a profound spiritual vision? Rosenzweig's famous suggestion that R, the historical redactor of the Torah, can be read as *Rabbenu* captures this thought beautifully.[12] But that thought allows us to say, as Rosenzweig himself was not quite willing to say, that *the Torah is in the end wholly God's teaching*, even if it arose in bits and pieces, by way of human authors whose immediate purpose was a profane one. Modern historical accounts leave ample logical space for the Bible to be attributed to God; they do not require us to turn to wordless encounter theology.

We can say much the same about the supposed advantages of wordless encounter theology for halakhic change. On the one hand, declaring the entire Torah to be a midrash on a wordless experience of God is not sufficient to remove the Torah's authority. A traditionalist may say that this midrash is *the closest we can come* to figuring out what God wants of us, or that the value of the halakhic system lies in what it has done for the Jewish people, not in its divine origin, and that that is enough to treat it with unqualified reverence. On the other hand, we can make good arguments for halakhic change even if we maintain that God spoke every word of the Torah. For to say that the Torah is God's word does not tell us what those words *mean*, nor that that meaning must be the same in every generation. All law codes change their practical meaning over time, as new circumstances arise and new beliefs change their adherents' idea of how to make best sense of them. The Talmud is a glorious example of how Jews who believed firmly in the Torah's divinity nevertheless adapted its practical import to the moral beliefs and communal

---

[12] Franz Rosenzweig, "The Unity of the Bible," in *Scripture and Translation*, eds. M. Buber and F. Rosenzweig, trans. L. Rosenwald with E. Fox (Bloomington: Indiana University Press, 1994).

needs of their time—often seeming well aware that that was what they were doing. Indeed, the more daring calls for autonomy among the Rabbis—the "not in heaven" story, for instance, or the story about Moses not understanding what was going on in the Beit Midrash[13]— appear to understand God's giving us the Torah as precisely an invitation to far-ranging, creative interpretation. And why should a supremely good Being, if that Being speaks at all, not speak for just this reason? Why should such a Being not *want* us to take His/Her/Its words as a spur to autonomy? (Genesis 18:17–25 is I think best read in exactly this way.) In any case, there is once again plenty of logical space for a firm commitment to the divinity of the Torah to go along with a commitment to halakhic change. We do not need wordless encounter theology for that.

VI

We might nevertheless want to endorse wordless encounter theology if we think it is coherent, spiritually attractive, and a helpful way of framing our Jewish commitments. It is none of these things, however. To begin with the Jewish problems and work backwards to the more general theological and philosophical ones:

a) *Wordless encounter theology is unsuited to Judaism, a supremely wordy religious tradition.* If one wants a sacred scripture that reflects or endorses silent encounter with a preconceptual, prelinguistic principle or force, one might best turn to the *Tao te Ching*. "The sage acts without action and teaches without talking," it says. Then, a bit later: "From nothingness to fullness and back again to nothingness, this formless form, this imageless image, cannot be grasped by mind or might." And again: "Something formless, complete in itself, ... provides for all things yet cannot be exhausted ... I do not know its name so I call it 'Tao.'"[14]

Or one might be impressed by the *Upanishads*, which speak of the ultimate point of human reconciliation with the universe as "that from which all words turn back and thoughts can never reach,"[15] or by

---

[13] B. *Menachot* 29b; *Baba Metzia* 59b.
[14] Lao Tzu, *Tao te Ching*, trans. J. Star, (New York: Penguin, 2001), 14–15, 37, 38. Fishbane's theology has strong affinities with this text. Compare: "Out of the depths, the Divine breaks into human consciousness, but it cannot be fixed or formulated." (*SA* 52). Or: "[I]n every feature of the world something of the unseeable face of God may be perceived, and something of the all-unsayable name of God may be named." (*SA* 54).
[15] "Taitiriya Upanishad" II.8–9, as translated by Eknath Easwaran in *The Upanishads*, (London: Penguin, 1987), 145. See also "Chandogya Upanishad," 14.4, 178.

Dharmakirti's *Fundamental Wisdom of the Middle Way*: "Action and misery having ceased, there is nirvana. Action and misery come from conceptual thought.... What language expresses is nonexistent."[16]

But the Torah? Why on earth would someone committed to wordless encounters with the divine turn to the Torah—or any other central part of the Jewish tradition? The God of the Torah creates the universe with words and inaugurates our role in the world by giving us the power of naming; the text then wends its voluble way through the adventures of clever and charismatic speakers such as Abraham and Jacob and Joseph to a dramatic climax in which God speaks to the entire Israelite people, which is followed by a stream of divine commands that fill most of the rest of the book. The great prophets speak for God in similar verbal outpourings, and the wisdom writers craft tales and poems and philosophical aphorisms with great attention to literary detail and no apparent anxiety about the limits of language. Taking a cue from these sources, perhaps, the Rabbis argue endlessly over how best to interpret all these stories and commands and aphorisms, delighting in every fine detail of their linguistic embodiment, and using those details as the ground for their points.

Moreover, Jews of all denominations do not worship just God, much less an ineffable "vastness" or object of wonder, but *the God Who created the universe*, or *the God Who took us out of Egypt*, or *the God Whose face is hidden from us*. Jews worship, that is, a God understood by way of propositions. It is of course not easy to interpret these propositions, and we often want to argue with them, or with the way others interpret them. But to engage in this work of interpretation and argument, we must immerse ourselves in language, not point to a mystical moment outside of language. Wordless encounter with an ineffable reality does not give us any point of entry into the discussions central to the Jewish tradition; it does not help us make sense of so much as what we *mean* by "God."

And even if one says, as some wordless encounter theologians may want to say, that the central religious moment to which they point may indeed be better expressed in writings such as the *Tao te Ching* but that the Torah is *our* sacred text and we should work within the tradition we

---

[16] Dharmakirti, "Examination of Self and Entities" (ch. xviii), verses 5 and 7, *The Fundamental Wisdom of the Middle Way*, trans. Jay Garfield (New York: Oxford University Press, 1995), 48–9.

have inherited, the presupposition of *this* claim—that religious commitment should be tied to family and tradition—is something that needs to be interpreted and assessed, criticized and defended. To worship *the God of our parents or people* is already to worship a God embedded in language, not a Being who transcends all words and concepts. *That* Being would surely also transcend all peoples and cultures, and their limited constructs.

Above all, of course, Jews worship *a God who commands them*.[17] But commands are irremediably linguistic. Fishbane tries valiantly to connect moments in which we experience "primordial forces" to commandment: these "charged moment[s]," he says:

> palpably call [...] to our elemental nature and conscience, directing us to: Remember, Do Something, or Have Sympathy; and to the extent that one can fix these revelations in one's mind through rituals of action and recollection, their moral charge remains, and the claim is continuous and does not fade (*SA* 20).

But the experiences of which Fishbane is speaking—of earthquakes and floods, birth and death, "monstrous" historical deeds—generally do not have clear normative implications over time. Yes, at the moment of an earthquake we should give aid, at the moment of a birth celebrate, at the moment of a death mourn. But *how* do we best raise children or remember our dead, or commemorate great natural and historical calamities? There is much debate over these things; they issue in no clear directive, nothing like a "command." And if we look at ancient Jewish history, whether the one recounted in the Bible or the one that, according to historical scholars, underlies the Bible, there is no obvious reason why we should respond to it by maintaining any form of traditional Jewish practice. We could just as easily take it: i) to show the foolishness and psychological contortions that come of centering religion around law rather than love, and become a Christian; ii) to show the barbarism and violence that come of tribal attachments, and become a Stoic or atheistic cosmopolitan; or iii) to show that Jews are always persecuted, often in the name of other people's universalistic ideologies, and become a secular, anti-humanistic nationalist. That none of these responses are normatively "Jewish" I would readily agree. But the case

---

[17] This is obviously true of Conservative and Orthodox Jews, but it is also true, if in a different way, of Reform Judaism. Hermann Cohen, Leo Baeck, and Arnold Jacob Wolf all wrote powerfully of the centrality of law and commandment to Judaism.

for that claim must be made, once again, by working out from biblical and rabbinic *texts*—not by trying to draw normativity from a silent, unconceptualized encounter.

b) *Wordless encounter theology is unsuited to monotheism.* One advantage of wordless encounter theology is supposed to be that it is better suited to the incorporeal, unlimited God of monotheism. A God who can speak, say its proponents, is a limited, corporeal god, like the "old man in the sky" of popular superstition or the anthropomorphic deities of ancient paganism. But is it any better to claim to "feel" God's presence by way of wonder and awe than to claim to hear God? Is it any less pagan to think one senses God at a stream, with Hesse, or stroking a horse, with Buber?[18] What is this "sensing" supposed to amount to? Do we smell or touch God, or become aware of God's shadow falling upon us? That would make the God of encounter theology *more* limited and pagan than the God Who is thought to speak through the Torah. But if we go in the other direction, insisting that "feel" and "sense" are mere metaphors, and that the wordless encounter in question has no literal sensory component,[19] then why continue to speak of an "encounter"? The God of wordless encounter theology is not supposed to be an abstraction whose existence can be demonstrated by philosophical argument—that is the rationalistic God from whom figures like Buber are fleeing—but a personal being Who can in some sense really *meet* us, as one person to another. Strip "encounter" of all sensory content and this claim falls empty; we can no longer even call it a metaphor.

Wordless encounter theologians may protest that they are not talking about a *direct* experience of God—just having a sense of wonder and awe, in response to various limited experiences, that opens us up to an awareness of the limitless whole underlying all experience. But even here, we are required either to take a literally sensory event to contain or betoken the presence of the limitless whole objectively (to spark our wonder and awe with good reason) or to treat our wonder and awe as an occasion for reflections that have nothing to do with *encountering* that whole at all. Either the wondrous and awful event really is a moment in which God is more than usually present, which would take us back to paganism, or it is just one of many things that

---

[18] See Hermann Hesse, *Siddhartha* (London: Penguin, 1999), 88–89, 92–96, and Martin Buber, *Between Man and Man* (Boston, MA: Beacon Press, 1955), 22–23.

[19] As Heschel sometimes does: "Is it possible to define the content of [a spiritual] experience? It is not a perception of a thing, of anything physical" (*GSM* 141–2).

might happen to inspire reflection on an impersonal limitless whole that does not "encounter" anybody. Neither route is suited to a Being personal enough to be *our* God but all-pervasive and incorporeal enough to be the God of the whole universe, rather than a limited nature deity like the spirit of a waterfall.

We may put this point in a different way by considering the purported objects of our wordless encounters. What makes wordless encounter theology intuitively appealing is that we often do feel we sense God's presence when standing at the Grand Canyon, or watching a glorious sunset. But is God supposed to be present *only* at these moments? How could the God of the entire universe be present only or even especially at these moments? Surely the all-embracing God of monotheism is equally present when we lose our keys, drive around Newark Airport, or hunt through the Chicago suburbs to find someone who will check our clothes for *shatnetz*. Surely the God of the entire universe is as much present in a tangle of hair or a plastic shopping bag as in the Grand Canyon. A deity we encounter just at special moments of natural grandeur would be a limited deity who belongs in a polytheistic pantheon, not a force or principle of goodness underlying or pervading the universe.

So we might go in the opposite direction and say that God can be encountered anywhere—even on the New Jersey Turnpike and certainly at a Chicago *shatnetz*-checker. But that threatens to empty the word "encounter" of meaning. If *everything* we do is an encounter with God, then we lose grip on the idea that an "encounter" might arouse a special kind of feeling in us, like wonder or awe, or resemble the silent communication that takes place when we lock eyes with another person. Once again, either we limit our encounters with the divine to moments that carry the everyday connotations of the word "encounter," and drift toward paganism, or we allow these encounters to range over every and any experience, and empty "encounter" of content.

"But is this not a problem shared by those who posit a speaking God? If we think God spoke at Sinai—or even throughout the process by which, on historical accounts, the Torah was produced—then are we not seeing God as appearing just at certain times and places? Is this not just as much a betrayal of monotheism, a limitation of God's presence to certain elements of the universe and not others?" The difference is that a God who can address us in language can make clear that and how His/Her/Its presence pervades the universe. The God of the Torah sets us laws that spread across our lives. When we eat, dress, make love, work and rest, give birth or die, even when we go to the bathroom, halakhah enables us to see our actions as bearing some relation to God's presence: as partaking of a world whose source is God, and every bit of which is upheld by, of concern to, or otherwise bound to God. Our encounter with God takes place by way of these laws, their interpretations, and the stories in which they are embedded: the linguistic whorl that generalizes the significance of moments of experience, and allows us to place them in the context of a general understanding of the universe. The central feature of language is precisely that it enables generalization, that it gives rise to general concepts—including the concept of "God." Sensation shorn of linguistic expression is by contrast bound to particulars: I see or feel or hear a *particular* tree or waterfall or reddening of the horizon. It is hard to see how, by way of sensation alone, we could ever move from the particulars with which we interact to a conception of a God as pervading or underlying every particular. That move would seem to require language. Which suggests that a purely non-linguistic theology will inevitably remain at a polytheistic or animistic level: it can never lead us to the idea of a single God structuring the universe. By way of language, I can find religious significance everywhere: on the Jersey Turnpike as well as at the waterfall. If I have to rely on my senses and feelings alone, I will not be able to do that.

c) *Wordless encounter theology is based on a philosophically untenable conception of language.* Wordless encounter theologians draw a sharp distinction between language and reality. Reality, including the reality of God, lies according to them beyond language; language is a human tool that only partially grasps, and bends to human use, what is out there. This is especially clear in Fishbane's *Sacred Attunement*. Fishbane tells us that "we can only orient ourselves in silence" to the "unsayable, and insensate, and utterly transcendent Giving" of concern to theology (*SA* 14). A bit later he says that language "channels the flow of a sometimes inchoate reality," enabling us "to build a life-world within the vastness." Every use of language "imprints trust in the power of words to carve a sphere of sense out of the limitless 'whole.' ... Only when words and works break down for one reason or another ... does the vastness return as a terrifying reality." (17) This dichotomy runs through the book. Reality consists in a "vastness,"[20] in

---

[20] Fishbane uses "God" more or less synonymously with "vastness": see, for example, 35.

the "unlimited" or "infinite", which we perceive when there is a "rupture" or "caesura" in the course of our ordinary experience. And the vastness "silences" us, is "mute," is not in itself "carve[d] up into verbal objects for practical use," not subjected to "our words" or "names" or "terms" (20, 39, 41). "We name things and thus try to 'have them' in our grasp"; "the vastness remains, always eluding our syntax and mental vigor" (50). All our names "have been wrought from the unfathomable unboundedness for human use, and thus do not reflect the ultimate truth" (51; compare also 52, 54, 59). In short there is a great divide, for Fishbane, between "vastness" or the "unfathomable unboundedness," and our words or names, which "carve up" what in itself is uncarved.

But from a philosophical perspective, this picture raises some questions:

i. "Vastness" and "unboundedness" and the rest are all words too—why suppose *they* capture reality in itself rather than carving it up for human use?
ii. Why suppose that reality in itself is "uncarved," has no intrinsic limits or bounds? If we know so little about reality in itself, how do we know this much?
iii. Why suppose that language is merely a human construct, a set of tools to make bits of reality usable for us? If we know so little about reality in itself, how do we know so much about the reality *of language*?

Fishbane has fallen into an old philosophical trap, in which one draws a line between the unknowable and the knowable but then—indeed in the very process of drawing the line—implies that one knows far too much, on one's own view, about the unknowable.[21]

To elaborate these points:

i) If we have no other good words for reality, then "vastness," "unboundedness," etc. also will not do. They cannot even serve as gestures or placeholders for an unknown since we have no idea (by hypothesis) what they are gesturing to and cannot put anything in their place. Moreover, these words have as specific, as limited, a role to play in ordinary language as do all other words. They

---

[21] Kant was perhaps the first philosopher to be accused of doing this—and he struggled hard to avoid it—in his account of "things-in-themselves" in the *Critique of Pure Reason*.

"carve" things up, if that is what words do, just like other words. We use "vastness," for instance, to make sure our fellow human beings appreciate the full size of something they might otherwise regard as small ("We need to recognize the vastness of this problem"), and "unboundedness" to fend off attempts to limit something: these words get their meaning from a set of dichotomies, rather than pointing beyond all dichotomies.

ii) If we cannot know the "ultimate truth" about reality, then we also cannot know whether it is an inchoate flow or instead carved up in a way that closely matches what we say about it. Philosophers today talk about "carving reality at its joints" and while debate continues to rage over whether we in fact do that, few would say that we know it cannot be done. Certainly, the mere fact that we *do* carve up reality when we speak about it is not enough to show that our carvings are arbitrary, that there are no natural kinds for us to grasp.

iii) If we do not know what the universe in itself is like, then we cannot assume we know what language in itself is like either. Language is after all something our species naturally produces, and exactly how that species functions is a question about reality, and depends on its interaction with its environment and not on what it thinks of itself alone. We cannot suppose we know all about ourselves by introspection: the limits on knowledge on which Fishbane insists are limits on self-knowledge as well. But then we cannot know that our language does *not* track the shape of reality. Nor indeed can we know that language serves human purposes: certainly not that that is all it does. Perhaps language has evolved naturally for no purpose. Or perhaps it has developed as part of God's plan for us, and serves to guide us toward other ends than the ones we consciously set for ourselves. Nothing Fishbane says can rule out these possibilities.

I have focused on Fishbane because he presents a particularly stark version of the dichotomy between the linguistic and the nonlinguistic. But Buber and Heschel and Gillman all rely on a similar dichotomy.[22] That dichotomy has in recent decades been pretty much dismantled, however, for reasons of the sort I have just sketched. As mentioned

---

[22] See, for instance, Martin Buber, *I and Thou* (New York: Simon & Schuster, (1970), 9, quoted above, *GSM* 108, 122–3, 131, and Gillman, *Sacred Fragments*, 79–80.

earlier, the romanticization of the nonlinguistic reached its height in early twentieth-century Europe. A very different picture of the relationship between language and reality emerged during the rest of the twentieth century. Among the most important framers of the new picture were the later Wittgenstein and the later Heidegger, criticizing their own earlier views.[23] The Hofmannsthal of the *Rosenkavalier*, *Ariadne auf Naxos*, and *Arabella* too seemed to think that nothing, not even the most mystical moments, was off-limits to language. And in the so-called "analytic" tradition of philosophy, the idea that linguistic meaning could be defined in terms of non-linguistic sense-data came to grief as it became clear that these data could not so much as be picked out, let alone matched up with sentences, except by means of language. Willard van Orman Quine, in his influential "Two Dogmas of Empiricism," showed that we need some sort of "conceptual scheme" to make sense of experience, and that the meaning of each sentence within the scheme depended on its relationship to other sentences, and only the scheme as a whole engaged with unprocessed bits of experience.[24] Donald Davidson took these points a step further, calling the very idea of a distinction between "scheme" and "content," between linguistic categories and unprocessed experience, "a third dogma of empiricism."[25] How, after all, are we to make sense of the unprocessed experience, even *as* unprocessed, without making use of linguistic categories? Davidson called for philosophers to give up "the concept of an uninterpreted reality, ... outside all [linguistic] schemes and science." The "dualism of scheme and content, of organizing system and something waiting to be organized," was, he said, a dogma that cannot be rendered intelligible.[26] Instead, we should recognize that what we take to be real is inextricably interwoven with the way we make sense of language, and that we cannot, consequently, make sense of an unverbalizable reality. This thought has become the basis for various programs of "direct realism," notably that of John McDowell. Not everyone in

---

[23] Writing in his own copy of *Being and Time*, Heidegger commented as follows, on a passage that attempted to found language on a prelinguistic signification: "Untrue. Language is not imposed, but *is* the primordial essence of truth as there." (*Being and Time*, trans. J. Stambaugh (Albany: SUNY Press, 1996), 82n.

[24] Willard van Orman Quine, "Two Dogmas of Empiricism," in *From a Logical Point of View* (New York: Harper, 1961).

[25] Donald Davidson, "On the Very Idea of a Conceptual Scheme," in *Inquiries into Truth and Interpretation* (Oxford: Clarendon Press, 1984), 189.

[26] Davidson, "On the Very Idea," 198, 189.

contemporary philosophy accepts such programs, but the idea of language as a medium through which we perceive reality but dimly, a screen or veil over the real world, has gone by the board.

VII

Relatedly, the idea that words are mere human "tools" has been subjected to sharp criticism. The later Heidegger is especially useful on this score. We think we control language but in fact it is closer to the truth to say that language controls *us*, according to Heidegger: "Man acts as though *he* were the shaper and master of language, while in fact *language* remains the master of man."[27] Language is not a mere means for expressing thoughts—as if we had fully formed non-linguistic thoughts and then just needed to bring them out—nor is it merely a means for "communication" (71, 144). Rather, "language alone brings what is, as something that is, into the Open for the first time" (71). Whatever exactly this means[28]—Heidegger is notoriously obscure—it fends off a purely instrumental conception of language, suggesting that language enables reality to appear to us, rather than just giving us tools to manipulate things.

And the suggestion that language consists of more than a set of tools is straightforwardly plausible. For to a great extent we do *not* control the meanings of our words. As I speak, a host of emotional associations may infuse my words and fill me with anger or delight, or choke me up, as much as they affect anyone I am trying to influence. My words are also shared by a large community, and therefore carry connotations, which I may be unaware of, due to the use of those words by other speakers. When George W. Bush described the war against the Taliban as a "crusade," he may not have been thinking about the connotations of that word—but was nevertheless taken, not inappropriately, to be calling for a new Christian war against Muslims. In private life, many of us

---

[27] Martin Heidegger, *Poetry, Language, Thought*, trans. A. Hofstadter (New York: HarperCollins, 2001), 144. All further quotations from Heidegger are from this collection.

[28] The point, I think, is that we get our ways of individuating things from language, along with the distinction between reality and illusion that these modes of individuation sustain, so can make no sense of "being" outside of a linguistic framework. This is not far from Davidson's point, in the essay cited above. For all their differences in style and training, Davidson and Heidegger have been seen by many as having strong philosophical affinities.

use "hot" or "queer" or "disabled" in ways that display an inept or incomplete grasp of their connotations, and are called to account for that usage regardless of our intentions.

Then there is the way that history shapes the words we use, regardless of our intentions (again, a point of particular concern to the later Heidegger). To take just a few flat-footed examples: "Pharisee" has long meant "hypocrite" to many, although it has begun to lose that connotation in recent years, as Christian scholars have begun to engage respectfully with rabbinic thought. Its air of anti-Judaism still hangs about it, however, and not infrequently pops up in public discourse. Nor is this sort of thing peculiar to words with moral or political implications. "Atom" has changed its meaning radically, from Lucretius' time to our own; "virus," "planet," and even "water" have also been re-shaped considerably by modern science. Over the course of this history, their exact meaning in various contexts has been unclear, and even today particular speakers may mean slightly different things by them, in accordance with their awareness of, and interest or lack of interest in evoking, their history. Particular listeners, too, will respond to the words they hear with varying levels of knowledge of their history. What exactly any given utterance does mean will therefore always be somewhat in flux, beyond the control of particular speakers or hearers. Language is densely layered with history, and no individual speaker can or does have a full grip on those layers. It is an expression and vehicle of everything that is beyond our control: of what Heidegger called our "thrownness."

We should bear in mind as well the simple fact that our intentions themselves are always linguistic, so language is always *prior* to our attempts to control the world, not a mere means for that control. Language is also prior to our attempts to find out what is in the world. It provides us with our modes of seeing and hearing, and interpreting what we see and hear, as well as the distinction between reality and illusion by which we determine which of our sensations are veridical. Words are not tools for analyzing what we perceive with our senses alone; they shape, rather, how we look and listen and what we look and listen for. Nor are they tools for helping us achieve purposes we have already set without language; once we have language, all our purposes are shaped by it.[29]

---

[29] Which is not to say that only linguistic creatures have purposes. But the purposes of a linguistic creature are broader, more nuanced, and in many other ways different from the purposes of a creature without language.

VIII

This picture is incomplete, however. Our purposes may be shaped by language but we also shape language *to* our purposes. Heidegger recognizes, indeed emphasizes, the point that has struck philosophers since Plato about words: that they are general categories for things, abstracting from the differences among the particulars around us, and projecting forms into the future that we hope will fit particulars we have not yet encountered. In this respect they express our attempt to put what we experience into some sort of intellectual order. They also express and figure in our attempts to order our actions. We can pattern our practices only if we can put them in words, to one another and ourselves, and we can have aims to reach for—particulars we have not yet achieved—only if we can characterize them generally enough to put a word to them. In all these ways, words are a supreme expression and vehicle of our freedom and thought: of what Heidegger calls our "projecting" of ourselves. (Human beings are, he says, "thrown project.")[30]

By speaking, then, we simultaneously create patterns to reflect and help us find our way through a universe and allow what is beyond us in that universe to jut through and claim those patterns; we attempt to make sense of and control our world only to find, often, that what we have said contains meanings that we did not intend, and that the consequences of what we have said are beyond our control. There could be no better site for our relationship to a God Who is both within us and beyond us: "within us," insofar as, in God's image, we rule over the world, reason about it, and attempt to subdue it; "beyond us," insofar as the world has always already shaped and claimed us, and can at any moment defeat our projects, or turn them to new and unexpected ends. I have argued elsewhere that God should be seen as a spirit of newness,[31] a force or principle, underlying the universe, that always holds out the possibility of making the world anew (*m'chadesh b'chol yom tamid ma'aseh b'reishit*). We prepare for this newness by establishing old patterns for the newness to break, a background of the expected against which it can stand out. Speech and halakhah are paradigms of that preparation—and halakhah is itself grounded on

---

[30] See Heidegger, *Poetry, Language, Thought*, 69n.
[31] "Faith in Newness," *Sh'ma*, September 2015. See also Hermann Cohen, *Religion of Reason Out of the Sources of Judaism*, trans. S. Kaplan (Atlanta, GA: Scholars Press, 1995), 63–6, and my introduction to Fleischacker (ed.), *Heidegger's Jewish Followers* (Pittsburgh: Duquesne University Press, 2008), 4–7.

speech. But the new can also occur *within* our speech: as we discover unexpected meanings, for good or ill, in what we have said, or heard from others. God thus appears *in* our speech as well as beyond it: and when God appears beyond speech, it is only by way of speech that we are able to recognize that appearance. Only a linguistic being can know what is wondrous about an unconsumed burning bush.

I am relying heavily here on Heidegger's account of language in "The Origin of the Work of Art."[32] Art is an "origin" of our ways of life, Heidegger argues there, because it presents us with a "world"—an ordered, deliberate way of acting and understanding—that is at the same time set back into the "earth": into the mysterious and uncontrolled. Sculpture is set into wood or stone, painting into color, music into tones, and these artworks do not merely "use up" their materials: they instead display, openly and proudly, their dependence on their materials, the importance to them of what lies beyond the artist's control. When we stare at the grain of the wood in a Nakashima bench, or the thick crust of paint in a Turner painting, these points make good sense. But what is the "earth" in a poem? One might think that literature, with its independence of materiality, is an anomalous case of art for Heidegger. On the contrary: "all art ... is ... essentially poetry," he insists. And the "earth" of poetry is language. If only we have "the right concept of language," he says—if we get away from the idea that it is primarily a means for communication and recognize that it instead "brings beings to word and to appearance" for the first time—we will see that it is just as "earthy," just as much beyond our control, as wood and stone and color. "In preparing the sayable," Heidegger writes, language "simultaneously brings the unsayable ... into the world." ("The Origin of the Work of Art," 71) As the prime vehicle of our attempts to control the world, language simultaneously brings out the limits of our ability to control that world. We find what we cannot say in the course of trying to say everything; we find what we cannot do when our speech fails to have the results we intended. And poetry revels in, delights in, this simultaneous control and relinquishing of control.[33]

But if so, then it should be clear why poetry is the perfect site for revelation. And the Torah is essentially a poem: an epic poem, telling

---

[32] Heidegger, "The Origin of the Work of Art."
[33] I elaborate this account of poetry in "Frustrated Contracts, Poetry, and Truth," *Raritan*, Spring, 1994, reprinted in Richard Eldridge ed. *Beyond Representation: Philosophy and Poetic Imagination* (Cambridge: Cambridge University Press, 1996).

a grand mythic tale of the origins of a people and their relationship to God, and manifesting itself in laws that reflect and flow from that tale.

IX

So the alternative to wordless encounter theology that I want to propose is one in which God encounters us, first and foremost, *in* language—not just, and not primarily, wordlessly. The aspects of language that are beyond our control can of course be explained naturalistically. Social scientists can and do put forward plausible explanations of the emotional, sociological, and historical factors about language that prevent individual speakers from fully mastering what they say. But it is perfectly reasonable for a religious believer to take these factors of language as, in addition, ways by which *God* shapes our world and destiny: vessels or vehicles through which God works. If God shapes nature and history, as the Jewish tradition believes, then God also shapes language. And if God can be present in trees and waterfalls and horses, then God can also be present in language: God can speak.

But where should we look for God in language? Everywhere? In principle, a monotheistic God, a God of all the universe, must be somehow present in all language. Still, the encounter theologians are right to say that we are most aware of God's presence when we come up against a mystery, something beyond our control and understanding, and especially when we encounter a mystery that seems to betoken a principle or force or being that might undergird or pervade the universe.

Moreover, the first thing we need to do in order to recognize such mystery in language is step back from the attempt to control some bit of language, suspend our confidence that we know what it means or implies. Which is to say: we need to humble ourselves to it, to let it guide or direct us—let it have authority over us. We need to allow God into our language if God is to speak to us. And we do that by giving some bit of language authority, directive power, over us.

Finally, if we stand in a religious tradition, we most resolutely humble ourselves if we let the tradition pick the bit of language that will have this authority over us, rather than trying to control that selection ourselves. We also form a community of religious believers this way—move beyond the arrogance of self-sufficient individuality.

All of which points, for Jews, to one clear bit of language as the primary site for us to encounter God: the Torah. Even modern Jews, renouncing the theologically and historically implausible story of God literally speaking to Moses on Sinai, must recognize the fact that the canonization of the Torah, the investing of that text with authority, was basic to the formation of our tradition. Perhaps that canonization reflects the traces of a powerful historical event, dimly recalled in the Sinai story; perhaps it came about because the Sinai story fitted well with the experience of Jews returning from Babylonian exile, as described in Ezra-Nehemiah;[34] perhaps it came about because the Sinai story simply spoke strongly to the ethical and spiritual imagination of Second Temple Jews. In any case, the text was canonized, and that set the stage for all the midrashim, rituals, legal codes, and theology that have defined the Jewish tradition for over two millennia. By embracing this canonization, we rejoin our tradition's particular form of humbling oneself before God. Jews encounter God, first and foremost, in the Torah. If we cannot encounter God there, we have no reason to expect such an encounter anywhere.

This returns us to a traditional Jewish view, but not on the basis of spurious claims to the effect that the Jewish people literally heard God at Sinai. Rather, the idea behind this return is that the one God of the universe, present somehow in or under everything we experience, must also be present in our language. And the Torah is the prime locus for our awareness of this presence simply because Jews have always taken it to be that locus; it is the vehicle by which we have let God in amongst us. Only by way of a text that we are willing to hear *as* God's voice can God speak to us at all: God can speak to us only when and where we are ready to listen.

One might of course not believe in God. I am not concerned here to offer arguments for God's existence, just to note that if one does not believe in God, one will not hold any view of how people encounter God. Nor is one likely to believe in Judaism.

One might also not believe in a personal God, just an abstract force or principle or substance that structures the universe. Then, too, one will not hold any view about how people encounter God. The idea of an "encounter" with an impersonal and omnipresent force is inept.

But *if* one believes that the universe is structured by a personal force or being, which can reasonably be thought of as supremely good and as loving us, then one can expect that force or being to structure our language as well as everything else. It is too simple to identify this force or being with what is mysterious as opposed to what is known or

---

[34] See my http://thetorah.com/two-models-for-accepting-the-torah/ for an elaboration of this suggestion about Ezra-Nehemiah.

under our control—a God who is in or works through everything must also be in or work through our capacity to know and to act—but we do tend to *feel* most strongly that we might be encountering a subjectivity other than our own, a Person outside ourselves, when we bump up against something mysterious, beyond our ken or mastery. Language itself partakes of the mysterious, however. Believers in a personal God should therefore be able to encounter that God in language. And Jewish believers should be able to encounter God in the language of the Torah: when they read or hear "I will be what I will be" and "Remember the sabbath" and "Do not wear cloth combining wool and linen."

Of course, what exactly God might *mean* by way of these things is a separate question. If, by hypothesis, they reflect something deeply mysterious, beyond our grasp, then what we take them to mean should be constantly in flux: they will require endless midrash, and endless reinterpretation of the directives they seem to give us. What an all-good Being, who loves all human beings and whom we can love, might mean by an expression or command is quite different from what a scribe or priest in ancient Israel might have meant, even if that scribe or priest is the immediate source of these words. Once we ascribe the Torah to God, we have *ipso facto* stripped it of its most straightforward meaning: we have opened it up to midrash. Taking the Torah's words to be divine rather than human is precisely an invitation to a fluid, ever-changing process of interpreting them.

But the essential step is for us to *take* the Torah to be divine; we cannot hear a bit of language as spoken by God unless we invest it with the capacity to be that. *We* sanctify texts and only then can God speak to us through them. We may compare this process to what happens, according to the Torah itself, when we build a tabernacle for the worship of God. *We* build it, *we* sanctify it, and only then can God dwell in it. Exactly the same is true of the language of the Torah. "Language is the house of Being,"[35] says the later Heidegger, and there could be no better metaphor for the Torah. The Torah is the house of God for us, but it becomes that if and only if we make it holy—if we invest it with sanctity, regard it as a way for God to address us. The sanctification of the tabernacle, in the Torah, requires us to treat all its parts with reverence, and never to use the whole for profane, daily purposes, let alone to mock or trample on it. Only then does it become a home of God, a space we can share with God. Sanctifying the Torah itself is similarly

---

[35] Martin Heidegger, *Pathmarks* (Cambridge: Cambridge University Press, 1998), 254.

to treat all its words with reverence, and to avoid employing it for our profane, daily purposes: to try always to learn from it rather than reading into it what we find it convenient to do, let alone mocking it or trampling on its demands. *We* make the Torah holy—we recognize and thereby establish its sanctity—but it then becomes speech that God can inhabit, speech we can share with God. Once we invest the Torah with authority, we can encounter God in it. On the literalist views common in many Orthodox communities, the Torah derives its authority from the fact that we long ago witnessed God speaking it. I am suggesting instead that *if* we invest the Torah with authority, God can speak to us today.[36] The Torah is not authoritative because it is divine; it is divine because it is authoritative.

In short, the view I am recommending would return us to the traditional Jewish idea that the Torah is God's word but not out of any historically naïve belief that God literally spoke it to Moses at Sinai. Rather, the view reflects an understanding of language as bearing God's presence in its mystery, as a meeting place for God and humanity rather than as a purely human product. This is a view that fits far better with the Jewish tradition, with personalist monotheism, and with philosophical understandings of the relationship between language and reality, than does wordless encounter theology. The central object of Jewish faith is that God speaks our language—*dibra Torah k'lashon bnei Adam*. This is what Christians would call a "mystery," to be sure: a paradox as great and of much the same kind as the Incarnation. But it is mysteries that distinguish revealed religions from the rational theology of philosophers. There is an irremediable paradox or mystery in the idea that an infinite, perfect being can enter our finite, highly imperfect lives—but without that paradox, there can be no personal God, and certainly not the personal God of Judaism.

X

The paradox must be addressed to reason. Only reason can perceive claims *as* paradoxical, and we need in any case to maintain our rational

---

[36] "Every day he who is worthy receives the Torah standing at Sinai; he hears the Torah from the mouth of the Lord."—Zohar, vol. I, p. 90a, as quoted in *GSM* 146. Ironically, Heschel himself sees the Torah this way, for all his critique of verbal revelation—and indeed puts the point beautifully: see *GSM* 171 and discussion in Held, *Abraham Joshua Heschel*, 97.

faculties in our religious commitments if we are to maintain our ability to grasp and use science, and to uphold a humanistic morality.[37] And the place for reason, in the account I am proposing, is oral Torah: the realm in which we adapt the written Torah to the particularities of our lives in various places and times. Oral Torah is the site in which halakhah is developed; it is also the site in which halakhah can change. The key to that change is the recognition that our ways of interpreting a divine text can be flexible even if the text itself is taken as fixed. I have argued elsewhere that revelation always consists in an interplay between an authoritative text and a fluid mode of interpreting that text.[38]

In the terms developed in this essay, we might put that point as follows: As we have seen, it is too simple to identify God just with what is unknown or mysterious. The one God of the entire universe must also be the source of our knowledge and agency—our autonomy. Jewish and Christian thinkers alike have long taken "the image of God" in which we were created to refer to our reason, or whatever else enables us to act morally.[39] Both Rabbi Akiva, in *Pirkei Avot*, and Maimonides, in *Hilchot Teshuvah*, speak of free will as "given" (*netunah*) to us: instilled in us by God.[40] One nice way of making room for this idea in the picture I have been sketching is to understand oral Torah as representing this gift of free will. Oral Torah will then express our autonomy, while the written Torah represents the unknown and uncontrollable to which that autonomy must respond. According to the story that gives us the name "Israel," we are a people that wrestles with God (Genesis 32:28). And we do that by trying to wrest meaning—different meanings, in different times and places—from the great Mosaic poem we set before ourselves as divine. In a robust sense, then, we can emphatically say that oral Torah was "given" at Sinai alongside the written Torah. But it was given as free will was given: as a fluid, ever-changing method or set of methods of interpretation,

---

[37] On these points, see parts I and II of my *Divine Teaching and the Way of the World* (Oxford: Oxford University Press, 2011) and chs. 1 and 2 of *The Good and the Good Book* (Oxford: Oxford University Press, 2015).

[38] I argue for this in *Divine Teaching*, part IV, ch. 6, and *The Good and the Good Book*, ch. 6.

[39] Adam Smith identifies the "impartial spectator" within us with the image of God: Smith, *Theory of Moral Sentiments* (Oxford: Oxford University Press, 1976), 128–30. That is not quite the same as reason, but Smith does mean it to be the basis of morality.

[40] *Pirkei Avot* 3:15; Maimonides, *Mishneh Torah*, Book I, "Hilchot Teshuvah" V:1.

perhaps even just a call to autonomous interpretation on our part, not as a fixed set of meanings for the divine words to which it is directed. And if "Sinai," as I have been suggesting, represents the process that took place historically when we canonized the Torah, we can translate this point about oral Torah by noting that canonization of the written Torah went inextricably along with the rise of oral modes of interpretation.[41] Fixing the written Torah as the word of God freed up its meaning to range widely, and to change over time. What God might plausibly mean by a set of words is after all very different from what a human author might mean by those same words.[42] It is implausible to think that an ancient Israelite priest or scribe might intend his words to be read in the light of modern liberalism, but it is not implausible to think that God might intend for us, today, to read them that way: God's communication is not circumscribed by place and time.

This view maps nicely onto a quite traditional understanding of the distinction between written and oral Torah. Written Torah is something that we receive, that we are given: we submit to it heteronomously. Oral Torah is by contrast something we develop actively: an expression of our freedom, our autonomy. But oral Torah defines the very contours of our submission to written Torah (what the Torah *is*, among other things), as well as its significance for us going forward. A moment of heteronomy is thus embedded in autonomy; we come to it autonomously and go from it autonomously. But the moment of heteronomy, of submission, is essential: else we will not be looking outwards, let alone to God, for the significance of our lives, merely constructing that significance out of our own resources.

So an oral Torah of some sort must always accompany the written Torah—ignoring that point was the error of the Karaites. Oral Torah in each generation should also look back with respect on the oral Torah of previous generations. If we need to interpret God's word with humility, we should start by treating our ancestors' understanding of that word with humility. Only by taking the

---

[41] See Moshe Halbertal, *People of the Book: Canon, Meaning and Authority* (Cambridge: Harvard University Press, 1997), 32–40.
[42] As the Rabbis famously say (BT Sanhedrin 34a), God speaks "as a hammer shatters rock": just as a rock shatters when hit with a hammer, so each word uttered by God "shatters" into many meanings.

interpretations of our ancestors as our starting point can we maintain a coherent sense of peoplehood across generations, moreover. A respect for tradition also has a variety of psychological and institutional benefits. It would be absurd to reinvent *tefillin* in every generation, or reopen the question of whether chicken may be eaten with milk. To insist that the oral Torah be free-flowing and creative is rather to insist, above all, that it be responsive to our central moral commitments: which change as societies come to new conceptions of gender roles, for instance, or of intercultural and interreligious relations. Immanuel Kant regarded autonomy as wholly expressed in morality. That may or may not be correct but moral demands are certainly its prime arena, and halakhah must meet those demands if it is, in any way, to reflect our autonomy.

Which brings us to a conception of revelation in which a fluid, open, and autonomous conception of oral Torah engages with an authoritative, fixed, written Torah. We encounter God in the Torah, we share its language with God, by moving back and forth between these autonomous and authoritative poles. Progressive Jewish theologians have given up too readily on authority; traditional Jewish theologians have given up too readily on autonomy. A conception of Torah as a space in which we share language with God can enable us to retain both poles.

XI

The Rabbis famously described the debates between Hillel and Shammai, because conducted with integrity, by saying "these and these are the words of the living God." But if we can say this of the words of Hillel and Shammai, why should we not say it of the words of the Torah? Indeed, I think this rabbinic saying reflects an implicit understanding of how God shares language with us that is quite close to the one I have presented.

Once again, to say that the words of the Torah are God's words is not to say that God is trying to tell us what a human being might try to tell us with those same words. On the contrary, it warns us against any straightforward or historicist interpretation of those words, and opens them up to meanings we could not plausibly attribute to their human sources. The dangers of taking the passage about the stubborn and rebellious son literally, and the way that our tradition has used midrash to skirt those dangers, is an example of these points.[43] We could and should do more to read the (apparent?) sexism and xenophobia of the Torah out of our tradition as well.

But as long as we realize that attributing the Torah to God should make us more vigilant, not less, about seeking admirable meanings for it, I see no reason—no moral reason, no philosophical reason, and no historical reason—not to attribute the *whole* Torah to God: every word and every letter of it, as Maimonides admonished us to do. We may be elated at the burning bush, bemused by the lists in *Numbers*, and horrified by the stubborn and rebellious son, but we can find religiously valuable meanings in all these passages: as our tradition has in fact long done. And anything less than this holistic reverence for the Torah, anything that splits it into more and less acceptable bits, takes away from its ability to teach us, to humble us, and thereby to enrich the ethical and spiritual sensibilities we bring to it. The Torah becomes less than a poem we admire, and far less than an object of sanctity, a space for encountering God. We preserve the sanctity of the Torah by preserving it whole. "These and these"—*all* the verses of the Torah—are the words of the living God. I know no more powerful way of encountering that God.

Selected Further Reading

Buber, Martin. *I and Thou.* Translated by W. Kaufmann. New York: Simon & Schuster, 1970.
Cohen, Hermann. *Religion of Reason Out of the Sources of Judaism.* Translated by S. Kaplan. Atlanta: Scholars Press, 1995.
Fishbane, Michael. *Sacred Attunement.* Chicago: University of Chicago Press, 2008.
Fleischacker, Samuel. *Divine Teaching and the Way of the World.* Oxford: Oxford University Press, 2011.
Fleischacker, Samuel. *The Good and the Good Book.* Oxford: Oxford University Press, 2015.
Gillman, Neil. *Sacred Fragments.* Philadelphia: Jewish Publication Society, 1990.
Gillman, Neil. *The Way Into Encountering God in Judaism.* Woodstock, VT: Jewish Lights Publishing, 2000.
Held, Shai. *Abraham Joshua Heschel: The Call of Transcendence.* Bloomington: Indiana University Press, 2013.
Levenson, Jon. *The Hebrew Bible, the Old Testament, and Historical Criticism.* Louisville, KY: Westminster John Knox Press, 1993.

---

[43] See b. Sanhedrin 68b–72a, and my discussion of this passage in *Divine Teaching and the Way of the World* (Oxford: Oxford Univeristy Press, 2011), 379–83.

Rosenzweig, Franz. *The Star of Redemption*. Translated by B. Galli. Madison, WI: University of Wisconsin Press, 2005.
Rosenzweig, Franz. "The Unity of the Bible." In *Scripture and Translation*. Edited by M. Buber, and F. Rosenzweig. Translated by L. Rosenwald with E. Fox. Bloomington: Indiana University Press, 1994.
Sommer, Benjamin. *Revelation and Authority*. New Haven, CT: Yale University Press, 2015.

19 A Constructive Jewish Theology of God and Perfect Goodness

JEROME YEHUDA GELLMAN

Jewish theology can be divided into two genres. One genre is that whose main focus is on the elucidation of Jewish theologies of those who have gone before or of concepts or periods in Jewish theology.[1] This genre is what appears, in outstanding contributions, in several chapters of this book. That is fitting and proper for a collection of this kind. An entirely different genre is constructive Jewish theology, which might have recourse to elements of the first genre, but whose aim is to construct Jewish theology for contemporary times. This might well require departure from what has come before or might yet confirm what has come before but from some new considerations and contemporary needs. This volume also contains a few fine chapters in constructive theology. What follows here is another contribution to contemporary constructive Jewish theology. In it I offer an understanding of what traditional Judaism demands of my philosophical concept of God. The primary sources for such a conception are the Hebrew Bible along with the rabbinic literature of Talmud and midrash. Secondarily are the later writings of Jewish philosophy and of the Jewish mystical literature, the Kabbalah. There is great diversity about God within that literature, however, so the task depends on selecting from that large literature what one finds most significant. While there is a dimension of personal choice, which causes me to write in first-person in what follows, I argue that there is reason for others to endorse the criterion I am about to propose for traditional Judaism. Others, Jews, Christians, and Moslems are invited to contribute their thoughts in response.

---

[1] Of course, focusing on a figure from the past does not preclude the aim of urging this figure's ideas for the present. We may presume that often that this is what motivates a philosopher to focus on a particular figure. My characterization of this genre, therefore, pertains to the main focus, and I agree that there can be fuzzy lines between this and the genre to follow.

Please note that agreeing with me on what traditional Judaism demands of the concept of God does not mean that you must believe that such a God exists or that such is your God. Recognizing that Judaism makes a particular demand does not in itself entail your having to accept that demand. You might have reasons for rejecting that demand. So, I will omit from this chapter any reasons from outside the tradition one might have for rejecting the God that I propose. In particular, I leave aside objections from the so-called "problem of evil." The latter does not challenge the fact that Judaism might demand a God of a certain nature but aims to reject that demand and that nature. As for objections from within the tradition, I leave such to further conversation as well as to individual differences in spiritual sensibilities. As for me, the God I see the Jewish tradition demanding of me is the God in which I believe, or try to believe, given the peaks and valleys of a serious religious life.

I

The Hebrew Bible is quite explicit about telling me to serve God with "all my heart and all my soul." Deuteronomy 6:5 says: "You shall love the LORD your God with all your heart, and with all your soul, and with all your might." Deuteronomy 30:6 says: "And the LORD your God will circumcise your heart and the heart of your offspring, so that you will love the LORD your God with all your heart and with all your soul." Deuteronomy 13:4 refers to God's testing the Israelites, "to know whether you indeed love the LORD your God with all your heart and soul."

Let us call love of God with all my heart and with all my soul, "maximal" or "utmost" love of God. Maximal love has two aspects. One is undertaking actions apt for creating maximal love of God. The second is where the *fulfillment* of such undertakings takes place, that is internal to the person, in the heart and in the soul.

The Hebrew Bible also tells me to serve God with all my heart and all my soul. Thus, Deuteronomy 10:12, 11:13, 26:16, and Joshua 22:5, and elsewhere.

I am also told to fear God. For example, Leviticus 15:13, 15:32, 25:17, and 19:14 repeat, "And you shall fear God," all in connection with commands to act with kindness to others. My tradition teaches me that there are two types of "fear" of God. One is fear of punishment and desire for reward. The other is more accurately described as *awe* of God. We are also told that fear of punishment and desire for reward is a lowly, immature form of attachment to God. We are not to serve God for reward but to serve God *not* for reward (*Mishnah* Avot 1:3). That is, I should wish *not* to receive a reward for serving God but to serve God for its own value.

Unavoidably, we must start with the lower fear, driven by our self-interests, but in time we are to leave that behind to replace it with the higher "fear"—the *awe* of God, a profound consciousness of God's grandeur. Biblical passages promising reward and threatening divine punishment thus have a two-layered stratum. In one layer they address people in their natural state of the lower fear. In another layer they are speaking, as Maimonides maintains, to persons motivated by a sense of God's grandeur, telling him or her that God will provide the environment enabling their higher form of awe to endure and flourish.[2] Or, as the Hasidic movement preferred, we are to take such passages metaphorically as pointing to God's providential goodness. In what follows I focus on awe of God, esteem of God's grandeur, as the favored fear of God.[3]

It is important to note that nowhere does the Hebrew Bible address to me a requirement to fear God with all my heart and all my soul. I am told marvelous things about fear of God, such as that fear of God is the "beginning of wisdom," (Psalms 111:10), and that fear of God endures forever (Psalms 19:19). But there is no injunction to have maximal or utmost fear of God. The injunction to fear God, explicitly in the Leviticus verses, occurs to motivate the observance of the divine precepts. An adequate degree of fear of God, then, will be what level generally serves sufficiently to motivate such observance.[4]

The contrast between the required degree of love and fear, respectively, is best marked by looking at Judaism's source for the most extreme act of fidelity to God—the giving up of one's life. Rabbinic

---

[2] For Maimonides on reward and punishment, see Menachem Kellner, *Must a Jew Believe Anything?*, 2nd ed. (Oxford and Portland, OR: The Littman Library of Jewish Civilization, 2006), 150–63.

[3] I subsume fear of God's punishment and desire for God's reward under the rubric of God's justice, which belongs with God's goodness. Here I will not be able to enter into the issue of combining God's justice with God's mercy, a not trivial topic.

[4] There are instances where the Hebrew Bible says to fear God and follows with saying to serve God with all of one's heart. However, we cannot infer from this that fear of God alone is to lead to serving God with maximal service. This is because that since maximalism occurs only with love of God and never explicitly with fear of God, it is most likely that the term "with all your heart" occurs in the Hebrew Bible as a synonym for love of God. Hence, to fear God and serve God with all one's heart is another way of saying to fear and love God.

literature establishes three situations in which one must give up one's life for God's will rather than agree to sin. These are when one is being forced to murder, to engage in illicit sexual acts, or to commit idolatry (Talmud Sanhedrin 74a).

This mandate follows not from the need to *fear* God, but from *love* of God. The Talmud, in *Mishnah* Berachot 9:5, commenting on the requirement to love God with all one's soul, says this: "With all your soul"—"even if God should take your soul," meaning even if God tells you to die for God's will. (As noted, the Talmud confines this to the three cardinal sins.) No such extreme action follows from our having to fear God. The directive to *fear* God does not require supreme fear, only a degree of fear that has what it takes to motivate us to do God's word in ordinary times, as it were, to do such actions as respecting the elderly, refraining from cheating, not cursing a deaf person, and the like (all from the Leviticus' link to fear of God). We are not told to give up our lives for fear of God. Love of God, though, has no limits.

In view of the above, I propose that the criterion for a *religiously* adequate conception of God in my tradition should be that God be such that it be most appropriate to love God with a love than which there can be no greater. Here we are talking about a being to whom maximal love is *most* appropriate and is *most* appropriate for *everyone* across the board and in *every* situation. Love of God is not context dependent but valid for all contexts and always.

The criterion of God being worthy of our utmost love plausibly yields a God suitable for the required degree of awe of God. This sounds credible since whatever being is most appropriate for maximal love likely will be more than adequate for being the object of the desired awe. A God who deserves my maximal love will most likely *ipso facto* be a God before whom I stand in awe. So, I take the criterion of maximal love to be the most fundamental for an adequate concept of God, trailing with it the appropriate degree of fear of God.[5] An adequate degree of awe

---

[5] William Wainwright, "Two (or Maybe One and a Half) Cheers for Perfect Being Theology," *Philo* 12 (2009): 228–51, takes the above Deuteronomy passages to be mandating unconstrained "devotion" to God. And, Wainwright suggests that unconstrained *devotion* is most appropriate only to a *perfect being*. A perfect being, here, is the classical conception of a being with an array of omni-attributes. Hence, Wainwright takes the appropriateness of offering maximal unconstrained devotion as a criterion of adequacy of a concept of God. And he advances that only a *perfect* being will merit that kind of devotion. Now, "devotion" is too wide a term to employ here for the verses in Deuteronomy that I have cited. Devotion can come from an array of motives, only one of which is love. Devotion can come from terror, from

of God should naturally ride piggyback (excuse the expression) on maximal love of God. Likewise, given that only regarding love of God am I told to engage all my soul and all my heart, it is plausible to assume that utmost service of God, noted above, also will be a function of love and not of fear. Since we are to love God with an unsurpassable love, we are to serve God to the utmost of our heart and soul.

Maximal love of God will have two features. It will entail gratitude and be grounded in perfect goodness. Gratitude does not yet yield maximal love. The ground of maximal love of God will have to involve God's essential character, a love of God because of the "whatness" of God. And so, I propose that a necessary and sufficient condition of God's being worthy of our utmost love is that God be a *perfectly good being*, in a sense I will now explain. And I propose that God as *a perfectly good being* properly induces in us the desired degree of awe. And it has what it takes to justify serving God with all our heart and soul. Since God's being a *perfectly good being* is an adequate concept of God for my religious life, and since God's being a *perfectly good being*, as I mean that, does not necessitate that God be a *perfect being, simpliciter*, it follows that for my religious tradition God need not be a perfect being *simpliciter*. Thus shall I argue.

II

My conception of a "perfectly good being" begins with having a *perfectly good character*. Richard Swinburne defines what he calls "perfect moral goodness" as "doing both the obligatory and supererogatory and doing nothing wrong or bad in other ways."[6] Obligatory good actions are those a person is under obligation to perform, while supererogatory good actions are those that go beyond obligation. Swinburne specifies further that a morally perfect being, "does whatever is of overriding importance that he should do."

Now, Swinburne's definition requires supplementation to fit my idea of a *perfectly good character*. That is because Swinburne confines his characterization solely to the *actions* of a moral person. That person

---

feelings of awe, or from having made a solemn promise to act with devotion. The above verses speak of *love* of God explicitly, and never do we find the same language regarding fear of God. Hence, I hinge the criterion of adequacy of a God-concept in my tradition on maximal love of God and not on devotion in general.

[6] Richard Swinburne, *The Coherence of Theism, Revised Edition* (Oxford: Clarendon Press, 1993), 185.

does certain sorts of things and refrains from *doing* other sorts of things. My person who has a perfectly good character, in distinction, must not only *act* in certain ways but must do so from proper moral sentiments. These moral sentiments are for me part of what it is to have a good moral character. So, a being who does the obligatory and supererogatory and does nothing wrong might *act* perfectly good, yet might lack the proper moral sentiments that we should require of one having a perfectly good character. At times one may be acting goodly from motivations of self-interest rather than for the sake of doing what is best for others or for society. It just might turn out that on those occasions what the person took to be in his self-interest was *also* coincidentally the right thing to do. For example, suppose I grab a knife away from a man on the street who is about to stab somebody, thereby saving the intended victim's life. I would have done a demonstrably "morally good act." But suppose I grabbed the knife from the assailant only because I recognized it as *my* knife, and I wanted it back. I really did not care whether I saved the poor guy. All that concerned me was getting back my favorite, pearl-handled, engraved knife. An act motivated by such self-regarding interest in this way would not be an act conforming to my idea of a perfectly good character, even if a good act. To have a perfectly good character requires always acting goodly *and* doing so with or from proper moral sentiment. Such moral sentiments will include things such as love, a sense of obligation, justice, and the like. (I leave working out the details for a later time.)

So, a perfectly good being has a perfectly good character. But, that is just the beginning. To be a perfectly good being, in my sense, one must also be perfect in *actualizing* the good intentions and sentiments of one's perfectly good character. This brings us back to Swinburne's good actions. This means being perfect *qua* having a perfectly good character. This requirement dictates several further attributes of a perfectly good being.

In my sense, a being with a perfectly good character will not yet be perfectly good unless it has all the *power* it needs to actualize its perfectly good character. It must have no logical limitations on its *ability* to *express* its perfectly good character. It must have, therefore, what I will call "perfect power for the good," or for short, "perfect good-power."

Next, a perfectly good being must have all the *knowledge* needed for perfect use of its goodness and power for the good. Let us call this "perfect good-knowledge." Perfect good-knowledge means knowing every proposition needed to actualize its perfectly good character and perfectly good power. Perfect good-knowledge should also include *intimate* perfect good-knowledge of what it is like for something conscious to be in various psychological states. With perfect good-knowledge one knows from the "inside," as it were, concerning sentient beings, what it is like to be a being of that kind, as well as what it is like to be *this* sentient being. So, one who is perfectly good knows from the inside what it is like to be me and what it is like to be you. Thus, even if the perfectly good being is never itself afraid, it should know what being afraid is like. This ensures full moral empathy when acting for the good.

Next, a being that is perfectly good will be able to do more good the longer it exists. So, it should exist forever to be perfectly good. Accordingly, I add that a perfectly good being exists forever. Some will think such a being will be everlasting in time, others that it must exist eternally out of time. In either case, there will be no time at which it is true to say that it does not exist.

Since one who is perfectly good has all the power and knowledge needed to use its perfectly good character, such a being will create and be sovereign over what it creates, thereby producing a reality toward which to be perfectly good. So, a perfectly good being will be the creator and sovereign of the world.

We would well believe that a perfectly good being must be in active relationship with the world and the creatures it creates. It must be responsive to the Creation. Some, including Richard Swinburne and Keith Ward, have argued extensively that such a being would have to exist in time for that to be the case.[7] Others, such as Eleonore Stump in her recent Aquinas Lecture, have argued that a being who is above or out of time can maintain active relations with the world.[8] Fortunately, to adopt relationality we need not decide between a being in time or out of time. There is also the possibility that it be out of time and enter time in the act of creation and subsequently in relating to the Creation. So, I will assume that one who is perfectly good is in active relations with the

---

[7] Richard Swinburne, "God and Time," in *Reasoned Faith* ed. Eleonore Stump (Ithaca: Cornell University Press, 1993), 204–22, and Keith Ward, *Christ and the Cosmos* (New York: Cambridge University Press, 2015), ch. 1.

[8] Eleonore Stump, *The God of the Bible and the God of the Philosophers* (Milwaukee, WI: Marquette University Press, 2016).

Creation and leave it open whether it is in or out of time, although my inclination is to the hybrid attribute of being both in and out of time.

So, *a perfectly good being* is, so far, a being with a perfectly good character, with perfect good-power, and perfect good-knowledge, existing always, the creator and sovereign of the world, and in active relationships with creation. Such a being deserves the requisite degree of awe, which might be less than maximal. And such a being will deserve trust with all your heart, as Proverbs 3:5 puts it.

III

It is time to contrast God as a perfectly *good* being with God as a *perfect* being, as commonly construed. I want to compare a perfectly good being with a perfect being regarding four attributes or characteristics: necessary existence, simplicity, omnipotence, and omniscience.

By necessary existence I mean metaphysically necessary in the sense of existing in every possible world. It is an open question for me whether a perfectly good being must have necessary existence. And that is because while the being who *is* the perfectly good being *might* be a metaphysically necessary being, it is not clear that it *need* be to be perfectly good. A perfectly good being might be deserving of my love with all my heart and all my soul, whether or not it be metaphysically necessary. It must be at least metaphysically *secure* in this world. I will then know that its love has endured and will endure forever. That requirement would be met by its being the sort of being that cannot come into or go out of existence. A being of that sort would be an *essentially* everlasting or eternal being, that is, one that is everlasting or eternal in every possible world in which it exists. And it would be a being that is essentially perfectly good, that is, perfectly good in every world in which it exists.

Simplicity is not a necessary attribute of a perfectly good being. To be so, it would have to contribute to the standing of that being as regards being most deserving of my maximal love. But it is hard to see how it would do that. The argument of Maimonides for God's simplicity is God's ontological independence. Maimonides needed God's simplicity to stop an infinite regress of causal dependence. That is because for him whatever was complex relied on something else that was the cause of the complex composition. But nowadays few believe that if God were compound there would be a chance of God falling apart or that complexity simply must be due to the sustaining act of another. So, for us, it would seem that God would be metaphysically secure even if complex. And as far as I know, there is no argument that would make simplicity a requirement of being a perfectly good being. Indeed, this might be an argument for no longer thinking of simplicity as an attribute of a perfect being either. In that case, simplicity would not afford a distinction between being perfectly good and being perfect *simpliciter*.

What about omnipotence? Must a perfectly good being be omnipotent? Conceptually, *perfect good-power* is different from omnipotence. Having perfect good-power, in my sense, does not mean that God can do everything possible, as, roughly, does omnipotence, only that God has whatever power is needed to fully implement God's perfectly good character. For all we know, this might be less than omnipotence. That is because there might be abilities or powers not needed by God to actualize his perfectly good character in any world in which God exists. Such abilities to act, then, would not be included in what I am calling "perfect good-power," as it would for omnipotence. I think we have no way of knowing whether there are such powers to be left out from a perfectly good being. Conceptually, at least, a distinction exists between omnipotence and perfect good-power. If the perfectly good being will be omnipotent that will not be because omnipotence is a perfection, but because it turns out that it must be omnipotent to be perfectly good. (See Part IV for more on omnipotence.)

Similarly, for omniscience. Do not confuse the concept of *perfect good-knowledge* with omniscience. Having perfect good-knowledge, in my sense, does not require that God know every true proposition, only that God knows whatever knowledge it takes to actualize God's perfectly good character. This may amount to omniscience, knowing all the truths there are to know. Or it might not. Perhaps there are truths a perfectly good being never needs to know to fully activate its perfect goodness. Perhaps there are propositions that are not relevant to doing any good in any world in which the perfectly good being exists. In that case what I am calling "perfect knowledge" will be less than omniscience. If the perfectly good being will be omniscient that will not be because omniscience is a perfection, but because it turns out that it must be omniscient to be perfectly good. Omniscience will turn out, whether we know it or not, to be metaphysically equivalent to having perfect good-knowledge. (See Part IV for more on omniscience.)

IV

In private communication, Mark Murphy has argued that a perfectly good being, in my terms, is perforce a perfect being. My response here to Murphy will help clarify my position on a perfectly good being versus a perfect being.

Murphy argues as follows:[9]

1) What makes it inappropriate to withhold love from a being are those being's excellences. (premise)
2) A being that is "perfectly good" [in my sense] but is not perfect is a being that lacks some excellences. (premise)
3) There will be some love that it is not inappropriate to withhold from a being that is perfectly good while failing to be perfect. (1, 2)
4) If there is some love that it is not inappropriate to withhold from a being, then one can, without error, withhold maximal love from that being. (premise)
5) If God is perfectly good but not perfect, then one can, without error, withhold maximal love from God. (3, 4)
6) One cannot, without error, withhold maximal love from God. (premise)
7) It is not the case that: God is perfectly good but not perfect. (5,6)

In reply, I find 1) to be problematic as stated. It can be understood in one of two ways:

> 1a) What makes it inappropriate to withhold love from a being is that being having all the excellences relevant to its being worthy of our maximal love.

and

> 1b) What makes it inappropriate to withhold love from a being is that being having all excellences.

I endorse 1a) as trivially true, but am less than tepid about accepting 1b). My skittishness regarding 1b) follows from my conviction that not every excellence is an occasion for generating maximal love, or even just plain love. For example, omnipotence and omniscience need not be a ground for love, per se. Being omnipotent might make one overwhelmingly impressive, perhaps, as a cosmic acrobat without equal, and so be

---

[9] I present this argument with the permission of Mark Murphy.

a superb excellence. But having omnipotence would not make one more *lovable* on top of the love due to one for having perfect good-power. Omnipotence might give us a big "Wow! Look at that!" "Amazing!"—but not a cause of love. Now, my perfect good-power *might* happen to turn out to be equivalent to omnipotence, because it turns out that there is no possible power never needed for doing good. In that case, the ground of the love-value of omnipotence will be due to its being metaphysically equivalent to being perfect in the service of a perfect-good character, not because it is omnipotence. The same for omniscience. That attribute might guarantee that God could win the jackpot on every possible quiz program, and so make God incredibly impressive. But I have grave reservations that this qualifies as relevant to God being worthy of my love with all my heart and all my soul.

Given that 1) is acceptable only as 1a), accordingly 2) is to be read as

2a) A being that is "perfectly good" [in my sense] but is not perfect is a being that lacks some excellences relevant to its being worthy of our maximal love.

Read as such, this premise is not acceptable. That follows from reasons similar to why I rejected 1b). And that is because, as I have argued just above, there are excellences that are not relevant to being worthy of our maximal love. So, a being can lack some excellences and still be worthy of our maximal love. So, 2a) is less than evident. In that case, the argument against my position lacks traction.

Another way I would reply to this argument would be to argue that there may be no excellences actually lacking to the perfectly good being, in my sense. With "excellences" here I focus on the classical excellences thought to make God perfect. Now, an attribute to be an excellence must have intrinsic value in and of itself (or else have only good extrinsic value). For example, having a perfectly good character counts as an excellence. Having a good character is intrinsically good and worthy. This is true even if the person is paralyzed and her ability to act goodly is greatly restricted. That she has a good character is an excellence she retains throughout.

Now, having lots of power and lots of knowledge is not *intrinsically* of value. This pair can *enable* much value if combined with a good character and can enable much *disvalue* when combined with an evil character. Having loads of power and knowledge will be deleterious if a being is quite evil. It would be far better for such a being to have less power and/or less knowledge rather than more. And of course, what applies to the pair together applies to each separately. Neither is intrinsically good nor intrinsically bad, alone or together. There is no value in knowledge for knowledge's sake. Cases that seem otherwise will be found to locate value in the knowledge in question for reasons, specific or general, beyond the very knowledge itself. And there is no value in power for power's sake.

The idea that knowledge or power are intrinsic excellences leads naturally to absurd claims. Listen to what Charles Hartshorne once wrote:

> We are told by an English writer that it is a question whether there be any "utterly senseless" or "unredeemed evil"? (sic) What would such a thing be like? I declare in all earnestness I have no idea. Any evil has some value from some perspective, for even to know it exists is to make it contributory to a good, *knowledge itself being a good*.[10]

Contra Hartshorne, no one should accept that there was anything good in the knowledge that Heinrich Himmler, head of the Nazi Gestapo and manager of Nazi exterminations camps, had that Hitler wanted to kill all the Jews. And nobody should think for a moment that there was a smidgen of good in a Catholic man in the Thirty Years' War knowing that the man standing opposite him was a Protestant and so had to be killed. But if you think that knowledge itself is good then you must believe such things. Similar thoughts apply to the idea that power in itself is an intrinsic good. It is not.

As for the possession of loads of power and knowledge, it would be best for us to wait patiently to hear more of the story. Now, when we *do* hear more, *the greatest contribution* we can hear that this pair makes to the excellence of a being would be if it were attached to a perfectly good character. That will give the power-knowledge pair its greatest possible value. But in that case, we need ascribe no more than what I have called "perfect good-power" and "perfect good-knowledge," perfect power and knowledge for the good. Omnipotence, including power for what makes for neutral states of affairs, and omniscience, including knowing propositions not needed for the good in any world in which God exists, would add nothing more of value to a perfectly good character than perfect good-power and perfect good-knowledge. Thus I am arguing in this second reply to Murphy, since neither knowledge nor power are good in themselves. The perfect value of power and knowledge can

---

[10] Charles Hartshorne, *A Natural Theology for Our Time* (La Salle, IL: Open Court, 1967), 81. My emphasis.

come only from adding them to a perfectly good character. And so, omnipotence and omniscience would add nothing more to perfection than perfect good-power and perfect good-knowledge. Beyond that there need be no further power or knowledge.

Some feminist thinkers, including Daphne Hampson and Mary Daly, have rejected massive power as an attribute of God, as reflecting a conception of God as male.[11] Having lots of power, they say, indicates a masculine, androcentric value. To think God has massive power is to set up a justifying model for male aspirations for power, to have the power to dominate others, including using male power to rule women.

This objection rests on the supposition that sheer power is being put forward as a "perfection" of God all by itself, in isolation from God's other attributes. If I am right, great power should be God's only together with God's perfectly good character. And it is only power for good. When considering power all by itself, indeed we should not think of it as a great good. So, when we attribute good-power together with perfectly good character, the divine model for humans, both male and female, is to use whatever power one has in a maximal way only for the good. The abuse of another cannot be the result of modeling oneself after a perfectly good God with perfect good-power. So, neither omnipotence nor omniscience are excellences in themselves and neither is simplicity. So, I conclude that there are no excellences missing from a perfectly good being. A perfectly good being is as perfect as they come.

Now 2a) is equivalent to:

> 2b) If a being is "perfectly good" [in my sense] but is not perfect, then it lacks some excellences relevant to its being worthy of our maximal love.

On my present thinking, this turns out to be trivially true because if I am right its antecedent is logically inconsistent. But then, by the same token, there cannot possibly *ever be* a being who is perfectly good and not perfect. So, there cannot be a proof that it is possible for a being to be perfectly good yet not perfect.

I think, therefore, that my position remains possible after this argument has been raised.

*

[11] See Daphne Hampson, "On Power and Gender," *Modern Theology* 4 (1988): 239 ff., and Mary Daly, *Beyond God the Father* (Boston, MA: Beacon Press, 1985), 20.

To believe in a perfectly good being is to relate to the world in an *ultimately* optimistic way, despite sadness, pain, and suffering. To believe that one who is perfectly good exists is to be convinced that the good is ontologically basic to reality and that evil is not, and that good wins out over evil. This conviction was behind the medievalists' characterization of evil as devoid of positive reality, a "privation," only an absence or corruption of good. Good for them was ontologically basic, evil was derivative. To believe in a perfectly good being is to acknowledge evil fully while being able to put the evil within a frame of reference in which it does not defeat you but is taken up into ultimate optimism.

Selected Further Reading

Daly, Mary. *Beyond God the Father*. Boston, MA: Beacon Press, 1985.
Gellman, Jerome. "The God of the Jews and the Jewish God." In *Routledge Companion to Theism*, 38–53. Edited by Charles Taliaferro, Victoria Harricosn, and Stewart Goetz. Abingdon-on-Thames: Routledge, 2012.
Gellman, Jerome Yehuda. *Perfect Goodness and the God of the Jews*. Boston, MA: Academic Studies Press, 2019.
Hampson, Daphna. "On Power and Gender." *Modern Theology* 4 (1988): 239 ff.
Harshorne, Charles. *A Natural Theology for Our Time*. La Salle, IL: Open Court, 1967.
Kellner, Menachem. *Must a Jew Believe Anything?* 2nd ed. Oxford and Portland, OR: The Littman Library of Jewish Civilization, 2006.
Stump, Eleonore. *The God of the Bible and the God of the Philosophers*. Milwaukee: Marquette University Press, 2016.
Swinburne, Richard. *The Coherence of Theism, Revised Edition*. Oxford: Clarendon Press, 1993.
Swinburne, Richard. "God and Time." In *Reasoned Faith*, 204–22. Edited by Eleonore Stump. Ithaca, NY: Cornell University Press, 1993.
Wainwright, William. "Two (or Maybe One and a Half) Cheers for Perfect Being Theology." *Philo* 12 (2009): 228–51
Ward, Keith. *Christ and the Cosmos*. New York: Cambridge University Press, 2015.

Index

Abelson, Joshua, 173
abortion, 310
Abraham, 56, 319, 357
Absolute, the, 283, 336, 401
Abulafia, Abraham, 158, 162, 178
acclamation rites, 88
Account of Creation, The, 159
Achilles, 252
acosmism, 205, 206, 209
Active Divinity, 175
Adler, Rachel
  on gender justice, 311, 312
  on halakhah, 300, 308
  on proactive halakhah, 309
  Ross and, 309
  on women as others, 297
Adon Olam
  the Aleinu and, 90, 92, 162
  the Ashrei and, 93
  contextual interpretation of, 89, 90
  Divine sovereignty and, 77, 90
  foci of, 91
  kingship in, 98
  monotheism and, 90, 92
  origins of, 91
  place in service of, 90
  Shaḥarit and, 94
  as theological introduction to the service, 91
  tiforah and, 92
  two sections of, 90
adonai, 154
aesthetics, 9, 229
affection, 140
After Auschwitz (Rubenstein), 268, 272, 273
afterlife, the, 129
Afterman, Adam, 7, 15

aggadah
  commandment and, 35
  covenant and, 27
  defined, 26
  God and, 34
  halakhah and, 26–30, 35
  method and, 27
  mitsvot and, 26
  phenomenology and, 37
  theological realism and, 397
  theology as, 36, 37
  Torah and, 28
aggadic midrashic literature, 224
aggadic theology, 398
Agus, Rabbi Jacob B., 332
Ahaz, 54
Akedah Theology, 300, 311
Akiva ben Yosef, 448
Albo, Joseph, 15
Aleinu, the
  Adon Olam and, 90, 91, 92
  the Amidah and, 93
  the Ashrei and, 93
  contextual interpretation of, 90
  in the daily liturgy, 93
  Divine sovereignty and, 78, 90, 93, 98
  foci of, 91
  kingship in, 98
  monotheism and, 90, 92
  redemption and, 79
  Shaḥarit and, 92, 94
  tiferet and, 92
  two stages of, 91
  Zechariah (book) and, 95
Alexandrov, Shmuel, 199
Alkabetz, Solomon, 89
Allah, 231
al-Ma'mūn, 105

467

al-Mansur, 105
Alston, William, 395, 396, 397, 400, 406, 420
Altizer, Thomas, 272
Amidah, the
 the Aleinu and, 79, 93
 the Ashrei and, 94
 in the daily liturgy, 100
 Divine worship in, 98
 kingship in, 97
 redemption and, 78, 87, 89
 Shaharit and, 94
 the Shema and, 80, 87
 theological program of, 78
Amos, 54
analytic philosophy, 8, 17, 38
"Ancient Holy One", 162
"Ancient of Days, The", 162
anthropocentrism, 332
anthropomorphism
 God as author and, 385
 the Godhead and, 168
 idolatry and, 125, 139
 of Kabbalists, 157
 Kant on, 386
 limitation of God and, 128
 sefirot and, 176
antinomianism, 145
apologetic theology, 219, 317
apophaticism, 398, 399, 417, 418
Arabella (Hofmannsthal), 439
Ariadne auf Naxos (Hofmannsthal), 439
Aristotle
 on God, 119
 on imitation, 139
 importance of for Jewish philosophy, 105
 Maimonides and, 22, 139, 143, 383
 on nature, 142
 theology and, 22
ascent, 156
Asher Yaṣar, 77
Ashrei, the
 the Aleinu and, 93
 in the daily liturgy, 93
 Divine kingship and, 78
 Divine sovereignty and, 93, 94
 Divine worship in, 98
 Pesquei DeZimra and, 94
 the Shema Liturgy and, 94
 structure of, 99

atomism, 215
Attah Hu, 98
attributes
 of God's actions, 139
 Kabbalists on, 150
 Maimonides on, 120
 model of prophets' conduct on, 140
 negative theology and, 375
 plurality and, 125
 as predicates of God, 122
Auschwitz
 belief in God and, 13
 as challenge to traditional Jewish theology, 273
 death of God and, 273
 God and, 268, 269, 287, 288
 God's power and, 292
 God's will and, 268
 Greenberg on, 284
 H. Jonas on, 294
 Jonas and, 289
 myth and, 288
 the Shema and, 34
 suffering and, 285
authenticity, 229
autonomy
 authority and, 450
 Buber on, 408
 freedom as, 277
 God and, 448
 halakhah and, 450
 morality and, 450
 in rabbinic literature, 431
 revelation and, 424
 Torah and, 241, 449
Avivi, Yosef, 206
Avoda Zara, 356, 361, 364, 367
Ayer, A. J., 393
Azriel of Gerona, 175

Babylonian Talmud, the, 10, 60
Back to the Sources (Holtz), 219
Bamberger, Bernard, 333
Barukh SheAmar, 78, 97
being, 240
Being and Time (Heidegger), 253, 427, 439
Beit Midrash, 431
Ben Bag Bag, 107
ben David, Abraham, 114
ben Gershon, Levi, 15

ben Nahman, Moses (Nahmanides), 165
ben Simeon, Rabbi Meir, 158
Benjamin, Mara, 221
Bereshit, 224
Bergson, Henri, 198, 252, 253
Berit Olam, 50, 51, 52, 53
Berkovits, Eliezer
  on the authority of Judaism, 275
  on confronting the Holocaust, 275
  on creation, 276
  on Divine self-denial, 281
  on Divine-human relationship, 400
  Fackenheim and, 325
  on the finite and the infinite, 323
  Greenberg and, 287
  H. Jonas and, 294
  on the hiddenness of God, 278
  Jonas and, 293
  Kant and, 277
  life of, 274
  on negative theology, 401
  on providence and the Holocaust, 283
  on revelation, 324
  theological realism of, 400–1
  on *tzimtzum*, 282
Besht, the, 202
Bi'ur Eser Sefirot, 175
Bible, the
  feminist midrash and, 306, 307
  midrash and, 219, 220
  midrashic analysis of, 226
  unity of God in, 169
Biblical law, 71
biblical theology, 2, 41, 42
Bildung, 214
bittul ha-yesh, 207
blood, 52
Blumenthal, David, 58
body, the, 77
Book of Beliefs and Opinions (Saadia), 132
Brill, Alan, 1, 7, 11, 352, 356
Buber, Martin
  Benjamin and, 221
  Berkovits and, 400
  biblical humanism and, 241
  on creation and redemption, 88
  Fackenheim and, 325
  hermeneutical theology of, 16
  on law, 305
  Levinas and, 239

on *mitsvah* and *halakhah*, 29
mysticism and, 11
negative theology and, 11
Plaskow and, 305
on redemption, 88
on revelation, 336, 426
theo-realism of, 407, 408
wordless encounter theology and, 427
Bultmann, Rudolf, 287
burning bush, the, 63
Bush, George W., 440
Byrne, Peter, 394

Cain and Abel, 70
Calvin, John, 395
care, 241, 255
Carver, Douglas, 393
Cassirer, Ernst, 223
categorical imperative, 201
causality, 117
Chabad Hasidic thought, 340
Challah, 52
chiasmus, 82
"Children in Egypt and the Theophany at the Sea, The" (Green), 220
Christian Bible, the, 43, 44
Christian dogmatic theology, 41
Christian feminist theology, 297
Christian Old Testament, 43
Christian Old Testament theology, 41
Christian scholasticism, 110
Christian theology
  biblical theology and, 41
  death of God movement in, 272
  influence of Greek philosophy on, 6
  language and, 6
  negative theology and, 336
  new covenant and, 43
  revelation and, 319, 320
  scholarly attention given to, 4
  syllogistic form of, 6
  systematic propositional form of, 6
Christian theology of religion, 363
Christianity
  antisemitism of, 369
  complementary relationship with Judaism of, 215
  crucifixion and, 74
  idolatry and, 360, 361
  Islam and, 362
  Kook on, 368

Christianity (cont.)
  Maimonides and, 361
  medieval Judaism and, 344
  Meiri on, 363
Chronicles, 48
Clooney, Francis, 363
"Cloud of Smoke, Pillar of Fire,"
  (Greenberg), 284
Codex Sinaiticus, 44
Codex Vaticanus, 44
Cohen, Hermann
  Ethical Monotheism and, 8
  Kant and, 198
  Maimonides and, 382, 389
  on morality and God, 382, 387–90
  negative theology and, 10
  religion of reason of, 200
  Rosenzweig and, 404
  Spinoza and, 199
  on transcendence and immanence, 177
  transcendental method of, 198
Cohen, Richard, 12, 16
Cohn Sherbok, Dan, 349
collective experience, 80
collective memory, 80
commandments. *See also* mitsvot
  aggadah and, 35
  authority of, 85
  Berit Olam and, 52
  covenant and, 26, 30, 286
  Fackenheim on, 325
  finite human nature and, 145
  Godhead and, 167
  God-human relationship and, 35, 36, 37
  gratitude and, 33, 34
  grounds for, 144
  halakhah and, 27, 35
  intention and, 23
  interhuman relationships and, 36
  Kabbalah and, 151, 155, 158
  knowledge of God and, 23
  limits to inquiry of, 145
  post-Holocaust, 286
  the Promised Land and, 137
  Recanati on, 166
  redemption and, 170
  revelation and, 24
  Saadia on, 132
  speculative theology and, 23
  speech and, 118

study of causes of, 143
word of God and, 29
Commentary on the Mishnah
  (Maimonides), 108, 119
common sense, 355, 395, 403
communication, 251
communion, 178, 179
community, 27, 30, 147, 236
comparative theology, 14
compassion, 65, 162, 257
complexity, 376
concealment, 190, 321
Conflicting Visions:Spiritual
  Possibilities of Modern Israel
  (Hartman), 349
Confrontation (Soloveitchik), 326
conscience, 240, 256, 260, 333, 433
consciousness
  creation and, 281
  deconstruction and, 15
  experience and, 211
  fear of God and, 455
  higher states of, 330
  historical events and, 330
  liturgy and, 94
  mystical union and, 206
  redemption and, 82
  religious realism and, 393
  revelation and, 318
  suffering and, 257
  tasks of the faithful and, 192
  tzadikim and, 209
constructive Jewish theology, 453
constructive theology, 18, 235, 453
contemporary Judaism, 9
contraception, 310
contraction, 76, 189, 293
conversation, 248, 249
Cordovero, Moses, 89, 173
correspondence theory of truth, 211
cosmic governance, 144
cosmic realism, 194
cosmological argument, the, 110, 126
covenant
  with Abraham, 319
  aggadah and, 27
  Auschwitz and, 285
  commandments and, 26
  creation and, 51
  the Decalogue and, 85
  existentialism and, 323

as forward-looking, 30
God and, 31, 33
in the Prophets, 53
interpretations of, 51, 53
Jesus and, 43
law and, 54
love and, 323
mysticism and, 150
the New Testament and, 43
the Old Testament and, 43
post-Holocaust, 285–87
priority of, 256
redemption and, 32
revelation and, 25, 44, 322
salvific grace and, 319
the *shema* and, 35, 87
the Shema and, 35, 87
Torah and, 25, 31, 319
covenant theology, 322, 323
Cover, Robert, 27, 300, 308, 309, 312
creation
  Berkovits on, 276
  covenant and, 51, 285
  defined, 31
  Divine law and, 143
  divine sovereignty and, 78, 88
  Divine sovereignty and, 78, 88
  existence of God and, 109
  Genesis and, 84
  God and, 35, 51, 138, 142
  God's precedence and, 119
  God's self-limitation and, 280
  the Hebrew language and, 159
  in the Torah, 132
  judging and, 133, 134, 142
  law and, 134, 135
  matter and form and, 283
  Mosaic prophecy and, 134
  Moses and, 142
  natural laws and, 4
  Platonic view of, 138
  prophecy and, 138
  redemption and, 88, 276, 277
  responsibility and, 281
  revelation and, 31, 88
  Rosenzweig on, 224
  Shabbat and, 52, 54
  the Shema and, 78
  in the Shema Liturgy, 81
  speech and, 236
  teleology and, 142
  tzimtzum and, 282
Crescas, Hasdai, 15, 109
critical realism, 394
Critique of Pure Reason (Kant), 387, 389, 437
Culture and Value (Wittgenstein), 413
cumulative revelation, 302, 303
Cyrus of Persia, 50, 56

daily liturgy, 79, 89, 92, 100
Daily Prayers, 86
Daly, Mary, 465
Daniel, 68, 70
Daniel (book), 48, 162
davar, 23
Davidson, Donald, 18, 439
Davidson, Herbert, 140
Day of Atonement. *See* Yom Kippur
death
  the Amidah and, 78
  creation and, 224
  the face and, 257
  love and, 227
  Rosenzweig on, 227
  transcendence and, 257
death camps
  as challenge to traditional Jewish theology, 273
  God and, 267, 288
  Greenberg on, 284, 285
  impact on theology of, 268
  myth and, 288
  theodicy and, 269
Decalogue, the, 84, 85, 86, 88, 89
deconstruction, 15
deism, 383
demiourgos, 138
democracy, 260, 261, 361
democratic socialism, 261
Derrida, Jacques, 15, 337
determinism, 193, 384
Deuteronomy, 72, 74, 84, 85, 139
devequt, 178
devotion, 241, 456
dialectic theology, 325, 326
dialogue
  Christian interest in, 348
  disputation and, 316
  God and Moses and, 28
  love and, 230, 231, 232, 233, 234, 237

dialogue (cont.)
  the other and, 249
  prayer and, 396
  revelation and, 216, 318, 342
  Theology of Religions and, 360
  thought and, 248
  Torah and, 29, 30, 234
  trust and, 230
diaspora, 186, 187, 203
dignity, 259, 286, 324
Dignity of Difference, The (Sacks), 349
Dirshuni (Weingarten-Mintz and Biala), 306
Discovery Seminar, 329
Divine communication, 118
Divine countenance, 228
Divine emanation, 149, 151, 206
Divine family, 171
Divine governance, 141, 142
Divine influence, 202
Divine law
  application of, 135
  authorship of, 135
  creation and, 143
  Moses and, 136, 137
  purposiveness of, 142
Divine light, 163
Divine names, 149, 152, 165
Divine sovereignty
  acknowledgement of, 98
  Adon Olam and, 77, 90
  the Aleinu and, 78, 90, 93, 98
  the Ashrei and, 93, 94
  creation and, 88
  the Decalogue and, 85
  redemption and, 81, 86, 88
  revelation and, 88, 97
  the Shema and, 81, 84, 89, 96, 97
  the Shema Liturgy and, 84, 87, 88, 96
Divine will, 117, 136
Divine wisdom, 174
Divine worship, 98
Divine-human encounter, the, 281, 282, 400, 401, 429
Divine-human relationship, the
  aggadic theology and, 398
  autonomy and, 408
  Berkovits on, 400
  Buber and Heschel on, 407
  Christianity and, 397
  Heschel on, 400
  prayer and, 403
  realism and, 397
  theo-realism and, 410
  understanding and, 410
  uniqueness of human nature and, 25
  universal human capacity for, 25
Doctrine of Revelation: A Narrative Approach (Fackre), 317
Dostoyevsky, Fyodor, 243
doubt, 202
dual-covenant theology, 215
Dulles, Avery, 317, 318
duration, 253, 261

Eclipse of God (Buber), 407
Ecstatic Kabbalah, 162
egoism, 242, 249, 255
ein sof
  contraction and, 189, 190
  Kook on, 207
  light of, 192
  mystical union and, 206
  paradoxical conceptualization of, 176
  Scholem on, 174
  sefirot and, 163, 172, 173–76
  Torah and, 189
  transcendence of, 174, 176
Eliade, Mircea, 271
Elijah Institute, the, 14
Elijah, Rabbi of Vilna, 191
Elohai, 77
Elohim, 65
emet, 80
empathy, 64, 73
encounter, 325
Engendering Judaism (Adler), 300
Enlightenment, the
  challenge to theology of, 3, 8
  influence on Jewish theology of, 7
  Kook on, 203
  medieval philosophy and, 8
  midrashic analysis of the Bible and, 226
  revelation and, 320
  Rosenzweig and, 223
Epicurus, 91
epistemology, 8, 12, 17, 222, 316, 395
eschaton, the, 79
esotericism, 107, 113
Esther (book), 48, 57
Esther, Queen, 257

eternal law, 147
Eternal, the, 230
eternity, 251–56
Ethical Monotheism, 7, 8
ethical politics, 258, 259, 260
ethics
    as care for others, 241
    contemporaneity of thought and, 246
    conversation and, 248
    dialogue and, 230
    as essence of Judaism, 8
    as first philosophy, 11, 246
    halakhah and, 27
    Isaiah and, 57
    Levinas and, 12, 16
    love and, 229
    as obligation, 239
    obligations to the other and, 241
    Post-Enlightenment Jewish theology and, 9
    primacy of, 239, 243, 245, 247, 258
    primacy of the other and, 242
    in the public sphere, 258
    relation to God as, 241
    religion as grounded in, 243
    responsibility and, 239
    revelation and, 225
    as source of meaning, 240
    suffering and, 257
    as surplus, 255
    Talmud and, 247
    time and, 254, 255
    transcendence and, 245, 247, 253
    as the ultimate event of being, 245
Euthyphro (Plato), 147
evil
    Adon Olam and, 91
    affection and, 140
    breaking of the vessels and, 196
    death camps and, 268, 269
    eternity and, 251
    exile and, 43
    freedom and, 279
    God and, 454
    God's power and, 292
    the Godhead and, 172
    good and, 278
    hiddenness of God and, 277, 281
    the Holocaust and, 275, 295
    in the Nevi'im, 47
    omnibenevolence and, 172

ontological status of, 466
    the other and, 249
    Platonic view of, 293
    Rubenstein on, 273
    Shekhinah and, 173
    spark-gathering and, 209
    value of, 464
evolution, 177, 178, 197, 333, 369
exclusivism, 361
exegesis
    Fishbane on, 220
    God and, 337
    Levinas on, 250
    revelation and, 321, 338, 340
    as strategy of Jewish theology, 6
exile
    burning bush and, 64
    depictions of God and, 69, 155
    in Ezra-Nehemiah, 445
    God's unity and, 197
    in the Historical Books, 45
    interpretation of the Torah and, 214
    Manasseh and, 49
    Messianic Aesthetics and, 237
    midrash and, 226
    in the Nevi'im, 47
    problem of evil and, 43
    punishment and, 54, 67
    Rabbis of the Great Assembly and, 69
    revelation and, 44
    sexual symbolism of, 170
    Shekhinah and, 170
    sin and, 53
    speech-thinking and, 216
Existence and Existents (Levinas), 256
Existentialism, 18
Exodus (book), 84, 276, 319, 381, 382
Exodus (event), 86, 279
expansion, 195
Expressionism, 428
Ezekiel (prophet), 49, 50, 54, 57
Ezra (prophet), 329
Ezra-Nehemiah (book), 48, 445

face, the, 255, 257
Fackenheim, Emil
    Berkovits and, 325
    Buber and, 325
    on the commandments, 325
    on the finite and the infinite, 323
    on freedom and revelation, 282

Fackenheim, Emil (cont.)
  Greenberg and, 287
  on Job, 57
  Jonas and, 293
  post-Holocaust theology and, 13
  on revelation, 325
Fackre, Gabriel, 317, 318, 332
Fagenblat, Michael, 12, 13
faith, 225, 316, 407, 410
Faith after the Holocaust (Berkovits), 275, 277, 279, 280, 281
falasifa, 111
falsafa, 111
fear, 454, 455
feminism, 303
feminist midrash
  development of, 305
  growing popularity of, 306, 307
  Lubitch on, 307
  orthodox approaches to, 306
  traditionalism of, 306
  Umansky on, 307
  women's otherness and, 302
feminist theology, 4, 9, 16
Feuerbach, Ludwig, 392
fictionalism, 409, 415–17, 419, 421
first cause, 112, 117, 128
Fishbane, Michael, 16, 220, 340, 425, 433
Fisher, Cass, 8, 17
Fleischacker, Sam, 8, 11, 18
form, 146
Francis, Saint, 250
Frank, Daniel, 4, 7
freedom
  as Divine image, 333
  authoritarian religion and, 244
  of choice between good and evil, 278
  covenant and, 285
  creation and, 281
  evil and, 279
  evolution and, 333
  God and, 75, 277, 281, 290, 322
  God's absence and, 279
  good and evil and, 278
  hiddenness of God and, 278, 280, 282
  as innate urge, 194
  language and, 442
  love and, 233
  nature and, 386
  necessity and, 196, 244
  Platonic view of, 293
  responsibility and, 242, 256, 277
  revelation and, 282, 423
  sanctification and, 276
  sin and, 389
  suffering and, 278
  Torah and, 449
freedom of will, 200
Fundamental Wisdom of the Middle Way (Dharmakirti), 432
future, the, 254, 255

Gadamer, Hans-Georg, 6, 20
Gaon, Saadia, 7, 114, 132, 144, 159
Garden of Eden, the, 55
Gellman, Yehudah, 8, 18, 405–6, 420
gender equality, 300
gender justice, 297, 310, 311, 312, 313
Genesis, 84
genocide, 221
genus, 126
German idealism, 198, 398
Geronese Kabbalah, 178
Gersonides, 15, 125–26, 379, 380
Gevura, 209
Gikatilla, Rabbi Joseph, 157
Gillman, Neil, 425
Gilson, Étienne, 326
Glaucon, 134
"God and Philosophy" (Levinas), 257
God
  as abusive parent, 58
  aggadah and, 34
  aggadic speculation about, 26
  anthropomorphism and, 113, 385
  Aristotelian conception of, 119
  as nature, 199
  attributes and, 120, 122, 125, 381
  aura of, 192
  capacity for restarint of, 68
  commandments and, 23
  covenant and, 31, 33
  creation and, 35, 51, 138, 142
  as creator, 134
  as debtor, 67
  divine failure of, 56
  Divine sovereignty of, 79
  emotion of, 140
  empathy and, 64, 73
  as emperor, 70
  esoteric description of, 154
  essential definition of, 121

ethics and, 241
evil and, 91, 172
exile and, 197
existence of, 108, 109, 378
as father, 66
freedom and, 75, 279, 281
as governor of the natural world, 135
in Greek philosophy, 156
Greek gods and, 69
hangings and, 72
historical view of, 69
as husband, 167
hyperlinguistic manifestation of, 179
images of, 15
imitation of, 139, 141, 142, 147
immanence of, 90
incorporeality of, 108, 112, 113, 139
as independent reality, 213
interventionist conceptions of, 118, 129
Isaiah and, 57
Jeremiah and, 57
as judge, 66
judgment and, 65
language and, 114, 123, 124, 409, 424, 444, 445
law and, 71, 72
love and, 63, 78, 218, 228, 234, 237, 454, 456
man as icon of, 152
in medieval Jewish thought, 153
mercy and, 65
in the Midrash, 60
mind of, 161
mitsvot and, 23
moral meaning of, 199
Moses and, 29, 30, 56, 135, 139
names of, 64, 164
nature and, 143
as necessary being, 75
negation and, 123
Neoplatonic conception of, 128
nous and, 161
as object of worship, 127–30
organs of, 157
panentheism and, 205
pantheism and, 205
perfection of, 74–76, 194
personalism and, 189
personalist conception of, 105, 129, 200

personality of, 66, 69, 119, 384
philosophy and, 130
prayer and, 90, 99
precedence of, 108, 119
process theology and, 202
as proper object of worship and praise, 109
proper representations of, 62
relation and, 150, 382, 388, 389
as relational subject, 60, 61, 65, 75
revelation and, 31, 281, 304, 318
righteousness of, 120, 122
Schopenhauer on, 205
scientific progress and, 203
sefirot and, 160
self-contraction of, 76
self-sufficiency of, 126
as slave, 67
soul of, 161
as source of eternal truth, 129
speculative theology and, 23
speech and, 115
as teacher, 66
the burning bush and, 63
the Holocaust and, 13, 34, 294
the Roman emperor and, 63
as Torah, 166
transcendence of, 90, 121, 193, 318, 388
as unity, 180
unity of, 108, 112, 120, 158, 169, 194, 365
unknowability of, 174
as unknowable, 175
as unmoved mover, 105
as vulnerable, 150
as warrior, 67
world and, 191
YHWH as personal name of, 165
anger and, 268
Auschwitz and, 268, 269, 285
death camps and, 267
death of, 268, 271
as historical agent, 269
as Holy Nothingness, 271
providence and, 274, 279
hiddenness of, 277, 324
self-limitation and, 280
history and, 290
tzimtzum and, 294
masculinity of, 298, 301

God (cont.)
  cumulative revelation and, 303
  in Catholic thought, 319
  covenantal love of, 323
  creative self-revelation and, 333
  exegesis and, 338
  validity of religions and, 364
  positive theology and, 375
  predication and, 376, 380
  logical priority of, 377
  assertion and, 378
  silence and, 380
  as source of morality, 380
  goodness of, 381
  knowledge and will of, 382, 384
  deism and, 383
  as author, 384
  morality and, 388
  human self-conception and, 389
  religious realism and, 393
  Divine-human encounter and, 400
  "God and Theoretical Entities: Their Cognitive Status" (Gellman), 406
  non-realist view of, 406
  I-thou relationship and, 408
  talking to and talking about, 408
  theological language and, 418
  as beyond speech, 424
  worship of, 432
  propositional understanding of, 432
  moments of presence of, 435
  halakhah and, 436
  transcendence and immanence of, 442
  newness and, 442
  Torah and, 444
  autonomy and, 448
  impartial spectator and, 448
  context and, 449
  maximal love of, 454, 456
  fear and, 454, 455
  power and, 465
  simplicity of, 460
God, Man and History (Berkovits), 280, 281, 400
Godhead, the
  anthropomorphism and, 168
  classical conceptions of God and, 153
  commandments and, 151
  ein sof and, 175
  emergence of notion of, 160
  evil and, 172
  the feminine and, 169
  femininity and, 197
  God's names and, 165
  Kabbalah and, 16
  man as extension of, 177
  middot and, 154
  neoplatonism and, 156, 163
  redemption and, 283
  sefirot and, 149, 154, 161, 171, 195
  Shekhinah and, 154, 170
  theurgy and, 150, 203
  Torah and, 167
  unity and, 169
  YHWH and, 165
Goshen-Gottstein, Alon, 14
Grand Inquisitor, the, 243
gratitude, 18, 34, 143, 457
Greek gods, 69
Green, Arthur, 220
Greenberg, Blu, 299, 307, 311
Greenberg, Irving, 284, 285–87, 354
Grüber, Heinrich, 267, 268
Guide of the Perplexed (Maimonides)
  on attributes of God, 122
  on dispassionate action, 141
  on emotions of God, 140
  idolatry and, 376
  on the incorporeality of God, 113
  on judging and creation, 133
  on law, 143
  pedagogical function of, 132
  significance of, 106
  on standing, 113

Habad, 191, 193, 194, 207
halakhah
  Adler on, 308
  aggadah and, 26–30, 35
  Akedah Theology and, 311
  autonomy and, 450
  commandments and, 35
  community and, 27
  defined, 26
  feminine identity and, 305
  feminism and, 299
  feminist midrash and, 307
  feminist theology and, 4
  gender bias of, 300
  gender equality and, 300, 307
  gender inequality and, 310
  gender justice and, 297, 310

God's presence and, 436
idolatry and, 356
justice and, 300
mitsvot and, 26
modernity and, 309
oral Torah and, 448
philosophical theology and, 22
revelation and, 327
Ross on, 312
solidarity and, 309
speech and, 442
theological realism and, 397
theology and, 3, 22, 38
theology of religions and, 345
Torah and, 28
tzadikim and, 207
women's inferior status in, 298
wordless encounter theology and, 429
halakhic Judaism, 356, 426
halakhic midrashic literature, 224
Halbertal, Moses, 15, 124, 363
Halevi, Judah, 10, 32, 115, 128, 221, 404
haluztim, 203
Hameiri, Rabbi Menachem, 359, 363–66
Hamilton, William, 272
Hampson, Daphna, 465
hangings, 71–74
Hartman, David, 349
Hartman, Tova, 299
Hartshorne, Charles, 464
Harvey, Warren Zev, 111
Hassidism
  bittul ha-yesh and, 207
  founding of, 203
  Habad and, 193
  Kabbalah and, 189, 190
  Kook on, 193, 194
  perfection of God and, 194
havurah, 223
Hayim, Rabbi of Volozhin, 167, 191, 192, 194, 195, 209
heaven, 240
Hebrew, 159, 165, 250
Hegel and the State (Rosenzweig), 214
Hegel, G. W. F.
  dialectical understanding of history of, 198
  on immanence and transcendence, 323
  Kook and, 198
  philosophy of history of, 221

Rubenstein and, 271
Spinoza and, 205, 323
on unity, 198
Heidegger, Martin
  on authenticity, 235
  on death, 257
  Jonas and, 287
  on language, 428, 439, 440, 441, 442, 446
  on projecting, 442
  Rosenzweig and, 217, 223
  thrownness and, 441
  on time, 253
  on the unsayable, 443
Hekhalot, 155, 165
Held, Shai, 427
heresy, 169, 176, 202
hermeneutical theology
  feminist theology and, 16
  Levinas and, 16
  positive theology and, 16
  in *The Star of Redemption*, 16
hermeneutics
  aesthetics and, 9
  analytic philosophy and, 17
  of Fishbane, 220
  legal and theological, 20
  models of revelation and, 318
  negative theology and, 3
  revelation and, 7
  Rosenzweig and, 7
  Torah and, 6
  trust and, 317
Heschel, Abraham Joshua
  Berkovits and, 400
  on the Bible, 24
  conjunction and prophecy and, 331
  on the feeling of God, 330
  logical positivism and, 407
  negative theology and, 11
  pre-linguistic experience and, 428
  on religious language, 411
  on revelation, 11, 425
Hesse, Hermann, 427
Hessed, 209
Hezekiah, 54
Hick, John, 351, 392, 394
Hilchot Teshuvah (Maimonides), 448
Hildesheimer, Esriel, 275
Hillel, 450
Himmler, Heinrich, 464

Hinduism, 357, 360
hineni, 251
historical memory, 301, 304, 305, 312, 429
historicism, 221
history, 78, 283, 290, 318, 322–25, 441
Hitler, Adolf, 13, 268, 269, 464
Hobbes, Thomas, 259
Hodu, the, 98
Hofmannsthal, Hugo von, 426
ḥokhmah, 166
holiness
  daily life and, 256
  dualism and, 251
  ethics and, 239
  failed expectations of, 56
  gathering sparks and, 197
  inclusiveness and, 203
  justice and, 54
  of Kook, 185
  maternal image of, 242
  negative theology and, 210
  Talmud and, 247
  temporality and, 256
  Torah and, 241
  tzadikim and, 209
  Zionism and, 187
Holocaust, the
  the book of Esther and, 57
  Christian interpretations of the Bible and, 44
  covenant and, 286
  God's absence during, 34
  the hiddenness of God and, 277
  as a human responsibility, 283
  impact on theology of, 268
  H. Jonas on, 291, 294
  as Shoah, 44
Holtz, Barry, 219, 220
hope, 225, 387
Hosea, 173
hukkim, 144
human goods, 141
human nature, 25, 135, 142, 145, 146
human rights, 9
human sciences, the, 244
humanity, 86, 91, 240
humility, 207, 390, 405, 444, 449
Husserl, Edmund, 11, 244, 252, 253

I and Thou (Buber), 427
ibn Ezra, Abraham, 61
ibn Gabbai, Rabbi Meir, 158
Idea of the Holy (Rudolf), 427
idealism, 227
Idel, Moshe, 162, 165, 175, 178
idolatry
  anthropomorphism and, 124, 139
  Christianity and, 360, 361
  Hinduism and, 360
  Maimonides on, 109, 125, 128
  matter and, 146
  negative theology and, 376
  other religions and, 356
  as sin, 362
  Torah and, 124
Idra Zuṭa, 162
Idrot, 162
imagination
  consciousness of God and, 191, 211
  fictionalism and, 416
  Lebens on, 417
  limitations of, 194
  liturgy and, 79
  Mosaic prophecy and, 118, 135, 248
  Torah and, 331
  transcendence and, 419
  Wittgenstein and, 421
  women and, 298
imitatio Dei, 139, 141
immanence, 90, 174
immanent, 176
inclusivism, 203, 351, 354, 362, 368
incorporeality, 108, 113, 120, 157
individual identity, 225
inerrancy, 328, 329
infinite, the, 173
intellectual frailty, 114, 124
intellectual intuition, 198
intelligibility, 239, 245, 247, 249, 250
International Rosenzweig Gesellschaft, the, 213
interreligious dialogue, 345, 348
intuition, 196, 211, 252, 410
Irshai, Ronit, 4, 9, 16
Isaac the Blind, Rabbi, 174
Isaiah (book), 278, 281
Isaiah (prophet), 49, 57
Islam, 344, 361, 362, 363, 368
Islamic philosophy, 111
Islamic theology, 231

Israel (people)
  as disciples of God, 66
  giving of Torah to, 319
  God's will and, 268
  liturgy and, 77
  metaphysical status of, 369
  particularity of, 357, 365
  redemption of, 86
  revelation and, 334
  the Shema and, 81
  Sinai and, 323
  theology of religions and, 345
  as wife, 167
Israel (state), 204, 306, 361

Jacobs, Rabbi Louis, 334, 425
James, William, 330
Jeremiah (book), 141
Jeremiah (prophet), 49, 50, 54, 57, 68, 70
Jeroboam, 57
Jerusalem, 57
Jerusalem (Mendelssohn), 319, 398
Jerusalem Talmud, the, 60
Jesus, 41, 43, 44, 248, 354
"Jew Who Wasn't There, The" (Adler), 297
Jewish Bible, the. See Tanak
Jewish biblical studies, 41
Jewish biblical theology, 42, 56, 58
Jewish Existentialism, 11
Jewish feminism
  halakhah and, 299, 300
  Kristeva and, 9
  law and, 9
  midrash and, 306, 307
  moral task of, 311
  origins of, 9, 312
  positive theology and, 300
  theological debates within, 312
Jewish feminist theology, 297, 298, 305
Jewish neoplatonism, 156
Jewish normativity, 23
Jewish philosophy, 15, 105
Jewish religious identity, 220
Jewish sectarianism, 236
Jewish theology, 1
  as *aggadah*, 37
  Biblical theology and, 2
  death camps and, 267
  Enlightenment and, 7
  epistemology and, 8

  genres of, 453
  German study of, 4–5
  as *halakhah*, 38
  as hermeneutical theology, 6
  influence of analytic philosophy on, 8
  influence of Greek philosophy on, 6
  influence of Kant for, 8
  influence of other religions on, 14
  Jewish feminism and, 9
  Kabbalah and, 16
  Kant and, 7
  medieval philosophy and, 7
  Messianic Aesthetics and, 216
  midrash and, 6
  modernity and, 4
  narrative forms of, 6
  negative theology and, 3, 9
  non-propositional forms of, 415
  normativity and, 23
  philosophy and, 7, 37
  positive theology and, 9
  revelation and, 425
  theological realism and, 414
  theological reference and, 421
Jewish-Christian relations, 237, 348
Job (book), 50, 220
Job (prophet), 57, 289, 290
Jonas, Hans
  Berkovits and, 293, 294
  Fackenheim and, 293
  on God and Auschwitz, 287
  on God and history, 290
  on omnipotence, 293
  Rubenstein and, 294
  Scholem and, 293
Josephus, 72
Judaism
  as anachronism, 254
  as care for others, 241
  demands of, 453
  negative theology and, 12, 14
  non-realist view of God and, 406
  place of theology in, 398
  as religion of reason, 8
  Theology of Religions and, 360
Judaism and Other Faiths (Cohn Sherbock), 349
Judaism and Other Religions:Models of Understanding (Brill), 316
judging, 133, 134, 142
judgment, 65, 209

justice
  analytic philosophy and, 38
  community and, 147
  difficulty of, 241
  as Divine mandate, 276
  ethical politics and, 259
  fear and, 455
  the future and, 254, 255
  halakhah and, 300
  holiness and, 54
  intelligibility and, 249
  law and, 134
  mercy and, 243
  morality and, 247, 254, 259, 260
  obligation and, 259
  the other and, 242
  redemption and, 225
  requirements of, 261
  salvation and, 350
  teleology and, 142

Kabbalah, 7, 10, 12, 15, 32, 111, 120, 159, 305, 306
  contemporary Jewish theology and, 16
  elements of, 152
  emergence of, 152
  German idealism and, 198
  on God as mercy, 65
  God and, 153
  Godhead and, 16
  importance of, 149
  Kook and, 369
  Lekhah Dodi and, 89
  medieval philosophy and, 7
  mitsvot and, 16
  modern philosophy and, 16
  morality and, 200
  mystical agnosticism of, 175
  negative theology and, 15
  revelation and, 24
  science and, 16
  theosophy and, 150
Kabbalah:New Perspectives (Idel), 178
Kabbalistic theosophy, 151, 160, 179
Kaddish, the, 98
Kafka, Franz, 427
Kalām, 111
Kant, Immanuel
  agnosticism of, 200
  on autonomy, 450
  Berkovits and, 277
  Cohen and, 199
  on God as author of the world, 383
  influence on Jewish theology of, 7, 8
  Levinas and, 243
  Maimonides and, 389
  metaphysical dualisms of, 244
  on morality and God, 382, 386–87
  on noumena and phenomena, 197
  on perfection of God, 386
  rationalism of, 244
  theological realism and, 392
  on things-in-themselves, 437
  on true religion and ecclesiastical faith, 243
Kaplan, Aryeh, 331
Kaplan, Lawrence, 141
Kaplan, Mordechai, 18
Kaufmann, Yehezkel, 344
Kavod, 168
Kellner, Menachem, 119
Kepnes, Steven, 213
keter, 151, 163, 206, 207, 209
Ketuvim, 47, 57
kiddush HaShem, 257
Kimelman, Reuven, 17
Kings, 49
kingship
  in the Aleinu, 91
  the Amidah and, 78, 97
  the Ashrei and, 78, 93
  in the High Holiday liturgy, 84
  the liturgy and, 96
  in the Pesquei DeZimra, 97
  the Shema Liturgy and, 84
  in Zechariah, 89
Klug, Brian, 339
Kogan, Michael, 349, 354
Kook, Rabbi Abraham Isaac
  against personalist interpretations of God, 200
  on the authority of Torah, 201
  on the categorical imperative, 201
  on divinity and morality, 200
  early Spinozism of, 193
  on *ein sof*, 207
  on Gentile monotheism, 200
  Habad and, 194
  on halakhah, 305
  inclusivism of, 368
  Kabbalah and, 369
  life of, 185

mysticism of, 16
pantheism and, 210
on the perfection of God, 194
pluralism of, 14, 366, 369
on prayer, 203
on revelation, 331
Ross and, 305
on *sefirot*, 206
Spinoza and, 202, 208
theodicy of modernity of, 203
on Theology of Religions, 366–70
on *tzadikim*, 207, 208, 209
Kristeva, Julia, 9
kulo hayav, 186
kulo zakkai, 186

Lamentation, 47
Lamentations, 57, 285
language
  authority and, 444
  control and, 440, 441
  encounter with God in, 444
  God and, 114, 123, 124, 445
  limits of, 436–40
  mystery and, 446
  negative theology and, 10
  poetry and, 443
  prophecy and, 249, 250
  purpose and, 442
  reality and, 436, 439
  silence and, 426
  Torah and, 114
  transcendence and, 426
  trust and, 436
  the unsayable and, 443
"Large Countenance, The", 162
law
  covenant and, 54
  creation and, 134, 135
  culture and, 308
  Divine origin of, 136
  freedom and, 277
  God and, 71, 72
  human nature and, 145
  Jewish feminism and, 9
  justice and, 134
  Maimonides on, 106
  Messianic Aesthetics and, 217
  Moses and, 143
  narrative and, 308, 309, 312
  nature and, 143

  pluralism and, 308
  punishment and, 54
  purposiveness of, 142, 143
  reason and, 110
  revelation and, 134, 304
  slavery and, 48
  study of, 143
  theology of religions and, 345
  Torah and, 46
laws of nature, 122
Laws of Noah, the, 14
leadership, 136
Lebens, Samuel, 417
Leibowitz, Yeshayahu, 129, 311, 327
Lekhah Dodi, 89
"Letter of Lord Chandos"
  (Hofmannsthal), 426
Letter to the Galatians (St. Paul), 72
Levenson, Jon, 55, 323
Levinas, Emmanuel
  on absolute truth, 338
  on adult and primitive religion, 243
  against dogmatism, 241
  against metaphysical dualism, 248
  on awakening, 257
  on being, 240
  biblical humanism of, 241
  Buber and, 239
  on the ceremonial, 255
  on the contemporaneity of thought, 246
  democracy of, 260
  on difficulty of ethics, 242
  on duration, 253
  ethical politics of, 259
  ethics and, 12
  on ethics and time, 253
  on ethics as trauma, 255
  on exegesis, 338
  focus of work of, 1
  on freedom and responsibility, 242
  on the future, 255
  on genuine religion, 241
  on God and ethics, 241
  hermeneutical theology and, 16
  on *hineni*, 250
  influence of works of, 246
  influences of, 253
  on intelligibility as proximity, 245
  on the irruption of ethics, 245
  on justice, 259, 261

Levinas, Emmanuel (cont.)
  Kant and, 243–46
  on language, 250
  messianic politics of, 260
  metaphysics and, 244, 245
  metaphysics of, 249
  on miracles, 251
  on mortality, 257
  on Mount Sinai, 255
  negative theology and, 11
  on obligations to the other, 241
  on perfection, 261
  phenomenology of, 244–46, 256
  Post-Enlightenment Jewish theology and, 9
  on the primacy of the other, 242
  on the primacy of ethics, 239
  on prophecy, 249
  on proximity, 249
  on Queen Esther, 257
  on responsibility, 239
  on revelation, 337, 338, 342
  revelation and, 16
  social justice and, 12
  on sociality, 258
  on speech, 249
  on suffering, 257
  Talmud and, 16
  Talmudic discourse of, 247
  theory of truth of, 248
  on thought, 248
  on *tikkun olam*, 257
  on time and eternity, 256
  on time and the other, 254
  on time and transcendence, 254
  on time as rupture, 255
  on the true and the good, 247
  on Zionism, 261
  Zionism of, 260, 261
Leviticus Rabbah, 398
Lichtenstein, Rabbi Aharon, 325
life, 52
Lilith, 172
Linevuchei Hador (Kook), 367, 370
Lithuanian Kabbalah, 189, 193, 195
Lithuanian Talmudism, 188
liturgical theology, 77
liturgy, 77, 94, 96, 237, 272
logical positivism, 392, 393, 400, 407
logos
  etymology of theology and, 22, 31
  in the Greek Septuagint, 23, 28
  negative theology and, 380
  reason and, 244
  revelation and, 25, 320
love
  apprehension and, 143
  communication of, 228
  community and, 236
  confession and, 231
  covenant and, 323
  death and, 227
  dialogue and, 230, 234
  ethics and, 229
  exegesis and, 338
  God and, 78, 218, 228, 237, 454, 456
  in Song of Songs, 228
  in the Midrash, 62
  midrashic analysis of, 227
  necessity and, 231
  the other and, 235
  as presence, 229
  remembrance and, 234
  revelation and, 224, 225, 227
  Rosenzweig on, 227–31
  in the Shema Liturgy, 78
  soul and, 454
  as speech act, 218, 229, 230
  speech acts and, 228
  speech and, 234
  the soul and, 233
  Torah and, 78, 237
  as transformative experience, 228
  trust and, 231
  tzadikim and, 208
  withholding of, 462
Lovers' Covenant, 309
Lubitch, Rivka, 307
Luria, Isaac, 271, 294
Luria, Rabbi Isaac, 189
Lurianic Kabbalah, 76, 162, 174, 188, 190, 271
Lurie, Yuval, 414

Mah Tovu, 90
Maimonides, Moses
  on anthropomorphism, 128
  anthropomorphism and, 385
  Aristotle and, 22, 139, 383
  attitude towards Christianity of, 358
  on attributes, 120, 122
  on autonomy, 448

on Christianity, 361
Christianity and, 361
Cohen and, 382, 389
on creation, 138
on descriptions of God, 123
on dispassionate action, 140
on emotions of God, 140
esotericism of, 107
on essential definition of God, 121
exclusivism of, 361
on the existence of God, 112
on fear of God, 455
on God as creator, 119
on God as author, 384
on God as object of worship, 127–30
on God's knowledge and will, 382
on God's organs, 157
on God's righteousness, 120, 122
on God's simplicity, 460
Halevi and, 115
on human goods, 141
on idolatry, 125
on imitation, 139
inclusivism of, 362
on the incorporeality of God, 113–16
influence on Kabbalists of, 157
Islam and, 361
Kant and, 389
on knowledge of God, 129
on the language of the Torah, 114
on law, 132
legitimation of other religions and, 357
on limits of the intellect, 385
on love, 143
medieval Jewish philosophy and, 105, 106
Meiri and, 364
on miracles, 110
moral meaning of God of, 199
on Moses, 134, 135
on multiplicity, 126
on negation, 123
negative theology of, 10, 189, 210, 375
Plato and, 379
pluralism of, 362
positive theology and, 375–82
on predicates of relation, 121
on prophecy, 117–18
on the rationality of the law, 144, 145
reason and, 111
Rosenzweig and, 404

on silence, 124
on societal order, 136
on the speech of God, 115
Spinoza and, 384
on standing, 113
on teaching Torah to Muslims and Christians, 362
theological language and, 418
Theology of Religions and, 361–63
thirteen principles of, 108
Torah and, 329
unity of God and, 162
Major Trends in Jewish Mysticism (Scholem), 271, 282
malkhut, 168, 206
Man is not Alone (Heschel), 407, 408
Manasseh, 49
Mann, Thomas, 82
Masorti, 425
materialism, 198
matter, 146
maximal love
 appropriateness of, 456
 devotion and, 457
 excellence and, 462, 463
 features of, 18, 454, 457
 perfectly good being and, 460, 465
 withholding of, 462
McDowell, John, 439
medieval Jewish philosophy, 105, 106, 188
medieval philosophy, 8, 180
medieval theology, 18
Meir, Rabbi, 73–74
Mendelssohn, Moses, 319, 398
mercy
 dispassionate action and, 139, 140
 Hessed and, 209
 justice and, 243, 455
 midot and, 154
 name of God and, 65
 negative theology and, 401
 the burning bush and, 63
 tzadikim and, 209
Merkavah, 155
Messengers of God (Wiesel), 220
Messiah
 arrival of, 186
 duration and, 261
 the Holocaust and, 274
 I. Greenberg on, 354

Messiah (cont.)
  Jesus as, 43, 44
  Kook on, 187
  politics and, 260
Messianic Aesthetics
  communal love and, 236
  community and, 236
  defined, 217
  exile and, 237
  as main issue for Jewish theology, 217
  speech-thinking and, 218
  universally open thought and, 236
  violence and, 229
messianic time, 255
Messianism, 193, 215, 217, 218
metaphysical dualism, 246, 247, 248, 253
method, 27
Methodological theology, 27
Micah, 50
midot, 154, 160
midrash (activity)
  defined, 219
  as distinct from theology, 415
  forms of, 219
  interpretation and, 450
  Jewish religious identity and, 220
  mystery and, 446
  renewal of, 221
  revelation and, 219
  Rosenzweig's renewal of, 223
  Torah as, 430
Midrash, the
  attentiveness to God in, 60
  on burial, 71
  on Cain and Abel, 70
  on the Divine name, 166
  on God as mercy, 65
  images of God in, 15
  on meaning of YHWH, 64
  the Mishnah and, 60
  names of God in, 64
  parables in, 63
  on proper representations of God, 61
  revelation and, 319
  sefirot and, 162
  the Talmud and, 60
midrashic analysis, 225
Minḥah, 92
miracles, 110
Mishnah, the
  on burial, 71
  on esoteric teachings, 107
  on hangings, 72
  images of God in, 15
  the Midrash and, 60
  the Talmud and, 60
mishpatim, 144
Mitnagdim, 191
mitsvot
  aggadah and, 26
  covenantal love and, 323
  the dead and, 256
  in the end of days, 201
  God and, 22
  halakhah and, 26
  Kabbalah and, 16
  performance of, 192
  personalist conceptions of God and, 129
  redemption and, 225
  Sinai and, 116
  Torah and, 26
  tzadikim and, 208
Mittleman, Alan, 413
Mizmor Le-Todah, 98
Models of Revelation (Dulles), 317
modern philosophy, 16
modernity
  challenges of, 273
  Expressionism and, 428
  halakhah and, 309
  interest in Jewish theology in, 4
  Kook and, 188
  midrash and, 223
  negative theology and, 12
  Rosenzweig and, 213, 221, 222
  theology of religions and, 344
monarchy, 55
monism, 205
monotheism
  Adon Olam and, 90, 92
  the Aleinu and, 79, 90, 91, 92
  Cohen on, 199
  Divine command and, 190
  encounter with God and, 435
  feminism and, 301, 303, 304
  Gentile versions of, 200
  historical memory of, 304
  in Jewish liturgy, 92
  ordinary and comprehensive views of, 194
  pantheism and, 387

personalism and, 447
uniqueness and, 387
wordless encounter theology and, 434
Moore, Andrew, 392, 395
morality
  Akedah Theology and, 311
  autonomy and, 450
  difficulty of, 241
  eternity and, 251
  ethical politics and, 259
  God as source of, 380, 388
  impartial spectator and, 448
  as imperative, 256
  justice and, 247, 254, 259, 260
  Kant on, 386
  Levinas on, 240, 241, 262
  linguistic, 406
  natural yearning for, 201
  the other and, 242
  perfection and, 200
  reason and, 448
  responsibility and, 260
  revelation and, 368
  as service to God, 243
  speech and, 249
  Theology of Religions and, 358
  Torah and, 36, 37
  validity of religions and, 368
Morality and Eros (Rubenstein), 271
Morgan, Michael, 13
Mosaic law, 135
Mosaic legislation, 137, 142, 144
Mosaic prophecy, 134, 135, 136, 141
Moses
  as author of the law, 135
  in the Beit Midrash, 431
  creation and, 142
  Divine law and, 136, 137
  Divine will and, 136
  encounter with the infinite of, 324
  genius of, 136
  God and, 56, 135
  as God's servant, 242
  imitation of God of, 139, 141
  as interpreter, 137
  Jesus and, 248
  as judge, 134
  judging and creation and, 133
  law and, 134, 143
  as lawgiver, 134
  as legislator, 135, 136

  as philosopher-king, 141
  relationship with God of, 29, 30
  revelation and, 44, 324, 328, 329
  revelation of, 331
  Spinoza's condemnation of, 248
  the burning bush and, 63
  as *tzadik*, 209
  wordless encounter theology and, 428
Moses und Aron (Schönberg), 427
Mount Sinai, 33, 44, 45, 223, 224, 256, 331, 403
Muffs, Yohanan, 415
multiplicity
  attributes and, 120
  corporeality of God and, 124
  Kabbalah and, 158
  language and, 126
  Maimonides on, 121
  negation and, 123
  of the physical realm, 156
  uniqueness of God and, 112
Murphy, Mark, 462
Musaf, 90
Mutakalimun, 215
mutakallimūn, 111
Myers, Jody, 306
mystical union
  Abulafia on, 178
  Afterman on, 16
  Cohen on, 388
  the Godhead and, 177
  Kabbalah and, 151
  Philo and, 178
  Scholem on, 177
  Torah study and, 179
  transformational nature of, 177
mysticism, 11, 128, 188, 359
myth
  after Auschwitz, 288
  as coping mechanism, 270
  of H. Jonas, 290, 292, 293
  Plato and, 290
  truth of, 272

narrative, 308, 309, 312, 313
national identity, 53
natural kinds, 438
natural law, 135
natural revelation, 336
natural theology, 332, 336, 392
nature, 78, 143, 255, 386

necessity
  freedom and, 196, 244
  the good and, 256
  love and, 231
  Maimonides and, 112
  perfection and, 75
  theological realism and, 403
negation, 123, 175, 377
negative theology
  after Maimonides, 15
  attributes and, 375
  Buber and, 11
  Cohen and, 10
  criticisms of, 378
  defined, 10
  Heschel and, 11
  humility and, 390
  idolatry and, 376
  Jewish culture and, 12
  Jewish Existentialism and, 11
  Jewish theology and, 3
  Kabbalah and, 15, 189
  language and, 10
  legacy of, 10
  Levinas and, 11
  Maimonides and, 10, 12, 210, 375
  modern Judaism and, 12, 14
  positive theology and, 15
  revelation and, 336
  Rosenzweig's rejection of, 402
  theological realism and, 392, 398, 401, 417
  Torah and, 15
Negative Theology as Jewish Modernity (Fagenblat), 12
Neoplatonism, 128, 163
Neshamah, 77
Neusner, Jacob, 220
Nevi'im, 47
New Testament, the, 41, 43, 46
New Thinking, 216, 218, 222
Newsom, Carol, 83
Nietzsche, Friedrich Wilhelm, 201, 273
Nine and a Half Mystics (Weiner), 271
nirvana, 432
Noachide commandments, 354, 355, 368
Noachide covenant, 354
nomos, 308, 309
Nomos and Narrative (Cover), 308, 312
nothingness
  ein sof and, 176
  God as, 271
  Kook on, 206
  of man before God, 324
  mystical union and, 179
  negative theology and, 336
  revelation and, 337
  in the *Tao te Ching*, 431
noumena, 8
nous, 156, 161
Novak, David, 4, 5, 358, 362
Numbers, 85

obligation, 239, 255, 259
olam, 50
Olam Haba, 108
Old Testament theology, 2, 41
Old Testament, the
  the Christian Bible and, 43
  Christian interpretations of, 44
  Christian theology and, 41
  linear progression of, 45–46
  the New Testament and, 46
  organization of, 44, 45
On Women and Judaism (Greenberg), 299, 307
oneness
  attributes and, 121
  H. Jonas on, 293
  Maimonides on, 108, 112
  multiplicity and, 123
  the Shema and, 81
  simplicity and, 376
ontology, 125
ontotheology, 386, 398, 401, 428
Open Secret (Wolfson), 176
Opening the Covenant (Kogan), 349
Oral Law, the, 137
organized religion, 186, 244
"Origin of the Work of Art, The" (Heidegger), 443
Orthodox feminism, 299, 300, 307
Orthodox Judaism, 345
other, the
  devotion and, 241
  evil and, 249
  justice and, 254
  love and, 230, 235
  responsibility and, 245
  responsibility to, 232
  soul and, 233
  spirituality and, 257

suffering and, 258
time and, 253–56
transcendence and, 240
vulnerability of, 242
women as, 301
Otherwise than Being or Beyond Essence (Levinas), 246
Otto, Rudolf, 427
overflow, 156
Ozick, Cynthia, 298, 299

Palestine, 26, 60, 79, 185, 366
pan-emanationism, 206, 209
panentheism, 205, 206, 210
pantheism
  Cohen on, 388
  Divine emanation and, 206
  Hegel on, 205
  Kook and, 205
  monotheism and, 387
  Spinoza and, 208
  as teleological ideal, 206
  in traditional Judaism, 205
Pardes Rimonim (Cordovero), 173
partzufim, 196, 198
Passover, 47, 170
past, the, 254, 255
Paul, Saint, 72
peace, 276
Pedaya, Haviva, 178
Pentateuch, the, 45, 54, 302 See Torah, the
Pereq Heleq, 108
perfectibility, 194, 196, 197, 198, 210
perfection
  the Absolute and, 401
  excellence and, 465
  of God of the Midrash, 74
  intellectual, 130, 141
  Kant on, 386
  Kook on, 194
  law and, 385
  in Lurianic Kabbalism, 196
  morality and, 200
  necessity and, 75
  omnipotence and, 461
  omniscience and, 461
  panentheism and, 210
  perfectibility and, 196, 197, 198, 210
  power and, 465
  prophecy and, 117

relational God and, 76
selfishness and, 261
theological realism and, 403
tzimtzum and, 76, 203
as universal urge, 203
perfectly good being
  belief in, 466
  defined, 460
  excellence and, 463, 465
  existence and, 459
  knowledge and, 458
  maximal love and, 18, 457
  necessary existence and, 460
  omnipotence and, 461
  omniscience and, 461
  perfect being and, 460, 462
  perfectly good character and, 457, 458
  simplicity and, 460
  sovereignty and, 459
  time and, 459
perfectly good character
  defined, 457
  excellence and, 463, 464
  knowledge and, 459
  omnipotence and, 461
  omniscience and, 461
  perfect moral goodness and, 457
  perfectly good being and, 458, 460
  power and, 458, 465
  sentiments and, 458
  sovereignty and, 459
personalism, 105, 189, 200, 447
Pesaḥ. See Passover
Pesikta de-Rav Kahana, 398
Pesuqei DeZimra, 90, 94, 95, 97, 98
Petuchowski, Jakob J., 335
Pharaoh, 67
phenomenological ethics, 233
phenomenology
  aggadah and, 37
  ethics and, 245
  Kant and, 244
  liturgy and, 94
  redemption and, 82
  Rosenzweig and, 223
Philo, 7, 64, 72, 178
philosopher-kings, 141
philosophical theology, 6, 22, 213, 235
philosophy
  ethics and, 247
  God of the Torah and, 130

philosophy (cont.)
　influence on Christian theology of, 6
　influence on Jewish theology of, 6, 7
　Rosenzweig and, 236
　theology and, 37
　Torah and, 111
philosophy of history
　Berkovits and, 276, 277, 280
　the Holocaust and, 275, 283
　Islam and, 362
　Rosenzweig and, 221
philosophy of language, 218
philosophy of religion, 392
pietism, 165, 188
Pirkei Avot, 137, 276, 448
Plantinga, Alvin, 395
Plaskow, Judith
　Buber and, 305
　on the masculine conception of God, 302
　on feminist midrash, 306
　on historical memory, 303, 312
　on Jewish feminist theology, 298
　on revelation, 301, 304
Plato, 290, 379, 442
Plotinus, 175
pluralism
　of Greenberg, 284
　of Hartman, 349
　inclusivism and, 354
　of Kook, 366, 369
　law and, 308
　of Maimonides, 362
　of Meiri, 364
　Theology of Religions and, 348, 365
　truth and, 354
　validity and, 353, 364
plurality, 125
poetry, 443
Porton, Gary, 219
positive theology
　after Maimonides, 15
　analytic philosophy and, 17
　constructive theology and, 18
　epistemology and, 17
　examples of in Hebrew Bible, 10
　existence of, 390
　hermeneutical theology and, 16
　Jewish feminism and, 300
　Kant and, 387
　Maimonides and, 375–82, 384

　negative theology and, 10, 14
　as part of a learning process, 378
　personhood and, 375
　reason and, 17
　revelation and, 18, 425
　Torah and, 15
Post-Enlightenment Jewish theology, 9
post-First Temple liturgy, 100
post-Holocaust theology, 13
post-Lurianic Kabbalah, 195
post-modernism, 235, 303
post-Temple liturgy, 100
potentiality, 112
power, 291
practice, 28
prayer, 90, 99, 203, 301
precedence, 119
predication
　Gersonides on, 379
　God and, 380
　God's simplicity and, 376
　negative theology and, 390
　simplicity and, 377
　theological reference and, 421
　truth and, 377
prime mover, 128
proactive halakhah, 308, 309
problem of evil, the, 129
process theology, 202
Promised Land, the, 137
prophecy, 117–18, 138, 250, 367
Prophets, 53
Proverbs, 50, 256
providence
　Berkovits on, 275, 276, 277
　freedom and, 279
　H. Jonas and, 294
　hiddenness of God and, 279
　the Holocaust and, 283
　immanence and, 90
　Kook on, 196, 202
　in Lithuanian Kabbalah, 195
　personalist conceptions of God and, 129
　validity of religions and, 364
proximity, 229, 241, 245, 249, 250, 258
Psalms, 57, 97, 99, 124, 225
public sphere, the, 258
punishment, 54, 72
purposiveness, 142, 143

Qohelet, 48, 50
Quine, Willard van Orman, 18, 439
Qumran, 83, 84, 86, 87

Rabad, 114
Rabbinic culture, 60
rabbinic Judaism, 116, 162, 180, 294
Rabbinic law, 64
rabbinic literature
    on Cain and Abel, 70
    feminist midrash and, 307
    on giving of the Torah, 319
    on God as husband and Israel as wife, 167
    on God's holy spirit, 156
    Hekhalot and, 155
    ḥokhmah and, 167
    Kabbalah and, 152
    Merkavah and, 155
    names of God in, 164, 165
    Sefer Yeṣirah and, 159
    Shekhinah in, 169
    supernal and mundane realms in, 155
    unity of God in, 169
    YHWH and, 65
Rabbinic liturgy, 86
rabbinic theology, 24, 84, 153, 397, 416
Rabbis, the, 60, 64, 65, 69
Race, Alan, 351
radical amazement, 409
Rahner, Karl, 332
Rambam. *See* Maimonides, Moses
Rashaz, 190, 191, 192, 209, 271
rational theology, 243
rationalism, 144, 145, 188, 223, 244
reading, 234
reality, 436, 437, 438, 439
realpolitik, 258
reason
    Kant on, 244
    law and, 110
    limits of, 145
    Maimonides' commitment to, 111
    nature and, 145
    paradox and, 447
    positive theology and, 17
    religion and, 111
    revelation and, 325, 326
Recanati, Rabbi Menachem, 166
reconciliation, 388, 431
Red Sea, the, 67, 261

redemption
    the Aleinu and, 79
    the Amidah and, 78, 79, 80, 87
    commandments and, 170
    covenant and, 32, 286, 287
    creation and, 88, 276, 277
    daily life and, 256
    defined, 32
    Divine sovereignty and, 81, 86, 88
    Exodus and, 84
    the future and, 86
    futurity of, 32
    the Godhead and, 283
    as a human task, 283
    of humanity, 86
    of Israel, 86
    Kook on, 204
    the past and, 86
    phenomenological analysis of, 82
    privileged status of Jewish people in, 211
    in Psalms, 225
    reconciliation and, 388
    revelation and, 82, 88
    the Shema and, 86
    in the Shema Liturgy, 81, 82
    shema liturgy and, 78
    speech and, 236
    tzadikim and, 208
Reid, Thomas, 395
relationship, 225
religion, 111, 243, 250, 412
"Religion and Reality" (Buber), 407
Religion within the Bounds of Reason Alone (Kant), 243
religious feminism, 309, 311
religious identity, 53, 56
religious language
    Heschel on, 411
    Jewish feminism and, 304, 305
    masculinity of God and, 298
    non-propositional forms of, 415
    theological realism and, 392
    theological reference and, 410
    theo-realism and, 411
    transcendence and, 419
    truth and, 395
    verificationist challenges to, 393
    Wittgenstein on, 399, 414
Religious Realism, 392, 393
Religious Realism (Carver), 393

religious Zionism, 204
"Remarks on Frazer's *Golden Bough*" (Wittgenstein), 412
remembrance, 234
repair, 196, 254
repentance, 204
Republic (Plato), 134
responsibility
　being and, 240
　Berkovits on, 276
　communication and, 251
　creation and, 281
　ethics and, 239
　the face and, 255
　forgiveness of sin and, 388
　freedom and, 242, 256, 277, 278
　genuine religion and, 241
　God and, 277
　hiddenness of God and, 278, 281
　the Holocaust and, 283
　morality and, 260
　to the other, 232
　primacy of, 247
　repair and, 254
　sanctification and, 276
　time and, 254
　transcendence and, 240
　as the ultimate event of being, 245
resurrection, 78
retribution, 364
revelation
　aggadah and, 26
　apophaticism and, 419
　autonomy and, 424
　Buber on, 426
　as central to Jewish theology, 24
　centrality of for Jewish theology, 24
　in Christian and Jewish thought, 319
　Christian interpretations of, 44
　consciousness and, 318
　covenant and, 25
　creation and, 31
　as creative self-revelation, 332
　as cumulative process, 302
　daily life and, 256
　decalogue and, 24
　defined, 31
　as the demand of the ethical, 339
　dialectical model of, 325–28
　divine communication and, 334
　Divine sovereignty and, 88, 97
　epistemology and, 316
　evangelicalism and, 318
　evolution and, 333
　as exegesis, 321
　exegesis and, 338, 340
　exile and, 44
　existential model of, 323
　experience of, 233
　experiential mystical model of, 330
　Fackenheim on, 325
　faith and, 316
　feminism and, 301, 304
　freedom and, 282
　God and, 318, 324
　as God's anthropology, 24
　God's speech and, 122
　of God's word, 24
　God's word and, 24
　as grounded in Israel, 334
　halakhah and, 26, 327
　hermeneutical model of, 337–41
　hermeneutics and, 7
　Heschel on, 11, 425
　hiddenness of God and, 281
　historical memory and, 304
　history and, 318, 322–25
　as a human awareness, 334
　humanistic approaches to, 318
　identity and, 54
　inerrancy and, 328
　Jesus and, 44
　Kabbalah on, 24
　of law, 134
　law and, 304
　Levinas and, 16, 337
　limits of human reason and, 326
　lived experience of, 228
　logos and, 320
　love and, 227, 338
　medieval thought and, 320
　midrash and, 219, 226, 319
　Midrash and, 219, 226, 319
　models of, 1, 318
　in modern Jewish theology, 1
　modern literature on, 317
　modern secular challenges to, 221
　morality and, 368
　Moses and, 44, 324
　Muslim concepts of, 319
　negative theology and, 336
　New Awareness model of, 332

as non-verbal encounter, 425
as normative demand, 328
nothingness and, 337
oral law and, 322
orthodox Judaism and, 303
particularity of, 365
pluralism and, 353
poetry and, 443
positive theology and, 425
practice and, 28
pre-modern approaches to, 320
as presence without content, 336
as present experience, 88
propositional model of, 328–30
in rabbinic tradition, 403
reason and, 325, 326, 448
redemption and, 82
Reform Judaism and, 321
Rosenzweig on, 218, 221, 225, 226, 237
Ross on, 302
sacred texts and, 423
salvation and, 353
in the Shema Liturgy, 81
the soul and, 340
as a speech act, 224
speech and, 115, 236
speech-thinking and, 215, 230
in *The Star of Redemption*, 222
as a supra-rational category, 324
the Enlightenment and, 320
as theological question, 317
theology and, 38
of Torah, 55
Torah and, 18, 202, 319, 320, 335, 447, 450
transcendence and, 318, 335
as transformation, 229
as universal phenomenon, 333
validity and, 353
without content, 335–37
Wittgenstein and, 424
Ricoeur, Paul, 6, 246, 316
righteousness, 120, 122
Rilke, Rainer Marie, 427
ritual
 challenges to, 272
 as coping mechanism, 270
 halakhah and, 345
 Kabbalah and, 167, 171
 Meiri and, 365

Messianic Aesthetics and, 236
Messianism and, 215
as speech act, 237
validity of religions and, 364
Romanticism, 18
Rosenberg, Rabbi Shagar-Shimon Gavriel, 340
Rosenkavalier (Hofmannsthal), 439
Rosenzweig Jahrbuch/Yearbook, 213
Rosenzweig, Franz
 on community, 225
 on the covenant, 31
 on exile, 237
 hermeneutics and, 7, 16
 life of, 214
 on love, 227–31
 Messianic Aesthetics of, 217, 236
 Messianism and, 218
 on midrash, 226
 midrash and, 221
 on *mitsvah* and *halakhah*, 29
 on revelation, 218
 on *Rabbenu*, 430
 theological realism of, 401–5
Rosenzweig's Bible:Reinventing Scripture for Jewish Modernity (Benjamin), 221
Rosh Hashanah, 66, 90
Rosh Hashanah Amidah, the, 79
Ross, Tamar
 Adler and, 309
 on the eternity of the Torah, 312
 on halakhah, 299
 on historical memory, 304
 Kook and, 305
 on the masculine conception of God, 302
 on religious forms of life, 413
 on revelation, 301, 304
Rubenstein, Richard
 on the death of God, 13, 271
 on God and the death camps, 267, 268–70
 Greenberg and, 287
 Grüber and, 267, 268
 H. Jonas and, 294
 Kabbalism of, 271
 Scholem and, 271
 Tillich and, 272
Rule of the Community, The, 87

Ruth (book), 47
Rynhold, Daniel, 7, 10

Sabbath Shirot, 83
Sabbath, the, 36, 170
Sacks, Jonathan, 349
Sacred Attunement (Fishbane), 425, 436
Sagi, Avi, 413
Salanter, Rabbi Israel, 257
salvation
  in Catholic thought, 319
  gratitude and, 34
  importance to Jewish theology of, 319
  Jesus and, 41, 44
  justice and, 350
  Kant on, 243
  Levinas on, 242
  in Lurianic Kabbalism, 197
  place in Judaism of, 350
  revelation and, 353
  selfishness and, 261
  Theology of Religions and, 350, 351
  truth and, 350
Samael, 172
Samuelson, Norbert, 222
sanctification
  ethical significance of, 257
  freedom and, 276
  hiddenness of God and, 278
  as a human task, 283
  human's need of God for, 389
  language and, 446
  redemption and, 277
Sanhedrin, 108
Schachter, Zalman, 271
Schelling, F. W. J., 198
Scholem, Gershom
  on communion, 178
  Ecstatic Kabbalah and, 162
  on *ein sof*, 174, 175
  on the emanation of divine energy, 149
  H. Jonas and, 293
  on mystical union, 15, 177
  on the nothingness of revelation, 337
  Rubenstein and, 271
  on *sefirot*, 171
Schönberg, Arnold, 427
Schopenhauer, Arthur, 198, 205
Schulweis, Harold M., 334
science, 16
Scott, Michael, 392

Second Chronicles, 49
Second Temple, the, 45, 64, 84, 100, 329
secular humanism, 223, 226
secular Zionism, 193
Seeskin, Kenneth, 7, 17, 418
Sefer Yeṣirah, 159, 160, 161, 174
sefirot
  anthropomorphism and, 176
  ben Simeon on, 158
  breaking of the vessels and, 196
  defined, 149
  Divine family and, 171
  dynamics of, 171
  ein sof and, 172, 173–76
  Godhead and, 160–64
  in post-Lurianic Kabbalah, 195
  the infinite and, 173
  Kook on, 206
  limbs of the human body and, 177
  YHWH and, 165
self-consciousness, 240, 241, 306
self-sufficiency, 126
Shabbat, 52, 54
Shaḥarit, 77, 90, 92, 94–96
Shammai, 450
Shavu'ot, 170
Shavuot, 47
Shechter, Jack, 53
Shekhinah
  bodily representation of, 161
  evil and, 172
  exile and, 170
  femininity of, 170
  as hypostatic mate of God, 168
  as lowest *sefirah*, 154
  malkhut and, 168
  Samael and, 173
  transformation of within Kabbalah, 168
Shema Liturgy, the
  the Ashrei and, 94
  chiastic structure of, 83, 86
  constituents of, 81
  Divine sovereignty and, 87, 88, 95
  origins of, 89
  Qumran and, 87
  Shaḥarit and, 94
  themes of, 84
Shema, the
  the Amidah and, 80, 87
  covenant and, 87
  as covenantal act, 34

creation and, 78
the Decalogue and, 85, 86, 88, 89
Divine sovereignty and, 79, 84, 89, 96, 97
the Exodus and, 86
hearing and, 250
love of God and, 18
Qumran and, 84
redemption and, 86
the Shema Liturgy and, 81, 83
structure of, 99
Zechariah (book) and, 89, 95
Shi'ur Qomah, 162
Shir ha Shirim
love and, 224, 228, 234, 236
midrashic analysis of, 226, 227
revelation and, 225
Rosenzweig on, 228, 233
speech-thinking and, 230
Shiur Qomah, 155
Shoah, the, 221
Shulchan Aruch, 256
Siddhartha (Hesse), 427
Siddur, the, 17, 77, 79
silence, 124, 127, 418, 426
Simon, Jules, 7, 16
simplicity, 376, 377, 460
sin
exile and, 53
fallenness and, 246
forgiveness of, 388, 389
giving up one's life and, 456
hanging and, 71, 72
idolatry and, 128, 362
as literal-mindedness, 331
repentance and, 204
Saul and, 55
theodicy and, 289
Sinaitic revelation, 116, 118, 323, 324, 333, 341
Six Day War, the, 275
skepticism, 128
slave law, 48, 55
slavery, 48
"Small Countenance", 162
Smith, Adam, 448
social justice, 9, 12
socialism, 9
sociality, 258
Socrates, 147
Sodom and Gomorrah, 56

Sofia, 168
solidarity, 287, 309
Solomon, 144, 250
Soloveitchik, Rabbi Joseph, 284, 311, 326
Song at the Sea, 97
song of Israel, the, 67
Song of Songs, 47, 58, 154, 167
Soskice, Janet, 415
soul, the
body and, 77, 244, 256
capacity for evaluation of, 232
concern for others and, 232
development of, 156
divinity of, 156
education of, 232
ethics and, 229
faith and, 407
fear and, 455
law and, 106
love and, 231, 232, 233, 338
love of God and, 454, 456, 457
in Lurianic Kabbalism, 197
morality and, 381
the other and, 233
reason and, 140
revelation and, 228, 340
ritual and, 171
sefirot and, 161
Shabbat and, 156
temporality and, 232
thought and, 248
speculative theology, 23
speech, 115–18, 236, 442
speech acts
authenticity of, 229
freedom and, 226
liturgy as, 237
love and, 228, 229, 230, 237
Messianism and, 215
midrash and, 225, 226
philosophy and theology and, 217
revelation and, 224
speech-thinking and, 228
universality of, 236
speech-act philosophy, 216, 217
speech-thinking, 215, 216, 218, 228, 230, 233
Spinoza, Baruch
anthropomorphism and, 385
Cohen and, 199

Spinoza, Baruch (cont.)
  on collapse of ancient Jewish
    Commonwealth, 259
  on God's knowledge and will, 384
  Hegel and, 205, 323
  on Jesus, 248
  Kook and, 202, 208
  Levinas and, 249
  Maimonides and, 384
  materialism of, 198
  on Moses, 248
  on nature, 142
  on necessity, 75
  on personality in God, 384
  on pure thought, 248
  on pure language, 250
  theological realism and, 18
spirituality
  diaspora and, 203
  Kabbalah and, 149
  Kook on, 16, 188, 211
  Levinas on, 257
  the other and, 257
  unity and multiplicity and, 156
spontaneity, 249, 286
Standing Again at Sinai (Plaskow), 299
Star of David, the, 215
Star of Redemption, The (Rosenzweig)
  on communal love, 236
  on death, 227
  Messianism and, 217
  midrash in, 222
  as midrashic speech act, 224
  negative theology in, 16
  on philosophy and theology, 217
  publication of, 214
  on revelation, 224
  revelation and, 222
  speech-thinking and, 216
  theological realism of, 402
Steigerung, 230, 232
Stern, Josef, 143
Strauss, Richard, 427
Stump, Eleonore, 459
suffering
  Auschwitz and, 285, 289
  embodiment and, 258
  ethics and, 12
  freedom and, 278
  of God, 73
  God's power and, 292
  hiddenness of God and, 279
  the Holocaust and, 275, 295
  of the innocent, 278
  Jerusalem as Bat Zion and, 57
  of Jesus, 74
  in H. Jonas' myth, 290
  justice and, 254
  moral significance of, 257
  the other and, 258
  responsibility and, 239, 241, 242
  theodicy and, 277
Sukkot, 48
Sweeney, Marvin, 2
Swinburne, Richard, 457, 459
"Symposium on Jewish Belief"
  (Rubenstein), 269
systematic theology, 60, 108, 152, 216,
  317, 332

Taḥanun, 100
Taliban, the, 440
Talmud, the
  adaptability of Torah and, 430
  feminist midrash and, 306, 307
  focus on daily life of, 256
  hiddenness of God and, 278
  irreverential tone of, 70
  Levinas on, 16
  on love of God, 456
  Meiri on, 363
  on the might of God, 68
  personalist God of, 128
  on showbread, 260
  on worker's wages, 259
Tanak
  anthropomorphic conception of God
    in, 113
  Berit Olam and, 50
  Christian Old Testament and, 43
  distinctive form of, 43
  diversity of viewpoint of, 48
  as foundational for Jewish thought, 42
  importance of for Jewish philosophy,
    105
  Jewish tradition and, 58
  monarchy in, 55
  personalist God of, 128
  speech in, 116
  standing and, 113
  structure of, 46–48
Tao te Ching, 431, 432

tefillin, 450
teleology, 142
temporality, 176, 225, 232, 256
Ten Commandments, the, 32
Tetragrammaton, the, 152, 164–66
theodicy
  Auschwitz and, 289
  death camps and, 268, 269
  free will and, 276
  God's power and, 292
  Job and, 289, 290
  H. Jonas and, 289, 291, 294
  Kook on, 203
  punishment and, 67
  sin and, 289
  suffering and, 277
theodicy of modernity, 203
theological instrumentalism, 405
theological language
  apophaticism and, 418, 421
  dialogue and, 231
  fictionalism and, 417
  heuristic function of, 418
  limits of, 401, 404, 410
  Maimonides and, 418
  Muffs on, 416
  non-propositional forms of, 415
  Rosenzweig and, 401, 403
  theological instrumentalism and, 405
  theological realism and, 17, 392, 396, 397–400
  theo-realism and, 409
  truth and, 416
theological realism, 403, 405, 418
  Berkovits and, 400–1
  common sense and, 404
  defined, 17, 392, 399
  epistemic humility and, 405
  in contemporary Jewish theology, 397
  knowledge condition of, 393–96
  linguistic morality and, 406
  medieval theology and, 18
  natural theology and, 392
  negative theology and, 392, 401, 417
  of Gellman, 405–6
  of Rosenzweig, 401–5
  principal claims of, 396
  Spinoza and, 18
  theological language and, 397–400
  theological reference and, 415, 420
  theo-realism and, 407

truth and, 397
Westphal on, 394, 395
Wittgenstein and, 412, 413, 414
"Theological Realism" (Gellman), 405
theological reference, 411, 415
  Gellman on, 420
  theological realism and, 420
Theological-Political Treatise (Spinoza), 259
theology
  aggadah as, 36
  as genuinely Jewish, 21
  coining of, 22
  definition of, 20, 21
  Enlightenment and, 8
  Enlightenment as challenge to, 3
  halakhah and, 3, 22
  Jewish interest in, 346
  modern universities and, 4
  philosophy and, 37
  practice of, 20
  revelation and, 38
Theology of Religions
  breadth of, 355
  challenges of, 360
  Chrisitan and Jewish versions of, 346–48
  complexity of, 353
  contemporary perspective of, 345
  defined, 344
  expansiveness of, 356
  idolatry and, 356, 357
  interreligious dialogue and, 348
  Israel and, 357
  Jewish-Christian relations and, 348
  Kook on, 366–70
  Maimonides and, 361–63
  Meiri and, 363
  morality and, 358
  the multiple concerns of, 350
  mysticism and, 359
  overlap with other areas of, 348, 349
  pluralism and, 348, 364, 365
  promise of, 360
  salvation and, 350
  systematic approach to, 355
  teachings and, 358
  tradition and, 356
  truth and, 350, 358
theo-realism, 407, 408, 410, 419

Theory of Intuition in Husserl's Phenomenology, The (Levinas), 246
theosophical Kabbalah, 162
theosophy, 149, 150, 171
theurgy, 150, 151, 168, 177, 203
Thiemann, Ronald, 337
things-in-themselves, 437
Thirty Years War, the, 464
tif'eret, 92, 165, 166
tiforah, 92
tikkun, 196
tikkun olam, 257
Tillich, Paul, 271, 272, 273, 332, 335
Timaeus (Plato), 138, 293
time
  in contemporary thought, 252
  eternity and, 251–56
  ethics and, 255
  Maimonides on, 119
  the Messiah and, 261
  nature and, 255
  the other and, 253–56
  responsibility and, 254
  transcendence and, 254
Time and the Other (Levinas), 256
Tiqqunei Zohar, 170
Tisha b'Av, 47
Tishby, Isaiah, 175, 178
Torah From Heaven (Heschel), 330
Torah im Derekh-Eretz, 275
Torah kelulah, 341
Torah min HaShamayim, 224, 339
Torah of the King, 55
Torah, the
  aggadah and, 28
  authority of, 201
  belief and, 339
  biblical humanism and, 241
  as central vehicle of Jewish theology, 6
  community and, 30
  context and, 27
  covenant and, 25, 31, 319
  creation and, 132
  cumulative revelation and, 302
  dialogue and, 29, 30
  the Divine name and, 165
  divinity of, 446
  ein sof and, 189
  as encounter with God, 326, 444
  exiles' interpretation of, 214
  faith and, 317
  feeling of God in, 330
  feminism and, 301, 303
  focus on daily life of, 257
  givenness of, 448
  giving to Israel of, 319
  God as, 166
  God's word and, 424
  the Godhead and, 167
  halakhah and, 28
  hermeneutical approaches to, 6
  hokhmah and, 166
  idolatry and, 124
  interpretation of, 202
  Kabbalah on, 24
  language and, 61, 114, 124
  law and, 46
  love and, 78, 237
  malkhut and, 166
  meaning of term, 46
  as midrash, 430
  mitsvot and, 26
  morality and, 36
  mystical union and, 179
  negative theology and, 15
  obligations to the other and, 241
  oral vs. written, 448
  philosophy and, 111
  in *Pirkei Avot*, 137
  positive theology and, 15
  reason and, 448
  remembrance and, 234
  rereading of, 250
  revelation and, 18, 32, 55, 223, 319, 320, 337
  speech-thinking and, 215
  study of, 192
  Talmud and, 247, 430
  the *Tao te Ching* and, 432
  tif'eret and, 166
  tzadikim and, 207, 208
  as word of God, 28, 29
  wordless encounter theology and, 428
  written and oral, 424
Toseftah, the, 71, 73
Totality and Infinity (Levinas), 245, 246, 250, 255, 256
tower of Babel, the, 52
Tractate Avot, 320
Tractate Sofrim, 329
Tractatus Logicus-Philosophicus (Wittgenstein), 427

transcendence
  Adon Olam and, 90
  being and, 240
  constriction of, 127
  death and, 257
  duration and, 253
  ethics and, 245, 247, 253
  God and, 318
  language and, 426
  law and, 144
  love and, 234
  Maimonides on, 126
  metaphysical dualism and, 251
  of *ein sof*, 176
  in organized religion, 244
  the other and, 240
  reciprocal, 179
  representation and, 419
  revelation and, 281, 335
  theological language and, 418
  time and, 254
  Torah and, 193
  in the *Zohar*, 174
Trigg, Roger, 397
trust
  dialogue and, 230
  hermeneutics and, 317
  Isaiah on, 50
  language and, 436
  love and, 231
  perfectly good character and, 460
  in rabbinic literature, 70
truth
  God and, 130
  Jewish thinkers' approaches to, 353
  literal, 378
  place in Judaism of, 351
  pluralism and, 354
  predication and, 377
  ranking of religions and, 368
  rational procedures and, 394
  salvation and, 350
  speech-thinking and, 216
  theological language and, 416
  theological realism and, 397, 406
  Theology of Religions and, 350, 358
  validity and, 353, 358
"Two Dogmas of Empiricism" (Quine), 439
Two Types of Faith (Buber), 408
tzadikim
  experience of infinity of, 209
  experience of non-being of, 208
  higher experience of holiness of, 208
  Kook on, 208
  of pre-Messianic times, 209
  pan emanationism and, 209
  power of, 208
  stages of the cosmos and, 210
  Torah and, 207
  tzimtzum and, 209
Tzimtzum
  allegorical interpretation of, 190
  Berkovits on, 282
  concealment and, 190
  creation and, 282
  ein sof and, 189
  events following, 196
  expansion and, 195
  German idealism and, 198
  H. Jonas and, 293
  hiddenness of God and, 280
  perfection and, 203
  as a spatial concept, 282
  tzadikim and, 209

Umansky, Ellen, 298
understanding, 81, 410
Understanding Rabbinic Midrash:Texts and Commentary (Porton), 219
Understanding the Sick and the Healthy (Rosenzweig), 402
unio mystica, 16, 174, 178, 206
uniqueness, 127
unity
  awareness of, 194
  contemporary thought and, 256
  God as, 180
  the Godhead and, 169
  incorporeality and, 113, 120
  Maimonides on, 108
  multiplicity and, 156
  of *ein sof*, 176
  in philosophy and Kabbalah, 158
  in philosophy and rabbinic literature, 169
universalism, 196, 332, 352
unmoved mover, 105, 112
Upanishads, the, 431

validity, 353, 358, 364, 367
Van Buren, Paul, 272

Vattimo, Gianni, 337
Verbin, Nehama, 416
violence, 82, 229, 244, 249, 433

Wainwright, William, 456
Ward, Keith, 459
Weinberg, Rabbi Yaakov, 328
Weinberg, Rabbi Yechiel, 274, 275
Weiner, Herbert, 271
Westphal, Merold, 393
Wettstein, Howard, 416
What is Midrash (Neusner), 220
Wiesel, Elie, 13, 220
will, 116
will of God, 50, 52
Wittgenstein, Ludwig, 339, 399, 411, 414, 428, 439
Wolfson, Elliot R., 164, 175, 176, 178, 179, 418
Wolfson, Harry, 379
Wolterstorff, Nicholas, 420
word of God, 23, 28, 29
wordless encounter theology
  appeal of, 435
  conception of language of, 436

critiques of, 429, 431
defined, 425
as dogma, 426
halakhah and, 429, 430
halakhic Judaism and, 426
monotheism and, 434
Moses and, 429
personalism and, 447
purported advantages of, 428
Schönberg and, 427
Torah and, 429
world, the, 191
worship, 129, 204

Yehie Khevod, 97, 98
YHWH, 64, 65, 154, 164–66
Yom Kippur, 55, 92, 164, 403

Zalman, Rabbi Shneur of Lyadi. *See* Rashaz
Zechariah (book), 86, 89, 95, 98
Zechariah (prophet), 50
Zedekiah, 54
Zeno's paradox, 252
Zionism, 9, 247, 260, 261
Zohar, 162, 170, 174, 317

Other Titles in the Series (continued from page ii)

THE HEBREW BIBLE/OLD TESTAMENT Edited by *Stephen B. Chapman* and *Marvin A. Sweeney*
HEBREW BIBLE AND ETHICS Edited by *C. L. Crouch*
THE JESUITS Edited by *Thomas Worcester*
JESUS Edited by *Markus Bockmuehl*
JUDAISM AND LAW Edited by *Christine Hayes*
C. S. LEWIS Edited by *Robert MacSwain* and *Michael Ward*
LIBERATION THEOLOGY Edited by *Chris Rowland*
MARTIN LUTHER Edited by *Donald K. McKim*
MEDIEVAL JEWISH PHILOSOPHY Edited by *Daniel H. Frank* and *Oliver Leaman*
MODERN JEWISH PHILOSOPHY Edited by *Michael L. Morgan* and *Peter Eli Gordon*
MOHAMMED Edited by *Jonathan E. Brockup*
THE NEW CAMBRIDGE COMPANION TO ST. PAUL Edited by *Bruce W. Longenecker*
NEW RELIGIOUS MOVEMENTS Edited by *Olav Hammer* and *Mikael Rothstein*
PENTECOSTALISM Edited by *Cecil M. Robeck, Jr* and *Amos Yong*
POSTMODERN THEOLOGY Edited by *Kevin J. Vanhoozer*
THE PROBLEM OF EVIL Edited by *Chad Meister* and *Paul K. Moser*
PURITANISM Edited by *John Coffey* and *Paul C. H. Lim*
QUAKERISM Edited by *Stephen W. Angell* and *Pink Dandelion*
THE QUR'AN Edited by *Jane Dammen McAuliffe*
KARL RAHNER Edited by *Declan Marmion* and *Mary E. Hines*
REFORMATION THEOLOGY Edited by *David Bagchi* and *David C. Steinmetz*
REFORMED THEOLOGY Edited by *Paul T. Nimmo* and *David A. S. Fergusson*
RELIGION AND TERRORISM Edited by *James R. Lewis*
RELIGIOUS EXPERIENCE Edited by *Paul K. Moser* and *Chad Meister*
RELIGIOUS STUDIES Edited by *Robert A. Orsi*
FREIDRICK SCHLEIERMACHER Edited by *Jacqueline Mariña*
SCIENCE AND RELIGION Edited by *Peter Harrison*
ST. PAUL Edited by *James D. G. Dunn*
SUFISM Edited by *Lloyd Ridgeon*
THE SUMMA THEOLOGIAE Edited by *Philip McCosker* and *Denys Turner*

THE TALMUD AND RABBINIC LITERATURE Edited by *Charlotte E. Fonrobert* and *Martin S. Jaffee*

THE TRINITY Edited by *Peter C. Phan*

HANS URS VON BALTHASAR Edited by *Edward T. Oakes* and *David Moss*

VATICAN II Edited by *Richard R. Gaillardetz*

JOHN WESLEY Edited by *Randy L. Maddox* and *Jason E. Vickers*

For EU product safety concerns, contact us at Calle de José Abascal, 56–1°, 28003 Madrid, Spain or eugpsr@cambridge.org.

www.ingramcontent.com/pod-product-compliance
Ingram Content Group UK Ltd.
Pitfield, Milton Keynes, MK11 3LW, UK
UKHW020241070625
459201UK00014B/189